THE
PENINSULA
QUESTION

THE
PENINSULA
QUESTION

*A Chronicle of the
Second Korean Nuclear Crisis*

YOICHI FUNABASHI

BROOKINGS INSTITUTION PRESS
Washington, D.C.

Library of Congress Cataloging-in-Publication data
Funabashi, Yoichi, 1944–
   The Peninsula question : a chronicle of the second Korean nuclear crisis / Yoichi
Funabashi.
      p.   cm.
   Summary: "Through interviews, gives a behind-the-scenes look at negotiations to
denuclearize the Korean peninsula. Offering multiple perspectives on the second Korean
nuclear crisis, provides a window of understanding on the historical, geopolitical, and
security concerns at play on the peninsula since 2002, paying special attention to China's
dealings with North Korea"—Provided by publisher.
   Includes bibliographical references and index.
   ISBN-13: 978-0-8157-3010-1 (cloth : alk. paper)
   ISBN-10: 0-8157-3010-1 (cloth : alk. paper)
   1. Nuclear disarmament—Korea (North) 2. Nuclear nonproliferation—Korea (North) 3.
Six-party Talk. 4. Korea (North)—Foreign relations—Korea (South) 5. Korea (South)—
Foreign relations—Korea (North) 6. Korea (North)—Foreign relations—China. 7.
China—Foreign relations—Korea (North) I. Title.

   JZ6009.K6F86 2007
   327.1'747095193—dc22   2007033083

                    1 3 5 7 9 8 6 4 2

The paper used in this publication meets minimum requirements of the
American National Standard for Information Sciences—Permanence of Paper
for Printed Library Materials: ANSI Z39.48-1992.

Typeset in Minion

Composition by Cynthia Stock
Silver Spring, Maryland

Printed by R. R. Donnelley
Harrisonburg, Virginia

CONTENTS

PREFACE

George Alexander Lensen's classic study of the geopolitics of major powers on the Korean Peninsula in the late nineteenth century, *Balance of Intrigue: International Rivalry in Korea and Manchuria, 1884–1899,* was aptly named.[1] Eventually, after much maneuvering among the rivals, the peninsula was annexed by Japan.

A century later, the Korean Peninsula has once again become a geopolitical arena in which the harsh strategic calculations of the major powers are playing out. The balance of power, which had been delicately maintained between the Western and the communist camps since the end of the Korean War, became shaky after the end of the cold war. The ideological foundation of North Korea was demolished, and the country's economy began to spiral toward total collapse. Chinese and Russian efforts to normalize diplomatic relations with South Korea deepened North Korea's sense of isolation. North Korea's founding father, Kim Il-sung, passed away. North Korea attempted to overcome those and other existential crises by driving itself to develop nuclear weapons, which inescapably brought confrontation with the United States.

The first North Korean nuclear crisis, in the early 1990s, brought the two countries very close to a military showdown, which was prevented only at the eleventh hour by President Jimmy Carter's visit to North Korea in June 1994. The crisis was resolved with the signing of the Agreed Framework by the two countries in October of the same year. North Korea agreed to freeze its production of plutonium in return for normalization of relations; as an added incentive, the United States, South Korea, Japan, and others were to provide energy assistance to North Korea. That was an attempt to prolong the state of truce. The first nuclear crisis on the Korean Peninsula is exhaustively recorded in *Going Critical: The First North Korean Nuclear Crisis.*[2]

The equilibrium thus achieved was short-lived. In June 2002, the United States revealed that it had obtained circumstantial evidence that North Korea had secretly pursued a plan to enrich uranium, rekindling the U.S.–North Korea conflict and bringing about the second North Korean nuclear showdown. It so happened that at that time Kim Jong-il was about to take a major gamble in order to advance his plans to reform North Korea's economy and improve relations with the world's major powers. However, the resurgence of U.S.–North Korean tension crippled Kim Jong-il's grand design.

Around that time the United States was pursuing its post-9/11 "war on terror." It had invaded Afghanistan in late 2001 and was in the midst of preparations for war with its next target, Saddam Hussein's regime in Iraq. Against that backdrop, a series of VIPs from other countries visited North Korea from fall 2002 through spring 2003: Prime Minister Junichiro Koizumi of Japan in September 2002; Assistant Secretary of State James Kelly of the United States in October; presidential envoy Lim Dong-won from South Korea and Putin's special envoy, Alexander Losyukov, from Russia in January 2003; and Vice Premier Qian Qichen of China in March 2003.

All of the visits were undertaken as separate responses by the leaders of those countries to the second Korean nuclear crisis. In the end, those individual responses merged into a multilateral consultation in which China played a major role. To cope with the crisis, China hosted a trilateral consultation among China, North Korea, and the United States in April 2003 and subsequently sponsored the six-party talks among those three nations plus South Korea, Japan, and Russia in August of the same year.

China continued to host the six-party talks, which took place in February 2004 (second round); June 2004 (third round); July, August, and September 2005 (fourth round); November 2005, December 2006, and February 2007 (fifth round); and March and July 2007 (sixth round). At the fourth round, participating members signed a joint statement that presented a framework for a package solution calling for North Korea's abolishment of its nuclear programs and normalization of relations between North Korea and the United States. However, the joint statement was not followed up with a concrete implementation plan, allowing North Korea to conduct a test launch of its ballistic missiles on July 5, 2006, and a nuclear test on October 9, 2006.

In response to those provocations, in July 2006 the UN Security Council adopted Resolution 1695, which imposed economic sanctions against North Korea, and in October it passed a stronger resolution, Resolution 1718, heightening tensions on the Korean Peninsula. But toward the end of 2006 and the beginning of 2007, a rapprochement was seen between North Korea and the United States, resulting in an agreement at the third session of the fifth round of the six-party talks in February 2007 on initial actions for implementing the joint statement of the fourth round of the six-party talks. It was agreed that

> The DPRK will shut down and seal for the purpose of eventual abandonment the Yongbyon nuclear facility, including the reprocessing facility, and invite back IAEA personnel to conduct all necessary monitoring and verifications as agreed between IAEA and the DPRK.[3]

Thus it appears that the second nuclear crisis on the Korean Peninsula, which lasted from the fall of 2002 through the end of 2006, has been tentatively "sealed." Those involved in the six-party talks stress that in the future the agreement will evolve into a "regional framework." At present, however, it should be reiterated that the agreement itself, at least in its initial stages, does not squarely address the issue of North Korea's possession of nuclear weapons. It is based merely on a fait accompli, that is, on North Korea's nuclear capability. The nations of the six-party talks seem to have avoided this tough issue and temporarily decided to focus on "nuclear programs," sidestepping "nuclear weapons." Eventually, that position will become unsustainable.

This book is a chronicle of the second nuclear crisis on the Korean Peninsula. It attempts to bring into the open the responses to that crisis of the parties concerned—Japan, the United States, Russia, South Korea, and China as well as North Korea itself—and to shed some light on the logic and emotions behind those responses.

The responses themselves raised countless questions. Why, for example, did the United States suddenly bring up the subject of the secret uranium enrichment program in North Korea in the summer of 2002? How did the U.S. government assess the information on the program provided by U.S. intelligence agencies? Did the government bring it up to derail the closer relationship between North and South Korea and cripple the attempt at normalization of diplomatic relations between North Korea and Japan? Why did the Bush administration, a known skeptic of the multilateral process, opt for a multilateral process, the six-party talks, to deal with the second nuclear crisis? Why did China abandon its persistent stance that the North Korean nuclear program was a bilateral issue between North Korea and the United States and agree to host the trilateral meeting and the six-party talks? Why did the United States more or less synchronize the disclosure of North Korea's money-laundering program through Banco Delta Asia with the drafting of the joint statement in September 2005? Why did North Korea agree with the wording of the joint statement of the six-party talks only to reject it within twenty-four hours? And how genuinely does South Korea oppose North Korea's nuclear capability? Does Seoul secretly wish for it because South Korea could inherit North Korea's program when the peninsula is unified in the future?

What about Japan? Why is Japan so persistent about the abduction issue? Does it hope to obstruct settlement of the North Korean nuclear issue in order to give itself an excuse to develop its own nuclear capabilities?

In this volume, I have attempted to respond to these questions as far as I can. But I was more intrigued by the issues underlying them. Why are there so many questions, including some that half-hint at the presence of some conspiracy? I find, beyond the nuclear crisis, geopolitical conflicts and divisions over the past that burden the future of the Korean Peninsula. Overcoming those divisions and the past, thus allowing for the eventual unification of the Korean Peninsula—that is the geopolitical drama of the Peninsula Question.

In the ensuing chapters, I highlight the following issues: The first part of the book explores how each of the parties engaged with North Korea during the second nuclear crisis, starting with Prime Minister Junichiro Koizumi's visits to Pyongyang in 2002 (chapter 1) and in 2004 (chapter 2). Discussion follows of U.S. presidential envoy James Kelly's visit to Pyongyang in 2002 (chapter 3) and the struggles within the Bush administration over how to engage North Korea after the collapse of the Agreed Framework (chapter 4). I then look to North Korea's neighbors, exploring first Russia's attempts to play the role of honest broker with Kim Jong-il (chapter 5), then Seoul's various attempts to keep its sunshine policy alive and how that policy differed under President Kim (chapter 6) and President Roh (chapter 7). I look at how China engaged with North Korea (chapter 8) and how the rise of China plays into the issue (chapter 9). The second part of the book looks at the convergence of the five parties in engaging with North Korea at the six-party talks (chapter 10) and the resulting joint statement following the fourth round (chapter 11). Finally, I examine North Korea's existential nuclear dilemma as Kim Jong-il's visits to China have transpired (chapter 12). An analysis of the dynamics of the second nuclear crisis is given in the conclusion (chapter 13).

The text of this volume covers developments up to the North Korean missile test of July 2006. I have attempted to incorporate newer developments that followed the nuclear test in the footnotes and in the discussion as appropriate. This geopolitical and nuclear drama is still in the making, and it might be quite some time before we see the end. I therefore decided to share with readers the results of my study of the four-year-long nuclear crisis at this stage.

YOICHI FUNABASHI
March 2007

ACKNOWLEDGMENTS

It is obvious, probably more so than with most other books, that this book would not have been completed without the generous cooperation and assistance of numerous individuals and institutions. On one hand, government officials, mostly from member countries of the six-party talks, granted me opportunities to interview them, sometimes repeatedly and sometimes over a long period of time. Readers will find their names in the list of interviewees at the end of this volume. Although I have occasionally benefited from the views of private scholars and other nongovernmental experts, I decided to include only those who were directly engaged in policymaking and implementation—that is, lawmakers and administrators, particularly diplomats, of the countries involved in the six-party talks. I refrained from including the names of those (mostly Chinese officials) who specifically declined to be listed and of those (mostly Chinese, Japanese, South Korean, and U.S. intelligence officers) who, in my judgment, would appreciate their identity not being disclosed. The North Korean diplomats who I interviewed agreed to be interviewed only if they remained anonymous.

My appreciation goes to the Brookings Institution for providing me with an office and highly competent research assistants for an entire year. Aside from Brookings's president, Strobe Talbott, former vice president James Steinberg, and vice president Carlos Pasqual, I am indebted to the following people at Brookings for their help throughout the process of researching and writing this book: Jeffrey A. Bader, Richard Bush, Jing Huang, Lim Wonhyuk, Yang Bojiang, Alexander Vorontsov, and Julia Cates. I am especially appreciative of the help provided by full-time research assistant Song Jiyoung from South Korea and part-time research assistant Ilya Brayman from Russia. Jiyoung in particular deserves a special word of thanks. Without her understanding of both Korean and English, I would not have been able to obtain and absorb the many documents and research materials that I was able to in such a short span of time. I am the proud owner of the Jiyoung memos on Korean Peninsula affairs, which she compiled everyday throughout the project. *Kamsahamnida,* Jiyoung, for your smile and devotion.

I am also grateful to the Japan Foundation Center for Global Partnership for its financial support of this year-long project at the Brookings Institution.

I also wish to express my deep gratitude to the *Asahi Shimbun* for having liberated me from my obligations as one of its columnists so that I could concentrate on researching and writing this book for one long year. In my Tokyo office, my research assistants—Arthur Lord, Daniel Sturgeon, and Rachel Amiya—supported my research by arranging interviews, collecting vital documents, and proofreading successive drafts of the manuscript. I learned a great deal from Dr. Li Hunan, who worked in my Tokyo office temporarily during my absence, particularly with respect to ethnic Koreans in China and China–North Korea relations.

The origins of this book lie in a joint lecture-seminar at the Graduate School of Public Policy, University of Tokyo, that I organized with Professor Kiichi Fujiwara in the summer of 2005. Case studies on the North Korean nuclear crisis that we conducted with the graduate students who enrolled served to develop the book's themes further. I learned a great deal from the students, who were willing to answer all of my questions, and I hope that I have given answers here to many of the questions that were left as my homework. I would like to take this opportunity to express my gratitude to Professor Fujiwara, teaching assistant Toru Sahashi, and our sixteen graduate students, four of whom were from China and South Korea.

THE
PENINSULA
QUESTION

CHAPTER ONE

PRIME MINISTER KOIZUMI'S VISIT TO NORTH KOREA

The *onigiri,* or rice balls, that were served for lunch were left on the table, as if they were some kind of offering. Prime Minister Junichiro Koizumi did not touch them at all.[1]

It was September 17, 2002, and Koizumi was sitting in a specially designated anteroom on the ground floor of the Paekhwawon (Hundred Flowers) Guest House in Pyongyang. It was a little past noon, and he had just finished a top-level talk with Chairman Kim Jong-il. Koizumi silently watched the Japan Broadcasting Corporation satellite TV news program that was reporting on the talk.

Armed North Korean police officers were occasionally seen outside the window. Inside the room, seated around the table with Koizumi, were Shinzo Abe, deputy cabinet secretary; Norimoto Takano, deputy minister for foreign affairs; Hitoshi Tanaka, director general of the Asian and Oceanian Affairs Bureau of the Ministry of Foreign Affairs (MOFA); Isao Iijima, personal secretary to the prime minister; and Kenji Hiramatsu, MOFA's director of the Northeast Asian Affairs Division. Koro Bessho, another secretary to the prime minister, seconded from MOFA, kept restlessly going in and out of the room.

"The TV is too loud," said Tanaka, but Iijima immediately shot back, "No, it's better this way." He instructed a foreign ministry official nearby to turn the volume even higher. When Koizumi started talking, however, the official immediately turned the volume lower. But Iijima, as if to say, "No, no," pointed his right index finger at his right ear and instructed the official to turn the volume up again.

"If the North Koreans won't acknowledge their wrongdoings," Tanaka said to Koizumi, "you have to push them." Abe pressed further: "Unless they disclose in full what took place and formally apologize for their wrongdoings, you should not sign the joint statement. If they don't do that, you should get up and leave." At Abe's last sentence, everyone fell silent. Takano broke the silence, agreeing, for the most part, with Abe: "We should consider not signing the statement if their attitude remains the same."

If in the scheduled afternoon session Kim Jong-il would not acknowledge that North Korea had abducted Japanese citizens and, accordingly, would not offer a formal apology, Koizumi could never sign what would become the Japan-DPRK Pyongyang Declaration. The summit would be a total failure.

Abe thought that they had no choice. The prime minister of Japan himself had come all the way from Tokyo to settle the issue directly with the leader of North Korea. Abe was convinced that the Japanese people would not endorse normalization of diplomatic relations with North Korea if Pyongyang did not apologize for the abductions now that, prior to the summit meeting, it had even disclosed the number of deceased among "the missing." Its actions were a state crime. He also was convinced that their conversation was bugged, but he hoped that Kim Jong-il was among those who could hear what he was saying. "First of all, we have to request a formal apology from Kim Jong-il," he thought. "That is the first order of business."[2] Abe was not alone in that wish. Koizumi simply said, "I'll say . . .," before resuming his silence.

Koizumi's visit to Pyongyang was a day trip. Pyongyang is only about a two-hour flight from Tokyo, and the trip took about fourteen hours altogether. Koizumi had two meetings scheduled, one in the morning and another in the afternoon. There was a short preparatory meeting just before the first meeting.

Earlier that morning, Koizumi had arisen at 5:00 a.m. in his temporary official residence in Higashi Gotanda, Tokyo. The government airplane took off from Haneda Airport at 6:46 a.m., carrying him and his entourage. Aboard, Koizumi reviewed the text of the Japan-DPRK Pyongyang Declaration, with which he was very pleased. "This is a very good document," he remarked. He also reread the message from President George W. Bush that U.S. Ambassador Howard Baker had presented to Yasuo Fukuda, chief cabinet secretary, the previous day. The message called for Koizumi's renewed attention to North Korea's enriched uranium program, referring to recent information from U.S. intelligence agencies. President Bush, however, requested that Koizumi not refer to that information in the Japan–North Korea summit talk.[3] Koizumi gave a thin smile. He thought that the United States was overreacting. He had no intention of normalizing diplomatic ties with North Korea if he had to depart from the Pyongyang Declaration. Nevertheless, he appreciated the message, which had the effect of reassuring him that President Bush was fully on his side.[4]

Koizumi's plane touched down at Pyongyang Sunan International Airport at 9:14 a.m. It was a perfect, clear autumn day. Kim Yong-nam, president of the presidium of the DPRK Supreme People's Assembly, was at the airport to welcome

Koizumi and his party. Koizumi slowly walked down the ramp to become the first Japanese prime minister to visit North Korea since the end of World War II.

At 10:00 a.m. sharp, Korean Central Television and the Voice of Korea reported on the arrival of the prime minister.[5] The Japanese delegation proceeded to the northern section of Pyongyang, where the Paekhwawon Guest House, believed to be the most prestigious of the more than 100 state guest houses in North Korea, is located. The Kumsusan Memorial Palace, where the body of the late Chairman Kim Il-sung lies in state, is nearby. Kim Jong-il held all of his summit talks at this guest house, including those with President Vladimir Putin of Russia in July 2000 and President Jiang Zemin of China in September 2001. Inside the guest house, on the left about 150 feet (50 meters) from the front entrance, are three conference rooms. The central room was chosen for this Japan-DPRK summit.

It was only several minutes before the first session of the summit meeting that the Japanese delegation was informed of the results of the North Korean "investigation" concerning the whereabouts of the Japanese abductees. Prior to the first session, a preparatory meeting was held in an annex building between Hitoshi Tanaka and Ma Chol-su, director of the Asian Affairs Department of North Korea's Foreign Ministry. During the meeting, Ma informed Tanaka that five of the abductees were still alive and that eight had died. Tanaka immediately requested that North Korea thoroughly examine and report on the causes and circumstances of the deaths of the eight abductees. In response, Ma promised that the North Korean Red Cross Society would dispatch the results of the investigation to the Japanese Red Cross Society. Ma chose to refer to the abductees as "the missing."

After the end of the preparatory meeting, Tanaka half ran to the main building. It was quite a distance. North Korea must have deliberately held the meeting in the remote annex building so that Prime Minister Koizumi would have to walk into the summit talk without ample time to review and analyze the North Korean information. Tanaka realized that the Japanese were caught in a trap, but it was too late to do anything about it.[6] He felt pressed. Upon entering the main building, he tripped on the thick carpet. Koizumi was shocked into silence when he heard Tanaka's report.

Kim Jong-il appeared wearing one of the khaki-colored military jackets, obviously of the best-quality cashmere, that he wears whenever he appears before his subjects or meets foreign dignitaries.[7] At the outset of the talk, Kim Jong-il expressed his appreciation to his guest, saying, "As the host, I regret that we had to make the prime minister of Japan come to Pyongyang so early in the morning in order to open a new chapter in the DPRK-Japan relationship." Continuing, he said, "I strongly hope that we can use this opportunity to begin a new, genuinely neighborly relationship between our two countries, thereby making the expression 'a country nearby, but remote' a saying of the past." He went on to praise the draft of the Pyongyang Declaration, which, if signed by the two leaders, would become the basic document for normalization of diplomatic relations between the two countries. Kim specifically referred to the contribution that Hitoshi Tanaka had made in drafting the document. During the subsequent talks, he mentioned Tanaka's name twice to express his appreciation for Tanaka's contribution. Hearing that, one of the Japanese delegates marveled at Kim Jong-il's diplomatic niceties. Kim Jong-il proudly emphasized that the secret negotiations between Japan and North Korea that had led to the meeting had been conducted without being leaked to the outside. He said that he himself had not mentioned the negotiations to anyone, not even the Chinese and the Russians.

"I, too, hope that the opportunity that this meeting presents will greatly advance bilateral relations between our two countries," Koizumi responded, repeating the word "opportunity," which Kim had used. Kim Jong-il continued to speak, occasionally dropping his eyes to read from a small memo pad in his hand. He looked a little stiff.

At the very beginning of the summit talk, Koizumi had raised the abduction issue. "We note that pertinent information was presented by the DPRK at the preparatory meeting immediately proceeding this session," he said. "However, I was utterly distressed by the information that was provided and, as the prime minister, who is ultimately responsible for the interests and security of the Japanese people, I must strongly protest. I cannot bear to imagine how the remaining family members will take the news."[8] Kim just listened silently. Abe observed that he looked unsure and less confident of himself, while Koizumi looked very stern.[9] Kim did not acknowledge Koizumi's remarks or offer an apology. Time ticked away, but Kim did not clarify his attitude regarding the abductions.

Toward the end of the first session, Koizumi raised the abduction issue once again: "I ask that you arrange a meeting for us with the surviving abductees. And I would like you to make an outright apology. In addition, I want you to provide information about the deceased abductees."

Kim listened, taking notes on a memo pad, then suggested, "Shall we take a break now?" The Japanese agreed, ending the first session, which had lasted for about one hour. Koizumi and his party were gravely discouraged by the first session, from which they had expected a much more satisfactory explanation of the abductions.

Diplomatic protocol normally would call for a lunch hosted by Chairman Kim after the morning session. However, when Koizumi had agreed to visit Pyongyang, he gave strict orders not to accept any North Korean offer to host lunch or dinner, even though he knew that the offer would be made; not to host a meal for a foreign dignitary who had traveled a long distance would be a breach of diplomatic protocol. Moreover, he knew that the host would lose face if the offer were declined. As a compromise, the North Koreans sounded out the possibility of hosting a working lunch. But that, too, was turned down by the Japanese, who explained to the North Koreans that "it is our prime minister's strong wish to make the visit a very practical event, eliminating diplomatic protocol as much as possible." Accordingly, a one-day visit without a luncheon was planned.[10] Koizumi had the abductions on his mind, a solemn and heavy issue.

Because it was totally uncertain how the abduction issue would evolve, Koizumi thought that it would be improper for the Japanese delegation to enjoy a gala reception or any other social activity at the summit. Expecting the worst possible outcome, he issued instructions that simple *onigiri* and Japanese tea be prepared for the delegation and transported to North Korea on the government plane. Koizumi's intuition proved to be accurate. All of the members of Japan's delegation had been distressed at the thought enjoying a lunch offered by the North Koreans after hearing of the death of eight abductees.

The afternoon session began at 2:00 p.m. Chairman Kim made the first remarks, reading a memo: "I would like to give an explanation about this matter. We have thoroughly investigated this matter, including by examining our government's role in it. Decades of adversarial relations between our two countries provided the background of this incident. It was, nevertheless, an appalling incident." With a humble attitude, Kim continued: "It is my understanding that this incident was initiated by special mission organizations in the 1970s and 1980s, driven by blindly motivated patriotism and misguided heroism. . . . I believe there were two reasons behind the abduction of Japanese citizens. First, the special mission organizations wanted to obtain native-Japanese instructors of the Japanese language. Second, the special mission organizations hoped to use abductees to penetrate into 'the South.' As soon as their scheme and deeds were brought to my attention, those who were responsible were punished. This kind of thing will never be repeated. I would like to take this opportunity to apologize straightforwardly for the regrettable conduct of those people. I will not allow that to happen again."[11]

The "South" that he mentioned was the Republic of Korea. Hearing Kim's comments, Koizumi thought that they contained too many undertones suggesting that Kim himself had not been aware of or involved in the incident. Nevertheless, he decided to sign the declaration then.[12] Both Kim and Kang Sok-ju, North Korea's first deputy minister for foreign affairs, who was seated next to Kim, kept staring fixedly at Koizumi, as if analyzing his facial expressions. Koizumi maintained a mild but strained demeanor throughout the meeting.

Koizumi also brought up the issue of the intrusion into Japanese territorial waters by mysterious vessels believed to be North Korean. On September 11, just before his visit to Pyongyang, Japanese authorities had raised a vessel that had exploded in Chinese waters in December 2001 after being chased by the

Japanese coast guard. "We ask for your guarantee that this kind of regrettable incident will not happen again in the future," Koizumi insisted. Chairman Kim once again responded without defiance: "We have thoroughly investigated this incident, and we have just learned what happened," he said. "I had absolutely no knowledge about this matter. Those vessels were used in training exercises that special mission units conducted independently. We have already identified the specific unit that was responsible for the misconduct. I wish to assure you that this kind of thing will never happen again in the future. We still have quite a number of those special mission units, but we wish to dissolve those remnants of the past."[13]

The afternoon session ended at 3:30 p.m. Kim Jong-il stood up to shake hands with all the members of the Japanese delegation. When he walked out of the room, Kim shook hands again, this time only with Iijima and Yasutake Tango, another secretary to the prime minister, seconded from the Ministry of Finance. Iijima found Kim's hand to be rough; he felt as if he were holding the toughened heel of a foot.[14] Then Kim disappeared into his outsized Mercedes. According to a Japanese diplomat who was present, it shot off immediately, roaring "as if it were in an F-1 race."[15] The Japanese delegation proceeded to the Koryo Hotel, where they relaxed for a while in the penthouse suite. The rest of the afternoon flew by, highlighted by the signing ceremony for the Pyongyang Declaration at 5:30 p.m. and a press conference at 6:30 p.m.

At the press conference, Prime Minister Koizumi began his remarks by saying "I feel heartbreaking grief about those abductees who lost their lives without coming home. I am utterly speechless when I imagine the tremendous grief their surviving family members must be experiencing." Continuing, he declared, "I have come to Pyongyang today in order to take a giant step toward building stable peace in this region, fully determined to prevent—at any cost—the recurrence of this kind of despicable conduct."

Back in Tokyo, Yasuo Fukuda, chief cabinet secretary, informed the families of the abductees of the grave news at 4:00 p.m. (There is no time difference between Tokyo and Pyongyang, as there is between Tokyo and Seoul.)

Relations between Japan and North Korea have been marked by occupation, isolation, and failed attempts at normalization. From 1905 to 1945, while occupying the Korean peninsula, the Japanese colonial government suppressed the Korean culture and language; the Japanese even forced the Koreans to take Japanese names. The occupation remains a defining event in the history of Korea. In North Korea, stories of Kim Il-sung fighting against Japanese colonizers are taught with great embellishment, while Japan's support of the United States in the Korean War and subsequent mistreatment of *zainichi*, ethnic Koreans living in Japan, have reinforced North Korea's resentment. Later, when Japan normalized relations with South Korea in 1965 and China in 1972, North Korea was simply ignored. Japan accepted South Korea's argument that it was the only legitimate government of Korea, and the United States provided security for Japan against North Korea.

However, with the end of the cold war, Japan made several attempts at normalizing relations with North Korea. Those efforts included visits to North Korea by several parliamentary delegations, but they often met with mixed results. Relations took a turn for the worse when in August 1998 North Korea test-fired a Taepodong-1 missile over Japan. The missile flew over northern Japan, landing in the Pacific Ocean. Suddenly, Japan's strange neighbor to the west was a serious security concern. However, while the security threat posed by North Korea was of great concern to policymakers and security experts, the primary focus of the Japanese people has been the abduction issue.

Claims that Japanese citizens had been kidnapped in the 1970s and 1980s by North Korean agents were at first treated as nothing more than a conspiracy theory. In 1980, when the *Sankei Shimbun* reported on the case of three people who went missing in the summer of 1978 under suspicious circumstances, the government and policymakers considered the report to be mere speculation. However, North Korean defectors confirmed the report in 1987 and again in 1993, stating that Japanese citizens had been abducted in order to train North Korean spies in the Japanese language and culture. Other motives include abducting Japanese in order to steal their identities or to silence those who had witnessed North Korean operatives. In 1977, An Myong-jin, a North Korean defector, described an abductee whom he had once met. His description was assumed to be of Megumi Yokota, a teenager kidnapped in 1977, and raised the profile of the reports.[16]

The charismatic Junichiro Koizumi, an atypical politician in Japan, was elected prime minister in April 2001 on a platform of government reform. As a populist politician, a break from the factional insiders of the past, he sought a political success to secure both his popularity and his legacy. Normalization of relations with North Korea proved to be a target ripe for a diplomatic breakthrough; it also presented an opportunity for Japan to put its colonial legacy to rest.

While, if successful, efforts to normalize relations with North Korea would bring great rewards, they also entailed great risks. One concern was how the United States would react, for it too was trying to denuclearize North Korea. Koizumi, however, elected to go it alone, keeping the United States in the dark about his intentions. Japanese prime ministers had rarely conducted an autonomous foreign policy separate from that of the United States, but that was exactly what Koizumi was doing when Japan began exploring the possibilities of a secret summit with a North Korean interlocutor. That was another way in which Koizumi broke with the past.

MR. X

Secret preparations for Koizumi's visit to North Korea had been under way since Hitoshi Tanaka became director general of MOFA's Asian and Oceanian Affairs Bureau in September 2001. Tanaka's first major project was Koizumi's visit to Beijing; Japan-China relations had been bumpy since China reacted strongly against Koizumi's visit to Yasukuni Shrine on August 13, 2001.[17] Koizumi's visit to Beijing took place in October, during which he visited the Marco Polo Bridge in a Beijing suburb, the site, in 1937, of the Marco Polo Bridge Incident, which triggered the Sino-Japanese War. He also visited the Chinese People's Resistance against Japanese Aggression War Memorial. Responding to questions during the press conference held that day, Koizumi said, "I walked through the exhibits, which made me wish to express both deep sorrow for the victims and my heartfelt apologies to the Chinese people. We must not repeat such a war again." At the museum, Koizumi offered flowers and, with a calligraphy brush, formed the characters for *chu-jo,* which roughly translates as "sincerity and magnanimity."[18]

At the beginning of the year a signal had arrived from North Korea regarding its wish to normalize bilateral relations with Japan. The North Koreans sounded the possibility of a bilateral summit talk involving Yoshiro Mori, who was then the prime minister. Only a few days before, across the Pacific Ocean, George W. Bush's victory in the U.S. presidential election had finally been confirmed. In January 2001, Hidenao Nakagawa, a former chief cabinet secretary, had a secret meeting in Singapore with North Korea's Kang Sok-ju, the first deputy minister for foreign affairs, which lasted nearly five hours. During the meeting, Kang stated that North Korea wished "to simultaneously settle both past-colonization issues and the 'humanitarian issue.'" "We intend to tackle this task with utmost sincerity," he added, suggesting a summit meeting between the two nations' leaders. The "humanitarian issue" referred to was the abduction issue.[19]

Several attempts at diplomatic normalization had been made during the 1990s, but the abduction issue was a stumbling block each time. Whenever the Japanese brought up the issue, North Korea denied the very existence of the abductees and reacted angrily, terminating the negotiations. In 1997, the Japanese government publicized a list of Japanese citizens believed to have been abducted by North Korea, and the abduction issue began to capture nationwide attention within Japan. Kang Sok-ju started to show a more flexible attitude by referring to the "humanitarian issue" in conjunction with the settlement of past-colonization issues. However, he did not refer to any means by which to arrive at a settlement. Moreover, he demanded what Mori described as "a huge amount" from Japan as compensation for settling past issues.[20]

The Japanese did not accept his demand. Nevertheless, dialogue between the Japanese Red Cross Society and the North Korean Red Cross Society—which encompassed "humanitarian issues," including the abduction issue, the return of the "Japanese wives," and food aid—was continued.[21] Simultaneously, secret negotiations were being carried out between the two governments. Kunihiko Makita, director general of MOFA's Asian and Oceanian Affairs Bureau and the predecessor of Hitoshi Tanaka, represented Japan, while Hwang Chul, a member of the standing committee of the Korean Asia-Pacific Peace Committee, represented North Korea. The Korean Asia-Pacific Peace Committee is an organization affiliated with the DPRK Workers' Party. Chaired at that time by Party Secretary Kim Yong-sun (now deceased), the committee had determined North Korea's policy toward Japan. Hwang was the right-hand man of Kim Yong-sun, and at one time he had served as Kim Il-sung's Japanese interpreter.[22]

The two men secretly contacted each other in Kuala Lumpur. Hwang was a veteran intelligence officer specializing in Japan. Early in August 2001, Hwang mentioned something odd during a consultation meeting with Makita in Kuala Lumpur. "If this deadlock continues," he warned, "there will be pressure inside my country to consider alternative methods, because the government will distrust my ability to accomplish anything." The Japanese interpreted that statement as a brinkmanship threat, paying little attention to it.

But Hwang was not present when consultations were held again on September 1 and 2. Representing North Korea instead was a fair-skinned man of medium height in his mid-forties. "I have been put in charge of the negotiations from now on," he politely informed the Japanese. "I hope we will have a good discussion." Similarly, Makita was replaced by Hitoshi Tanaka less than one month after that encounter.

Makita was a member of MOFA's so-called China School and therefore was regarded as a leader of the pro-China faction within the ministry. He was accused by pro-Taiwan members of the ruling Liberal Democratic Party (LDP) of having obstructed Japan's issuance of an entry visa to Lee Teng-hui, former president of the Republic of China, and of catering to the wishes of the People's Republic of China. As if being stoned out of town, Makita was appointed ambassador to Singapore. Meanwhile, Hwang simply disappeared. There were even rumors that he had been purged.

Tanaka met the new North Korean representative for the first time on November 17, 2001. All the Japanese, including Tanaka himself, considered the man gentle looking.[23] He later became known as "Mr. X." The meeting took place at the Swissotel in the vicinity of Labor Park in Dalian, China, a territory that had been leased to Imperial Russia late in the nineteenth century. Labor Park was built during that period. The representatives used the hotel's penthouse suite on the thirty-fifth floor, from which they could look out the window down on the Dalian railway station. They also could glimpse, further away on the right, between nearby skyscrapers, Dalian Harbor. After that first meeting, Dalian was the site of frequent secret meetings between Tanaka and X, although they used different hotels each time, respecting the wishes of the North Koreans. Also, because to rent a conference room would call undesired attention to their meetings, they always used a hotel suite, bringing in sofas, extra chairs, and a slightly oversized table.

The North Korean party did not arrive in a group; its members always came one by one. Inside the suite, they would always sit with their backs to the windows. The Japanese thought that it was unrealistic to fear that someone would sneak a look into a room on the thirty-fifth floor, but the North Koreans also asked that the room's curtains be closed before the talks began. Consequently, the meetings were always held with the sunlight blocked out.

X introduced himself as Kim Chul, a high-ranking member of the National Defense Commission. According to the North Korean constitution, "The National Defense Commission is the sovereignty's supreme guiding institution and the comprehensive managing institution for military affairs," and its very name strikes fear in the hearts of the North Korean people. The chairman of the commission is Kim Jong-il.

Tanaka presented his business card, but he did not receive X's card in return. X's subordinates addressed him as *Shiljangnim*, meaning "Mr. General Manager"; they never addressed him by his name. The preliminary consultation thus commenced with the Japanese uncertain of the real name of North Korea's top representative. But it may not have mattered what his real name was, because in North Korea a person's name is more an ID number or a code used within the system than proof of personal identity. The Japanese decided that X's conduct and the outcome of the negotiations would be more important than X's real name.

"This is the first time for me to engage in negotiations with a foreign government," X said at the outset. "But I am sure that you, Mr. Tanaka, are an old pro." When they were about to leave the negotiation table, X gave Tanaka his office and cell phone numbers. "These are my phone numbers," he said. "Please do not hesitate to contact me any time."

Once, at a later negotiation meeting, X remarked, "I am a military man." Tanaka took that as the truth. He had tried to narrow down X's background, deducing that there was no doubt that he was a military person, probably "a staff technocrat affiliated with the military, perhaps belonging to the reformist group." Tanaka found X to be quite different from the other Foreign Ministry or Workers' Party types whom he had previously encountered.[24] X was normally accompanied by two deputies and an interpreter. In sharp contrast to the fair-skinned X, the two deputies were deeply tanned. It is said that in North Korea high-ranking members of the Workers' Party or the National Defense Commission are, for the most part, fair-skinned people.[25] Moreover, X did not smoke, while both deputies would hastily light up their cigarettes when X left the room.

Although Tanaka tried various tricks to find out about X's career and background, X almost never talked about himself. He once subtly implied that his daughter went to a prestigious women's university, but he did not identify the university. One time he also said that he had been stationed in a francophone African country, but there was no way to verify that. However, X did understand French, and one time he actually told something like a joke in French.

CHECKING CREDIBILITY

All things considered, it was not the true identity or credentials of X that mattered. What mattered was his credibility—whether he was directly connected to Kim Jong-il and whether he was in a position to actually carry out whatever would be agreed on by the two sides. X repeatedly emphasized that he was his country's "sole route of negotiations with Japan." He seemed to be sending the message that North Korea would refrain from using other routes, such as the Workers' Party or the General Association of Korean Residents in Japan (Chosen Soren or simply Soren), and that therefore Japan should follow suit by negotiating only through him. To Tanaka and the Japanese, his words implied that he was delivering direct instructions to them from Kim Jong-il. But if that was indeed the case, it would be all the more important to confirm X's credibility. That would be the Japanese delegation's first priority.

At that time, Japan's vice minister for foreign affairs was Yoshiji Nogami. Nogami instructed Hitoshi Tanaka to ask the North Koreans to give him some "souvenir," by which Nogami meant some evidence of North Korea's sincerity that Tanaka could take back to Japan.[26] (Later Nogami and Foreign Minister Makiko Tanaka would clash and both of them would be forced to resign, following the traditional Japanese practice of punishing both parties to a fight. Nogami resigned as vice minister at the end of January 2002.)

However, in December 2001, almost immediately after the secret consultations had commenced, an unidentified vessel apparently was deliberately sunk by its crew just offshore of Amami-Oshima Island after being fired on by a Japanese coast guard ship for having violated Japan's territorial waters north of Okinawa. The ship seemingly self-destructed, exploding in Chinese territorial waters after being chased by Japan's coast guard. There was a strong suspicion that the mystery boat was a North Korean vessel. Tanaka demanded an explanation from X, who turned a deaf ear, saying, "My republic had nothing to do with it. Is there any evidence that it did?" Tanaka subsequently requested a further investigation into the incident but decided not to pursue the issue.

Although Tanaka refrained from referring to a "souvenir," he demanded that his counterpart "show some evidence of North Korea's sincere desire to improve relations with Japan and to settle the abduction issue."

The first evidence of North Korea's sincerity came in the form of the release of Takashi Sugishima, formerly a reporter with the *Nihon Keizai Shimbun,* who had been detained by North Korean authorities as a suspected spy. After retiring from the *Nihon Keizai Shimbun* in 1999, Sugishima entered North Korea in November of the same year, only to be arrested five days later. His activities, such as taking photos and making tape recordings, had aroused North Korean suspicions, and he was closely watched. After his arrest, the Korean Central News Agency reported that "the results of the investigation clearly prove that his espionage was conducted under a carefully worked out plan of the relevant organ of Japan and the South Korean authorities and obviously what he did was anti-DPRK espionage."[27]

Tanaka demanded that Sugishima be released. Because Japan's major concern was settlement of the abduction issue, a conclusive test of X's influence and credibility would be whether X could actually arrange for the release of an openly detained person. If Sugishima could not be released, there would be no hope of saving the abductees. "Show us first how much influence you have," Tanaka said to X. "Next, show us how seriously and sincerely you wish to promote the normalization of bilateral relations. But first we request the unconditional release of Mr. Sugishima." Negotiations toward that goal took place toward the end of 2001 and the beginning of 2002, and Sugishima was released on February 12, 2002. North Korea attached no conditions to his release. The timing coincided with the sixtieth birthday (February 16) of Kim Jong-il as well as with a trip to Japan, Korea, and China by President George W. Bush, who in his State of the Union address at the end of January had denounced North Korea as part of "an axis of evil." Bush arrived in Japan for a summit talk with Koizumi on February 18.

X passed the first test of his credibility. He could and did deliver. It also was obvious that he was well connected to North Korea's leaders. How directly he was connected to Kim Jong-il—whether he reported directly to Kim or through a superior who talked directly with Kim—remained uncertain. X rarely said, "I will ask Pyongyang's opinion," or "Let me take this back and respond later." Instead, he often made decisions on the spot, indicating that he had been given the discretionary authority to do so. X also was very well informed, making the Japanese wonder whether he was a member of a department that was a central clearinghouse for intelligence information.

The Japanese also were paying renewed attention to the tone of North Korean media reports concerning Japan and observed that criticism of Japan had been toned down since January 2002. There was hardly any criticism of Prime Minister Koizumi.[28] And in March 2002 a new development arose concerning the abductions. It was reported in the Japanese media that a former wife of one of the "Yodo-go" group, which hijacked a Japan Air Lines plane in 1970, had admitted to the police that the group, most of whom were residing in North Korea, had been responsible for planning and carrying out the abduction of a certain Keiko Arimoto, who had been officially registered by the Japanese government as an abduction victim. The woman admitted that she also was involved in the kidnapping.[29]

In 1970, nine members of the Japanese Red Army, which aimed for a worldwide revolution, had hijacked Fukuoka-bound JAL flight 351 (nicknamed Yodo-go) after it took off from Haneda Airport in Tokyo. It was the first airplane hijacking to take place in Japan. The plane first landed in Fukuoka and then flew to Gimpo International Airport, in South Korea, where the hijackers released all 129 hostages. The hijackers then had the plane fly to Pyongyang.[30] In response to the woman's confession, Japan's National Police Agency formally recognized Keiko Arimoto as a new North Korean abduction victim and set up a special team to investigate her case. In addition, Prime Minister Koizumi met with family members of the abduction victims and declared, "We will not negotiate to normalize diplomatic relations unless the abduction issue is satisfactorily settled." Koizumi set up a special task force consisting of deputy directors from relevant agencies, headed by Shinzo Abe, deputy chief cabinet secretary.[31] Backed by the heightened political attention and sensitivity to the abduction issue within Japan, Hitoshi Tanaka strongly demanded information about the abductees from the North Koreans.

On the evening of March 22, the Korean Central News Agency, while emphasizing that North Korea "was never engaged in the kidnapping or abduction of Keiko Arimoto," announced that the spokesperson of the North Korean Red Cross Society admitted that North Korea had "decided to continue the investigation into 'those missing'"[32] On that particular day, leaders of Japan and the Republic of Korea met in Seoul, and it was obvious that North Korea had timed the announcement to coincide with that particular meeting. That was the second piece of "evidence" that the North Koreans offered in response to Tanaka's request for assurance of their sincerity.

The remaining issue was whether a date for discussions between the Red Cross societies of the two countries could be promptly set. X suggested that the discussions should take place toward the end of April. That could be interpreted as a third piece of "evidence."

But Tanaka was not satisfied with the three pieces of evidence. He attempted further to have appropriate representatives of the North Korean Foreign Ministry directly involved in the upcoming Red Cross discussions in order to make the meetings more official. He suggested that North Korea's first deputy foreign minister, Kang Sok-ju, who was believed to be a close confidant of Kim Jong-il, participate in one of the sessions. X avoided answering on the spot, but he said that they would consider that proposal. Soon thereafter, X conveyed North Korea's consent.

On April 6, 2002, the secret meeting was held in Kuala Lumpur, with Kang in attendance. X and Kang did not come together. Kang arrived by himself, while X was accompanied by two deputies, as usual. During the discussion, only Kang spoke; X remained silent. What Kang said was essentially the same as what X had said earlier. He criticized the immorality of Japan's colonization of Korea prior to World War II and loudly demanded compensation. During the discussion, Kang and X did not exchange any words. Although X remained in the room for a while after the meeting, Kang left the room immediately after the discussion. Tanaka noted that the two men seemed to keep each other at arm's length, but that might have been a precaution that the North Koreans had taken so that the two would not exchange any honorific expressions or use modes of speech that would make the nature of their relationship clear to the Japanese. The important discovery for Japan was that X was capable of having Kang sent to the negotiation table. That would have been impossible unless X had direct access to Kim Jong-il.

At the same time that Hitoshi Tanaka was checking X's credibility, X was checking Tanaka's. The North Koreans must have been coolly observing Tanaka to see how influential he really was. Tanaka knew that his counterpart would never negotiate earnestly unless Tanaka could prove that he too was capable of fulfilling whatever commitments he made and that he was directly connected to Japan's top leadership. With that in mind, Tanaka decided to visit the office of the prime minister frequently. According to the daily prime minister's log, as reported in the *Asahi Shimbun,* Tanaka met with Koizumi more than eighty times in the prime minister's office from September 2001 to September 2002. (In contrast, the director general of MOFA's Bureau of North American Affairs met Koizumi twenty-five times at the latter's office during the same period.) Tanaka's maneuver to get extensive exposure through the newspaper's reports of the prime minister's daily log was intended to show the North Koreans that he could meet and talk with the Japanese prime minister whenever and wherever he wished. Tanaka also told X so directly. "Please read the Japanese newspapers carefully," he said. "If you look at the daily records of the prime minister's log for Friday and Monday, the days before and after I met with you, you'll find my name there."[33]

Nevertheless, it was not at all easy for the two to build mutual confidence. Initially, X did not hide his bewilderment about Koizumi as the political leader of Japan. He candidly asked, "What are Prime Minister Koizumi's real views?" Koizumi seemed to be a right-wing politician. In his campaign to become prime minister, for example, he had said that it was the prime minister's duty to visit Yasukuni Shrine, and then, moreover, he had actually done so. And yet Koizumi seemed determined to promote normalization of diplomatic relations between Japan and North Korea, which the right wing would surely find repugnant. Was he serious and sincere, or did he have some ulterior motive?

The Yasukuni Shrine issue is deeply intertwined with complicated and delicate history issues between Japan and the Korean Peninsula. X once confessed, "This is a private matter, but my grandfather was killed by the Japanese, so I hold deep resentment toward Japan," and he also mentioned that his grandmother had a Japanese name. He did not disclose the name and Tanaka did not pursue the issue. During the period when Imperial Japan occupied Korea, Koreans were forced to give up their names and use Japanese names instead, and it was recorded that close to 80 percent of Koreans changed their names. X also repeatedly raised the issue of Koreans having been uprooted and moved to Japan to serve as forced labor. "Japan moved 6 million Koreans to Japan for use as forced labor, and the Koreans had to undergo unbearable humiliation there," X said. "How will Japan take responsibility for what it did to these people?" Japan had indeed conscripted a large number of Korean citizens in what the Japanese called a "civilian draft" in order to supply labor to labor-deficient Japanese companies. There are various accounts regarding the number of Koreans who were transported for that purpose.[34] The North Koreans had previously referred to a figure of 8.4 million, but this was the first time that 6 million had been mentioned. X never offered evidence supporting that claim. But Tanaka decided to let his counterpart speak his mind, and he refrained from questioning X and antagonizing him about it.

NEGOTIATIONS IN DANGER OF COLLAPSE

Only once did X bring up an irrelevant issue in the course of a discussion. That was the bankruptcy of the Chogin Tokyo Credit Union (better known in Japan by its abbreviated form, Chogin). Toward the end of 2001, the Tokyo District Prosecutor's Office indicted a former treasurer of the General Association of Korean Residents in Japan (Chosen Soren) on suspicion of embezzlement in conjunction with the diversion of funds from Chogin, a financial institution run by North Korean residents in Japan. As a result, the Japanese government had to inject ¥600 billion in public funds into Chogin branches throughout Japan in order to save Chogin from bankruptcy. Japanese investigative authorities suspected that Chogin funds illegally diverted by Chosen Soren may have been sent to North Korea, which also would have been illegal. The authorities carried out an investigation, suspecting that behind Chogin was Chosen Soren, behind which, in turn, was North Korea.[35]

North Korea was very nervous about the investigation, and X asked repeatedly whether there was anything that the Japanese could do to interfere with it. He looked desperate, but he did not seem to care how he looked. Each time he raised the issue, Tanaka spurned his request: "It should be obvious to you that there is absolutely nothing we can do about this issue," he said. "Besides, that is not a subject of our negotiations." It was quite obvious that X kept on raising the issue because of instructions from above.

By spring of 2002, both sides were able to confirm the scenario for negotiations on normalization of the two nations' diplomatic relations. It was agreed that on the surface the abduction issue would be handled through dialogue between the two Red Cross societies, but in reality possible solutions would be pursued through the secret meetings between Tanaka and X. The approach would be to narrow the differences first, then pass the results upward for discussion at meetings of senior officials, then at ministerial-level meetings, and, hopefully, eventually at the summit-talk level.

Nonetheless, it was not easy to prepare a framework for achieving concrete solutions. Tanaka insisted that the negotiations would not move forward until, first, North Korea acknowledged the abductions, disclosed all pertinent information relating thereto, and released and returned all the surviving abductees; second, Kim Jong-il apologized for the abductions; and third, all of those responsible for the abductions were properly punished. Talks on economic assistance could start only after those prerequisites were fulfilled. Without a satisfactory explanation of the abduction issue, Japan's Diet would never approve an appropriation for economic aid to North Korea. As for Prime Minister Koizumi's visit to Pyongyang, if it were conceivable at all, it would not be possible unless North Korea were to provide satisfactory information about the abductees.

X, in turn, persisted in his stance that settlement of the abduction issue would be difficult unless Japan explicitly indicated the amount of compensation that it would pay to North Korea, a condition that Japan would never accept. The argument about the abductions went around and around in circles. Occasionally, there were Zen-like exchanges between X and Tanaka. X would say, "Japan can't see the forest for the trees," and Tanaka would retort, "But the forest is made of the trees." In the course of this go-round, X seemed to become suspicious of Tanaka, who kept bringing up the abductions.

Tanaka referred to the possibility of a visit to Pyongyang by Koizumi as only one of the possible scenarios. At the outset, Tanaka had presented X with Japan's three basic conditions for entering into negotiations and requested North Korea's acceptance of them: first, participants in the negotiations would speak in their private capacities and could always retract their statements; second, any secret agreements that they reached must, without exception, be confirmed through formal channels; and third, strict confidentiality must be observed throughout the entire process.[36] In the course of negotiations with X, Tanaka never looked down to read from or to check the papers that he brought with him, in that way sending the message that he did not wish to be constrained by what had been written on paper. Moreover, he wished to emphasize the conditions of retraction at will and strict confidentiality. The suggestion that Koizumi might visit

Pyongyang was, therefore, nothing more than a remark by Tanaka in his personal capacity and one that could be withdrawn at any time.

On May 8, 2002, five North Korean nationals attempted to rush into the Japanese Consulate in Shenyang, China, but Chinese security police detained them. A Japanese member of a nongovernmental organization who was there took a video of armed Chinese policemen grabbing five asylum seekers and whisking them off the consulate property, a scene that was broadcast by all the TV stations in Japan. The Japanese government protested to the Chinese government on the grounds that the Chinese action constituted a violation of the Vienna Treaty provision regarding the inviolability of diplomatic properties. China replied that the security policemen merely had been preventing unknown persons from intruding into the Japanese Consulate and thus had been protecting the security of the diplomatic premises. The tension between the two countries immediately heightened.

The next round of secret negotiations between Tanaka and X was scheduled to be held toward the end of the same week, on May 11 and 12. But on May 10 the Japanese requested that the meeting be postponed by one week, until May 18 and 19. The North Koreans were furious at having to reschedule at such a late date, especially because they had already arrived in Beijing, where the negotiations were to take place. But the rescheduling could not be avoided. Tanaka was in Japan, fully occupied in dealing with the tense situation with China, making it absolutely impossible for him to sneak out to Beijing. This was the first discordant incident in the previously unhampered negotiations.

Throughout the Shenyang incident, Japan's Ministry of Foreign Affairs was a target of highly critical public opinion because of the ministry's de facto policy of rejection of the asylum seekers, and some critics demanded that Tanaka be fired. That was the first trying time that he had experienced since becoming director general. On the rescheduled dates of May 18 and 19, the Japanese and North Korean negotiators met in Shanghai. Hoping to prepare an environment that would make it easier for China to release the detained escapees, Tanaka asked X to persuade North Korea to urgently but secretly convey its intention not to disagree with the decision of the Chinese and Japanese governments on how to deal with the asylum seekers. At that request, X grinned but remained silent. In two weeks, the Chinese government released the five escapees, who subsequently went to the Republic of Korea via the Philippines. The North Korean media simply ignored the incident.

Toward the end of their two-day consultation, X suddenly and unilaterally declared that the next round of negotiations would be canceled. That was the first time that that sort of thing had happened. In response to Japan's demand for an explanation, X simply referred to "domestic reasons." Tanaka stretched his imagination, speculating that perhaps, among other possibilities, North Korea was revising its position regarding the normalization of diplomatic relations, but he had no clue as to what was really happening.

Bilateral negotiations were next held on June 1 and 2 in Dalian. In that round, X demanded much more forcefully than before that Japan's prime minister visit North Korea. X even declared that further discussions would be a waste of time unless he were to receive a firm commitment from Tanaka regarding such a visit. Tanaka, on the other hand, did not change his original stance: a visit to Pyongyang by the prime minister would be inconceivable without satisfactory information from North Korea concerning the abductees.

X did not hide his annoyance, and his suspicions regarding Japan's intentions appeared to have deepened. "So, that was it, just as I suspected," he might well have been thinking. "Their only purpose in negotiating was to draw as much information as possible from us about the abductees, using Koizumi's visit as bait." X then accused Tanaka of trying to deceive him and proclaimed, "We have no recourse but to terminate these negotiations."

Tanaka calmly responded, "That is fine with us."

Both sides had tried to wrap a rope around the other and tie it up, so to speak, like a spider ensnaring an insect caught in its web. Although in the course of the negotiations there had been moments of human warmth, those were past.

Koizumi's Decision to Visit Pyongyang

The very next day, on June 3, Tanaka related to Koizumi the essence of what had happened. "I am prepared to visit North Korea even though they haven't provided us with satisfactory information about the abductees," Koizumi responded. "If they will provide that information only if I visit them, I can go along with that."[37]

Thus, for the first time during the negotiation process, Tanaka was in a position in which he could use the "Pyongyang visit" card. However, he did not do so immediately. Rather, he waited for two weeks, after which time the North Koreans telephoned to say that they wished to resume the negotiations. It seemed that they had started worrying that Japan might withdraw altogether from attempts at normalization. It was then agreed that the next round of talks would be on July 6 and 7, again in Dalian.

Shortly thereafter, on July 1, North Korea announced the launching of a series of "economic measures," including the suspension of price controls. The Japanese conjectured that the reason for the sudden change in North Korea's attitude—which X might have referred to previously as "domestic reasons"— was that the North Koreans realized that diplomatic normalization and economic cooperation with Japan were essential to the success of their economic reforms.

The negotiations were entering a crucial stage. This time the bargaining took place with Koizumi's Pyongyang visit as a given. Tanaka demanded, as a prerequisite to the visit, that North Korea acknowledge and apologize for the abductions as well as provide truthful information about the abductees and firm assurance that they would be released.

X did not refuse his demands outright. "As a scenario, they are within the bounds of possibilities," he conceded. Tanaka followed up by requesting X to convey directly to Kim Jong-il the essence of the Japanese conditions; moreover, he requested that they be incorporated in the draft of the Pyongyang Declaration. X adamantly rejected that request, saying that it would be Kim Jong-il himself who would determine what would be incorporated in the declaration. Nonetheless, he carefully chose his words to give the impression that information about the abductees could be disclosed if and when Koizumi visited Pyongyang. At the same time, X adamantly insisted that the draft explicitly include the amount of Japan's compensation for its colonization of Korea and "drafting" of laborers. Tanaka adamantly refused to specify any such amount. X stressed that North Korea had to have some idea of the size of the compensation in order to proceed toward normalization of relations, and he once again requested that an amount be indicated.

Tanaka pushed back. "We can't do that," he said. "If no compensation amount means no visit, then that's that."

X nevertheless remained obsessed with the amount of compensation. "As long as you explicitly tell us the specific amount," he would say, "it does not have to be included in the declaration." Tanaka refused that request point blank. He was under strict orders from Koizumi not to mention any amount whatsoever. "Don't compromise there at any cost," Koizumi had told him. "Just repeat 'We can't.'"[38] Koizumi had vowed never to repeat Shin Kanemaru's mistake.[39]

So, between "Give us information about the abductees" and "Tell us the amount," the discussion went round and round in circles, while time ticked away.

On one occasion, X, looking desperate, said, "The worst that could happen to you is dismissal. My situation is much more serious. My life might be at stake."

It was during a short talk toward the final stage of the negotiations, when Koizumi's visit became more or less confirmed, that both sides brought up the possibility of exchanging special envoys. There were some indications that X was considering Kang Sok-ju as the DPRK candidate. Tanaka also thought that exchanging special envoys might not be such a bad idea. Believing that a former foreign minister in whom he had long placed his personal trust would make an ideal envoy, he brought the idea to Koizumi. However, Koizumi showed no interest whatsoever. He curtly replied, "If we send a politician as special envoy, he will surely make concessions, whoever we send." Besides, he continued, "Politicians talk"—as if he were not one of them.[40] The idea of a special envoy was shelved.

More obstacles were waiting for the Japanese. There was the unsettled issue of salvaging a mystery vessel that had been scuttled toward the end of the previous year, described earlier in this chapter.[41] China cautioned Japan to exercise restraint in dealing with North Korea. However, because the vessel went down in Chinese waters, this was also an issue outstanding between China and Japan. The Japanese government decided to raise the ship on June 21. To make matters worse, on June 29, North Korean and South Korean soldiers exchanged gunfire on the Yellow Sea, heightening the tensions over North Korea. It was conceivable that when the Japanese government decided to salvage the vessel, North Korea would react with strong displeasure. But the North Koreans did not make any fuss about it.

On July 12, 2002, Tanaka briefed Koizumi on the result of his negotiations with X, to which Koizumi replied, "Stay the course." That was a clear indication that Koizumi had peremptorily made up his mind to visit North Korea.

In July 2002, the secret negotiations entered the last stretch. At a ministerial meeting at the ASEAN Regional Forum (ARF) held in Brunei, Foreign Minister Yoriko Kawaguchi met Foreign Minister Paek Nam-sun of North Korea. A joint statement circulated after the talk explicitly described the abduction issue as a "pending humanitarian issue."[42] Two years earlier, Foreign Minister Paek, in a meeting with Yohei Kono, Japan's foreign minister at that time, had strongly opposed such wording. Thus, the joint statement reflected a sea change in North Korea's position.

On August 18 and 19, discussions between the Japanese and North Korean Red Cross societies were held in Pyongyang. During the meetings, the North Koreans explained that they had been investigating the whereabouts of the missing Japanese nationals much more deeply and comprehensively than before, and they promised to further expedite the investigation.

On August 25 and 26, also in Pyongyang, a meeting among the directors general of the foreign ministries of the two countries was convened. Tanaka participated in the meeting, and on August 25 he paid a courtesy visit to Prime Minister Hong Song-nam to convey Koizumi's message to Kim Jong-il. This message read, "We will sincerely tackle the normalization issue and other unresolved issues involving our countries. We expect nothing less than the same from your side."[43] Hong tried to maintain composure while pretending to comprehend the situation, which he obviously did not grasp at all. The key players were X and Kang Sok-ju.[44]

Tanaka and the other members of the Japanese delegation subsequently visited the North Korean Foreign Ministry to pay a courtesy visit to Kang Sok-ju. Kang told Tanaka that Kim Jong-il had already read Koizumi's message and had instructed Kang to convey his reaction: "The message was very encouraging, and I wish to express my gratitude to Prime Minister Koizumi." Kang proudly added, "This is a message sent directly from Chairman Kim aboard his train in

Siberia."[45] At that time, Kim Jong-il was on his way home from a summit talk with President Putin in Vladivostok.

After the courtesy visit, without being informed of his destination, Tanaka was taken by car to a mansion where negotiations were resumed over dinner. A small group made up of Tanaka, Kang Sok-ju, X, and a few others participated. Kang again demanded an explicit indication of the amount of compensation; Tanaka again refused. Kang next referred to an amount that North Korea demanded as reparation, to which Tanaka refused to respond. The amount Kang referred to was said to be a round figure in excess of $10 billion. Tanaka found out that Kang had known the details and implications of the previous exchanges between Tanaka and X. Tanaka was again reminded that within the North Korean foreign ministry only Kang was in direct contact with Kim Jong-il.

JAPAN'S "PIED PIPER OF HAMELIN"

It was in 1987 that Tanaka was first involved with North Korea, when, as MOFA's director of Northeast Asian affairs, he had to deal with the aftermath of the downing of a Korean Airline (KAL) jet due to an on-board explosion. The jet, bound for Seoul, disappeared off Burma after taking off from Baghdad. Prior to that, when it touched down in Abu Dhabi, a couple had gotten off who were found to possess forged Japanese passports. While being interrogated, the two attempted to poison themselves. The man died, but the woman survived. The woman, named Kim Hyon-hui, was taken to Seoul. The South Korean government subsequently announced that the KAL flight had been sabotaged by two North Korean agents.

Tanaka flew to Seoul and interviewed Kim Hyon-hui. He felt a shiver of fear upon learning that North Korea had attempted to entangle Japan in the sabotage. North Korean agents could have posed as South Koreans if their sole aim was to blow up a KAL airplane, but they had impersonated Japanese so that the explosion would seem to be a Japanese terrorist attack on South Korea. Tanaka sensed in that attempt the deep-seated animosity that the Korean people felt toward Japan.[46]

Kim Hyon-hui's testimony led to the discovery of the existence of a Lee Eun-hye, a Japanese woman who had been Kim's Japanese instructor. In 1991, Japan's National Police Agency declared that there was a strong possibility that Lee Eun-hye actually was Yaeko Taguchi, a Japanese national who was believed to have been abducted by North Korea. In 1997, the Japanese government officially recognized Lee Eun-hye as Yaeko Taguchi and a victim of North Korean abduction.[47]

A nuclear crisis involving North Korea then erupted, continuing into 1994. It was the largest security crisis yet faced by postwar Japan. North Korea threatened Japan, South Korea, and the United States, saying that it could and would make

Seoul a "sea of fire." In response, the Japanese government, led by Nobuo Ishihara, deputy chief cabinet secretary, conducted simulations of North Korean invasions of South Korea. As a result, it became sadly obvious that Japan was not prepared for such a scenario and had no deterrent to use in such a situation. Tanaka, as director of policy coordination in MOFA's Foreign Policy Bureau, engaged himself in preparing a "crisis management plan."[48]

The nuclear crisis was temporarily contained by the signing of the U.S.-DPRK Agreed Framework, which proposed providing North Korea with light-water reactors if it would halt its nuclear programs. Tanaka participated in the launching of the Korean Peninsula Energy Development Organization (KEDO), an international organization created to arrange for provision of the reactors to North Korea.

Another major task for Tanaka as MOFA's director of policy coordination was to handle Japan's efforts to come to terms with its history. In 1995, the Japanese government, commemorating the fiftieth anniversary of the end of World War II, launched three major initiatives, one after another: the Peace, Friendship, and Exchange Initiative; a statement by the prime minister expressing remorse and apologizing for Japan's past wrongdoings; and establishment of the Asian Women's Fund.[49] Tanaka was involved in all three of the initiatives, and during the negotiations with X, he tried both to share with X a sense of their being mutual stakeholders in peaceful coexistence between the two countries and to assure X that he had gone through a similar process before. He was convinced that normalization of DPRK-Japan relations would be inconceivable unless they shared the same vision of regional order, in which both sides could coexist peacefully.

Tanaka used to say, "We've got to prepare a way out"—that is, prepare an exit strategy. In his vision of the future, Japan and the United States would normalize diplomatic ties with North Korea in exchange for the latter's abandonment of its nuclear program. Negotiations for normalization between Japan and North Korea would be linked to the framework of regional multilateral processes, and the abduction issue would be settled within the context of those processes. After both sides went through all the processes, they would suddenly realize that they had already gotten out of the maze of intransigence and hostility.

Tanaka negotiated hard down to the last minute before Koizumi's visit to make North Korea agree to disclose information about the abductees. But if his efforts did not succeed, Tanaka was prepared to shift the focus of the negotiations in order to obtain as many concessions as possible from North Korea, such as North Korea's agreement both to allow Japan to achieve "settlement of the past" through economic cooperation and to engage in a regular bilateral security dialogue. He was, in other words, pursuing a comprehensive, multifaceted approach—a "grand bargain."[50]

In order to advance that grand bargain, however, a series of smaller bargains had to be made in one way or another with people and groups that had vested interests in domestic decisionmaking in Japan. After Tanaka's first meeting with X on November 17, 2001, Tanaka suggested to Yoshiji Nogami, vice minister at the Ministry of Foreign Affairs, that Tanaka be authorized to pursue secret negotiations toward achieving diplomatic normalization. In spite of his usual aggressiveness, Nogami was, for once, cautious. "This is too much for MOFA," he told Tanaka. But Nogami continued to go over possible scenarios. It would be too risky for MOFA bureaucrats to suggest the idea to their superiors, because it would become an easy target of the conservative elements in the legislature, who would not welcome the normalization of diplomatic relations with North Korea. If that occurred, there was a strong possibility that Prime Minister Koizumi would not accept the idea because of the political risk that it might involve. It would be one thing if MOFA made a suggestion in response to inquiries from high above, but if the proposal originated with MOFA, the ministry might be forced to take full blame if the proposed activities did not yield the expected fruit.

Besides, there was the "Makiko issue." At that time, Makiko Tanaka was Japan's foreign minister, and she and the ministry were in a showdown over personnel and budgetary matters. If Hitoshi Tanaka reported secret negotiations with North Korea to Makiko Tanaka, she might leak the information, making the negotiations impossible. The United States would intervene to kill the plan.[51]

Hitoshi Tanaka was in close consultation with Yasuo Fukuda, chief cabinet secretary, and Teijiro Furukawa, deputy chief cabinet secretary. Furukawa, who sat at the top of Japan's central bureaucracy, had been in charge of the administrative functions of the office of the prime minister since 1995, serving five prime ministers, including Koizumi. During his tenure, he had dealt with such difficult issues as the Hanshin-Awaji earthquake in Kobe, the sarin gas attack in the Tokyo subway system, relocation of the U.S. Marine Corps Futenma Air Base in Okinawa, and reorganization of the central bureaucracy.[52] Fukuda also had instructed Tanaka to consult with Furukawa before deciding anything. He said, "When it comes to the prime minister's visit to North Korea, a great many matters will be involved, including the handling of the abduction issue and domestic politics. If Furukawa said he had not been informed, that would be the end of it. However, if one could get Furukawa involved, he could become a protective shield if something unexpected happened."[53] Fukuda had immeasurable faith in Furukawa.

When Furukawa heard what Tanaka had to say, he said, "Mr. Tanaka, there is something called a cause. And normalization of diplomatic relations with North Korea is a cause."[54] If the abducted Japanese nationals, or at least some of them, were believed to be alive in North Korea, bringing back as many of them as possible—an act taken to protect the lives and property of Japanese citizens—would be a cause. Creating peace in Northeast Asia by normalizing relations with North Korea would be another.[55] Tanaka did not always report everything to Furukawa, but he once confessed to Furukawa that he could breathe freely when he was in Furukawa's office. When Tanaka was deeply discouraged by the stalling of the negotiations in May through June of 2002, Furukawa was there to cheer him up.[56]

Now that Tanaka's idea was endorsed by Furukawa, the head of Japan's entire bureaucracy, Tanaka was able to bring the proposal to conduct secret negotiations to the attention of Prime Minister Koizumi as a possible prime minister's initiative. Hearing Tanaka's report in late 2001, Koizumi explicitly ordered Tanaka to proceed but to maintain strict confidentiality, which Koizumi believed to be more essential when dealing with an autocratic state like North Korea than with other nations. Koizumi instructed Fukuda to confine knowledge of the proposal to essential individuals only and to have the Foreign Ministry take responsibility for ensuring that its personnel maintained secrecy.

The thorny issue was what to do with Deputy Chief Cabinet Secretary Shinzo Abe. It would be difficult to keep Abe out of the scheme, because he had been zealously tackling the abduction issue. But Koizumi was of the opinion that Abe could be informed of the secret negotiations with North Korea after Koizumi's visit to Pyongyang was officially announced on August 30. Fukuda did not consider it proper to do that, so he persuaded Koizumi that Abe should be informed before the official announcement. As a result, Abe was briefed about the secret negotiations by Fukuda on August 29, one day before the official announcement.

In January 2002, Vice Minister Nogami resigned, and he was succeeded by Yukio Takeuchi. In the course of "passing the baton," Nogami informed Takeuchi about the plan. Takeuchi remarked to Nogami, "Hitoshi Tanaka is scary. He acts like the pied piper of Hamelin. If you follow his lead, charmed by his pied pipe, you might end up in the river."[57] The secret plan of Tanaka, the pied piper, was limited to a very small number of people, namely Koizumi, Fukuda, and Furukawa and Bessho at the office of the prime minister and Nogami (and, later, Takeuchi) and Kenji Hiramatsu at MOFA. When Yoriko Kawaguchi succeeded Makiko Tanaka as foreign minister, she, too, joined the club.

It was toward the end of August 2002 that Tanaka finally informed the directors general of MOFA's major bureaus of the secret negotiations for normalizing diplomatic relations with North Korea. On the evening of August 21, Takeuchi called to his office Shotaro Yachi, director general of the Foreign Policy Bureau; Ichiro Fujisaki, director general of the North American Affairs Bureau; Shin Ebihara, director general of the Treaties Bureau; and Hitoshi Tanaka. Takeuchi said, "I apologize for having gone this far without informing you earlier. I'd like you to know, however, that we have had the prime minister's consent regarding this." The draft of the Pyongyang Declaration was distributed among those present. Takeuchi asked Tanaka to explain further. Tanaka apologized again before starting the explanation.

After the briefing, Yachi asked, "What about the settlement of the abduction issue? This draft does not directly refer to the abductions. Will we allow this?" Tanaka replied, "Please leave it to me. I have already obtained the prime minister's approval." Then Ebihara asked, "How did you explain this to the United States?" Tanaka replied, "We need to start working on that. Richard Armitage is coming to Tokyo in one week to attend the U.S.-Japan Strategic Dialogue, and Mr. Takeuchi can brief him directly then."

After that, Takeuchi's office was filled with a heavy silence.[58] There was no further discussion.

THE JAPAN-DPRK PYONGYANG DECLARATION

By the time that Koizumi's plan to visit Pyongyang was announced, the full text of the draft of the Pyongyang Declaration had been prepared. At the earlier debriefing in Takeuchi's office, Tanaka had assured the other officials that "the prime minister has already approved the substance of this draft." In order to complete the draft, however, they had to have the cooperation of MOFA's Treaties Bureau (later renamed the International Legal Affairs Bureau).

Among the Japanese present at the meeting of senior officials held in Pyongyang on August 25 and 26 were MOFA's Keiichi Hayashi, the Treaties Bureau's deputy director general, and Naoko Saiki, director of the Treaties Bureau's Regulations Division. While it was originally planned that they would conduct the fine-tuning of the Pyongyang Declaration during this visit, they had to postpone it because they had more to discuss on the abduction and the compensation issues. Consequently, officials from the Treaties Bureau had no role to play while in Pyongyang.

Senior officials of the Treaties Bureau became angry, suspecting that Tanaka did not wish to expose his counterpart, X, to senior officials of other bureaus. The Treaties Bureau director general, Ebihara, protested to Tanaka, declaring, "The Treaties Bureau will take no part in this task." Tanaka disagreed with the Treaties Bureau's argument. He was of the view that the Treaties Bureau's task in this endeavor was to attend to technical details regarding treaty obligations and their relationship to those in other treaties and not to interfere with the substance of the negotiations.

Perhaps partly because of Ebihara's outburst, Takao Akiba, director of MOFA's Treaty Division, was invited to participate in the bilateral finalization of the draft, which took place in Beijing after the August 30 announcement of Koizumi's upcoming Pyongyang visit.[59]

The Pyongyang Declaration consists of four articles. The first article expresses a strong determination to "make every possible effort for early normalization of relations." The North Koreans had suggested that the declaration be called a "declaration concerning diplomatic normalization." They wanted to follow the path of the Japan-China Joint Declaration of 1972, which immediately led to the normalization of bilateral diplomatic relations, by giving the declaration a name that would have a great impact. The Japanese, however, insisted that the declaration remain a declaration of political intention on the part of both Japan and North Korea to strive for normalization in the future; they did not want to declare, with great fanfare, that relations had been normalized. In the end, the Japanese position was adopted on this particular issue.

What did the "early" in "early normalization" mean? North Korea had conveyed to Japan its wish to achieve normalization within the year 2002. Although that was a highly unrealistic goal, there was a moment of enthusiasm within Japan in the immediate afterglow of the announcement of Koizumi's visit, when the Japanese leadership hoped to complete the negotiations within the year in order to ratify the draft treaty in the Diet's 2003 ordinary session. Although the North Koreans strongly insisted on setting a specific deadline, the Japanese refused to do so. Koizumi and Tanaka shared the vague idea that if everything worked out as planned, normalization could be accomplished within one or two years.

Fukuda was much more cautious. Recounting those days, he said, "It took fourteen years [through seven rounds of negotiations from 1951 to 1965] for Japan to finally sign the Japan-ROK Basic Treaty. Therefore, I thought we could also take time to normalize relations with North Korea." "We also had to consider the apprehension of some in the U.S. government concerning the speed of the normalization process," he continued. "However, if we told the North Koreans outright that we would not hurry to conclude the negotiations, they would not respond positively. It is common sense to set a time limit in this kind of negotiation, but we dared not do that. Taking all these things into consideration, we inserted the word 'early' in the declaration. It was intended to mean 'as early as necessary conditions are made ready.'"[60]

The second article states that "the Japanese regard, in a spirit of humility, the fact of history that Japan caused tremendous damage and suffering to the people of Korea through its colonial rule in the past, and express deep remorse and heartfelt apology." Japan has a heavy responsibility for its role in the history of the Korean peninsula. It had failed to sufficiently express its remorse and sense of responsibility in the earlier Japan-ROK Basic Treaty, and that failure had long left Koreans with ill feelings toward Japan. In contrast, the Pyongyang Declaration is very clear and explicit. That part of the declaration was modeled after a 1995 statement by Prime Minister Tomiichi Murayama (widely known as the Murayama Statement) to commemorate the fiftieth anniversary of the end of World War II:

"During a certain period in the not too distant past, Japan . . . caused tremendous damage and suffering to the people of many countries, particularly to those of Asian nations. . . . I regard, in a spirit of humility, these irrefutable facts of history, and express here once again my feelings of deep remorse and state my heartfelt apology."[61]

"Apology" was the word that the North Koreans were obsessed with most. They had envisioned using Koizumi's visit as a political show; after all, the prime minister of a U.S. ally was coming to Pyongyang to apologize. However, Japan, although it recognized well the necessity for an apology, insisted on the apology being directed to the Korean people; it could never be an apology to the North Korean government.[62] The North Koreans translated the Japanese word *owabi* (apology) as the Korean word for "atonement."[63] *Owabi* is not atonement, which could imply legal responsibility. The issue was not a simple matter of translation; it concerned a decision having a clear political intention.

Nevertheless, Japan, fully aware of the implications, did not oppose the Korean translation. For one thing, in the Japan–Republic of Korea Joint Declaration, which President Kim Dae-jung and Prime Minister Keizo Obuchi announced in 1998, the South Korean government had translated the Japanese *owabi* to mean *atonement,* and North Korea knew of that maneuver. Japan decided, as with the declaration of 1998, that "this Korean word for *atonement* is not used here to imply legal responsibility. As a matter of fact, in the Pyongyang Declaration, North Korea agreed to 'mutually waive all its property and claims' and agreed to accept economic cooperation in place of compensation."[64]

It should be noted that there actually was some uneasiness and opposition within the Japanese government over the inclusion of an "apology" to North Korea in an official document. When Tanaka debriefed a small number of high-ranking MOFA officials in late August, Shin Ebihara, director general of the Treaties Bureau, challenged him. "Of all the countries with which Japan has bilateral relations, the Republic of Korea has been the only one to which Japan apologized formally in an official document," he said. "We decided to include 'apology' in that official document because we truly wished to build a future-oriented relationship with the Republic of Korea. Are you sure that North Korea deserves the same treatment?" Ebihara, as personal secretary to Prime Minister Keizo Obuchi, had been heavily involved in the drafting of the "apology document" published by the Japanese government on the occasion of the Japan-ROK Summit of 1998, the so-called "Japan-ROK reconciliation summit." Ebihara further charged, "That this expression is the same as the expression used in the Murayama Statement is not good enough." Tanaka brushed aside Ebihara's challenge, simply saying, "I have already obtained the prime minister's approval concerning this matter."[65]

Ebihara was not the only one who was apprehensive about "apology." After Koizumi's trip, Tanaka visited Masahiko Komura, foreign minister at the time of the Japan-ROK reconciliation summit, to report on the trip. "Although I support the Pyongyang Declaration on the whole, I cannot agree with the insertion of the apology," Komura told him. "Why did you apologize to North Korea in the official document, when we have not yet apologized to China?" Tanaka replied, "Japan fought a war with China, but Japan colonized the Korean peninsula." "You are wrong," Komura retorted. "We included an apology in the Japan-ROK Joint Statement of 1998 because Kim Dae-jung had promised, for the sake of a future-oriented relationship with Japan, that the Republic of Korea would never bring up the history issue if Japan agreed to apologize in the official document. Jiang Zemin did not offer the same promise, and that's why we have not apologized to China in the official document."[66]

Although the Pyongyang Declaration states that "the Japanese regard, in a spirit of humility, the facts of history," implying Japan's historical responsibility, the Japanese persisted in the view that the wording in no way pointed to legal responsibility. At the same time, the wording matched the refusal of the North Koreans to include in the declaration their "apologies" regarding the abductions of Japanese citizens. They insisted, instead, on stating that "it would take appropriate measures so that these regrettable incidents . . . will never happen in the future."

The second article of the declaration also clearly states that Japan will provide North Korea with economic assistance after normalization of relations. During preliminary negotiations with X, Tanaka stressed the significance of economic cooperation, citing as examples Japan's earlier successful economic cooperation with China and Vietnam. In that exchange, Tanaka took time to explain repeatedly that economic assistance would be provided on a project basis and that Japan would provide North Korea goods and services but not cash. X had for a while come close to accepting the economic assistance proposal but then, probably under strong pressure from above, reverted to persisting in demanding the inclusion of "reparations" and "compensation."[67]

In the negotiations leading to normalization of Japan-ROK relations, both sides had agreed on economic aid totaling US$500 million. When Shin Kanemaru, LDP strongman, visited Pyongyang in 1990, it was rumored that he might offer economic aid on the order of US$8 billion to US$8.5 billion. In the negotiations with the North Koreans, while they referred to an "amount over $10 billion," the Japanese consistently refused even to negotiate on the issue; the Pyongyang Declaration therefore contained no specific figure. Neither was there any backroom deal or subtle oral agreement. The Japanese had been consistent on the matter from the beginning to the end. Yasuo Fukuda later stated that "there had been rumors of strange figures with respect to the amount of compensation or economic cooperation. Economic cooperation with North Korea would not be implemented by simply providing X amount of cash in the vicinity of a few trillion yen. We were extra careful when we drafted the economic cooperation portion of the declaration, and I think it is well written. I also was surprised when North Korea agreed to it."[68]

The declaration stipulates that economic cooperation will begin after diplomatic normalization, but it would be difficult to normalize the relationship unless outstanding issues—including the abductions and North Korea's missile launchings and nuclear development program—were settled. In the context of the entire document, the portion on economic cooperation was almost disproportionately specific. The North Koreans made Japan present a specific framework for economic cooperation because Japan failed to include an amount for reparations and compensation. The Japanese, however, by providing very specific descriptions, aimed to stress that they would provide only economic assistance, not reparations or compensation.[69]

The third paragraph of the second article concerns confirmation of the principle of mutual waiver of all claims, providing that "when the bilateral relationship is normalized both Japan and the DPRK would mutually waive all their property and claims and those of their nationals that had arisen from causes that occurred before August 15, 1945." In the Pyongyang Declaration, the words "reparations" and "compensation" were not used at all; instead, "mutual waiver of claims" was made a basic principle. That, too, was modeled after the Japan-ROK Basic Treaty. Customarily "reparations" is understood to refer to the demands that the victor in a war places on the loser for payment of the victor's wartime expenditures; "compensation" to refer to payments to war victims; and "property claims" to refer to a war victim's right to request payment of unpaid wages and other amounts due.

In history classes in North Korea, it is taught that "in the 1930s, the Korean Liberation Army, under the leadership of General Kim Il-sung, began fighting a war against Japan, winning the war after fifteen years of struggle."[70] But Japan took the stance that Japan and Korea had not fought a war. Japan had claimed, as evidence of that, that neither government on the Korean peninsula was a signatory to the San Francisco Treaty and that the United States had not recognized the Republic of Korea as one of the victors in World War II. In terms of the financial settlement of postwar responsibilities, Japan had adopted an across-the-board "waiver of claims" between states as settlement instead of compensation to individual victims of the war. In this particular exchange, North Korea accepted the Japanese stance.

The North Koreans tried to connect "deep remorse and heartfelt apology" in the second article with "economic cooperation," which appeared later in the same article. They wished to structure the article so that Japan's promise of economic cooperation would look like a token of apology—the logical consequence of an apology by the Japanese prime minister. Tanaka, therefore, strongly opposed connecting the two parts. In the end, the two elements were separated in two different paragraphs.

The Japanese highly approved the second article's agreement concerning waiver of claims. From the Japanese viewpoint, that statement foreclosed the possibility of any future North Korean demands for reparations or compensation. In the summit meeting, Kim Jong-il himself said, "I am prepared to decide on the compensation issue from a broader perspective. I am in agreement with the prime minister's suggestion to continue the negotiations according to the Japanese formula," making it explicit that he intended to make a concession to the Japanese.[71] However, at the Japan–North Korea bilateral negotiations held in Beijing in February 2006, the North Koreans insisted that they had agreed only to waive their property claims, not the right to compensation of individuals such as victims, although the declaration did not include compensation to individual victims.[72] On that occasion, the North Koreans referred to individuals' right to reparations, such as for the so-called wartime comfort women, but did not include the state's right to reparations.

There was the possibility, however, that in the course of discussions on the scale of economic cooperation, North Korea would resume its demand for compensation to individual victims instead of compensation to the country. But even if such a demand had been accepted, it would not have been altogether certain that the compensation would find its way to individual victims, because the North Korean government had made it clear that it would not approve individual compensation. Furthermore, regime change in North Korea was not impossible, either. It was not inconceivable that individual North Koreans would demand personal compensation in the future.

The last sentence in the second article reads, "Both sides decided that they would sincerely discuss the issue of the status of Korean residents in Japan and the issue of cultural property." The North Koreans attached great importance to this sentence. The Japanese interpreted the North Korean attitude not as a wish to upgrade the general legal status of Korean residents in Japan but as an attempt, in anticipation of the investigation and prosecution of the Chogin Tokyo Credit Union matter, to prevent "oppressive" actions by the Japanese government in the form of economic sanctions.[73]

OUTSTANDING ISSUES OF CONCERN RELATING TO THE LIVES AND SECURITY OF JAPANESE NATIONALS

The third article of the declaration was written with the abduction issue in mind. It states that "the DPRK side confirmed that it would take appropriate measures so that these regrettable incidents, which took place under the abnormal bilateral relationship, would never happen in the future." There was no mention of abductions. X appealed for Japanese understanding, asking Japan to agree "not to include such dishonorable behavior as abductions in the Japan-DPRK Pyongyang Declaration, which will have a long life." "That is not acceptable," Tanaka responded. "If the North Koreans wish to use an abstract expression here, we demand that you honor your commitment to make Chairman Kim Jong-il squarely acknowledge the issue and to apologize in person to Prime Minister Koizumi."[74]

Throughout the 1990s, North Korea had adamantly denied that any abductions had taken place and the existence of any abductees. Often the meeting immediately broke up when the Japanese side used the "A" word. In 1999, former prime minister of Japan Tomiichi Murayama visited Pyongyang and met with North Korea's Japan-handler, Kim Yong-sun. When Japan raised the abduction issue, Kim shot back, "Why do you Japanese always talk to us of abductions? What about the case of a political leader kidnapped by the South [Kim Dae-jung]? Do you use the word 'abduction' in that case too? Just stop using the word."[75]

The Japanese had to find a different expression, but it would have to be an expression that would still clearly point to abductions. In the past, the North Koreans had used such expressions as "humanitarian issues" and "outstanding humanitarian issues," which the Japanese were reluctant to accept because they were too broad and too vague. The North Koreans then suggested a slightly more focused expression, "the missing Japanese," which Japan opposed, insisting that they could not "sit at a negotiating table dealing with such an obscure matter as 'the missing.'" In the end, they agreed to the phrase "outstanding issues of concern related to the lives and security of Japanese nationals." The Japanese decided to interpret Kim Jong-il's explicit reference to the conduct of the North Korean special mission organizations, whose purpose was to secure native speakers of Japanese and penetrate to South Korea, as recognition of the past abductions.

The fourth article of the declaration states that "both sides confirmed that, for an overall resolution of the nuclear issues on the Korean Peninsula, they would comply with all related international agreements. Both sides also confirmed the necessity of resolving security problems including nuclear and missile issues by promoting dialogues among countries concerned." During the secret negotiations, Tanaka stressed the special concern about nuclear development felt by the Japanese people, who had been the first victims of a nuclear weapon. He repeatedly pointed out that "abductions, missiles, and nuclear development will be huge obstructions to Japan-DPRK diplomatic normalization and economic cooperation."[76]

"All related international agreements" included the Nuclear Non-Proliferation Treaty (NPT), which North Korea signed in 1987; the International Atomic

Energy Safeguards Agreement, which North Korea signed in 1992; the January 1992 North-South Joint Declaration on Denuclearization of the Korean Peninsula; and the Agreed Framework between the United States and North Korea, signed in 1994. Both sides confirmed that they would comply with the agreements. The Japanese were thinking about the North Korean enriched uranium program, which the United States had informed Japan about before the negotiations, and Japan wanted to warn North Korea that the program might violate the spirit of all the agreements. Although Japan and the United States did not go over the wording of the Pyongyang Declaration line by line, they had occasion to exchange general views with each other. The Japanese, in consultation with the United States, decided to insert the phrase "Both sides confirmed . . . they would comply with all related international agreements," noting the North Korean enriched uranium program.[77]

Koizumi had to make up his mind whether he would pursue normalization with North Korea in spite of its secret highly enriched uranium (HEU) program. Yukio Takeuchi, vice minister of MOFA, queried Koizumi specifically on this point. Koizumi's determination did not waver. "I will go to Pyongyang as planned whatever secret program they have been seeking."[78]

Tanaka insisted that the nuclear and missile issues should be addressed in the Pyongyang Declaration, but X persisted in maintaining the DPRK's traditional position that the issues were U.S.–North Korea bilateral issues; hence no progress was made. Nevertheless, the Japanese pushed further, although the North Koreans resisted, claiming that it would be difficult to address issues that concerned the military. In the end, however, the North Koreans agreed to include these two issues in the declaration, provided that the DPRK's supreme leader would endorse them.

The Bush administration did not feel uncomfortable with the declaration. Assistant Secretary of State James Kelly clarified this point later: "The Japanese government did not ignore concerns about the Pyongyang Declaration. It clearly emphasized nuclear weapons more so than I would have before. Even though we didn't want Koizumi to make a position, we did want him to be mindful that these weapons will continue to be a great big problem. The Pyongyang Declaration was a perfectly legitimate way to do that."[79]

The nuclear situation on the Korean Peninsula was not an issue that Japan and North Korea could settle by themselves. It was an issue for all the "countries concerned," including the United States, that called for policy coordination among those countries. The Pyongyang Declaration confirmed that point. The Japanese were envisioning a multilateral framework, such as the six-party talks, regarding peace and stability on the Korean Peninsula. In fact, Tanaka made a suggestion to X regarding six-party talks, but X expressed reluctance: "The time is not ripe yet for that," he said.[80] The North Koreans suggested instead the statement "Both sides also confirmed the necessity of resolving . . . problems . . . by promoting dialogue among countries concerned," which was included in the declaration.[81]

North Korea had traditionally been highly suspicious of a multilateral framework for ensuring peace and stability on the Korean Peninsula. It had steadfastly maintained that the issue of war and peace was essentially an issue between two countries that had fought the Korean War: the United States and North Korea. The Japanese, therefore, found it significant that North Korea had accepted a multilateral framework by "promoting dialogue among countries concerned."[82] In the subsequent summit meeting with Kim Jong-il, Koizumi reiterated the significance of this portion of the declaration. "It is important to prepare a forum for dialogue among the six countries concerned in order to promote confidence building," he said. "We ask for your cooperation." In response, Kim Jong-il said, "It is my view that a forum for confidence-building dialogues will be prepared as the relations among concerned countries become normalized. Our republic is prepared to participate in such a forum." Koizumi interpreted that response as "not an agreement nor a disagreement, but a cautious stance."[83]

It should be noted, however, that the multilateral framework envisioned by the Japanese was, as a high-ranking MOFA official in charge of Northeast Asian affairs in those days confessed, "a loose forum to facilitate confidence building, something similar to a Northeast Asian version of the ASEAN Regional Forum." The concept was different from that of the subsequent six-party talks, which were designed primarily to make North Korea abandon its nuclear program.[84] Reflected in the Pyongyang Declaration was the determination that agreements in the declaration should be placed within the overall framework of international agreements concerning the comprehensive settlement of all the issues regarding the Korean Peninsula. By introducing cooperation with all the countries concerned, the declaration gave those agreements the potential to develop from mere bilateral arrangements into regional and, further, international frameworks. That potential was partially fulfilled when the Joint Statement of the Fourth Round of the Six-Party Talks, adopted in September 2005, referred to the Pyongyang Declaration as a norm of conduct for Japan and North Korea.

The Japanese hoped that the Pyongyang Declaration would be the starting point of a deterrent process that imposed some kind of constraints on the behavior of North Korea and Japan toward each other.[85] The declaration thus came to have a dual nature: on one hand, it was an instrument to facilitate evolution toward the multilateral framework of the six-party talks; on the other hand, it would be a function of that framework, expanding or shrinking depending on the framework's success or lack thereof.

Immediately following the paragraphs in Article 4 of the declaration came this statement: "The DPRK side expressed its intention that, pursuant to the spirit of this Declaration, it would further maintain the moratorium on missile launching in and after 2003." The Japanese, touching on North Korea's launching of a Tae-podong-1 missile over the Japanese archipelago in 1998 and the resulting shock to and backlash from the Japanese people, had stressed to the North Koreans that the missile issue was an extremely serious issue for Japan. Among all the countries in Northeast Asia, Japan was and remains the country most sensitive to the issue of North Korean missiles. In a U.S.–North Korea joint communiqué issued in October 2000 following consultations begun in 1999, North Korea promised that it "would not launch any kind of long-range missiles during the duration of the bilateral consultations on the missile issue."

In fact, the Japanese government had asked the U.S. government whether the Rodong missile was included in the long-range missiles referred to in the U.S.–North Korea joint communiqué, and the United States said that it was. The Japanese government regarded the reference to the "moratorium on missile launching in and after 2003" in the Pyongyang Declaration as a part of the regime of international agreements, including the U.S.–North Korea joint communiqué, concerning North Korea's missile launching.

In May 2002, Kim Jong-il had announced to the visiting heads of EU governments that North Korea would maintain the moratorium on long-range missile launching until the end of 2003. The Pyongyang Declaration disclosed North Korea's "intention" to further extend that moratorium. It should be noted, however, that although North Korea had made promises to the United States and the EU about long-range missiles, the Pyongyang Declaration formally states that North Korea would maintain the moratorium on missile launching.

The Japanese had raised the missile issue in previous bilateral negotiations, including those of April 2000 and August 2000. On those occasions, the Japanese requested that North Korea abandon the development, production, deployment, test launching, and all other activities relating to the Rodong missile. The North Koreans brushed aside the Japanese request, claiming that the issue was a topic to be discussed bilaterally between North Korea and the United States. In those negotiations, therefore, the discussions about missiles did nothing but register Japan's concerns. It was in the Pyongyang Declaration that North Korea made a concrete promise for the first time. But the sentence concerning that moratorium covered only the launching of missiles and did not mention development, production, or export of missiles. The wording also did not specify whether the Rodong missile, capable of reaching almost all of Japan, was included in the moratorium. But the Japanese decided that detailed specification of the target of the moratorium was not necessary, given the U.S.-Japan common understanding that the Rodong was included among the long-range missiles.[86]

Following the four articles, the Pyongyang Declaration includes, after a blank line, one more sentence: "Both sides decided that they would discuss issues relating to security." The Japanese deliberately requested that this particular sentence be separated from the four articles in order to emphasize the understanding between the two parties regarding the need to have consultations on all security-related issues, including nuclear development and missiles. The Japanese aimed to stress their determination that Japan and North Korea continue to negotiate not only on the abduction issue and the normalization of diplomatic relations, but also on security as the occasion demanded. The Japanese also wanted to confirm that security issues such as nuclear development and missiles were issues not only between the United States and North Korea but also between Japan and North Korea. In the end, Japan was able to obtain a concession from North Korea on this point.[87] Based on this clause of the Pyongyang Declaration, diplomatic normalization negotiations between Japan and North Korea at the beginning of 2006 dealt simultaneously with the abduction and security issues.[88]

The Pyongyang Declaration was signed by Junichiro Koizumi as prime minister of Japan and by Kim Jong-il as chairman of the DPRK National Defense Commission. It was the second solemn international agreement that Kim Jong-il had signed, the first being the ROK-DPRK Joint Declaration of June 2000. North Korea later issued a postage stamp that featured a photo of the Japan-DPRK signing ceremony. The *Korea Encyclopedia*, published in North Korea, describes the Pyongyang Declaration as follows:

> A declaration to settle Japan's improper past conduct toward Korea and to realize diplomatic normalization. It was concluded as the result of our beloved leader Comrade Kim Jong-il meeting with the visiting Japanese prime minister on September 17, Juche 91 [2002]. It is composed of four articles, declaring that both countries would resume talks toward diplomatic normalization and that Japan would repent and deeply apologize for the damage and suffering it had imposed on the Korean people.[89]

Koizumi was not even identified by name; he was referred to merely as the "Japanese prime minister."

Although it might seem that Japan had gained more from the negotiations, winning a concession regarding reparations and compensation, North Korea also gained a great deal, including Japan's apologies for its past misdeeds, a visit to North Korea by Japan's prime minister, and a road map for diplomatic normalization. One of the Japanese officials who had been directly involved in the negotiations later offered the following assessment: "It was more or less an even match."[90]

Throughout the entire process of drafting the Pyongyang Declaration, at least as far as the text of the declaration was concerned, the North Koreans never presented even one piece of paper, until the very end. It had constantly been the Japanese who presented written drafts. The North Koreans typically offered only critical comments, which the Japanese typically rebutted. One of the Japanese negotiators commented, "This was a highly unusual case of diplomatic negotiations."[91]

BACKLASH OVER THE ABDUCTION ISSUE

How many abduction victims did Koizumi expect to rescue when he decided to visit Pyongyang? First of all, how many victims did he expect to still be alive in North Korea? In fact, Koizumi felt certain that not all of them were dead; otherwise North Korea would not have invited him, the prime minister of Japan, to Pyongyang to talk about the normalization of diplomatic relations. Koizumi interpreted North Korea's highly positive attitude toward his visit as evidence that at least some of the abductees had survived.[92]

During the secret negotiations with Mr. X, Tanaka had gotten the impression that North Korea would offer some information about the abductees either during or immediately prior to the summit talk. But not until the end of the negotiations did X disclose how many had died and how many were still alive. If every one of the abductees had been alive and well, the North Koreans would not have had to be so cautious or so secretive about information concerning them. Because the North Koreans were so closemouthed, Tanaka felt sure that at least some of the abductees were dead. "If that was the case," he wondered, "should Koizumi still visit Pyongyang?"

If Koizumi decided against the visit because too many abductees were dead, the whereabouts of the surviving abductees might never be known. The prime minister's next move might even decide whether those who were still alive would survive. This, then, was a matter of human lives that called for extremely prudent judgment. To be sure, diplomatic normalization between the two countries was a strategic issue that could lead to a peaceful Northeast Asia. But, at the same time, the negotiations were also a struggle to settle a humanitarian issue on which the lives of at least a few people might well depend.

Of course, Japan would have to take a firm stand in the negotiations concerning the abductees, but, at the same time, if Japan demanded too many details, the lives of the surviving abductees might be adversely affected. There was a strong possibility that the people watching the abductees were "those kinds of people"—those who were affiliated with North Korea's special mission organizations. Depending on how the negotiations went, the people who were monitoring the abductees might feel that their security was threatened, which might result in their harming the abductees in one way or another. During negotiations with X, Tanaka repeatedly stressed that only the truth would eliminate the problem. "Therefore," he said, "we beg you not to twist the truth at this stage. And we ask that you guarantee the safety of the surviving abductees."[93]

Tanaka attempted throughout the negotiations with X to obtain even bits and pieces of information about the abductees, but always in vain. In any case, if the information had been provided, it might have made the situation all the more complicated. For example, if specific information about the fate of the abductees had been leaked beforehand, it was quite possible that domestic pressure would have forced Koizumi to give up his plan.[94] By that time, of all the victims, Megumi Yokota and Keiko Arimoto in particular had become symbols of the tragedy. Thirteen-year-old Yokota had gone missing in Niigata City in 1977 and twenty-three-year-old Arimoto in London, where she had been studying, in 1982. Whether the two were alive would have a great impact on public opinion in Japan. If it became publicly known that some of the abductees, including those two, were dead, emotional opposition to the Pyongyang visit might erupt, making it impossible for Koizumi to go. If that happened, the dream of diplomatic normalization and all the other positive developments would go up in smoke. That was, perhaps, what North Korea was most worried about and why the North Koreans never disclosed any information about the abductees until the very end of the negotiations.

The Japanese finally decided that there was no way to obtain the information other than for Prime Minister Koizumi to visit Pyongyang and to request it directly from Kim Jong-il. But the question was whether it would be appropriate for the prime minister of a sovereign nation to go to obtain such information.[95] It was a serious dilemma that called for an eleventh-hour decision. Along the way, Tanaka asked Koizumi about what he would do if the abductees were dead, and Koizumi replied, "I still will go." His determination was firm.[96]

Later, during a session of the Diet, Koizumi, in response to a question, said, "The negotiations about the abductions would not have achieved a breakthrough if left to government officials. I had come to believe that there would be no progress without a direct talk at the top level."[97] Koizumi decided to take an enormous risk—the risk of being told that some abductees were dead while trying to persuade the public to support his normalization policy. The breakthrough therefore would come from a comprehensive approach, an approach that Tanaka called a "grand bargain."[98]

Perhaps Koizumi had no real alternative in deciding whether to visit Pyongyang. Some people would criticize him because he visited Pyongyang knowing that some abductees were dead; others would criticize him because he visited Pyongyang without knowing anything about the dead abductees. Either way, he probably would be bashed. It was a risk that he had to take.

On that particular point, Yasuo Fukuda later reminisced,

I thought that the prime minister had to go to Pyongyang if any of the abductees were alive. It would have been a different story, though, if all of them were dead. I felt sorry for the prime minister and sympathized with his agony. But if we missed this chance, I didn't know when, or if, the next chance would come. A politician sometimes has to hit a ball even if he knows it is a bad ball. Otherwise, I thought, what is the politician for to begin with? The prime minister went ahead and visited Pyongyang because, through a narrow window of opportunity, we had been able to obtain a certain assurance about the abductees. We were prepared for a situation in which, depending on the fate of the abductees, the prime minister might come home without signing the Pyongyang Declaration."[99]

The reference to the "fate of the abductees" included the worst-case scenario—no survivors; "without signing the Pyongyang Declaration" referred to the prime minister's response if the worst-case scenario were to become reality.

It seems, in retrospect, that Koizumi had hoped that with the return of the surviving abductees he could begin a big push toward diplomatic normalization.[100] However, as Masahiko Komura, a former foreign minister, had correctly pointed out immediately after the Pyongyang summit, the Japanese people were driven much more by sorrow and anger over the deaths of abductees than by happiness that some abductees were still alive.[101] People were especially furious about the deaths of Megumi Yokota and Keiko Arimoto.

Two days after Koizumi's visit, the National Association for the Rescue of Japanese Kidnapped by North Korea (NARKN) released an urgent statement claiming that "the official announcement about the dead and surviving abductees is not based on any objective grounds." The statement continued: "The information about the fate of the abductees is utterly ungrounded. There is a strong possibility that the eight who are said to be deceased are actually alive. However, because the Japanese government has informed their families that those eight are dead, there has emerged the danger that they actually will be disposed of."[102]

Since the very day that Koizumi visited Pyongyang, a chorus of acrimonious attacks had been directed at the Japanese government, particularly at the Ministry of Foreign Affairs. Didn't the government just uncritically swallow the North Koreans' information about the dead and pass it on to their families? Didn't it inform the mass media of the deaths of the eight abductees as if that were an established fact? Didn't the government keep secret a certain portion of the "whereabouts list" presented by North Korea? These and many other suspicions and criticisms erupted.

The "whereabouts list" was a piece of paper, written in Korean, containing the supposed date, place, and cause of death for each of the eight deceased abductees; it had been presented by the North Koreans at the end of the preliminary meeting immediately preceding the morning session of the summit talk on September 17. The list included the names of the following people: Megumi Yokota,

Keiko Arimoto, Tôru Ishioka, Kaoru Matsuki, Shuichi Ichikawa, Rumiko Masumoto, Yaeko Taguchi, and Tadaaki Hara. It had the adverse effect of magnifying the suspicions of the Japanese people about the cause and circumstances of the deaths as well as the way that North Korea had conducted its investigation.

Many questions and suspicions have arisen about the list of five living abductees as well. Why did North Korea include in the list Hitomi Soga, who was not among the abductees on the list prepared by Japan? Was it because North Korea needed to increase the number of survivors in order to present a slightly more balanced list in terms of deceased and surviving abductees? Did North Korea aim to emphasize its "sincerity" in order to pave the way for an easier "final settlement?" Or was it actually Charles Jenkins, the American husband of Hitomi Soga, that North Korea intended to release, together with Hitomi, so that it could initiate talks with the United States?[103] Jenkins had defected to North Korea in January 1965, when he was a U.S. Army sergeant stationed in a U.S. military camp along the demilitarized zone (DMZ), in order to avoid being transferred to the battlefront in Vietnam. He crossed the DMZ and entered North Korea, where he later married the abducted Hitomi Soga.

The denouncements of MOFA especially took the form of personal attacks on Hitoshi Tanaka, who had paved the way for Koizumi's visit to Pyongyang. On September 26, when Tanaka tried to answer a question asked by Issui Miura, an LDP member of the House of Councilors, about the future direction of investigations concerning the abduction victims, he broke into tears, overcome with emotion. He started by saying, "I haven't gotten over the shock and sorrow that I felt when I was told that eight abductees were already dead."[104] Tanaka sobbed as if his emotional faucet had been accidentally turned on, thereby giving Tanaka bashers an additional reason to criticize him: he was a bureaucrat who had cried in a Diet session. The Japanese government, pressured by hardening public opinion, announced early in October that its basic policy was to "give the abduction issue the highest priority."[105]

North Korea's enriched uranium program was another factor that propelled the abduction issue to the top of the list for the Japanese government. On October 6, at the official residence of the U.S. ambassador to Japan, Yasuo Fukuda and Foreign Minister Kawaguchi met with James Kelly, the U.S. assistant secretary of state, who had just visited North Korea. Kelly informed them of the shocking news that North Korea had acknowledged the existence of its enriched uranium nuclear development program. If that news were to become known to the public, U.S.-DPRK and Japan-DPRK relations might immediately become strained, which, in turn, might make it impossible for the five abductees (the four on the list prepared by Japan, plus Hitomi Soga) to return to Japan.[106] Deciding that it was urgent to hurry the return of the abductees, Tanaka contacted X and convinced him to accept the idea of their "temporary return."[107]

On October 15 a Japanese government plane carrying the five abduction victims touched down at Haneda International Airport, two days before the U.S. Department of State announced on the morning of October 17 (the evening of October 16 by U.S. Eastern standard time) that North Korea had admitted the existence of its enriched uranium project. Aboard the plane were Kaoru Hasuike, Yukiko Okudo, Yasushi Chimura, Fukie Hamamoto, and Hitomi Soga. Their emotional reunions with their respective families in Japan were widely covered by the mass media, leaving deep impressions on people all across Japan.

Japan had promised North Korea that the five were being "returned to Japan temporarily" and that their "stay" was estimated to be seven to ten days. That promise became another target of public criticism. To make the situation worse for the Japanese government, it was revealed that the government had set aside an allowance for the five to buy souvenirs to take with them when they returned to North Korea. Although the attacks took a variety of forms—including nagging about the "cold and heartless MOFA," particularly its North Korea–sympathizing Asian and Oceanian Affairs Bureau, and accusations about Tanaka's misjudgments and mishandling of the affair—beneath them was a strong undercurrent of deep distrust of the Japanese government, particularly MOFA, for having consistently ignored the abduction issue too long and shown a lack of compassion for the abduction victims and their families.

Inside the government, a clash of opinions between Fukuda and Abe became apparent. Fukuda insisted that they were obliged to send the five back to North Korea because MOFA had obtained North Korea's agreement on the basis of a "temporary return." He pointed out that if Japan did not return the five, the North Korean government might use their remaining family members in North Korea as bargaining chips—in effect, as hostages. He contended that the government had to make some other arrangement so that the families of the five could join them at some unspecified future time in returning to Japan.[108]

Abe, in contrast, took the position that Japan should not return the five.[109] His logic was that "it would be abdication of a sovereign nation's responsibility to leave to the individuals the decision about whether they should go back to North Korea or stay in Japan permanently."[110] On October 24, at the prime minister's office, Fukuda said to Abe, "You insist that we should not let them go back. But what about the five themselves? What does each one of them want to do?" Hearing from Abe that their wishes were not known, Fukuda instructed Abe to contact every one of them immediately, by telephone if necessary. A few hours later, Abe reported to Fukuda that it had been confirmed "that none of the five intends to go back to Pyongyang."

Subsequently, Prime Minister Koizumi was joined in his office by Fukuda, Abe, Kiminari Ueno (a deputy chief cabinet secretary), Tanaka, and a few others to finalize the government's position not to return the five to North Korea.

Koizumi was presented with two options, return or not return. He decided not to return.[111]

At a press conference after the decision was made, Fukuda announced, "We will not return the five to North Korea, and we will obtain the return of their family members." One MOFA official who was seconded to the prime minister's office at that time said, on reflection, "When I served in the prime minister's office, that was the only issue that had to be brought to the prime minister in that fashion because his subordinates were unable to agree on a decision among themselves." He vividly remembered a remark that Deputy Chief Cabinet Secretary Teijiro Furukawa let drop at the meeting. "If we return the five to North Korea and no progress is made after that," Furukawa said, "the Koizumi government surely will topple. We will all be forced to resign."[112]

In response to Japan's announcement, the North Korean government vehemently protested what it regarded as a "broken promise" on the part of the Japanese government. North Korea's anger about being taken advantage of by the Japanese government remained long afterward. It should be noted, however, that the "temporary return" itself was, in a sense, a product of mutual deception. The five abduction victims had been fully aware before they departed Pyongyang that the North Korean government would never approve their departure unless it was for a "temporary return" to Japan. The five therefore chose to return temporarily. The North Koreans, on the other hand, claimed that it was their "free will" to return to Japan temporarily and that therefore they had to be returned to North Korea.

Japan knew that, in truth, the five "temporary returnees" would never want to go back to Pyongyang. However, for them to openly acknowledge their true wishes might jeopardize the safety of their family members remaining in North Korea. The Japanese government had no choice but to announce that it was the government's decision not to return the five without mentioning the wishes of the returnees.[113]

Japan-DPRK relations subsequently degenerated. Tensions between the two countries were heightened, aggravating U.S.-DPRK tension over North Korea's enriched uranium project, an issue whose resolution was interdependent with that of the abduction issue.

As a matter of fact, on October 16 (U.S. Eastern standard time), Park Kil-yon, North Korea's permanent representative to the United Nations, had invited Charles Pritchard, the U.S. special envoy for negotiations with North Korea, and David Straub, country director for Korean affairs at the Department of State, to North Korea's permanent mission, where he made the following statement:

> The Japanese government had informed DPRK that there could be no Japan-DPRK normalization talks that did not include a discussion of the

DPRK's covert uranium enrichment program. This action clearly shows that the U.S. government has already launched a campaign of pressure against North Korea concerning HEU issue. Now that the Unites States has instigated Japan and made the issue public, it leaves us no other choice but to make the issue public ourselves.[114]

Park also warned, "We will use 'physical means,' not words," but he did not clarify what was meant by "physical means." On the evening of the same day, Department of State spokesperson Richard Boucher was forced to announce, due to a leak to *USA Today,* that North Korea had admitted the existence of the uranium enrichment program to the visiting Kelly delegation. U.S. ambassador to Tokyo Howard Baker immediately communicated the North Koreans' response to the Japanese government.[115]

At the Japan-DPRK negotiations in Kuala Lumpur, on October 30, North Korea described the Pyongyang Declaration as "the first significant positive development in the 100-year history of Korea-Japan relations," and proposed promoting normalization of diplomatic relations and economic cooperation between the two nations. But Japan said that settlement of the abduction and nuclear issues would be its top priorities. Japan's ambassador, Katsuya Suzuki, stressing the importance of the "human emotions of family members," demanded that the abduction issue be settled on a fundamental level, but North Korea never changed its stance. To quote Ambassador Jong Thae-hwa, "This issue has been essentially settled. I believe it has already been resolved."[116] The two governments' positions remained as far apart as before. As the year ended, the prospects for Japan-DPRK relations were not bright.

"DUALISTIC DIPLOMACY"

After the Koizumi-Kim talks, Tanaka held secret meetings with X in order to achieve a breakthrough regarding the return of the abductees, but he could not find a way to end the impasse. It seemed to Tanaka that X had rapidly been losing his extraordinary influence—that the unilateral decision of the Japanese government to change the "return" status of the five abductees from temporary to permanent had weakened X's position in North Korea. X accused Japan of breaking its promise, saying, "I am deeply hurt." While Tanaka tried to explain that in Japan there was a certain thing called public opinion, X confessed his anguish: "I can no longer propose, at my discretion, a scenario for bilateral normalization," he said.

On February 22 and 23, 2003, Tanaka met X for the first time in a while, in Dalian. The nuclear crisis had deepened. All of the Japan–North Korea, North Korea–U.S., and South and North Korea plans had crumbled. X sighed repeatedly.

When Tanaka finally asked when they should get together again, X gave an ambiguous reply. These turned out to be Tanaka's last secret negotiations with X in a third country.[117] At the beginning of 2003, North Korea had announced its intention to withdraw from the NPT, giving rise to the second nuclear crisis involving North Korea, which triggered the move toward the six-party talks under the U.S.-China initiative. The year 2003 slipped away, but Japan could not find any solution to the abduction issue.

At the beginning of 2004 Koizumi began to consider visiting Pyongyang one more time in order to try to achieve the return of the returned abductees' family members who still remained in North Korea. Koizumi was irritated by the lack of progress and felt that there would be no breakthrough if the issue was left to MOFA; in his eyes, MOFA was thwarting any progress. Recalling those days, Koizumi said, "It was around New Year's Day that I started thinking that we must obtain the return of the family members as soon as possible. However, MOFA was, in contrast, very cautious."[118] Around that time, a variety of rumors had reached his ears, including claims that MOFA's pipeline through X was "clogged," that it looked as if Kim Jong-il had "written off X and started using his Ministry of Foreign Affairs instead," and that in order "to move things along," the government would have to take "a different route."[119]

Koizumi also was approached by a few people who seemed to be connected to North Korea in one way or other, suggesting direct talks with Kim Jong-il as a means of achieving a breakthrough. But Koizumi turned down all of them, saying, "If you want direct talks, go through Tanaka."[120]

Fukuda keenly understood and shared Koizumi's feeling of irritation. He instructed Tanaka to "do something," but no remarkable progress was made.[121] However, toward the end of 2003, the North Koreans made a new move. At the request of North Korea, two senior members of the Federation of Diet Members for Early Rescue of Japanese Nationals Abducted by North Korea—Japanese Lower House members Katsuei Hirasawa, of the LDP, and Jin Matsubara, of the Democratic Party of Japan (DPJ)—met in Beijing with North Korea's Ambassador Jong Thae-hwa, who had been in charge of Japan-DPRK negotiations. In the course of the discussions, Jong offered to release the family members of the returned abductees on the condition that the five returnees came to Pyongyang to get them.

Moreover, the North Korean government granted Japanese officials permission to interview a Japanese male who had been arrested on suspicion of possession of narcotics. His case—plus the case of a thirty-one-year-old Japanese woman, a former member of the Aum Shinrikyo cult (which was later renamed Aleph) who had earlier "defected" to North Korea but now announced her wish to return to Japan—required MOFA to dispatch officials to Pyongyang for negotiations. That was the first contact between the two governments in the fifteen months since October 2002. The timing of these developments coincided with that of North Korea's consideration of participating in a second round of six-party talks.[122] North Korea had started to show some interest in a barter involving a freeze of its nuclear program in exchange for compensation. The Japanese interpreted these indications as a sign that North Korea was seeking a chance to resume negotiations with Japan.[123]

In addition, X had resurfaced. In a telephone conversation with Tanaka, X promised to set up a meeting between Tanaka and Kang Sok-ju, North Korea's first deputy minister of Foreign Affairs. In February 2004, Deputy Minister for Foreign Affairs Hitoshi Tanaka and Mitoji Yabunaka, director general of MOFA's Asian and Oceanian Affairs Bureau, flew to Pyongyang. In consideration of the negative feelings toward Tanaka among family members of the abduction victims, Tanaka had requested that Fukuda not make him the chief of the delegation, and MOFA designated Yabunaka instead. But the Korean Central News Agency reported that Tanaka was the leader of the group.[124]

In Pyongyang, X visited the Japanese delegation at the Koryo Hotel, where they were staying. They met X in the hotel penthouse and Tanaka introduced Yabunaka to X. But X did not show up later at the reception hosted by Deputy Foreign Minister Kim Yong-il or at the talks with Kang Sok-ju. It seemed that X had decided to observe from behind the scenes how things would develop.[125]

The negotiations with Kang at the North Korean Foreign Ministry produced no meaningful results. At the outset, Kang denounced the amendment, only two days earlier, of Japan's Foreign Exchange and Foreign Trade Control Law, saying, angrily, that it "was the result of a conspiracy by a right-wing faction in Japan."[126] The amendment enabled Japan to impose economic sanctions on North Korea on its own, independent of the UN Security Council. Although the timing was merely coincidental, North Korea seemed to suspect that Japan deliberately sent Tanaka and Yabunaka to North Korea after the law had been amended. Kang continued to criticize the amendment. "This is an attempt to constrain North Korea by force," he declared.

Although North Korea's Foreign Ministry had earlier conveyed to the nation's top leaders the ministry's prediction that the amendment would never be enacted, it was approved by both houses of the Diet, causing the ministry officials to lose face. The Japanese suspected that Kang's blow-up was an attempt, by stressing conspiracy on the part of the Japanese, to provide an excuse for the North Korean foreign ministry's misjudgment.[127]

The Japanese handed Prime Minister Koizumi's message to Kang Sok-ju, stating that the return of the eight family members of the five abduction returnees would be Koizumi's top priority. "If North Korea would release the family members of the five returnees, the stage for diplomatic normalization would be set," said Yabunaka. Kang retorted, "It was the Japanese who broke their promise. First return the five returnees to Pyongyang. After that, if they wish to go back to Japan, they can go." Thus, the discussion went around and around in circles.

When Kang accusingly demanded to be told why the Japanese would so strongly oppose the "temporary return" formula, Yabunaka counterattacked, "Because we in Japan feel that North Korea is treating the abduction victims as hostages."[128] Yabunaka told Kang that, to the Japanese people, the North Korean announcement that ten abductees had either died or had never entered North Korea was unconvincing and unsatisfactory, and he once again demanded the honest disclosure of information about their fate. Kang simply brushed him off: "What can we do about an issue that has already been settled?"

In this February 2004 meeting, Kang also told the Japanese delegation that the U.S. accusation that North Korea had an uranium enrichment program was totally unfounded, following his declaration with a round of criticism of the United States.[129] The Japanese had been prepared to offer to dispatch an appropriate, high-ranking government official to Pyongyang to receive the eight family members of the returned abductees, depending on North Korea's attitude, but North Korea's unapproachable stance discouraged the Japanese from making the offer until the end of the negotiations.[130]

At a debriefing at MOFA after the team came back from Pyongyang, Tanaka described the negotiations as "the most unpleasant discussions."[131] Tanaka's irritation was directed not only at North Korea's stance, particularly Kang Sok-ju's attitude, but also at the unexpected derailing of the scenario for normalization that he had painstakingly constructed through a series of secret negotiations. At the end of the negotiations in Pyongyang, Kang put his arm around Tanaka's shoulder and said, "Next time, let's talk about the future, okay?"[132] Although Tanaka replied, "Yes, let's do that," his heart sank.

Looking down from the top floor of the Koryo Hotel, the Japanese could see large flakes of snow falling incessantly, covering the entire city of Pyongyang in a white blanket. On one of those winter mornings, Kim Jong-il had praised Pyongyang's snow-covered beauty and ordered that no one sweep the snow away.[133] Outside the window lay a white, chilly expanse that seemed to symbolize the environment surrounding the relationship between Japan and North Korea. There had been no contact between the Japanese and DPRK governments for sixteen long months, and the feeling of emptiness caused by noncommunication had become increasingly acute.

This experience made clear, if nothing else, that the conventional negotiation pipeline would lead nowhere. Koizumi was deeply frustrated.[134] In the spring of 2004, the frustrated Koizumi was approached by the pro-Pyongyang General Association of Korean Residents in Japan (Chosen Soren) with a proposition. Ho

Jong Man, Soren's top leader, had already contacted Isao Iijima, a personal aide to Koizumi. "Prime Minister Koizumi is the only one we can trust," he said. "We wish to pursue normalization talks with him through you."

On April 28, Koizumi called Tanaka to his office. Fukuda already was there. Koizumi said, "We have received an offer from Chosen Soren to return the family members of the five abduction victims if I again visit Pyongyang. I want you to confirm this offer and make the necessary preparations." Fukuda and Tanaka knew that, by "make the necessary preparations," Koizumi meant that they should attend to the details and logistics, because Koizumi had already agreed that he would again talk directly with Kim. Fukuda pleaded for caution, saying, "We should go back to the basics. If we can get all the family members returned to Japan, that will be good, of course. But we should keep in mind that negotiations with North Korea will continue for a long time in the future. If at this point we do something that deviates from the proper course, that might cause problems for future negotiations, and we might have to pay for that." Fukuda added, "We should have MOFA negotiate formally with North Korea one more time. Can't we forget that offer?"

Koizumi shot back, "No, we can't." Turning to Tanaka, Koizumi said, "Go and determine if this is a real offer. If not, we can always cancel." Tanaka replied, "Let's work out conceptually how to make this feasible . . . . Please put your project on hold and let us take over from now on." Tanaka gave a final push, asking Koizumi if he would leave it to Tanaka, to which Koizumi nodded his consent. "But," he said, "It is not as if we have to stick to this new offer at any cost."

What mattered to Koizumi was whether the new opportunity could actually result in progress or not. It was not whether the offer was good or bad; if it would not move things forward there was no reason to stick to it. Tanaka repeated his question, "Will you leave it to me, then?" Turning to Fukuda, Tanaka asked, "We will join the negotiations from now on. Now, do we have your consent?" Fukuda nodded by way of agreement, albeit grudging.[135]

By this time, bits and pieces of information about "dubious" activities in the prime minister's office had caught the attention of top-echelon MOFA leaders. Two days before the Koizumi-Fukuda-Tanaka consultation, MOFA vice minister Takeuchi tested the waters in a conversation with Fukuda, saying, "We have detected some mysterious activities in the prime minister's office. Isn't he working through an alternative channel on another visit to Pyongyang?" In fact, the information had already reached Takeuchi's ears that Chosen Soren had been working with the prime minister's office to pave the way for the prime minister to visit Pyongyang once again. But Fukuda confidently replied, "No, he isn't. That's impossible." Takeuchi was relieved to see how self-assured Fukuda seemed.[136]

Tanaka, too, had sensed strange goings-on in the prime minister's office. When he, together with Yabunaka, met Koizumi on April 27, he looked Koizumi in the eye. "Is there anything we should be aware of?" he asked. Koizumi simply relied, "No. Nothing."

Foreign Minister Yoriko Kawaguchi asked Fukuda the same question that Takeuchi had asked and got the same reply. Fukuda was apprehensive about other channels to North Korea intervening in the normalization negotiations. He was quite displeased, in fact, that Taku Yamazaki, the former vice president of the Liberal Democratic Party, and Katsuei Hirasawa of the House of Representatives had contacted Ambassador Jong Thae-hwa, North Korea's chief negotiator with Japan, in Dalian in April of that year. Fukuda suggested to Koizumi that the only route of communication with North Korea should be through the Foreign Ministry. And yet Fukuda continued to hear of information being passed along a "different route" and "behind the scenes."

Three times, Fukuda had asked Koizumi, "I've heard rumors of a new route. You're not involved in it, are you?" Each time Koizumi had answered, "I've never heard of it."[137] However, Koizumi later acknowledged that he had communicated with North Korea through Chosen Soren; moreover, Koizumi suggested that the new route should be used in the future. It was later revealed that Koizumi had already conveyed his intention to visit Pyongyang again through that route.

It was a humiliating experience for both Fukuda and Tanaka, who had been secretly working on a plan to dispatch Deputy Chief Cabinet Secretary Hiroyuki Hosoda to Pyongyang to receive the eight family members of the returned abductees. As mentioned earlier, they were actually considering proposing this plan during the negotiations with Kang Sok-ju in February, but North Korea's unapproachable stance made Tanaka decide not to present the proposal. But, without their knowledge, Koizumi had already conveyed to North Korea his intention to revisit Pyongyang. Even though Tanaka had no choice but to accept Koizumi's unilateral initiative, he was very upset inside.

On the next day, Tanaka received an urgent message that Koizumi wanted Tanaka to phone him. When Tanaka called, Koizumi was furious. He said, "Make no mistake. I am the prime minister. As long as I take full responsibility in negotiations with North Korea through my channel, this is the only diplomatic route we should pursue. You can't accuse your prime minister of being the source of dualistic diplomacy." It was obvious that Koizumi had somehow overheard that Tanaka was complaining about the risk of "dualistic diplomacy." Tanaka answered, with deliberate composure, "Yes, sir. I understand, sir." But that did not calm Koizumi or lessen his fury.[138]

That was not the first time that Koizumi had yelled at Tanaka. It had happened earlier, on December 25, Christmas Day, of 2003. Tanaka went straight from Narita Airport to see Koizumi after consultations in Beijing with Wang Yi, China's vice foreign minister. Meeting Koizumi, Tanaka enumerated the problems that Koizumi's annual visits to Yasukuni Shrine were creating in Japan's relations with China and South Korea. "Are you saying I should not visit Yasukuni Shrine because China told me not to?" Koizumi demanded. "I go to Yasukuni as a private person. From a long-term perspective, it is necessary for China to have this experience." It sounded as if Koizumi was suggesting that China had to learn a lesson so that it would not use the history card anymore and that that was why he kept visiting Yasukuni. When Tanaka further stressed the problems with the visits to Yasukuni, Koizumi at last burst into a fit of anger.[139]

On May 4, 2004, Tanaka and Yabunaka flew to Beijing to negotiate with Ambassador Jong Thae-hwa, North Korea's chief negotiator with Japan, regarding steps to be taken toward Koizumi's next visit to Pyongyang. During the consultation, the North Koreans said that they were prepared to return the family members of the abductees. They seemed to be talking about the five children of the Hasuikes and the Chimuras, but they did not make clear what would happen to Charles Jenkins and his and Hitomi Soga's two children.

Immediately before the North Koreans' statement, the Japanese government had said that it was prepared to offer humanitarian aid to the victims of the April 24, 2004, explosion at Ryongchon Railway Station as well as to provide food aid to the North Korean people as requested by the United Nations. Responding to the offer, North Korea asked Japan to provide the maximum possible amount of rice, which is more expensive than wheat and corn, and referred to the specific amount of aid that it wished to receive. The amount was larger than what the Japanese had considered by tenfold.[140] Nevertheless, after Tanaka returned to Japan, he reported to Fukuda that the children of the Hasuikes and Chimuras were likely to be returned, adding, "I think we can manage to strike a deal."

Hearing Tanaka's report, Fukuda thought to himself, "Now I can resign." It had recently been revealed that at one point in the past he had failed to pay his required national pension premiums, forcing Fukuda to make the issue his first priority for a few days after the revelation. On May 7, Yasuo Fukuda resigned as chief cabinet secretary. At what became his last press conference as chief cabinet secretary, Fukuda apologized, saying, "Of all people, I myself have fueled people's distrust in politics." Fukuda's resignation was a blow to Koizumi because Fukuda was the central pillar of the Koizumi government, and he necessarily affected its policies toward North Korea. The foothold that had been established and the framework that had been constructed for normalizing bilateral diplomatic relations became shaky.

On the very day that Fukuda resigned, Koizumi told Hiroyuki Hosoda, who had succeeded Fukuda as chief cabinet secretary, to "engage in negotiations with North Korea on the assumption that I will again visit Pyongyang. If the negotiations are successful, I will do that. I am sure I can gain the understanding of the abduction victims and of the nation as a whole."[141]

His instructions were based on the impression that the Japanese had received during the Beijing consultations on May 4 and 5. However, no determination had yet been made as to what to do about Charles Jenkins. Koizumi had privately decided that after he again arrived in Pyongyang he would try, face-to-face, to persuade Jenkins to come to Japan. Whether Jenkins would be released had become delicately entangled with the issue of Japan's food aid to North Korea.

Although the Japanese were planning to offer food aid based primarily on wheat and corn, the North Koreans, noting how tasty Japanese rice was, demanded rice. The Japanese tried to reject the request. However, in the end Japan agreed that rice would be added to the package of wheat and corn, for a total package of 250,000 tons of grain. (However, after Koizumi's second visit on May 22, the Korean Central News Agency reported that Koizumi "assured the DPRK side that Japan would . . . supply 250,000 tons of rice and medicament worth 10 million U.S. dollars.")[142]

Before dawn on May 14, Song Il-ho, vice director, Asian Affairs Department of North Korea's Ministry of Foreign Affairs, contacted the Japanese Foreign Ministry to inform them that Kim Jong-il had formally announced that he would welcome Koizumi's visit on May 22. The message also said that by the time that Koizumi arrived in Pyongyang, North Korea would have persuaded Jenkins to depart for Japan.[143] The same morning, the Japanese government formally decided that Prime Minister Koizumi would return to North Korea.

CHAPTER TWO

KOIZUMI AGAIN
VISITS PYONGYANG

It was a beautiful spring day at the Taedonggang Guest House in Pyongyang. Outside, thousands of fluffy willow seeds were in the air—not falling, not flying, just floating in the air. In ancient days, Pyongyang was called Ryugyong, Capital of Willows. It was May 22, 2004. Japanese prime minister Junichiro Koizumi was soon to meet with North Korean leader Kim Jong-il for the second time, a little less than two years since their first meeting on September 17, 2002.

A solitary clock—flat, golden, and shiny—was on the table. The clock had a face on each side, and both the Japanese and North Korean leaders, seated on opposite sides of the table, kept staring at the clock. One of the members of the Japanese delegation suspected, just for a moment, that the clock might be a secret recording device.

At the outset, Kim Jong-il criticized Japan for "dragging up the abduction issue, which had already been settled." He also told the Japanese that he had been disappointed by the lack of improvement in the Japan-DPRK bilateral relationship after the signing of the Pyongyang Declaration.[1] "I was hoping," he said, "that a head of government would have more influence, commensurate with his position, even in a democratic state." "Head of government" in the North Korean context meant "supreme leader." The Japanese were a little surprised at Kim Jong-il's comment, because he seemed to understand the limits to an elected leader's power in a democracy, although he obviously hoped that Koizumi would deliver more.[2] One might have detected some sarcasm in his remark.

It was amazing that Kim Jong-il had ever apologized for the abduction of Japanese nationals, as he did during the first meeting, to the former colonizer of his country. It was a voluntary acknowledgment, on the part of the leader of North Korea, that the country was in a desperate state.

The Japanese had heard that after the earlier summit talk people in Pyongyang were complaining that "our beloved leader has been deceived by Koizumi."[3] Although on the surface the comment seems like a denouncement of Koizumi, it might actually reflect some displeasure with Kim Jong-il for having allowed himself to be deceived. If it had such a thorny aspect, Kim's authority would be further diminished if he did not do something to remedy the situation. Moreover, less and less food had been available for rationing in North Korea,[4] so it would not be at all surprising if the North Koreans wanted it to look as if Koizumi undertook his second visit to apologize and, as a token of penitence, to offer food aid.[5]

However, when Koizumi arrived in Pyongyang, he was wearing a blue ribbon on his lapel, a symbol of the "blue ribbon campaign" in Japan to rescue the abduction victims.[6] As with his first visit, negotiations on the abduction issue were conducted without any official ceremonies. Regarding the return of the abductees and their families, Kim Jong-il declared, "Everyone should do as they wish. There is no need to create another set of separated families." The Japanese realized then that the family members of the abductees would be allowed to go to Japan. Koizumi immediately responded, "I'll bring home all eight of them."

Kim Jong-il asked Kang Sok-ju, who was at his side, "Jenkins is here, isn't he?" Kang replied that he was. Kim then turned to Koizumi. "Five may go home with you," he said. "The three Jenkinses also are allowed to go, but I have been informed that Jenkins has his own opinion about this. Why don't you ask him yourself after the meeting? He can do whatever he wishes to do. If he does not want to go to Japan, you can meet him in Beijing or somewhere in Russia, or wherever it's convenient for you." The Japanese learned then that Charles Jenkins was there at the guest house.

Koizumi demanded that a satisfactory investigation be conducted of the fate of the ten missing persons who North Korea claimed were deceased or for whom there supposedly was no record of entry into North Korea. Continuing, he declared that if Japan were to learn of the abduction of any other Japanese people, the Japanese government would repeat its demand for thorough investigations. Koizumi also requested North Korea to hand over to Japan the remaining members of the "Yodo-go" group that had hijacked JAL flight 351 in 1970. The hijackers had obtained political asylum in North Korea after the incident, and they were suspected of being involved in the subsequent abductions.[7]

Kim Jong-il replied, "If you are so insistent, I am prepared to go back to the drawing board and order a reinvestigation of the fate of the ten missing persons. If you doubt our sincerity, you are welcome to participate in the investigation." Everyone in the Japanese delegation took note of Kim's reference to "going back to the drawing board."[8] Kim, however, added, "I am tired of playing the role of the bad man in a poorly scripted play"—a bad man who was further reprimanded even after he had apologized. He was protesting that it was preposterous for the Japanese to force him to play that role and then wait to see how the Japanese would react.

It had been twenty months since the two leaders met for the first Japan-DPRK summit talk. During those months, the international situation surrounding the two countries had changed greatly. North Korea's secret enriched uranium program had been exposed, triggering a second Korean nuclear crisis. The United States had invaded Iraq to oust Saddam Hussein from power and now, after the collapse of the regime, it occupied Iraq.

In addition to his statement about the return of abductees, Koizumi had another message that he wanted to convey to Kim Jong-il during his visit: it was his unchanged wish and intention to normalize diplomatic relations between Japan and North Korea. He wanted to make the current talks a turning point in the normalization negotiations—to "convert Japan-DPRK relations from adversarial relations to friendly relations, from conflict to cooperation"—and he stressed the importance of settling the nuclear issue in order to achieve that goal. "North Korea has more to gain from dismantling its nuclear weapons than from possessing them," Koizumi said, adding that "having a guarantee of security within the framework of the six-party talks would be more promising than possessing nuclear weapons, since the framework also includes China and Russia."[9]

"We should not let this opportunity slip away," Koizumi declared, pressing further. His deliberate manner of speaking was in marked contrast to that of Kim Jong-il, who, once he started to speak, had a tendency to speak rapidly. Referring to Libya's announcement that it would abandon its nuclear development program, Koizumi repeated his demand that North Korea give up its program too. Kim Jong-il brushed him off. "We are no Libya," he said. "We are advanced in nuclear development; Libya is not."[10] One could detect Kim's pride in the fact that North Korea, unlike Libya, already was capable of developing a nuclear program.

In December 2003, the United States and the United Kingdom had concluded an agreement with Colonel Muammar al-Qaddafi, Libya's leader, that, in return for Libya's abandonment of its nuclear development program, they would not try to topple his government. The agreement later became widely praised as "the Libyan Model" of nuclear nonproliferation, and political observers wondered whether the same model could be applied to North Korea.

Kim continued, saying, "I am of the opinion that nuclear development is good for nothing. We really did not want to engage in nuclear development. But the United States' continuation of hostile policies toward us left us no choice." In addition, Kim noted that "the ultimate goal is to denuclearize the Korean peninsula. If a nation freezes its nuclear development program, it will be subject to verification." The Japanese interpreted Kim's comment as indicating both his view of a nuclear freeze as a first step toward denuclearization and his willingness to accept inspections by the IAEA (International Atomic Energy Agency) after denuclearization.

"You do not have any objection to our conveying your comment to President Bush, do you?" asked Koizumi.

Kim answered, "By all means, please do."

Kim Jong-il repeated his wish, which he had expressed at the first summit talk with Koizumi, to improve North Korea's relations with the United States. "I wish to sing and dance with Bush until I lose my voice," he said. "And I want all of you to be good accompanists. If we have a six-member orchestra, our duet will be successful."[11] During the first Japan-DPRK summit talk, Kim would not commit himself to a multilateral consultation plan, such as the six-party consultations that Koizumi had mentioned. This time, Kim likened the parties to the members of an orchestra, playing in harmony.

During the summit talk, Kim Jong-il repeatedly referred to the Japan-DPRK Pyongyang Declaration.[12] The Japanese took that as Kim's expression of his pride in having been directly involved in drafting the document, as well as a reminder to Koizumi that he, too, could not back away from its spirit. The talk was over in about ninety minutes, after which Koizumi and Kim walked out of the room and shook hands by way of farewell. Kim Jong-il then walked away at a brisk pace. It seemed that he wanted to give an impression of being perfectly composed. He was surrounded by a circle of bodyguards, and the group, including Kim, flowed in unison into an oversized Mercedes Benz.

After the talk, Koizumi was led to a room on the second floor of the government guest house where he met Charles Jenkins and his two daughters, twenty-year-old Roberta Mika and eighteen-year-old Brinda Carol. "Hitomi-san is waiting for you," Koizumi said to Jenkins, who was seated across the table. "I heard that she has purchased three sets of *futon* for you. I will do my very best to enable the four of you to live together as a family."

Following their conversation, Koizumi gave Mika a letter that Hitomi Soga had entrusted to him, saying, "This is from your mother." Next, Koizumi gave the family a SONY video recorder that contained a video of Hitomi talking to them. As soon as they saw the video, the girls began to cry. Mika, the elder daughter, pleaded with Koizumi in Korean: "Thanks to our great beloved general, I am now a college student," she said. "Please keep your promise and return our mother to us now. We will then discuss and decide what we will do next."

Koizumi responded, "We cannot possibly return your mother to the country that abducted her in the first place."

"But her house and her family are in this country," said Mika.

"I have come here to arrange the reunion of Hitomi-san with the three of you," replied Koizumi.

Jenkins cut into the conversation, speaking in English, "It's as if my wife has been kidnapped by Japan."

"You're wrong," Koizumi responded. "Your wife does not want to return to North Korea. She wants all of you to come to Japan instead. Come with me. Let's all go back to Japan. As long as you are on Japanese territory, the U.S. government cannot do anything to you."

But Jenkins refused. "If I go to Japan," he said, "I will be arrested by the U.S. Army and then deported to the United States, where I will be shot to death. The U.S. is a dangerous country."

Koizumi persisted. "I assure you that I will do my very best personally to settle the issue with the United States," he promised.

Yabunaka then tore a page from the interpreter's notebook and wrote in English: "The Prime Minister of Japan will assure you that he will do the utmost so that you can live together happily with Mrs. Jenkins in Japan."[13] Yabunaka passed the paper to Tanaka, who passed it to Koizumi, who once again said, "I assure you," showing the paper to Jenkins.

That action, however, did not produce the expected reaction from Jenkins. "I am truly grateful for the assurance from the Japanese prime minister himself," he said. "But what I really need is a guarantee from the president of the United States." Nonetheless, he stashed the paper protectively in the chest pocket of his jacket.[14] Meanwhile, Brinda kept sobbing.

Koizumi changed his tactics a little. "Chairman Kim Jong-il told me that the three of you could go to Japan," he said. "He proposed 'a reunion in Beijing or somewhere else.'" To that Jenkins responded by saying, "Actually, that was the idea that I proposed to Chairman Kim earlier. I welcome the proposition."[15]

That was as far as they could go at the time. Koizumi and his party failed to persuade Jenkins, in whom Koizumi sensed "something like raw fear."[16] It did not seem to be only the fear of facing a U.S. military firing squad; it must have included a fear of some unspoken threat from the North Korean authorities. It was later revealed that Jenkins had been convinced that the North Koreans were listening to their conversation, so when he spoke he was speaking to them. The Japanese were aware of that possibility, and Yabunaka tried to communicate Koizumi's assurances without making any vocal reference to them through the English note that Koizumi handed to Jenkins.

Jenkins and his two daughters had been taken to the guest house at about 9:00 o'clock that morning. For about three hours after that, before they finally met Koizumi, four high-ranking officials took turns going into their room to try to persuade them not to go to Japan. At the last stretch, even Deputy Foreign Minister Kim Yong-il came to talk to them. None of them said, "Don't go to Japan." Instead, they said something along the lines of "If you choose to go with the Japanese delegation to the airport, you'll go in a different vehicle, not the delegation's bus." And, as Jenkins later wrote in his memoir, "somewhere on its way to the airport, our vehicle would have been split off from the delegates' bus. The North Korean authorities would later have explained to the Japanese that the Jenkins had a sudden change of heart. Meanwhile, our vehicle would have disappeared somewhere known to no one." Late on the day that Jenkins turned down Koizumi's proposal, Jenkins was told by North Korean authorities that "our beloved general was greatly pleased by your conduct."[17]

Later on the same day, at Pyongyang Sunam International Airport, the five children of the Hasuikes and Chimuras were to depart for Japan on a second government plane, following Koizumi's plane. After boarding, Koizumi said to Yabunaka, "Have all the children gotten on board?" When Yabunaka replied that he had not yet received confirmation, Koizumi said, "If they haven't, don't leave Pyongyang."

Yabunaka rushed down the ramp and returned to the airport building. In a few minutes he returned and reported to Koizumi that all of the children were now on board.[18] At first the five children were to board before the Japanese delegation boarded their plane, but departure procedures for the five took longer than expected, causing a delay. Yabunaka asked Kim Yong-il, who was there to see the party off, to expedite the process.[19]

On the same day in Japan, members of the Kazoku-kai (Association of the Families of Victims Kidnapped by North Korea), the Sukuu-kai (National Association for the Rescue of Japanese Kidnapped by North Korea), and the Rachi-Giren (Parliamentary League for Early Repatriation of Japanese Citizens Kidnapped by North Korea) got together to wait for the outcome of the Koizumi-Kim talks. When they heard that there had been no noteworthy breakthrough, the room was filled with sighs of disappointment and angry comments:

"Was that all they got, even with an offer of food aid?" one person asked scornfully. "Everybody knows that economic sanctions are the only way to make the North Koreans get serious," added another. "Why did the government tell them from the beginning that there wouldn't be any? Does it really want to settle this issue?"

Shigeru Yokota, chairman of the Kazoku-kai, severely criticized the outcome as "the worst possible result that we could imagine." Takeo Hiranuma, president of Rachi-Giren and Japan's former METI minister, said bluntly, "This is unacceptable. This is far less than one should expect from a visit of the prime minister himself. It doesn't take a prime minister to achieve this outcome. Even I could have done it."[20]

When the government plane touched down at Haneda Airport, Ichiro Aizawa, the senior vice minister for foreign affairs, was waiting at the foot of the exit ramp to welcome the returning children and their parents. Aizawa warned Koizumi that the members of the three organizations were in a foul mood and might severely criticize him. "Please give a very brief report and leave the meeting room quickly," Aizawa asked, referring to the debriefing session that had been planned by the government for the family members of the abductees. Aizawa did not plan to let the prime minister become a captive target of the family members' verbal abuse, unable to leave the room gracefully. But Koizumi replied, "I think we should make it open. I'm sure some members will bring tape recorders. If so, it won't make any difference if we shut out the TV crews."

"Let them speak their minds," he added. "I'll respond to every one of them until the very end."[21]

After Koizumi's first visit to North Korea in 2002, Hitoshi Tanaka and MOFA had been the target of all the criticism. Koizumi was like Teflon—nothing stuck to him. This time, however, Koizumi offered himself as the target. The media, who had expected to be allowed to stay in the debriefing room for only the initial three minutes, stayed throughout the debriefing, which lasted about one hour, covering the entire proceeding. Harsh words were heard from the family members of those whose fate was announced as unknown:

"You let Kim Jong-il trick you twice," exclaimed one relative. "Don't you have any pride?" "Things couldn't be any worse," interjected another. "You seem to place more weight on implementing the Pyongyang Declaration than on settling the abduction issue." "You're nothing more than an errand boy," added someone else.[22]

TV stations all over Japan broadcast the videotape of Koizumi patiently enduring the cross-fire. Almost instantly, waves of protest from viewers hit the Kazoku-kai office:

"How come there were no words of thanks to the prime minister?"

"You just keep on accusing the prime minister!"

"What about a few words of welcome for the five returnees?"[23]

The next day, opinion polls conducted by the *Asahi Shimbun* and *Mainichi Shimbun* showed that Koizumi's popularity had risen by 9 percentage points and 11 percentage points, respectively.[24] This was "Koizumi magic" at its best: first creating an imaginary enemy and then engaging in a daring fight with this "enemy," thereby increasing one's popularity with the public. This time, Kazoku-kai was set up as the imaginary enemy.

Some time later, Koizumi was heard to say, contentedly, "I was chewed up, wasn't I? As they say, though, too much water drowns the miller."[25] The previous day's debriefing was a sweeping triumph of another Koizumi performance—Koizumi's theatrical politics at its most effective.

DIALOGUE AND PRESSURE

Nevertheless, Koizumi's second visit to Pyongyang was criticized liberally from many corners, in many ways:

—It was interpreted as an attempt to gain more votes at the Upper House election to be held on July 11.

—It was criticized for giving North Korea the incorrect impression that Japan was in a rush to normalize diplomatic relations.

—It was criticized for lack of adequate preparation and groundwork, leaving the outcome of the summit talk to chance.

—It suggested that Japan had two or even three channels of diplomacy.

—Policies toward a country like North Korea require dialogue as well as pressure—a carrot-and-stick approach—but Japan's dealings with North Korea entailed a simple offer of carrots.

—A meeting that had been intended to advance a strategic plan for creating peace in Northeast Asia through normalization of Japan-DPRK relations was downgraded to a tactical bargaining session over money and rice.

The criticism that inadequate preparations for Koizumi's visit left the outcome to chance included the idea that it had been wrong, in terms of both diplomatic protocol and Japan's honor, for the Japanese prime minister to have gone to Pyongyang twice, both times without formal protocols. If a politician tried to take a diplomatic initiative vis-à-vis a country like North Korea, he or she would have no choice but to visit the country to exercise his or her diplomatic skills on that country's turf. Meanwhile, the other country would never put its cards on the table until the politician arrived; that country's officials would just say, "You will be pleased if you come." The visiting politician would know what was inside the box, so to speak, only upon making the visit. One might call this the "black-box diplomacy" of North Korea.[26] Koizumi was criticized for having fallen for a diplomatic trick.

The criticism that Koizumi's government had two or even three sources of foreign policies was based on the fact that in order to pave the way for Koizumi's second visit to Pyongyang, contacts between the two countries occurred simultaneously through three different channels that sometimes intertwined. The first channel was between Tanaka/Yabunaka and X. The second was between the LDP's former vice president, Taku Yamazaki, and Katsuei Hirasawa, of the House of Representatives, on one side and the ambassador in charge of negotiations with Japan, Jong Thae-hwa, on the other. The third channel was between the prime minister's office and the top leadership of Chosen Soren (General Association of Korean Residents in Japan).[27]

Because there had been no diplomatic relations between Japan and North Korea, North Korea had repeatedly approached instead the political parties in Japan—particularly the long-time ruling party, the LDP—and, using its contacts with the various parties as leverage, attempted to make the Japanese government accept whatever agreements North Korea had concluded with the parties. Thus, numerous delegations from different parties had gone to North

Korea, where they had made half-baked promises that later created controversy in Japan. That pattern was repeated over and over. In those cases, Chosen Soren often played the role of a back channel contact with North Korea, but what Tanaka aimed at through his secret negotiations with X was to make back channel contacts a thing of the past. To use the expression of a veteran Japanese diplomat whose duties centered on Japan's policies regarding the Korean Peninsula, he attempted to "slough off Japan-DPRK relations based on money and rice."[28]

However, the traditional back channel was used once again to arrange Koizumi's second visit to Pyongyang. North Korea had made it clear to the Japanese that it was comparing the three channels to determine which would yield the largest return; in doing so, North Korea got a second visit from Koizumi and a pledge of 250,000 tons of food. Fukuda was convinced that the Pyongyang Declaration had been possible because Japan had excluded North Korea's back-channel contacts—Chosen Soren types and "Japan handlers" in Pyongyang's Ministry of Foreign Affairs—from the negotiations; because of that, he was all the more disturbed by the revival of back channel communications.[29] Fukuda's split with Koizumi over the prime minister's second visit was another factor in Fukuda's sudden resignation.

Regarding the need for "dialogue and pressure," a rift erupted among Japanese government officials. The government had taken the stance that it had to engage in dialogue with as well as apply pressure on North Korea with respect to the nuclear and the abduction issues. However, even within the government there were various views on the proper proportions of the two types of action. The feud could be characterized as one between the "pressure school," which would not hesitate to impose economic sanctions on North Korea, and the "dialogue school," which insisted on patiently engaging North Korea in dialogue based on the Pyongyang Declaration. The debate was further intensified by frustration over the bleak prospects for the return of the abduction victims at the time of North Korea's withdrawal from the NPT in January 2003.

The rift resurfaced on the occasion of Koizumi's visit to the United States in May 2003. A heated argument arose between Shinzo Abe and Hitoshi Tanaka, in the presence of Koizumi, while they were en route to the United States. The prime minister was determined to state, in the upcoming summit talk with President Bush, that "both dialogue and pressure are indispensable for peacefully settling the North Korean issues." The argument between Abe and Tanaka was over whether Koizumi should use the word *pressure* in the post-summit press conference.

"If the prime minister refers to *pressure*, it's quite possible that all of North Korea will explode in fury," said Tanaka. "They'll take all of our messages negatively."

"No country, in the entire history of the world, has exploded in fury as one," Abe retorted. "Of course we should use the word *pressure*."

"It goes without saying that dialogue and negotiations are inconceivable without some sort of pressure mechanism in the background," Tanaka responded. "And indeed the tough U.S. stance on North Korea made the Pyongyang Declaration possible. But it's equally inconceivable to start a dialogue with another nation by declaring that we'll put pressure on it."[30]

Both of them agreed on the need for pressure; the question was how open Japan should be about applying pressure. While Tanaka insisted on its discreet, behind-the-scenes application, Abe felt that pressure should be applied openly. In this argument, Koizumi supported Abe, and it was decided that both dialogue and pressure would be explicitly mentioned in the post-summit press conference.

The balance between dialogue and pressure and the timing of their use became an issue again on the occasion of Koizumi's second visit to Pyongyang in May 2004. Did the amendment of Japan's Foreign Exchange and Foreign Trade Control Law, aimed at allowing economic sanctions against North Korea, really contribute to increasing Japan's bargaining power vis-à-vis Pyongyang? Did the amendment enable the return of the family members of the abduction victims? Or was it the 250,000 tons of food aid that was really decisive? The bilateral negotiations in February of that year did not produce any remarkable results. Could that be attributed, at least in part, to the possibility of economic sanctions raised by the amendment?

It was quite possible, in fact, that Kang Sok-ju's unapproachable attitude during the February negotiations had been his defiant way of emphasizing that North Korea would never compromise under the threat of pressure.[31] And because at that time Koizumi had not allowed Tanaka and Yabunaka to use his Pyongyang visit as a bargaining card, the North Koreans must have seen no chance of a positive outcome of the negotiations. Sheer pressure alone would not promote dialogue, because it would not give the other party any incentive to engage in dialogue. At the same time, the hard reality was that it was impossible to move North Korea without pressure. It was also undeniable that North Korea felt pressured by the amendment, which the Diet had passed in February, as if to coincide with Japan's negotiations with North Korea that month.

Koizumi's second visit to Pyongyang ultimately resulted in the return of eight (initially five) family members of the abductees to Japan.[32] As a result, Koizumi's second visit acquired a quality somewhat similar to that of a humanitarian mission. Nevertheless, there was no progress concerning the abduction issue, and from that time to the present bilateral normalization negotiations have stagnated. In November 2004, Yabunaka flew to Pyongyang to have working-level consultations with his North Korean counterpart concerning the results of the reinvestigation of the fate of the other missing Japanese believed to have been abducted by North Korea. After renewing their investigation, the North Koreans admitted that they discovered that the death certificates that they had presented earlier were forgeries. Regarding Megumi Yokota, the North Koreans claimed that the date of death was April 13, 1994, not March 13, 1993, as previously stated, saying that they found that she had been repeatedly in and out of a mental hospital after April 13, 1993.[33]

Following the reinvestigation, in December 2004 North Korea told the Japanese government that eight of the missing people had died and that two had never entered North Korea. After examining the physical evidence and records of testimony accompanying the December report from North Korea, the Japanese government concluded that "the North Korean explanation was utterly groundless." Accordingly, Chief Cabinet Secretary Hiroyuki Hosoda protested strongly.[34]

The North Koreans had obtained what they called the "remains of Megumi Yokota" from a Kim Chol-jun, allegedly her husband, and gave them to the Japanese government. After a thorough examination, however, the Japanese government announced that the remains contained DNA of someone other than Megumi Yokota. Public opinion in Japan toward North Korea hardened, and voices demanding economic sanctions against North Korea became louder.

Special abduction issue committees of both the upper and lower houses of the Diet adopted a resolution requesting the government to consider imposing aggressive economic sanctions against North Korea. The resolution was extremely critical of North Korea, stating that "the insincere response of North Korea has gravely offended our country's dignity and played on the feelings of the abduction victims." In light of the statement in the Pyongyang Declaration that "both sides . . . would sincerely tackle outstanding problems between Japan and the DPRK," sanction advocates stressed that North Korea's conduct in presenting a total stranger's remains as those of an abduction victim was extremely insincere.

This development put the Foreign Ministry in a more difficult position. Within the ministry, views were split, but Foreign Minister Nobutaka Machimura decided to apply economic sanctions against North Korea. When he had received the report from the National Police Agency that a DNA test had confirmed with 99 percent, if not 100 percent, certainty that the remains were not those of Megumi Yokota, Machimura shook with rage. "The North Koreans had the nerve to ridicule us like this," he thought. "If we don't put pressure on them now, when do we?"[35]

During the six-party talks, China and South Korea had requested Japan's prudence regarding sanctions, while the United States remained neutral, leaving the matter to Japan's discretion. Machimura repeatedly stressed to Koizumi the need to apply economic sanctions against North Korea. "Whether we apply full-scale sanctions or not, I think we should faithfully convey the anger of the Japanese people," he said. "But diplomacy toward diplomatic normalization with North Korea has been started at your initiative, Mr. Prime Minister. So in the end we must leave the final judgment to you."

Koizumi repeated what he had previously said in response to similar remarks: "The relationship with North Korea entails both dialogue and pressure. As for pressure on North Korea, the less visible the better. We don't want blatant sanctions." For just an instant, Machimura thought of further challenging Koizumi, even if it meant losing his job. But at the last minute he held himself in check, reminding himself that a cabinet member does not interfere with a diplomatic initiative of the prime minister.[36]

In fact, during the summit talk at the time of Koizumi's second visit to Pyongyang in May, Koizumi had promised Kim Jong-il that Japan would not impose economic sanctions on North Korea. During the talk, Kim Jong-il repeatedly referred to the Pyongyang Declaration and announced that "as long as Japan complies with the Pyongyang Declaration, North Korea will not pose any threat to Japan. No need to worry." Koizumi responded in kind: "As long as North Korea complies with the declaration and observes the moratorium on missile launching, Japan will not impose economic sanctions on North Korea."[37] Some time later, Koizumi explained his promise to Kim Jong-il:

> We didn't have to use the term "economic sanctions." "Dialogue and pressure" would be much more appropriate. Economic sanctions is a broad concept. One can apply pressure, including economic pressure, when necessary, without resorting to economic sanctions. To begin with, we must be sensitive when we use the term "economic sanctions." North Korea claims that it would regard economic sanctions as a declaration of war.[38]

Thus, Koizumi remained cautious with regard to applying unilateral economic sanctions against North Korea, which, in any case, could be expected to have only limited adverse effects. What Koizumi was most concerned about was whether Japan was really ready to deal with the consequences if North Korea did in fact respond to Japan's economic sanctions as a declaration of war.

Less than one week after Koizumi became prime minister, four aliens—believed to be Kim Jong-nam, the eldest son of Kim Jong-il, and his family—were detained by Japanese immigration authorities for violating Japan's passport law when they tried to enter Japan in May 2001 in order to visit Tokyo Disneyland.[39] The group had arrived at Narita Airport on the afternoon of May 1 on Flight JAL 712 from Singapore, but their Dominican Republic passports were found to have been forged. In fact, both the police and the immigration authorities had been informed by their respective sources of the arrival of "a male who resembles Kim Jong-nam." Although the police had considered tailing the group while they were in Japan, the immigration authorities were determined to detain them. There was no communication or coordination between the two authorities; each believed that it had exclusive information.[40] The information on the detention of "a male who resembles Kim Jong-nam" was conveyed to Koizumi that evening.

The following morning Foreign Minister Makiko Tanaka and Yutaka Kawashima, the administrative vice minister for Foreign Affairs, discussed the handling of the situation. Tanaka said, emphatically:

> Get them out of Japan immediately. . . . Deport them before the mass media learn about their presence. . . . We might be attacked by North Korean missiles if we don't. . . . We can erase the record of the illegal entry, can't we? . . . You can do something about their passports, can't you?[41]

Her comments suggested that the foreign minister was recommending that the group be secretly deported, bypassing the standard procedure, which was to issue a written order to deport. In other words, the foreign minister of Japan was suggesting that the government resort to an extralegal measure. Later that day, Teijiro Furukawa, the deputy chief cabinet secretary, convened a meeting at the prime minister's office of officials from the relevant agencies in order to decide whether to deport the detainees or seek criminal penalties against them. The meeting became mainly an exchange between the National Police Agency and the Ministry of Justice:

> *National Police Agency*: Bring charges against the four, and provide us with the immigration information.

> *Ministry of Justice:* It was an ordinary illegal entry that should be properly handled by deporting the offenders.

> *National Police Agency:* The records show that they had previously attempted to make illegal entries. Let's investigate them. We need to find out who they are, anyway.[42]

At that point a Ministry of Foreign Affairs official cut in to point out that there were about ten Japanese nationals residing in North Korea at that time, calling the officials' attention to the need to take into consideration the influence that any decision might have on their fate. The officials failed to come to an agreement.[43] Consequently, Chief Cabinet Secretary Fukuda convened a second meeting that evening, at which the officials eventually decided to initiate action for a forced deportation. It was also decided that the four aliens would be deported to China, respecting the request of the "male who resembles Kim Jong-nam," and Kawashima asked the Chinese ambassador to Japan to receive them.[44]

Throughout the incident, the Japanese continued to call the illegal male alien "a male who resembles Kim Jong-nam," deliberately obscuring his true identity (he was, in fact, Kim Jong-nam). Meanwhile, North Korea kept silent.[45] Koizumi was convinced that Japan had no choice but to forcibly deport the four people in accordance with Japanese law. Koizumi kept saying, "Japan won't be able to withstand the various complications that will result if we take any other action.

The Japanese people and Japanese public opinion are not prepared to meet the challenge squarely. That's why it's better to let them go." He added:

> We are not trained to carry out the kind of diplomacy that utilizes hostages to force an opponent to accept our terms. In fact, we are not capable of doing that. To take the four as hostages and to force North Korea to comply? North Korea is not that kind of country. Japan cannot maneuver using hostages, while North Korea won't even hear of some of its important members being taken hostage. We are a democratic country. North Korea is a dictatorship.[46]

On May 4, the detainees boarded an All Nippon Airways flight and departed for Beijing. They were given the entire upper business-class deck and were accompanied by officials of Japan's Foreign Ministry and immigration authorities. After the plane landed in Beijing, they were escorted to the VIP room at the airport.[47]

The controversy over the economic sanctions against North Korea was rekindled by the incident concerning the false remains of Megumi Yokota, but ultimately the Japanese government decided not to resort to sanctions. In the Diet, however, the voices demanding economic sanctions became increasingly louder, and the Koizumi government was criticized severely for its inaction. Some criticism went so far as to say that the Koizumi government's diplomacy toward North Korea had deteriorated to the point that it existed merely to defend the Pyongyang Declaration. Concerning Koizumi's promise not to resort to economic sanctions while North Korea complied with the Pyongyang Declaration, the critics claimed that North Korea had already violated the declaration the moment it announced its nuclear capability. Foreign Minister Machimura had to withstand their criticisms and many others.[48]

Angered by the result of the DNA analysis conducted by the Japanese government, North Korea demanded the return of the remains. Separate DNA analyses also revealed that it was highly likely that Megumi Yokota's husband was a South Korean national, Kim Young-nam, who had been abducted in the late 1970s.[49]

A CAUSE FOR A NATION

After both of Koizumi's visits to North Korea, the approval rating of Koizumi's cabinet rose significantly. An opinion poll taken by the *Asahi Shimbun* on September 18, 2002, immediately after the first visit, showed that the cabinet's rating shot up to 61 percent from 51 percent in late August. The poll also revealed that 81 percent of respondents gave a positive evaluation to the summit talk and that 58 percent approved of normalizing relations with North Korea.[50] However, as the Japanese public's interest in the abduction issue increased, the public became more cautious about normalization. An *Asahi Shimbun* poll taken on

October 5 and 6 revealed a near-perfect split of views regarding normalization, with 44 percent of respondents approving and 43 percent opposing it.[51] A poll taken on May 23, 2004, immediately after Koizumi's second visit, showed that 67 percent of respondents approved of that visit, and it showed that his cabinet's approval rating also increased, to 54 percent from 45 percent.[52]

Koizumi's style—often called "Koizumi theatrics"—resembled that of an action movie hero. To the Japanese people, Koizumi might have looked like the Lone Ranger, voicing a hearty "Hi Ho, Silver! Away!" as he rushed to the rescue of the children of the abductees. But the same theatrics might have blurred the most important reason for Koizumi's visit to Pyongyang and, what is more fundamental, for his effort to expedite the normalization process in the first place. It also could be said that Koizumi himself had not convincingly explained his reasons to the Japanese people.

After he returned from his second visit to Pyongyang, Koizumi shared his convictions with his fellow members at a Diet session, quoting a Meiji-era foreign minister, Munemitsu Mutsu, who once said, "I genuinely believe that there was no other way." Munemitsu Mutsu, who served in the second Hirobumi Ito cabinet of 1892, successfully concluded the Sino-Japanese Peace Treaty (Treaty of Shimonoseki) after the end of the Sino-Japanese War in 1895. Koizumi said, "After puzzling over Japan's true national interest, Mutsu must have reached the conclusion that anyone else would have found that there was no alternative if he or she thoroughly considered the country's national interest. I fully share the spirit of that statement."[53] It should be obvious, however, that although Koizumi might have laid bare his true feelings, doing so did not constitute a presentation of his grand design for normalization of relations with North Korea.

Assessments of the outcome of Koizumi's Pyongyang visits and the normalization negotiations varied. After Koizumi's first visit, the prime minister's inner circle made the rather self-serving claim that Koizumi had gotten nearly everything that he wanted except information about the abductees.[54] As time went by, however, such self-aggrandizing appraisals ceased to be heard. Instead, harsher evaluations predominated, assessing the trips and normalization attempts as failures. Comments heard among politicians and diplomats in Tokyo revealed quite a few problems with the negotiations and Japan's foreign policy after the Pyongyang visits:

—The scenario for normalization was not thoroughly prepared and was too hastily pursued.

—The government should have realized more accurately the difficulty of accomplishing normalization without settling the nuclear program issue.

—Before visiting Pyongyang, the government should have consulted more thoroughly with the U.S. government on the approach to take regarding North Korea's nuclear development program.

—The government should have had more thorough discussions with the U.S. government on the handling of the highly enriched uranium issue so that the two countries could coordinate their respective policies after James Kelly came back from his visit to North Korea.

—The United States should have extended its suspension of shipments of heavy fuel oil supplies to North Korea under the KEDO framework, not terminated them, in order to prevent resumption of North Korea's nuclear fuel reprocessing program.

—The government should have decided beforehand how to finalize settlement of the abduction issue once Kim Jong-il apologized.

—The government should have made it clear to North Korea that it was inconceivable to have abduction victims "return home temporarily," and it should have negotiated with Pyongyang to ensure that it shared that understanding.

Such comments did not necessarily mean that the Koizumi government had failed to attend to the issues raised. Indeed, even its critics acknowledged that there were many issues that Koizumi and his lieutenants tried their best to address throughout the process, only to obtain inadequate results.

Although there is almost no way to know how North Korea had actually evaluated developments after Koizumi's visits, one North Korean diplomat said that

> while we were convinced that the United States would surely try to obstruct our normalization, Japan was full of confidence that they knew how to handle the United States. In the end, however, the situation evolved as we had feared it would. The United States tried to interfere with the movement toward normalization by dispatching James Kelly to Pyongyang. Furthermore, while we had been deeply apprehensive about the Japanese reactions toward the outcome of the abduction issue, Japan failed to appreciate how seriously negative the people's reactions would be.[55]

In October 2002, the United States had sent a government delegation led by James Kelly, assistant secretary of state, to Pyongyang. During that visit, Kelly confronted the North Koreans with U.S. suspicions about North Korea's secret development of enriched uranium, triggering the second Korean nuclear crisis (this incident is discussed in more detail in chapter 3).

In fact, X also showed great concern about the reaction of the Japanese people to the abduction issue, and he repeatedly asked for Tanaka's views. "If we ever admit having abducted Japanese people, won't Japanese public opinion toward my country worsen even more?" he asked Hitoshi Tanaka on one occasion. "In a democratic country like Japan, you can't hide anything from the people," Tanaka responded. "If North Korea admits it had abducted Japanese nationals in the past, anti–North Korean sentiment would inevitably increase, at least temporarily. But if North Korea were to express remorse and sincerely attend to the issue, public opinion within Japan would calm down in time. In the end, North Korea should be aware that it has more to gain from an admission than to lose."[56]

Beyond a doubt, North Korea was much more concerned about negative reactions within Japan than the Japanese were. That was in part because North Korea did not disclose the death of eight of the abductees until the very last minute. As Teijiro Furukawa reminisced, "What was really crucial was that the list of the deceased included Megumi Yokota and that all those listed were too young to die." The tragedy of Megumi Yokota might well have been the most significant factor in forming Japanese public opinion toward North Korea.[57]

Much graver issues than specific tactical and technical shortcomings affected how well-prepared Japan had been regarding the normalization process, including the strategic plan, the diplomatic apparatus, public opinion, and, most of all, the political leadership to achieve normalization.

To begin with, what kind of strategic calculations were behind the Koizumi government's drive toward normalizing Japan-DPRK diplomatic relations? In fact, it was North Korea that had taken the initiative to bring about Koizumi's visit to Pyongyang and start the process toward normalization. Before he became prime minister, he had had only a very vague notion, if any at all, concerning the specifics involved in normalization. But it is beyond doubt that Koizumi firmly grabbed the chance when it was presented to him. Although to initiate negotiations with North Korea regarding diplomatic normalization, which was a minefield in domestic politics, would have been impossible without effective teamwork by Koizumi, Yasuo Fukuda, Teijiro Furukawa, and Hitoshi Tanaka, it is beyond doubt that Koizumi's decisiveness and tenacity was a critical factor in the entire process.

In terms of a vision, however, Fukuda was much clearer than Koizumi was. Fukuda once said:

I have always wished to improve Japan's relations with such neighboring countries as Russia, China, and North Korea. Besides, Japan has not concluded a peace treaty with Russia and North Korea. I have always wanted to do something about this situation, not to pass it on to the next generation as homework. A little mischief by such a tiny country like North Korea can delay the development of the Sea of Japan Basin. This is where Japan will have to exercise leadership and where I have thought it could.[58]

Since Japan's defeat in World War II, the nation's foreign policy toward its Asian neighbors has always been designed to enhance confidence and reconciliation, starting with the payment of war reparations, followed by normalization of diplomatic relations, and then by economic cooperation, mainly through provision of official development assistance (ODA). In Japan's postwar diplomacy,

North Korea alone had been left out; it has been the only country in the world with which Japan has not had formal diplomatic relations.

Since Japan's postwar diplomacy has had to rely on the nation's economic power—the Japanese Constitution prohibits the use of military force—it often is regarded as a mercantile diplomacy. However, it also should be noted that Japan's postwar diplomacy has been characterized by Japan's persistent quest to overcome the past. Relations with Southeast Asian countries, South Korea, and China have all been pursued within that context. Japan already had envisioned applying the same postwar diplomacy to North Korea, thereby further stabilizing relations with China and South Korea, and when possible, contributing to a framework for East Asian peace and stability that would involve the United States.

For example, Prime Minister Keizo Obuchi had once pursued the possibility of launching six-party consultations as a framework for peace and security in Northeast Asia. He proposed his scheme to President Bill Clinton in a summit talk in September 1998, but Clinton did not show much interest in his proposal, partly because at that time the United States was working on a four-party consultation among the two Koreas, China, and the United States. Although ROK president Kim Dae-jung endorsed Koizumi's idea, it appeared that the United States interpreted it as an abrupt intervention by Obuchi, driven by Japanese self-interest and Japan's need to save face as a regional actor.[59] In contrast, Hitoshi Tanaka's scheme for Japan-DPRK normalization featured the following four objectives:

—North Korea's abandonment of its nuclear development program

—Settlement of the abduction issue

—Japan's engagement and participation in the construction of a multilateral framework for peace in Northeast Asia

—Japan's coming to terms with its past history.

Tanaka's plan for normalization of Japan-DPRK relations included a strategically and chronologically multilayered structure that "could take care of Japan's security, facilitate the process of North-South reconciliation on the Korean Peninsula, and thereby complete Japan's attempt to heal the wounds of war."[60] In order to achieve that goal, Japan had to deal actively with all of the issues above as a responsible partner. Tanaka thought that although Japan had had to put up with playing the role of a U.S. subcontractor in the U.S.-North Korea Agreed Framework, this time Japan could and should actively participate as a major party in constructing a framework.

For Fukuda and Tanaka, Japan's strategic plan for normalizing relations with the DPRK was a scenario for "greater peace"; Furukawa regarded it as "a cause." Fukuda described the practical feasibility of the plan in the following way:

> The Pyongyang Declaration has given an incentive to China, Russia, and South Korea to actively engage in the Six-Party Talks. The declaration's

explicit announcement by Japan of economic cooperation with North Korea must have encouraged these countries to participate in Six-Party Talks, because they realized that they could now depend on funds provided through Japan's economic cooperation. The significance of the Pyongyang Declaration was, even from this angle, formidable.[61]

Kenji Hiramatsu, director of MOFA's Northeast Asian Affairs Division, had been engaged in preparing the groundwork for normalization negotiations under Hitoshi Tanaka. He thought that at the start of the negotiations there was an awareness of the need to "break the traditional pattern of Japan-DPRK negotiations, actually affect the bilateral relations, and, thereby, guarantee Japan's security."[62] He did not directly refer to the abduction and history issues that were among Tanaka's four objectives listed above; instead, Hiramatsu pointed to the need to reconstruct Japan's foreign policy process by taking steps to "break the traditional pattern of Japan-DPRK negotiations." That statement made it clear that the traditional informal actors would be replaced by major diplomatic players in the government and MOFA. It also called for building a structure whereby Japan and North Korea could talk about normalizing their relations and ensuring security and begin negotiations toward future normalization. In that sense, the secret consultations between Hitoshi Tanaka and X were a major turning point.

One might wonder why X entered the Japan-DPRK negotiations in the first place. Why did he appear only in negotiations with Japan? And why wasn't there someone like X in the negotiations with the United States? A high-ranking MOFA official has speculated that Kim Jong-il had interposed X as his proxy so that Kim could monopolize control of the economic cooperation (or compensation) from Japan that would accompany normalization. That official interprets the entry of X as a step by Kim Jong-il himself to help ensure that North Korea obtained the largest possible economic benefit from the negotiations.[63] Yet another MOFA official who had dealt with X conjectured that Kim Jong-il had granted X special authority after North Korea realized that settlement of the abduction issue would be a prerequisite for normalization:

It would be heavy work to settle the abduction issue. You would have to take up the unfortunate task of investigating what the special mission organizations had done, a task that a mere civilian bureaucrat or a diplomat could not successfully discharge. It would be necessary to assign to this job someone who had proper institutional backup.[64]

Another factor that may have had some significance was that X had a National Defense Commission background. In fact, from 2001 through 2002 the United States was approached several times regarding secret negotiations, and one or two of the proposals were identified as coming from the National Defense Commission.

At least two came through religious leaders, who passed on suggestions made to them to the White House and Department of State. None of the contacts were pursued. James Kelly recalled that "there were indeed a few approaches through various persons, including Dr. Billy Graham. The National Defense Commission was behind at least some of these."[65] It is quite conceivable that, under special orders from Kim Jong-il, the commission approached the United States and Japan through back channels almost simultaneously.

Another aspect of the "reconstruction of Japan's foreign policy process" turned out to be the revitalization of MOFA itself. In fact, diplomats such as Yukio Takeuchi and Hitoshi Tanaka, who had been engaged in the Japan-DPRK normalization negotiations, had a hidden agenda—to revitalize the Foreign Ministry through the process. In those days, the ministry, which had come under public scrutiny due to a series of scandals, including one involving diversion of funds, was engaged in an endless war of attrition with Makiko Tanaka, newly appointed foreign minister of the Koizumi cabinet. Makiko Tanaka once called the ministry an "abode of demons," a phrase that took wings of its own, deepening people's suspicion and distrust of MOFA.

Toward the end of October 2001, when Hitoshi Tanaka was about to attend his first meeting with X, Makiko Tanaka demanded the replacement of Akitaka Saiki, director of MOFA's Personnel Division, whom Makiko disliked. She locked herself in the Personnel Division office and demanded that a female clerk who happened to be there input into a computer a letter of appointment to replace Saiki. She occupied the room for ninety minutes, ignoring the wailing of the clerk. Japan's foreign policy apparatus was thus shaky, and, as a result, Japan's foreign policy continued to meander. Regarding that time, Fukuda reminisced:

> I personally wanted to break the overall diplomatic deadlock, or at least break a hole in the coop that the Japanese felt that they were locked in. Looking around, Japan's foreign relations were deadlocked everywhere. The stalemate situations included the Takeshima Island issue with the Republic of Korea, the rise of China and the feud with China over Yasukuni Shrine, the Northern Territories issue with Russia, and on and on and on. That's why I wanted to advance the normalization of relations with North Korea, which would provide Japan with a great opportunity to contribute to the stability of Northeast Asia. I believe that the prime minister's visit to Pyongyang made the Japanese people feel that something was moving and that Japan might be overcoming its deadlock with North Korea.

He continued:

> There also was chaos within MOFA. I ordered that the entire staff, starting with the vice minister and director general of the Foreign Policy Bureau,

work as one to put the ministry back on its feet. But everyone was standing in everyone else's way. Thus, I thought this normalization drive would also provide a golden opportunity to revitalize MOFA."[66]

THE POLITICS OF "RESTORING JAPAN"

Meanwhile, a sea change was occurring with respect to the Korean Peninsula. Each and every one of various major developments throughout the region and the world had the potential to change the future of the Korean Peninsula, including the nuclear crisis in North Korea; the rise of China; social upheaval approaching the level of a revolution in the Republic of Korea; Japan's quest to be a "normal country" and a world political power; turmoil in Russia and its ambition to be an energy superpower; turbulence in the United States after 9/11; U.S. fear of the proliferation of weapons of mass destruction; and transformation of the military/overseas presence of the United States—to mention a few.

Simply put, changes of seismic proportions were taking place in the strategic environment in Northeast Asia. Consequently, Japan was faced with the challenge of envisioning an appropriate framework for regional order and building constructive relations with its neighbors. Koizumi's visit to Pyongyang and attempts to normalize diplomatic relations with North Korea together were to be the starting point of Japan's strategic response to that challenge, which was designed to take advantage of the new trends in the international environment. More precisely, Koizumi's diplomacy skillfully utilized the United States' uncompromising stance toward North Korea, on one hand, and South Korea's more conciliatory attitude toward North Korea, on the other.

The hard-line U.S. stance toward North Korea, adopted after the inauguration of President George W. Bush and especially evident after the 9/11 terrorist attacks in the United States, had the effect of causing North Korea to devote more attention to Japan, which in time led to North Korea's more conciliatory attitude toward Japan. During the course of the secret negotiations with Hitoshi Tanaka, X was full of apprehension about U.S. hostility to and pressure on North Korea, as well as about U.S. aggressiveness in general after 9/11. X repeatedly asked for Tanaka's view on U.S. intentions and strategies. The Japanese were made to realize more than once or twice that North Korea felt threatened by the United States, which it feared was not just a "paper tiger." The Japanese, including Tanaka, surmised that North Korea hoped to obtain a higher level of security from the United States by proceeding with normalization negotiations with Japan.

X repeatedly said to Tanaka, "We don't have a pipeline with the United States like the one we have with your country. That's why we can't have a dialogue with the United States like we do with you." At the time of the first Japan–North Korea summit talk Kim Jong-il himself was heard to say, "We truly wish to proceed toward normalization of relations with the United States as we have done with Japan this time. Unfortunately, in the case of the United States it is not possible to apply the same method of multiple informal consultations."[67] His comment was meant to praise the secret negotiations between X and Tanaka, but it also might well have reflected his irritation about the lack of progress in U.S.-DPRK dialogue.

Japan's decision to dispatch its Self-Defense Forces to Iraq, further tightening the U.S.-Japan alliance, also must have affected North Korea's approach to Japan. Under the circumstances, it was infeasible for North Korea to try to make a diplomatic maneuver to drive a wedge into the U.S.-Japan alliance, which had been cemented by the Bush-Koizumi partnership.

It should be pointed out that in South Korea, President Kim Dae-jung (and his successor, Roh Moo-hyun) openly welcomed Japan's rapprochement with North Korea and expressed very favorable views regarding Koizumi's visit to Pyongyang. But that change of heart became possible only in the late 1990s. The situation was quite different during the cold war era, when South Korea would have seen any attempt by Japan to normalize relations with the DPRK, South Korea's enemy, as an unforgivable act. The situation remained basically unchanged even after the end of the cold war.

Under the "Northern Diplomacy" of President Roh Tae-woo, South Korea hoped to normalize relations with China and Russia; at the same time, the nature of its relations with North Korea became more pragmatic than before. In response, North Korea pursued a "Southern Diplomacy," sending an enticing hint to Japan to promote normalization. However, South Korea opposed Japan's "Northern Diplomacy" vis-à-vis North Korea. South Korean opposition was expressed, in typical fashion, through vehement protests against the normalization negotiations undertaken in 1990 during a visit to North Korea by a delegation of Japanese Diet members led by Shin Kanemaru.

In October 1995, in reference to Japan-DPRK rapprochement, including Japan's provision of rice, President Kim Young-sam stated that "if Japan advances its relations with North Korea over our heads, the people of the Republic of Korea might get the impression that Japan is obstructing the reunification of Korea," and Japan stopped making further moves in that direction.[68] The situation in those days can be compared to a chase scene in a movie: When Japan steps on the gas to get to North Korea faster, a police cruiser, the Republic of Korea, races to intercept Japan from behind, its siren blaring. On overtaking Japan, the ROK yells loudly, "Pull over! Pull over!" and Japan applies the brakes.

Through his "sunshine policy," President Kim Dae-jung removed the yoke imposed on Japan. "If it had not been for the sunshine policy, it would have been impossible for Prime Minister Koizumi to visit Pyongyang," Hitoshi Tanaka said later. "His visit was made possible by the policy change in the Republic of Korea."[69]

Nevertheless, it was U.S.-DPRK relations, not U.S.-Japan relations or Japan-ROK relations, that eventually decided the direction of Japan's DPRK normalization efforts. Although the tension between the United States and North Korea had surely led to the move toward normalization between Japan and North Korea, full normalization would be impossible without an improvement in U.S.-DPRK relations and, more accurately, some lessening of the fundamental tension between the U.S. and the DPRK over North Korea's nuclear activities. That presented the greatest dilemma that Koizumi had to face with respect to normalization of Japan-DPRK relations.

Koizumi's visit to Pyongyang was the starting point of the march toward normalization. The visit was the greatest bargaining card that Japan had, and Koizumi was willing to take the risk of being used as a bargaining card. By going to Pyongyang himself, he succeeded in obtaining both information about the abductees and apologies from Kim Jong-il. He also succeeded in persuading North Korea, following the pattern of the Japan-ROK agreement, to give up its demand for compensation and, instead, to accept an offer of economic cooperation that would become effective only after normalization of the two nations' relations. He further succeeded in obtaining a North Korean moratorium on missile launching after 2003. Moreover, he succeeded in reaching an agreement that the nuclear and missile issues would be pursued within a framework of multilateral consultations. The greatest fruit of the Koizumi government's North Korean diplomacy was, arguably, the signing of the Japan-DPRK Pyongyang Declaration. In spite of public criticism of the normalization endeavor triggered by the abduction issue, the Koizumi government continued to negotiate with North Korea from a basic position that emphasized, first, North Korean compliance with the Pyongyang Declaration; second, a comprehensive framework for a package settlement; and third, composed and rational responses by North Korea. Even though the Diet had enacted the law permitting the imposition of economic sanctions on North Korea, the government restrained itself from actually implementing it. Koizumi repeatedly emphasized that point.[70]

Any future evaluation of Koizumi's visit to Pyongyang, the signing of the Pyongyang Declaration, and the Japan-DPRK normalization process will have to take into consideration, in addition to the results just mentioned, the future development of the framework for the settlement of the nuclear and abduction issues and the future direction that the six-party talks take toward denuclearization and peace and stability on the Korean Peninsula.

JAPAN AS A "NORMAL COUNTRY"

But the gravest challenge to Japan may not come from any threats by North Korea, or U.S. intervention, or China's attitude toward Japan, or South Korean sentiments about the Japanese, but from within Japan. Today in Japan one can see a fierce quest for a new national identity. It was greatly stimulated by the performance of Prime Minister Koizumi, who, in a way, penetrated into "enemy territory" and rescued the abduction victims. To many in Japan, that was the action of a strong leader, a break with the miserable tradition of a sovereign nation that could not even protect its citizens' lives and property. Koizumi's image was reinforced by his repeated visits to Yasukuni Shrine despite repeated protests from China. Again, to many in Japan, Koizumi was a strong leader who defied China, which has repeatedly slighted Japan, for example, by intruding into Japan's territorial waters with its submarines and by blocking Japan's bid for a permanent seat on the UN Security Council.

The Japanese people also found it refreshing when Koizumi suddenly announced his intention to visit Pyongyang without consulting the United States. Here was a Japanese leader who tried not only to pursue his own foreign policy independent of the United States but moreover to pursue Japan's true independence from the United States itself. One reason why most Japanese people consistently supported normalization of Japan-DPRK relations despite being very angry about the abduction issue was Koizumi's forthright manner of advancing Japan's foreign policy independent of the United States. Nonetheless, it was Koizumi's very close relations with the U.S. president that gave him substantial latitude to advance independent policies.

The new brand of Japanese politics that was born in the Koizumi era was the result of a search for answers to various questions related to Japan's national identity: "How do we restore and reintegrate our country, whose present has been torn from its past?" "What is Japan all about?" "What kind of a country should Japan aspire to be?"

One can call this "the politics of restoring Japan," and the quest to reunite families torn by the abductions by retrieving the abductees became its symbol. One could detect here a hint of a victim mentality among the Japanese people, which must have been somewhat cathartic because, throughout the postwar era, Japan had been consistently accused of being a victimizer in World War II.

Or one can call it "normal country" nationalism, whereby Japan is yearning to be a "normal country" but is frustrated and exhausted by attacks from China and Korea because of Japan's past. This was seen in the theatrics of Prime Minister Koizumi's visits to Yasukuni Shrine, controversies over Japan's textbook descriptions of "comfort women," and challenges to the Tokyo Tribunal as "victor's justice" and to other historical legacies. The abduction issue resonated with the new political sentiments and dynamics in Japan.

In any case, this surge of national identity politics washed away Koizumi's policy of promoting normalization with North Korea. Japan-DPRK normalization was to be the undertaking of a lifetime for Yasuo Fukuda, who had "felt elated as a man" to devote himself to it and who deeply regrets its failure. "Nevertheless, we missed the goal," he said. "We failed to become the one to turn the page of history."[71]

A GAME OF HARDBALL

In the summer of 2002, everything was going well, following the scenario that Hitoshi Tanaka had mapped out. There was, however, one question left to be answered: When should Japan reveal to the United States what it had been doing vis à vis North Korea, so that Japan could secure U.S. support? One MOFA official who used to work with Tanaka admitted that "Tanaka was very much concerned in those days about the proper timing for informing the United States."[72] Tanaka had been instructed by Yasuo Fukuda to inform the United States before the announcement of Koizumi's visit to Pyongyang.

In early July 2002, Tanaka flew to Washington to meet with Richard Armitage and Assistant Secretary of State James Kelly. Tanaka had been convinced that the United States would interfere after he informed them of Koizumi's plan to visit Pyongyang. Aware that he was about to step into "a power game, a game of hardball," he decided to set up an explanation that would foreclose U.S. opposition; at the least, he must not present the United States with an excuse to interfere.[73] In order to do that, he thought that it would be best to keep the secret until the very last minute, when Koizumi would inform Bush directly. Bush's approval was considered to be likely, given the honeymoon relations between the two leaders at the time.

Accordingly, when Tanaka informed Armitage of Japan's basic stance toward normalization of Japan-DPRK relations, he hinted only that some VIP might fly to Pyongyang from Japan. He did not disclose that the plan was for Koizumi himself to visit Pyongyang. In reply, Armitage said, "Japan has bilateral issues with North Korea, so it would be only natural for Japan to address those issues," thereby approving Japan's initiative toward normalization with North Korea.[74]

But normalization involved issues—most notably security issues, particularly the nuclear and missile issues—that could not be dealt with by Japan and North Korea alone. Fukuda had urged Tanaka to visit the United States because he was convinced that "in light of the nuclear issues involved, we are obliged to inform the United States of the prime minister's planned visit to Pyongyang."[75] Nevertheless, Tanaka did not utter a word about the prime minister's visit because he had not received any instructions to do so from Koizumi himself. In fact, Koizumi was extremely strict about maintaining confidentiality. Yoriko Kawaguchi, who served as foreign minister in the Koizumi cabinet, reminisced:

> Prime Minister Koizumi was very strict; in fact, in regard to confidentiality he was the most strict legislator that I have ever known. We did not

receive his instructions to inform the United States of his plan until the very end. Even if I had thought it would be prudent to inform the U.S. government via the Japanese Embassy in Washington, D.C., I could not even send a telegraph to the embassy, because it had been decided not to inform even the director general of the MOFA's North American Bureau.[76]

On this point, Koizumi once explained, saying, "There are elements, both in the United States and Japan, that wish to derail the attempts at Japan-DPRK normalization. That's why I could not disclose my plan until the very end."[77]

On August 27, Japan informed the U.S. government of Koizumi's intention to visit North Korea. Koizumi invited Richard Armitage and Howard Baker, the U.S. ambassador to Japan, to the prime minister's office. Armitage was visiting Japan with James Kelly for the U.S.-Japan Strategic Dialogue with Yukio Takeuchi, vice minister for foreign affairs. In terms of protocol, it was rather unusual for a deputy secretary of state, such as Armitage, to personally visit the prime minister, who is at a much higher level.

Armitage was amicable when he walked into the prime minister's office, through the anteroom used for Koizumi's personal aides.[78] Koizumi personally disclosed to Armitage his intention to visit Pyongyang and requested U.S. cooperation, immediately adding, "We'll deal with the nuclear issue in close consultation with the United States. We are well aware of the U.S. position." Armitage noted that there were "other developments [regarding North Korea's development of nuclear power], so you might want to be a little cautious," catching Koizumi's attention. That was a tacit reference to North Korea's secret HEU (highly enriched uranium) program, but Armitage did not use the term on this occasion.[79]

At 8:30 p.m. on the same day, Chief Cabinet Secretary Yasuo Fukuda invited Armitage, Kelly, and Michael Green, director of Asian affairs at the National Security Council, to a meeting at the Hotel Okura in Tokyo. Hitoshi Tanaka, who had just come back via Beijing from consultations at the director general–level in Pyongyang, rushed from the airport to join the group. Fukuda told his guests that he wanted to see them before further advancing the process toward diplomatic normalization with North Korea, which would require settlement of security issues, including the nuclear issue. Tanaka briefed the American participants about the prime minister's planned trip. As Tanaka went on, neither Armitage nor Kelly said a word; their silence was deafening. When Tanaka was finished, Armitage said, referring to the United States' stand on Japan's initiative, "It depends on how the president takes this news," thereby avoiding giving a response on the spot. He said that he himself would inform Secretary of State Colin Powell, adding that, in consideration of the high degree of confidentiality of the matter, he would use a secure telephone line instead of sending a diplomatic telegraph.[80] Toward the end of the meeting, Tanaka said, "We hope that the U.S. government accepts in a positive way Prime Minister Koizumi's plan to visit North Korea and our efforts toward diplomatic normalization with that country." After the American guests left the room, Tanaka was heard to murmur, "That might be hard for the United States to swallow."

On the evening of August 28, Prime Minister Koizumi made a direct phone call to President Bush. Although an interpreter was needed, calling appropriate MOFA directors general and official interpreters into the prime minister's office would attract the attention of the media. Koizumi therefore called Koro Bessho, a personal aide who had been seconded to the prime minister from MOFA, from the adjacent anteroom and used him as the interpreter. In the phone conversation, Koizumi informed Bush that he would start negotiations toward diplomatic normalization with North Korea. Bush said, "That's good. I support your decision," to which Koizumi replied, "Thank you."[81]

Prior to the telephone conversation, Koizumi had consulted with Fukuda as to whether he should ask for Bush's support for his initiative, but in the end he decided against it lest he appear to be asking for U.S. approval. Koizumi need not have worried, because Bush voluntarily expressed his full support of Koizumi's initiative.

On the afternoon of August 30, Chief Cabinet Secretary Fukuda publicly announced Prime Minister Koizumi's plan to visit North Korea. The U.S. government had been formally informed three days earlier, by way of Koizumi's meeting with Armitage and Baker. The Japanese government had followed the example of the ROK government, which in June 2000 had notified the U.S. government of the summit talk between the two Koreas three days before the official announcement. Incidentally, the South Korean government had informed the Japanese government one day before the ROK's official announcement, and the Japanese government, following suit, informed the ROK government of the proposed visit on August 29, one day before Japan's official announcement.[82] After the Republic of Korea, the Japanese government subsequently secretly notified the Chinese and Russian governments. Koizumi gave instructions that the information should not be leaked by the governments of either country.[83]

Although Armitage had reported Koizumi's plan to Secretary of State Powell by electronic means, after Koizumi's direct briefing he reported directly to Powell on what he had heard from Koizumi. Powell immediately telephoned President Bush, who said that he trusted Koizumi.[84]

Bush had come to share Armitage's solid trust of Koizumi, who had firmly supported Bush's war on terror after the 9/11 attacks. Recalling their sentiments, Armitage said, "Koizumi would not trade our equities away. We believed him."[85]

But surely there were a variety of "noises" around the president. As Armitage noted, "'There are many voices in my father's house.' It's like a saying out of the

Bible: 'There are many rooms in my Father's house.'"[86] For one thing, there was surprise that Japan had adopted and was implementing foreign policy independently, without having given notice to the U.S. government. While some American officials were deeply impressed by what could be termed the "diplomatic acrobatics" by which the Japanese government, through the medium of Mr. X, had conducted its dealings with Kim Jong-il, others did not react calmly to Japan's engaging in those acrobatics for about one year without U.S. knowledge. They were not only surprised but also a bit insulted that they were informed only at the very end. Japan traditionally had been passive in its foreign policy, and the Japanese government had hardly ever initiated any foreign policy independently. To some Americans, it seemed as if Japan had all of a sudden begun to disregard the U.S. government's wishes.

When Hitoshi Tanaka informed Kelly of X's existence, Kelly had said, as if by reflex, that the U.S. should conduct a credibility check of X. Tanaka politely declined the offer, saying that "it would be messy if U.S. intelligence were to come into the picture. Besides, it's his behavior that matters. So we've done our own credibility check by observing his behavior."[87] Some Japanese officials suspected that nevertheless a U.S. intelligence agency secretly attempted to find out X's true identity. One official disclosed that he thought that "our telephone conversations with X might have been tapped by the American side."

On the occasion of the director general–level consultations, a minor argument arose among the Japanese delegation over how to communicate with MOFA headquarters from Pyongyang on how to settle some final details of Koizumi's visit. Yoriko Kawaguchi, Japan's foreign minister at the time, later reminisced, "It might sound silly, but we were not able to use a secure line to send the report from Pyongyang. We should have given more thought to the intelligence side, but we didn't think much about it." She also said that "there was speculation that the United States, through its intelligence activities, had known about Japan's secret negotiations with North Korea."[88]

On one occasion, Armitage directly asked Vice Minister Takeuchi, his counterpart in the Japan-U.S. Strategic Dialogue, "Yukio, do you have any idea what kind of a man this X is?" "I've been informed about X," Takeuchi responded, "but I don't know his real name. Even if I was told, I can't remember Korean names. But we have verified that X is directly connected to Kim Jong-il. As a matter of fact, X recently said something that cannot be stated without Kim Jong-il's consent." Takeuchi was referring to X's informing the Japanese of North Korea's decision to declare its withdrawal from the Non-Proliferation Treaty prior to its official announcement.[89]

At one point, a staff member of a U.S. intelligence agency tried to obtain information about X's true identity from the Japanese, but the Japanese kept their guard high. One U.S. intelligence officer later remarked, with a wry smile,

"When the Japanese demanded more information on North Korea's HEU, I demanded more information on X in return. But they refused."[90]

In 2005, a senior official of the U.S. Department of State said, with some agitation:

> Japan definitely contributed to the creation of the six-party talks. Japan has taken some very good action. But the point is that you more or less came up with the idea of normalization negotiations, but we just never had much confidence in that X or whoever this secret interlocutor, or whoever the hell he was.[91]

Meanwhile, the Japanese embassy in the United States had been communicating to Tokyo all the dissonant noises heard in Washington, among them remarks such as "Japan should not have resorted to underhanded tactics " and the warning that North Korea was "not the kind of country that behaves when it's provided with money or dialogue." Another objection was that Japan should not have let "all the money talks precede everything else. You have to address the security issues."

Hearing the complaints, Ryozo Kato, Japan's ambassador to the United States, became deeply apprehensive that the Japanese government had not consulted in enough depth with the U.S. government about Koizumi's visit and the normalization negotiations with North Korea. He communicated his grave concerns to MOFA headquarters:

> Make no mistake. Japan-DPRK normalization is not the same as Japan-ROK normalization. What then is the fundamental difference? It concerns the security issues. We didn't have to pay any attention to security issues in the case of Japan-ROK normalization because both nations were allies of the United States. But that's not the case with North Korea, which continues to threaten Japan through its nuclear program, missiles, conventional forces, and mysterious vessels. No normalization is possible unless these issues are resolved.[92]

These were the very issues that, throughout the secret negotiations, the Japanese had raised with North Korea and checked North Korea's responses thereto; the Japan-DPRK Pyongyang Declaration was the outcome of the process. The embassy in Washington, however, was completely out of the loop. The inflow of information from Tokyo did not improve much even after the secret announcement of Koizumi's visit to Pyongyang, to the extent that Kato first learned about North Korea's HEU directly from Richard Armitage after he came back to the United States, even though Armitage had provided the Japanese government pertinent information about it while he was in Japan. In fact, for unknown reasons, the information that Armitage provided was completely missing from the record of his Tokyo remarks that MOFA headquarters telegraphed to the embassy in Washington.[93]

An Intelligence Game

There was one more issue that had been troubling Hitoshi Tanaka during the summer of 2002: the revelation of North Korea's HEU program. The U.S. government had informed the Japanese government that a U.S. intelligence agency had detected the secret development of highly enriched uranium in North Korea, which could result in a showdown between the United States and North Korea and thereby derail the Japan-DPRK normalization negotiations. Some Japanese officials even suspected that the United States had deliberately notified Japan of North Korea's HEU program in the last stretch of the preparations for Koizumi's visit to Pyongyang in order to obstruct or at least to rein in the negotiations.

Weariness with the United States was especially strongly felt among some Japanese officials at MOFA's Northeast Asian Affairs Division, which had been in charge of the secret negotiations. Arata Fujii, who succeeded Kenji Hiramatsu as director of the division in July 2003, remarked:

> When Shin Kanemaru was about to visit North Korea, Secretary James Baker communicated to us the United States' concern about North Korea's nuclear development program. It was eventually proven that the U.S. apprehension was well-founded, but we were tempted to ask the United States why it had not informed us a little earlier of what it had known. We were tempted to believe that whenever Japan tried to make a move, the United States would be there to obstruct it.[94]

Fujii also had in mind an episode that occurred in the fall of 1990, when Shin Kanemaru, a powerful LDP legislator, and Makoto Tanabe, an influential member of the Japan Socialist Party, visited Pyongyang to discuss the normalization of Japan-DPRK relations with Kim Il-sung. It was the first attempt by Japan and North Korea to promote normalization since the end of the cold war, but further progress stopped, at least in part because Secretary of State James Baker cried foul play because of North Korea's nuclear development program.

In November 1991, Baker sent a secret telegraph to Secretary of Defense Dick Cheney regarding the program and normalization talks:

> Concerning Japan's negotiations with North Korea to normalize relations, Tokyo's terms have hardened significantly. The new Miyazawa government has moved Tokyo's position close to our own: normalization and economic aid require not just signing and implementing the IAEA full-scope safeguards agreement, but also foregoing a reprocessing capability. Some

Japanese bureaucrats might seek to nibble away at this position, but we should hold them to it. We must continue to work in tandem with Japan on this issue.[95]

Baker's telegram expressed his satisfaction with the effects of U.S. interference.

Japan was puzzled by U.S. actions during the Clinton administration too. Toward the end of the administration, the U.S. government had strongly requested that the Japanese government ban the export to North Korea of centrifugal separator parts. Although the Japanese government requested that the United States provide information to justify the export ban, the U.S. government failed to do so. Nevertheless, Japan restricted the export of the applicable parts to North Korea.[96]

In those days, the Clinton administration had been harshly criticized by the Republican-dominated Congress for its policies toward North Korea. In March 1999, a North Korea Advisory Group composed of conservative Republican members of the House of Representatives published a report later known as the Gilman Report. It warned of "North Korea's efforts to acquire uranium technologies, that is, a second path to nuclear weapons," and criticized the Clinton administration, saying "[T]he Clinton Administration did not succeed in negotiating a deal with North Korea that would ban such efforts. It is inexplicable and inexcusable."[97] It is quite possible that those criticisms were behind the Clinton administration's request that Japan ban the export of parts to North Korea. Later it seemed that the United States had lost interest in the issue. Why, then, did the United States suddenly raise the issue again in the summer of 2002?[98]

The Japanese government believed that U.S. policies toward North Korea might have been affected by the eruption of post-9/11 arguments for "preventive and preemptive strikes" and "regime change" made by influential players in the Bush administration such as Vice President Dick Cheney and Secretary of Defense Donald Rumsfeld. The Japanese paid extra attention to the statements of Rumsfeld, who had openly called North Korea a "terrorist regime, teetering on the verge of collapse."[99] Immediately before the Koizumi-Kim talks, Rumsfeld had said, emphatically: "[W]e do know that they [North Korea] are one of the world's worst proliferators, particularly with ballistic missile technologies. We know they're a country that has been aggressively developing nuclear weapons and has nuclear weapons."[100] His real aim was "regime change" in North Korea.[101]

When Foreign Minister Yoriko Kawaguchi visited the United States just before Koizumi's trip to Pyongyang in September, Rumsfeld conveyed to her the U.S. concern about North Korea's secret HEU program and the problems associated with it. About that conversation, one Department of Defense official remarked:

Rumsfeld was apprehensive about Koizumi visiting North Korea without having a proper understanding of the seriousness of this issue, which would have an adverse effect on the U.S.-Japan alliance. Before the meeting started, Rumsfeld expressed his wish to directly convey this message to Kawaguchi. First, we had a small group meeting and the Japanese side started talking about the PCB contamination around the Sagami Depot in Sagamihara City used by the U.S. military. Not knowing anything about what was being talked about, Rumsfeld was in a bad mood. After a while, the meeting was transformed to a tête-à-tête talk between Rumsfeld and Kawaguchi even without an interpreter. I understand Rumsfeld conveyed the United States' concerns to Kawaguchi in quite a severe tone.[102]

Both in the U.S.-Japan summit talk in New York on September 12, 2002, and in the talks between the foreign minister and the secretary of state that followed, the U.S. government called more explicitly for caution on the part of the Japanese government. In the summit talk with Bush, Koizumi explained the aim of his visit to North Korea and expressed his hope for future U.S.–North Korea consultations. In response, Bush pointed to North Korea's nuclear programs and its expansion of its missile capabilities and said, "To me, Kim Jong-il has no good points. He is one of the worst human beings in the world." Referring to a memo in his hand and keeping a very serious expression on his face, Bush said, "We are interested in weapons of mass destruction, missiles, and conventional forces in North Korea." But he added:

We are well aware that this issue cannot easily be settled by military means. Although North Korea is a member of the "axis of evil," we need to take a different approach to this country from that for the other axis countries. It is crucial to make Kim Jong-il act rationally and not to make him feel cornered. I very much hope that Prime Minister Koizumi's visit to Pyongyang will be a big help in that direction.

Bush then laughingly said to Koizumi, "You should play the good cop," and half-jokingly expressed his willingness to play the bad cop. Bush added, as if to reassure Koizumi, "I wholeheartedly welcome Prime Minister Koizumi's plan to visit North Korea." Although the Japanese had previously been informed that the enriched uranium issue might be brought up at the summit talk, Bush did not touch on the issue directly.[103]

During the foreign ministers meeting between Powell and Kawaguchi, however, the United States was more forthcoming about the enriched uranium issue, saying that the United States had obtained "new information." A high-ranking U.S. official added, "We were concerned that Mr. Koizumi might be embarrassed if he went to Pyongyang unaware of that."[104]

Nevertheless, the way that the United States handled the HEU issue with one of its most trusted allies was clumsy at best. At the U.S.-Japan foreign ministers meeting on the occasion of the ASEAN Regional Forum (ARF) in Brunei on July 31, 2002, the U.S. government put a feeler out to the Japanese government for the first time regarding North Korea's HEU program. In the course of the meeting, Secretary of State Colin Powell told Foreign Minister Yoriko Kawaguchi, "There is a serious problem regarding North Korean nuclear development. At this stage, our intelligence agencies are still trying to finalize their findings and there is a lot that we have not yet found out. But we are very much concerned."[105] Powell deliberately used the obscure expression "serious problem." Kawaguchi later reminisced, "Because it was about intelligence activities, it was not very definite, and I could not fully grasp all the facts."[106]

Actually, Powell had a reason for being deliberately obscure, as he later disclosed:

I thought it would be premature to notify Japan and South Korea about North Korea's HEU program. We were planning to raise that issue directly with North Korea at the time of James Kelly's visit to Pyongyang. And, as rude as it might sound, we were worried about the risk of this information being leaked if it were shared with Japan and ROK too soon.[107]

It was no secret that the U.S. administration did not trust Japan's safeguards with respect to intelligence. The Armitage Report of 2000 suggested several steps that Japan should take to improve intelligence cooperation with the United States, including a recommendation that Japanese leaders "win public and political support for a new law to protect classified information."[108] As one senior U.S. administration official later said, "With no law protecting classified information, and proven irresponsibility of some (not many) officials and politicians, there is a long standing reluctance among U.S. intelligence officials to share truly sensitive information."[109]

Kelly later disclosed that when he and Powell visited Brunei, he had informed Hitoshi Tanaka that what Powell had called "suspicious nuclear development" was actually North Korea's uranium enrichment program. Tanaka did not remember the incident, but Kelly remembered that Tanaka "just smoked a cigarette." At that point, Tanaka had not informed Kelly of Prime Minister Koizumi's plan to visit Pyongyang.[110]

On August 24–28, 2002, just before Armitage and his party arrived in Japan to attend the U.S.-Japan Strategic Dialogue, Under Secretary of State John Bolton, whose duties centered on arms control and nonproliferation of weapons of mass destruction, visited Japan and then South Korea. While in Japan, Bolton shared his analysis of North Korea's nuclear capacity in a briefing with top MOFA officials, including Vice Minister Yukio Takeuchi. Bolton only touched on North

Korea's "secret nuclear development" and did not refer to the most recent assessment by a U.S. intelligence agency, but the paper that he had prepared for the briefing mentioned North Korea's uranium enrichment program.[111] It was when Bolton was on his way to Narita Airport that a high-ranking U.S. official informed him by phone of Koizumi's plan to visit Pyongyang.[112]

It should be noted that the United States had informed the Japanese government of the HEU program in North Korea before it learned of Koizumi's planned visit to North Korea. It is obvious therefore that the U.S. government did not rush to try to upset Koizumi's plan by feeding Japan the information before he made the trip. One U.S. intelligence officer noted that, as a matter of fact,

[i]t would have been impossible to withhold such critical intelligence so as to release it at a specific time. What really happened at that particular time was that various intelligence agencies—after months of meticulous work collecting, analyzing, and selecting the best information—had finally come to a conclusion at that particular time. In the background were the 9/11 attacks, after which all the U.S. intelligence agencies launched efforts to reassess North Korea's nuclear capacity. And it was in the summer of the subsequent year that we came up with the results of our reassessment work, which happened to coincide with the timing of the groundwork for Koizumi's visit.[113]

The same U.S. intelligence officer explained:

We did receive requests from the Japanese government for more detailed information. But it should be understood that verification of intelligence is time-consuming work. We base our judgment, first of all, on the need to protect the sources of information. We verify each piece of information one by one from the viewpoint of whether it threatens the source of the information, and we have to do that in cooperation with our government's policy people. It is time-consuming work.[114]

Corroborating the preceding comments, a high-ranking U.S. official stated that "we tried to verify those results, but we could not complete the work in time for Koizumi's visit. It was only immediately before Kelly's visit to Pyongyang that we had finally confirmed the information."[115]

In short, it was by sheer coincidence that the intelligence was passed on to Japan at that particular time, and it was because verification of the intelligence took a long time that the U.S. government could not give the Japanese government a detailed briefing. Besides, the U.S. government and intelligence agencies were preoccupied with Iraq at the time.[116] The U.S. government requested that the Japanese government proceed with the prime minister's visit and normalization of negotiations with North Korea, keeping the HEU issue in mind. When the

Japanese asked whether they could raise the issue with their North Korean counterparts, the United States responded negatively, citing "intelligence reasons." The Japanese had no choice but to ask that in that case the "United States government directly negotiate with North Korea on the HEU issue."[117]

On the occasion of the meeting of the Trilateral Coordination and Oversight Group (TCOG) in Seoul in early September 2002, Hitoshi Tanaka had an argument with James Kelly. When Kelly reminded Tanaka that the North Korean nuclear and missile issues would not be problems for the United States alone, Tanaka responded, "They directly affect Japan. They are as serious to us as they are to the United States." When Kelly then expressed "concern" that the Japan-DPRK normalization negotiations did not squarely address the issues, Tanaka retorted, "If you are so apprehensive about this, why don't you go to Pyongyang yourself and raise those issues?"[118]

One high-ranking Japanese official later commented on that argument, his remarks colored by anger:

> Who can bring up a subject at a summit talk when the only thing you have is the suspicion of a foreign intelligence agency, without any evidence to back it up? Do you think you can say to your counterpart [North Korea] something like "According to the CIA, you seem to be doing something naughty"? That kind of diplomacy is simply unthinkable.
>
> If we were to do that, then the counterpart would surely ask if we were just a running dog of the United States. Do we just repeat like a parrot what we are told by the United States? The important thing was for Japan to conduct diplomacy so as to obtain concessions from North Korea in order to pave the way for eventual peace, even if that called for some negotiations with the United States, wasn't it?[119]

While it is obvious that the United States did not bring up the HEU issue in order to obstruct Japan's attempt to normalize relations with North Korea, that does not necessarily mean that the United States totally favored normalization. Lawrence Wilkerson, who was Secretary of State Powell's chief of staff, later noted that there were two schools of thoughts within the U.S. government about Koizumi's visit to Pyongyang:

> On the one hand, there were those who didn't like the visit because that would make it more difficult for us to put pressure on North Korea, while there were also those who evaluated this visit positively, hoping that it would give North Korea an incentive to move toward reform. Secretary Powell belonged to the second school. However, you should know that the evaluation of Koizumi's visit was not necessarily strictly split between the

moderates and the neoconservatives. Some neoconservatives actually hoped that it would lead to peaceful evolution from the bottom up.[120]

"Peaceful evolution" entails a softer version of regime change, through economic and social pluralization by way of economic reform, that leads to political reform and eventually to democratization. Perhaps most apprehensive in the U.S. government about Japan's normalization negotiations with North Korea was the Department of Defense, along with sections in other departments that were concerned with nuclear nonproliferation. According to Stephen Yates, who was in charge of East Asian affairs at Cheney's office, Vice President Cheney reacted ambivalently to the information about Koizumi's visit:

> Because the abduction issue was such a great issue within Japan, we were worried that Japan might go ahead with normalization when this issue was settled, leaving the nuclear issue unresolved. It would be possible, then, that the United States and Japan might get out step with each other vis-à-vis North Korea.[121]

One Department of State official who was concerned with nuclear nonproliferation said, "I think there was concern that Japan was going to move too far forward and essentially would give North Korea $10 billion that North Korea would then in turn use for its WMD program."[122] The U.S. government felt that it was necessary to explicitly communicate its concerns to the Japanese government before Koizumi visited North Korea, but it did not express its opposition to the proposed visit.

When a U.S. ambassador to a major Asian country visited the White House to meet Steven Hadley, the deputy national security adviser, at the time of Koizumi's Pyongyang visit, he was given the Pyongyang Declaration, which had just been released, by Michael Green, director of East Asian affairs. The ambassador later said, "Condi [Rice] came into the meeting unexpectedly. . . . I can tell you that everybody's reaction [to the declaration] was positive." Needless to say, the positive reaction was attributable to the declaration's explicit references to the nuclear and missile issues.[123]

Richard Armitage also recalled that "we had no intention to obstruct the prime minister's visit to Pyongyang." He added:

> [T]he whole idea was to warn Mr. Koizumi that you must do what you have to do for Japan, but don't get too far out in front, don't say too many glowing things about Korea, because someday in the future, matters that would be complicating for Japan could become public. . . . [I]f Koizumi got himself "pregnant" and then the HEU became known, he would look silly. That was the fear.[124]

That fear proved unfounded, because, in the words of Armitage, "The prime minister actually handled himself pretty well during his visit to Pyongyang."

James Kelly, looking back, said, "if . . . an active diplomatic role [that Japan plays] . . . won't mesh exactly with American interests as defined on that particular day, that doesn't bother me. I'm convinced that in the end the convergence of American-Japanese interests is large enough so that Japan's role is not going to come off badly."[125]

Nevertheless, it is beyond doubt that some Japanese became displeased with and distrustful of the United States, which, in their eyes, tried to restrain Japan's active diplomatic initiative. It should be noted, however, that the Bush administration did not systematically attempt to derail Japan's drive toward normalization of relations with North Korea. Lawrence Wilkerson later addressed that point, with obvious cynicism: "To derail Japan's normalization with North Korea? This administration is too incompetent to do such a big job. It is so disorganized that it can't accomplish anything. It's so incompetent that it can't even lay a plot. To me this is more horrifying."[126]

Nevertheless, the Bush government was watching Koizumi's Pyongyang visit soberly. Although it was willing to let Koizumi do what he wanted to do without interfering, it was convinced that normalization would not be easy with the abduction issue standing in the way. Bush administration officials who had not necessarily been in harmony with each other regarding U.S. policies toward North Korea were strangely in unison on that point.

"TANAKA MAKES ME NERVOUS"

Japanese diplomats who were concerned with Japan's diplomacy toward Asian countries shared a sense of distrust of the United States.

In the autumn of 2000, after Secretary of State Madeleine Albright's visit to North Korea was decided on, the Clinton administration urged the Japanese government to hasten its own normalization of relations with North Korea, saying that the "president will eventually go to North Korea, too. Japan might be left out if you don't do something about it." As it turned out, Albright's visit to Pyongyang was harshly criticized in the United States, and Clinton's plan to visit burst like a bubble. The Japanese saw the U.S. policy toward North Korea as shaped by political ambitions and opportunism, which it found troubling. At the launching of the Korean Peninsula Energy Development Organization (KEDO) in 1994, the Clinton administration had enthusiastically solicited Japan's support of KEDO, and the Japanese government had bent over backward to help. However, when objections erupted in Japan to providing financial assistance for KEDO after North Korea launched its Taepodong missile, the administration had the nerve to give the Japanese government a lecture on Northeast Asian security.

When the Bush administration succeeded the Clinton administration, it immediately started criticizing KEDO and the Agreed Framework of 1994 and adopted instead a highly irrational, ideological diplomacy toward North Korea described as "anything but Clinton (ABC)." Yukio Takeuchi and Hitoshi Tanaka, who had participated in the launching of KEDO and who had directly dealt with the North Korean nuclear crisis, found the American inclination to think it only natural for all policies to change when the government changes insupportable.[127]

Another source of the distrust of the United States within the Japanese government was its suspicion that the United States did not have full confidence in Japan as an ally. Although the U.S. government had encouraged Japan to grow into an equal partner in their alliance, it discouraged Japan when Japan planned to launch its own intelligence satellite and when Japan tried to become deeply involved in regional cooperation in East Asia. Although the U.S. government had openly announced that it would no longer apply *gaiatsu* (external pressure) on Japan because their bilateral relationship had become one between two equal "adults," it nonetheless maneuvered behind the scenes to affect Japanese policy by inducing Japanese politicians whose views corresponded to those of the United States to apply internal pressure.

In the spring of 2004, on the occasion of the Japan-U.S. Strategic Dialogue, Hitoshi Tanaka and Richard Armitage got into an argument. "We wish the United States would stop applying pressure on Japan by saying things like 'Show the flag,' during the Afghan War, and 'boots on the ground,' during the Iraq War," Tanaka remarked.

Armitage retorted, "But it was you and your colleagues who asked us to put pressure on Japan in order to expedite domestic reforms. I remember that clearly."

"That might have been the case in the past," Tanaka replied. "But times have changed."[128]

Armitage and Tanaka seemed to keep each other at a respectful distance. Armitage always regarded Tanaka as "a Japanese patriot. . . . And I thought he was a good friend of the U.S.-Japan alliance." But he also thought that Tanaka was "not as good a friend as he should have been."[129]

Similarly, Tanaka valued highly Armitage's contribution to strengthening the U.S.-Japan alliance, but he also was proud of his own contribution. He therefore could not figure out why the people around Armitage kept him at a distance, as if he were not a friend of the United States. However, Tanaka's ill-at-ease feeling might have been due to the inclination within the Japanese government, in particular the pro-American school within MOFA, to rely on the United States and Armitage for virtually everything. Tanaka felt that Japan's diplomatic subservience to the United States, which seemed to be the expression of an inherited gene in postwar-Japanese politics and diplomacy, had convinced the United States that Japan would quietly follow whatever path the United States took. In Tanaka's view, if that was indeed the case, then the United States had underestimated Japan. At one informal gathering among colleagues, Tanaka burst out, "We don't have to ask for U.S. approval every time that we come up with a foreign policy initiative. Japan is not a protectorate of the United States."[130]

Tanaka and a few other MOFA officials who had been directly involved in implementing Japan's foreign policy toward North Korea shared the conviction that Japan was the master of its own foreign policy, particularly toward East Asia, and that it was capable of acting on it own.[131] However, their quest for a more independent diplomacy was based in part on one other factor, that is, the weakening of the U.S. foreign policy system, particularly the striking decline of the power of MOFA's counterpart, the Department of State. During the Bush administration, actions of various components of the administration have not been well coordinated, so much so that agreements made only with the Department of State could easily be overturned later.

Apprehension that the United States might do something over Japan's head was also rooted in concern about intra- and interdepartmental rivalries and power struggles, within both the American and Japanese bureaucracies.[132] A U.S. agency might well do something that would put its Japanese counterpart on the defensive in order to reduce the influence of a rival of the U.S. agency. Or a U.S. agency might try to obstruct a policy that a rival U.S. agency and that agency's Japanese counterpart were trying to promote. From the viewpoint of the Pentagon and hardliners in other parts of the U.S. government concerned with nuclear nonproliferation, Japan's MOFA and the "North Korean engagement school" of the U.S. Department of State were two of a kind, colluding to maintain KEDO and the Agreed Framework. A high-ranking U.S. official remarked:

> We need to bid farewell to the old school of North Korean policies promoted by the likes of Tanaka, Takeuchi, and Pritchard. The core of their policies remains the provision of the light-water reactors to North Korea that in the Clinton era were agreed upon under the Agreed Framework. We should not hang on to such a derailed program.[133]

Under such circumstances, it was extremely difficult to explain Japan's intentions and to obtain U.S. approval. One high-ranking Japanese official reminisced, "When we are told to do this or that by a government that cannot make any decision because of disagreement among its departments, we can't possibly say we will do so. Therefore, we had no choice but to present a fait accompli regarding the prime minister's visit to Pyongyang."[134]

There were reasons to suppose that the United States suspected that MOFA, and Hitoshi Tanaka in particular, had deliberately withheld information from Koizumi about the significance and danger of North Korea's HEU program.[135]

That suspicion was one of the reasons that Bush entrusted U.S. Ambassador Howard Baker to deliver his message to Koizumi (via Yasuo Fukuda) on September 16, 2002, as described in chapter 1. One senior U.S. official later confided:

> Although we had repeatedly explained to the Japanese government the significance of this issue during the summit talk in New York and on other occasions, we talked in general terms. We felt the need to provide more focused information to get the Japanese government's attention on the issue. Because if we gave the Japanese MOFA a letter they could leak it, we decided to send one to Ambassador Baker as an "Eyes only for the Ambassador to Tokyo" cable and have him personally hand it to Koizumi. It was a case of "But you need to know this is the case before you see him."[136]

It should be recognized that the essence of the issue was the conflict between Japan and the United States over the desirable shape of their bilateral alliance. Tanaka's strong request to the U.S. government for intelligence information about North Korea's HEU program came from his concern about the status of the alliance. "I requested the intelligence because it would affect the essence of the alliance, namely, the trust in the relationship," he once said. "North Korean nuclear development is a vital security issue for Japan. If the assessment of the intelligence has changed, this needs to be explained to us to our satisfaction."[137] Tanaka repeatedly demanded that the United States provide more information.

When, after James Kelly's visit to Pyongyang in early October 2002, the U.S. government publicly announced that North Korea had acknowledged its secret development of highly enriched uranium, the Japanese government requested the verbatim report of the exchange between Kelly and Kang Sok-ju, but the U.S. government rejected the request.[138] The Japanese suspected that this rejection reflected the United States' lack of trust in Japan and the immature nature of the U.S.-Japan alliance.

At the same time, the U.S. government was trying to evaluate, in the context of the U.S.-Japan alliance, Japan's initiative for normalization of relations with the DPRK and the secret diplomacy associated with it.

An old hand in the U.S. government's dealings with the Far East admitted, "We were worried about the stark absence of a sense of danger on the part of the Japanese government when it was very obvious that North Korea intended to split the alliance."[139] As Tanaka's distrust of the Bush government's North Korean policy deepened, U.S. officials concerned with East Asia policy became more vocal in expressing their doubts about Tanaka and MOFA's Bureau of Asian and Oceanian Affairs. "Tanaka makes me nervous," one of them once said.[140]

The Japanese had always wondered why the United States was so extremely resentful of Japan's independent conduct of foreign diplomacy. Hitoshi Tanaka himself was of the following view:

I think it has the same psychological root as the theory of a "free ride" with respect to security. At the bottom of Americans' minds must be the sentiment that it is unforgivable for a U.S. ally to negotiate with the enemy while American soldiers are defending allies at the risk of their own lives.[141]

Quite a few years back, Tanaka visited Washington for the first time after being appointed director of Northeast Asian affairs in 1988. In a conversation with Tanaka, William Clark, the director of Japanese affairs at the Department of State, half-jokingly said, "Tanaka-san, please don't go over our heads on Korean Peninsula affairs."[142] Before his new appointment, Tanaka had been serving as director of MOFA's Second North America Division, dealing directly with the U.S. Trade Representative for bilateral trade negotiations rather than with the Department of State. Some people in the Department of State were not pleased with that situation. Clark seemingly tried a pick-off throw, so to speak, knowing that Tanaka had been interested in the normalization of Japan's relations with North Korea. Clark wore an amicable smile, but his eyes were not smiling. In the summer of 2002, Tanaka still remembered those eyes from the summer of 1988.

CASTING THE VOTE

Prime Minister Koizumi was not satisfied with just taking an independent diplomatic initiative to which the United States could not say no. Taking advantage of the serious U.S. concern about the HEU program, he tried to persuade the U.S. government to say yes to having its own direct dialogue with North Korea. On September 19, after Koizumi came back from Pyongyang, he telephoned Bush. Koizumi conveyed to Bush Kim Jong-il's message that North Korea was prepared to engage in direct dialogue with the United States, to which Bush responded, "We would like to give it full consideration." Koizumi pushed on, asking Bush to "please consider sending a high-level delegation to North Korea."[143] Two weeks after Koizumi's visit, a U.S. delegation headed by Assistant Secretary of State James Kelly visited Pyongyang. One can only wonder whether Koizumi's efforts had anything to do with it.

In those days, the Bush administration was split into two schools in terms of its North Korea policy, the "engagement school" and the "confrontation school." The engagement school, including Secretary of State Powell, wanted to use Koizumi's Pyongyang visit as leverage to steer the United States in the direction of direct dialogue with North Korea and toward a policy of engagement with North Korea. In contrast, the confrontation school, including the Pentagon, Vice President Cheney, and Under Secretary of State John Bolton, had taken a position opposing both any U.S. visit to Pyongyang and any direct dialogue with North Korea. If the Japanese government had consulted the U.S. government prior to Koizumi's visit, the planned trip might have been killed by the confrontation school. That was precisely why Hitoshi Tanaka did not inform the U.S. government of the prime minister's plan earlier. At the same time, the engagement school members would have worried about the possible negative effect on their engagement policy if the U.S. government had been informed of Koizumi's plan and a controversy had arisen as a result.

Moreover, the war with Iraq had become subtly intertwined with the North Korean issues. The remark by Wilkerson quoted earlier, that the neoconservative group was not necessarily opposed to Koizumi's visit, might have been related to the fact that the group had already set up a game plan around Iraq and so genuinely wished to avoid the emergence of a nuclear crisis in North Korea at that stage. Their cautious stance vis-à-vis North Korea was clearly expressed in Bush's remark in New York during his talk with Koizumi on September 12: "Although North Korea is a member of the 'axis of evil,' we need to take a different approach to this country from that for the other axis countries."

From that point on, North Korea and Iraq came to represent bargaining chips for Japan and the United States. Japan's support of the U.S. war against Iraq could be traded for U.S. support of Koizumi's visit, and U.S. support of the normalization of Japan-DPRK relations could be traded for Japanese support of the U.S. occupation of Iraq. However, there was, in fact, no such bargaining. Nevertheless, it seemed beyond doubt that the Bush administration had decided to take a positive view of Koizumi's initiative in the hope that the Koizumi government would cooperate with U.S. policies concerning Iraq and, more generally, the Middle East. Koizumi did not rush to support the United States in Iraq because his attempts to normalize relations with North Korea had agitated the United States. It would be more accurate to say that Japan had offered its cooperation regarding U.S. actions toward Iraq hoping—and calculating—that the United States would in return support normalization of Japan-DPRK relations as the basis for peace and stability on the Korean Peninsula—and thereby would demonstrate to North Korea that the U.S.-Japan alliance was still healthy.[144]

Among all of these factors, Koizumi's gentle prodding of Bush had the effect of pushing back the engagement school within the Bush administration. The role that Japan played in helping to set the stage for the U.S.-DPRK foreign ministers' talk in Brunei on July 31, 2002, was one example of that. When Hitoshi Tanaka visited Washington in early July 2002, Richard Armitage talked about the awkward position of the Department of State in the Bush administration with regard to U.S. policy toward North Korea. Opposition to Kelly's visit to Pyongyang was still quite strong within the administration, and it would be awkward for Secretary Powell to ask North Korea's foreign minister Paek Nam-sun to help facilitate James Kelly's visit. After hearing Armitage's explanation, Tanaka asked, "Would it help Kelly's visit if North Korea were to apologize about the

Yellow Sea incident?" Armitage responded that it would. Tanaka then asked, "If North Korea were to apologize, would that make the U.S.-DPRK foreign minister talks possible?" Again, Armitage responded that it would.[145]

Based on that exchange and Armitage's commitment, Tanaka tried to persuade X to make North Korea apologize at the earliest possible opportunity. North Korea subsequently made an announcement to "express remorse," which in turn served to accelerate both the Japan-DPRK and the U.S.-DPRK foreign minister talks. Marginal though the Japanese influence or impact might have been, it turned out to have been crucial in shifting the Bush administration's approach toward North Korea, which had been going nowhere.

Around that time Foreign Minister Yoriko Kawaguchi visited Washington and met with Condoleezza Rice at the White House. In the course of their discussions, Rice was called by the president and left the room. While Rice was out, Kawaguchi asked James Moriarty and Michael Green of the East Asian Division of the National Security Council (NSC), "Should I ask about Jim Kelly going to North Korea?"

"Why don't you ask her?" Green responded. "In fact, why don't you tell her exactly what you think? She respects your opinion. You should tell her exactly what you think." When Rice came back in, Kawaguchi said, "What do you think about going to North Korea? Don't you think it's time to go?" Rice replied, "Yes, I think you're right."[146] Both Moriarty and Green silently shouted "Yes!" Immediately after they returned from the West Wing to their office in the Eisenhower Executive Office Building, they called James Kelly to inform him that his visit to North Korea had been approved.

Meanwhile, John Bolton, Vice President Cheney, and the Pentagon were still trying to prevent Kelly's visit to North Korea.[147] As Michael Green explained later, "The U.S. government was in a state of gridlock concerning the pros and cons of Kelly's visit to Pyongyang when Koizumi suggested to Bush that Kelly should go. Thus, in a sense, Koizumi cast the deciding vote."[148] Had it not been for Koizumi's then-planned visit to Pyongyang, the talks about Kelly's visit to Pyongyang would not have been resumed. Had it not been for Koizumi's phone call to Bush, Kelly might never have visited North Korea. It seemed, therefore, that Koizumi's diplomacy had accomplished a great deal. At the time, no one even dreamed that Kelly's visit would later have an adverse effect.

CHAPTER THREE

HEU Program

It was past 5:00 p.m. on October 4, 2002, in a conference room of the DPRK Supreme People's Assembly in Pyongyang. Outside, it already was dark. On the front wall of the spacious room, whose ceiling was at least thirty feet (ten meters) high, hung gigantic portraits of Kim Il-sung and Kim Jong-il. Kang Sok-ju, North Korea's first deputy minister of foreign affairs, walked into the room, after having had his guest, James Kelly, U.S. assistant secretary of state for East Asia and Pacific affairs, wait for him for quite some time. He was barely seated when he declared bluntly, "I don't think it matters who goes first."

During more than thirty years of dealing with Asian affairs, Kelly had never met a high-ranking Asian official who began a meeting in such a manner with an unacquainted guest who had traveled a long distance to attend. Kelly responded, "Well, Mr. Vice Minister, if that is your wish, we have no objection. Please go ahead."

No sooner had Kelly finished than Kang Sok-ju started talking, referring to a memo that listed talking points.

> I am here today representing the party and the government of the Democratic People's Republic of Korea. From last night until early this morning, we held a very important meeting that included representatives of all the relevant ministries, the military, defense production agencies, and the nuclear power agency. Let me state at the outset that what I am going to say today is the consensus achieved in that meeting.[1]

Kang began his presentation in a confident and penetrating voice. North Korea's delegation included Deputy Foreign Minister Kim Gye-gwan but no uniformed military officers. Kang criticized in a harsh tone what he called the "hostile policies" of the Bush administration toward North Korea, starting with its failure to adequately provide light-water reactors as promised by the Korean Peninsula Energy Development Organization (KEDO). "The Bush administration has referred to our Republic as part of an 'axis of evil,'" he said. "And, according to the *New York Times*, the United States government includes our Republic in a list of countries targeted for possible nuclear attack under the United States' Nuclear Posture Review (NPR)."[2]

Kang added, sarcastically: "We are a part of the axis of evil and you are a gentleman. This is our relationship. We cannot discuss matters like gentlemen. If we disarm ourselves because of U.S. pressure, then we will become like Yugoslavia or Afghanistan's Taliban, to be beaten to death."[3]

Kang's words constituted an accusation that the United States had violated the spirit of the Agreed Framework that the United States and DPRK had signed in 1994. In that document, the United States pledged that it would provide "formal assurances" to the DPRK that "the United States would not use or threaten to use nuclear weapons against North Korea.[4] Kang kept up his monologue of criticism of the United States for what seemed to be an eternity. In the course of his talk, Kang touched on the HEU issue, saying, "What is wrong with us having our own uranium enrichment program? We are entitled to possess our own HEU, and we are bound to produce more powerful weapons than that."[5]

Kelly jotted down something on a piece of paper and quietly handed it to Ambassador Charles L. "Jack" Pritchard, President Bush's special envoy for negotiations with North Korea, who was seated next to Kelly. The memo said, "Jack, do you hear what I'm hearing?"[6] Kang was the first to touch on the HEU issue. Kelly intervened here, saying, "In order not to misunderstand the point you have just made, please repeat your remark one more time."

Kang continued, "The hostile policies of the U.S. administration have left us with no choice but to pursue such a program. This is intended to be nothing but a deterrent against the United States' hostile policies toward us."

"North Korea had been pursuing such a program long before President Bush's election," Kelly replied.[7] Kang had no response.

This was the last of several meetings that Kelly had held in Pyongyang since he and his delegation arrived the day before, when they had a meeting with Kim Gye-gwan, followed by a dinner that Kim hosted. Earlier on the second day, they had had another meeting with Kim Gye-gwan and a meeting later in the afternoon with Kim Yong-nam, president of the Presidium of the Supreme People's Assembly. They met with Kang last.

The U.S. delegation consisted of eight members, including James Kelly; Jack Pritchard; Michael Green, director of East Asian affairs at the National Security Council; Mary Tighe, acting deputy assistant secretary of defense; David Straub, director of Korean affairs at the State Department; and Michael Dunn, an Air

Force major general and deputy director of strategic operations for the Joint Chiefs of Staff.

In the course of the discussion, Kang repeatedly referred to North Korea's uranium enrichment program. He also said that North Korea "considered the Agreed Framework 'nullified,'" due to misconduct on the part of the United States.[8] Then he added, "Some in our government, however, insist that we should negotiate with the United States, using our program as leverage." Kang continued, "If the United States ceases its hostile policies toward North Korea, we are prepared to make the efforts necessary to reduce the United States' concerns about our nuclear development program."[9] In terms of ceasing its hostile policies toward North Korea, Kang insisted that the United States should take the following specific measures:

—Recognize the sovereignty of the DPRK.

—Enter into a mutual nonaggression treaty with the DPRK.

—Not interfere with North Korean economic development (that is, by lifting embargoes on exports to North Korea and not blocking Japan and South Korea from normalizing relations with North Korea).

—Compensate the DPRK for the delay in constructing light-water reactors.

Kang added, "It is conceivable that the settlement could be made via summit-level negotiations."[10]

By this time almost fifty minutes had passed since the start of the meeting. "If you're pushing inducements to settle the issue," Kelly said, "this is going to be most unwelcome news in Washington and there's nothing more to talk about here." Kelly then stood up to leave. Stunned, other members of the U.S. delegation also stood up, staring at each other and shaking their heads.[11] Kang Sok-ju and the North Korean party, also stunned, just stared at the Americans.[12] But they rushed to the door and formed a row. With smiles on their faces, they shook hands with each and every member of the U.S. delegation, saying, "Thank you. Please come again" and "Thank you, we look forward to further discussions. Thank you."[13]

In the summer of that year (2002), a U.S. intelligence agency reported to top policymakers its conclusion that North Korea had been secretly developing its uranium enrichment program beyond the experimental level. It concluded that if that indeed was the case, then obviously the program was geared toward the development of nuclear weapons. Members of the intelligence agency had given Kelly a briefing on this and other new information before he went to Pyongyang.[14]

It was during the George H. W. Bush administration that U.S. intelligence agencies discovered that North Korea was developing a plutonium-type nuclear weapon in Yongbyon, some 150 miles (90 kilometers) north of Pyongyang.[15] In January 1992, North Korea signed the IAEA safeguards agreement but delayed allowing inspectors into the country, raising suspicions about its intentions. In May 1992, Hans Blix confirmed that North Korea was processing spent fuel into plutonium, although in tiny amounts. The Clinton administration brought that information to the attention of the UN Security Council. In March 1994, North Korea announced its withdrawal from the Nuclear Nonproliferation Treaty (NPT), and the UN Security Council started preparing economic sanctions against North Korea. In addition, the U.S. government started planning a military attack on the North Korean nuclear facility.

Thus, from the spring through the summer of 1994, the Korean Peninsula was on the verge of a major military crisis for the first time since the end of the Korean War. The crisis was avoided at the last minute by a talk between Kim Il-sung and President Jimmy Carter, who visited Pyongyang in June 1994. In October of that year, the United States and North Korea signed the Agreed Framework. The 1994 crisis was about reprocessing spent nuclear fuel to make plutonium. If North Korea now had a secret uranium enrichment program, it would be a matter of grave concern for the international community.

The U.S. delegation went back to the Koryo Hotel, where it was staying in Pyongyang, and in the lobby discussed the next step that it should take. The delegates were scheduled to meet the British chargé d'affaires and attend a reception to be hosted by the Swedish ambassador in the evening, but they had a little time. In light of the importance and urgency of what Kelly had heard from the North Koreans, he decided that he had to report immediately to Washington.[16] Ideally, the U.S. delegation would have departed from Pyongyang and sent its report on the meeting by telegraph from the airplane. However, because the U.S. delegation had already agreed with the North Korean authorities that the plane was to depart the next day, the party had to stay one more night in Pyongyang. Therefore it was decided that the U.S. team would ask the British embassy in Pyongyang to send the telegram to Washington, and they telephoned U.K. chargé d'affaires James Hoare. Within fifteen minutes of the call, two Range Rovers flying the Union Jack drove into the hotel driveway, carrying James Hoare and his staff. Seeing Hoare—white-haired, white-bearded, and chubby—in a pair of Birkenstock clogs, one of the U.S. delegation thought, "Little bearded guy, looks like Santa Claus."[17] Hoare was both a professional diplomat and an academic expert, having a Ph.D. in Korean Peninsula affairs.

After Kelly and his associates arrived at the British embassy, they were taken to a room where three of the U.S. members who were proficient in Korean—and their interpreter—compared notes with each other as well as with the notes in English taken by the non–Korean speaking delegation members who had taken notes from the North Korean interpreter's version of Kang's presentation.[18] They then drafted the telegram, which after some time was sent to Washington through the wiretap-free line at the embassy. Before the telegram was sent, Kelly looked at it in draft form and instructed that it be divided into two parts—a "transcript" that set forth what was said between the two parties and "comments" that included descriptions of the atmosphere at the meeting and the U.S. delegates' impressions.[19]

That took longer than expected and the delegates had to excuse themselves from attending the reception at the Swedish embassy.[20] In theory, the U.S. delegation could have used the secure line at the Swedish embassy, which was allowed to contact North Korea on behalf of the United States, which did not have diplomatic relations with North Korea. The Swedish embassy was older and better equipped than the British embassy, and its wiretap-free facilities were far superior. But the British embassy in Pyongyang had been informed earlier by the British Foreign Office in London that the U.S. government had requested contact information for the British embassy in Pyongyang and permission for the U.S. delegation to use the embassy's communications lines in case of emergency.

The biggest problem was that none of the laptop computers at the British embassy, including Hoare's, was equipped with a wiretap-prevention mechanism, and no one in the U.S. delegation had brought a laptop with such a device. The U.S. team had no choice but to borrow Hoare's computer. But communications sent using his computer could be tapped by the North Koreans, and the embassy building itself was not constructed so as to be safe from eavesdropping. Moreover, the embassy was surrounded by several suspicious-looking buildings, making it extremely easy for the North Koreans to monitor the embassy's communications if they wished to do so.

At that point, Hoare began to have a strange feeling. Although he did not easily accept conspiracy theories, in this particular situation he felt forced to suspect that there might have been some hidden motive behind Kelly's visit. He thought that the U.S. delegation might actually be going through all this trouble deliberately, hoping that the North Koreans were eavesdropping in order to emphasize dramatically what a crucial failure Kelly's visit to North Korea had been.[21]

In fact, Hoare was imagining things. The FBI had not allowed Kelly's delegation to bring along laptops equipped with anti-wiretapping devices, reasoning that if somehow the North Korean authorities were to get hold of one of the U.S. computers, the North Koreans could have obtained classified materials from it.[22]

"SHOW US THE EVIDENCE"

In any event, Kelly was surprised by the 180-degree change in North Korea's attitude in just one day. On the afternoon of October 3, Kelly's group had met with Kim Gye-gwan in Conference Room 2 on the ground floor of the Ministry of Foreign Affairs. The room was spacious, with portraits of Kim Il-sung and Kim Jong-il looking down on a shiny teak table.

Kelly started the discussion by stating that the Bush administration had taken the policy of entering into negotiations with North Korea "without attaching any precondition, and whenever and wherever that would be possible." The U.S. government was prepared to take a "bold approach" in order to improve its bilateral relations with North Korea. This was a policy that President Bush had developed in close consultation with U.S. allies. If North Korea would alter its behavior on a range of important issues, the United States would be ready to take significant economic and diplomatic steps to improve the lives of the North Korean people. Kelly then announced, "However, given the fresh information of nuclear weapons development efforts, this approach is no longer possible without action on your part." He continued: "The U.S. knows the program has been aggressively implemented and it was a serious violation of international agreements. I will now ask the North Korean government to weigh its response carefully." Kelly spoke clearly, as if he were reading, word for word, prepared talking points. He added, "Unless you provide us with a satisfactory explanation regarding this matter and abolish this program immediately, the United States government cannot and will not continue its policy of engagement with North Korea."[23] Kelly concluded by saying, "Since we have raised a variety of issues, we do not intend to ask for your immediate reactions here. Please give them careful thought before giving us your answers."[24]

Kim Gye-gwan looked a little stunned. Despite his attempt to keep his normal poker face, he could not hide an expression of bewilderment.[25] Nevertheless, he immediately regained his composure and suggested a coffee break. He probably had decided that responding to Kelly's points would be beyond his discretion and that he needed to report to his superior.[26]

Coming back from the break, Kim Gye-gwan became highly aggressive, as if his personality had changed. "We have no such program as the one that you have charged," he declared. "That is a fiction fabricated by our enemy to denounce us."[27] He added, "It was another false accusation, like the charge the U.S. had made in August 1998 that North Korea had a secret underground facility at Kumchang-ri."[28] His last comment referred to an incident that took place in the summer of 1998. The United States government had received intelligence information about secret subterranean nuclear facilities in Kumchang-ri, in the countryside north of Pyongyang, and it sent a team of State Department experts to North Korea in May 1999 to independently verify the information.[29] North Korea accepted the verification team in exchange for 50,000 tons of food aid, which North Korea characterized as an "admission fee." But the only thing the team found, in return for its expensive admission fee, was a gigantic underground tunnel complex, which was embarrassing for the United States. One intelligence officer somewhat self-mockingly described it as "the world's largest underground parking garage."[30]

Kelly emphasized that North Korea's uranium enrichment program violated several international accords and that it would cause grave concern worldwide. Included among those accords was the Agreed Framework that the United States and North Korea signed in 1994, under which the United States was to assist North Korea in constructing two light-water reactors in return for Pyongyang's abandonment of its nuclear development program. It was agreed that while the reactors were being constructed, North Korea would freeze its nuclear development program and the United States would provide heavy [fuel] oil to North Korea. North Korea promised to consistently undertake measures to implement the North-South Joint Declaration on the Denuclearization of the Korean Peninsula—which, in part, forbade both Koreas from reprocessing or enriching uranium—in return for "formal assurances" from the United States that it would not use or threaten to use nuclear weapons against North Korea.[31] Kelly also stressed that North Korea's nuclear development activities would certainly have an adverse effect on economic exchanges with Japan and South Korea.

Kim retorted, "It is the United States that has been obstructing our economic exchanges with Japan and South Korea," charging, in particular, that the United States had been obstructing Japan's attempts at normalization of its relations with North Korea, including by trying to prevent Koizumi's Pyongyang visit, which had preceded Kelly's visit.[32]

In his presentation, James Kelly insisted that North Korea should, first, terminate its uranium enrichment program and do so in a transparent and verifiable way and second, maintain the freeze on plutonium separation, as provided by the Agreed Framework.[33]

Kim demanded, "If you insist that we are developing HEU, show us the evidence."

"The reason that countries often enter into uranium enrichment programs is because they are more easily concealed than plutonium programs," Kelly responded, "and if I were to give you all that information, it might make it easier for you to conceal it."[34]

That evening, a welcoming reception in honor of Kelly and his group was held in one of the North Korean government's guest houses in the suburbs of Pyongyang. It was a luxurious affair, consisting altogether of eleven courses and generous quantities of Heineken beer, French wine, and Irish whiskey.

Kim Gye-gwan stood up to give the first toast. "We could make great progress in these talks," he said, "if only we could exclude the DOD and JCS [Joint Chiefs of Staff] representatives. Then we could get down to business."[35] By that remark, Kim might have been expressing his apprehension about the U.S. military and hardliners in the Pentagon who had been obstructing the normalization of U.S.-DPRK relations. Or could he have been expressing his sympathy as a fellow diplomat who had to suffer his own North Korean hardliners? Although Jack Pritchard, judging from Kim's facial expression and gestures, interpreted his words as a half-joking comment, Tighe's body language conveyed silent protest. The Americans just stared at each other as if to say that they would not take such criticism.[36]

Kim proposed several toasts, but the Americans hardly touched their glasses, although some, including Straub, lifted their glasses a few inches from the table.

Prior to their departure for Pyongyang, Kelly was told that the team could shake hands with the North Koreans. The trickier part of the protocol was whether the team should be allowed to raise their glasses for a toast at the dinner. Kelly shared his uneasiness with the team about the toast; he did not want to give the North Koreans a chance to take a photo.[37] Kelly remembered that Brent Scowcroft, George H. W. Bush's national security adviser, had been harshly criticized "for playing footsy" when pictures of him exchanging toasts with his Chinese hosts were circulated in the press after he had secretly visited China after the Tiananmen Square incident in 1989. Kelly was determined not to repeat that mistake.[38] However, when it came time for Kelly to respond to Kim's toast, he replied with a toast.[39]

In fact, it had not been decided before the group left for Pyongyang whether the delegates would go to the evening reception; it was only after they had arrived that they received permission to attend.[40] Dunn noticed that all the North Korean government officials seated at his table wore Rolex watches. When, half-jokingly, Dunn asked whether the watches were fakes, the North Koreans looked rather upset and proudly replied, "These are gifts from our dear general."[41]

On the next day, October 4, prior to the talk with Kang Sok-ju, Kelly and his group paid a courtesy visit to Kim Yong-nam, president of the Presidium of the DPRK Supreme People's Assembly. Dunn wore his formal Class A military uniform, which clearly indicated that he was a major general. Military personnel of every country show respect to other military personnel, and normally they physically show their respect by saluting. But no sentry in any of the government buildings he visited saluted him.

Kim Yong-nam was very courteous, perhaps to the point of excess. Their discussion dealt mainly with economic affairs. "He must be reading from the talking points that were delivered before yesterday's meeting with Kim Gye-gwan," Kelly thought to himself.[42] A uniformed general who was seated behind Kim Yong-nam was staring at the U.S. delegation with an angry expression on his face; throughout the meeting, he focused primarily on General Michael Dunn. To Kelly, the North Koreans' behavior amounted to "a pantomime theater of nasty faces" intended to convey the North Korean military's willingness to fight with the United States.[43] Dunn stared back at the officers, eye to eye, for quite some time.

On October 5, Kelly and the U.S. delegation left for the airport in several cars. Handlers from the Foreign Ministry accompanied them. "When do you think you'll come to Pyongyang again?" they kept asking. "When will we continue this discussion?"[44] The delegation flew from Pyongyang directly to Osan, South Korea, on a C-21. In order not to fly in North Korea's Air Defense Identification Zone, the C-21 first flew to the Yellow Sea and then back to the Korean Peninsula, the reverse of the route it took going to North Korea.

When the delegation arrived at the U.S. embassy in Seoul, they reviewed several English-language newspapers, where they found an article about Yang Bin, a Chinese businessman who had been entrusted by Kim Jong-il with the development of a special economic zone in Sinuiju City, on the North Korea–China border. The article stated that he had been arrested by the Chinese authorities on October 4 and was being investigated by the police for alleged illegal business practices.[45] From Kim Jong-il's viewpoint, the news was troublesome, because within a day or two Kelly would raise thorny questions regarding this new development. It was a double blow for Kim, since the arrival of the U.S. delegation in Pyongyang—to which Kim had been looking forward as an opportunity for direct negotiation with the United States—had yielded little fruit. Moreover, the future prospects for the development of the special economic zone, which had been entrusted to Yang Bin, had suddenly become bleak. Kelly was laughing when he said, "Boy, Kim Jong-il is having a bad day."[46]

Back in Seoul, Kelly's party had a series of meetings with high-ranking ROK government officials, including Choi Sung-hong, minister for foreign affairs and trade, and Lim Dong-won, President Kim Dae-jung's special assistant in charge of foreign affairs, security, and unification. When Kelly told them that North Korea had not denied the existence of the HEU program, everyone, Lim Dong-won in particular, looked stunned. "At first he was shocked, his face was a little bit shocked," one of the U.S. delegates observed. "And then [his expression] was one of sadness. And then it was one of—he decided clearly not to believe it."[47]

When Kelly had stopped in Seoul on his way to Pyongyang, he had secretly informed the top leaders of the Kim Dae-jung government that he would raise the HEU issue in Pyongyang. At that time, the South Koreans were concerned that that issue would lead to a U.S.-DPRK showdown. Kelly's body language had been stiff as he literally read the talking points to Lim and others in the meeting, although Kelly and Lim usually had had lunch together to freely exchange views and notes when Kelly visited Seoul before.[48] After Kelly returned from Pyongyang, the South Koreans were depressed to hear that their concerns had been justified.

Before Kelly flew to Pyongyang, Bush himself had placed a phone call to Kim Dae-jung to inform him of Kelly's planned trip. Kim had been extremely pleased by the news, and expectations among South Koreans had been raised; the disappointment with the outcome of the visit was therefore all the greater.[49] From the beginning to the end of Kelly's debriefing, Lim did not change his skeptical expression. He also mentioned that in the past, misunderstandings had repeatedly occurred in negotiations with North Korea because of somewhat inaccurate translations of what was said. "I hope you're not making the same mistake as the one with the Kumchang-ri incident," Lim said to Kelly.[50]

NORTH KOREA'S "NCND" POLICY

For North Korea, Kelly's accusation about the HEU program was like a surprise attack. The Korean Central News Agency reported on October 3 that Kelly was "the highest official of the U.S. administration ever to visit the DPRK since the visit paid by Albright, secretary of state of the former Clinton administration, in October 2000 as a special envoy of the president."[51] In an editorial, Pyongyang Broadcasting stressed, "We will make an effort to improve relations even with a hostile country as long as it respects our right to self-determination and abandons its hostile policies toward us."[52] One could read between the lines North Korea's hope that the trend toward détente in Japan-DPRK relations would also extend to U.S.-DPRK relations.

James Hoare, the United Kingdom's chargé d'affaires to North Korea, had a habit of attempting to persuade North Korean diplomats that they should talk with the United States instead of stubbornly challenging them. They would respond that although they had attempted to engage in talks several times, the United States had not shown any interest. Nonetheless, the North Koreans had been looking forward to Kelly's visit, hoping that it might lead to a breakthrough.[53] The very fact that North Korea allowed Kelly's group to fly directly from South Korea on board a military airplane indicated eloquently how high its expectations were.

However, North Korea was cornered by what looked almost like an ultimatum. On October 7, the North Korean Foreign Ministry loudly criticized Kelly for "raising 'issues of concern' [and] taking a high-handed and arrogant attitude." Continuing its denunciation of the United States, the ministry claimed that "the U.S.-raised 'issues of concern' are nothing but a product of its hostile policy towards the DPRK."[54] From that point on, the expression "high-handed and arrogant" became the stock description for Kelly.

In fact, no adjective was farther from describing the real James Kelly, who had been nicknamed "Buddha" by his colleagues in the Bureau of East Asian and Pacific Affairs at the U.S. State Department. The nickname described Kelly's calm manner as well as his air of magnanimity, though it also implied that he was difficult to fathom.[55]

When Kelly reported to his senior colleagues at the State Department in Washington about the outcome of his visit, Armitage's first reaction was to ask, "Did Kang really say that?"[56] Secretary of State Powell also seemed to be taken aback. "Did they really say they had it?" he asked, raising his voice at the end of the sentence.[57] When Powell reported North Korea's response to President Bush,

Bush expressed disbelief: "What? Did they admit it?"[58] As one U.S. official later said, "All of us were at a loss as to what to do, because we had no doubt that North Korea would deny it as it had always done in the past."[59] Both the pro-engagement school, including Powell, which advocated dialogue with North Korea, and the confrontation school, including Cheney, were equally shocked.

Although the U.S. government briefed the Japanese and South Korean governments on the gist of the Kelly–Kang Sok-ju talk, it did not make the contents of the talk public. It still gave some consideration, a little optimistic thought, to the need to "try to keep this quiet as long as possible and give the North Koreans an opportunity to come back . . . and say they will dismantle HEU and come back into the Agreed Framework."[60] However, the U.S. government learned that someone had leaked the gist of the Kelly-Kang talk and that it would be reported in the next day's issue of USA Today.[61] Consequently, on the evening of October 16 the U.S. government issued an urgent press statement through Richard Boucher, spokesman of the U.S. State Department:

> Assistant Secretary James A. Kelly and his delegation advised the North Koreans that we had recently acquired information that indicates that North Korea has a program to enrich uranium for nuclear weapons, in violation of the Agreed Framework and other agreements. North Korean officials acknowledged that they have such a program. The North Koreans attempted to blame the United States and said that they considered the Agreed Framework nullified.[62]

Two weeks later, however, the North Korean government made an announcement denying the existence of the program that they had acknowledged earlier. On October 25, the Korean Central News Agency reported:

> [T]he DPRK made itself very clear to the special envoy of the U.S. President that the DPRK was entitled to possess not only nuclear weapon but any type of weapon more powerful than that so as to defend its sovereignty and right to existence from the ever-growing nuclear threat by the U.S.[63]

The announcement stated that the United States had deliberately misinterpreted North Korea's message, officially denying that North Korea had acknowledged the existence of the HEU program. Had Kang Sok-ju acknowledged the existence of the program or had he denied that it existed? The reactions of the two sides became increasingly exacerbated as they battled over what he had in fact said.

On November 14, 2002, the executive board of KEDO announced that "heavy fuel oil deliveries will be suspended beginning with the December shipment. Future shipments will depend on North Korea's concrete and credible actions to dismantle completely its highly enriched uranium program."[64] North Korea implemented a series of countermeasures triggered by the announcement, one after another:

—On December 12, 2002, the North Korean government announced that it would immediately resume operation of its nuclear facilities and construction of nuclear facilities on which work had been frozen.

—On December 21, North Korea removed all the surveillance cameras and seals from its nuclear facilities.

—On December 31, the IAEA's inspectors, who had been stationed in North Korea since 1994, were expelled and left the country immediately.

—On January 10, 2003, North Korea withdrew from the Nuclear Non-Proliferation Treaty (NPT).

—On February 12, the IAEA decided to refer the North Korean issue to the UN Security Council, marking the beginning of the second nuclear crisis on the Korean Peninsula.

What had gone wrong?

During the Kelly-Kang talk, Kang's remarks were translated into English by a North Korean interpreter, Choi Son-hui, while Kelly's remarks were translated into Korean by a U.S. interpreter, Tong Kim. Choi Son-hui was known as something of a character among U.S. officials who had been dealing with North Korea. Jack Pritchard once witnessed a rather bizarre incident involving Choi. When Charles Kartman was negotiating with Kim Gye-gwan at the United States UN Mission building in New York, Choi started shaking her head at the American interpreter's interpretation saying, "No, no." Her behavior was rather unusual in itself, but the next moment Choi stood up and left the table as if to say, "This is absurd. I can't take it any longer." Nevertheless, Kim did not say anything to restrain her, relying on the U.S. interpreter for the rest of the session.[65] This episode resulted in speculation that Choi might be a daughter of a high-ranking North Korean official. During a U.S.-DPRK conference in 1994, Joel Wit, a U.S. coordinator in negotiations leading to the Agreed Framework, heard from Choi that she had learned English by reading Eric Segal's *Love Story*.[66] Although some doubted the accuracy of the rather uneven quality of her interpretation, others pointed out that it was her mood rather than her English ability that was uneven.[67]

In contrast, Tong Kim is a U.S. citizen of Korean ancestry and a veteran interpreter at the State Department; he is so meticulous that some people regard him as almost obsessive. He also has opinions of his own on policy matters, and some desk people at the State Department find him troublesome.[68] The U.S. delegation also included David Straub, State Department director of Korean affairs and a Korea expert fluent in the language, and Jack Pritchard, a weathered veteran of U.S.-DPRK negotiations.

After the announcement of October 25, the North Korean government stressed that during the talk with Kelly it had referred to its "right to possess nuclear weapons" and not to the fact that it possessed such weapons, and it accused the U.S. delegation of having deliberately misunderstood and misinterpreted North

Korea's position. The issue of errors of interpretation was also raised by the South Korean government. On the day before North Korea made its announcement denying the existence of the HEU program, South Korean unification minister Jeong Se-hyun, upon returning from Pyongyang, told the press that "Kelly might have misunderstood the North Koreans' remarks or cut off the head and tail of their remarks," resulting in a case of "cultural misunderstanding."[69]

But the fact of the matter was that it was not an error on the part of the interpreters or a "cultural misunderstanding." Kang Sok-ju's remark itself was from the beginning extremely tricky, so tricky in fact that three Korean-language experts in the U.S. delegation had a hard time determining what Kang had actually said, arguing among themselves, memo pads in hand.[70] In the talk with Kelly, Kang never explicitly declared that North Korea "had" or "had been developing" an HEU program, but he never explicitly denied that North Korea had such a program, either.[71] Moreover, Michael Dunn recalled that Kang had said that "we in the Foreign Ministry were surprised that there was indeed this program: we did have this program, and the military was running it."[72]

Dunn had the impression that Kang was speaking on the assumption that North Korea did have the program, and he was not the only member of the U.S. delegation who had that impression.[73] One of them reminisced, "Kang sounded like he was saying that everybody else present knew almost nothing about the case, but that he did."[74] Another U.S. member, reflecting on the atmosphere of the meeting and his impressions during the talk, thought that Kang Sok-ju deliberately tried to make the United States realize that North Korea did have an HEU program. He added that Kang was so agitated that his words skidded a bit, admitting the existence of the HEU program.[75]

A senior State Department official who later read the transcript of the talk got the following impression:

> When I first read the transcript, I thought Kang Sok-ju was presenting two entirely different stories. I thought his words could be interpreted either way, but I was more inclined to understand it as meaning that North Korea had the right to possess uranium enrichment. Therefore, when the U.S. government announced that North Korea had admitted the existence of the program, I thought that we had jumped to that conclusion.[76]

In retrospect, it is quite conceivable that when Kang spoke with Kelly, Kang had deliberately chosen an expression that could be interpreted either as "right to possess" or "come to possess." It was reported that when the North Korean government later telegraphed official instructions to its ambassadors to inform their respective host government of the gist of the Kang-Kelly talk, some countries were told that North Korea had "come to possess" HEU, while others were told that it had the "right to possess" it. A U.S. State Department official later said,

"They must have deliberately made the wording of the official instructions obscure."[77]

It was highly likely that Kang Sok-ju had adopted a "neither confirm nor deny" (NCND) policy from the very beginning. Throughout the night after the Kelly-Kim talk, the North Koreans must have discussed among themselves how to react to the situation, and Kang Sok-ju must have approached Kim Jong-il for final instructions. Given that the United States knew of the HEU program, the North Koreans might have decided to improvise a game plan in which they would use that knowledge as a bargaining card to lure the United States into settling issues at the highest level, through a DPRK-U.S. summit talk. For that purpose, it was best to adopt a "neither confirm nor deny" policy, leaving the facts obscure. Regarding this issue, Powell said:

> They are masters of their language, and so we always triple translated everything and then had another guy look at it, and there could be no doubt that they said "Yeah, we have it. What about it?" This is beyond doubt.[78]

A senior official of the Blue House (the residence of the president of South Korea) concurred with Powell's view, saying that the problem was not one of interpretation. "The North Koreans meant exactly what Kang Sok-ju had said," he observed, "and the U.S. understood exactly what it heard from Kang."[79]

Michael Dunn vividly remembered that when Kang Sok-ju told Kelly that North Korea was entitled to have an HEU program and that the country planned to develop weapons more powerful than nuclear weapons, all the North Koreans seated behind Kang smiled. They continued to smile until the end of the meeting and "almost as if . . . having rehearsed the whole negotiation."[80] In retrospect, that might have been a type of wooing by intimidation—silent mass calisthenics of a sort intended to propose DPRK-U.S. negotiations.

Everyone present on the U.S. side, including Kelly, Pritchard, Green, and Straub, thought that it was impossible to interpret what Kang Sok-ju said as anything other than an admission of the existence of an HEU program in North Korea. Jack Pritchard, another member of the U.S. delegation, analyzed the situation as follows:

> Much has been made, after the fact, of the actual language of Kang's admission of the HEU program. While there was no precise, irrefutable statement—a smoking gun—many factors led all eight members of the U.S. delegation to reach the conclusion that Kang had effectively and defiantly admitted to having an HEU program.[81]

Don Oberdorfer, a veteran American journalist and well-respected Korean specialist who visited North Korea after Kelly's group, had a chance to discuss this issue with appropriate North Korean officials. He later reported that the North Korean officials implied the existence of the HEU program but, at the same time, ambiguously denied its existence.[82] It was highly likely that North Korea insisted that it, too, was entitled to adopt the same NCND policy concerning the existence of nuclear weapons overseas that the United States traditionally had adopted, thereby strongly implying that it had become nuclear capable. Kelly later said that "the DPRK essentially took an NCND position."[83]

Why, then, did North Korea later deny having nuclear weapons? One member of Kelly's delegation said:

> Kelly did not disclose if the U.S. had discovered the location of the HEU facilities, but he was very good at giving the impression that it had. The North Koreans, assuming that the U.S. already knew where the facility was, thought it had no choice but to acknowledge its existence. However, the North Koreans became convinced that the United States did not know the location of the facility. So they decided to deny that the program existed.[84]

James Kelly had a similar view. "Only later," he said, "when it became clear that this was a major tactical error that was resulting in massive international criticism, did D.P.R.K. officials first begin to suggest that the United States had misunderstood its statements, and later still that the United States had lied about them."[85]

One thing was certain: when Kang Sok-ju was confronted with the allegation concerning the development of a uranium enrichment program, he decided to use it as leverage to lure the United States into bilateral negotiations with North Korea. Kang seemed to have become insistent about once again striking a deal with the United States. He might have aspired to force the United States to accept a deal, just as he had done once before by using plutonium development as leverage. The Agreed Framework of 1994 was a diplomatic victory for Kang Sok-ju. By merely freezing its nuclear programs, North Korea was able to obtain a U.S. commitment to provide light-water reactors. Thus, it was able to kill two birds with one stone: it was allowed to preserve its nuclear capability in a frozen state and, for agreeing to the freeze, it was rewarded with light-water reactors. "The Agreed Framework was a great success story for Kang Sok-ju," said one Russian diplomat who was involved with Korean Peninsula affairs and who had a series of dealings with Kang. "Therefore, when Kelly brought up the issue of uranium enrichment, Kang must have sensed the emergence of a second windfall."[86]

If that was indeed the case, Kang's decision to take an NCND stance was quite understandable. Total rejection was tantamount to abandoning the chance to get a possible second windfall. But the United States had no intention of accepting such a deal. Moreover, by making a statement that could be interpreted as an admission of possession of HEU, Kang caused a violent reaction in Washington. After hearing the U.S. response to Kelly's report, Kang must have realized that he had made a tactical error.

BODY LANGUAGE

It took the Bush administration more than eighteen months after taking office in January 2001 to dispatch Kelly to North Korea. During that time, U.S. policy toward North Korea had gone through a series of ups and downs. At a joint press briefing with the Swedish foreign minister on March 6, 2001, the day before President Kim Dae-jung, president of the Republic of Korea, was to arrive in Washington, Secretary of State Colin Powell said, "We want to make sure that our North Korea policy is totally synchronized with what our South Korean friends are doing. . . . We do plan to engage with North Korea to pick up where President Clinton and his administration left off."[87] The next morning, Powell made the same remarks at breakfast with Kim Dae-jung. Powell's remarks were interpreted both as the Bush administration's intention to continue, in essence, the Clinton administration's North Korean policy and as an endorsement of Kim Dae-jung's "Sunshine Policy" toward North Korea.

However, President Bush's attitude toward North Korea was totally different in his talk with Kim Dae-jung on March 7.[88] With Vice President Cheney at his side, Bush suddenly started to criticize Kim Jong-il. "He simply cannot be trusted," he said.[89] Bush was very blunt: "When you make an agreement with a country that is secretive, how do you—how are you aware as to whether or not they're keeping the terms of the agreement."[90] Bush also urged that Seoul not make any prospective reciprocal visit of Kim Jong-il to Seoul—which Kim Dae-jung indicated that he expected to occur at the end of June, around the first anniversary of the North-South Joint Declaration—an occasion for issuing a North-South peace declaration.[91]

His personal feeling of repulsion for Kim Jong-il as a person and for his dictatorship notwithstanding, Bush was sending a signal to North Korea that the U.S. government would pursue pro-engagement policies vis-à-vis North Korea. A joint U.S.-ROK statement released after the Bush-Kim summit stated, "President Bush expressed support for the Republic of Korea's government's policy of engagement with North Korea and President Kim's leading role in resolving inter-Korean issues."[92] As Deputy Assistant Secretary of State Thomas Hubbard (who later became U.S. ambassador to South Korea) said, "The substance of the summit talk was not bad, and we reaffirmed the United States' willingness to stick with the Agreed Framework so long as the North Koreans did. . . . [T]he body language of that visit was . . . very unfortunate."[93]

That "body language" must have included the fact that in effect President Bush had corrected Powell's remarks, giving the impression that the Bush administration's policy toward North Korea had not only been in flux but also was disputed internally. Powell's remark after his breakfast with Kim Dae-jung had immediately been reported by the media. At the White House, an emergency meeting was held among Bush, Vice President Cheney, White House chief of staff Andrew Card, and the communications director, Karen Hughes. It was decided that Powell's remarks could be interpreted as praise of the Agreed Framework as it was, that the Agreed Framework had to be transformed into a verifiable agreement, and that therefore Powell's remarks had to be corrected immediately.[94] When Powell later walked into the Oval Office, Bush asked him to rectify his earlier remarks. Looking bewildered, Powell asked Bush, "What do you mean?" Nevertheless, later that day Powell made an announcement revising his remarks.[95]

Powell tried to cover it up, saying "I got a little too far forward on my skis."[96] From the White House's point of view, however, Powell's earlier statement was more than that; it was a serious error. To begin with, Bush was not favorably disposed to Kim Dae-jung's visit to the United States, but despite the White House's misgivings, Kim had insisted that he should visit Washington before the visit of the Japanese prime minister.[97] Before Kim's trip, Bush had talked with him by phone. Hearing Kim's endless praise of the correctness of his own sunshine policy toward North Korea, Bush held the phone away from his head, covered the mouthpiece and mouthed to Pritchard, "Who does this guy think he is?"[98]

In engaging with North Korea, the Bush administration did not pick up where the Clinton administration had left off. Instead, it started with a review of what Bush's predecessor had done that lasted until June 2001. On June 6, the U.S. government announced a new policy agenda toward North Korea, including

—improved implementation of the Agreed Framework relating to North Korea's nuclear activities

—verifiable constraints on North Korea's missile programs and a ban on its export of missiles

—a less-threatening conventional military posture on the part of North Korea.

In other words, the United States had decided to aim at comprehensively eliminating all North Korean threats, from both nuclear and conventional weapons, including missiles.

Bush instructed his national security team to "undertake serious discussions with North Korea on a broad agenda" based on the administration's new policy.[99] Bush tried to emphasize how his North Korean policies differed from those of the Clinton administration, particularly in regard to limits on missiles, where the latter had failed. Nevertheless, the Bush administration retained the earlier dialogue option, announcing that the United States was prepared to negotiate "without conditions and virtually whenever and wherever the North Koreans wanted it."[100] The new policy was called the "bold approach."

The central figures in the earlier review of the Clinton administration's North Korea policy were Thomas Hubbard, deputy assistant secretary of state, and Robert Joseph, senior director for nonproliferation, counterproliferation, and homeland defense for the National Security Council (NSC). The two of them reviewed the Clinton administration's policy from the perspective of regional security on one hand and nonproliferation of weapons of mass destruction (WMDs) on the other, contributing their respective suggestions. Hubbard and his group thought that the Agreed Framework, though it was inadequate, brought with it various positive effects due to the freezing of North Korea's nuclear development program; they also thought that the Bush administration should continue the pro-engagement policy. In contrast, Joseph and his group found the Agreed Framework useless and felt that there was no need to engage or negotiate with North Korea. The gap between the two factions was so wide that they had a hard time finding any common ground.[101]

The "review" thus produced was therefore a product of compromise; nonetheless, the Agreed Framework somehow survived the review. Hubbard described the outcome as follows: "That June 6 statement reaffirmed our willingness to follow the Agreed Framework approach but it was wrapped in some body language that was ... much more harsh."[102] So, at one point Pritchard met Lee Hyong-chol, North Korea's permanent representative to the United Nations, and told him that the United States was prepared to negotiate with North Korea, "whenever, wherever, and without any precondition," but North Korea did not show any interest in the offer.

At the outset of the Bush administration, the State Department insisted that it should maintain the channel of contact with the North Korean mission to the United Nations in New York that it had long relied on, but the nuclear nonproliferation section of the White House rejected that idea. Accordingly, early in 2001 the U.S. government unilaterally abolished the "New York channel." In response, North Korea insisted that it would not enter into negotiations with the United States unless it was compensated for the damage done by the U.S. severance of the communications channel. Time ticked away, then, on September 11, the terrorist attacks occurred.

One of the effects of the 9/11 attacks was to cause the United States to reconsider the results of the earlier review of its policies concerning North Korea. Toward the end of January 2002, Bush identified North Korea as a member of the "axis of evil," along with Iraq and Iran. In March, American news media reported on a confidential portion of the Nuclear Posture Review (NPR) that the Bush administration had prepared as a guideline for the use of nuclear weapons in case of an emergency. The NPR listed seven countries as potential targets of a nuclear attack; North Korea was first on the list, followed by Iraq, Iran, Syria, Libya, China, and Russia.[103] In September 2002, the Bush administration issued the National Security Strategy of the United States, which stated that "in the past decade North Korea has become the world's principal purveyor of ballistic missiles, and has tested increasingly capable missiles while developing its own WMD arsenal. . . . We must be prepared to stop rogue states and their terrorist clients before they are able to threaten or use weapons of mass destruction against the United States and our allies and friends."[104]

No Intention to Attack North Korea

However, the Bush administration did not abandon its pro-engagement policy toward North Korea. In February 2002, Bush visited South Korea and had a third summit meeting with Kim Dae-jung in Seoul. During the talk, Kim Dae-jung referred to the Clinton administration's emergency scenario, which projected the loss of 1 million people in the event of an attack, and he earnestly stressed that war must be avoided at any cost. "No South Korean, including myself, praises the North Korean regime," Kim said. "But we cannot openly denounce it, either. It will not be wise to try to change it by force. I beg for your understanding on this particular point."[105] In the course of the discussion, Kim Dae-jung expressed his apprehension about the concept of the "axis of evil." He continued, saying:

> Diplomacy is not about who is good and who is bad. It is about national interests and peace. Ronald Reagan might have called the Soviet Union an evil empire, but he engaged in constructive dialogue with Mikhail Gorbachev. North Korea invaded South Korea, but the United States signed an armistice with the invader, and somehow this has enabled us to maintain peace on the peninsula for the past 50 years. Nothing is solved by just saying that North Korea is evil.[106]

When Kim Dae-jung was talking about Reagan, Bush nodded his head repeatedly and said, "We have no intention of invading North Korea," words that had not been included in the talking points prepared for the talk.[107] The summit tête-à-tête was originally planned to be about fifteen minutes long, but the two leaders kept talking for an hour.

At the joint press conference after the summit talk, Bush said, "President Kim reminded me a little bit about American history," mentioning the account that Kim had related regarding Reagan's achievements. Consequently, Bush explicitly declared, "We have no intention of invading North Korea." He added, "We're purely defensive. And the reason we have to be defensive is because there is a threatening position on the DMZ."[108]

During Bush's visit to the Republic of Korea, he went to Panmunjeom, located on the military border between North Korea and South Korea, and flew over the DMZ in a helicopter. "No wonder I think they're evil," Bush said when told that the ax that a North Korean soldier had used to kill two American soldiers in 1976 was on display in a museum on the north side of the border.[109]

After having lunch with American soldiers stationed along the DMZ, Bush visited Dorasan Station, the northernmost station on the South Korean side of the Gyeongui Line, the rail line that had been bisected into North Korean and South Korean segments. Kim Dae-jung accompanied Bush. At Dorasan Station, Bush made a speech in which he said the following:

> President Kim has just showed me a road he built—a road for peace. And he's shown me where that road abruptly ends, right here at the DMZ. That road has the potential to bring the peoples on both sides of this divided land together, and for the good of all the Korean people, the North should finish it.[110]

In the first draft of the speech, prepared by a White House speechwriter, "railroad" was used instead of "road," and the draft concluded with a plea: "Complete the construction of this railroad." But Defense Secretary Donald Rumsfeld opposed the reference to the railroad because he feared that the completion of a trans-peninsula railroad might jeopardize the mission of the U.S. troops stationed in South Korea. North and South Korea had started preparations to reconnect the divided Gyeongui Line, but that required removal of the landmines inside the DMZ. The U.S. Department of Defense was displeased by South Korea's unilateral undermining of the very foundation of the armistice agreement without sufficient consultation with the U.S. troops in South Korea. Rumsfeld, instead, requested a speech to echo the famous "Tear Down This Wall" speech by President Reagan in Berlin in 1987: "General Secretary Gorbachev, if you seek peace, if you seek prosperity for the Soviet Union and Eastern Europe, if you seek liberalization: Come here to this gate. Mr. Gorbachev, open this gate. Mr. Gorbachev—Mr. Gorbachev, tear down this wall!"[111]

Rumsfeld's idea was to make Bush's speech end with "Mr. Kim Jong-il, tear down this wall." But the problem was that the physical wall to be torn down was a tank trap built by the Americans; it would have been preposterous to ask North Korea to tear it down. The alternative that the White House suggested was to end the speech with "Finish this railroad," which would surely resonate with the South Korean people's wishes. But Rumsfeld would not accept the reference to a railroad, saying, "I'm not going to approve any of it. They're not building that railroad." In the end, "road" was used instead of "railroad."[112]

Actually, one portion of the speech prepared by the White House was changed after Bush arrived in Seoul; at the last minute, the reference to the "evil" regime in North Korea was dropped from the text, at the urging of Kim Dae-jung during the summit talk with Bush. That proved that the South Korean government had secretly obtained from the U.S. government a draft of the Dorasan speech.[113]

The next morning, all the South Korean media reported Bush's remark that "The United States has no intention to invade North Korea" as the top news. When told of that, Bush said, disbelief on his face, "Is that news?"[114]

In April 2002, North Korea signaled that it would welcome a visit to Pyongyang by a U.S. delegation, and the State Department immediately started to study the possibility of sending a delegation the following month.[115] However, it proved to be difficult to reconcile various opinions within the U.S. government regarding who would be the presidential envoy. Although it would have been natural for Jack Pritchard, ambassador and special envoy for negotiations with North Korea and U.S. representative to the Korean Peninsula Energy Development Organization, to head the delegation, he was not well-liked among those who were concerned with the nonproliferation of WMDs. To them, "Pritchard [was] a carryover from the Clinton administration, too soft on North Korea and untrustworthy."[116] Thus, several of them—including Stephen Hadley, deputy national security adviser; Paul Wolfowitz, deputy secretary of defense; Richard Armitage, deputy secretary of state; Lewis "Scooter" Libby, chief of staff for Vice President Dick Cheney; and James Kelly—got together to discuss who should be presidential envoy. Essentially, they all pointed at each other, saying "You go." "No, you go." "No, you go." Finally all the others agreed that Kelly should go, and Kelly said, "Okay, I'll do it."[117] In a way, Kelly was the default choice. There was tacit agreement on the need to ensure that someone other than Jack Pritchard was the presidential envoy, and yet nobody wanted to volunteer.[118]

On June 25, the U.S. government notified North Korea's permanent mission to the United Nations that it was prepared to dispatch a delegation on July 10; the message was conveyed on June 27.[119] But then, on June 29, a shootout erupted between North Korean and South Korean patrol vessels on the Yellow Sea, and the U.S. government decided to postpone the trip. On July 25, however, the North Korean government sent the South Korean government a message by telephone, saying, "Feeling regretful for the unforeseen armed clash that occurred in the West Sea [Yellow Sea] recently, we are of the view that both sides should make joint efforts to prevent the recurrence of similar incidents in future."[120] That was followed by a statement by the spokesman of North Korea's Foreign Ministry that "The DPRK side accepted the U.S. recent proposal to send its special envoy to Pyongyang to explain its stand on the resumption of the dialogue."[121]

It was in that context that U.S. Secretary of State Colin Powell and North Korean foreign minister Paek Nam-sun engaged in dialogue over coffee on the sidelines during the ministerial conference at the ASEAN Regional Forum (ARF) in Bandar Seri Begawan, Brunei, on July 31. Arriving at the conference site, an aide to Powell sent a message to Paek's staff, saying, "Powell is having coffee in the delegates' lounge. Please join him if you wish."[122] Paek immediately accepted the invitation, and the two foreign ministers had a fifteen-minute chat,[123] during which Powell said, "We have a particular issue that we have to discuss," and repeated three times that "all of the provisions about nuclear programs stipulated by the Agreed Framework needed to be strictly honored." Five note-takers from both the United States and North Korea recorded that remark.[124] Powell then said, "We are going to send Kelly to North Korea to directly discuss this issue. When Mr. Kelly comes, he will tell you why we have concerns, but he will also tell you what we're prepared to do if we can deal with these concerns." Although Powell declared that "North Korea was given prior notice" of the message by the Kelly delegation, his words were so subtle that it was uncertain how well Paek understood what Powell's intentions were.[125]

The plan for Kelly's visit succeeded in clearing one hurdle only to be confronted by another: the U.S. intelligence community's assessment of North Korea's uranium enrichment program, as a result of which the conflict of opinions within the administration concerning the proposed visit was revived with intensified fierceness. Powell had told Paek on July 31 that Kelly would visit Pyongyang, but the date still needed to be set and what Kelly would say about the uranium enrichment program had to be decided. Those who favored Kelly's visit insisted that because the United States did not yet have complete information, it did not need to decide whether what North Korea was doing violated the Agreed Framework. They also stressed that the United States did not need to bring up this issue itself. On the other side, those who initially opposed Kelly's visit insisted that the Agreed Framework no longer needed to be maintained because North Korea's development of HEU constituted a serious violation of the agreement.[126]

As the two camps within the Bush administration continued to argue, the summer of 2002 passed with no decision on the date or game plan for Kelly's visit. On August 30 the Japanese government announced that Prime Minister Koizumi planned to visit Pyongyang. The announcement had the effect of giving momentum to the dispatch of a U.S. delegation to North Korea, and on September 25, the Bush administration also announced that it would dispatch a delegation to Pyongyang. It remained to be decided, however, how to handle the HEU issue and how to raise the issue with North Korea in the first place.

Regarding the latter point there were two widely different views. One school considered it unwise to confront North Korea when a confrontation might inadvertently help North Korea to conceal whatever it had. The State Department's

Bureau of East Asia and Pacific Affairs was the chief advocate of that position. Although this school admitted the seriousness of North Korea's HEU program, it advocated a "comprehensive HEU settlement," aiming to settle the issue by incorporating what President Bush had proposed as a "bold approach."

The other school stressed the importance of nipping the HEU program in the bud by directly confronting North Korea with the existing intelligence information. The chief advocates of this view included John Bolton, NSC staff concerned with nonproliferation of WMDs, Cheney, and the Pentagon. Particularly vocal among them were four mid-level staff members of various agencies who formulated the school's theoretical framework: Mark Groombridge (Bolton's office), John Rood (NSC), Samantha Ravitch (Cheney's office), and Jody Green (Pentagon).[127] They insisted that North Korea's uranium enrichment program was a center-front issue, qualitatively different from other issues, and that they had to base their position on the undeniable fact that uranium enrichment was a clear violation of the Agreed Framework. They therefore contended that the HEU issue had to be settled first.[128]

The strategy paper for the Pyongyang visit was drafted and edited by James Kelly himself, based on discussions with each involved government agency. It was then submitted to the National Security Council at the White House. Although that kind of draft is normally commented on by officials at the assistant secretary level, Rumsfeld and Paul Wolfowitz themselves faxed handwritten comments regarding this particular draft. They called for continuing with the "bold approach"; nevertheless, they said, "Now that we know of the existence of the HEU, we cannot go on as if nothing has happened."[129]

In the end, the second school prevailed, and it was decided that Kelly's delegation would raise the HEU issue head on. According to a State Department official, domestic political considerations may also have been a factor—that is, it would be politically disadvantageous to be later accused by Congress for failing to achieve anything if Kelly's delegation did not raise the issue with North Korea.[130] However, Kelly reminisced later that it would have been inconceivable not to raise the uranium enrichment issue after July.[131]

In January 2003, some time after North Korea's withdrawal from the NPT, a U.S. spy satellite detected several trucks arriving at the fuel-rod storage site in Yongbyon. It was strongly suspected that the trucks went there to pick up rods in order to move them to a reprocessing plant. Robert J. Einhorn, a former nonproliferation official in the Clinton administration, observed that "the North Koreans may be taking a fatal step," if what was detected was the first indication that reprocessing had been resumed.[132] Toward the end of February, the U.S. intelligence community confirmed that North Korea had resumed operation of its graphite-moderated five-megawatt nuclear reactor.

A MID-AIR CONFRONTATION

In February 2003, President Roh Moo-hyun took office in South Korea. The Bush administration had a new partner in Seoul, ambitious but inexperienced. Then, on March 2, a week after the inauguration, a bizarre incident occurred. Four armed North Korean jets (two MiG-29s and two MiG 23s) intercepted a U.S. Air Force RC-135V/W Rivet Joint reconnaissance aircraft and flew alongside it for about twenty minutes over the Sea of Japan/East Sea.[133] At one point one of the North Korean jet fighters came to within less than fifty feet (sixteen meters) of the U.S. plane. The MiGs were armed with heat-seeking air-to-air missiles.[134]

The main mission of the RC-135 was to detect any North Korean preparations for its next missile test that could not be detected by reconnaissance satellite by monitoring communications to and from the facilities involved, communications that would increase just before a missile test. After the launching of the anti-ship missile one week before, the Pentagon had deployed the RC-135 to Kadena Air Base on Okinawa, Japan, from its usual base on the mainland United States, believing that North Korea would be testing a longer-range ballistic missile.[135] The RC-135 had taken off from Kadena Air Base.

The incident reminded the world of the USS Pueblo incident of January 1968 and the shooting down of a U.S. EC-121 reconnaissance aircraft over the Sea of Japan/East Sea in April 1969.[136] For what became its last mission, the RC-135 was scouting the eastern seaboard of North Korea, and it received fuel midair from a KC-135.[137] The North Korean government had repeatedly warned the U.S. government about the RC-135 for several days before the attempt to intercept it was made on March 2, 2003:

> The plane belonging to the U.S. Forces took off from its overseas base at around 9:30 Monday morning. It illegally intruded into the air above the territorial waters of the DPRK between Musudan and Wonsan bay in the East Sea and spied on the DPRK for hours, supported by a KC-135 refueling tanker.
>
> This reconnaissance plane made shuttle flights in the air above the same territorial waters of the DPRK for more than 10 hours on Feb. 21, 22, and 23 to spy on important targets along the east coast of the DPRK.
>
> This is a premeditated move to find an opportunity to mount a preemptive attack on the DPRK.[138]

The "overseas base" was Kadena Air Base on Okinawa. By specifying the exact time that the RC-135 had taken off, the North Koreans must have wanted to tell the United States that they knew everything that the United States was conspiring to do. Musudan was known to be the location of the launch site of the North Korean Taepodong ballistic missile.[139]

In response, the U.S. government protested what it referred to as North Korean provocation. The Pentagon claimed that the North Korean fighters tried to force the U.S. aircraft to land in North Korean territory.[140] Within the Pentagon there were a variety of views regarding the incident:

—North Korea might be trying to limit U.S. air reconnaissance activities, which had been intensified after U.S.-DPRK tension had worsened.

—North Korea might also be sending a warning about the U.S.-ROK joint military exercise that was to start on March 4 and, at the same time, to restrain the United States from sending the North Korean nuclear issue to the UN Security Council.

—The North Korean fighters might have mistakenly approached the RC-135 because North Korea had believed that it was attempting to intercept a WC-135 that had been monitoring North Korea's spent fuel reprocessing facilities.[141]

A Department of Defense official concerned with Korean Peninsula matters confessed that he was truly appalled by the incident. No jet fighter guzzled as much jet fuel as the MiG-29, and the North Korean Air Force was so short of jet fuel that it could not afford to have satisfactory flight exercises. Nevertheless, the North Korean pilots who had intercepted the RC-135 had obviously been well-trained, and they had detected the flight route and the timing accurately enough to fly far over the Sea of Japan/East Sea. The U.S. Department of Defense was so impressed that some of its officials speculated that China must have fed the flight route and timing information to the North Korean pilots, who must have been secretly trained by the Chinese air force.[142] One senior Pentagon official later stated:

> Clearly the objective was to divert the aircraft and to capture it, not unlike the Pueblo incident. . . . [I]t was very carefully practiced ahead of time. . . . [T]here was also some increased rhetoric beforehand. . . . [I]f they had successfully diverted the aircraft, they would have been able to claim that they had been complaining about U.S. intrusiveness and surveillance for several weeks beforehand, and this was just them asserting their rights, which they had already announced they were going to do.
>
> The question for us then became what was their intention once they would have captured the aircraft. I think it would have been to draw and force us to engage them in a direct dialogue, to embarrass us in the process, to gain points with our allies in the Republic of Korea, and to embarrass us in front of Japan.[143]

Some observers suspected that "they were trying to scare the WC-135s to stay away so that the plutonium would be harder to smell."[144] Others speculated that North Korea might have been inspired by the April 2001 forced landing of a U.S. reconnaissance aircraft by Chinese fighters when the reconnaissance airplane was on a mission over Hainan Island and might have been trying to emulate China.[145] The Hainan Island incident was the first diplomatic challenge that the Bush administration had to face. Although it temporarily strained U.S.-China relations, a prompt and appropriate response by Secretary of State Colin Powell succeeded in turning the incident into the start of more stable bilateral relations.

Was North Korea really inspired by the Hainan Island incident and did it attempt to use the RC-135 incident as an opportunity to "try to get a senior [U.S.] negotiator to come and to try to get concessions"? One senior White House official observed, "This clearly was not a deed of a cowboy pilot like the Chinese pilot during the Hainan Island incident, which was caused by the pilot's personal adventurism. The North Korean interception clearly was carried out under instruction from the top military echelon."[146] A senior Pentagon official agreed with that view: "They had no experience in interceptions at that distance off the North Korean coast. So it was something that was ordered at the national level."[147]

President Roh Moo-hyun insisted that the incident was well within the scope of an ordinary military exercise, and he pleaded for U.S. restraint, saying, "I am urging the United States not to go too far."[148]

A ROSETTA STONE

What did the United States learn about North Korea's uranium enrichment program (UEP)? When did the United States find out about the program? These questions were later raised over and over again. More specifically:

—How advanced did the United States think that the North Korean uranium enrichment program was? Was it still at the research stage or already at the production level? Was North Korea still collecting necessary parts and materials, or had it already completed the system? Or, indeed, had it already been in operation for some time? Was the United States able to specify the location of the facilities?

—Although the United States confronted North Korea with the allegation that its uranium enrichment program actually was an HEU program for developing nuclear weapons, did the United States confirm that the program was indeed an HEU program?

—Although the United States had since 1999 or 2000 suspected that North Korea had a uranium enrichment program, why did the United States suddenly bring the issue to the forefront in the summer of 2002? Was there any ulterior motive?

The first clue the United States received about North Korea's uranium enrichment program was provided by South Korea in 1997, during the Clinton administration.[149] At that time, the program was considered to be for research purposes.[150] In the fall of 1998, South Korea passed on to the United States HUMINT (human intelligence), which the ROK's intelligence community had painstakingly collected, that indicated that North Korean nuclear physicists had visited Islamabad, Pakistan. Consequently, suspicions that Pakistan and the DPRK were cooperating on nuclear development deepened.[151] After Bush took office, South Korean intelligence agencies picked up strong evidence that North Korea was buying components for uranium enrichment, and they passed the evidence to the United States.[152]

North Korea's rapid accumulation of uranium enrichment technology was attributable to Dr. Abdul Qadeer Khan of Pakistan, who had provided North Korea with both a blueprint and a prototype of a centrifugal separator. Khan was instrumental in the success of Pakistan's atomic test in 1998, thereby earning the title of "father of Pakistan's nuclear bomb." In the 1970s, Khan had been an engineer in an affiliate company of Urenco, an English-Dutch uranium-enrichment joint venture, and it was believed that he had obtained the plan for a centrifugal separator during that period. Khan subsequently became engaged in nuclear development activities in his homeland.

North Korea and Pakistan had maintained a close relationship since Prime Minister Benazir Bhutto of Pakistan visited Pyongyang in December 1993. Bhutto later said in an interview with the *Asahi Shimbun* that she had been able to "obtain technology for a long-range missile."[153] In return, North Korea obtained from Pakistan something that was similarly valuable—uranium enrichment technology. Bhutto was accompanied to North Korea by Khan,[154] a step that later led to the secret nuclear cooperation between Pakistan and North Korea.[155] At a later stage, Pakistan made a secret deal with North Korea to provide, instead of financial compensation for North Korean–made missiles, a prototype of and an assembly plan for a centrifugal separator to enrich uranium. (Pakistan nevertheless also provided some monetary compensation.) According to Hwang Jang-yop, a former theoretician of the *Juche* ideology in North Korea who defected to South Korea in 1997, the missile/nuclear technology deal took place in the summer of 1996. It is believed that actual payment began in 1997.[156] Centrifugal separators began to be transported to North Korea in 1998.

A senior U.S. administration official said the following regarding the Pakistani–North Korean nuclear connection:

During 1998 and 1999, a total of twenty units of different sizes of two types of centrifugal separators, P1 and P2, arrived in North Korea from Pakistan. All of them were for demonstration purposes [prototypes]. Before long the Clinton administration noticed what was happening. The reinforced aluminum pipe that they procured was 268 millimeters thick. It was not a kid's toy.

Subsequently, the number of centrifugal separators procured by North Korea steadily increased. Also, there was information that a German vessel had transported from France as many as 3,000 or 4,000 units of centrifugal separator materials [high-strength aluminum tubes]. Those items on that German vessel were confiscated as a result of a maritime inspection. Adding this and that, I think North Korea might have ordered close to 10,000 separators, although it is estimated that North Korea did not obtain one-third of those 10,000.[157]

The P1 and P2 were formally the Pakistan 1 and Pakistan 2, centrifugal separators manufactured by Urenco. The P1 is equipped with a rotor made of aluminum, while the P2 uses a special steel alloy.[158] The items on the German vessel bound for North Korea were 214 German-made reinforced aluminum tubes weighing a total of twenty-two tons. Although the cargo was addressed to Shenyang Aircraft Manufacturing Co. Ltd., China, it was actually bound for North Korea.[159] In April 2003, nine days after the vessel left the port of Hamburg, security officers of France, Germany, and Egypt boarded the vessel and confiscated the aluminum tubes.[160] In November of the same year, representatives of Urenco testified in a German court that the confiscated aluminum tubes had been manufactured precisely according to the specifications for Urenco's centrifugal separators.

In 2001, after the 9/11 terrorist attacks, the United States formed a united front against terrorism with Pakistan, lifting the economic sanctions that it had imposed on the latter. The Pakistani government consequently began to provide evidence regarding its secret deal with North Korea, such as receipts and other documents, based on the confession of A. Q. Khan. According to a senior U.S. administration official, however, the information provided by the Pakistani government was "no major source of new intelligence. It was more of a validation of what we already knew."[161] This official was of the opinion that the basic body of information had already been more or less consolidated, using HUMINT from South Korea and U.S. intelligence from satellites and other signals intelligence (SIGINT).[162] Nevertheless, it was beyond doubt that the disclosure of the international nuclear black market started by Khan greatly contributed to the investigation of North Korea's uranium enrichment program.

One of the important pieces of information provided by Pakistan was the "shopping list" that A. Q. Khan had given to North Korea for its HEU program, which, according to a senior U.S. administration official, perfectly matched North Korea's materials procurement list. The same official likened the bringing to light of the North Korean HEU program to the deciphering of the Rosetta Stone:

There had been a suspicion earlier that North Korea had HEU. Bob Gallucci was among those who had such a suspicion. But it had always remained a grey zone until our intelligence people discovered the deciphering code. They went back, they got all the backlog of intel, human intelligence, all kinds of intelligence they had. And they put together an incredibly clear picture that nobody disagreed with. It was not a black and white thing. It was an increasing crescendo. . . . It was like the Rosetta Stone.[163]

During the Clinton administration, Robert Gallucci was an ambassador at large with the State Department and the key U.S. player, Kang Sok-ju's counterpart, in negotiating the Agreed Framework. The Agreed Framework requires both North Korea and South Korea to implement the North-South Joint Denuclearization Declaration, which prohibits both sides from maintaining any reprocessing or enrichment capability; Gallucci told North Korea that therefore uranium enrichment would be a violation of the Agreed Framework. Gallucci testified before Congress in December 1994 that "if there were ever any move to enrich, we would argue they were not in compliance with the Agreed Framework."[164]

When did the United States find out about North Korea's uranium enrichment program? By the end of the Clinton administration, the United States had accumulated quite a lot of intelligence about uranium enrichment in North Korea; in 1999, for example, the U.S. Department of Energy reported that "North Korea is at the first stage of a uranium enrichment program, in cooperation with Pakistan."[165] It should be noted, however, that the top policymakers in the Clinton administration "were not aware of HEU" because the United States had been pursuing a pro-engagement policy toward North Korea, exemplified by the attempt, even until the very end of the presidential election campaign in 2000, to pursue the possibility of a Clinton visit to North Korea. Information concerning the issue was limited to "the administration's lower level of the intelligence community."[166]

Similarly, the Bush administration initially had not paid much attention to the issue. For example, it did not ask the intelligence community for new information for its review, on June 6, 2001, of U.S. policy regarding North Korea.[167] According to Richard Armitage, it was only in February 2002 that a full-fledged assessment of intelligence concerning North Korea's HEU program was begun. As he testified before the Senate Foreign Relations Committee, "It was about a month or so in front of Mr. Kelly's visit to Pyongyang that we got what we felt was incontrovertible evidence of a production program of highly enriched uranium."[168] A task force regarding the North Korean HEU program was set up, led by Robert Wolpole, a senior analyst in charge of nuclear nonproliferation activities at the Central Intelligence Agency (CIA). The task force received the entire backlog of intelligence that the U.S. government had about North Korea's nuclear program in general, with a special focus on the HEU program in particular. The task force reexamined and reassessed the intelligence and evidence that had already been accumulated in order to extract the relevant "historical evidence"[169] and ultimately made a critically important finding in reviewing the radio communications that had been tapped. They took notice of exchanges such as "We ordered twenty boxes of cherries," and "Twenty boxes of cherries have arrived," conjecturing that the "cherries" actually were centrifugal separators.[170] During the June–July period of 2002, the intelligence community submitted the National Intelligence Estimate (NIE) to the administration's policymakers.[171]

On July 19, top leaders at the State Department, including Powell, decided to accept the NIE assessment, and they discussed its policy implications. It was decided that because of the Yellow Sea incident, they had no choice but to postpone Kelly's visit to North Korea again. At the White House the following week, a cabinet meeting was held in which Powell took up the NIE assessment and stressed that the issue had to be settled before the administration pursued its "bold approach" toward North Korea.[172] When Powell met Paek Nam-sun toward the end of July, his remarks were based on the position that he had taken during that cabinet meeting.[173]

The U.S. intelligence community's assessment of nuclear development in North Korea at the time can be summarized as follows:

—North Korea has embarked on a large-scale, covert effort to establish the capability to produce uranium enrichment for nuclear weapons.

—This effort has clearly been under way for several years, although the United States has only recently become aware of its scope.

—North Korea decided by late 2000 to pursue a production-scale uranium enrichment program and is now constructing a centrifuge enrichment plant.

—Since 1999, a North Korean organization has acquired special lubricants and epoxies that are used in the assembly of Urenco/Pakistani-type centrifuges. These acquisitions indicate that the North was involved in centrifuge R&D at that time.

—By late 2000, North Korea began seeking these items in much larger quantities. In addition, it began seeking large quantities of specialty equipment and parts that are used in centrifuge enrichment plants.

—By mid-2002, North Korea had acquired at least enough specialty metal to make the outer casings for more than 2,600 of the larger Urenco/Pakistani-type centrifuges.

—An enrichment plant of this size can produce enough HEU for two to three nuclear weapons per year when fully operational.

—North Korea has been acquiring the materials to produce centrifuges and construct the plant, which could produce enough highly enriched uranium for a nuclear weapon by late 2004.

—There are indications the plant may be underground, but the United States does not know the location.[174]

Stephen Yates of Vice President Cheney's office described that assessment as "not necessarily a slam dunk but overwhelming circumstantial evidence that tells us for sure they're pursuing this."[175]

When it came to the crucial point of how advanced the North Korean uranium enrichment program was, however, many points remained obscure:

—How many separators had already been installed on the cascade?

—How much uranium 235 had been concentrated? Was the amount sufficient to enable production of nuclear weapons?

—Had North Korea succeeded in producing nuclear devices?

There was a good possibility that North Korea had achieved the ability to produce not only so-called "yellow cake" (refined) uranium but also uranium hexafluoride. The Bush administration suspected that the two tons of uranium hexafluoride that had been included in the WMD materials that Libya had abandoned could have been produced by North Korea.[176] (It should be noted, however, that the intelligence agencies' assessments in 2002 did not touch on North Korea's ability to produce uranium hexafluoride.)[177]

It was also beyond doubt that North Korea had obtained centrifugal separators from Pakistan and other sources. The pattern of procurement of the devices clearly revealed where they had come from. It had been believed that of the centrifugal separators that North Korea had obtained from Pakistan, the P2s had been unfinished products and production parts, while the P1s were finished products. There was some intelligence indicating that North Korea had also obtained some P3s, which were more advanced, although that had not been confirmed.[178]

Many of the parts and materials that North Korea ordered were confiscated en route and never got to North Korea. Some parts and materials that were indispensable for operating the centrifugal separators also were missing. For instance, the International Institute for Strategic Studies (IISS) in London concluded that North Korea had not obtained such key materials as a special steel alloy and bearings that were essential for manufacturing the rotor for a centrifugal separator.[179] The rotor, spinning at high speed inside a centrifugal separator, plays a crucial role in the uranium enrichment process and greatly affects the quality of the resulting enriched uranium. Even if all the necessary parts and materials were obtained and the necessary infrastructure was prepared, the assembly and operation of a centrifugal separator required sophisticated production management technology. Did North Korea have such technology? Moreover, North Korea was handicapped with regard to the power required to operate the devices. There was serious doubt within the State Department over whether North Korea was capable of supplying, on a sustained basis, the amount of electricity necessary to operate centrifugal separators.[180]

There were differences of views regarding North Korea's nuclear capability even within the intelligence community. In fact, some intelligence analysts in the State Department's Bureau of Intelligence and Research (INR) questioned the validity of the conclusions drawn, taking more cautious views. They pointed out that two key questions remained unanswered: first, when did North Korea start the enrichment program? Second, how far had it advanced? Furthermore, the United States had not even been able to specify the location of the program's facilities.[181]

A senior U.S. administration official used the following metaphor to explain how the Bush administration perceived the existence of North Korea's uranium enrichment program at the time:

> [W]e had their shopping list; we caught them buying 99 percent of it, 98 percent. . . . [T]hey were buying chocolate chips, and flour, and butter, and everything for chocolate chip cookies. . . . We didn't know where their kitchen was, and we didn't know if they had actually started baking or were just mixing the dough.[182]

The "cookies" had not yet been baked at that time, but the U.S. government concluded that North Korea had plans to bake them. A senior U.S. administration official reminisced:

> Judging from each and every angle, it became obvious that North Korea was aiming to produce HEU. Nobody knew how highly enriched their uranium enrichment was, but the centrifugal separators were not being used for a simple uranium enrichment program or for medical purposes. It was beyond doubt that the North Koreans were aiming for HEU. We were very certain of their aim.[183]

As Mitchell Reiss and Robert Gallucci stressed in their *Foreign Affairs* article, it was difficult to believe that North Korea had been undertaking uranium enrichment simply to develop low enriched uranium for civilian use.[184]

In conclusion, it was beyond doubt that North Korea had pursued uranium enrichment perhaps at least since the late 1990s. As President Pervez Musharraf later revealed in his autobiography, A. Q. Khan's assistance was critical in helping North Korea to develop its weapons program, not only in providing centrifuges but also in training nuclear engineers.[185] It was a deadly serious, systematic national project.

As for HEU, it would be more natural to conclude that North Korea was aiming to develop weapons grade HEU. It should also be obvious that that was and perhaps still is North Korea's aim. But what about North Korea's capability in that regard? How much uranium has it actually enriched? How much uranium enrichment capacity does it have? Is its uranium really HEU? At least in the fall of 2002, the Bush administration did not have any solid evidence or intelligence to answer those critical questions.

Intelligence concerning the HEU program has since remained obscure. After the failure to discover WMDs in Iraq became politicized in the summer of 2004, Condoleezza Rice and some of her advisers visited the CIA in order to pose some hard questions regarding the intelligence concerning North Korea's nuclear development program. On that occasion she was told that the estimates for when North Korea's uranium enrichment program would go into full operation were based on several assumptions, including one regarding the level of North Korea's uranium enrichment technology. The assumption was that "if they're that good at plutonium, and you apply that same level of expertise to HEU," then it could be assumed they were pretty far along. If that particular assumption was removed from the assessment, the time estimate would have a wider range because the United States did not really know how good North Korea's technology was.[186]

In February 2005, the Bush administration dispatched two NSC staff members, Michael Green, senior director for Asian affairs, and William Tobey, director of nonproliferation policy, to Japan, China, and South Korea. Their mission was to brief the top policy people in those nations on the North Korea policy of the second-term Bush administration and to share the U.S. concern about the possibility that North Korea was transferring nuclear materials overseas. Before they departed, members of the Bush administration discussed internally how they should refer to the North Korean uranium enrichment program. They decided to use the term "UEP" (uranium enrichment program) or "enriched uranium technology" instead of "HEU program."[187]

THREE THEORIES

What was North Korea's intention in having a uranium enrichment program? It must have been obvious that disclosure of such a violation of the Agreed Framework would lead to severe sanctions from the United States. In the worst-case scenario, it was conceivable that the UN Security Council might impose an embargo on exports to North Korea. Why did North Korea undertake such a risky venture?

Three perhaps overlapping explanations seem plausible: the deterrence theory; the buying time theory; and the insurance theory. Kang Sok-ju had told Kelly that North Korea needed a nuclear deterrent to counter the Bush administration's hostile policies toward his country, but Kelly immediately refuted that argument then and there. It was believed that North Korea had launched its uranium enrichment program long before Bush entered the White House. Joseph Bermudez Jr., an American scholar specializing in North Korea, stated in 1999 that North Korea had been deeply interested in uranium enrichment since the late 1980s.[188] A veteran U.S. government intelligence analyst said:

> I suspect that North Korea started to study the possibility of a uranium enrichment program in the 1987–88 period . . . although it was probably after the impact of the Gulf War in 1991 that North Korea became serious about that. Intimidated by the annihilation caused by the United States' cruise missiles and high-tech pinpoint attacks, the North Koreans must have been reminded how vulnerable were their plutonium-type nuclear development facilities in Yongbyon, which were fully exposed.[189]

North Korea's fear that the United States would topple its regime by force if it did not possess nuclear weapons capability must have deepened; North Korea then might have decided to push the development of a plutonium-type nuclear facility in Yongbyon, temporally shelving the uranium enrichment program.[190] It has been estimated that North Korea started HEU development in the mid-1990s, but it is quite possible that it started a little earlier than that.[191] Because North Korea signed the Agreed Framework, however, it had to freeze operation of its plutonium-related facilities in Yongbyon; some observers in the United States suspected that North Korea therefore might have reactivated and vigorously pursued its hitherto-shelved uranium enrichment program.[192] North Korea's connection with Pakistan would have facilitated that decision.

On April 6, 2003, a spokesperson for North Korea's Foreign Ministry issued the following statement:

> The Iraqi war shows that to allow disarming through inspection does not help avert the war but rather sparks it. . . . Only a physical deterrence force, a tremendous military-deterrence force powerful enough to decisively beat back an attack . . . can avert war and protect the security of the country and the nation. This is a lesson drawn from the Iraqi war.[193]

Shortly after that announcement, Li Gun, a North Korean representative at the China-DPRK-U.S. trilateral meeting held in Beijing in April 2003, told his counterpart in the DPRK-U.S. talk, half threateningly, "We have already completed reprocessing of nuclear spent fuel. We are now able to demonstrate, produce, and transfer nuclear weapons to other countries." That kind of rhetoric must have resulted from fear brought home by the Iraq war and the fall of Baghdad.[194] Regarding the remarks by Kang Sok-ju and Li Gun, a North Korean diplomat later confessed, "The important thing was to let the United States know that we have nuclear capability. By those remarks, we aimed to have the United States change its policies toward us."[195]

In summary, North Korea overstretched itself to appear, in the eyes of the United States, to be a nuclear power or at least to be capable of nuclear deterrence.

It attempted to obtain one more deterrence card in addition to that of the spent fuel reprocessing program, which was frozen under the Agreed Framework and which was vulnerable because it was fully exposed to military satellites. Kelly concluded that "North Korea wanted to enrich uranium in order to win the United States' respect and wanted to develop a retaliatory capability that could not easily be interfered with."[196] North Korea's principal aim was, therefore, to develop nuclear deterrence.

Another possible explanation is that North Korea wanted to buy time. Perhaps it never had intended to abandon its nuclear development program. According to this view, North Korea agreed to the construction of two light-water reactors under the Agreed Framework only to buy time to secretly continue its nuclear development activities and reinforce its nuclear capability. Meanwhile, it could advance the development of HEU, which was, by its nature, easier to conceal. Regarding HEU development, Kelly later said, "I'm convinced the main reason they did this is because it's much more easily concealed."[197]

For North Korea, nuclear development was not something that it could give up in return for normalization of diplomatic relations or for economic assistance. It had been a forty-year-long core project for national security on which the regime's and the nation's survival hinged. In addition, the military needed to make up for North Korea's disadvantage in conventional forces vis-à-vis South Korea and to maintain its own prestige.

Hwang Jang-yop once disclosed that Kim Jong-il and his entourage had made comments that slighted the significance of the Agreed Framework immediately after signing the agreement. In October 1994, Kang Sok-ju came back from the signing of the Agreed Framework in Geneva and reported to Kim Jong-il. When, during their meeting, defense procurement czar Chung Byong-ho said, "According to the Geneva agreement we have to allow inspectors in within five or six years, and currently we have no alternatives," Kim Jong-il responded, "Then we have no option but to declare that we possess nuclear weapons and to confront the United States." Hwang Jang-yop also testified, "Kim Jong-il had no intention of complying with the NPT. He once said, 'We shouldn't have signed the treaty and we shouldn't have accepted inspections in the first place.' And he added, 'We do not accept inspection of our biochemical weapons.'"[198] Kim Il-sung had not been dead for three months when North Korea signed the Agreed Framework. A senior U.S. administration official expressed skepticism of North Korea, saying, "They clearly had a plan in 1995 to rev this up, to compensate for freezing the plutonium.... Kang Sok-ju and the rest of the leadership had a plan to build up their nuclear deterrent while its plutonium was frozen."[199]

Nor was it altogether certain how sincerely the United States had intended to comply with the agreement, particularly with regard to its duty to provide North Korea with light-water reactors. At the time, most of the senior members of the

Clinton administration, including Vice President Al Gore and Anthony Lake, the national security adviser, speculated that Kim Jong-il's regime would collapse before the light-water reactors were completed.[200] Thus, the United States, too, was buying time. Kim Jong-il must have been fully aware of the intentions of the United States and must have worked out his own scheme for buying time.

The third and last possible explanation lies in the theory of insurance—that is, North Korea was buying insurance to protect itself against not only military but also political threats. It is conceivable that North Korea had held a pessimistic view of the future of the Agreed Framework from the time that it signed the agreement in 1994. About one month after the signing, midterm elections were held in the United States, and the Republicans made major gains. During the campaign, the Republicans had criticized the Agreed Framework as a performance by the Clinton White House designed to produce a diplomatic coup. After emerging victorious from the election, the party increased its criticism of the agreement, crippling hopes for normalization of DPRK-U.S. relations.

In September 1996, a North Korean submarine crossed into South Korean waters, triggering a gunfight with South Korean forces. The incident took place while the two Koreas' representatives to the UN were in negotiations regarding the mutual opening of liaison offices. In addition, public opinion in the United States toward KEDO's construction of nuclear reactors in North Korea was becoming increasingly critical. North Korea, after considering these factors, must have concluded that the Agreed Framework could collapse and that the United States was seriously considering attacking North Korea's nuclear facilities. North Korea also might have started its uranium enrichment program as insurance against the surgical annihilation of its plutonium facilities by the U.S. military. "HEU may have been pursued as a fallback in case of emergency," Kelly later said.[201]

It is important also to consider the domestic political situation in North Korea in those days. North Korea's military probably was most staunchly opposed to signing the Agreed Framework. A senior U.S. administration official observed, "It is quite conceivable that North Korea started full-fledged development of uranium enrichment as an alternative nuclear development in order that the military would approve of the signing of the Agreed Framework."[202] But some observers have wondered whether relations between Kim Jong-il and the military were of the sort to allow or require bargaining and negotiating. It is noteworthy, however, that Kim Jong-il said to Madeleine Albright, who visited North Korea in the fall of 2000, "If we are properly guaranteed by the United States that our security will not be threatened, I can persuade the military that the United States is no longer a threat, which will make it easier to reroute the military budget toward the general economy and other areas."[203]

It would be natural to relate the country's nuclear development strategy to the intentions of the military and the need to maintain a proper relationship with the military. Doing so could have been an insurance policy for Kim Jong-il in order to maintain his authority.

An Intelligence Gap

Although there were repeated schisms and conflicts within the Bush administration regarding its North Korea policy, the administration's policymakers almost unanimously endorsed the intelligence assessment of North Korea's HEU program. Kelly later said, "American intelligence, with unusual unanimity, assessed that North Korea was pursuing a large-scale covert program."[204] Even Jack Pritchard, who had resigned in August 2003 to protest the Bush administration's lack of a North Korea policy, said:

> When the intelligence community made a fuss about secret nuclear development in Kumchang-ri, I challenged it because I didn't find the evidence convincing enough. Intelligence people still insisted that they were right. But this time, I don't have any doubt. They came up with enough evidence.[205]

In response to Kang Sok-ju's remarks admitting the HEU program during James Kelly's visit to Pyongyang, Kelly stressed that the U.S. administration had "taken careful steps and confirmed the real intention" behind the remarks.[206] Because the U.S. intelligence community had always underestimated North Korea's missile development capability in the 1980s, misjudging its amazing speed, Kelly had since then cautioned himself and his staff not to underestimate North Korea's ability to master a technology, including the technology relating to uranium enrichment.[207]

However, the governments of Japan and South Korea did not necessarily share the U.S. assessment concerning North Korea's uranium enrichment program. Secretary of State Colin Powell later said, "[Japan, South Korea, and China] never were quite as persuaded as we were that the North Koreans were doing this [HEU]," and he attributed the perception gap to the difficulties that the United States had to face in dealing with the North Korean nuclear issue.[208]

Initially there was skepticism in both Japan and South Korea about the very existence of HEU in North Korea. It was clearly reflected in the facial expressions of both Lim Dong-won, a presidential aide to Kim Dae-jung in charge of foreign affairs, security, and unification, and Hitoshi Tanaka, director general of MOFA's Bureau of Asian and Oceanian Affairs, when Kelly told them of Kang Sok-ju's "acknowledgment" of the HEU program.

Subsequently, in various countries there arose, in addition to doubt regarding the existence of the program, suspicion regarding the U.S. timing of its disclosure. From 2000 through 2002, Kim Jong-il launched what could be called "smile diplomacy" toward South Korea, Russia, China, and Japan, and, particularly in the summer of 2002, both Japan and South Korea were about to accelerate implementation of their pro-engagement policies toward North Korea. At that particular time the Bush administration started raising the HEU issue and confronting North Korea, making many officials in other countries suspect that the United States had an ulterior motive. As pointed out in chapter 2, Japan shared that suspicion and secretly prepared for Koizumi's visit to Pyongyang and normalization of diplomatic relations with North Korea. Moreover, both Japan and South Korea were displeased with the inadequacy of the briefings by U.S. intelligence agencies, and the two countries even suspected that the U.S. government might be using the briefings in a rather arbitrary fashion in order to dramatize the North Korean crisis.

The Trilateral Coordination and Oversight Group (TCOG) meeting held in Tokyo in November 2002 presented an opportunity for Japan and South Korea to raise, vis-à-vis the United States, the HEU issue. When Kelly said that it was "the U.S. view that North Korea should never and will never receive a light-water reactor," Hitoshi Tanaka, the Japanese representative, and Lee Tae-sik, the ROK representative, criticized his comment, and Tanaka in particular pushed back very hard, challenging the validity of the U.S. intelligence concerning the HEU program. One member of the U.S. delegation felt that Tanaka should not have gone that far in front of the South Koreans, later remarking, "That was not so helpful."[209] Both South Korea and Japan asked the U.S. government to provide a detailed transcript of the exchange between James Kelly and Kang Sok-ju. Yukio Takeuchi, vice minister for foreign affairs, and Lim Dong-won separately conveyed that request to senior U.S. administration officials, but both were turned down.[210] Some U.S. officials hesitated to share intelligence with Japan and South Korea on the grounds that one or both might leak the information. Although it is almost needless to say that hesitance was especially strong among the intelligence community, there also was conflict within the U.S. intelligence community, particularly between the CIA's Weapons Intelligence, Non-Proliferation, and Arms Control Unit (WINPAC) and its Asia-Pacific, Latin America, and Africa (APLAA) Division. According to a senior U.S. administration official, "When APLAA said we must share this [intelligence] with the allies, WINPAC people would say, 'No, we mustn't. We have to protect the source of the intelligence.'"[211]

At the beginning of 2003, U.S. government intelligence experts started providing full-fledged briefings to Japan and South Korea,[212] but a senior ROK government official found the briefings to be "sketchy and inconclusive."[213] Although South Korea had distrusted U.S. intelligence since the Kumchang-ri incident, it began to genuinely suspect U.S. credibility since the Bush administration had misled the world concerning the existence of weapons of mass destruction in Iraq in order to justify the U.S. invasion.[214]

Japan, South Korea, and other concerned nations started to voice their suspicions about the explanations given by the United States regarding its assessment of North Korea's nuclear capability. In 1993, for instance, the U.S. intelligence community concluded that North Korea had produced enough plutonium to produce one or two nuclear weapons. After the Bush administration took over, however, the U.S. government's assessment changed. In August 2001, for example, John MacLaughlin, deputy director of the CIA, suddenly declared that North Korea possessed at least one or two nuclear weapons. The initial conclusion that North Korea had the ability to produce one or two atomic weapons was transformed into the claim that in fact it already had done so.[215]

In April 2004, the U.S. intelligence community modified its assessment of North Korea's nuclear capability, saying that the country possessed eight nuclear weapons, assuming that it had reprocessed all of the 8,000 fuel rods it possessed. That assumption was based on an analysis of residual plutonium by-products found on the clothes of an American nuclear physicist who had visited the Yongbyon facility.[216] The U.S. revision of the earlier assessment roughly coincided with the timing of Vice President Cheney's visit to China, Japan, and South Korea. According to a senior Japanese government official, Japanese officials were "surprised, because when we compared notes with our American counterparts in preparation for Cheney's visit, the United States' assessment of North Korea's nuclear capability had jumped from 'one or two nuclear weapons' to 'eight nuclear weapons,'" and the Japanese government wondered about U.S. intentions.[217]

Some South Korean officials claimed that the second nuclear crisis involving North Korea had been triggered by South Korea's provision of intelligence on North Korea's uranium enrichment program to the United States. South Korea subsequently stopped feeding the United States information about the program, afraid that the United States might use it for political purposes.[218] Cooperation between the United States and South Korea on intelligence matters had been very smooth during the Kim Dae-jung era, partly because President Kim, who believed that there should be no secrets within the U.S.–South Korea alliance, had instructed Lim Dong-won not to hide anything from the United States.[219] But the situation had changed drastically since then.

China, too, was half-doubtful when the United States briefed it about the HEU program. When Under Secretary of State John Bolton visited Beijing to give the Chinese government a background briefing, Vice Foreign Minister Wang Yi requested that the evidence be presented at the outset. But Bolton refused to present any evidence, saying that "to do so might cause a variety of problems."[220] The Chinese government got the impression from Bolton's response that the United States did not have a grasp of the total picture, and it has held that attitude since then. In June 2004, Zhou Wengzhong, China's vice foreign minister (who became the Chinese ambassador to the United States in April 2005) said, "We know nothing about the uranium program. We don't know whether it exists. So far, the United States has not presented convincing evidence concerning this program."[221]

In contrast, however, ROK foreign minister Yoon Young-kwan, referring to the assessment of the HEU program in the early months of 2003, said, "We didn't take any official action about the validity of that argument."[222] Similarly, in Japan, a top-level official concerned with arms control and nuclear nonproliferation later said, "At first we were quite doubtful, but in the winter of 2002–03 we became convinced of the accuracy of the information."[223] That conviction was further reinforced by A. Q. Khan's confession that he had provided North Korea, Iran, and Libya with nuclear technology and the repeated confirmation of that fact by Pakistani president Pervez Musharraf in his autobiography.[224]

When Chung Dong-young, South Korea's unification minister, visited Washington in the summer of 2004, he told a U.S. government official with whom he met that "when I talked with my North Korean counterparts, I explicitly told them that it would be difficult for South Korea to provide North Korea with economic assistance if North Korea did not include its HEU program in the list of nuclear programs to be abolished."[225] Similarly, from around that time, Chinese diplomats started saying that they did not disagree with the U.S. analysis and conclusions regarding the existence of a uranium enrichment program in North Korea. "Whether it is plutonium or uranium," a senior Chinese government official said, "North Korea must not possess nuclear weapons. That is the most important point."[226]

Nevertheless, both China and South Korea have refrained from clarifying their position on the question of whether the uranium enrichment program of North Korea actually involved HEU. A Chinese diplomat said, "Regarding the North Korean nuclear issue, plutonium is a problem, while uranium is a question."[227] It should be noted, however, that many of the remarks from China and South Korea might have been affected by diplomatic considerations, specifically the importance, in view of the then-imminent six-party talks, of not agitating North Korea. That may have been the case particularly with China, which was to host the six-party talks. As one Chinese diplomat confessed later, "China was wary that, if China were to swallow what the United States insisted on, the United States might urge China to further pressure North Korea."[228]

When considering the U.S. intelligence, one should be aware of several "biases," including professional and bureaucratic bias on the part of the intelligence agencies as well as political bias on the part of the policymakers who use the intelligence. One example of professional bias is what can be termed the "worst-case scenario syndrome." People in the intelligence business have a professional and bureaucratic tendency to emphasize, as a matter of self-protection, the negative aspects of information. But it is not merely to protect their career or organization; it derives also from a sense of responsibility and professional ethics that require anyone who is involved professionally with national security or the personal security of individuals to be cautious enough to prepare for the worst. General James Clapper, who was director of the Defense Intelligence Agency during the 1994 North Korean nuclear crisis, later said, "Personally, as opposed to institutionally, I was skeptical that they ever had a bomb. We didn't have smoking-gun evidence either way. But you build a case for a range of possibilities. In a case like North Korea, you have to apply the most conservative approach, the worst-case scenario."[229]

Another professional bias is the "passing-the-burden-of-proof-to-someone-else" syndrome. This often appears when the conclusions of an intelligence agency concerning a piece of information are challenged—for example, "If you insist, show me evidence that we're wrong. If you can, we'll start all over again. If you can't, shut up and listen."[230]

When doubt was raised regarding Pakistan's involvement in the exportation of uranium enrichment technology to North Korea, Defense Secretary Donald Rumsfeld said, "You can't prove a negative." While North Korea might not have advanced to being able to produce highly enriched uranium, nobody could prove that North Korea did not have an HEU program. It might have been possible to say that the U.S. claims were not trustworthy, but it was not possible to disprove those claims.[231]

A third bias, part professional and part political, may be termed the "exorbitance-of-the-anti-proliferation-faction" syndrome. Counterproliferationists such as John Bolton and Robert Joseph, being overzealous about pursuing policy issues, oftentimes clashed with professional intelligence people. John Bolton's office received the first information concerning North Korea's uranium enrichment program on June 23, 2002; however, at the time it was "raw data."[232] His office subsequently requested the intelligence community to present it expeditiously in the form of a National Intelligence Estimate, in consideration of its significance. However, some administration officials suspected that Bolton just wanted to get the more formal result out as soon as possible in order to demolish the Agreed Framework.[233]

When Bolton's nomination as U.S. ambassador to the UN was being considered in 2005, Bolton was repeatedly criticized for putting political pressure on intelligence analysts. Robert L. Hutchings, former chairman of the National Intelligence Council, later said, "This is not just about the behavior of a few individuals, but is about a culture that permitted them to continue trying to skew intelligence to suit their policy agenda." He continued, "When policy officials come back day after day with the same complaint and the same instruction to dig deeper for evidence to support their preformed conclusions, that is politicization."[234]

Interestingly, the counterproliferationists have built a very intimate relationship with the anti-proliferation experts within the intelligence community. Admittedly, to a certain extent that attitude is necessary for people who are engaged in intelligence, whose job it is to prevent crises. One State Department intelligence analyst has pointed out, however, that while they might pay attention to analysis and evaluation by anti-proliferation experts within the intelligence community, they tend to slight intelligence provided by region specialists.

This phenomenon goes beyond the issue of intelligence and represents a distinctive characteristic of decisionmaking by the Bush administration. On the surface, the Bush administration stresses the importance of its alliances, and it has attempted to elevate its alliances with Japan and South Korea to "alliances for the peace and stability of the world." In reality, however, as James Kelly later said, "the slighting of alliance relations by Cheney and Bob Joseph" had become a major obstruction for the administration's policy regarding North Korea.[235]

Last is sheer political bias and, unique to the Bush administration, what can be termed the "Cheney-Rumsfeld-cabal syndrome." At the time Dick Cheney and Donald Rumsfeld had a decisive hand in decisions regarding foreign policy and national security that must have added a significant degree of bias to U.S. intelligence. A U.S. government intelligence analyst later related:

> Those two people are intelligence skeptics. They firmly believe that protection of one's skin and hedges against risk are the primary concerns of intelligence agencies and, therefore, that the agencies always undersell the intelligence. They think that when an intelligence agency cautiously says "yes" without negating the suspicion outright, the agency actually is giving a substantially firm "yes." When an intelligence agency says "five," they suspect that the number should actually be eight. When intelligence people say they have rather firm evidence of uranium enrichment development in North Korea, those two become convinced of the certainty of the program and make a big deal about it.[236]

Although intelligence agency personnel may be inclined to favor the worst-case scenario in order to save their own skins, so to speak, they do have a tendency to undersell intelligence to politicians and political appointees in the decisionmaking circle. They know that politicians and political appointees have a strong inclination to maneuver intelligence for political ends, often making a mountain out of a molehill. World-wise Washington insiders such as Cheney and Rumsfeld knew how to exploit the bureaucratic calculations of intelligence agency personnel.

CHAPTER FOUR

THE COLLAPSE OF THE AGREED FRAMEWORK

It became difficult for the pro-engagement school in the Bush administration to promote dialogue with North Korea after James Kelly's delegation came home with Pyongyang's acknowledgment of its pursuit of highly enriched uranium. Moreover, Kang Sok-ju had gone so far as to declare the Agreed Framework invalid. The confrontation school, consequently, reveled in its triumph.[1] On hearing Kelly's report from Colin Powell, Rumsfeld hit the desk and declared, "Jim Kelly is an American hero."[2] Kelly's stock was very high (though it did not last long with Rumsfeld).

The offices of John Bolton, Robert Joseph, and Dick Cheney reiterated their demand to nullify the Agreed Framework. It became extremely difficult even for expert regional desk officers at the Department of State and the White House—those who belonged to the pro-engagement school—to suggest any need for maintaining the agreement. According to Lawrence Wilkerson, Powell's chief of staff, Powell found himself in the same situation.[3] Nevertheless, the pro-engagement school held to the position that there was no reason to nullify the Agreed Framework. Conflict and confusion lingered within the Bush administration.

On the occasion of the APEC summit meeting held in Mexico toward the end of October 2002, conflicting views concerning the status of the Agreed Framework, voiced by anonymous officials of the Bush administration, were reported by newspapers as if those views had been expressed in an open forum. On October 25, the *Washington Post* reported a senior Department of State official's remark that "the Bush administration does not yet consider the 1994 agreement with North Korea dead."[4] But the very next day the *Post* quoted a Bush administration official who said, "What that person said [yesterday] . . . may represent his view, the Department of State view, but it does not represent the administration view." The same administration official, who was conjectured to be affiliated with the White House, continued to say that the State Department official's remarks "represented a Department of State in revolt."[5] The situation was nothing short of abnormal.

The feud between the two schools became further aggravated over the U.S. obligation under the Agreed Framework to provide heavy oil to North Korea. The confrontation school insisted on immediate and full termination of the agreement to provide oil; the pro-engagement school insisted on a temporary suspension so that they could observe its consequences.

Over the weekend of November 8 and 9, 2002, the United States, Japan, and South Korea held a Trilateral Coordination and Oversight Group (TCOG) meeting in Tokyo. In a joint statement, they called for North Korea to "dismantle this program [to enrich uranium for nuclear weapons] in a prompt and verifiable manner."[6] However, they did not agree on what to do with the delivery of heavy fuel oil. Kelly informed Hitoshi Tanaka and Lee Tae-sik, TCOG representatives for Japan and South Korea, of the Bush administration's likely decision to freeze shipments, but both Tanaka and Lee cautioned against it. The ship bound for North Korea with the November shipment of oil had started to slow its pace to avoid entering North Korea's territorial waters before November 14, the date of the next Korean Peninsula Energy Development Organization (KEDO) Board meeting.

Kelly told Tanaka and Lee that he personally had no problem with the November delivery, but he added that the confrontationist school within the administration was arguing for invalidation of the agreement and total suspension of the shipments. He suggested that it would help the engagement school win the battle over the November delivery if Japan and South Korea would support the suspension of the December and January shipments, which Tanaka and Lee reluctantly endorsed.

The KEDO board was very reluctant to vote for suspension. "It was entirely a U.S. decision, and it was really forced on the board. It was a very uncomfortable KEDO executive board meeting," related Robert Carlin, who was senior policy adviser at KEDO from 2002 to 2006.[7]

According to Carlin, there was a feeling among many KEDO board members that they should "cut off the fuel oil but not do it formally and publicly, because [they] were afraid that it would provoke the North Koreans and precipitate a crisis." Carlin continued:

> And so what we wanted to do was simply stop the fuel oil deliveries, the North Koreans would "get the message" . . . but we would give ourselves space for diplomatic maneuver. . . . None of us [the engagement school] were committed, per se, to LWR. But this was the last channel that was open to the North Koreans, in the middle of a "gathering storm."[8]

However, Washington was adamant. "Washington wanted a public, very formal decisive step where they could show that they had taken, sort of, retaliatory actions," Carlin said. Throughout the meetings, the influence from Washington was obvious. Carlin related later:

> Jack Pritchard, KEDO executive board member representing the United States, was getting instructions from Washington. . . . he would be sitting and we would be talking about the wording of the resolution, and suddenly he would get a phone call and have to get up, get out of the room and consult with somebody because they wanted another "wording change." So the other delegates understood that this was being dictated from D.C.[9]

What hurt the pro-engagement school at the time was more vocal criticism by members of Congress regarding the Agreed Framework and its requirement that the United States supply heavy oil to North Korea. According to a senior U.S. administration official, "politically and bureaucratically, it became hard to disagree with cutting off the [heavy fuel oil]. For Japan and Korea, too."[10] Thus, whether to provide heavy oil to North Korea, or more precisely, how to describe the suspension of shipments, temporary or permanent, had become a political litmus test demarcating the pro-engagement school from the confrontation school.[11]

In the end, the confrontation school prevailed. The decisive factors were a trio of beliefs:

—"North Korea has a uranium enrichment program and has acknowledged as much."

—"North Korea has violated the Agreed Framework."

—"North Korea has deceived us."

One senior U.S. administration official has described the fragmented state of the U.S. government's decisionmaking at the time as follows:

> It was like Yugoslavia falling apart. There was no cohesion. Everybody retreated to their original positions. The Asia people retreated to protecting alliances, and the proliferation people retreated to attacking the Agreed Framework. The "neocons" retreated to pressuring and isolating North Korea. . . . The Department of State's Korea experts—Pritchard, the Korea desk—they retreated to bilateral negotiations. . . . Everyone retreated to their own little fiefdoms, and the policy broke into pieces.[12]

Although the Bush administration decided to stop supplying heavy oil, nobody had any idea of what to do next. If anyone were to raise the issue of what to do next, he or she might be criticized for being too soft on North Korea, which is how the confrontation school characterized the pro-engagement school.[13]

Moreover, although the shipment of heavy oil was suspended, the confrontation school's true target was cancellation of the U.S. obligation under the Agreed

Framework to construct light-water reactors in North Korea. In the end, it was decided at the subsequent meeting of the NSC Principals' Committee (PC), the cabinet-level interagency forum for consideration of policy issues affecting national security, that North Korea would never get light-water reactors. Nobody disagreed, not even Powell.[14] At that point, the Bush administration officially abandoned the Agreed Framework.

However, immediately following the KEDO board's announcement of the U.S. decision to suspend delivery of heavy oil to North Korea, the DPRK started taking a series of retaliatory actions, one after another, that were well beyond U.S. expectations. The United States was spurred to take new action. In December 2002, Condoleezza Rice, the national security adviser, instructed National Security Council (NSC) staff to suggest several policy options. Three alternatives were suggested for further examination of their comparative merits: an "international approach," a "tailored-containment approach," and a "regime change approach."[15]

The international approach sought to persuade North Korea to abandon its nuclear weapons—not just to agree to freeze production—through diplomacy. The Agreed Framework would not be jettisoned but maintained with substantial modification. This approach, which was formulated by Michael Green, also aimed at deepening U.S. cooperation with Japan and South Korea and promoting policy coordination with China. The Department of State, except Bolton's office, was agreeable to this approach.

The tailored-containment approach could be called, alternatively, the "strangulation" approach. It aimed to threaten North Korea in order to further isolate it, exposing it to constant political and economic stress. Under this approach, maximum pressure would be exerted not only by the United States but by the international community as a whole in order to weaken North Korea's position and, eventually, to make Pyongyang abandon its nuclear development activities.[16] This approach was formulated by Robert Joseph, senior director for nonproliferation at the National Security Council, and his deputy, John Rood.

The regime change approach, which was based on the assumption that North Korea would never give up its nuclear development activities as long as Kim Jong-il was in power, aimed to end the regime, through various means. This approach was formulated by J. D. Crouch, assistant secretary of defense, and it had the support of Dick Cheney and Donald Rumsfeld. Although initially only the neocons were strongly inclined toward regime change, it became more widely supported as the fear of future terrorism involving the use of weapons of mass destruction became increasingly widespread after 9/11. North Korea was regarded as a potential source of such terrorism.

The pro-engagement school suspected that the regime change approach was a "straw man," set up by the advocates of the tailored-containment approach.

When a policy option is presented to the U.S. president, it often is submitted as one of a set of three options. When three are presented as a group, the one in the middle—between the two extremes—often looks best. To the advocates of the international approach, it was conceivable that the advocates of the tailored-containment approach deliberately introduced the unrealistic regime change option so that the tailored-containment approach would fall in the middle, enhancing its chance of being adopted. Their suspicion was reinforced by the fact that Condoleezza Rice herself had been inclined toward the tailored-containment approach. When Rice proposed the three options to Bush, however, Bush chose the international approach.[17]

The next step was to elaborate the international approach into specific policies. Rice instructed the NSC staff to study how it could be implemented. "The only idea the Department of State has is to go back to bilateral negotiations and the Agreed Framework, and that's not going to work," she said, and she ordered them not to tell the Department of State about the study.[18] For the first time, the Bush administration opted for an international approach to handling the issue of North Korea's nuclear development activities—and for a multilateral approach at that.

Passive Aggressive

For the most part, it was the Department of State that formulated the Bush administration's policies toward North Korea. At the top were Secretary of State Colin Powell and Deputy Secretary Richard Armitage, both of whom had fought in the Vietnam War. Powell was chairman of the Joint Chiefs of Staff at the time of the Gulf War, and the victory in that war made him an instant national hero. Bush, in order to persuade Powell to work for his administration, gave him special treatment. Nevertheless, or maybe because of that, the White House staff remained wary of Powell. They suspected him of pursuing his own mission and defining a role for himself that was quite independent of the president.

Powell concluded that the Agreed Framework that the Clinton administration had entered into with North Korea had achieved certain positive outcomes. At least it had succeeded in freezing North Korea's nuclear reprocessing activities at Yongbyon—in the preceding eight years, North Korea had not produced any additional plutonium. But as long as the facility remained in North Korea, production of nuclear material could be restarted at any time. In Powell's judgment, freezing production, which would seal the "genie" in the bottle, was inadequate, so he proposed instead "taking the bottle out of the country"—getting North Korea to agree to abandon its program. The burden of proof that it had done so would fall on the North Koreans.[19]

In order to get North Korea to agree, however, the United States itself would have to make substantial concessions. Therefore, if the United States planned to negotiate with North Korea, it should be prepared to discuss at least the possibility of normalizing diplomatic relations and cooperating on economic issues. It had to be a give-and-take deal—to give more to take more. Armitage was convinced that in order to accomplish that, the United States had to adopt a more flexible diplomatic approach.

Among the Bush administration's political appointees, Richard Armitage was perhaps one of the best informed on the North Korean nuclear issue. In March 1999, Armitage coauthored, with Paul Wolfowitz, who later joined the Bush administration as deputy secretary of defense, "A Comprehensive Approach to North Korea." The report points out that although the Agreed Framework might have been a necessary measure for freezing plutonium production in North Korea, it had never been a sufficient measure. In order to make the Agreed Framework a sufficient measure, the report proposed that the United States take the following actions in relation to North Korea's nuclear program and missiles:

—To put a credible mechanism in place to increase the on-going transparency of the present site but not to limit it to that site, which the IAEA had demanded to inspect in the past

—To adopt a new agreement providing for early removal from North Korea of the spent nuclear fuel currently in storage at Yongbyon

—To try to intercept shipments of missile exports if they continue and the United States can identify them, making it clear that the United States will act under its right to self-defense as established under the UN Charter

—To make it clear that if an agreement is not reached through negotiation, the United States will intercept North Korean missile exports on the open seas.[20]

Assistant Secretary of State James Kelly and later Assistant Secretary of State Christopher Hill were given primary responsibility for the North Korean nuclear issue. Kelly, a graduate of the U.S. Naval Academy, was a captain in the U.S. Navy before he joined the Reagan administration in the 1980s, and he stayed on for the first two months of the George H. W. Bush administration in early 1989. During that time he worked consistently on East Asian policy. He was president of the Pacific Forum CSIS, a Hawaii-based think tank specializing in East Asian security policies, and now serves as a senior adviser there. Christopher Hill is a career diplomat, having worked for Assistant Secretary of State Richard Holbrooke, who successfully concluded peace negotiations concerning the Balkans during the Clinton administration. After serving as U.S. ambassador to Poland and later to South Korea, Hill was promoted to assistant secretary of state.

The position of ambassador and special envoy for negotiations with North Korea was assumed by Charles "Jack" Pritchard and subsequently by Joseph DeTrani, special envoy for six-party talks. Pritchard spent twenty-eight years in the U.S. Army, where he worked in the Office of the Secretary of Defense as country director for Japan and also as U.S. Army attaché at the U.S. embassy in Tokyo. He joined the National Security Council in 1996 as director of Asian affairs during the Clinton administration. Pritchard stayed on in 2001 under the Bush administration but in the summer of 2003 resigned in protest of Bush administration policies. DeTrani, a former Air Force officer, worked his way up at the CIA through various posts, including director of East Asia operations and executive assistant to the Director of Central Intelligence. He spoke both French and Chinese fluently.[21]

On the working level, David Straub was director of Korean affairs at the Department of State's Bureau of East Asian and Pacific Affairs, followed by James Foster. Straub, who is fluent in Korean, is a Korean affairs specialist who once served as a counselor at the U.S. embassy in Seoul. Foster has a Ph.D. in Japan studies from Kyoto University and once served as a counselor at the U.S. embassy in Tokyo.

When planning policies regarding the North Korean nuclear issue, Secretary of State Powell often heard the views not only of department officials at the Bureau of East Asian and Pacific Affairs but also of those at the Policy Planning Staff. At the Policy Planning Staff, Richard Haass and Mitchell Reiss worked on the theoretical framework of the pro-engagement policy and multilateral diplomacy in light of the six-party talks. All the engagement policies drafted by the Department of State were discussed in interagency consultations organized by the department. In the course of consultations, the views of the White House and the Pentagon concerning the drafts were bound to be interjected. At the White House, Vice President Dick Cheney and Robert Joseph in particular were highly skeptical about the pro-engagement approach to North Korea, as was Under Secretary of Defense Douglas Feith. At the Department of State, Under Secretary John Bolton shared their skepticism.

Many of the skeptics belonged to a group categorized as "neocons" (neoconservatives). The neocons believe that there is a dichotomy between Good and Evil in international politics, and they worship the power of the United States, which they believe represents the Good. They believe in the containment and conversion of what they regard as evil states, and they do not hesitate to resort to preemptive strikes or even preventive attacks to nip in the bud any perceived threats from evil states. There are no formal criteria regarding who is a neocon and who is not. Armitage has included Cheney's staff, Rumsfeld's staff, and Rumsfeld himself among the neocons. Others draw finer distinctions.[22]

Dick Cheney's office, which had close to fifteen staff specializing in foreign policy, was sometimes referred to as a "mini NSC."[23] No other vice president has ever had such a large foreign policy staff. Cheney's chief of staff and assistant for national security affairs was I. Lewis "Scooter" Libby, who was typical of the neocons in the Bush administration.[24] To the regional desk people at the Department of State, the phrase "Cheney's office" always gave rise to a special creepy feeling. One NSC senior staff member later said, "Cheney sat there like a sphinx. . . . [T]hey didn't know what the vice president thought, except for 'Scooter' Libby and one or two others."[25] Nor did anyone know what kind of political chemical reactions might occur inside Cheney's office. Policies that were agreed on during interagency consultations were often watered down or even rejected by Cheney's office, which was a "black box" inside the Bush administration.[26]

Cheney receives an intelligence briefing in the Oval Office together with Bush at 8:00 a.m. every morning. He eats lunch alone with the president every Thursday, and he talks alone with the president for a long time every day.[27] In addition to his closeness and his access to the president, his "passive-aggressive" posture was an added cause of fear among Washington insiders. Cheney always listened to you with a smile on his face, but when something displeased him, he would stab you in the back.[28] Lawrence Wilkerson, chief of staff to Secretary of State Colin Powell, pointed to Dick Cheney as the source of the Bush administration's lack of a North Korean policy. "At the time of Kelly's visit to Pyongyang," Wilkerson later said, "even though Kelly's visit was decided at the Cabinet level, the vice president talked to the president alone and let the words come from the president. The vice president did it very carefully." He continued, "The Secretary of State sometimes would say, 'Somebody got to the President after I did.' Well, it's not very difficult to figure out who. . . . [T]he main impediment to Colin Powell was the vice president of the United States."[29] In the autumn of 2005, Wilkerson openly criticized Cheney and Rumsfeld, calling them leaders of "a secretive, little-known cabal"—words that stirred a lot of controversy.[30]

Cheney had worked as a staff member under Rumsfeld in the 1970s, when he became chief of staff for President Ford. When Rumsfeld was appointed secretary of defense, Cheney took over Rumsfeld's position. Cheney later was elected to the House of Representatives and became secretary of defense in the administration of George H. W. Bush. He also managed Halliburton Energy Services, Inc., a multinational defense-industry company, as chief executive officer and chairman. Even with such background information, it is difficult to pin down the philosophy and policy direction that Cheney's office subscribes to. One former staff member of Cheney's office whose duties centered on foreign affairs admits, "Although Cheney raised a number of questions about all the policies, it is highly unlikely that he had any alternatives in mind."[31] That comment dovetails with a remark by Wilkerson: "There was one major difference between us and the Cheney crowd. While we always attempted to formulate a coherent policy, it was always politics from the beginning to the end at Cheney's office."[32]

There was a period after 9/11 when Cheney's inherently pessimistic nature harmonized with the widespread pessimism among Americans at the time. When Cheney said, regarding the danger of WMDs and terrorism combined, "The risks of inaction are far greater than the risk of action," he touched the hearts of many.[33] Cheney's politics, however, were driven by fear. One senior U.S. administration official later said, "I have always felt that his relentless pessimism was unsustainable. After a while, people want more than fear, they want a positive vision, and that was not his strong suit"[34] Cheney's basic attitude toward North Korea was that because that country was not trustworthy, there was no room or need for negotiation or dialogue. Hence his famous dictum: "We don't negotiate with evil, we defeat it."[35] As Donald Gregg, chairman of the Korea Society and a long-time friend of Bush's father, noted in an interview in the PBS program *Frontline*, "[the administration has] never had a policy. It's had an attitude."[36]

Although the Department of State's pro-engagement school was mortally afraid of Cheney's office, it detested like the plague the office of Under Secretary of State John Bolton. Bolton was assistant secretary of state for international organizations, charged with responsibility for UN policies, under the first President Bush before joining the conservative think tank American Enterprise Institute (AEI). When Bolton was appointed under secretary of state, he was rumored to be an "assassin that Cheney hired to control Powell."[37] Famous Boltonisms include this: "There is no such thing as the United Nations. There is an organization, which is composed of member governments.... There's simply a group of member governments who, if they have the political will, every once in a while, to protect international peace and security, they're able to do it.... When the United States leads, the United Nations will follow. When it suits our interests to do so, we will lead. When it does not suit our interests to do so, we will not."[38] And this: "If I were redoing the Security Council today, I'd have one permanent member, because that's the real reflection of the distribution of power in the world—the United States."[39] And it was this UN critic who became the U.S. permanent representative to the United Nations in the Bush administration's second term. When, in a *New York Times* interview in the winter of 2002, Bolton was asked about conflicting signals from the Bush administration concerning North Korea, he strode over to a bookshelf, pulled off a volume and slapped it on the table. It was *The End of North Korea*, a 1999 book by Nicholas Eberstadt, Bolton's former colleague at the AEI. Bolton solemnly declared, "That is our policy."[40]

In the summer of 2003, when the six-party talks were about to begin, those in the Bush administration who opposed the talks tried to have Bolton head the U.S. delegation, but to no avail.[41] A little earlier, in a speech in Seoul, Bolton had referred to Kim Jong-il almost forty times without using an honorific.[42] In response, a furious North Korea called Bolton "human scum."[43] It was obvious that Bolton intended to obstruct the six-party talks. One of his staffers admitted later that Bolton thought the six-party talks deserved to be trashed; according to this person, Bolton believed conferencing with North Korea was like "screwing a square peg in a round hole."[44] Bolton's Seoul speech made the pro-engagement school of the Department of State equally furious. "It was not only insubordinate to his immediate boss, the Secretary of State," one senior official said, expressing his anger, "but also insubordinate to the President."[45] As if having had too much of Bolton, another senior official of the Department of State said:

> When North Korea called him human scum, actually it was not too much off the mark of how he was perceived here. The junior staff people at his office have the nerve to add "Ph.D." to their names on e-mail, apparently emulating what Bolton does himself. If he wants to write that title so much, we would say he should write "John Bolton, PhS." The last "hS," of course, stands for "human scum."[46]

Even Armitage had a hard time handling Bolton. "Bolton stuck his nose into everything," he said. "He was very opposed to any negotiations with North Korea. If I ever caught him being troublesome, and I'd slap him, he would respond and obey. But he's very difficult to catch."[47]

WATCHERS AND THE WATCHERS OF WATCHERS

One cannot talk about the Bush administration's diplomacy without considering the impact of the 9/11 terrorist attacks. As a result of those attacks, the Bush administration became something like a cyborg government. The United States jumped into a "long war" with international terrorists; in the process, the power of the Pentagon became overblown, exceeding that of policymakers. Leading the Pentagon was the champion of bureaucratic wrestling in Washington, Donald Rumsfeld, who had been captain of the wrestling team when he was a student at Princeton. According to a top Pentagon official, Rumsfeld's world view is highly "Hobbesian," filled with life-or-death struggles.[48] In that sense his world view might not be very far from that of Kim Jong-il.

In January 1998, the U.S. Congress set up the Commission to Assess the Ballistic Missile Threat to the United States, referred to as the Rumsfeld Commission because it was chaired by Donald Rumsfeld, to review U.S. missile defense policy. The commission's report warned of growing ballistic missile threats and broke with previous intelligence estimates by predicting earlier threats. Just six weeks after the report was released, North Korea proved the commission right with its August 1998 test launch. Both the importance of missile defense and Rumsfeld's status increased greatly. Further, the report identified Iran, Iraq, and North Korea as three "worrisome countries" and warned about "newer, developing threats" from them.[49] The report can be seen as a preview of what later developed into the idea of the "axis of evil."

Rumsfeld advocated regime change. At one point he wrote a memo in which he said that "the United States, in cooperation with China, should topple the Kim Jong-il regime."[50] The Department of State opposed the proposal, which therefore was never released publicly, although it was leaked. It is obvious from the memo that Rumsfeld was strongly obsessed with the regime change approach, despite the multilateral approach that the Bush administration had adopted vis-à-vis the North Korean nuclear issue.[51]

Paul Wolfowitz was a representative figure of the neocons in the Bush administration. He strongly advocated going to war with Iraq. He enthusiastically pushed for the democratization of Iraq through occupation by multilateral forces and ultimately for the extension of the occupation, which he expected to lead to the democratization of the greater Middle East. Wolfowitz referred by way of example to the success of the occupation of Japan and Japan's subsequent democratization after World War II. Wolfowitz firmly believes in Wilsonian idealism and interventionism. For instance, at an interagency consultation prior to the first round of six-party talks in August 2003, he suggested that North Korean humanitarian issues, such as the situation of North Korean refugees in China, should be included in the agenda.[52]

Directly in charge of East Asian security at the Pentagon was Richard Lawless, the deputy under secretary of defense. In the 1970s Lawless had been stationed in Seoul as a young CIA officer during the Park Chung-hee government, and he distinguished himself by finding out about the nuclear weapons development program that President Park had secretly initiated. Although at the time Lawless was in a rank-and-file position, he picked up clues from casual conversations during the daily information exchanges inside the embassy. Donald Gregg, then CIA station chief in Seoul, assigned him to follow up on what he had heard. Gregg had no doubt that Japan would have no choice but to develop nuclear weapons if South Korea obtained them; South Korea, therefore, would never be allowed to possess them.[53]

Within three months Lawless made a great discovery: the Park government had set up a secret group deep within the Blue House (the ROK presidential office) to direct the development of nuclear weapons. Lawless succeeded in obtaining an abundance of confidential documents from a member of the group. Following the disclosure of such decisive evidence, the Park government had no choice but to yield to the U.S. demand to abandon its nuclear development activities. It was Rumsfeld, secretary of defense in the Gerald Ford administration, who visited Seoul to hand the ultimatum to the Park government, saying, "The United States will review the entire relationship with the Republic of Korea unless it abandons nuclear development."[54]

The veiled enmity between opposing camps within the Bush administration regarding U.S. policy toward North Korea often took the form of interagency conflict between the Department of State and the Pentagon, particularly in the form of a personal feud between Powell and Armitage on one side and Rumsfeld on the other.

Lawrence Wilkerson, who had served under Richard Haass as associate director and member of the Policy Planning Staff before he was appointed Powell's chief of staff, had an experience that serves as a good illustration of the interagency feuding. Under its first director, George Kennan, the Policy Planning Staff had maintained informal exchanges of views with the staff of the chairman of the Joint Chiefs of Staff. When Haass instructed Wilkerson to reestablish the informal exchanges, Wilkerson had a colonel in mind with whom it would be best to do that. When Wilkerson approached the colonel, he was very excited, and they started meeting twice a month. After some time, Wilkerson found that the colonel always had to sneak into the Department of State as if he were a ninja. When Wilkerson asked him why he was "having to sneak over," the colonel whispered, "Oh, you don't understand. If they knew that we were coming over here, we'd be in big trouble." Two months after that conversation, the colonel said apologetically to Wilkerson, "I can't come anymore. I've been forbidden to come over here."

When Wilkerson asked, "Can I come to the Pentagon?" the colonel replied, "Well, yes, you can come to the Pentagon, but you've got to be cleared through this, that, and the other, and so forth and so on." After their conversation, Wilkerson decided to take his team to the Pentagon, where they had the next few meetings. But each time they had to go through such cumbersome procedures that, in the end, they stopped going. Wilkerson had the following to say:

> What I discovered in the meetings we did have was that more often than not, with regards to policy, and particularly in regards to policy on the [Korean] peninsula, the Joint Staff was in sync with us. . . . North Korea was deterred. And that's fine. Let's leave it that way. . . . [M]ost people believe that Kim Jong-il was the last one of the Kims. They weren't going to be able to hold it together much past him. And then we might have to deal with a problem. But let's not rush it.[55]

To be sure, confusion in the Bush administration over its policies regarding North Korea could not be attributed solely to the feud between Powell and Armitage on the one side and Cheney and Rumsfeld on the other. As one senior administration official has pointed out, on the day-to-day decisionmaking level, "it was more of a conflict between the regionalists and the nonproliferators rather than a feud between the Department of State and the Pentagon."[56] The regionalists and nonproliferators had head-on collisions at virtually every possible opportunity, including Kelly's Pyongyang visit, the evaluation of the Agreed Framework, discussion of the wisdom of continuing to provide North Korea with heavy oil, the three-party negotiations in the spring of 2003, and the subsequent six-party talks.

Representative figures for the "counterproliferationists" were John Bolton and Robert Joseph. Joseph had been responsible for nonproliferation efforts at the NSC before he was appointed to succeed Bolton as under secretary of state. Joseph regarded nonproliferation as a "counterforce," and he believed in a "counterforce" strategy to complement strategic deterrence. The "counterforce" included U.S. nuclear capability. To Joseph, North Korea, Iran, and China posed threats in terms of political regime, as did the proliferation of missiles in general. "We simply can't wait until [proliferation] occurs before we protect ourselves," he would argue. "If nukes are outlawed, only outlaws will have nukes," he would say. "The Bush policy is to worry about the outlaws rather than the nukes."[57] In terms of policies regarding North Korea, Joseph advocated the tailored-containment approach, as previously mentioned. He believed that strengthening the containment of North Korea would cause the regime to collapse from within.

The counterproliferationists also voiced their opinions regarding the North Korean nuclear issue from a global perspective, in terms of such matters as arms control, nuclear nonproliferation, and missile defense. They frequently rationalized their intervention in regional strategies by saying that "no exceptional treatment is allowed, so that there will be no problem in the global implementation of policies." Joseph and Bolton formed an informal network with Douglas Feith, under secretary of defense for policy; J. D. Crouch, assistant secretary of defense for international security policy; and Eric Edelman of the Vice President's Office. These men, except for John Bolton, represented either the stated view or were sympathetic to such views, particularly those of Cheney and Rumsfeld.[58] One senior official of the Department of State bitterly complained:

> Even though those neocons were not directly in charge of the negotiations, they had the ability to block what they didn't like. When they can't have their way, they immediately start maneuvering behind the scene, including leaking intelligence to the press. Look how much argument went round and round and got nowhere. We wasted eighteen months—eighteen months![59]

Those eighteen months represented the time between the beginning of the Bush administration and Kelly's visit to North Korea.

When the six-party talks began, the U.S. delegation became a mixed bag of members of both the pro-engagement school and the confrontation school, or regionalists and counterproliferationists. The confrontation school was represented by Bolton's office, the White House's NSC nonproliferation office, Cheney's office, and the mid-level directors of various divisions of the Pentagon. Armitage later said, with a wry smile, "So we were somewhat like an old Soviet trade delegation traveling to Western Europe; you had principals, you had watchers, and you had watchers to watch the watchers."[60]

CONFUSION IN THE DECISIONMAKING PROCESS

On March 31, 2003, at a meeting in New York, Pak Gil-yon, North Korea's permanent representative to the United Nations, told Jack Pritchard and David Straub that North Korea had *restarted* reprocessing spent fuel rods. The two Americans rushed to LaGuardia Airport by taxi after the talk with the North Koreans, and during the ride they communicated the intelligence to their seniors at the Department of State by phone.[61] A senior administration official reported that the Department of State did not convey the information to the White House;[62] another senior administration official reported that White House staff in charge of East Asian affairs learned of it from South Korea.[63] Condoleezza Rice became furious. A senior White House official later remarked, "It's one thing to keep it away from DOD or the vice president's office, but they kept it away from the White House, from the president. . . . [T]hat really damaged the credibility of the Department of State leadership in the eyes of the White House."[64] After the incident, "a big gap start[ed] to grow between Rice and Hadley and Powell" and the White House started to negotiate directly with the Blue House.[65]

Confusion in the decisionmaking process was due also to weak policy coordination by the White House's National Security Council. Wilkerson observed:

> The National Security Council, in light of what the 1947 National Security Act and what the framers of the act intended it to do, was utterly dysfunctional. Part of this dysfunction was the inability of the national security adviser, Dr. Rice, to discipline the system. But a larger part was the very deft maneuvering by both the vice president and the secretary of defense to stop us from doing anything that they felt would be against their wishes. In scheduled Policy Coordinating Committee meetings, deputies' meetings, and even principals' meetings—nothing would ever come to fruition. It would either get stopped, [or] get sidetracked by members of the vice president's staff or by the vice president himself.[66]

At the press conference announcing Condoleezza Rice's appointment as national security adviser, she introduced herself as a person who grew up in Birmingham, Alabama, a southern city where racial prejudice against African Americans was severe. She was eight years old when she lost a friend in the 1963 bombing of the Sixteenth Street Baptist Church in Birmingham, a major incident in the history of the civil rights movement in the United States. Speaking about the bombing, she said:

> I did not see it happen, but I heard it happen and I felt it happen, just a few blocks away at my father's church. It is a sound that I will never forget, that will forever reverberate in my ears. That bomb took the lives of four young girls, including my friend and playmate Denise McNair. The crime was

calculated, not random. It was meant to suck the hope out of young lives, bury their aspirations, and ensure that old fears would be propelled forward into the next generation. . . . But those fears were not propelled forward. Those terrorists failed.[67]

Rice had fought both prejudice against African Americans and prejudice against women. She skipped grades one and seven, and entered the University of Denver when she was fifteen years old. At first she aspired to be a pianist, but she changed her major to Soviet-Russian studies and eventually concentrated on the study of diplomacy and strategy after hearing a lecture by a Czech diplomat and defector, Professor Joseph Korbel, father of former secretary of state Madeleine Albright. In 1989, national security adviser Brent Scowcroft hired her as director of Soviet and Eastern European affairs at the NSC. After the Clinton administration took power, Rice became provost of Stanford University. She has expressed the following views on China and North Korea:

> China is a potential threat to the stability of Asia and the Pacific. . . . In order to contain China's power, the United States must strengthen its relations with Japan. . . .
>
> These regimes [in North Korea and Iraq] are living on borrowed time, so there need be no sense of panic about them. Rather the first line of defense should be a clear and classical statement of deterrence.[68]

She is a member of the traditional balance-of-power school of diplomacy, along with others such as Henry Kissinger and Brent Scowcroft. However, when the United States became deeply committed to the war on terror following the 9/11 terrorist attacks, Rice's inclination toward the neocon line also was strengthened.

In terms of U.S. policy toward North Korea, Rice became attracted to the tailored-containment approach advocated by Robert Joseph. Although the views of the White House's department in charge of East Asian affairs often differed from those of Cheney's office and the counterproliferationists—and although from time to time the relations between the two sides became strained—White House relations with the pro-engagement school of the Department of State sometimes became delicate. One NSC staff member once described the White House's irritation toward the Department of State as follows: "While Wolfowitz may be wrong sometimes, he has a strategy. In contrast, all the Department of State talks about is to engage in dialogue. Engagement is a mere modality, and it is no strategy. You cannot beat something with nothing."[69]

Rice's lieutenant, deputy national security adviser Stephen Hadley, was a lawyer by training, having graduated from Yale Law School. For thirty years or so, he had been involved with national defense issues. During the Reagan administration, Hadley served as a legal counselor to the independent counsel for Iran-Contra matters and later served in the George H. W. Bush administration as assistant secretary of defense in charge of international security policies under Secretary of Defense Cheney. Although he was out of government during the Clinton administration, he wrote a paper that advocated including among policy options the use of nuclear weapons as a deterrent against biochemical weapons. Having long-standing relations with Cheney, Hadley often is regarded as one of the neocons, but actually he is a pragmatist. In the second-term Bush administration, he was promoted to the national security adviser position vacated by Condoleezza Rice.

The position of senior director in charge of East Asian affairs under Condoleezza Rice had been passed down from Torkel Patterson to James Moriarty and then to Michael Green. Patterson, due to his Navy background, was strong in strategic thinking. After serving for many years in Japan with the Navy and later working in many Japan-related positions in the Pentagon, such as senior country director for Japan at the Pentagon and director of Asian affairs on the National Security Council staff, he was appointed personal aide to Howard Baker, the U.S. ambassador to Japan, and later deputy assistant secretary of state in charge of South Asian affairs. Moriarty was a career diplomat and a China expert. After leaving his White House position, he was appointed U.S. ambassador to Nepal. Michael Green was an academic who, using his highly fluent Japanese, had succeeded in building relationships of mutual trust with a number of Japanese politicians and bureaucrats. When Green was named senior director, Georgetown University professor Victor Cha, a leading scholar of Northeast Asian affairs, Japan-U.S.-ROK policy coordination in particular, took over Green's post. Both Green and Cha, being up-and-coming scholars of international politics, took an approach that attempted to reconstruct the Northeast Asian regional order, taking into account both reality (power equates with consolidation of alliances) and ideas (peace among democratic nations). But, of course, the ultimate responsibility rested with President Bush.

Bush's attitude toward North Korea was full of contradictions. Toward the end of 2002, one senior White House official said of those contradictions, "Bush understands pretty well that Powell's dialogue is able to operate thanks to Rumsfeld's hard-line. He has good judgment."[70]

Another senior White House official later described Bush's approach as "a hybrid" between the international approach and the tailored-containment approach.[71] But it might be closer to the truth to say that two different, incongruous visions of North Korea existed within Bush's mind. Although he knew intellectually that a more international and multilateral approach was needed to make North Korea abandon its nuclear program, he felt in his heart that the United States should not negotiate with such an evil regime, which really had to be toppled. Bush did not hesitate to call Kim Jong-il "a tyrant," "a pygmy," and "that man." He went even further: "I loathe Kim Jong-il. I've got a visceral reaction to this guy because he is starving his people."[72] (North Korea did not remain silent, either. On August 23, 2004, a spokesperson of the North Korean Foreign Ministry retorted to Bush's labeling Kim Jong-il as a tyrant by saying, "Bush is a tyrant that puts Hitler into the shade and his group of such tyrants is a typical gang of political gangsters."[73] The *Rodong Shinmun* responded too, saying that "Bush is the world's worst fascist dictator, a first-class war maniac and Hitler, Junior, who is jerking his hands stained with blood of innocent people."[74])

It also might be said that inside Bush were two different Bushes.[75] That might have been at the bottom of the Bush administration's attitude toward North Korea. A senior Department of State official analyzed the situation as follows: "The Bush administration's policy toward North Korea is more accurately described as ambivalent rather than incoherent."[76] Wilkerson said that Bush's judgment was clouded by his "Texas cowboy" mentality; by his moral scrupulousness, which forbade him to deal with tyrants; and by his sentiment that he could not do anything resembling what Bill Clinton had done.[77] In the eyes of ROK president Kim Dae Jung, Bush's attitude toward North Korea gave an impression of "capriciousness."[78] A former senior Bush administration official who resigned in the middle of Bush's first term had the following to say:[79]

> President Bush was apprehensive that promotion of the engagement policy with North Korea might create an image of association with Clinton. To be sure, President Bush occasionally hinted at his support of the engagement policy, but he was only trying to appear more flexible. He had never been flexible. When someone must be blamed for the barrenness of the North Korean policy of the Bush administration, it is obvious that the president himself certainly was responsible.[80]

James Kelly found fault with a president who "would never calm these dogs outside the door.[81]

THE "ANYTHING BUT CLINTON" NORTH KOREA POLICY

There were, naturally, wide differences in the world views as well as the policy measures of the pro-engagement school and the confrontation school, or the regionalists and counterproliferationists, but the two groups did share certain views, for instance, regarding the "anything but Clinton" (ABC) approach. Ideology set aside, not a small number of career diplomats at the Department of State felt uncomfortable with the way that the Clinton administration had conducted its North Korea policy. One veteran diplomat long associated with East Asia, who characterized himself as nonpartisan, said:

They were probably convinced that they would be succeeded by another Democratic administration. But it was obvious in the autumn of 2000 that a compromise with North Korea on the missile issue was impossible. I was once approached by one of that administration's political appointees with a request for ideas for the next Democratic government's North Korean policy. It was as if they were carried away by Pyongyang fever.[82]

Another career diplomat, a specialist in East Asian affairs, also made a similar observation: "If the Clinton administration had not been possessed by excessive ambition, the grab of historical legacy, and if there had been a smoother transition between administrations, it would have been quite conceivable that the Bush administration might from the beginning have pursued a policy much more similar to that of the Clinton approach."[83]

The differences between the Clinton administration and the Bush administration with respect to North Korea can be summarized as follows:

—The Bush administration wished to revise and, if possible, to abrogate the Agreed Framework.

—The Bush administration did not set up a "red line" that could not be overstepped.

—The Bush administration's policy was formulated while the United States was planning and later was engaged in a war in Iraq.

It should be pointed out that both the pro-engagement school and the confrontation school shared the view that the Agreed Framework had many problems. James Kelly had argued for continuing with the Agreed Framework and KEDO organization but against providing large light-water reactors to North Korea, which he viewed as "unrealistic."[84] In his first testimony at a congressional hearing after becoming assistant secretary of state, Kelly said that the following two objectives had to be accomplished in order to improve and implement the Agreed Framework:

—To have North Korea agree to accept special inspections by the IAEA as soon as possible

—To confirm the schedule for and method of transporting used nuclear fuel out of North Korea and to expedite the disposal of the fuel.[85]

The Bush administration, attributing the failure of the Clinton administration's North Korea policy to an inadequate inspection regime, demanded what Bush called a "complete verification" of North Korea. That concept was initially introduced in the six-party talks as "complete, verifiable, and irreversible dismantlement" (CVID). In addition to the inadequacy of the inspection regime, a number of problems that needed to be remedied were found in the Agreed Framework.

Nevertheless, the Agreed Framework at least made North Korea freeze its plutonium production. In addition, it prevented a military clash, which in 1994 seemed imminent, over the issue. It was often referred to as the "least bad option."[86] Powell insisted that the merits, as well as the problems, of the Agreed Framework must be appreciated. Stressing the point, he said to Bush:

> You know, President Clinton, Bill Perry, all those folks did manage to cap Yongbyon. I mean nothing came out of there for years. And they got a moratorium on missile shooting. So don't just say it was all bad. The trouble is that they came up with a new program.[87]

What prompted the shift from "modification" of the Agreed Framework to "abrogation" was the information provided in the summer of 2002 by a U.S. intelligence agency concerning North Korea's secret HEU program. The members of the confrontation school got excited, John Bolton not the least. "This was the smoking gun," he exalted. One of his staff said, "It took the wind out of my sails."[88] However, the information included a disclaimer saying that it was "still preliminary data." And, indeed, it was raw data. Bolton's office, however, insisted that the intelligence should be used in formulating policy because the matter was too urgent to wait for completion of the usual type of intelligence assessment.[89]

The policy to be formulated would terminate the Agreed Framework. The confrontation school, including Cheney's staff, urged that this tidbit of intelligence be adopted in an NIE, probably in the hope of finally and completely burying the Agreed Framework. One senior Department of State official later said, "There was a political intention to take this opportunity to annihilate Clinton, who had boasted of the Agreed Framework as a great diplomatic achievement."[90] Accordingly, in a press conference on March 6, 2003, President Bush said, "My predecessor, in a good-faith effort, entered into a framework agreement. The United States honored its side of the agreement; North Korea didn't. While we felt the agreement was in force, North Korea was enriching uranium."[91] Bush was saying that the United States felt betrayed by the Agreed Framework.

It was quite possible, however, that North Korea also felt betrayed by the Agreed Framework. There was a long delay in the construction of the promised light-water reactors, and the Clinton administration did almost nothing to improve relations with North Korea until it sent Secretary of State Madeleine Albright to Pyongyang. The formal assurances in the Agreed Framework that the United States would neither use nor threaten to use nuclear weapons against North Korea had become highly dubious with the introduction of the post-9/11 preemptive strike doctrine, at least in the North Koreans' eyes. The move toward modification or abrogation of the Agreed Framework reflected the depth of the mutual distrust between the United States and North Korea. By the time that James Kelly visited Pyongyang, the Agreed Framework was as solid as a cracked clay statue.

In contrast to the Clinton administration, the Bush administration did not draw a red line and explicitly indicate to North Korea that if it overstepped the line, grave consequences would result. In the case of the Clinton administration, reprocessing of plutonium nuclear fuel rods was believed to be the red line. Samuel Berger, who was national security adviser to President Clinton, said later, "While we made it clear that extracting plutonium from nuclear fuel was a red line, the Bush administration remains obscure about the red line."[92] Even when, in December 2002, North Korea communicated to the United States its intention to reprocess nuclear fuel rods, the Bush administration made no response. On December 29, 2002, Colin Powell appeared on TV talk shows on one major network after another. NBC's *Meet the Press* aired the following exchange between Tim Russert and Powell:

> Russert: "But we cannot let North Korea begin to sell or ship nuclear bombs."
>
> Powell: "This, I think, would be a red line that would definitely be crossed."[93]

In April 2003, only three months after the broadcast, Li Gun threatened James Kelly at the trilateral consultations in Beijing, saying, "We will not hesitate to demonstrate, transfer, or further develop nuclear weapons," but the Bush administration did not interpret that statement as a crossing of the red line.[94] According to Richard Armitage, the administration did not set up a red line for several reasons:

—Recurrence of a North Korean attempt at intimidation by launching missiles, as with the 1998 launch of a Taepodong missile, was highly unlikely (reduced threat of direct North Korean military action).

—The United States did not want to tie its own hands by setting up a red line, believing it was better to keep North Korea guessing at what the U.S. red line was (U.S. wish to avoid limiting its freedom of action).

—A red-line policy required close consultation with allies, and it was highly doubtful that the South Koreans would have accepted such a policy (difficulty of international cooperation.).[95]

What about nuclear testing, then? Hwang Jang-yop, the highest-ranking defector from North Korea, once testified that North Korea had atomic weapons but that it had not carried out any subterranean nuclear tests because the North Korean Foreign Ministry warned against doing so.[96] While the accuracy of

Hwang's intelligence has to be discounted substantially, like many other of his statements, Armitage agreed that North Korea would not carry out nuclear testing:

> If they would have detonated a weapon, they would have squandered all the progress they have made with the South entirely. They would have made it much more difficult for the Chinese to keep the spigot of oil and fuel [open]. So I never felt they were going to test it. When David Sanger was writing in the *New York Times* they're going to test it, I never believed it.[97]

The Bush administration has not officially made its position clear vis-à-vis North Korean nuclear tests. Underlying the decision not to set a red line was the administration's psychological aversion to negotiations with North Korea; setting a red line itself could lead to engagement with North Korea, so it was best avoided. One senior White House official related, "Steve Hadley put it at one point, 'If you create a red line, the North Koreans will be really happy, and then they'll drive right through it.'"[98] The result was an extremely passive approach.

It was around the summer of 2002 that the Bush administration started to examine the pros and cons of a military attack on Iraq, and the decision to invade later gravely affected the administration's policy toward North Korea. The Bush administration had paved the way for U.S.-DPRK dialogue at the time of the talks between Powell and Paek Nam-sun in Brunei toward the end of July. On board the homebound government plane, however, Powell was preoccupied with the Iraq issue. The neocons had already launched a large-scale campaign to expedite a war with Iraq. North Korea policy had been obstructed by a series of events, starting with the Yellow Sea incident, then the HEU issue, then the military action in Iraq, one after another. Kelly later said, "It was obvious to me that North Korea was interesting but Iraq was what was on his mind."[99]

In October, domestic pressure for an invasion of Iraq heightened in the United States. In less than two weeks, from October 4, when Kelly visited Pyongyang, to October 16, when Department of State spokesperson Boucher announced North Korea's acknowledgment of an enriched uranium program, the U.S. government narrowed down the options on Iraq, explained its decisions to congressional leaders, and consulted with its allies. It was only a few hours before Boucher's announcement that Bush had signed the Authorization for Use of Military Force against Iraq Resolution of 2002, a joint resolution of Congress granting the president the power to take military action against Iraq. Both Houses of Congress had passed the resolution the week before. Bush signed it into law on October 16, 2002.[100] Meanwhile, Bush had been briefed by the Pentagon on a detailed plan for the military attack against Iraq.[101]

Because of those developments, no one wanted the U.S. relations with North Korea to deteriorate, creating a crisis. Kelly later said that, just before he visited

Pyongyang, "my instructions in October 2002 were to quietly advise DPRK that we knew that they had a major uranium enrichment process going on, and that program had to end before the broad negotiation. . . . I did not even seek a reply, and if one was offered [I] was to take it back for consideration."[102]

The instruction to "quietly advise DPRK" seemed to embody the Bush administration's wish to avoid a crisis. Even Rumsfeld, despite his belligerent attitude, actually remained cautious about taking military action against North Korea. At one point he said, "North Korea is a threat, to be sure, but it's a different kind of threat, one that, for now at least, can be handled through diplomacy, and differently."[103] Although the U.S. government officially maintained that it would not exclude any options, including a military option, vis-à-vis North Korea, it could not envision any effective "military solution" with North Korea, as it thought that it could in the case with Iraq. Armitage later related: "We didn't want to tie our own hands into following some course of action or other when we had other problems—Afghanistan from September 2001, Iraq in 2003—and so it was better to keep them guessing about our red line."[104]

In other words, the United States wanted to buy time, putting off any North Korean crisis as much as possible in order to prepare for and execute the war with Iraq. The Bush administration tried in a variety of ways to explain its rationale for not taking military action against North Korea when it did against Iraq:

—North Korea has not used weapons of mass destruction against its own people or its neighbors.

—North Korea has never violated a UN Security Council resolution.

—North Korea is not accused of being connected to international terrorists, at least at present.

—Regional powers, particularly China, are capable of containing North Korea's development of nuclear weapons.[105]

But the actual reason was none other than the difficulty of using military might against North Korea effectively. One senior U.S. administration official pointed out the following reasons why military action against North Korea had been judged to be more difficult in 2003 than in 1994, when the Clinton administration had considered taking military action:

—In 1994, it was known that all the nuclear facilities were concentrated in Yongbyon, which presented a clear military target. In 2003, North Korea had already acquired nuclear capability; moreover, it was unknown where the uranium enrichment program was being pursued.

—In 1994, ROK President Kim Young-sam took an extremely hard line toward North Korea, whereas in 2003 President Roh Moo-hyon seemed to be accommodating North Korea.

—In 1994, North Korea had just succeeded in launching a Rodong missile into the Sea of Japan/East Sea, while in 2003 North Korea deployed 200 Rodong missiles, making military action against North Korea difficult.[106]

In the spring of 2003, the Democrats began to harshly criticize the Bush administration's "cautious attitude" toward the North Korean nuclear crisis. For example, Senator Robert Byrd, a veteran member of Congress from West Virginia, warned, "North Korea today poses a much more imminent threat on the United States than Iraq does." Similarly, Senator Tom Daschle of South Dakota, demanding an early settlement through bilateral negotiations between the United States and North Korea, said, "[T]he White House continues to sit back and watch, playing down the threat and, apparently, playing for time."[107] The two were, in short, criticizing the Bush administration for downplaying the North Korean nuclear crisis in order to start a war with Iraq, which both of them opposed. However, after the decision to attack Iraq was made, the Bush administration deepened its logical as well as its sentimental inclination to believe that a victory in the Iraq war would put strong pressure on North Korea. One senior U.S. administration official observed:

> North Korea has always been—and the debate about North Korea has always been—derivative of the Iraq thing, for better or worse. . . . We thought that successful military operations in Iraq would provide us with strong leverage against North Korea. And indeed the military operations were quite successful at the beginning. Nobody predicted that it would be as messy as it actually became.[108]

In fact, the Iraq war might have played a certain role in drawing North Korea to the table for the trilateral negotiations in April 2003. The fact that Kim Jong-il never appeared in public between February and April of 2003 reflected his fear of a U.S. military attack. Nevertheless, the threat of military attack posed by the Iraq war was not strong enough to force North Korea to abandon its nuclear program. On the contrary, the Iraq war might have renewed North Korea's fear of attack, reinforcing its perceived need for a nuclear deterrent against the United States.[109]

"ABC" (anything but Clinton) was a stock expression among those within the Bush administration. Although using it might have contributed to a sense of emotional community, it actually obstructed the formulation of logical and rational alternative policies. Seeming to acknowledge that effect, Condoleezza Rice said at a meeting with her staff, "We are not going to criticize the Clinton administration. At the beginning, when we said we would continue the Agreed Framework, we did not know there was an HEU program, either. We will not criticize the Clinton administration."[110]

A MULTILATERAL APPROACH

The most outstanding difference between the North Korea policy of the Clinton administration and that of the Bush administration was that the latter pursued a multilateral approach to the nuclear issue based on collaboration with Japan and South Korea as well as cooperation with China. The central person within the Bush administration who consistently pursued a multilateral approach to issues related to the Korean Peninsula was Richard Haass, director of the Department of State's Policy Planning Staff. Rather than focusing only on settling the North Korean nuclear crisis, Haass envisioned a broader scheme of confidence-building measures designed to promote peace and stability on the Korean Peninsula and eventually in Northeast Asia as a whole.[111] However, when the nuclear crisis deepened further after Kelly's visit to Pyongyang, the scheme became more focused on the crisis, and its specifics became visible around the time of the U.S.-China summit talk in October 2002.

Quite a number of schemes emerged, only to be abandoned one after another. Initially, Powell envisioned a multilateral group that would include the five permanent members of the UN Security Council plus North and South Korea, Japan, Australia, and the EU.[112] Rice, however, had studied the possibility of establishing a multilateral group similar to the "contact group" consisting of the United States, the United Kingdom, Germany, Russia, and Italy that had negotiated the peace plan with the Milosevic government of Yugoslavia. That possibility was one of the reasons why Anthony Banbury, senior director for human rights and international operations on the National Security Council, was added to Rice's study group.[113] Banbury had held a variety of human rights and humanitarian assistance positions, including with the UN Protection Force/Peace Force in Yugoslavia.

The Rice model called for collaboration among five countries—Japan, the ROK, China, the United States, and Russia—to develop a joint plan for negotiating with North Korea. What was envisioned was a five-to-one negotiation dynamics model.[114] In the end, it was decided to establish a multilateral framework involving the United States, China, and North Korea, which was later expanded to include a total of six countries.

Why did the Bush administration, which had been criticized for its unilateralism, pursue a multilateral approach vis-à-vis North Korea? To begin with, the Bush administration had a strong aversion to engaging in bilateral negotiations with North Korea, knowing that it would be difficult to exercise bargaining pressure in bilateral negotiations. The ultimate U.S. bargaining card was military power, but the United States had no intention of resorting to a military solution. One senior U.S. administration official had the following observation:

Since the United States had long imposed economic sanctions on North Korea, the only threat that the United States could exercise on North Korea was a military one. Taking advantage of this military threat from the United States, North Korea would artificially create a crisis situation in order to induce negotiations with the United States. At the same time, North Korea would try to involve South Korea in order to apply extra pressure on the United States.[115]

The United States did not want that to happen, especially because it was rushing toward war with Iraq at the time. The Bush administration, looking for new leverage, came up with the idea of a U.S. initiative to construct a multilateral framework that would put pressure on North Korea.

The administration decided to use its alliance relations with Japan and South Korea to pursue the idea more fully. The notion of using U.S. relations with Japan and South Korea to induce North Korea to abandon its nuclear program was also incorporated in the administration's "review" of North Korea policy in June 2001.[116] Scott Snyder, an expert on Korean Peninsula affairs, noted "just how important it is that any approach toward North Korea involve Japan and South Korea; excluding these two countries was perhaps the biggest mistake made by the Clinton administration, and they remain weak links that North Korea has consistently tried to exploit."[117]

The Clinton administration failed to treat Japan and South Korea as equal negotiating parties in the Agreed Framework process or to include Japan in the four-party talks among the United States, China, and the two Koreas that began in 1997. However, although the Agreed Framework was an agreement between the United States and North Korea, specific measures were to be implemented through multilateral cooperation, in which Japan and South Korea were involved, and through the Korean Peninsula Energy Development Organization. The United States alone could not bear the cost, especially that of the construction of light-water reactors. Nevertheless, the contributions of Japan and South Korea were hidden beneath the surface, providing the infrastructure of the framework. That was attributable primarily to North Korea's obsession with the U.S.-DPRK initiative.

But the Bush administration decided to highlight multilateral cooperation with Japan and South Korea, through which it aimed to further consolidate Japan-ROK-U.S. cooperation. The administration intended to involve both Japan and South Korea from the very beginning in order to avoid giving them any reason for discontent, which would give North Korea an incentive to play a divide-and-conquer game with the three allies.[118]

Another new idea that the Bush administration adopted was to rely on China to play a certain role. Previously, neither the Agreed Framework nor KEDO called for Chinese participation. But the Bush administration was determined to have China contribute, too. In October 2002, on the occasion of the U.S.-China summit talk with President Jiang Zemin held at Bush's home at Crawford Ranch, President Bush requested Chinese cooperation to promote the denuclearization of North Korea. Because Jiang responded positively to his request, a foundation was established for U.S.-China cooperation concerning the North Korean nuclear issue. The Bush administration saw the foundation as new leverage that it could apply against North Korea.

Robert Gallucci, assistant secretary of state in the Clinton administration and the U.S. negotiator at the time of the Agreed Framework, was said to have once referred to the North Korean style of negotiating as "pay per view."[119] Whatever North Korea agreed to do, whether to participate in a conference, receive an overseas delegation, approve a new proposition, or modify a proposal, it demanded compensation for its actions.

The same senior U.S. administration official who had referred to Galluci's "pay-per-view" characterization continued, saying, "You know, pay them a lot to sort of learn a little bit about the nuclear program. They wanted to leverage for that. We knew that. We knew that very clearly from the experience of the Agreed Framework and from everything they said."[120] North Korea had gained a lot from the Clinton administration by using plutonium reprocessing as bait, and it looked as if Pyongyang intended to gain a lot from the Bush administration by using uranium enrichment the same way.

However, key people in the Bush administration felt they had had enough of that kind of diplomatic play. In addition, the administration realized that it had to consider domestic political views regarding U.S.-DPRK bilateral negotiations. "There is no political advantage to promoting U.S.-DPRK relations," one senior White House official said. "On the contrary, we are simply criticized domestically. There is absolutely no political support base in the United States for better U.S.-DPRK relations." He added, "While we have to promise to do something, all that the North Koreans promise is to do nothing. It simply doesn't pay."[121]

More specifically, while North Korea merely promised not to pursue nuclear development, the United States had to promise North Korea normalization of diplomatic relations, economic assistance, and energy assistance, an exchange that the U.S. Congress would not swallow easily. Therefore, from the domestic political view, too, the Bush administration felt pressured to involve other concerned nations in the risks and costs of negotiations with North Korea.

Chapter 11, which focuses on the six-party talks, considers more thoroughly how successful the Bush administration's multilateral approach has been. It is sufficient to point out here that the development of a multilateral approach as a new form of leverage to use against North Korea did not proceed as fast or as far as had been expected initially. In particular, the shift in the relations between the two Koreas toward "cooperation and conciliation" following changes in South Korea's domestic politics made it difficult to advance cooperation among Japan, the United States, and South Korea. Although the Bush administration stressed the importance of cooperation among the three nations, it felt that the Trilateral Coordination and Oversight Group—which was a by-product of the crisis management and policy coordination efforts of the United States, Japan, and South Korea in response to the first North Korean nuclear crisis—had become too formal.

In the meantime, the emergence of the multilateral approach provided the confrontation school with another reason to characterize U.S.-DPRK bilateral negotiations as useless. It also provided the United States with an excuse to buy time and postpone making a bold decision concerning the settlement of the North Korean nuclear issue. The psychological inclination toward postponement was not confined to the confrontation school. One senior official of the U.S. administration concluded that not only Cheney and Rumsfeld but also Powell and Armitage were subconsciously hesitant to fully engage with North Korea:

> Cheney didn't believe in direct dialogue with North Korea, and he insisted on shaking it off. Rice and Hadley in the White House were essentially inclined to postpone such engagement. Even Powell or Armitage was not an exception. Everyone tried to avoid direct engagement with North Korea. It would have been quite another story, though, if North Korea had really intended to negotiate with the United States.[122]

It can be said that the Bush administration's multilateral approach was confined to being a tactical concept. The administration maintained a passive attitude, advocating a multilateral approach not because it believed in the advantages of a multilateral approach, but because it did not like the bilateral approach and because it disliked Clinton, who had pursued a bilateral approach. Or perhaps, more than anything else, administration officials simply were too absorbed with Iraq and had no choice but to opt for a multilateral approach. A senior U.S. administration official later said, "Cheney and Rumsfeld and those guys agreed to the six-party-talks because they wanted some place to park the North Korean problem until they dealt with Iraq."[123]

A FOREIGN POLICY WITHOUT DIPLOMACY

The Bush administration's policy and its diplomatic stance toward North Korea were problematic in many ways. Members of the administration who were directly in charge of North Korea policy themselves have, in retrospect, admitted as much. At the time of Kelly's visit to North Korea, one of Kelly's delegation pointed out a problem in the U.S. negotiating technique. "Kelly and Kang Sok-ju met without a third party," he said. "As a result, it soon became a chicken-or-egg argument. That was a tactical mistake." He added, "In addition, although we gave the Japanese and South Korean governments briefings about the intelligence concerning the HEU, our clumsy presentations led these governments to suspect that the U.S. government might have been manipulating the intelligence. That had to be avoided."[124] Another member of the Kelly delegation noted that it was a mistake for Kelly to leave the table. He reminisced:

> The North Koreans were obviously upset. Therefore, Kelly should have proposed a break then and there and resumed the meeting after both sides cooled down. We could even have started the meeting with how we interpreted their argument, asking for their clarification. However, Kelly immediately stood up and left the table as soon as he heard Kang Sok-ju's response. I must say Kelly was too impatient then.[125]

Richard Armitage noted that the United States should have sent a smaller delegation so that Kelly could have meetings with the North Koreans that were more private: "We should have gone like any other delegation and had Kelly meet privately with them."[126]

However, it should be pointed out that Kelly's discretion with respect to how to conduct the meetings was extremely limited. Cheney's office and Robert Joseph had predetermined everything that Kelly could say or do, and Kelly was being watched to see whether he was faithfully following directions. When Kelly led the U.S. delegation to the six-party talks in Beijing, he was heard to say, "A trained monkey who can speak English could do this job."[127] According to Armitage, "There was no difference, in a way, between the leader of the North Korean delegation and Jim Kelly, because Jim Kelly was tied up."[128] He wished that Kelly had been allowed more room for flexibility in the negotiations.

Thomas Hubbard, former U.S. ambassador to Seoul and a veteran diplomat who had been in charge of negotiations with North Korea in the 1990s, has pointed out four mistakes in the Bush administration's North Korean policies:

> We should have maintained contact with the North Koreans . . . so that once we had our policy in line we could begin to engage with them, and instead we almost created circumstances in which the North Koreans wanted us to pay them to go back to the table. . . . We had already paid to get to the table in the Clinton administration and we had to pay again. . . . That was a very significant mistake.
>
> We should have given a lot more careful thought to just how the North Koreans might react [when we confronted them with the intelligence concerning the HEU] and how we did this in such a way that . . . we started a process of trying to eliminate those programs.

> We should have . . . continued to have monitored there in Yongbyon, so that they didn't start reprocessing.
>
> Another mistake was effectively allowing the TCOG to wither on the vine.[129]

Self-criticism also was heard concerning the premature decision to embargo the supply of heavy oil to North Korea after the HEU program was brought to light. One senior U.S. administration official remarked, "But I think that the biggest mistake we made was just saying 'Because they violated it, we stop.' Without thinking through how it affects the next stage of the game. . . . And what happened, of course, was they started reprocessing."[130] Moreover, the very introduction of the HEU issue was criticized:

> In retrospect, we made a tactical error when Kelly visited Pyongyang. We should have refrained from confronting the North Koreans with the HEU issue and instead should have concentrated on negotiations regarding the plutonium. As for the HEU, we had the option to wait for the intelligence to be substantiated before confronting the North Koreans.
>
> The intelligence concerning the HEU might have been a good call. But the problem was how to respond to it in policy terms. In this respect, we must say Kelly's visit was a failure. We should not have used that intelligence to confront North Korea.[131]

Those comments stress that Kelly's delegation should have first negotiated with North Korea about the issue of plutonium. However, Kelly did not share that view. "But it's a big black box," Kelly said. "And in 2002, it may have been logical to expect that we would learn much more about this as time went on, but what was clear is that this was just not a minor addition . . . but a major addition to their nuclear capabilities."[132] Kelly was not alone in his view. Mitchell Reiss and Robert Gallucci also criticized the idea of starting with negotiations on plutonium: "To focus solely on the more visible plutonium program would mean turning a blind eye to a parallel program that has the potential to provide North Korea with a covert, steady supply of fissile material for the fabrication of nuclear weapons or export to terrorist groups."[133]

Certainly, North Korea carried a lot of the blame for the showdown and confrontation between Washington and Pyongyang in the fall of 2002. However, Kelly's visit to Pyongyang was the greatest "lost opportunity" with respect to the North Korea policy of the Bush administration's first term. And more lost opportunities would follow. Although the Bush administration had launched a multilateral approach vis-à-vis North Korea, it failed to use that approach fully. As Hubbard said, "What was most challenging in formulating the North Korean policy? It was the disunity within the U.S. government."[134] That view was widely shared by most of the members of the administration who were engaged in policy formulation.

As "lost opportunities" and "lost time" passed by, U.S. foreign policy also drifted. In February 2003, Armitage testified before the U.S. Senate Committee on Foreign Relations:

> As President Bush said during his visit to South Korea last year, the United States has no intention of invading North Korea.... President Bush ... has repeatedly said that when it comes to defending our nation, all options must remain on the table. . . . [I]n this case, at this time, we believe that diplomacy is our best option.[135]

In short, Armitage declared that it was the season for diplomacy. A little while after, a Democratic senator called Armitage to say, "I saw the president after that, but the president said to us 'That wasn't my policy.'" Armitage answered, "You watch. It will be the policy." It was later revealed that someone in the White House had deliberately misinterpreted Armitage's testimony as being a harbinger of U.S.-DPRK bilateral negotiations and whispered it in the president's ear. Bush was displeased.[136] There was a strong possibility that this someone, believing that diplomacy would automatically entail U.S.-DPRK bilateral negotiations, had aimed to weaken the position of the pro-engagement school. Throughout the Bush administration, diplomacy has always remained fragile and frail. On that point, Armitage had the following to say: "For [the] vice president and secretary of defense, it doesn't matter who assumes the position that Kelly ended up with. Be it Kelly or Hill, [the] vice president and defense secretary will hate anyone who is in charge of diplomacy and negotiations." He added, "While I believe diplomacy is the art of letting other guys have your way, they think diplomacy is weakness."[137]

Similarly, David Straub, a career diplomat devoted to relations with Korea, observed: "For the neocons, North Korea is an evil regime full of vicious behavior. Therefore, to them, bargaining with such an evil regime is itself vicious." He added:

> They [the neocons] believe that from the bottom of their heart, and that is somewhat understandable. After all, the North Korean government is a horrible regime. Having said that, can the neocons' method achieve what we wish to pursue? The answer will have to be no. And the neocons have never asked this question of themselves.[138]

For Straub, working for the Bush administration on the battlefront with North Korea was an extremely mentally exhausting experience. Straub's syndrome was described as "battle fatigue" by another State Department person who regards himself as a "neocon." And the "neocon" said that he too had been exhausted, both mentally and physically, by the endless struggles within the administration. Exhaustion, then, was felt by both the pro-engagement and the confrontation school. The same person added, "I joked with . . . my friends in Japan's Ministry of Foreign Affairs. I said, 'I really feel sorry for you guys and your budgets, because now you guys have to take two sets of Washington officials out to lunch.'"[139]

But for the Bush administration, having "two governments in one" was no joke. The resulting battle fatigue robbed many people of their motivation and initiative. Straub resigned from the Department of State in April 2006, terminating his long diplomatic career. All he wanted to do was to go home to Kentucky and stay, a decision he reached after repeatedly asking himself the same questions: "Preoccupied with internal struggles one after another, what good can this government accomplish? Is this really a government? What is the meaning of working as a diplomat for such a government?"[140]

CHAPTER FIVE

RUSSIA AS HONEST BROKER?

On January 18, 2003, Alexander P. Losyukov, deputy foreign minister of Russia, visited Pyongyang. He had never expected the Pyongyang winter to be so cold. As a Russian, he was used to cold winters; in fact, he did not much mind the cold outdoors, at least compared with that inside buildings, where the cold seeped into every joint of his body. None of the government offices or conference rooms in Pyongyang were heated. At night, few lights were seen on the streets of Pyongyang. Paekhwawon Guest House, where the delegation was staying, had its own idiosyncrasies; for example, one could phone in to the guest house but not out. However, the guest house was comfortably heated, and both cold and hot water gushed out when one turned on the faucet.

Losyukov had visited North Korea twice before. The first time was in November 1984, when he accompanied Mikhail Kapitsa, first deputy foreign minister, in order to negotiate a border-crossing treaty between the USSR and North Korea. Russia today shares only a 16-kilometer border with North Korea, a negligible distance compared with the 1,400 kilometers between China and North Korea. It is the shortest border that Russia shares with a foreign nation, but the area is a strategically important location where the borders of China, Russia, and North Korea meet at the mouth of the Tumen River.

The negotiations went well, and the Russian delegation was given an opportunity to meet Chairman Kim Il-sung and Kim Jong-il, then secretary of the DPRK Workers' Party. It was the first time that Losyukov met Kim Jong-il, who was then forty-two years old. During the summer of 1984, Kim Jong-il had accompanied Kim Il-sung to Moscow. Losyukov also accompanied Vladimir Putin when he visited North Korea in July 2000. The 2003 visit, in the middle of winter, was Losyukov's third.

The delegation was first met by Jo Myong-rok, first vice chairman of the National Defense Commission. Jo was a military man who enjoyed the deep confidence of Kim Jong-il. In June 2000, he had delivered a farewell speech to Kim Dae-jung on the occasion of the visit of ROK president Kim Dae-jung to North Korea. On October 10 of that year, Jo had visited the White House as Kim Jong-il's special envoy. Jo, being a military man, wore his uniform. He handed to President Clinton a leather-bound personal letter from Kim, reportedly including his proposals for détente on the Korean Peninsula.[1]

On January 19, 2003, the Russian delegation met Jo Chang-dok, the vice premier; Choe Tae-bok, chairman of the Supreme People's Assembly and party secretary in charge of international affairs; and Kung Sok-ung, deputy foreign minister in charge of Russian affairs, one after another.[2] A meeting with Foreign Minister Paek Nam-sun also had been scheduled, but it was canceled because of Paek's health.

The Russian delegation subsequently met Kang Sok-ju, first deputy foreign minister, at the state guest house. At that meeting, Kang talked about the meeting that he had had with James Kelly, the U.S. assistant secretary of state in early October 2002.[3] Kang complained at length about how Kelly had unfairly denounced North Korea as having overstepped certain limits, how North Korea consequently had had to give some kind of negative response, and, moreover, how ungracious Kelly had been. After accepting some of Kang's points, Losyukov pointed out that nevertheless it remained quite fuzzy how North Korea intended to respond to the U.S. allegations and what North Korea intended to do in the future. He suggested that North Korea should be more open in disclosing its intentions. Losyukov proposed that if North Korea indeed did not possess nuclear weapons, Pyongyang should explain its stance to the whole world in easily understood language. It could say, for example, that North Korea did not possess nuclear weapons and did not want to inflict damage on its neighbors. It could state that North Korea was developing nuclear power because it needed energy. It could point out that as a poor country, North Korea needed assistance from other nations, and that it had no intention of confronting the international community.

Russia was quite weary of North Korea's behavior. When North Korea withdrew from the Nuclear Non-Proliferation Treaty (NPT), Russia immediately expressed "deep concern."[4] On the same day, President Putin emphasized that Russia was firmly committed to the denuclearization of the Korean Peninsula. At the same time, Putin also noted that the DPRK's leadership had "left the door open for negotiations," stressing the Russian position that the crisis could be resolved peacefully.[5] Indeed, Losyukov had gone to North Korea to communicate Russia's proposal for resolving the crisis peacefully, a "package solution" based on three pillars:

—Ensuring the non-nuclear status of the Korean Peninsula through strict observance by all parties involved of their obligations stemming from other international arrangements, including the 1994 Agreed Framework

—Conducting constructive bilateral and multilateral talks among the parties concerned so that, among other results, the DPRK might obtain guarantees of its security

—Resuming humanitarian and economic programs that previously operated on the Korean Peninsula.[6]

Kang Sok-ju did not give even cursory consideration to the proposal. Maintaining a rigid stance, he insisted as usual that the nuclear issue was basically a bilateral issue between the United States and the DPRK.[7] Losyukov, emphasizing the importance of multilateral negotiations for the resolution of the North Korean nuclear issue, tried to lure Kang into a consultation among six countries (the two Koreas, the United States, China, Japan, and Russia), but Kang did not take the bait.

Losyukov had brought with him a personal message from President Putin, addressed to Kim Jong-il, in which Putin gave his views on the situation on the Korean Peninsula. On the second day of his visit, Losyukov telephoned the headquarters of the Russian Foreign Ministry to inform officials there that he might not be able to hand Putin's message directly to Kim Jong-il because a meeting with Kim seemed highly unlikely. On returning to the guest house from a morning meeting on January 20, the third and final day of the delegation's visit, Losyukov and Andrei Karlov, the Russian ambassador to North Korea, found people there that they were not accustomed to seeing. Moreover, there was a general stir in the guest house. Karlov murmured, "This might be a sign that something is happening."[8]

After fifteen minutes passed, they were abruptly informed that they were to see Kim Jong-il in half an hour. In the Kim Il-sung era, Kim never had failed to meet a special envoy who brought a personal letter from a Soviet political leader, although Kim would not see the envoy if he brought only a verbal message. That protocol, however, had deteriorated during the Kim Jong-il regime, and on several occasions Kim would not see a Russian envoy even when he carried a personal letter.[9] So, although there had been a good chance that Losyukov would meet Kim Jong-il, it was not at all certain.

The North Koreans asked Losyukov about the contents of Putin's letter and then asked him to give it to them. But Losyukov emphasized that he had been instructed to hand it directly to the Supreme Leader, and he refused.[10] If Kim's aides were to see the letter first, they might decide that it was not worth the trouble to let him meet with Kim Jong-il. Losyukov had been instructed to bring the letter back to Russia if he could not give it to Kim Jong-il directly.

This visit to North Korea had long been planned as a routine part of the annual consultations at the deputy minister level between the governments of Russia and the DPRK.[11] The eruption of the second Korean nuclear crisis, however, made it necessary to hastily upgrade Losyukov's position to that of Putin's special envoy so that the delegation could discuss the nuclear issue with North Korea. Losyukov became the first foreign emissary that Kim Jong-il had met with since the crisis erupted. The meeting between Kim and Losyukov lasted for six hours, including lunch. During the meeting, Losyukov raised a question:

> Why wouldn't you explain to the world that you don't have atomic bombs or something like that, and that you don't want to have them and be more precise in order to bring about a better mood from the outside world, even some assistance? Remove some fears that other countries entertain about your position?

Kim Jong-il replied, smilingly, "Probably you are right. One day in the future, probably we'll do that. But this is not yet the time. We have to wait." Losyukov then went to the core of the issue:

> If Russia can offer a multilateral guarantee of North Korea's security, you do not need to further develop nuclear weapons, do you? The major issue is [your concern about] an imminent American attack or some kind of occupation or punishment if you do not honor the agreement. Why not pursue a scheme of a security guarantee by which five nations will prevent the United States from threatening your security?[12]

Losyukov elaborated further on this scheme:

> If a guarantee by five nations is hard to come by, probably a bilateral guarantee by China and Russia would be a good guarantee not to allow that kind of treatment [from the U.S.] . . . even if the United States hypothetically wished to punish North Korea until it discloses and cancels its nuclear program, I don't think the United States will do something that would go against a joint Russian-Chinese obligation.[13]

Kim Jong-il rejected that idea. "We do not need any guarantees from Russia or China, because they are friendly countries," he said. "We believe them. We trust them. But our problem is with the United States, and it is exactly from the United States that we want some guarantees or some obligations." In the course of that exchange, one of the Russian delegation members got the impression that Kim Jong-il actually understood Russian to a certain extent, but he never spoke a word of Russian in the meeting.[14]

After the meeting, all the members of the Russian delegation and the staff of the Russian embassy were invited to a lunch hosted by Kim Jong-il at Paekhwawon Guest House. Leading the Russian delegation were Losyukov; Valery Sukhinin, first deputy director general of Asian affairs, who acted as the interpreter during the meeting; and Ambassador Andrei Karlov.

In 1968 Losyukov had entered what was then the Soviet Ministry of Foreign Affairs, and he began his diplomatic career at the Soviet embassy in Afghanistan, where he mastered Pashto, the Iranian-based language of the Pashtuns in Afghanistan. When the Soviets invaded Afghanistan, he was stationed at the Soviet embassy in Washington. As mentioned above, Losyukov became an aide to Deputy Foreign Minister Kapitsa in the mid-1980s. Kapitsa, who had worked at the Soviet embassy in China during World War II, was one of the most respected Soviet diplomats, and he was also a China scholar. It was an honor for Losyukov to be chosen to assist Kapitsa. After the demise of the Soviet Union, Losyukov served as the Russian ambassador to New Zealand and subsequently to Australia. He was appointed deputy foreign minister in charge of Asian and Pacific affairs in March 2000. When the six-party talks began in August 2003, Losyukov was chosen to represent Russia. Being a pragmatic and humorous man, Losyukov was well liked by the diplomats of the United States, Japan, and South Korea. When Losyukov was appointed Russia's ambassador to Japan in 2004, Alexander Alekseev succeeded him as deputy foreign minister in charge of Asian and Pacific affairs.

In what has become an established pattern, Russian diplomats concerned with North Korean affairs study at Kim Il-sung University in Pyongyang and are posted to Pyongyang for a lengthy assignment afterward. Among those diplomats were, in addition to Valery Sukhinin, Alexander Timonin, deputy director general of the First Asian Bureau; Georgy Toloraya; and Alexander Minaev, counselor at the Russian embassy in Seoul. Sukhinin is an expert on Korean affairs. Being one of the best masters of the Korean language within Russia's Foreign Ministry, he had long taught Korean at the Moscow State Institute of International Relations (MGIMO), a training institute for diplomats, while serving in various positions at the ministry. He was the interpreter at the three summit talks between Putin and Kim Jong-il.

Karlov, too, is a Korean affairs expert. After serving at the Russian embassy in Pyongyang as a first secretary, he was posted to South Korea. In 2000 he was appointed the Russian ambassador to North Korea, where he is known to be the only ambassador who can manage to meet with Kim Jong-il.

Traditionally, China and Japan have been the most important countries in the East Asian Bureau of the Russian Foreign Ministry. But the ministry has produced some diplomat/scholars with deep knowledge of Korean affairs, such as former deputy minister Georgy Kunadze, a renowned Japan specialist who later served as Russian ambassador to Seoul. When Losyukov was deputy foreign minister, Evgeny Afanashev and Sukhinin were director general and deputy director general of the First Asian Affairs Bureau, respectively, in charge of Korean Peninsula affairs.

The Kremlin hardly interferes with day-to-day diplomacy except when it involves top leaders, such as when Putin visited North Korea and Kim Jong-il visited Russia. As far as Russian policies toward the Korean Peninsula are concerned, the director general of the first Asian Affairs Bureau has full de facto authority. Coordination with the Kremlin is done through a presidential aide seconded by the Foreign Ministry. Since Putin became president, the authority of the Kremlin has been enhanced significantly. In 2003, the Kremlin decided to strengthen its control of the "power ministries" (the offices of the secret police, military, interior, justice, prosecution, and tax) and at the same time to get a better grip on foreign policy, which resulted in a reduction in the number of director generals.[15]

DIFFERENT KINDS OF WEAPONS

On January 21, 2003, Losyukov left Pyongyang and arrived in Beijing, where he spent the night. He learned from an article in the January 20 issue of the *New York Times* that, at the request of the U.S. Central Intelligence Agency, Russian intelligence officers had secretly placed inside the Russian embassy in Pyongyang sophisticated equipment to detect krypton emissions.[16] Krypton is a byproduct of fission of either plutonium or uranium.[17] Based on the timing of the release of the news, Losyukov suspected it was intended to coincide with his visit to North Korea. He also wondered if there were some in the Bush administration who were not happy with Russian activities vis-à-vis North Korea.[18]

The Russian intelligence authorities immediately announced that Russia was not conducting any covert activity in North Korea; nevertheless, it did not confirm or deny the presence of detection devices within the Russian embassy in Pyongyang.[19] Losyukov told the Russian media in Beijing that a certain degree of optimism was warranted regarding the solution of problems when the countries concerned were prepared to address the problems, but he did not forget to add that that would be just a first step toward the solution.[20] On his way home to Moscow, Losyukov had a variety of thoughts:

> We should give North Korea a chance. If we are carried away solely by U.S. policy, we will end up facing extremely dangerous consequences. If we keep on applying pressure on North Korea without any way out, the nation might implode. Being desperate, it might even engage in military adventurism.

Nevertheless, it was unimaginable that North Korea possessed any means of delivering a nuclear device that would pose a threat to the United States. Other thoughts occurred to Losyukov:

> North Korea is not a direct threat. It should be the first priority to have them stop saying anything about their military means. If, despite our advice, they do not stop referring to their military capabilities, then we will have to improvise stricter measures for them.[21]

In other words, Losyukov decided that Russia should take a two-step approach to dealing with the North Koreans: give them a chance, but take stricter measures if they refuse to comply with certain requests.

What remained fuzzy was the existence of the highly enriched uranium that the United States accused North Korea of possessing. The U.S. government offered China and Russia a background briefing about the HEU program in North Korea after it had done the same for Japan and the ROK, but Russia remained dubious even after the briefing. Losyukov himself remained doubtful, too. He reminisced, "I didn't want to believe entirely in the American accusation, because at that time they were not giving any plausible explanation . . . they were just words, accusing North Korea of this and that . . . not convincing at all."[22]

The Russians were convinced that North Korea was far from possessing the scientific and technical capability to enrich uranium. That conviction was based on their own past experiences with North Korea. In early September of 1990, Soviet foreign minister Eduard Shevardnadze had visited Pyongyang and informed North Korean government leaders, including Foreign Minister Kim Yong-nam, that the Soviet Union was establishing diplomatic ties with South Korea. When he attempted to "convince the leaders of North Korea that the forthcoming establishment of diplomatic ties between the Soviet Union and South Korea would serve to overcome division and reunite the country," there was a violent reaction from the North Koreans.[23] Vladimir O. Rakhamanin, one of the accompanying Russian diplomats, later said:

> The North Koreans became furious. . . . [They] used three different threats to dissuade the Soviet Union from establishing diplomatic ties with South Korea. First, they threatened to officially recognize three Baltic states (Estonia, Latvia, and Lithuania) as independent from the Soviet Union. Second, they threatened to support Japan's claims to the four Kurile Islands. Third, they threatened to produce different kinds of military weapons, i.e., nuclear weapons.[24]

To produce different kinds of weapons was the only threat to which Shevardnadze reacted. He warned the North Koreans that such a course of action was extremely dangerous and adventurist, "bound to bring about unpredictable consequences."[25] After returning home, Shevardnadze instructed officials there to expedite the process of diplomatic normalization with South Korea. As a result, the establishment of diplomatic relations with South Korea was advanced from January 1, 1991, as originally scheduled, to September 30, 1990.

The North Koreans discussed their meeting with Shevardnadze in a September 19, 1990, editorial in the government organ *Minju Chosun (Democratic Korea)* and disclosed that they had handed to the Soviets a memorandum concerning North Korea's views regarding diplomatic relations between the Soviet

Union and South Korea. The editorial criticized the Soviets because, along with the United States, the Soviet Union had been responsible for dividing the Korean Peninsula after World War II and claimed that therefore its establishment of diplomatic ties with South Korea was fundamentally different from its establishment of ties with other countries. North Korea subsequently declared that if the Soviet Union were to establish diplomatic ties with South Korea, that would amount to the de facto nullification of the DPRK-USSR alliance treaty, leaving North Korea no choice but to search for an alternative method of procuring the small number of weapons that traditionally had been supplied to North Korea through the alliance.[26]

The Soviet Union relayed to the Japanese government the information that North Korea had presented to Shevardnadze to the effect that it would pursue its own nuclear program if ROK-USSR diplomatic relations were normalized, which the Soviets interpreted as a reference to nuclear weapons, not just peaceful uses of nuclear energy.[27] Although one senior official concerned with the Korean Peninsula at the Russian Foreign Ministry remembered that the North Korean remarks did not seem necessarily to specify nuclear weapons, Georgy Kunadze testified that at the time the Soviet Union thought that they did.[28] The Soviet Union subsequently ordered twenty Soviet engineers who had been working at North Korea's nuclear and missile facilities to return to the USSR.[29] At the same time, the Soviet Union secretly investigated whether North Korea was capable of producing nuclear weapons. It concluded

> that North Korea possessed a small amount of plutonium, but that it would not be enough to produce a nuclear weapon. If North Korea aggressively pursued its nuclear development program, it could obtain the capability to reprocess plutonium and it might be able to process enough weapons-grade plutonium to produce one or two nuclear weapons per year.... [I]t was quite infeasible for North Korea to enrich uranium, not only because of that nation's technological deficiency but also because of a shortage of the electric power that would be required.[30]

These sober views concerning North Korea's technical capabilities were passed on to a succession of Soviet/Russian governments. A Russian diplomat who was well-experienced regarding Korean Peninsula affairs had the following to say on this point:

> It is only my speculation, but they might have attempted to develop something military in nature. Given the level of their economic and technological developments, however, it was impossible for them to produce a functional nuclear weapon. They must have been developing a nuclear device only to enhance their bargaining position.[31]

There are some in Russia, however, who are greatly alarmed by the reinforcement of North Korea's nuclear capabilities. Government officials involved with nuclear nonproliferation are more strongly inclined to be concerned. Russia, along with the United States, is one of the world's two leading nuclear powers, and it has had a strong interest in nuclear nonproliferation. Proliferation would automatically threaten Russia's vested interests as a nuclear weapons repository state and its authority in the area of nuclear weapons. Russian nonproliferationists therefore have views similar to those of their American counterparts such as John Bolton and Robert Joseph.[32]

The U.S. government "regionalists" concerned with Northeast Asia have hardly engaged in policy consultations with Russian officials concerning the North Korean nuclear issue. More often than not, those discussions have been led by John Bolton in the case of the Department of State and by Robert Joseph in the case of the White House, both of whom have also been engaged in negotiations with Russia on the issue of the latter's withdrawal from the ABM Treaty. Their Russian counterparts often are nonproliferation specialists in the government, not regional specialists at the Russian Foreign Ministry. Regarding the interaction between Bolton and the Russians, one senior U.S. government official later said, "Bolton always played hardball on the North Korean nuclear issue. While the Asians were terrified of him, the Russians kind of respected him. . . . He was respectful of the Russians, too."[33]

In addition, the U.S. nonproliferationists, including Bolton, were convinced that the final stage of verification of North Korean nuclear dismantlement could be carried out only in cooperation with the Russians. Regarding that, one senior U.S. administration official said:

> Because they [U.S. nonproliferationists] had engaged in nuclear arms control activities with the Russians, they knew how that worked. . . . They knew how to work on this with the Russians. They'd never done this with the Chinese, and Japan and Korea aren't nuclear weapons powers and thus probably could not be involved in the actual verification. . . . Bolton's people thought that with regard to the dismantlement process, Russia, as a repository state, eventually would be playing a key role . . . and the Russians were positive about this role, too.[34]

It should be noted, however, that one Russian Foreign Ministry official involved with Korean Peninsula affairs murmured that the Russian nonproliferationists had been "noisy" even though they had no independent intelligence regarding uranium enrichment by North Korea.[35]

At the same time, Russia has been exporting nuclear power plants and fuel under the supervision of the nation's Ministry for Atomic Energy, and it has had a strong interest in the commercial aspects of nuclear development. That poses a dilemma for Russia. In Russia, the Ministry for Atomic Energy supervises nuclear development for both civilian and military uses. In the realm of civilian use of atomic energy alone, the ministry oversees ten operational nuclear power plants, ten nuclear reactor producers, and thirteen nuclear fuel recycling facilities. But because nuclear disarmament proceeded rapidly after the end of the cold war, the nation's budget for nuclear development for military use has been drastically reduced—so much so, in fact, that the budget for dismantling nuclear warheads is twice the size of that for producing warheads.

In addition, the Russian government must underwrite the livelihood of the 800,000 residents in the military-like nuclear facility cities, which are isolated and closed to the outside for security reasons; that requires as much funding as can be raised in the civilian sector, which in turn requires that Russia increase its exports.[36]

The Russian Ministry for Atomic Energy holds North Korea's nuclear development capabilities in low esteem. According to Alexander Rumyantsev, Russia's minister of atomic energy, North Korea was fifty years away from creating nuclear weapons in 2003. In January 2003, he said that "as far as we know the situation with the nuclear program in North Korea, there are no weapons technologies there."[37] He also pointed out that North Korea declares only peaceful intent in its nuclear program.[38] In other words, Russia was in denial about the dangers posed by North Korea's nuclear weapons program, and it was convinced that even if North Korea did possess nuclear weapons, they would not be directed toward Russia. Russia's foreign and security policy therefore did not give very high priority to North Korea.[39]

Nevertheless, Russia has been firmly determined not to allow North Korea to possess nuclear weapons. Russia has been a nuclear power for many years, and during the cold war that gave the country the status of superpower. It has been compatible with Russia's national interest to uphold nonproliferation pacts, including the Nuclear Non-Proliferation Treaty. Russia has taken the position that North Korea's possession of nuclear weapons would not only weaken the pacts but also induce nuclear arms and missile defense races in Northeast Asia. That would be against Russia's national interests. The North Korean threat against Russia, however, would be an indirect, not a direct, one.

It should be pointed out that underlying Russia's low esteem of North Korea's nuclear development capabilities has been Russia's wish to discourage the United States from using North Korea's supposed nuclear capability as an excuse for developing a missile defense system. When the HEU issue erupted, the initial Russian reaction included both suspicion of U.S. motives and denial regarding North Korea's nuclear development activities. Hearing the Russian reaction,

Alexander Vershbow, the U.S. ambassador to Russia, remarked, "We think Russia has got to get past the denial stage and join us in putting pressure [on Pyongyang]."[40] After Losyukov visited Pyongyang, Russia tried to consult with the United States regarding the North Korean crisis, but the United States showed no interest. Underlying the U.S. attitude, at least in part, was that Russia had initially formally denied the existence of the HEU program.[41]

RUSSIAN ABSTENTION

On the same day—January 21, 2003—that Losyukov stopped in Beijing on the way home from Pyongyang, John Bolton departed for Seoul after a series of meetings with leaders of the Chinese government. Losyukov saw a report in which Bolton was quoted as saying, "In my conversations in Beijing and in Secretary Powell's conversations in New York with China's Foreign Minister Tang Jiaxuan, the Chinese did not object to bringing the matter [of North Korea's nuclear development activities] to the Security Council."[42] When Losyukov requested Chinese verification of the report, they responded that "China has not heard anything of the sort."[43]

Actually, the United States had confidentially hinted to China that even if it brought the issue to the UN Security Council, it would limit itself to calling for a warning to North Korea.[44] That was because the United States wanted China's cooperation in promoting a multilateral approach to settling the issue. In Vienna, the board of governors of the International Atomic Energy Agency (IAEA) had already started deliberations on whether to raise with the UN Security Council North Korea's expulsion of the IAEA inspectors and its declaration that it would withdraw from the NPT. The statute of the IAEA provides that its board of governors should bring to the UN Security Council a member state's failure to comply with its obligations under its Safeguards Agreement with the IAEA. By that time, the IAEA had already brought the North Korean nuclear issue to the Security Council twice. The first time was in April 1993, immediately after North Korea declared its intention to withdraw from the NPT. North Korea later decided to accept the IAEA inspectors, only to reject them again, which forced the IAEA board to bring the matter to the Security Council for a second time, in March 1994. Economic sanctions against North Korea were discussed on the second occasion, but no resolution regarding sanctions was adopted. Instead, in October 1994, the Agreed Framework between the United States and the DPRK was signed, the result of bilateral negotiations between the two nations.

Losyukov, after meeting the North Korean ambassador to Russia before visiting Pyongyang, had said that "it is a must to learn what the DPRK's concerns are based on and to eliminate them. Only after that is it legitimate to expect Pyongyang to take actions that will alleviate the concerns of the international community. . . .Without a detailed analysis, it is inexpedient to call an IAEA meeting only to make demands."[45] He added, "The North Koreans announced that they would approve IAEA inspections within their territory under certain circumstances. But they demanded a guarantee of their security from the United States as a prerequisite." With that comment, Losyukov showed his reluctance to raise the North Korean nuclear issue with the UN Security Council.[46]

On February 12, 2003, the IAEA board of governors held an emergency meeting at IAEA headquarters in Vienna to discuss the North Korean nuclear issue. In the resolution subsequently submitted to the UN Security Council, the board of governors stated that "the DPRK has not undertaken to co-operate urgently and fully with the Agency," despite the board's January resolution requiring North Korea to again open its nuclear facilities to IAEA inspectors and to abandon its programs related to nuclear weapons development and uranium enrichment. The February resolution also expressed "deep concern" that North Korea's behavior would bring grave consequences to the NPT regime. At the same time, however, the resolution emphasized the IAEA board's "desire for a peaceful resolution of the DPRK nuclear issue and its support for diplomatic means to that end," showing special consideration to Russia, China, and other parties that had emphasized the importance of dialogue with North Korea. The resolution was adopted 31-0, with two abstentions (Cuba and Russia).[47]

The Russian delegation explained why it had abstained in the vote: "Referring this issue to the UN Security Council right now was, in Russia's view, a premature and counterproductive step [that did not encourage] . . . a peaceful resolution of the prevailing situation on the Korean Peninsula, including the DPRK nuclear problem." After the resolution was adopted, the Russian Foreign Ministry announced that it stood "firmly for resolving the crisis around the DPRK nuclear program solely by politico-diplomatic means."[48]

While China did not clarify its position until immediately before the voting, it eventually supported the resolution. Japan and the United States also supported the resolution, while South Korea could not vote because it was not a member country of the board of governors.[49]

Russia's "Sphere of Attention"

Losyukov's visit to North Korea was the most timely and most active foreign policy initiative among the few measures that Russia had taken vis-à-vis the second Korean nuclear crisis. Losyukov has said that "the Korean Peninsula has never been dropped from the sphere of Russian attention," but that comment is not necessarily accurate.[50] During the 1990s, Russian interest in North Korea steadily declined. In the Gorbachev era, particularly after September 1990, when diplomatic ties between South Korea and the USSR were established, the USSR (and later Russia) completely lost influence over North Korea. The next Russian government, led by Yeltsin, further emphasized foreign relations with South Korea—and a West-oriented diplomacy inherited from the Gorbachev government—inclining Russia further toward non-engagement with North Korea. Accordingly, North Korea disappeared from Russia's "sphere of attention" strategically, economically, and ideologically.

At the same time, North Korea's tendency to ignore Russia also increased. North Korea did not want Russia to participate in either the Korean Peninsula Energy Development Organization (KEDO), which was established to overcome the first North Korean nuclear crisis in the 1990s, or the four-party talks among the United States, China, and the two Koreas. When in March 1994 Russia proposed eight-party talks (involving the five permanent members of the UN Security Council, the two Koreas, and Japan), North Korea rejected the proposal. It was reported that the North Koreans remarked to the Russian delegation that they did not like that the Russians talked to them "in the same manner as the United States" did. In the end, the proposal for eight-party talks went nowhere.[51]

Russia was losing its footing as a concerned party regarding North Korea. As Russia became more inclined toward the West and South Korea, it lost influence over North Korea, which, ironically, reduced Russia's strategic value to the West and South Korea. As a result, Russia came to be ignored in the designing of multilateral frameworks.[52]

The same dynamics also diminished Russia's influence on South Korea. Moreover, as rapprochement between the two Koreas began to develop after the installation of the Kim Dae-jung government, a new dynamic emerged by which Russia's reduced (increased) influence on North Korea would reduce (increase) its influence on South Korea. The new dynamic also pushed Russia out of the orbit of influence concerning the Korean Peninsula in general.

When Vladimir Putin was elected president of Russia in 2000, the above-mentioned long-term decline of Russian influence was halted. Putin attempted to change Russia's policy toward the Korean Peninsula, claiming, "The Korean Peninsula is integral to Russia's national interest, both historically and geopolitically." In February 2000, the DPRK-USSR Treaty of Friendship, Cooperation, and Mutual Assistance, which had been inherited from the Soviets, was replaced by the newly signed DPRK-Russia Treaty of Friendship, Good Neighborliness, and Cooperation. At the signing of the treaty, Russian foreign minister Igor Ivanov declared, "Our two countries from now on will put an end to a ten-year-long period of cooling relations."[53] A veteran Russian diplomat once quipped, referring to a new Russian policy toward the Korean Peninsula under Putin, "If Bush's policy toward North Korea is 'Anything but Clinton,' Putin's could be 'Anything but Yeltsin.'"[54] The most dramatic manifestation of the change in Russian policy was Putin's visit to North Korea in July 2000. It was the first visit by a leader of Russia, including leaders during the Soviet era, since the birth of North Korea. One Russian diplomat who attended the talks between Putin and Kim Jong-il recalled:

> Up until then, neither Stalin nor Brezhnev nor any other leader of the Soviet Union had visited North Korea. Summit talks had always been held in Moscow. But Putin made a breakthrough concerning this practice by visiting Pyongyang and unpretentiously talking with Kim Jong-il. This behavior must have charmed Kim Jong-il.[55]

Putin's visit, in retrospect, became the starting point of a series of subsequent events, including Kim Jong-il's visit to Russia in August 2001 and the Russia-DPRK summit talk in Vladivostok in July 2002.

In the same period, between 2000 and 2002, Kim Jong-il pursued an aggressive schedule of diplomatic events, beginning with his visit to China (May 2000), followed by the ROK-DPRK summit talks (June 2000), the DPRK-Russia summit talks (July 2000), the visit of U.S. Secretary of State Albright to North Korea (October 2000), the establishment of diplomatic ties with the European Union and Canada (2001), his visit to Russia (24 days in July–August 2001), and the Japan-DPRK summit talk (September 2002).

By scheduling his visit to Pyongyang to occur immediately before the G-8 Okinawa summit, Putin highlighted his debut at the G-8. During the Okinawa summit, Putin described Kim Jong-il as "a modern man" and praised both Kim's ability to objectively observe world affairs and his flexibility. He also mentioned that, during the Russia-DPRK summit talk, Kim Jong-il had referred to a plan by which North Korea would terminate its missile-launching experiments in exchange for Russia's assistance with launching a satellite.[56]

In Okinawa, Putin disclosed to U.S. President Clinton that Kim Jong-il had told him that North Korea had been prepared to accept an agreement on missiles similar to the 1994 Agreed Framework, which called for U.S. economic assistance to North Korea in return for the latter's freezing of the production and export of missiles. Samuel Berger, national security adviser under Clinton, noted that Putin's remark had provided an important clue for the development of U.S. policy prior to Secretary Albright's visit to North Korea in the autumn of 2000.[57]

The two ends of the new axis of Russian policy toward North Korea advocated by Putin were "energy" and "railways." This policy was an economic development strategy that encompassed the following:

—developing Siberian oil and natural gas reserves and constructing pipelines for transport

—promoting regional development in Northeast Asia as well as in Siberia and Russia's Far East region by connecting the Trans-Siberian Railway with the Trans-Korean Railway

—providing assistance to achieve economic development and reform in North Korea.

Losyukov, with the consent of President Kim Dae-jung, proposed a plan by which Russia and South Korea would construct hydraulic power plants in North Korea instead of the light-water reactors offered by KEDO.[58] The eight-point statement issued after the Russia-DPRK summit talk in August 2001 proposed an "Iron Silk Road" project that would connect the Trans-Siberian Railway and the Trans-Korean Railway.[59] But the proposed Russian projects would never be launched unless the North Korean nuclear issues were settled; besides, Russia lacked the funds to take the lead in implementing the projects.

Another new factor in Russia's policy toward North Korea was that Putin and Kim Jong-il seemed to be personally compatible. Russian diplomats would say, for instance, that Putin's successful visit to North Korea in the summer of 2000 was attributable to the fact that the two leaders were "on the same wavelength." As mentioned earlier, Putin informed the leaders of the G-8 countries how sensible Kim Jong-il was, a view that he repeated to Prime Minister Junichiro Koizumi in an attempt to create a tailwind to aid normalization of diplomatic relations between Japan and North Korea.[60]

In Konstantin Pulikovsky's book *The Orient Express: Through Russia with Kim Jong-il,* the author, a former career military officer, describes the frank relationship between Putin and Kim Jong-il. Pulikovsky accompanied Kim on the latter's train trip to Moscow in the summer of 2001. In the book, he relates a story of an unexpected invitation for dinner with President Putin at his Kremlin apartment. Pulikovsky described the effect of the dinner on Kim by saying:

> The unscheduled meeting left an unforgettable impression on Kim Jong-Il. Everything was simple and homey. It is as if the dinner in the apartment of Vladimir Vladimirovich changed the nature of Kim Jong-Il. Until that time he somehow contained his own emotions. However, after Moscow, he became more open-minded, trustful, and kind. . . . For me it seemed that they became real friends.[61]

Pulikovsky noted that after this meeting, the Western media stopped writing about Kim as a "demonic dictator" and more as a human being. Kim Jong-il reminisced about the dinner throughout his return journey to Pyongyang. "If I am treated diplomatically, I become a diplomat myself," he said. "But Putin was sincere with me, and I opened my heart to him."[62] With regard to "opening hearts" and personal "wavelengths," it was reported that Kim had been almost obsessively interested in Putin's KGB background and that Putin had pleased Kim with a played-up version of his personal history.[63] That could mean, on the other hand, that it was actually Kim Jong-il who had been eager to please Putin, letting him talk on his favorite subject.

Putin's KGB career was a source of personal identity and pride. In *First Person: An Astonishingly Frank Self-Portrait by Russia's President Vladimir Putin*, which was compiled from interviews with Putin, he boasts of a conversation that he had with Henry Kissinger. When Kissinger visited St. Petersburg, he had a chance to chat with Putin, through an interpreter, during a car ride. In the course of the conversation, Kissinger wanted to know about Putin's background as an intelligence officer. After hearing a somewhat humble reply from Putin, Kissinger said, "All decent people got their start in intelligence. I did, too."[64]

A Russian diplomat in charge of Russian Far East matters observed that if there was indeed some personal harmony between Putin and Kim Jong-il, it must have been rooted in more psychological factors. "We Russians do not oppress him," he said. "We do not look down on him. Although Kim fears China and the United States, he can relax with Russia. His familiarity with Russian certainly helps, too." The Russian diplomat added:

> But, more fundamentally, it must have something to do with the thinness of North Korea's relations with Russia. The two countries used to be allies, but now they are neither friends nor foes. To begin with, Russia does not provide economic assistance to North Korea, which makes Russia fundamentally different from China, on which North Korea depends for economic survival. And although China hosts the six-party talks, Russia is not burdened with such a heavy responsibility. Besides, North Koreans think that Russia, as a former communist country itself, must appreciate the problems that North Koreans are suffering from.[65]

But the most fundamental factor in the relationship between Russia and North Korea has to be North Korea's fear of China. For North Korea, Russia is a buffer to absorb the impact of China. Russia is, in that respect, just a card that North Korea uses to keep China in check. After the China-DPRK-U.S. trilateral meeting in Beijing in April 2003, it was reported that Kim Jong-il sent a personal letter to Putin requesting his assistance in facilitating DPRK-U.S. dialogue.[66] The message insinuated, to China, that it was Russia and not China that North Korea counted on as mediator.

In the summer of 2003, both the United States and China were busy with behind-the-scene negotiations to realize six-party talks. On July 30, President Bush told President Hu Jintao in a telephone conversation that it would be important for both of their countries to have Japan, South Korea, and Russia participate in the process. It was also revealed that Bush had requested Hu to repeatedly impress on Kim Jong-il that it would be against North Korea's national interests to possess nuclear weapons.[67] On the following day, July 31, Pak Ui-chun, the North Korean ambassador to Russia, conveyed to Yuri Fedotov, Russia's deputy foreign minister, North Korea's decision to "support a multilateral negotiation among six countries, including Russia." Furthermore, North Korea requested that Russia, not the host, China, announce the decision.

It was rumored that North Korea had sweet-talked Russia by expressing its wish that the six-party talks be held in Moscow instead of Beijing.[68] North Korea was very apprehensive regarding the possibility of collusion between China and the United States over the Korean Peninsula, and injecting Russia into the process was an attempt to form a certain counterbalance to any such collusion.[69] Actually, at the same time, Russia was apprehensive regarding North Korea. As one veteran Russian diplomat has said, "Kim Jong-il uses the Russian card. We are aware of it and we let him use it. And he knows that we know it."[70]

"HONEST BROKER" DIPLOMACY

Russia continued to spread the idea that it enjoyed special relations with the DPRK based on its easy access to Kim Jong-il; Russia also attempted to create a new niche for itself in the role of "honest broker" in international politics concerning the Korean Peninsula. The onset of the Bush administration in the United States provided Russia with a unique opportunity to play that role, because the Bush administration heightened North Korea's sense of fear and isolation. The administration also made South Korea's government, which had been pursuing its sunshine policy with North Korea, uneasy.

As the tension between the United States and North Korea increased following Bush's reference, in the spring of 2002, to North Korea as part of the "axis of evil," Russia's presence also increased. In May 2002, the *Kommersant-Daily* reported, "Russia was the only party that could bring the United States and North Korea closer to a dialogue, because even China did not have such a capability, due to the Sino-U.S. dispute over Taiwan."[71]

Russia dispatched Deputy Foreign Minister Losyukov to Japan in late April and Foreign Minister Igor Ivanov to North Korea in June and the United States in July, to work behind the scenes. According to the Russian media, the fruits of their diplomatic efforts became visible as early as that summer. The media mentioned such happenings as North Korea's apology to South Korea about the Yellow Sea incident immediately after Ivanov's visit to Pyongyang[72] and the successful launching of U.S.-DPRK foreign minister talks on the occasion of the ASEAN Regional Forum (ARF) conference in Brunei toward the end of July.[73]

Moreover, Foreign Minister Ivanov approached Foreign Minister Choi Sung-hong of South Korea during the Brunei meeting to offer to set up a talk between the two Korean foreign ministers. Choi declined the offer in a roundabout way.[74] One high-ranking ROK official later described Russia's "mediator" diplomacy in Brunei as follows: "Russian diplomacy is to always attend a party without an invitation, with a spoon in one's pocket, always asking to sit at the best table."[75]

Russia also was active in mediating between Japan and North Korea. During the Japan-Russia summit talk on the occasion of the G-8 summit held in Kananaskis, Canada, in late June 2002, Putin referred to the situation on the Korean Peninsula. In response, Koizumi explained the status of Japan-DPRK relations, including the abduction issue, and requested Putin to convey Japan's position to North Korea.[76] At the Japan-Russia summit talk in January 2003, Koizumi expressed gratitude for Russia's help with resolving the abduction issue and requested further cooperation from Russia toward that end. However, it remains highly questionable how sincerely Russia had tried to influence the North Korean government on the issue.[77]

During the first Japan-DPRK summit talk in September 2002, Prime Minister Koizumi referred to Putin's contribution to facilitating direct dialogue between Koizumi and Kim Jong-il. Kim replied, "We have never mentioned anything to the Chinese or Russians about the secret negotiations between our two countries."[78] Kim probably intended to emphasize to Koizumi that North Korea was not the kind of country that could be easily moved by an outsider. North Korea might also have been wary of Russia's excessive boasting of its role and contributions as an "honest broker."

Russia also attempted to sell its role as an honest broker to the United States. About one month after Losyukov's visit to Pyongyang in January 2003, Losyukov went to Seoul to attend the inauguration of President Roh Moo-hyun. On the day of the inauguration, Roh met guests from Japan, the United States, China, and Russia. Losyukov was the guest from Russia whom Roh met. On the evening of the same day, Losyukov had a talk at the Russian embassy in Seoul with U.S. Assistant Secretary of State James Kelly and Michael Green, director of East Asian affairs for the National Security Council, both of whom had accompanied Secretary of State Powell to Seoul.

Losyukov was in high spirits. He was boasting that of any nation Russia had the best relationship with Kim Jong-il: Russia had a "pipeline" to the leadership, and in order to maintain that pipeline, which the Americans might need later on, the Russians were going to say things that would not be pleasing to the Americans' ears; nevertheless, the Americans should appreciate Russia's efforts because the Russians were the only ones who could actually talk to Kim Jong-il. They were very proud of the fact that their ambassador was actually able, sometimes, to speak with Kim Jong-il, while the Chinese ambassador was not. But Losyukov did not forget to add that not only North Korea but also the United States had to make concessions in order to resolve the North Korean nuclear issue.[79]

Losyukov used to say that Russia was not playing the role of "middleman" but that of "honest broker."[80] As long as North Korea claimed that the nuclear issue was a bilateral issue between the United States and North Korea—and therefore would not talk with any "middleman"—Losyukov might have decided against using the term. In addition, in Russia the word "middleman" evoked the image of a merchant engaged in petty commerce. The use of the term "honest broker" instead might have been based in part on the psychological need to maintain Russia's superpower image; Russia could not be slighted as a mere middleman.[81] Meanwhile, the United States was observing Russia's "honest broker" diplomacy somewhat incredulously. From the end of 2002 through the spring of 2003, the Bush administration had been in the process of replacing the U.S.-DPRK bilateral dialogue of the Clinton days with a multilateral approach. Nevertheless, Russia persisted in asserting that the North Korean nuclear issue had to be settled through bilateral negotiations between the United States and North Korea. One senior White House official remarked:

> Putin sent the president a letter.... [I]n the letter, Putin proposed that the United States basically make some concessions to North Korea in exchange for denuclearization. And . . . the concession would be the building of a pipeline from Siberia, through North Korea, to South Korea, to provide energy to Japan and South Korea.... We ignored it, because we weren't sure if it was Putin, or it was economic interests, or what? It was totally unhelpful and there was no way the United States was going to do that.[82]

Condoleezza Rice, national security adviser to the president, regarded the Russians' attitude as "uncooperative." She was of the opinion that Russia should not be included immediately in the multilateral framework that the United States and other nations had been working on. Her position was not to invite Russia as long as it insisted that the North Korean nuclear issue should be settled through bilateral negotiations but to include Russia in the multilateral framework as soon as it recognized the nuclear problem as a "regional issue."[83]

Therefore, when Powell envisioned a multilateral forum among ten countries, including Russia, Rice ignored his idea. Rice seemed to be convinced that nothing short of hardball would work on the Russians. Under President George H. W. Bush, she was put in charge of Russian affairs at the National Security Council. In 1989, in the twilight of the Gorbachev regime, Boris Yeltsin, Communist Party secretary of Moscow, visited the United States. Yeltsin, who was spotlighted as the leader of democratization in Russia, was known for his harsh criticism of Gorbachev. When Yeltsin requested a meeting with President Bush, the White House decided, in consideration of Gorbachev, to invite Yeltsin to the White House on the pretext of meeting with Brent Scowcroft, national security adviser to the president—a meeting during which the president just happened to drop in.

It was Rice who welcomed Yeltsin at the White House. When Yeltsin requested reassurance that he was going to meet President Bush, Rice told Yeltsin that it would be Scowcroft who would meet him. When the furious Yeltsin declared that he would not move an inch if he were not guaranteed that he would meet the president, Rice coolly said to Yeltsin, "If you do not intend to see Scowcroft, please go back to your hotel immediately."[84]

Although Russia was excited that the time for Russia's "honest broker" diplomacy had arrived, the second Korean nuclear crisis shook up the "special relations" between Russia and North Korea. It also led the "personal friendship" between Putin and Kim Jong-il to a dead end. The Russian reaction to the crisis was, as mentioned earlier, pursuit of a "package solution" consisting of the denuclearization of North Korea, a security assurance for North Korea from the parties concerned, and humanitarian assistance. But North Korea did not react at all. Instead, it persisted with its fundamental position—that the nuclear issue was a bilateral issue between it and the United States.

The United States, too, lacked interest in the Russian proposition. Although Losyukov considered a follow-up trip to Washington to convince the United States of its merits, the trip never materialized.[85] The United States and China later took the initiative in creating a multilateral framework, and when the trilateral meeting was held in April 2003, Russia had to take a backseat role. The "honest broker" was deprived of a stage on which it could act.

The next best thing that Russia could do was to push itself into the multilateral framework that had been established by the United States and China. Russia had earlier had the bitter experience of being excluded from the four-party talks held in Geneva in the late 1990s among the two Koreas, the United States, and China. When in 1996 Foreign Minister Evgenii Primakov of Russia met Foreign Minister Gong Ro-myong of the ROK in Moscow, Primakov exploded. "It doesn't make sense that Russia is excluded from the four-party talks," he exclaimed. "Who in the world do they think really fought the Korean War?" Hearing that, Gong thought, "He's letting the cat out of the bag."[86]

The Soviet Union had kept its de facto participation in the Korean War a state secret. It was quite some time after the end of the cold war that that fact had gradually been exposed. According to Konstantin Pulikovsky, "In all, Soviet pilots flew 63,000 sorties during the war and engaged in 1,790 dogfights, in which 1,309 enemy planes, including 1,097 combat planes, were shot down. Two hundred twelve were shot down by anti-aircraft artillery. Soviet air formations lost 335 MiGs and 120 MiG pilots. Our general loss reached 315 people, including 168 officers and 147 sergeants and soldiers." Although the United States knew of the Soviets' involvement during the war, it feigned ignorance in order to avoid the possibility of a third world war.[87]

Russia's exclusion from the four-party talks was an error on the part of the Yeltsin government, which had failed to secure Chinese support, that Putin would not allow to be repeated. Accordingly, on May 27, 2003, Putin had a talk with Hu Jintao at the Kremlin, and the two leaders signed the Joint Declaration of the

Russian Federation and the People's Republic of China. Although the declaration stresses the importance of "a nuclear-free status of the Korean Peninsula and observance there of a regime of nonproliferation of weapons of mass destruction," it declares that "simultaneously the security of the DPRK must be guaranteed and favorable conditions must be established for its socioeconomic development." It also declares, intending to restrict the United States, that "the scenario of power pressure or the use of force to resolve the problems existing there are unacceptable."[88] A few days earlier, leaders of the United States and Japan had announced a joint statement that claimed that those two countries would take tough measures against North Korea if need be, increasing the pressure on North Korea.[89] It was obvious that the Russia-China joint declaration was announced with full awareness of the U.S.-Japan joint declaration.

At the same time, Russia approached Japan, which also had been excluded from the earlier multilateral framework, suggesting a coalition between the two countries. Being excluded from the four-party talks remained a bitter experience for Japan, too, but Japan did not show any interest in a coalition with Russia.[90] In the end, Russia had no option but to lobby the United States, and the U.S.-Russia summit talk in June 2003 provided Russia with an opportunity. At the meeting, the leaders of the two countries agreed on the need to stop nuclear development in Iran, and, using strong language, they demanded denuclearization of the Korean Peninsula, saying, "We strongly urge North Korea to visibly, verifiably, and irreversibly dismantle its nuclear weapons program."[91] During the course of the discussions, Putin, concurring with Bush when Bush emphasized that denuclearization of the Korean Peninsula was a regional instead of a bilateral issue, announced that Russia had been prepared to participate in a regional dialogue on the problem. After the meeting, the Bush administration became inclined to include Russia in the multilateral framework.[92]

Russia's approach to the United States and China did bear some fruit. In mid-July 2003, when Deputy Foreign Minister Dai Bingguo of China visited North Korea and later the United States to lay the groundwork for the six-party talks, Dai spoke with Secretary of State Powell. In response to Powell's reference to a five-party scheme, Dai strongly emphasized that Russia also should be included. Powell accepted the suggestion, and Russia's participation in the multilateral framework was formally finalized.[93]

It should be noted, however, that the United States did not regard Russia's role as an "honest broker" to be very important in the multilateral approach because the core of the approach, as the Bush administration envisioned it, would be the presentation of a united front of a small number of concerned countries vis-à-vis North Korea. To begin with, few in the United States actively advocated Russia's participation, fearing that it might give North Korea, China, and Russia an opportunity to form a "troika."[94] Nevertheless, the United States decided that it would be more beneficial to include Russia in the multilateral framework because, first, it would look bad in the international community to exclude a permanent member of the UN Security Council and second, it would be easier for the UN Security Council to threaten North Korea with economic sanctions if multilateral negotiations including Russia did not work out. One senior U.S. government official has described the Russian stance at the time as follows:

> The Russians wanted the United State to make concessions to North Korea in a bilateral approach, while it insisted on every involved party providing bait instead of pressure in the multilateral approach. We ignored all of them. But we did not intend to eternally exclude Russia, which was, after all, a nuclear superpower and a permanent member of the UN Security Council.[95]

Nevertheless, the greatest barrier to Russia's "honest broker" diplomacy might have been its lack of influence on North Korea. Access to Kim Jong-il did not automatically mean influence on Kim. Aleksei Arbatov, a member of the Duma from the liberal Yabloko Party and vice chairman of the Duma's Defense Committee, shared with news media the following insight concerning Kim Jong-il's visit to Russia in 2001:

> His trip did not promote dialogue between North Korea and South Korea. It probably made it difficult for Russia to have a dialogue with the United States or South Korea, too. If Russia attempts to use the North Korean card in its relations with the United States, Russia will be caught in a classic trap of diplomacy. Realistically, it is Kim Jong-il that is using the Russian card vis-à-vis the United States, China, and South Korea. The tail is wagging the dog.[96]

RUSSIA AND THE U.S. MILITARY PRESENCE IN KOREA

The logic of Putin's North Korea policy with respect to Russia's national interest and strategy can be summarized as follows:

—For Russia, as a nuclear superpower, to maintain and promote nuclear nonproliferation and, as a permanent member of the UN Security Council, to facilitate multilateral approaches to the issue of nonproliferation in coordination with the United Nations

—To neutralize the influence of the United States and China by ensuring peace and stability on the Korean Peninsula through a multilateral approach

—To maintain and develop peace and stability in Northeast Asia and to promote regional economic development based on energy and railroads, fields in which Russia excels.

Russia decided that a multilateral framework and multilateral approach were most conducive to its purposes because Russia was not endowed with the national strength, particularly the economic power, to single-handedly sustain its dominance and influence. Russia therefore decided to buy time, maintaining its involvement in efforts to promote peace and stability on the Korean Peninsula and Northeast Asia as a whole and skillfully employing its current diplomatic assets and resources so that the country could return to the front stage at some time in the future. The "honest broker" diplomacy was an expression of that decision; in that respect, it could be said that Russia had succeeded in carrying out its diplomacy.

It also could be said that Russia had been aware of both the potential and the limits of its "honest broker" strategy. As one Russian diplomat concerned with the Russian Far East said, "The role of 'honest broker' might be important, but it is not decisive."[97] Moreover, Russians, particularly those of the urban and cosmopolitan segments of society, seemed to feel uncomfortable with the Russian leadership embracing Kim Jong-il. For example, Russia's view of Kim Jong-il's "special train diplomacy" was complex.

Russian journalist Andrei Kolesnikov has said that he was reminded by Kim's diplomacy of a train, described in a Solzhenitsyn novel, going to the detention facilities in Siberia. He wrote in his *Kommersant Daily* column, under the headline "Chattanuga-chuchkhe":

> Comrade Kim followed a very Russian route, so to speak. He was "transported" through Russia. But what was the point of this tour of the Russian Federation? What was the result, except a broken schedule or malfunctioning suburban trains and cynical outrage about the needs of a private person? What was that? Reeducation of a dictator concerning the example of a former empire moving toward the shining heights of capitalism? Or an unacceptably overextended diplomatic trick? Or was it for Russian foreign policy the building of the diplomatic equivalent of a railroad sidetrack? We saw our past . . . . [A] while ago there was a big nation that wept in chorus at the burial of Stalin and had a huge crowd at Trubnaya. Quite similar to Korea, isn't it? . . . We showed Kim the future; we looked at the past. I hope we didn't like it.[98]

It is hard to imagine that Russia will remain satisfied for long with its role as "honest broker" vis-à-vis the future of the Korean Peninsula. Russia will again attempt to project its distinctive presence in the geopolitics of the Korean Peninsula and Northeast Asia, converting its oil, natural gas, and other energy resources into diplomatic resources. When that day comes, how should Russia interpret and relate the U.S. military presence on the peninsula and the unification of the two Koreas with Russia's grand strategy for the region? That is a critical question that Russia, like any other participant in the six-party talks, must bear in mind when dealing with the North Korean nuclear issue.

Today Russia does not oppose the presence of the U.S. military in the Far East, as it did during the Soviet era. Russia knows that the U.S. presence is no longer intended to counter a threat from Russia. Losyukov related, "Russia's view is that the American presence in the Pacific plays a stabilizing role . . . it can be reconfigured, but at the same time, it has a stabilizing effect and it will continue to have a stabilizing effect for some years."[99] At the same time, Russia must also consider the risk that the U.S. military presence around Russian borders imposes on Russia's security.

In the post 9/11 war on terror, the United States and Russia have found a common enemy in international terrorism and radical Islam. Nevertheless, when the United States constructed military bases for its forces in Central Asia, Russia felt uncomfortable and threatened. Maintaining the borders between the former Soviet Union and its former allies and ensuring the stability of the regions involved, whether Central Asia or Northeast Asia, present significant security challenges for Russia. Alexander Zhebin, a Russian expert on North Korea, has criticized the United States, saying, "Washington's appeals to Moscow and Beijing to take part in certain multilateral efforts with the ultimate aim of liquidating the DPRK look somewhat arrogant. The Russians and the Chinese actually are being called upon to help create the conditions for bringing American soldiers right up to their own borders."[100] That sentiment is quite widely shared in Russia.

Igor Rogachev, Russia's former ambassador to China, has expressed the opinion that "the United States should consider withdrawing American troops out of South Korea at some time in the future. It seems advisable to do so in relation to the creation of the multilateral framework for the six-party talks."[101] North Korea has consistently demanded the withdrawal of U.S troops from South Korea and has asked Russia to support its position. Russia has taken the position that it understands North Korea's position. The eight-point statement agreed upon at the DPRK-Russia summit talk in August 2001 also stated that Russia understood the North Korean position, which was that the withdrawal of U.S. troops from South Korea was of the utmost urgency if the peace and stability of the Korean Peninsula and Northeast Asia were to be ensured.

However, every once in a while one can detect a slightly different nuance in Kim Jong-il's remarks. On the occasion of the ROK-DPRK summit talk in June 2000, for example, Kim Jong-il agreed with Kim Dae-jung, who had emphasized the need for a U.S. military presence even after reunification, and subsequently disclosed that North Korea had already communicated that view to the United States as early as in 1992. That communication referred to what Kim Yong-sun, director of international affairs of the DPRK Workers' Party, had directly told

U.S. Under Secretary of State Arnold Kantor when Kim visited the United States to discuss the first North Korean nuclear crisis. At that time it was reported that Kim Yong-sun had emphasized the importance of the U.S. presence to counter Japan's influence.[102] At the same time, however, Kim Jong-il said, through Kim Yong-sun, that "the role of American troops on the peninsula should be changed. Rather than defending the South against the North . . . they should have a peace-keeping purpose." [103]

Russia's former deputy foreign minister Georgy Kunadze remarked in June 2006 that "the U.S. troops stationed in South Korea are, in a sense, hostages of the South Korean government. Because of this military presence, the United States has not been able to take military action against North Korea, which has been very favorable for surrounding countries." He continued, "The North Koreans say in informal conversations that they would accept the continued presence of American troops in South Korea after reunification. This could be a lure to bring the United States to the table for normalization negotiations."[104]

In contrast, Alexander Zhebin concluded that "North Korea might find the presence of neutral American troops as a kind of peacekeeping force that is desirable because the withdrawal of U.S. troops from South Korea could sharpen the rivalry over the Korean Peninsula among superpowers." Zhebin, however, criticized North Korea for its double standard: "Moscow has been displeased by North Korea because, although it has requested the Soviet Union and subsequently Russia to support its demand for the withdrawal of American troops from South Korea, it has secretly been looking for an alternative solution."[105]

In addition, Russia has been wary of China's rise and the rapid expansion of China's influence in Northeast Asia. It also has repeatedly expressed concern about the decline of the Russian population in Siberia and in the Russian Far East, as well as about the pressure of the Chinese population there. Inside Russia, some have started to think that in the long run China's politico-military ambitions might become a greater threat to Russia than the U.S. military presence on the Korean Peninsula.[106]

At present, the "China as threat" view remains a minority position. However, when the Chinese influence in Northeast Asia expands in the future, Russia might rely more on the United States to counterbalance the Chinese influence. According to Losyukov, "We think that neither country should be dictating its terms in the region—neither the United States nor China."[107] It is quite likely that, on the global level, Russia, in cooperation with China and the EU, will try to restrain U.S. unilateral dominance while, on the Northeast Asia regional level, it will cooperate with the United States to check the rise of China.

Among the participants at the six-party talks, Russia has explicitly expressed its support of the reunification of the two Koreas. One veteran Russian diplomat and long-time observer of Korean Peninsula affairs remarked that "among the members of the Six-Party Talks, Russia is probably the least negative toward unification." He continued:

> Although China and Japan might be apprehensive about unification, that does not bother the United States or Russia very much. For the United States, the greatest concern will be whether it can maintain its military presence there after unification. Russia does not care whether the United States retains a military presence in a unified Korea, because we have no allergy to its military presence. We have no fear.[108]

Georgy Kunadze echoed this view. "If it happened, unified Korea will be extremely anti-Japanese. That will be the only unifying factor between Northerners and Southerners. Japan and China as well certainly want Korea to be divided. That's not our case."[109]

Yet other Russians have expressed somewhat different views. For example, according to Yuri Vanin of the Institute of Oriental Studies, "the Korean Peninsula is a bridge connecting Eurasia and the Pacific. In order to prevent conflicts there, a multilateral framework for unification, peace, and stability is essential. A unified Korea must be neutral."[110] Common to the two views is the belief that the raison d'etre for having American troops in South Korea will be gone when the two Koreas are reunified, making it possible to weaken the U.S. military presence there. If that is the case, the balance will be tipped against Japan. In other words, a reunified Korea will be a countervailing force against Japan. However, which direction the 70 million people of a unified Korea will take remains highly uncertain. One Russian diplomat stationed in Seoul observed:

> Putin exercises strict control on radical nationalists in Russia, that is, those eccentric ones in the KGB. This is to sustain Russia as a multiracial nation. When the two Koreas are unified, however, who will guarantee multiethnicity there? More likely, a monolithic group of 70 million nationalists will emerge there. Isn't this prospect horrifying? Some day, probably, we will miss Kim Jong-il.[111]

SECURITY ASSURANCE

The largest selling point of Losyukov's "package solution" was the security assurance to North Korea. From the day the proposal was announced, whenever Russia tried to persuade North Korea to denuclearize itself, the package always included security assurance. In June 2004, after the third round of the six-party talks failed to produce any positive outcome, Putin dispatched Foreign Minister Sergey Lavrov to Pyongyang, where Russia again proposed a solution combining a freeze on North Korea's nuclear development with a security assurance and economic cooperation. (At the same time, Russia proposed trilateral negotiations among the two Koreas and Russia.)[112] The two ideas have become so associated that "security assurance" has become something like boilerplate text that is always included in every Russian proposal regarding North Korean denuclearization.

What does this "security assurance" guarantee? On January 19, 2003, one day before Losyukov met Kim Jong-il, the Korean Central News Agency criticized the United States for "turning aside the DPRK's fair and aboveboard proposal for settling the issue in a peaceful way through the conclusion of a nonaggression treaty with the United States and clamoring for any 'countermeasures.'"[113] It was obvious that North Korea wished to conclude a nonaggression treaty with the United States, but the United States had no such intention. In the U.S. system, a nonaggression treaty can be entered into only with a diplomatically recognized sovereign nation, after which it must be ratified by the U.S. Senate. It was hard to imagine that the United States would officially recognize North Korea as a sovereign nation before it abolished its nuclear weapons program. Some in the Bush administration suspected that North Korea's persistence regarding a nonaggression treaty might be attributable to the Soviet training of those who had conceived the idea.[114] Whenever a nonaggression treaty is mentioned, anyone knowledgeable with contemporary world history would think of the USSR-German Nonaggression Pact (Molotov-Ribbentrop Pact).

However, if it is not possible to reward North Korea with full-scale recognition, the United States might be able to treat North Korea as a state-like entity with which it can enter into a nonaggression treaty. For example, something similar to the Taiwan Relations Act could be used. Although the United States does not recognize Taiwan as an independent state, it is obliged to offer Taiwan defense cooperation in order to maintain Taiwan's defense infrastructure. The Taiwan Relations Act is a purely domestic law of the United States that prescribes that duty.

Another alternative would be to entrust the security assurance function to a third country. According to Henry Kissinger, because the Nixon administration was desperate to extricate itself from Vietnam, it informally proposed to the USSR an elaborate formula for ending the conflict that involved the USSR as a third party to guarantee the security of South Vietnam. But the proposal failed to impress the USSR, and it was quickly dropped.[115] In a similar formula, a country that could guarantee North Korea's security would be China, but China might be reluctant to take up the role of chief guarantor.[116] As a matter of fact, China deliberately attempted to erase any suggestion of a military obligation from the alliance treaty that it signed with North Korea in 1961. China does not seem to have any intention of single-handedly guaranteeing North Korea's security. Even if it does, the other countries concerned might feel uncomfortable granting

China such a monopolistic position. It also remains highly doubtful that North Korea would accept such a formula.[117]

The Soviet–North Korea Treaty of Friendship, Cooperation, and Mutual Assistance was concluded between the two countries in 1961, at the height of the cold war, in response to the May 16, 1961, military coup d'etat in South Korea and the revising of the U.S.-Japan Security Treaty of 1960. The end of the cold war and the demise of the Soviet Union, however, caused the DPRK-Soviet alliance to collapse.[118] In 1992, President Boris Yeltsin said that the 1961 Soviet–North Korea treaty existed only on paper.[119] Then, in 1993, Deputy Foreign Minister Georgy Kunadze visited North Korea and unilaterally declared that Russia would assist North Korea only if the latter were attacked by a foreign power, without North Korea's provocation.

In 1996, the Soviet–North Korea Treaty of Friendship, Cooperation, and Mutual Assistance expired. In its place, the new Treaty of Friendship, Good Neighborliness, and Cooperation was signed in 2000, but it did not include mutual duties for automatic military intervention, stipulating instead that in the case of an emergency each party should contact the other without delay.[120] The new treaty did not call for mutual "defense" or "assistance" but for mere "contact." Moreover, it has been said that at the signing of the new treaty, North Korea requested the assurance of a "nuclear umbrella" from Russia as in the 1961 treaty, but Russia rejected the request.[121]

In this connection, a North Korean diplomat once described an episode that occurred in January 1968, during the Vietnam War. The USS *Pueblo*, a U.S. Navy vessel involved in an intelligence mission off the coast of North Korea, was captured by North Korea, resulting in greatly heightened tensions between the two countries. The North Korean diplomat was in elementary school in Pyongyang at the time. People repeatedly chanted what Kim Il-sung had said: "Retaliation to retaliation. All-out war to all-out war." He remembered that many people evacuated to relatives' homes in the countryside and that the people who remained in Pyongyang stood by with backpacks filled with food and first-aid kits. No lights were allowed on at night. Although North Korea's relations with China were so strained during the Great Cultural Revolution that in September 1967 China recalled its ambassador to North Korea, China fully supported North Korea's conduct regarding the USS *Pueblo*, triggering an improvement in their bilateral relations.

But the situation with the Soviet Union was different. "The Soviets panicked and rushed to tell us 'Just return the *Pueblo* crew members home immediately. What are you going to do if a war actually erupts?' That was all they had to say," the same North Korean diplomat related.[122] But Russia has a bitter memory that is quite different from the North Korean version. Alexander Zhebin wrote that at the time of the *Pueblo* incident, "Pyongyang tried to develop relations with

Washington in disregard of Moscow's interests."[123] According to Zhebin, the North Korean tactic of first creating a crisis and then using the crisis as leverage to negotiate directly with the United States, totally ignoring the security and interests of its neighbors, was nothing new.

Nonetheless, it is equally uncertain how deeply China would commit itself to assuring North Korean security. China, too, had initially regarded the North Korean nuclear issue as essentially a U.S.-DPRK bilateral concern and had taken the position that the United States should first respond to the security concerns of North Korea. Although North Korea and China had signed the DPRK-China Treaty of Friendship, Cooperation, and Mutual Assistance in 1961, their bilateral relations cooled after the normalization of China-ROK diplomatic relations in 1992. Unlike Russia, China did not let its treaty with the DPRK expire, and in July 2001 China celebrated the fortieth anniversary of the pact, sending delegations to North Korea. Nevertheless, China has cautiously avoided linking any guarantee of North Korean security to the treaty.[124]

Losyukov, before visiting North Korea, had a chance to discuss with Chinese leaders "more privately than officially" his "package solution." In the end, he thought that the Chinese had responded favorably to his suggestion. But it is hard to imagine that China had any renewed interest in guaranteeing North Korea's security. One Russian diplomat observed: "During the Korean War, Mao Zedong sent his son [Mao Anying] to fight on the Korean side, and he was killed. Can you imagine that now the son of Hu Jintao or Jiang Zemin or the like would go to a war front in North Korea?" He added, "It is understandable that the North Koreans realize that the main thing that they can rely on is their own strength . . . not words, not international agreements, international law . . . but the strength of the country, of the state."[125]

The weakest point of Losyukov's proposal, however, was that North Korea would not trust Russia even if Russia were to offer North Korea a security assurance. Losyukov's proposed solution also was weakened by the fact that Russia failed to lure China into the arrangement. North Korea must have concluded that what Russia, China, and South Korea called security assurance was merely lip service. In fact, the North Korean ambassador to China has said, "If the countries concerned are worried about the nuclear security of the Korean Peninsula, they had better persuade the United States to provide us with a security assurance. If they say they can't do that, I hope they shut their mouths."[126]

On January 11, 2003, before Losyukov's visit to North Korea, Foreign Minister Igor Ivanov met Secretary of State Colin Powell and tried to secure U.S. endorsement of the package settlement scheme, but Powell declined. That was another weak point of Russia's "security assurance" initiative. In addition, however, Losyukov's proposal, including the security assurance, was criticized by not a small number of Russians. The critics insisted that a decision to present the proposal to other countries should have been made only after a thorough study of whether giving such a guarantee would be compatible with Russia's national interests. To begin with, why should Russia guarantee North Korea's security? "Let those whose actions have resulted in creating the present situation [that is, the United States] provide the guarantees," the critics said.[127]

Looking back later, Losyukov said that he believes that "if North Korea truly wanted to obtain a genuine guarantee, they would have agreed with my proposal."[128] He regards his proposal as a "lost opportunity" for North Korea.

Did North Korea really want to obtain a genuine guarantee? The selling point of Losyukov's proposal was that it would restrain the United States by having Russia and China provide North Korea with an assurance of security. But Kim Jong-il brushed the idea aside, saying, "There is no need for that, because China and Russia are friendly nations." However, even though China and Russia are allied with North Korea as "friendly nations," North Korea has pursued its nuclear options. Mitchell Reiss, director of the U.S. Department of State's Policy Planning Staff, commented: "Are we to believe that it will surrender its tangible nuclear weapons program for an intangible promise of security? North Korea must recognize that the very best guarantee of its security is not a piece of paper, but a strategic determination to join the mainstream of the region—with all of the myriad trade, diplomatic, and cultural contacts this would entail."[129]

North Korea has not offered a convincing explanation of its logic. Did North Korea try to secure its regime and legitimacy by obtaining security assurance from the United States? The security assurance that the Bush administration would give in return for North Korea's abandonment of its nuclear program was a guarantee only within the multilateral framework of the six-party talks. Why would a guarantee within a multilateral framework be any less valuable in conferring legitimacy than a unilateral guarantee from the U.S.? It was uncertain how much that would improve the legitimacy of the North Korean state and its current regime.

Although North Korea frequently speaks of "security assurance," perhaps it has not been able to decide how to connect two strategic courses of action—on one hand, dismantling its nuclear weapons and programs and, on the other, initiating economic reform and opening. (This point is further elaborated in chapter 12.) The Bush administration made public its commitment to provide security assurances to North Korea in Bangkok in October 2003. North Korea simply ignored it. A senior Department of State official expressed his dismay with North Korea's behavior, saying, "We gave you this and now you switch it."[130] Concerning the ambiguity of North Korea's demand for "security assurance," a Chinese diplomat involved with the six-party talks remarked:

In China we have an expression, *jieti fahui,* which roughly means to express one's opinion or, by taking advantage of an unrelated opportunity, to do something one has wanted to do. The North Korean demand for security assurance somehow reminds me of this expression. . . .

The North Korean government once said that no country except itself can guarantee its security. And it said this after the United States had agreed to provide North Korea with a security assurance. I myself was puzzled how serious North Korea was about a security assurance. Needless to say, the United States was furious.[131]

In August 2003, prior to the first round of the six-party talks, a North Korean delegation, including the deputy foreign minister, visited Moscow for routine consultations on the deputy minister level. The Russian Foreign Ministry took the party to the ministry's historic archives, where the party stopped in front of the display of a copy of the 1939 Treaty of Nonaggression between Germany and the Union of Soviet Socialist Republics. North Korea's deputy foreign minister said, "So, this is the Molotov-Ribbentrop Pact, isn't it?" and stared at it for a while. He murmured, "Even having a treaty—not just a declaration or a letter, but an official treaty—doesn't represent to us a guarantee of smooth relations between two countries. So how can we just rely on the words of the Americans?"[132]

CHAPTER SIX

BROTHERHOOD

Lim Dong-won flew to Pyongyang on January 27, 2003, aboard the presidential plane. Lim was President Kim Dae-jung's special adviser for foreign, security, and unification policies, and he had worked behind the scenes running the historic summit talk between leaders of the two Koreas in June 2000.

Lim had visited Pyongyang several times before as a secret emissary or presidential special envoy, but this visit would be his last as an envoy. Kim Dae-jung's administration was to end in one month, and President Kim had dispatched Lim and his delegation to assure North Korea that the Roh Moo-hyun administration would be a like-minded successor to the Kim government and that Kim's sunshine policy would be continuously upheld. The delegation consisted of eight members, including Yim Sung-joon, who was senior secretary to the president, in charge of foreign and security policies, and Lee Jong-seok, a North Korea expert at an independent think tank, the Sejong Institute.

Yim Sung-joon was appointed to the senior secretary position at the Blue House (the executive office and official residence of the president of South Korea) at the time of a cabinet reshuffling in January 2002, when he had been an assistant minister at the Ministry of Foreign Affairs and Trade. He was a career diplomat who, as the ROK representative to the Trilateral Coordination and Oversight Group (TCOG), had long been concerned with North Korean nuclear issues.

Lee Jong-seok, on the other hand, was an up-and-coming scholar and expert on the North Korea Workers' Party and Kim Il-sung. Lim, highly appreciative of Lee's talent as a policy professional and of his future prospects, had included Lee in the South Korean delegation to the North-South summit of June 2000. Since then, Lim and Lee had maintained a comradely relationship.

Although the meeting with Kim Jong-il had not been on the agenda before-hand, that did not set off any alarms, inasmuch as last-minute changes were not unusual in the case of North Korea. Lim Dong-won had requested the visit to Pyongyang as the presidential special envoy, and the North Koreans granted his request. The South Koreans expected the acceptance of their request to mean that Kim Jong-il would meet the delegation automatically.[1]

Lim's title was a special one given to him by the president when Lim accompanied President Kim to the North-South summit talk in June 2000. No such position was provided for in South Korea's government organizational chart; it was improvised so that Lim's official title, director of the National Intelligence Service, would not be used. North Korea had long demanded the scrapping of South Korea's National Intelligence Service and refused to deal with it.[2]

The National Intelligence Service's previous incarnation had been as the Korean Central Intelligence Agency (KCIA), which was renamed the Agency for National Security Planning in 1981. It was given its current name in 1999. When Lim had to resign as unification minister by parliamentary resolution in September 2001, President Kim revived the position of special adviser to the president and appointed Lim to that position. This time, Lim also was made presidential special envoy, and he was given the role of directly handing to Kim Jong-il a personal letter from President Kim Dae-jung.

During the South Korean delegation's three-day stay in North Korea, from January 27 through January 29, the members met twice with Kim Yong-sun, secretary in charge of relations with South Korea for the United Front Department of the Korean Workers' Party, who later became director of international affairs. They also paid a courtesy visit to Kim Yong-nam, president of the Presidium of the DPRK Supreme People's Assembly. President Kim's letter to Kim Jong-il was handed to Kim Yong-sun.[3]

Pyongyang was in the middle of a cold winter, and the temperature dropped to twenty degrees below zero Celsius. At the beginning of the plenary conference attended by Kim Yong-sun at the Paekhwawon Guest House on January 27, Kim Yong-sun started by saying the following:

> We didn't get the oil and so we couldn't heat the buildings as much as we wanted, and this guest house has had no heating for many many days, but if heating facilities just over night, you cannot get the heat high enough, so they started to heat the guest house ten days ago.

One member of the South Korean delegation was surprised to see the long underwear underneath Kim Yong-sun's shirtsleeve. He said, "He was wearing very thick underwear, something like my grandpa used to wear. I was convinced that his offices also were not heated."

Soon after the discussion started, it turned into a heated exchange about the second Korean nuclear crisis, which had become all the more serious after Kelly's visit to North Korea. In President Bush's State of the Union speech on January 28, he once again severely criticized Kim Jong-il's regime for "leaving its people living in fear and starvation," and he stressed that the United States and other countries concerned would not be "blackmailed" into granting concessions to North Korea because of its nuclear weapons development. One day earlier, the Korean Central News Agency issued a strong alert, declaring that "the situation on the Korean Peninsula is deteriorating so rapidly that an armed clash might break out any time."[4] Lim Dong-won repeatedly warned that North Korean nuclear development could result in war, which "must be avoided at any cost. A peaceful settlement should be pursued." However, the North Koreans would not soften their posture, claiming that "the hostile policies of the United States toward North Korea are the root cause of all the problems."

Lim made the following three points to emphasize the grave international implications of North Korea's uranium enrichment program. These points were also stressed in President Kim's personal letter.

—South Korea is deeply concerned about the uranium enrichment program that the United States has claimed that North Korea has. If North Korea has such a program, Pyongyang should terminate it and verify the dismantlement of all related facilities.

—It is highly likely that this issue will be sent to the UN Security Council, which might decide on economic sanctions against North Korea. That has not yet happened only because South Korea acted to delay the UN Security Council's move to debate the issue. Pyongyang therefore should not miss the opportunity to take action as indicated above while it is still possible.

—A nonaggression treaty with the United States, as demanded by North Korea, would be nearly impossible to conclude, even if the Bush administration wanted to negotiate one, because it would have to be ratified by the U.S. Senate, which is dominated by Republicans. Realistically, a written nonaggression prom-ise backed by multilateral guarantees would be appropriate.[5]

Lim was very straightforward when he said:

North Korea should recognize that the Bush administration's North Korea policy is totally different from that of the Clinton administration. . . .The outgoing Kim Dae-jung government has no residual political influence. North Korea has no choice but to promptly take proper actions to facili-tate dialogue with the United States.

To these candid bits of advice from Lim, Kim Yong-sun sullenly retorted,

It was none other than the United States that degraded the Agreed Frame-work to a mere piece of paper. . . .Your comments represent nothing but the American position. Did you come all the way here to tell us such nonsense?

Kim Yong-sun even raised his voice, saying, "We said we could prove that we do not possess nuclear weapons through verification if the United States does not threaten us with its own nuclear weapons, didn't we?"[6]

While other issues, such as reconnecting the severed railways and roads between the North and South and reuniting separated families, also were discussed, almost no tangible results were achieved.[7]

On the evening of January 27, Chang Song-taek, senior deputy director of organizational leadership of the Korean Workers' Party and a brother-in-law and a confidant of Kim Jong-il, hosted, in a different guest house, a welcoming reception for the delegation. Chang Song-taek had just visited South Korea in October of the previous year as a member of a North Korean economic mission. He was in a good mood, drinking toast after toast with every member of the South Korean delegation, saying, "I wish to repay you, even if only a little, for the great favors I received in Seoul. Drink as much as you can." But nothing substantial was discussed during the dinner.[8]

The delegation did not meet Kim Jong-il on the first day in Pyongyang, but members hoped that they would see him the next day. On the second day, however, the delegation received an unexpected announcement: "Since the Great General is visiting local areas giving important instructions, he will not see you this time." (In North Korea, Kim Jong-il is called Great General, while his late father, Kim Il-sung, is called Great Leader.) On hearing the announcement, the members of the delegation were speechless, but the impact of the news was strongest on Lim Dong-won. Lim already had secretly met with Kim Jong-il several times. In order to complete the groundwork for the historic North-South summit talk in June 2000, Lim had secretly visited Pyongyang and met with Kim Jong-il in May. Although the prior consultations concerning the agenda of the summit meeting had almost been completed, the very important issue of exactly what should be talked about at the meeting had not been settled. Kim Dae-jung instructed Lim not only to settle the issue but also to meticulously observe Kim Jong-il—his temperament, ideas, manner of speaking, and behavior. On that occasion, Lim was able to monopolize Kim Jong-il for nearly five hours, including supper. When Lim briefed Kim Jong-il on the gist of Kim Dae-jung's talking points in detail, Kim had listened very attentively.

Lim visited Pyongyang again in April 2002 as presidential envoy, this time through Panmunjeom, and again met Kim Jong-il. It should be recalled that in late January of that year President Bush delivered what later became known as his "axis of evil" speech, which was followed in February by his visit to South Korea. The situation relating to the Korean Peninsula had been evolving rapidly since George W. Bush became president, and Kim Dae-jung dispatched Lim to Pyongyang to have him exchange views with the North Korean government on inter-Korea relations, DPRK-U.S. relations, and Japan-DPRK relations.

During the discussions, Lim explained that when Bush visited South Korea he had made it clear that the United States would not invade North Korea. Lim stressed that now that Bush's preemptive strike doctrine was not to be applied to the Korean Peninsula, North Korea should engage in dialogue with the Unites States and, to facilitate dialogue, should accept the visit of U.S. special envoy Charles Pritchard. Although Kim Yong-sun was not very receptive to the idea, Kim Jong-il, with whom a separate meeting was set up at the last minute, unceremoniously accepted Lim's suggestion and agreed to officially announce North Korea's intention to receive the U.S. special envoy.[9]

On the same occasion, Lim also encouraged North Korea to improve its relations with Japan. More specifically, he suggested the following to facilitate normalization of diplomatic relations with Japan:

—North Korea should acknowledge the abduction of Japanese nationals as the deed of a radical minority element in North Korea in the past and should settle the issue.

—North Korea should expel the radicals suspected of carrying out the hijacking of JAL flight 351 (Yodo-go) in order to induce the United States to lift economic sanctions against North Korea and to make it possible for North Korea to receive loans from international organizations, including the World Bank.[10]

—North Korea should compromise concerning its requests for compensation for Japan's colonial rule, following the example of South Korea.[11]

Although Kim Jong-il brushed off the abduction issue as something that North Korea had no knowledge of, he, too, emphasized the importance of normalization of relations with Japan. In fact, it was revealed later that Kim Jong-il had already assigned "Mr. X" to carry out secret negotiations with Japan toward eventual normalization.

During Lim's visit, both sides reached agreement concerning such issues as promoting economic cooperation, reconnecting the severed railway between the North and South, constructing a special industrial site in Kaesong, reuniting separated families (the fourth such reunion), and sending a North Korean economic mission to South Korea.[12] However, Lim could not obtain Kim Jong-il's agreement to visit Seoul in return for Kim Dae-jung's visit to Pyongyang, which had been the hidden agenda of Lim Dong-won's visit.[13]

Lim Dong-won found Kim Jong-il to be well-versed in South Korea's popular culture, and Kim highly praised the hit movie *Gongdong gyeongbi guyeok JSA* (*Joint Security Area*). The film, directed by Park Chan-wook and released in South Korea in September 2000, was another North-South "brotherhood" film. Lim, however, had not yet seen the movie.[14]

"WAKEUP CALL"

Despite past accomplishments, in January 2003 Lim was not allowed to pay even a courtesy visit to Kim Jong-il. Lim wondered why. Could it be that North Korea had suddenly downgraded its treatment of the Lim delegation because the message that it had brought turned out to be much tougher on North Korea?

The Kim Dae-jung government had hoped to improve the deteriorating relations between the United States and North Korea by facilitating dialogue between the two nations. To paraphrase a member of the delegation, "The Kim Dae-jung government wanted to warm the sub-zero American attitude toward North Korea at least to above zero," and it hoped to make the most of the current visit for that purpose. Moreover, because the South Korean presidential election happened to coincide with the North Korean nuclear crisis in December, the Kim Dae-jung government had had to interrupt not only its contacts with North Korea concerning the issue but also the trilateral policy consultations among the United States, South Korea, and Japan, a step that was deemed to be especially dangerous. South Korea wished to improve the situation.

Prior to Lim's visit, the South Korean government had dispatched Yim Sung-joon to Washington to explain its intentions to Condoleezza Rice, President Bush's national security adviser, as well as to Richard Armitage, deputy secretary of state, and to secure their understanding. During the meeting with Armitage, Secretary of State Powell also joined the conversation. Although Armitage did not openly oppose South Korea's initiative, he remained rather cautious about it.[15] Immediately after Lim's visit to Pyongyang, Armitage testified before the Senate Foreign Relations Committee that "during his meetings with North Korean officials last week, Special Envoy Lim emphasized the international community's grave concerns about the North's nuclear weapons program, and he urged the North to respond to those concerns." Armitage praised Lim's role highly and testified that the Bush administration strongly supported Lim's visit to North Korea.[16] But in fact, the administration had not given as much outright support to the visit as Armitage had indicated in his testimony.

It might have appeared to the North Koreans as if the United States and South Korea had joined together to pressure North Korea. Alternatively, the North Koreans' attitude might have hardened when they realized that the major item on the agenda during Lim's visit had been the North Korean nuclear issue. Pyongyang had consistently taken the position that the nuclear issue was a strategic issue to be negotiated between itself and the United States, not something to be discussed with South Korea. In making preparations for Lim's visit, Yim Sung-joon, judging that it was essential to exchange views on the nuclear issue with North Korea's top diplomat, requested an appointment with Kang Sok-ju, even though it was unusual for diplomats on either side to participate in any of the

North-South negotiations. But the request was turned down. The North Koreans explained that because the South Korean delegation had been hosted by the Korean Workers' Party for discussions about North-South relations, an appointment could not be set up with the Foreign Ministry, which had nothing to do with North-South relations. Consequently, an appointment was made for Yim Sung-joon with Lim Dong-ok, first deputy director of the United Front Department of the Korean Workers' Party.[17]

The real reason behind the delegation's inability to obtain the desired appointments probably was that the Kim Dae-jung government was soon to be succeeded by a new government; it reflected how little the North Koreans expected from meeting with the special envoy of a president who was leaving office in a little over three weeks. Some suspected that Lim's trip was designed to institutionalize the back channel to Pyongyang for Kim Dae-jung's group after they left office and particularly to ensure that the summit between Kim Jong-il and Roh Moo-hyun would be held.[18] And perhaps Pyongyang suspected it too. Needless to say, both Kim Dae-jung and Lim Dong-won had been fully aware of that sobering fact, which was why they had included in the delegation Lee Jong-seok, who was expected to assume a key post in the incoming Roh Moo-hyun government. By including both Lim and Lee to symbolize the nature of the transition from Kim Dae-jung to Roh Moo-hyun, the Kim Dae-jung government aimed to reassure North Korea that Kim's sunshine policy would be continued.

During the visit, Lee Jong-seok participated in meetings as a "representative of the incoming president." On January 29, the last day of the visit, Lee met with Kim Yong-sun apart from the delegation and conveyed the following message from the incoming president of South Korea: "The North Korean nuclear issue has to be settled promptly, and South Korea is prepared to extend greater cooperation toward the North. Only this will benefit the future development of the Democratic People's Republic of Korea." Lim did not attend the meeting with Kim Yong-sun; Lee instead explained how Roh Moo-hyun perceived the situation.[19]

The North Koreans, on the other hand, had been greatly encouraged by Roh's victory over Lee Hoi-chang of the Grand National (Han Nara) Party, but that was totally unrelated to how North Korea assessed Roh as a person. North Korea informed the South Korean delegation that it had been very displeased by the criticism of their "beloved leader" by Roh Moo-hyun, who had critically referred to human rights practices in North Korea during an interview with CNN.[20] In answering a question by CNN's Mike Chinoy, Roh had said, "I also don't like the attitude of North Korea, and I also am uncomfortable [with] having dialogues with North Korea. I myself [am a] human rights lawyer and I have some issues with North Korea's deplorable human rights practices. I think Chairman Kim Jong-il is partly responsible for this." His criticism of North Korea's human rights situation, which was reported worldwide, caused further repercussions, even though Roh had immediately added that he wished to have a frank and candid talk with Kim Jong-il: "If the other party is evil or a bad person, we need to have dialogue with him. . . . I am also a straightforward and a frank person, to the point of being called dangerous."[21]

The Bush administration was very pleased with Roh's reference to the human rights situation in North Korea, and it was even more pleased by North Korea's criticism of Roh's remarks. A White House staffer said, after Lim Dong-won's visit, "That was . . . Lee Jong-seok's and the new team's wakeup call about North Korea. They are still very idealistic about North Korea, but that was nice, from our perspective, that was a good thing."[22]

Lee Jong-seok later recalled Roh's remarks, noting that "President Roh had first made some negative remarks and then added that dialogue had to be carried out notwithstanding. But only the initial negative part was emphasized."[23] The North Korean criticism was a reminder to the incoming government that it should not have referred to the North Korean human rights issue unnecessarily.

The South Korean media were highly critical of the outcome of Lim's visit to North Korea. They denounced North Korea and, at the same time, criticized the Kim Dae-jung government:

> What perplexes and enrages us even more was the returning envoy's remark. "Rather than disappointed, I just feel unsatisfied" that President Kim's letter had to be delivered indirectly. Mr. Lim was still trying to embrace the North, but he had no consideration for our people's anger and shame. It made us wonder if the envoy was working for the South or the North.[24]

One member of the delegation later commented:

> North Korea is not a country governed on the basis of personal emotional feelings. It coolly decides on the basis of strategy and tactics. Rather than being nice to the outgoing Kim Dae-jung government, the North Koreans must have decided to play hard-to-get so as to gain a better bargaining position vis-à-vis the incoming Roh Moo-hyun government . . . and at the last minute they made a very, very cold decision not to see Lim Dong-won."[25]

One senior Blue House official later claimed that Kim Dae-jung's obsession with having Kim Jong-il pay a return visit to Seoul clouded his judgment:

> Kim Dae-jung wanted to be in the spotlight once more before he retired. He really wanted to have Kim Jong-il come to Seoul and to hold a second round of North-South summit talks. But that was such an unrealistic dream. From Kim Jong-il's perspective, he would gain nothing by meeting a special envoy

of the outgoing president. Participation in a North-South summit talk was the greatest bargaining card Kim Jong-il held vis-à-vis South Korea. Why should he give it up for an outgoing South Korean president?[26]

Kim Dae-jung was outraged by the outcome, of which he had never even dreamed:

Kim Jong-il had said he would see my special envoy. But once I dispatched one, he wouldn't see him, even though he was bringing with him my personal letter. Kim Jong-il ignores international customs, diplomatic protocol, and even courtesy. Moreover, he hasn't even mentioned anything about a return visit.[27]

Kim Dae-jung made those remarks almost three years after Lim's visit to Pyongyang, and, as if overtaken by anger when he remembered the incident, he had to strain his voice to say that much. Although it seemed that Kim Dae-jung had been informed that Kim Jong-il had agreed to meet Kim Dae-jung's envoy, North Korea had not made any such commitment. Lim Dong-won's last visit to Pyongyang turned out to be a one-sided courtship.[28] As the second Korean nuclear crisis deepened, it was not just Kim Dae-jung's government that was in its twilight; his sunshine policy was, too.

THE TRANSITION TEAM

Special quarters emerged suddenly on the fourth floor of the newly built headquarters of the Ministry of Foreign Affairs and Trade in Seoul. Roh Moo-hyun, who had just been elected president of South Korea on December 19, 2002, had set up a transition team, and the team's unification, foreign, and security policies subcommittee began its deliberations there. The subcommittee included four members: Yoon Young-kwan, a professor at Seoul National University; Lee Jong-seok, a fellow at the Sejong Institute; Suh Joo-seok, a research fellow on North Korean affairs at the Center for Security Strategies, Korea Institute of Defense Analysis; and Suh Dong-man, a professor at Sangji University. Yoon had just turned fifty years old, while the other three were in their mid to late forties.

Yoon Young-kwan was a well-known scholar of international politics. He had a Ph.D. from Johns Hopkins University in the United States, and he had been an assistant professor at the University of California, Davis, before becoming a professor at Seoul National University in 1990. He also was president of the Future Strategy Institute, a think tank of progressive scholars. Lee Jong-seok obtained his Ph.D. at Sungkyunkwan University in Seoul, and in 1994, with a recommendation from Lim Dong-won, he joined the Sejong Institute, where he served as director of North-South relations studies. He had accompanied President Kim

Dae-jung as a member of the South Korean delegation when Kim visited Pyongyang in June 2000.

Suh Joo-seok obtained his Ph.D. in political science at Seoul National University. He had served as a research fellow in North Korean affairs and had been in charge of North Korean military affairs at the Security Strategy Center of the Korea Institute of Defense Analysis. He also was an expert on both the Soviet Union (later Russia) and national defense.

Suh Dong-man obtained an M.A. and a Ph.D. from the University of Tokyo. In 1997 he became a professor at the Institute of Foreign Affairs and National Security, and he is now a professor at Sangji University in Wonju City.

Wi Sung-lac, an assistant to the foreign minister, was seconded to the group as staff director from the Ministry of Foreign Affairs and Trade. Wi had been posted in the United States and Russia, and he had worked at the Blue House during the Kim Young-sam and Kim Dae-jung governments. Wi also was a classmate of Yoon Young-kwan in the Department of International Relations at Seoul National University. In addition, staff members were seconded from the Ministry of Foreign Affairs and Trade, the Ministry of National Defense, and the Ministry of Unification as well as from the National Intelligence Service, making the group a formidable size. Among the staff from the Foreign Ministry was Lee Jong-hun, director of educational affairs at the Institute of Foreign Affairs and National Security, the research and training arm of the Foreign Ministry. Lee Jong-hun had been a devout supporter of Roh Moo-hyun even before the presidential election, and he became a representative figure of the *nosamo* (People Who Love Roh) diplomats who emerged after Roh took office.[29]

A special subcommittee was created to address the North Korean nuclear issue specifically and attached to the unification, foreign, and security policies subcommittee. The special subcommittee consisted of four members of the latter subcommittee, plus Moon Chung-in, a professor at Yonsei University. Moon Chung-in was a political scientist who had earned a Ph.D. from the University of Maryland in 1984. After teaching at the University of Kentucky, Williams College, and the University of California at San Diego, he became a professor of comparative politics at Yonsei University in Seoul.

In the winter of 2001, Yoon Young-kwan received a telephone call out of the blue from the secretary of Roh Moo-hyun, who was then running for president, telling Yoon that Roh wished to see him. When Yoon met Roh for the first time, the meeting lasted more than two and a half hours, during which Yoon was impressed by Roh's unpretentious, frank attitude. Roh asked for Yoon's help in drafting his foreign policy proposals, but Yoon, being a professor at a national university, could not openly participate in the campaign of a presidential candidate. It was later agreed that Yoon would play the role of a covert foreign policy adviser to Roh.[30] Roh also brought Suh Dong-man, Lee Jong-seok, and Suh Joo-seok onto his team.

After Roh was elected, Yoon was asked to head the newly created subcommittee on unification, foreign, and security policies. For nearly two months, until President Roh's inauguration on February 25, 2003, the subcommittee worked out the foreign policy strategy of the Roh Moo-hyun government in its quarters at the Ministry of Foreign Affairs and Trade building. Each member of the subcommittee was placed in charge of a specific government agency: Yoon, Ministry of Foreign Affairs and Trade; Lee, Unification Ministry; Suh Joo-seok, Ministry of Defense; and Suh Dong-man, National Intelligence Service. The subcommittee coordinated with the North Korean Nuclear Task Force in drafting the Roh government's position regarding North Korea's nuclear program.

All four members shared the view that South Korea's policies toward the United States were outdated. Long dominated by the conservative Grand National Party, South Korea's U.S. policy overall had been an extremely anti-communist legacy of the cold war. It reflected nothing but blind obedience to the United States, and the Korean people had long wanted to graduate from their total dependence on the United States.[31]

The first meeting of the subcommittee, which focused on the North Korean nuclear issue, was held on Christmas Eve 2002. Roh himself participated in the meeting. "We will settle the North Korean nuclear issue peacefully through negotiation," he said. "This will be the very foundation of all the unification, foreign, and security policies of my government."[32]

Roh's attention was focused on that single issue. However, in order to achieve his goal, his government had to be prepared to deal with two other issues: first, how to prevent North Korea from possessing nuclear weapons and second, how to restrain the United States from taking military action against North Korea. It also would be essential for South Korea itself to find the most appropriate solutions through its own initiatives. Those three elements guided the Roh government's North Korea policy.[33]

The Kim Dae-jung government's policy toward North Korea also was based on a commitment to diplomatic negotiations. Especially after the United States started taking a stricter stance toward North Korea due to the revelation regarding the North Korean HEU in October 2002, the Kim Dae-jung government had no choice but to make the issue its top priority. At the Japan-U.S.-ROK summit talks during the APEC summit in Los Cabos, Mexico, on October 26, 2002, President Kim stressed to both Bush and Koizumi the importance of searching for a solution of the North Korean nuclear issue through dialogue, and a "commitment to resolve this matter peacefully" was made in the joint statement issued after the talks.

The joint statement also noted that the North-South dialogue between the two Koreas and the negotiations toward normalization of diplomatic relations between Japan and North Korea could provide an important channel for peaceful settlement of the nuclear issue. All in all, what Kim Dae-jung had insisted on was, to a considerable extent, adopted in the joint statement, although the "settlement through dialogue" wording that the South Koreans had strongly insisted on was not included.[34] South Korea wanted to incorporate the phrase to promote direct dialogue between the United States and North Korea, among other reasons. But the United States adamantly rejected it, asking why it should engage in dialogue with a country that had violated the Agreed Framework and secretly developed HEU.

When, at the Japan-U.S.-ROK summit talk, President Bush stated that settlement through peaceful means was desirable, President Kim asked him whether peaceful means included applying pressure on North Korea. Although Kim had intended to restrain Bush from rushing to initiate UN sanctions, Bush brushed aside Kim's concerns.[35] The Bush administration had consistently pursued a policy of "putting all the options on the table" vis-à-vis North Korea's nuclear program, including UN sanctions and even military action.

Roh repeatedly stressed that the U.S. "all options" policy was absolutely unacceptable. Roh also wanted to spell out more explicitly the "proactive role" that South Korea wanted to play in the effort to settle the North Korean nuclear issue. Lee Jong-seok and Suh Joo-seok identified South Korea's "proactive role" as "converting North Korea and the environment of Northeast Asia from an unpredictable one to a predictable one." In other words, instead of focusing on being prepared for a military solution because of the unpredictability of the situation on the Korean Peninsual, Roh advocated proactive engagement to ensure that nothing would happen that would make a military solution necessary.[36]

The four members of the subcommittee on unification, foreign, and security policies achieved almost perfect agreement among themselves as far as the objectives and principles of the Roh government's policies were concerned. However, when it came to which specific measures to take to pursue those objectives and principles, the views of the four never converged. As the discussions deepened, the subcommittee's views became polarized, giving rise to the Yoon Young-kwan line and the Lee Jong-seok line.

Yoon advocated closer policy coordination with the United States. He thought that as the relations between South Korea and the United States deepened further, South Korea would be able to influence U.S. foreign policy and, along the way, convince the United States to adopt a more realistic policy toward North Korea, leading to greater engagement. Yoon stressed that although that approach might seem to be a long detour, it would be, after all, the quickest way to accomplish their goals.

Lee Jong-seok remained highly skeptical of Yoon's optimism. Lee's view was that since the true objective of the United States seemed to be regime change in North Korea, it would be difficult to promote policy coordination with the United States. What South Korea had to do instead was to graduate from dependence on the United States and pursue a more autonomous foreign policy. Lee further argued that South Korea should make the best use of China's influence on North Korea.

However, all four members were in full agreement on not letting the United States freely mount a military attack against North Korea. The fear that the United States might again "rush to readopt a hard line against North Korea, as it had done in 1994," as described by one of the members, was shared by all.[37] In 1994, while the Clinton administration attempted to settle the North Korean nuclear crisis diplomatically, it also explored the possibility of a "military option" to bomb the nuclear facilities near Yongbyon or to destroy them by using precision-guided weapons. During the course of the U.S. examination of its options, Secretary of Defense William Perry decided that it would be possible to destroy the Yongbyon nuclear facilities without any danger of a radiation leak at the level of that in Chernobyl, and he submitted to the president the idea of a military attack as a viable option.[38] As it turned out, the Agreed Framework was signed, and the United States did not have to take the military option. But as Perry later pointed out, "We were about to give the president a choice between a disastrous option—allowing North Korea to get a nuclear arsenal . . . and an unpalatable option, blocking this development, but thereby risking a destructive non-nuclear war."[39]

At the time, the incumbent President Kim Young-sam also consistently stressed to the United States that it "would never be allowed to start bombing on our soil."[40] Despite his intense hatred of North Korea (no doubt attributable to the murder of his mother by North Korean soldiers during the Korea War), he would not give even one inch in the argument for a military attack on the nuclear facilities around Yongbyon. "As long as I am the president, I will not mobilize any one of our 600,000 troops," he said. "I cannot afford to commit a crime against our history and our people."[41] He had a heated argument with Clinton, who had announced to Kim by phone that the United States would deploy an aircraft carrier and seven U.S. Navy destroyers off the eastern seaboard of North Korea. That argument lasted forty minutes. Kim told Clinton that Seoul would be a "sea of fire" if U.S. forces attacked North Korea, in which case Kim, "as com-mander-in-chief of the South Korean army," would not "send one single mem-ber of South Korea's 650,000 armed forces into battle."[42]

Regarding the same incident, Roh Moo-hyun once referred to a 2002 Korean television program, "U.S. Military Operation in Yongbyon 1994." The program attempted to reveal that the United States, without consulting at all with South Korea, had unilaterally planned a self-serving military operation that could have endangered the lives of numerous South Korean citizens. Roh said he had been deeply impressed by the program. "As long as I am president," he avowed, "this kind of thing will never be tolerated."[43]

At the time, many South Koreans, including Roh Moo-hyun, indeed were convinced that the United States planned to attack North Korea in 1994 without consulting South Korea, a conviction that Thomas Hubbard, then the U.S. ambassador to Seoul, later referred to as a "new myth."[44]

"OPERATION PRESIDENT'S PERSONAL LETTER"

Soon after the transition team was formed, Roh Moo-hyun invited five members of the subcommittee to lunch. During lunch, Yoon Young-kwan and Moon Chung-in stressed the importance of maintaining the ROK's alliance with the United States, while Lee Jong-seok and Suh Dong-man insisted on the need to review the alliance. "How much longer do we have to put up with this kind of relationship?" they asked. "We should take a much stronger position toward the United States." Yoon retorted, "Do you have an alternative?" To back his position, Yoon presented the following arguments:

—If the United States decided on military action, it would act with or without South Korea's agreement.

—The best way to prevent unilateral U.S. military action would be to cooperate with the United States so that South Korea could "meddle" in the details of its plans.

—If South Korea opposed military action until the very end and the United States nevertheless took military action, the alliance would be fractured and a military conflict would erupt on the Korean Peninsula.

—If, in contrast, the United States gave up the idea of military action because of South Korea's opposition, the United States would ditch its alliance with South Korea. What would South Korea gain from that? How would Seoul cope with North Korea if that happened?

—The best approach would be to let diplomacy play its role. South Korea had no viable alternative to working with the United States.

In contrast, Lee and Suh Dong-man insisted on the importance of taking a national approach to North-South relations and a regional approach in Northeast Asia. To begin with, they declared, North Korea had started developing nuclear weapons as a countermeasure to the U.S. threat; that action was not directed at South Korea. Therefore, if the United States would guarantee North Korea's security and would normalize diplomatic relations with Pyongyang, it would be conceivable to denuclearize North Korea through negotiations. It would not be wise, they said, to put pressure on North Korea in international forums such as the International Atomic Energy Agency (IAEA) or the United Nations, because that would push North Korea deeper into a corner. South Korea should maintain its pro-engagement policy and continue North-South dialogue, but it should be cautious vis-à-vis the "internationalization" of the North Korean nuclear issue. Nevertheless, at the same time, the possibility of trilateral cooperation with Japan and China should be further explored.

The key would be China's role—that is, South Korea should fully utilize China's rising economic power and influence to stabilize and, eventually, to denuclearize North Korea. Lee and Suh believed that in order to elicit a positive influence from China, it would be essential for South Korea to develop a more balanced relationship with the United States, Japan, and China, rather than relying heavily on its alliance with the United States or the Japan-U.S.-ROK framework. South Korea then would be able to restrain North Korea from engaging in any eccentric activities and to persuade the United States to accept a peaceful settlement of the North Korean nuclear issue.

In response, Yoon retorted that Lee and Suh's arguments overestimated the role that China could play. If South Korea were to turn toward China to that extent, Seoul would run the great risk of displeasing the United States. Instead, he argued, South Korea should firmly maintain the U.S.-ROK alliance and should consolidate Japan-U.S.-ROK cooperation in order to achieve a more sustainable stability on the peninsula. Yoon repeatedly stressed the importance of the Japan-U.S.-ROK policy coordination regime in particular, including the Trilateral Coordination and Oversight Group.[45]

Soon after the subcommittee was formed, Yoon was informed by Suh Joo-seok of calls to include Lee Jong-seok in the Lim Dong-won delegation. That would be like a sack race, in which the contestants hobble from the start to the finish line, their freedom of movement curtailed by the sack around their legs. Yoon was not happy to receive the news:

> When you start up a new government, you should not do something that will restrict your hand in regard to the nation's most important diplomatic as well as domestic political issue concerning North Korea. It would be especially unwise to include in the delegation someone who will occupy a key position in the new government.

Yoon could not figure out the reasoning behind the decision to dispatch a delegation to North Korea. He believed that the new Roh government should, while supporting the objectives of the sunshine policy, form its own approach to the policy rather than just stick to what the Kim Dae-jung government had done.[46] Nevertheless, the decision had already been made and confirmed by Kim Dae-jung and Roh Moo-hyun, and there was nothing that anyone could do about it.[47]

Roh Moo-hyun took another initiative: sending his personal delegation to major countries. The delegation consisted of the members of the presidential transition team together with South Korea's leading parliamentarians. They were sent to countries of major importance to South Korea to communicate the new president's diplomatic philosophy to the leaders of those countries and to get their feedback. Yoon was sent to the United States; Lee Jong-seok to China; Suh Dong-man to Japan; and Suh Joo-seok to Russia. The delegation to Washington, which was led by Minister of Parliament Chung Dae-chul and included Moon Chung-in, met in succession with Defense Secretary Donald Rumsfeld, Secretary of State Colin Powell, Vice President Dick Cheney, and Stephen Hadley, the deputy national security adviser to the president.

During the meeting at the Pentagon, Rumsfeld mentioned an adjustment to the size and location of American troops in South Korea. Hadley referred to a plan for a multilateral framework such as a ten-party talk involving the P-5 countries (United States, Russia, Britain, France, and China), the two Koreas, Japan, Australia, and the European Union. "If North Korea refuses to negotiate, the other nine countries will get together and apply pressure on North Korea," Hadley said. Moon Chung-in retorted, "That would backfire. Instead, we need bilateral consultation between the U.S. and North Korea. We came here to appeal to you to have bilateral talks."[48] As Yoon and the other members of the ROK delegation engaged in one discussion after another, they agreed on two fundamental principles: first, that North Korea was a dialogue partner, not a threat, and no military action should be taken against North Korea; second, that there would be zero tolerance of any North Korean nuclear development activities.[49]

Some of the new initiatives explored by the presidential transition team were actually pursued by the new government. One was "Operation Personal Letter," in which South Korea was to convince Bush to send a letter to Kim Jong-il. This initiative was intended to explore the possibility of mutual concessions between the United States and North Korea—that is, to make Kim Jong-il promise to abandon nuclear development in return for Bush's promise not to attack North Korea militarily. If successful, the scheme also envisioned allowing North Korea to produce plutonium, provided that it was for peaceful uses, under international supervision.[50]

Soon after the Roh government assumed power, Lee Jong-seok secretly sounded out the U.S. response to the personal letter initiative, and he repeatedly asked the United States to consider the idea when he visited the United States. Some U.S. administration officials showed interest in the scheme, and some had even drafted a letter for Bush to send to Kim Jong-il. However, they realized that the opening salutation was a big problem. How should Kim Jong-il be addressed?

To encourage adoption of the Agreed Framework, President Clinton had sent a personal letter to Kim Jong-il in which Clinton addressed Kim as "His Excellency Kim Jong-il, Supreme Leader of the Democratic People's Republic of Korea." Despite the fact that the United States did not have diplomatic relations with North Korea, addressing Kim in that manner signified an American president's de facto recognition of North Korea as a sovereign nation and of Kim as its legitimate leader.[51]

The question was whether the Bush administration should follow suit. It should be remembered that, for the most part, the top echelon of the Bush administration was obsessed with the "anything but Clinton" doctrine. To follow Clinton's lead would be a nonstarter. How about "Dear Mr. Kim Jong-il"? Or "Dear Chairman Kim Jong-il," inasmuch as he was chairman of the National Defense Commission? Should "dear" be used when President Bush openly said that he loathed Kim? And first of all, who was going to persuade Bush to write such a letter? Although White House staff talked about the letter with a certain interest, the senior people there showed absolutely no interest in the scheme, which was made a pending matter.[52]

The year 2003 began with the deepening of the second Korean nuclear crisis and heightened tensions in anticipation of a U.S. military attack on Iraq. South Korea received mixed messages from the United States—sometimes Seoul heard a "pro-engagement" argument that advocated the settlement of the North Korean nuclear issue through dialogue, sometimes a hard-liner argument with no reservations on the use of force. On January 15, President Bush declared that the United States would pursue a "bold initiative" including provision of energy and food supplies to North Korea if Pyongyang would abandon its nuclear weapons program.[53] But Bush also announced that "all options are on the table," including the option of a military attack on North Korea. On February 8, Bush made a telephone call to Jiang Zemin requesting China's cooperation toward settling the nuclear issue. In the press conference after the call, Bush once again clarified that he had not given up the military option vis-à-vis North Korea.[54]

Defense Secretary Rumsfeld boasted that the U.S. military was capable of fighting in two major regional conflicts at once: one against Iraq and one against North Korea.[55] Around that time the U.S. Air Force transferred twenty-four B-1 and B-52 bombers—nuclear-capable bombers—to Anderson Air Force Base in Guam.[56] Rumsfeld, while emphasizing that the move should not be interpreted as aggressive, threatening, or hostile, complacently said, "As the situation with respect to Iraq becomes somewhat tense, it seems to me that it's appropriate for the United States to look around the globe and say 'Where might someone think of taking advantage of the situation with respect to Iraq?'" It was obvious that by "someone" he meant North Korea.[57]

After that announcement, North Korea became extremely nervous about being attacked by the United States under the guise of an attack on Iraq. On February 12, the IAEA resolved to send the North Korean nuclear issue to the UN Security Council. On that very day, Kim Jong-il met with a Russian delegation, which had brought gifts from President Putin. For close to fifty days after the meeting, Kim Jong-il did not appear in public. His next public appearance was on April 3, when he attended an awards ceremony at the Kim Hyong Jik Military Medical University of the Korean People's Army.[58]

PASSING THE BATON

On February 23, 2003, President Kim Dae-jung opened his final cabinet meeting, which ended up being a twenty-five-minute-long monologue by Kim. In the course of his talk, Kim Dae-jung earnestly shared his views with his cabinet members, saying that in order for South Korea to survive it had to strike a good balance between its relationship with the United States and its relationship with North Korea. "With a small country like Korea, diplomacy is crucial," he said. "We don't have the luxury of committing any minor mistakes in diplomacy."[59]

All of Kim Dae-jung's cabinet members listened to this poignant message, lowering their heads. One of them, Foreign Minister Choi Sung-hong, remembered that President Kim had once said that he held Otto von Bismarck, Germany's first chancellor, in the highest esteem. Kim had praised the subtlety of Bismarckian diplomacy, which had enabled Germany to improve its relations with neighboring countries, paying close attention to all the details.[60] Kim Dae-jung might have felt that he could retire from the presidency with peace of mind. After all, in the past five years he had accomplished a diplomatic miracle: simultaneously managing and improving South Korea's relations with all of its neighboring countries, including Japan, China, Russia, and North Korea as well as the United States.

After the cabinet meeting, Kim Dae-jung made a nationally televised speech in which he said, in part:

> The Korea-U.S. alliance has been of benefit to both countries, and therefore anti-American or anti-Korean feeling should be avoided.
>
> A road has been finally opened through the Demilitarized Zone. This marks the dynamic start of inter-Korean economic integration, which is leading North Koreans to switch their distrust and hostility [of South Korea] to understanding and envy.... Give your support to President Roh. The policies of inter-Korean reconciliation and cooperation and his reform agenda regarding public participation should succeed.[61]

His last function as head of state was to receive a courtesy visit by Vice Premier Qian Qichen of China.

On February 24, 2003, one day before President Roh Moo-hyun's inauguration, North Korea launched an anti-ship missile that landed in the Sea of Japan/East Sea, some forty miles (sixty kilometers) off Hamgyong-Namdo, North Korea. It was a tactical missile, not a ballistic one like the Taepodong. The spokesperson for South Korea's Ministry of Defense coolly announced, "We are trying to determine whether the launch was part of the North Korean military's regular training exercises or a test of its arsenal of anti-ship missiles."[62] The Japanese government took the position that the launching did not violate the Japan-DPRK Pyongyang Declaration, in which North Korea expressed "its intent that it would maintain the moratorium on missile launching in and after 2003."[63] Both the Japanese and South Korean governments wanted to avoid overreacting to the incident.

At midnight on February 25, the giant bell in Seoul's Bosingak Belfry, a bell tower of the ancient Lee Dynasty, rang out thirty-three times, echoing in the bitter chill of the night. Thirty-three was the number of Korean representatives who on March 1, 1919, signed the document declaring Korea's independence from Japanese colonial rule.

At 11:00 a.m. on February 25, the inauguration ceremony for Roh Moo-hyun, the sixteenth president of the Republic of Korea, commenced at the National Assembly in Yoido, Seoul. Roh took the oath of office and then delivered his speech, "A New Take-off toward an Age of Peace and Prosperity." In the speech, Roh developed new geopolitical possibilities for the Korean Peninsula, saying, in part:

> The Age of Northeast Asia is fast approaching. . . . The Korean Peninsula is located at the heart of the region. It is a big bridge linking China and Japan, the continent, and the ocean. Such a geopolitical characteristic has often caused pain for us in the past. Today, however, this same feature offers us an opportunity. Indeed, it demands that we play a pivotal role in the Age of Northeast Asia in the 21st century.[64]

Roh followed up with his "policy for peace and prosperity," which further reinforced the Kim Dae-jung government's sunshine policy, and laid out the new policy's four guiding principles: to resolve all pending issues through dialogue; to build mutual trust and to uphold reciprocity; to actively cooperate internationally, on the premise that South Korea and North Korea are the two main actors in inter-Korean relations; and to enhance transparency, expand citizen participation, and secure bipartisan support for the new policy toward North Korea.

Regarding North Korea's nuclear development program, Roh maintained that "Pyongyang must abandon nuclear development" and that it was "up to Pyongyang whether to go ahead and obtain nuclear weapons or to gain both guarantees for the security of its regime and international economic support." At the same time, Roh said, "I would like to emphasize again that the North Korean nuclear issue should be resolved peacefully through dialogue. Military tension in any form should not be heightened."[65]

Roh Moo-hyun's policy vis-à-vis the North Korean nuclear issue was based on the following three principles:

—no tolerance of any nuclear development activity by North Korea

—pursuit of a peaceful settlement of the issue through dialogue

—South Korea's active involvement in resolving the issue.[66]

Roh thereby stressed again that South Korea regarded North Korea as a dialogue partner, not as a threat, and that South Korea would not take any military action against North Korea. In addition, Roh's policy for peace and prosperity further clarified the intention of the new government to adopt a wider perspective on Northeast Asia rather than confine its view to the Korean Peninsula; moreover, when formulating and implementing policies regarding North Korea, it would make the most of opportunities to cooperate and coordinate with the other countries concerned—the United States, Japan, China, and Russia. The plan was to achieve peace with North Korea as a step toward ensuring peace in all of Northeast Asia, in cooperation with other regional powers, instead of relying solely on the U.S.-ROK relationship. It also defined South Korea as a Northeast Asian hub and attempted to claim a much more positive role in the region for South Korea.

On that day, Roh met four foreign dignitaries at the Blue House: Prime Minister Junichiro Koizumi of Japan, U.S. Secretary of State Colin Powell, Vice Premier Qian Qichen of China, and Deputy Foreign Minister Alexander Losyukov of Russia.

The North Korean media reported without commentary that President-elect Roh Moo-hyun of the Millennium Democratic Party officially took office. The Korean Workers' Party newspaper *Rodong Sinmun*, for instance, covered the story in a short article on page 5 on February 26. Nevertheless, North Korea's coverage of the event was quite an improvement over its coverage of Kim Dae-jung's inauguration, which was not mentioned until three days after the ceremony— and only in the form of criticism of the inaugural speech, with no mention of his name.[67]

The transition from the Kim Dae-jung government to the Roh Moo-hyun government was not a simple change of regime. It signified the raising of the curtain on a type of "managed social revolution" intended to pursue the reorganization of the social structure and the replacement of the elite class in response to revolts by a wide range of the alienated public in post–World War II South Korean society.[68] The very first policy issue that the Roh government pursued was relocation of the capital and approval of the following four bills by the National Assembly:

—repeal of the National Security Law

—revision of the existing Private School Law

—enactment of a new Newspaper Law

—initiation of an inquiry concerning the truth regarding historical incidents in modern Korea.

All of the bills reflected the passion of those who, in an effort to break with the past, had pushed Roh Moo-hyun into power.

For the most part, the break with the past took the form of identifying people who had collaborated with the postwar military governments—or with the U.S. government, which had supported those governments—or who had collaborated with the pre-war Japanese colonial government or pro-Japanese elements in order to erase their influence once and for all. The antipathy of the alienated elements of Korean society toward the mainstream was focused at several specific targets, including, most notably, offices of public prosecutors, the Ministry of Foreign Affairs and Trade, the National Intelligence Agency, the central government's bureaucracy as a whole, three major daily newspapers (*Chosun Ilbo, Joong-An Ilbo*, and *Dong-A Ilbo*), the *chaebol* (industrial conglomerates), political parties, and politicians. The GNP (Grand National Party), the opposition party, claimed that this movement, led by Roh, evoked in time a nationwide emotional reaction not unlike that in China during the Great Cultural Revolution, promoting factionalism and leaving deep schisms within Korean society.[69] Kim Hee-sang, who later joined the Roh Moo-hyun Blue House as a presidential adviser for national defense, reminisced:

> The current situation reminds me of the time when the entire country was divided into Right and Left when establishing a government right after the liberation from Japanese colonialism in 1945. . . . [T]he entire population is divided between liberals and conservatives, and between pro–North Korea groups and ultranationalists, and those groups are distrustful of each other, filled with hatred as sharp as a knife.[70]

Roh Moo-hyun himself was an embodiment of the social revolution—that is, he had consciously represented the alienated elements in Korean society. Born in 1946, the youngest of five children in a poor peasant family, Roh graduated from a business high school and passed the national bar examination without going to college. After serving as a district judge, Roh began his practice as a lawyer. During the democratization movement of the 1980s, he defended students who had been tortured, among his other activities. Hand-picked by the opposition leader Kim Young-sam, Roh ran for the National Assembly in 1988, gaining elected office for the first time. He became nationally known for his spirited criticism of the Chun Doo-hwan government. Roh later joined Kim Dae-jung's camp and served as minister of maritime affairs and fisheries.

In the early stages of the presidential election in 2002, it was pointed out that about 70 percent of the candidates—including Lee Hoi-chang of the Grand National Party, who had fought Roh to the end for the presidency—had Seoul National University backgrounds but that Roh was not a Seoul National University graduate. In fact, the last educational institution he had attended was a business high school, although in a Confucian society an elite education is considered an essential attribute of a leader.

Many in Roh's brain trust and many of his campaign activists had joined the student revolts against the oppression of the military government during the 1980s, and quite a number of them had actually been imprisoned. Unlike the older generations, who had looked upon the United States as their savior for having fought on their side during the Korean War, this generation regarded the United States as a patron of military governments. An explosion of anti-American sentiment triggered by a June 2002 incident in which two Korean junior high school girls were accidentally killed by a U.S. military armored vehicle became a tailwind for Roh's candidacy.

According to a Gallup Korea survey taken in December 2002, 54 percent of the respondents had a negative image of the United States, more than triple the 15 percent of 1994. Anti-American attitudes were especially prevalent among Koreans in their twenties and thirties, of whom 76 percent and 67 percent, respectively, held a negative view of the United States. In contrast, the share of those having a positive image of North Korea—because its people are of the same ethnicity— went up to 47 percent, exceeding by 10 percent the percentage of those holding a positive view of the United States.[71] The survey results revealed that anti-American sentiment increased directly in proportion to pro–North Korean sentiment.

Although South Koreans as a whole considered North Korea to be less of a threat, the United States began to feel more threatened by North Korea, from the standpoint of proliferation of weapons of mass destruction and the post-9/11 war against terrorism. The gap between the perceptions of the two countries regarding the threat posed by North Korea found its expression after President Kim Dae-jung met with President Bush for the first time in March 2001 at the White House, when many South Koreans began to see the presence of U.S. troops in South Korea and President Bush as an impediment to cooperation between the two Koreas, improvement of North Korea's behavior, and progress toward unification. The tendency to make the United States a scapegoat was particularly evident among younger South Koreans.[72]

Accordingly, South Korean sympathy increased toward North Korea, which had squarely confronted the United States. Because South Koreans could not find a satisfactory way to express their own anti-American sentiments, they found North Korea's anti-American posture and rhetoric strangely satisfying and therapeutic.

To many who supported Roh Moo-hyun, the United States had backed up the detested military governments in the past and delayed democratization in South Korea. It was the United States, not North Korea, that had obstructed the reunification of North and South and had damaged South Korea's sovereignty, independence, and pride. It should be noted, however, that the anti-American mood

Blame USA

that had raised Roh to the presidency was somewhat different from the earlier, more left-wing, ideological anti-Americanism. This time it was based on national pride, backed up by South Korea's economy, the world's twelfth-largest; the outstanding performance of South Korea–based global enterprises such as Samsung; and South Korea's ascendance to the final four in the 2002 FIFA World Cup soccer games. Discontent and frustration built up among the many Koreans who believed that the United States did not grant South Korea the recognition that its international status warranted. In addition, because Roh supporters believed that the "Seoul establishment," the South Korean ruling class, was without exception pro-American, their animosity toward the establishment also found expression in antipathy toward the United States.[73]

In a public debate with Lee Hoi-chang toward the end of the presidential campaign, Roh stressed that he had "no intention of kowtowing to the U.S."[74] He also called for the "maturation and advancement" of the bilateral alliance, distinguishing himself from Lee, who had been called "a blind follower of the United States."[75] Traditionally, presidential candidates in South Korea appealed to the electorate on the basis of their ability to maintain good relations with the United States. But Roh took the opposite approach—he cashed in on the anti-American sentiment among voters, clinching the presidency and signifying that Korean politics had entered an entirely new dimension.

Roh's own attitude toward the United States also was complex. In 1990, he signed a petition demanding the withdrawal of American troops from South Korea, but he modified his position during the presidential campaign, saying, "There are some negative views, but I believe the stationing of U.S. troops is necessary for the sake of our national interests. I believe the U.S. forces should stay here even after the establishment of peace and unification on the peninsula so they can preserve the balance of power in Northeast Asia"[76]

However, it was believed that Roh's true wish was genuine independence from the United States. Prior to becoming president, he once said that if the United States and North Korea engaged in armed conflict, South Korea would mediate between the two rather than automatically join the U.S. camp—a position that stirred quite a controversy. More specifically, he said, "We should proudly say we will not side with North Korea or the United States."[77] In an *Asahi Shimbun* interview about one month before his inauguration, Roh brushed off an argument that South Korean youth had turned anti-U.S., saying:

> It would be an inaccurate oversimplification to define these people as anti-American. What these people truly wish is for South Korea to have an autonomous and more equal-footed relationship with the United States.... It is in fact more problematic that some in South Korea overreact and define this trend as anti-American.[78]

It seems accurate to say that Roh's anti-American sentiment was directed more toward the pro-American elements in South Korea rather than toward the United States itself. Even after he took office, Roh was heard to say, "I feel troubled when I see that there are Koreans who possess a more pro-American way of thinking than Americans themselves."[79]

That sentiment was shared by many of the staff who had entered the Blue House with Roh, of whom more than 40 percent had taken part in the anti-dictatorship movement in the 1970s and 1980s.[80] When the Roh government took over, there was a mass exodus of those who had been in charge of relations with the United States in postwar South Korea. U.S. Assistant Secretary of State James Kelly was made acutely aware of that fact during his two visits to South Korea around that time. In February 2002, when President Bush visited, Kelly was present at a reception held in Bush's honor. Kelly found many of the 300 guests to be his acquaintances, including a number of Americans and Japanese, and he found some fifty to sixty people that he had known long and well.

On February 25, 2003, a year after the previous reception, he was present at Roh's inaugural reception at the Blue House. While there were some foreign guests here and there, the room was full of Koreans, and he saw only two people that he had known before. Korean was spoken almost exclusively. In the good old days of the Seoul establishment, almost everyone spoke English; they even spoke in English with each other when English-speaking foreigners were present. Kelly had the deep impression that that era was over and that it would never return.[81]

ADVISING THE PRESIDENT:
INTERNATIONALISTS VERSUS NATIONALISTS

Yoon Young-kwan, the minister for foreign affairs and trade, and Lee Jong-seok, the deputy secretary of the National Security Council, were to be the central figures in formulating the Roh government's foreign and security policies. Yoon had visited Pyongyang in 2000 as a member of a South Korean church–related NGO that had been providing milk to North Koreans in need (the aim of the delegation was to determine whether the milk had actually reached its intended recipients). At one point, as the delegation took an escalator to get to the subway in Pyongyang, Yoon found a young man squatting on the escalator. Looking closely, Yoon saw that the man was counting U.S. dollar bills. They were all one-dollar bills. Yoon thought he was witnessing the beginning of the dollarization of the North Korean economy. He was struck by the premonition that something was changing.[82]

Yoon supported Kim Dae-jung's sunshine policy toward North Korea. He believed in its objective—to create an environment for peace both on the Korean Peninsula and in Northeast Asia overall through mutual engagement and dialogue between the two Koreas. He was clearly opposed to Seoul's traditional North Korea policy, which was set by conservative elites who were subservient to the United States and who would not even acknowledge the end of the cold war. But Yoon felt uncomfortable with the sunshine policy's methods. For one thing, the sunshine policy tended to approach every aspect of North-South relations from the perspective of the interests of all Koreans as members of the same ethnic group, subjugating all other policy goals. Yoon believed, however, that relations between the two Koreas had to be pursued rationally from the viewpoint of South Korea's national interest. Second, and related to the first point, engagement and dialogue with North Korea had to be shifted to a more principled and a value-based footing. In other words, Yoon thought an approach that was more compatible with universal values should be pursued; human rights, for instance, should be an important element. The sunshine policy seemed to have resulted in North-South dialogue merely for the sake of North-South dialogue. Yoon insisted that the possibility of putting the North-South dialogue in a more international context should be pursued instead. He challenged the conventional view, which maintained that North Korea would never give up its nuclear options, that it would never pursue reform and openness, and that the only remedy for North Korea was regime change. Yoon argued instead that

—if the other nations concerned addressed the nuclear issue in a more comprehensive manner, North Korea might give up its nuclear options. That could be done through normalization of diplomatic relations between North Korea and the United States and between North Korea and Japan, which would deprive North Korea of the incentive to arm itself with nuclear weapons. North Korea's acceptance of verification would be one test of whether the scheme would succeed.

—to promote reform and openness requires political stability and foreign assistance. Because North Korea is isolated internationally, its suspension of domestic price controls in July 2002 caused hyperinflation due to shortages of goods. A comprehensive solution must be developed that incorporates all aspects of military, foreign, and economic policies.

—if North Korea's regime crisis and its nuclear crisis were addressed simultaneously, a road might be opened to peace and stability in Northeast Asia, including North Korea, as well as to cooperation and reconciliation between the two Koreas. Thus, that is the approach that South Korea should take.[83]

As for specific approaches, Yoon first envisioned promoting policy coordination between South Korea and Japan, which could work together to soften the U.S. hard-line attitude toward North Korea. In fact, the Trilateral Coordination and Oversight Group, launched in 1999, along with other organizations, played this function. Second, he envisioned maintaining closer relations with China and encouraging China to engage more deeply with North Korea. He was careful, however, not to overestimate China's role. In fact, he wished that the United

States would host the six-party talks instead of China.[84] Third, Yoon believed that the North-South dialogue should be continued and developed further; the Unification Ministry should be the main actor in that endeavor.

Yoon proposed a new set of engagement policies incorporating the three elements above and named his approach the "third path." At first glance, Yoon's approach to the North-South issue and to U.S.–South Korea relations might give the impression of being a heavily internationalist strategy, but it was backed by a sober realism based on the international environment surrounding South Korea. He was quoted as saying:

> If we weaken our alliance relationship with the United States, probably China or North Korea will not pay as much attention as before. . . . We lose our leverage if we weaken our alliance relationship with the United States. If that happens, I think we might be facing the danger of being bypassed.[85]

In contrast, Lee Jong-seok's approach to North-South and U.S.–South Korea relations was a blend of nationalism and idealism. Lee advocated continuing and further developing the sunshine policy. He believed that the relationship between North Korea and South Korea differed from an ordinary international relationship, and his concept of the national interest differed accordingly. Lee argued against Yoon's position, saying that in terms of relations between the two Koreas, the national interest should be perceived from the longer-term and strategic vantage points of the "Korean race" and "unification." Lee, therefore, did not subscribe to Yoon's "third path."

Lee also remained cool regarding cooperation among Japan, the United States, and South Korea. His master's thesis was a study of Kim Il-sung's anti-Japan partisan activities in which Lee vividly portrayed how superior Kim Il-sung had been as a military leader. In his study Lee emulated the "internal logic" approach used by left-wing West German scholars, which had been advocated by Professor Song Du-yul of the Free University of Berlin in regard to East Germany. Instead of seeing North Korea through the lens of anti-communist ideology, he advocated first understanding North Korea through its own internal logic. Lee's approach was harshly criticized by experts on North Korea who were in the conservative camp, including Shin Il-chul, a professor emeritus at Korea University.

Nevertheless, nobody, including those whose ideological convictions differed from Lee's, would deny that Lee Jong-seok was the foremost expert on Kim Il-sung and North Korean politics. It was Lim Dong-won who had discovered Lee Jong-seok, who had been a low-key research fellow at the Sejong Institute, and took Lee with him to the North Korea–South Korea summit talk in Pyongyang in June 2000.

After the summit talk, Lee produced a paper in which he praised the North-South summit, which "paved the way for lasting peace and unification of the

Korean Peninsula." He stressed that in order to consolidate the outcome of the summit, South Koreans must nurture "a culture of coexistence." Lee continued to stress that point:

> The agreements reached between the two Koreas can be likened to fragile glassware prone to breakage even with careful handling. To prevent disputes along the Military Demarcation Line and sea boundaries and to respond properly to any situation, the two sides should install a military hotline and promote confidence-building between the two militaries. At the same time, domestic efforts should be made to develop a nationwide consensus to not unnecessarily offend the North.
>
> The recent summit has served to restore the leading roles of North and South Korea. It has moderated the hitherto significant influence of the United States. This is the very point that might concern Washington. In this regard, South Korea must reassure the United States that the U.S.-led Perry process and the international process characterized by the summit talks are not contradictory but rather complementary.
>
> South Koreans who have called on the other side to change have changed only slightly themselves, so slightly that they cannot sense the change that has already occurred on the other side. . . . The National Security Law and various other laws that have served to maintain the Cold War system on the Korean Peninsula must be carefully reviewed. In education . . . a new emphasis is needed, replacing enmity toward the North Korean people with a sense of brotherliness.[86]

In the early days at the Blue House, Lee was called a "Blue House Taliban." He was regarded as an advocate of North-South brotherhood, a North Korean–South Korean reconciliation supremacist, or as an "independence" fundamentalist. But Lee was no simple ideologue.

Among the several policy intellectuals that had joined the nucleus of the Roh Moo-hyun government, it was Lee Jong-seok, a mere research fellow from a think tank, and not renowned scholars like Ra Jong-il, Yoon Young-kwan, or Han Sung-joo, that survived in the Roh Moo-hyun government. Thomas Hubbard, the U.S. ambassador to Seoul, later said, "[Those scholars] got eaten alive by Lee Jong-seok."[87] One senior South Korean government official has said that Lee's strength was his "proximity to the president," as well as his "talent for explaining complicated matters in plain language to the president." Another senior official pointed out that Lee was a "keen observer of the president's mind."[88] Yet another senior official attributed Lee's survival to loyalty.

Although all of those factors must have helped, it was the reorganization of Korea's National Security Council (KNSC) immediately after the start of the Roh Moo-hyun government, particularly the reinforcement of its secretariat, that enhanced Lee's position in the government. Upon appointing Lee Jong-seok as the KNSC's deputy secretary, President Roh announced the upgrading of the function of the KNSC secretariat from that of a coordinating body to that of "efficiently facilitating substantive national security operations from a comprehensive perspective." (Suh Joo-seok was appointed KNSC's director of strategic planning.) At the same time, the position of KNSC executive secretary was raised from its traditional vice-minister level to minister level and the secretariat staff was increased from twelve members during the Kim Dae-jung government to forty-five. Moreover, new mandates, such as mid- to long-term policy planning and integration of intelligence, were added to the KNSC's traditional tasks relating to security policies and crisis management.

MOODY'S RATING

Stock market reaction

An issue of more immediate urgency for the government was South Korea's ranking by an American credit-rating agency, Moody's Investor Service. Moody's informed the South Korean government on February 11, 2003, that it had downgraded South Korea's credit rating from "positive" to "negative" by two grades. South Korea's rating had been upgraded several times after it finally overcame the effects of the 1997–98 Asian financial crisis. Moody's cited the "uncertainties of the nuclear crisis" as the reason for the current downgrading.[89]

In the stock markets, shares of Korean companies already had been subject to stop-loss selling due to apprehension about the North Korean nuclear issue, the rise of anti-Americanism, and the possibility of a U.S. military attack on North Korea. The stock markets became jittery, especially toward the end of 2002, when Donald Rumsfeld referred to possible simultaneous wars with Iraq and North Korea, and they became even more jittery when, on January 10, 2003, North Korea announced its withdrawal from the Nuclear Non-Proliferation Treaty. (At the end of the first quarter of 2003, U.S. investment in South Korea had declined by 70 percent since the previous year.)[90] The memory that the Asian economic crisis of 1997–98 had wiped away all of the Kim Young-sam government's achievements was still fresh in people's minds.

In April 2003, the Roh government sent to the United States a delegation headed by Kim Jin-pyo, deputy prime minister and minister of finance and economy, who was accompanied by Ban Ki-moon, foreign policy adviser to the president, and Cha Young-koo, assistant minister of defense. On Wall Street, the delegation met Robert Rubin, former secretary of the treasury, and John Thain, president and CEO of Goldman Sachs, as well as the heads of credit-rating agencies, including Moody's and Standard & Poor's, to explain the current situation in South Korea and future prospects for the country. Hoping to relieve their concerns regarding the North Korean nuclear issue, Cha Young-koo declared,

"North Korea does not want to possess nuclear weapons; it just hopes to use that issue as a tool for economic negotiations with the United States."[91] Kim Jin-pyo addressed 300 Wall Street analysts, emphasizing that "what matters most for easing tensions with North Korea is a continuation of the solid alliance between the United States and Korea" and adding that "our government's decision to send troops to Iraq is a tangible demonstration that our commitment to the alliance matches words with deeds."[92] South Korea had just decided to dispatch 700 military personnel, including medical personnel, to Iraq.

Ban Ki-moon went to Washington to visit the White House and to the Department of State to request help in restoring South Korea's image and creditworthiness. In short, Ban was asking the U.S. government to assure Moody's that there would be no war.[93] After talking with Ban and getting clearance from the White House legal counsel, the White House's director of East Asian affairs, Michael Green, contacted Moody's. Moody's explained to Green that investors' trust in South Korea had been damaged by the unpredictability of North Korea's behavior and investors' belief that the U.S.-ROK alliance was at an end.[94]

ROH MOO-HYUN MEETS LINCOLN

South Korea's relations with the United States was the biggest foreign policy challenge that the Roh Moo-hyun government had to face. How should it distance itself from the anti-American rhetoric that it had used for its own political advantage, most notably during the presidential campaign in 2002? In early January 2003, Roh announced that "U.S. forces are essential now for the stability of the Korean Peninsula, and they will continue to be essential in the future." When North Korea launched a missile and North Korean fighters attempted to intercept a U.S. military aircraft in February and March of 2003, respectively, the Roh government became more concerned about North Korea.[95]

This renewed realization of the importance of the U.S.-ROK alliance was clearly reflected in Roh's appointment to key foreign and security policy positions of seasoned practitioners who emphasized relations with the United States. Roh appointed Ra Jong-yil as his national security adviser (and executive secretary of Korea's National Security Council), Ban Ki-moon as presidential adviser for foreign affairs, and Kim Hee-sang as adviser to the president regarding national defense.

Ra Jong-yil, who had a Ph.D. from Cambridge University, was a professor at Kyung Hee University. He became involved in policy affairs when he became a member of Kim Dae-jung's brain trust when Kim ran, in vain, for president in 1992. When Kim became president in 1998, Ra was appointed first director of the Korean National Intelligence Service and, subsequently, as ambassador to the United Kingdom. When he was invited to a dinner hosted by Stephen Bosworth, the U.S. ambassador to South Korea, at the ambassador's official residence, Ra took Roh Moo-hyun with him as his guest. That was the first time that Roh entered not only the U.S. ambassador's residence, but also the American world, so to speak. During the dinner, Roh praised Ra, calling Ra his old mentor.[96]

Ban Ki-moon was a career diplomat who had served in various posts, including as director general of the North American Affairs Bureau and as ambassador to Austria. In 2000, he was appointed as deputy minister for foreign affairs and trade. During the first North Korean nuclear crisis in 1993–94, Ban was a minister-counselor in Washington working to coordinate the ROK's policies toward North Korea with those of the U.S. government. He was a veteran diplomat whose knowledge and insight regarding the United States was formidable.[97]

Kim Hee-sang was a lieutenant general in the Korean Army Reserve. Being a professional soldier, Kim served as deputy commander of the First Army before he became president of the Korea National Defense University in 2000. Kim subsequently joined the Rand Corporation in the United States and had just returned to South Korea toward the end of 2002.

All three had studied in either the United States or the United Kingdom, and Ban and Kim had previously worked in the Blue House. All three were regarded as moderates. Of the three, both Ban and Kim, particularly Kim, might have been closer to the position of the conservatives. Kim had openly criticized the sunshine policy of the Kim Dae-jung government. "Sunshine must be shed on the people of North Korea," he declared. "It has shed light only on the North Korean leadership and regime. . . . It is doubtful that the Sunshine Policy has . . . . decreas[ed] tension, deterred war, and reduce[ed] heavy conventional military forces."[98]

In April 2003, President Roh appointed as ambassador to the United States Han Sung-joo, a professor at Korea University, who had served as foreign minister in the Kim Young-sam government. If there really was a political class such as the one that James Kelly called the "Seoul establishment," Han Sung-joo, an outstanding intellectual with intimate knowledge of the United States, was most representative of that class. Although people around Roh were not comfortable with the president's choice and some adamantly opposed the appointment, Roh persisted.

In fact, Roh was entirely preoccupied with how to make his first visit to the United States a success. The last trip, by his predecessor, Kim Dae-jung, in March 2001 turned out to be a miserable failure, and it was harshly criticized in the South Korean media. In order not to repeat that mistake, Roh had to build a personal relationship with President Bush; the question was how best to do it. It so happened then that President Bush's father, former president George H. W. Bush, visited Seoul. Roh invited the senior Bush to a dinner that was also attended by Thomas Hubbard, the U.S. ambassador to South Korea; Lee Kun-hee, chairman and CEO of the Samsung Group; and Ra Jong-yil. Throughout the dinner, Roh enthusiastically asked for tips to building a personal relationship with President Bush. The senior Bush advised Roh that it was "best to be frank and candid. He likes unpretentious exchanges."[99] Thomas Hubbard, who witnessed the exchange, later remarked, with an ironic smile, "It was sort of an odd vision of a former president briefing the Korean president on how to deal with his son, the current president."[100]

On May 13, 2003, Roh Moo-hyun visited Washington. It was his first visit to the United States. Roh was a fan of Abraham Lincoln, and on the day of his arrival, Roh visited the Lincoln Memorial. When he ran for the presidency in 2001, Roh published a book titled *Roh Moo-hyun Meets Lincoln* in Korean. When Roh failed to win in the April 2000 general election, he recalled reading Lincoln's second inaugural address:

> How can I describe the thrilling inspiration that I felt when I read his speech? At that moment, I had an exciting reunion with Lincoln, like Gandhi who experienced a moment of truth in an icy-cold waiting room after being thrown out of a train by a segregationist, and Paul, who dramatically met with Jesus on a hot and sandy path to Damascus.[101]

Both Lincoln and Roh grew up in poverty and became self-taught lawyers. They both experienced the loss of their seat in the legislature after having been elected to public office. Having experienced hardships similar to those of Lincoln, Roh was inspired by Lincoln's life. In Lincoln's second inaugural speech, he referred to the need for reconciliation between the North and the South, which Roh noted:

> On the verge of his victory in the Civil War, he tried not to mention anything about victory or defeat. He did not brand the South as the enemy, nor divided the North and South with such expressions as "justice and injustice" or "good and evil." He just talked about reconciliation and love. . . . Both read the same Bible and pray to the same God.[102]

Roh himself must have been referring to North and South Korea.

It should be noted, however, that Roh has been criticized for taking Lincoln's words and deeds out of their original context and using them to suit his own needs and interests, thereby exploiting his "encounter with Lincoln" for political advantage. When some time later he was asked about human rights issues in North Korea, Roh again turned to Lincoln for his answer:

> I do understand that President Lincoln was quite slow in liberating the slaves in the United States. And this was because the President, if he took the lead in this issue, he thought that America would be divided in opinion, and this would be very serious. . . . President Lincoln's first priority was unity among the states of America. . . . I think that this is quite similar to

the position that we are taking when it comes to North Korean human rights issues.[103]

Prior to the summit with President Bush, Roh was interviewed by the *New York Times*. In the interview he admitted that his earlier signing of a declaration calling for the removal of American troops from the Korean Peninsula was a mistake.[104] The Roh-Bush U.S.–South Korea summit took place on May 14, 2003. Roh's presentation focused solely on how to dissuade the United States from engaging in a military attack on North Korea, and as he talked he occasionally referred to a thick briefing book that he held in his hands. After letting Roh talk for quite some time, Bush said that the United States was not considering a military attack on North Korea. "Then my book is all wrong," Roh replied, pushing it away. Subsequently, the talk became a free exchange of views.[105]

Prior to the summit, however, the drafting of a joint statement by the two nations ran into rough water. The U.S. side said that "All options are on the table" should be inserted in the statement, clarifying that "all options" included military action. Robert Joseph of the White House strongly demanded inclusion of that wording. James Moriarty and Michael Green agreed that it was appropriate to put strong pressure on North Korea, and together they negotiated with the South Koreans in order to get the sentence inserted.[106]

However, the South Koreans opposed including the phrase, which they thought would provoke North Korea. The South Koreans tried to convince the U.S. side that "it would be wise to stay away from extreme wording in order to make North Korea and the Northeast Asian environment more predictable." But the U.S. side would not give in, insisting that "the president will not compromise on this point." The South Koreans also refused to give an inch. "Our president will not accept the military option, no matter what," they declared, because "accepting this phrase would shake to its foundation the peaceful solution approach that the Roh government has taken from the very beginning."[107]

Drafting of the joint statement was carried out in Washington by members of the White House staff and of South Korea's Ministry of Foreign Affairs and Trade. During the process, the South Korean embassy informed the drafting team, "This is a serious matter. A group of Taliban is coming from the Blue House." One of the Taliban thus joined the drafting team, maintaining an uncompromising stand against any wording that implied "military option." Then the embassy relayed the information that the matter was getting even more serious: "A big shot Taliban is coming."[108] That turned out to be Suh Joo-seok, director of the Strategic Planning Staff of Korea's National Security Council. Suh was the right-hand man of Lee Jong-seok, deputy secretary of the KNSC.

In the end, the two sides agreed on the following wording: "While noting that increased threats to peace and stability on the peninsula would require consideration of further steps, they expressed confidence that a peaceful resolution can be achieved."[109] That implied, albeit indirectly, that a military solution would not be pursued. The term "further steps" was a much less provocative expression than "tougher measures," which was included in the joint statement of the U.S.-Japan summit that took place nine days after the U.S.–South Korea summit.

The South Koreans made a big fuss about their diplomatic triumph in excluding the military option, but on the U.S. side it was said that no one was serious about the military option. Looking back, one senior U.S. administration official remarked, "Everyone at the Blue House, including Roh, simply assumed that the United States would take military action against North Korea. The staff people at the Blue House must have planted this idea in Roh's mind."[110]

The joint statement also said that "[Bush and Roh] welcomed the role played by China at the April 23–25 trilateral talks in Beijing" and emphasized that "they agreed that the Republic of Korea and Japan are essential for a successful and comprehensive settlement."[111] The trilateral talks were held toward the end of April among the United States, China, and North Korea in an attempt to settle the North Korean nuclear issue. Criticism had erupted in South Korea against a multilateral approach to a Korean Peninsula issue that did not include South Korea. Roh himself was of the view that the North Korean nuclear issue should be settled pragmatically through bilateral negotiations between the United States and North Korea and should not be unnecessarily multilateralized. Therefore, when the trilateral consultation began to take form, he took the position that South Korea did not have to participate.[112]

However, Foreign Minister Yoon Young-kwan was of the opinion that South Korea must participate. When he met Secretary of State Powell in Washington toward the end of March 2003, Yoon, while appreciating the importance of the trilateral scheme, expressed concern about the exclusion of South Korea.[113] Powell responded, "Under ordinary circumstances, it should be a five-country consultation including Japan and South Korea. However, when China says it can host only a trilateral consultation at this time, we must respect that. But if Japan and South Korea oppose this formula, we will not pursue it any longer." Although Powell had agreed that the first consultation would be a trilateral affair, Yoon understood that he would not agree with a scheme that excluded Japan and South Korea in any future consultations. After Yoon came back from Washington, he had to face strong criticism at the National Assembly for allowing a trilateral consultation without South Korea's participation. But because the content of the Powell-Yoon talk was a diplomatic secret, he could not disclose it at the National Assembly.[114]

CHAPTER SEVEN

South Korea as Balancer?

Bush was in high spirits. The United States had attacked Iraq in March, occupied Baghdad in April, and declared victory in May. Once the occupation of Iraq started, however, a series of problems erupted. The United States alone could not maintain stability or even public order in Iraq, and therefore the reconstruction of Iraq could not proceed as planned. International cooperation became indispensable, and in response, the Roh Moo-hyun government dispatched some 700 medical corps personnel to Iraq. But because public order deteriorated further over the summer of 2003, the U.S. government began to request its allies and other friendly nations to dispatch troops to Iraq or reinforce troops already there. The United States stressed in particular that it would appreciate receiving troops that could accomplish a mission self-sufficiently.[1]

South Korea also was asked to send reinforcements. Roh Moo-hyun was not enthusiastic about the idea. Even when the dispatch of the medical corps was decided at the National Assembly, he implied in his speech that South Korea should put priority on maintaining the U.S.–South Korean alliance instead of on maintaining the moral high ground, thereby displeasing the Bush administration.[2] It was as if Roh was saying that Bush had gone to war for the wrong cause.

But South Korea could not ignore a strong request from the United States. Although the Blue House was reluctant to comply, it hoped that, at least, South Korea's dispatch of troops to Iraq would lead to a more flexible policy toward North Korea on the part of the United States.

It so happened that Foreign Minister Yoon Young-kwan was going to New York for a meeting of the UN General Assembly in the autumn, and the Roh government hoped that Yoon could meet Powell at that time and persuade the United States to reciprocate as desired by South Korea. If the United States would take a more flexible stance in the six-party talks on the North Korean nuclear issue, which had begun that August, South Korea would send reinforcements. It was, so to speak, a conditional offer.[3] Yoon had just met Powell in Washington in early September. Powell as well as Condoleezza Rice was favorably disposed toward Yoon, who impressed both as an earnest and reliable gentleman; Powell even took Yoon to the White House for a twenty-minute talk with President Bush. Bush was in a good mood, and his first words were "How is my friend doing?" It was the first time in a decade that a South Korean foreign minister had met with a U.S. president at the White House, the previous time being when Foreign Minister Han Sung-joo met with President Clinton in 1993.[4]

When South Korea requested a meeting between Powell and Yoon in New York, the United States was perplexed, because the two had met just a few weeks before. To begin with, the U.S. secretary of state was extremely busy during the U.N. General Assembly meeting. Nevertheless, a meeting was set for September 26. When the two got together, Yoon handed to Powell a book, *Crisis on the Korean Peninsula*, that Yoon had read aboard the airplane to New York. The coauthors were senior fellows at the Brookings Institution, an independent think tank in Washington, and they were critical of the Bush administration's North Korean policy.[5] Handing the book to Powell, Yoon said:

> I read this book. The North Korean nuclear issue is a comprehensive issue in which all other elements are intermingled, including economic, diplomatic, and military dimensions. It is difficult to single out the nuclear issue and to resolve it separately. I find that this book explains this point quite well.

While Powell looked a little displeased, Yoon continued to say, as if reading a memo:[6]

> President Roh has been facing a difficult political situation . . . [H]e has been facing strong opposition [to dispatching troops to Iraq] from his own constituents . . . [I]t might be easier for him to pursue a policy of cooperation with the United States in terms of Iraq if the United States can take some measures that can be regarded by the Korean people as a kind of change to a more-flexible attitude than before.[7]

As he listened, Powell's expression hardened, and he curtly told Yoon, "This is not how allies deal with each other."[8]

The talk thus came to an awkward ending. Powell was not pleased; moreover, he suspected that "Operation Linkage," Yoon's proposal to link the dispatch of South Korean troops to Iraq with the U.S. stance toward North Korea, might be Yoon's own idea.[9] But Powell guessed wrong. Yoon was only implementing President Roh's directive to try to persuade the United States to soften its policy toward North Korea, using the troop dispatch to Iraq as leverage.

In a press conference with journalists from Busan and other southern Korean cities on September 26, the same day that Yoon Young-kwan departed for the United States, Roh Moo-hyun had said that "under uncertain circumstances, such as the crisis that loomed in January due to North Korea's nuclear ambitions, it will be difficult to convince the people that an unconditional dispatch of our troops to Iraq is justified." He added that if more troops were to be sent, there should be "something predictable about the Korean Peninsula's stability, indicated, for example, by how the United States and North Korea will enter the six-way talks concerning the North Korean nuclear problem." His intention was obviously to link South Korea's dispatch of troops to Iraq with U.S. policy toward North Korea.[10] At the time, as Roh's presidential aide Yoo Ihn-tae later said, "Everyone in the Blue House, including President Roh and myself, coupled these two issues."[11]

In contrast, Yoon Young-kwan himself was highly skeptical of "Operation Linkage." He firmly believed that an alliance should be based on trust and shared values such as freedom and democracy. "If we can build a trust relationship in that way," Yoon thought, "probably we can ask for help on this issue or that issue . . . rather freely." He did not believe that the relationship should be one in which each request was bargained for individually, but as long as that was the directive of the president, it had to be carried out.[12] So although the top leadership of the Ministry of Foreign Affairs and Trade, including Yoon, remained negative about "Operation Linkage," the Blue House, particularly the secretariat of Korea's National Security Council (KNSC), pressed ahead forcefully, citing the "presidential directive." The Foreign Ministry therefore asked the Blue House to develop talking points, on which Yoon's presentation in New York was based.

A few days after the Yoon-Powell talk, the Roh government obtained information that top leaders of the Bush government, starting with Powell, were angry about South Korea's Iraq–North Korea proposal. Accordingly, the Blue House acted to distance itself from the issue. The Blue House spokesman told the press, "President Roh will not tie one thing to the other as a package deal . . . [T]he deployment issue will be handled separately from the relocation plan for U.S. bases here or the U.S. stance on North Korea's nuclear program."[13] The Blue House insisted that the message itself was appropriate and that it was Yoon's presentation that was problematic. That assertion was followed by an accusation concerning the supposedly poor quality of the English translation of the talking points. In response, the official in charge at the Foreign Ministry examined the translation, comparing it word for word with the original, but found no short-comings. Eventually, the Blue House complacently admitted, "We did say 'glue them together,' thinking of light glue. We never imagined that Yoon would use industrial-strength glue instead."[14]

Yoon, however, did make one miscalculation, which was to present Powell with the book *Crisis on the Korean Peninsula*. Powell later recalled, with a wry smile, the exchange with Yoon:

> He tries this, 'Here, why don't you read this book by Mr. O'Hanlon,' and they [South Korean officials] start linking things. And I said no . . . I didn't even sense it was an approach from his government as opposed to his personal approach . . . it just came at the wrong time in the wrong way.[15]

At the time, South Korean defense authorities were considering dispatching a minimum of 5,000 troops and a maximum of 12,000 troops to Iraq as reinforcements. The ideal was about 7,000 soldiers; in the Blue House, too, defense policy adviser Kim Hee-sang insisted on 7,000 soldiers.[16] Although ordinarily there are approximately 10,000 troops in a light-infantry brigade, 7,000 was deemed a sufficient number if South Korea would dispatch an artillery brigade, a tank brigade, and some other heavy combat troops. South Korea's Defense Ministry had originally envisioned dispatching only ordinary combat troops.

Yoon Young-kwan, Ra Jong-il, and Ban Ki-moon turned out to be the key players in the debate. Yoon offered President Roh the following advice:

—It is important to cooperate with the U.S. government when it requires our help, although it might be politically difficult domestically. That will further strengthen U.S.–South Korean relations. That is in our national interest.

—At the time of the Korean War, we benefited greatly from foreign assistance, including that of the United States and some other Western countries. It is time for us to repay the favor.[17]

In advocating reinforcements at the KNSC meeting, Yoon was joined by Ra Jong-yil and Ban Ki-moon. In contrast, a more cautious argument was advocated by Unification Minister Jeong Se-hyun in the cabinet and by Yoo Ihn-tae of the Blue House staff. They argued:

—Because the legitimacy of the Iraq War itself was highly questionable, it would be difficult to justify the dispatch of Korean troops to join in that war.

—Dispatching troops would make the president's domestic political position very difficult.

Lee Jong-seok remained silent on the issue, listening attentively to what the others had to say. President Roh, who usually preached his views with enthusiasm, remained uncharacteristically silent.[18] Nevertheless, even the more cautious elements were, as Yoo put it, "not opposed to the dispatch. Everyone knew that South Korea had to dispatch more troops sooner or later."[19] Roh himself also was aware of the need to dispatch more troops.

At the same time, the Blue House was urged to smooth relations with the U.S. administration, whose attitude had hardened after Yoon's Iraq–North Korea proposal. Accordingly, the Blue House sent Ra Jong-yil, the president's senior security adviser, to Washington to explain the circumstances surrounding the linkage proposition.[20] In addition, Ra entrusted to Condoleezza Rice a personal letter from President Roh to President Bush, in which Roh wrote that "Seoul, despite its difficult circumstances, is seriously considering the U.S. request that we send more troops to Iraq."[21]

THE DECISION TO SEND MORE TROOPS

Meanwhile, voices opposing the second dispatch of troops to Iraq were becoming increasingly loud throughout South Korea. On October 17, 2003, President Roh met representatives of South Korean NGOs to discuss the issue. In the course of the meeting, Roh said that he would "take extreme caution in deciding whether to send troops to Iraq" and that he would "respect public opinion."[22] The following morning, October 18, Roh announced his troop dispatch plan. The announcement, however, did not include any important details, such as the scale, mission, location, and timing of the dispatch. The South Korean government also decided to provide an additional US$200 million in free assistance for the rehabilitation of Iraq over the 2004–07 period. Behind that decision were two considerations: the adoption on October 16 of a new resolution by the UN Security Council to dispatch multilateral forces to Iraq and the upcoming U.S.–South Korea summit, which was scheduled for October 20 during the APEC Summit in Bangkok.

On the day of the announcement, Roh flew to Bangkok for the APEC summit. Students and NGO activists staged rallies to protest the troop dispatch.[23] Almost without exception, the people who opposed the dispatch had voted for Roh in the presidential election, and to them, Roh's decision to dispatch more troops to Iraq was a betrayal.[24]

On October 20, during his talk with President Roh in Bangkok, President Bush praised Roh's decision and said, "ROK's dispatch of troops to Iraq will . . . serve as an opportunity to increase South Korea's prestige in the international community."[25] When Roh asked for Bush's opinion on the mission and the scale of the South Korean reinforcements, Bush simply replied, "The more you can dispatch, the more appreciative we will be."[26] In the course of their discussion, Bush announced that the United States would consider offering an assurance of security to North Korea, the first explicit sign of flexibility that the United States had shown on this issue. Behind his remark was Powell's personal effort to persuade Bush to concede.[27] Although the U.S. government had expressed displeasure at South Korea's attempt to link its troop dispatch with U.S. North Korea policy, a proposal that the Bush administration had denounced as "absurd," a senior White House official later said that "in the end, the South Korean troop dispatch and the U.S. response to North Korea became linked."[28]

Once the South Korean government decided to dispatch more troops to Iraq, it had to determine the scale, role, and mission; specific destination; and timing of the dispatch. Although the United States had not specified a particular number of reinforcements, it attempted to convey its preference through various channels. The U.S. government was highly encouraged by the Turkish government's announcement in early October that its cabinet had decided to dispatch 10,000 troops, which would be the third-largest contingent in Iraq, exceeded only by U.S. and U.K. forces. The United States therefore implied to South Korea that the dispatch of something between 3,000 and 5,000 troops was expected, but then Turkey canceled its dispatch due to strong domestic opposition. Discouraged and frustrated, the U.S. government raised its expectations of South Korea all the more.

South Korea wanted to find out what the Bush administration's true wishes were. In early November, it dispatched Deputy Foreign Minister Lee Soo-hyuk, Assistant Deputy Defense Minister Cha Young-koo, and Suh Joo-seok, director of strategic planning at KNSC, to Washington. Some senior officials of the Ministry of National Defense had hinted to the United States that South Korea was prepared to dispatch a formidable number of combat troops to Iraq, and the Blue House was apprehensive that their personal views might be misinterpreted as the government's official decision. It therefore was decided to send a tripartite team of representatives from the Blue House, the Ministry of Foreign Affairs and Trade, and the Ministry of National Defense to make explicit South Korea's intentions with regard to not only the number of troops to be dispatched but also the role and mission of the troops.

The Blue House was highly distrustful of the Ministry of National Defense, which, in the eyes of the Blue House, had blindly followed instructions from the Pentagon. Accordingly, the Blue House sent Lee Soo-hyuk, who had served as a South Korean representative at the six-party talks and was believed to be on the same wavelength as the president, and Lee Jong-seok as central members of the delegation; Suh Joo-seok was sent as "watchman," as a Pentagon official put it.[29] During the talks, Suh Joo-seok never said a word.

The delegation had meetings with senior staff at the White House, the Department of Defense, and the Department of State, one after another. At the White House meeting, Stephen Hadley praised South Korea's troops as being as good as North Atlantic Treaty Organization (NATO) troops and hinted that the U.S. expected a contribution from South Korea that was comparable to that of NATO.[30] In the meeting at the Department of Defense, Deputy Under Secretary Richard Lawless followed up by saying, "We are asking none other than South Korea. We would like you to be prepared to dispatch a division." In response, Lee Soo-hyuk, emphasizing the strategic significance of South Korea's dispatch of its forces to Iraq, proposed sending 500 to 1,000 troops, which a senior U.S.

administration official later called "such a small figure that we thought we had misheard Lee."[31]

The U.S. was puzzled. In close cooperation with South Korea's Ministry of National Defense, the U.S. Central Command as well as the Pentagon had already estimated the level of South Korea's reinforcements. Given their estimate, the United States had hoped that South Korea would dispatch a brigade of 5,000 to 7,000 troops, if not a full division of 10,000 to 15,000 troops.[32]

The United States had been informed by South Korea's Ministry of National Defense that Lee Soo-hyuk might deliberately suggest an extremely small number in the hope of buying the United States' favor at a bargain rate and thereby pleasing President Roh.[33] At every meeting, Lee Soo-hyuk tried to find out the "bare minimum" of reinforcements that would satisfy the United States; he even pursued the question in the corridors after the meetings were over. But he got nothing but obscure answers.[34]

However, the United States gave South Korea a variety of hints, mentioning the "Polish dispatch model" and "at least a brigade, and as much as a division."[35] The Polish dispatch model was a combat force on the scale of a division that could defend itself without the help of other forces. The Polish division was a multilateral force composed of 2,500 to 3,000 Polish Army soldiers and 5,000 to 8,000 soldiers from eighteen other countries, under the command of a Polish two-star general. Normally, a military division consists of 10,000 to 12,000 troops, but in South Korea it can range from 3,000 to 12,000 troops. Typically, a mobilized division is commanded by a brigadier general (one star), while a regular division is commanded by a major general (two stars).[36]

Next to be decided was whether South Korea should dispatch combat troops or a noncombatant force. After the Roh government made the decision to dispatch reinforcements, the opposition shifted its target to the dispatch of *combat* troops. That was the target of not only the NGOs but also the ruling party (Uri Party) as well as some staff members of the Blue House, some of whom reportedly threatened to resign if combat troops were dispatched.[37] Although the United States preferred that South Korea dispatch combat forces, Lee Jong-seok tried to lead the public to approve the dispatch of noncombatant troops, stressing that South Korea would dispatch troops not to stabilize the region but to contribute to peace and reconstruction.[38]

South Korea also had to decide where in Iraq to send its reinforcements. Because the United States had been forced to redeploy its 101st Airborne Division, which had been stationed in Mosul, it hoped that the vacuum would be filled by South Korean troops, and South Korea initially decided to send its troops there.[39] However, learning that Mosul might become a combat zone, South Korea changed the destination to Irbil, Kurdistan, in northern Iraq.

On November 11, Roh Moo-hyun himself convened a meeting of the standing committee of Korea's National Security Council in order to review the report of the second survey mission that it had dispatched to Iraq and to exchange views concerning the dispatch of reinforcements. The committee decided that the role of South Korea's troops would be to assist in the reconstruction of Iraq, not to maintain peace and order, which would have required combat troops. During the meeting, Defense Minister Cho Young-kil said that "it would be appropriate to dispatch 3,000 troops," but his voice was so soft that no one heard him. When Cho repeated "3,000 troops," Roh asked, "Is that enough? Are you sure?" Cho assured Roh that is was, and Roh looked relieved and pleased.[40] The committee decided that South Korea would send a 3,000-strong division, commanded by a major general.[41] After the meeting, the Blue House announced that Roh Moo-hyun had presented the KNSC standing committee with guidelines for the dispatch, including the stipulation that the number of additional Korean troops to be dispatched to Iraq should not exceed 3,000 and that the foremost task of the Korean unit was to help with reconstruction efforts in Iraq; maintaining security would be the responsibility of the Iraqi police and military. It was also announced that "these instructions were given based on the results of the recent consultations between Korea and U.S. in Washington."[42]

Immediately following the announcement, U.S. Secretary of Defense Donald Rumsfeld visited Seoul to meet with Defense Minister Cho Young-kil during the thirty-fifth ROK-U.S. Security Consultative Meeting (SCM). The joint communiqué issued after the meeting stated that "Secretary Rumsfeld expressed his appreciation for President Roh Moo-hyun's decision to provide additional forces in Iraq and $260 million in Iraq reconstruction funds from 2003 to 2007."[43] But in fact Rumsfeld was very disappointed. He complained to General Leon LaPorte, commander of the U.S. forces in South Korea, "How can South Korea just send 3,000?" LaPorte answered, "Even 3,000 is [a] very hard decision for South Korea."[44]

From the beginning of the conflict over reinforcements, Lee Jong-seok found it inevitable that South Korea would have to dispatch additional forces. Nevertheless, he wanted South Korea to send no more than the minimum number of troops that would be acceptable to the United States, and he came up with the number 3,000. A senior Blue House official revealed that that was the figure that Lee had in mind when the Roh government decided on October 18 to send reinforcements to Iraq, but the same official added that "that was Lee's personal opinion. President Roh had not yet decided on the number of troops to be dispatched at that time."[45]

As explained earlier, in the South Korean military system, 3,000 troops is the equivalent of a mobilized division. In fact, that was one of the numbers that the Ministry of National Defense had originally considered. It should be noted, however, that the 3,000 troops being considered by the Ministry of National Defense were "3,000 heavily armed, self-reliant troops." Lee's proposition called for 3,000 lightly armed, noncombatant troops. But it also was decided to appoint a two-star general—a person one rank higher than a brigadier general, who normally commands a reserve mobilized division—as the commander of the noncombatant troops, giving the reinforcements the appearance of a regular division. Lee Jong-seok later said:

> Some in the U.S. administration were not too happy that we specified the mission and the role of reinforcements to reconstruction of the peace. But ten days later, the U.S. government formally welcomed the South Korean government decision and expressed its gratitude.[46]

Although it was true that the United States expressed its appreciation of South Korea's decision, it did so as if it was swallowing something that was not to its liking. It could have been irritation at the delay of the decision and the dispatch rather than the mission of the reinforcements. It was one year after the announcement, in the period from September through November 2004, that the South Korean troops actually departed for Iraq.

YOON YOUNG-KWAN RESIGNS

The greatest political challenge that Roh had faced since he became president was having to decide whether to dispatch troops to Iraq. Although he made his decision, it was not cost free.

Toward the end of 2003, Roh made several grumbling comments about his foreign and security affairs team. He said, loudly enough to suggest that he wished to be heard, that Foreign Minister Yoon was too focused on maintaining good relations with the United States. At the same time, he was heard to remark that "no ministry can do such a job in place of the National Security Council."[47] It was obvious that Roh was actually praising the KNSC's deputy secretary general, Lee Jong-seok, which could be interpreted as criticizing Yoon and the Ministry of Foreign Affairs and Trade.

On Christmas Eve 2003, the director of a Foreign Ministry division concerned with U.S. relations, perhaps under the influence of a few drinks, was overheard criticizing the Roh government. "This government has been dominated by the immature Blue House Taliban," he reportedly said. "Thanks to them, our foreign policy is a mess."[48] That remark was written down and leaked to the Blue House, whereupon the Blue House leadership became furious. From the very start, the progressive elements that entered the Blue House at the start of the Roh government, including the "386 Generation," had a tendency to look down on the diplomats who traditionally had attended to policies toward the United States as shady, pro-American fellows. The Blue House and the Foreign Ministry had differing opinions on all matters, from the dispatch of troops to Iraq to relocating the U.S. military base in Yongsan. It was even reported that seventeen Foreign Ministry officials, including directors general, had been targeted for review by the Blue House.

The situation was complicated even further by internal feuding within the Foreign Ministry. There had been a conflict between the North American Affairs Bureau and the Treaties Bureau over the issue of the relocation of the U.S. military base in Yongsan. While both bureaus agreed that the relocation of U.S. bases had to be ratified by the National Assembly, it was more a matter of national pride and self-respect to the Treaties Bureau. In particular, Lee Jong-hun, the director of the Treaty Division of the Treaties Bureau, who became a representative *nosamo* ("People who love Roh") diplomat within the Foreign Ministry, strongly insisted on the need for ratification.[49]

On January 14, 2004, Roh Moo-hyun announced in a press conference that opponents of government policies had leaked intelligence information, pointing a finger at the Foreign Ministry. The very next day, Yoon Young-kwan tendered his resignation, which Roh accepted. In his farewell speech to the senior members of the Foreign Ministry, Yoon made discreet criticisms of President Roh Moo-hyun's aides, who Yoon said had tried to steer the country on a nationalist, independent course. "Korea does not exist in an international vacuum," he said. "It exists in relation to other countries, and our national interest must be found in this reality.... Some in the government, as well as the people and opinion leaders, do not seem to recognize this."[50] Finally, Yoon told the members of his audience to remain strong: "I hope you will undertake diplomacy like the bamboo tree, never breaking even in the middle of a raging storm."[51]

Although, on the record, Yoon resigned, taking responsibility for deficient supervision and control of the Foreign Ministry, his resignation was reported by the media as a de facto dismissal. One senior government official who was in the Blue House at the time later disclosed what happened:

> Believing the Foreign Ministry to be a stubborn and conservative bureaucracy, President Roh must have wanted to introduce a new breeze in the ministry. That was why he appointed Yoon as Minister for Foreign Affairs and Trade. But the handling of the troop dispatch to Iraq might have given Roh the impression that Yoon would not be able to change the Foreign Ministry that much. This might be a case of going native. That must be why Roh wanted to replace Yoon.[52]

In his brief farewell speech, Yoon criticized those who "try to steer the country on a nationalist diplomatic course," which was interpreted as criticism of Lee Jong-seok, who had advocated a self-reliant approach to national defense. Yoon, in contrast, advocated pursuit of the national interest in an international context. He denounced adopting a stiff foreign policy stance, emphasizing that to stress only self-reliance and independence in an age of rapid globalization was an anachronism, a holdover from the days when South Korea had been paranoid due to constant pressure from abroad. Yoon believed that South Korean foreign policy had to graduate from that orientation, which was "held by some at the NSC."[53]

Rather than being differences in approach to specific policies, the differences between Yoon and Lee on foreign affairs were rooted in their fundamentally different world views. It should be noted, however, that some observers attributed Yoon's dismissal to his professorial attitude toward the president, in addition to such problems as doubts about his administrative capabilities and differences in policies and philosophies.

RELOCATION, TRANSFER, REDUCTION

Immediately after taking office, the Roh government had to face the second North Korean nuclear crisis and the Iraq war, two incidents that forced both the United States and South Korea to confront the difficult issue of relocating some of the U.S. forces stationed in South Korea.

In April 2003, the two governments launched the Future of the ROK-U.S. Alliance Policy Initiative (FOTA) to study the restructuring of U.S. bases in South Korea. Following discussions, it was agreed that Yongsan Garrison, a U.S. military base in Seoul, would be moved elsewhere. In Japan, 70 percent of the U.S. military bases are concentrated in Okinawa, far from the capital, Tokyo, but the U.S. military bases in South Korea are concentrated within and around the capital city of Seoul. Yongsan Garrison has been a symbol of the U.S. military presence in South Korea. To the north stands Namsan, to the south of which runs the Han River—a sought-after "mountain at the back, facing water" location, according to *feng shui.*

Yongsan, located in the center of Seoul, has served as a base for foreign troops for more than 120 years. The first foreign troops stationed there were 3,000 Qing Dynasty soldiers in 1882. In 1904, during the Russo-Japanese War, the Japanese Imperial Army built military barracks in Yongsan, and after the annexation of the Korean Peninsula by Imperial Japan in 1910 it became the site of the Imperial Army Headquarters. After the Republic of Korea gained independence in 1945, 15,000 troops of the 7th Division of the U.S. Army took over the Japanese barracks, and in time the site developed into the headquarters of U.S. Forces Korea, the U.S. military forces in South Korea.

President Roh, in his speech on August 15, 2004, commemorating the fifty-ninth anniversary of Liberation Day (the day of national independence in the Republic of Korea), noted that negotiations between South Korea and the United

States over the relocation of the U.S. military garrison in Yongsan had dragged on for more than ten years. He then boasted, "This piece of land in the center of Seoul, which has served as a base for foreign troops for more than 120 years, has finally been returned to Koreans."[54]

Return of the U.S. military base in Yongsan was a matter of deep pride to the Korean people. Nevertheless, in exchange for the return of Yongsan base, the United States proposed relocating the U.S. Army's 2nd Division (12,500 troops), which was stationed along the DMZ. It was suggested that, first, numerous U.S. military bases scattered north of the Han River would be combined into Camp Casey and Camp Red Cloud, and second, that the thus-integrated Second Division would be relocated to south of the Han River.

The restructuring of the U.S. military presence in South Korea was in fact the core of the East Asian Strategic Initiative (EASI) that Secretary of Defense Dick Cheney and Under Secretary of State Paul Wolfowitz had launched pursuant to a congressional request during the George H. W. Bush administration in the early 1990s. The initiative was postponed when the first North Korean nuclear crisis erupted, and what the U.S. proposed to the Roh government was a rehash of the EASI restructuring plan.[55] Nevertheless, for the Roh government it was an abrupt proposal that shook up the Blue House.

Some in the Blue House even suspected that Rumsfeld, by coupling the relocation of the U.S. Army's 2nd Division with the return of the Yongsan military base, might have been attempting to get revenge for the anti-U.S. demonstrations and anti-U.S.-base movement in South Korea by forcing South Korea to bear the cost of relocating the U.S. troops. In addition, the South Korean government was deeply worried that the United States might be planning not only the southward transfer of the 2nd Division but also a simultaneous reduction in forces. It kept receiving information hinting at that possibility from sources close to the U.S. Department of Defense; a remark on February 25, 2003, by Deputy Under Secretary of Defense Richard Lawless was the first such hint. Lawless was visiting South Korea to attend President Roh Moo-hyun's inauguration when he whispered to Ban Ki-moon, foreign policy adviser to the president, that the United States was planning to "transfer and reduce the 2nd Division."[56]

During the dinner with former president George H. W. Bush mentioned in chapter 6, before Roh's first trip to the United States in 2003, Roh complained that his government was bewildered by Defense Secretary Rumsfeld's abrupt announcement on March 6 at the Pentagon of the withdrawal from South Korea of a division-scale unit of U.S. forces.[57] Knowing that the withdrawal had been effected single-handedly by the Pentagon without consulting with the White House or the Department of State, Roh, so to speak, told on Rumsfeld. As soon as George W. H. Bush came home, he called his son and told him, "[T]his plan to pull the troops out is really making the Koreans nervous! We've got to be really careful."[58]

Upon receiving his father's phone call, President Bush called Condoleezza Rice to the Oval Office to discuss how to handle the issue, and they agreed that they should not allow Rumsfeld to have his own way. They also agreed that the FOTA needed to be controlled by the White House. In several weeks a meeting was held that included Stephen Hadley, assistant to the president for national security affairs; Douglas Feith, under secretary of defense; and Richard Armitage, deputy secretary of state. At one point, Feith said, "In this modern day of transformation, we don't need large numbers of troops. We can do more with less." Armitage and Hadley, however, pointed out that "Iraq has proven you wrong."[59] In the end, it was agreed that the Pentagon would proceed with the reorganization of the U.S. forces in South Korea in consultation with the White House and the Department of State, and that there would be no unilateral announcement on the issue.

The relocation of the U.S. military bases also was a major topic, along with the North Korean nuclear issue, at the U.S.-ROK summit in May 2003 in Washington. Although Roh asked that the relocation of the 2nd Division be put off until the nuclear issue was settled, Bush did not give Roh a clear answer. He only promised that the United States would pay attention to the implications of relocation for South Korean politics, and he requested that South Korea study the relocation plan carefully.

The joint statement issued after this summit meeting indicates that the two leaders agreed on the following objectives of base relocation:

—To modernize the U.S.-ROK alliance, taking advantage of technology to transform both nations' forces

—To work out plans to consolidate U.S. forces around key hubs and to relocate the Yongsan Garrison at an early date

—To continue expanding the role of the ROK armed forces in defending the Korean Peninsula.[60]

After the end of the cold war, the United States repeatedly attempted to restructure its armed forces in South Korea. However, it always hesitated to do so because of the threat from North Korea, and the South Korean government always discouraged it from doing so.

The U.S. military bases scattered along the DMZ to the north of the Han River in Seoul were highly vulnerable to attack from North Korea if an armed conflict were to break out, a fact that worked to deter both sides from using military force. While the arrangement was called a "trip wire," it in fact made hostages of the U.S. troops stationed there. But because the sunshine policy promoted cooperation and reconciliation between North and South Korea, and because the North-South summit in June 2000 resulted in the psychological warming of South Korea toward North Korea, intimidation from the North diminished. As a result, the attitude of South Koreans toward having U.S. forces on their soil also changed. In addition, South Korea pointed out to the United States that urban growth in the once isolated but now populated areas surrounding the bases was constraining routine training of combat-ready forces—another reason to move away from the DMZ. In particular, the eruption of anti-American sentiment triggered by the death of two middle-school girls in an accident involving U.S. soldiers once again brought home to both South Korean and U.S. authorities the sensitivity of the continued presence of U.S. military forces in Seoul.[61]

To Be Abandoned, To Be Entrapped

Soon after the Roh government took office, it published a paper entitled "Peace, Prosperity, and National Security—A Vision of the Security Policy of a Participatory Government." Its major thrust was that during its time in office, the Roh government would construct the foundation for a "cooperative self-reliant defense" that would give the same weight to self-reliant defense as to the U.S.–South Korea alliance. Behind the new policy initiative were several changes in the circumstances surrounding the Korean Peninsula:

—The U.S. policy toward the Korean Peninsula was becoming unpredictable.

—The South Korean people had become more confident in envisioning and realizing a future for the peninsula.

—It is necessary to prevent North Korea from calling South Korea a puppet of the United States.

The new policy initiative was based on the new conviction that North Korea could be changed and that South Korea could play a major role in effecting the change. It also was based on South Koreans' newly acquired confidence that South Korea was now influential enough to independently prevent war on the peninsula.

In 2004, Lee Jong-seok told high-ranking officials of the Ministry of National Defense that the "main enemy" reference to North Korea was outdated and that, as a matter of policy, it needed to be dropped. The Defense Ministry was strongly opposed to doing so; in fact, a poll taken among army officers and soldiers revealed that 85 percent of them believed that the government should retain the terminology.[62] In the process of scrapping the "main enemy" wording, the Roh government prepared new guidelines concerning the threat from North Korea in which it declared that "North Korea's nuclear development is the gravest threat, while North Korea itself is no longer a threat."[63]

Out went the "main enemy" concept and in came the concept of self-reliant defense. The need to "break from the past," which held special meaning in the Roh government, was seen to apply to foreign, security, and unification policies as well as to domestic issues, and the U.S.–South Korea alliance may also have come to be seen as another part of a despicable past that had to be discarded.

Under the Status-of-Forces Agreement (SOFA), which clarifies the rights and duties of the U.S. military forces in South Korea, South Korea has been treated as if it were a tributary state of the United States. In addition, the United States had monopolized wartime operational control and command authority. The Blue House had been urged to break away from such symbols of the past.

There were external as well as internal pressures for restructuring the U.S. forces, including the following:

—Forward deployment of the U.S. forces along the DMZ with North Korea was outdated. Because North Korea could no longer maintain its traditional military posture and capability due to the economic crisis, it concentrated on creating an "asymmetrical threat" by specializing in long-range anti-aircraft guns, missiles, and special operations forces. In view of the shift, it was not very meaningful to station U.S. troops on the front line.

—Quicker global deployment of the U.S. forces became possible due to the advances of the "Revolution in the Military Affairs" (RMA). It was inefficient to station as many as 37,000 troops in South Korea to defend only that country.

—In order to respond to the rise of nationalist antipathy toward U.S. military bases, something had to be done to reduce their "footprint."[64]

There was one final factor: it became necessary for the United States to redeploy to Iraq and Afghanistan the forces stationed in South Korea. But out of concern over South Korea's possible reaction, it was decided that the transfer would be kept top secret for the time being.

In the summer of 2003, the United States formally notified South Korea that it would transfer the 2nd Division to Iraq, a decision that came as a greater second shock to South Koreans than the announcement of the division's relocation. In the first plan that Rumsfeld presented to the White House, the troops to be stationed in South Korea were to rotate among divisions. Suspecting that the Department of Defense might actually have intended to permanently reduce the U.S. troops stationed in South Korea, which would have an adverse effect on the U.S.–South Korea alliance, officials at the White House conducted hearings with offices other than the Department of Defense. Richard Armitage strongly opposed the abrupt dispatch of the 2nd Division to Iraq, which would result in a permanent reduction in forces in Korea. He feared sending the "wrong signal" to North Korea, but Bush endorsed Rumsfeld's plan. Consequently, Hadley had to contact Ban Ki-moon of the Blue House to explain the administration's intentions. Before he gave Ban the explanation, the United States transferred some of its bombers on the mainland to Guam in order not to give a "wrong signal" to North Korea.[65]

The decision to transfer the 2nd Division to Iraq came almost back-to-back with the U.S. request that South Korea dispatch more troops to Iraq.[66] South Korea could have argued that it had become difficult to dispatch reinforcements to Iraq because its home defense was more vulnerable due to the transfer. However, the Department of Defense and the U.S. military much preferred transferring the battle-ready 2nd Division to Iraq to having South Korea dispatch a South Korean division. If South Korea raised that argument, the United States might say, "Okay. We'd rather have our brigade," and quietly expand the scale of the transfer of the 2nd Division.[67]

When the division was actually transferred to Iraq, both the U.S. and South Korean governments explained that it became possible to transfer the U.S. forces deployed along the DMZ because South Korea itself had strengthened its deterrent ability vis-à-vis North Korea. But that did not eliminate the uneasiness on the part of South Korea.

At the SCM in October 2004, the United States and South Korea agreed that the U.S. forces in South Korea would be reduced from the current 37,000 to 25,000 in 2008. On that occasion, Rumsfeld commented on the proposed transfer of the U.S. troops to overseas duty, saying that the United States was aware of South Korea's apprehension and promising that the U.S. government would give full consideration to South Korea's unique security situation. He also warned that it would be wrong for anyone to interpret the transfer as a manifestation of U.S. weakness. It was obvious that he had North Korea in mind.[68]

Rumsfeld's effort to restructure the U.S. forces in South Korea was based on a number of factors. Besides worship of the so-called Revolution in Military Affairs (RMA), it included an anti-army sentiment and ideological antipathy toward Roh Moo-hyun's liberalism that was actually widely shared in the Pentagon. For quite some time, the suggestion that the U.S.–South Korea alliance should be ranked lower than the U.S.-Japan and U.S.-Australia alliances had been openly discussed in the Pentagon. When the U.S. government conducted a comprehensive review of its East Asia policy in 2003 through the beginning of 2004, the Department of Defense proposed downgrading the U.S.–South Korea alliance by one rank, but it had been overridden by strong opposition from the Department of State, the National Security Council, and the Joint Chiefs of Staff.[69] At the same time, the Department of Defense encouraged South Korea to expand its defense capability. The downgrading of the U.S.–South Korea alliance and the self-sufficiency and expansion of the South Korean military role were flip sides of a coin. Rumsfeld used to say to the South Koreans, "You guys are enablers [of the upgrading or downgrading of the alliance]."[70]

South Korea turned the U.S. position to its own advantage. In October 2005 it requested the transfer of command relations and wartime operations control to the South Korean military. It was a *jujitsu* diplomatic move that took advantage of the opponent's momentum. When South Korea proposed a two-year consultation to draw a roadmap for the transfer of command and control, Rumsfeld made a counter-proposal. "If you want them so much," he asked, "why don't we start the consultation right away?"[71] This time it was Rumsfeld who used the *jujitsu* move.

The joint communiqué issued after the thirty-sixth annual U.S.-ROK Security Consultative Meeting states that "the Minister and the Secretary agreed to appropriately accelerate discussions on command relations and wartime operational control."[72] While the United States wanted to "accelerate" the process, South Korea wished to proceed gradually and "appropriately" and had to force a compromise to add "appropriately" to the joint communiqué. The tug-of-war between "accelerate" and "appropriately" was about the timing of the transfer: South Korea proposed making it effective in 2010; the United States suggested 2009.

Although the Roh government advocated self-reliant national defense, it was more of a slogan than anything; the idea lacked a sound financial and organizational basis. In this instance, a cool-headed, logical calculation of South Korea's position and the national defense capability was overridden by nationalist sentiment and South Korea's political desire to be a full-fledged sovereign state. What was absent in many of the U.S.–South Korean consultations at the time was an approach that encouraged the joint pursuit of military and defense goals and the development of a shared vision of peace, stability, and order on the Korean Peninsula and in Northeast Asia as a whole.

Rumsfeld had been heard to say more than once that "if you don't want U.S. forces stationed in South Korea, we can withdraw immediately."[73] The implied threat left the South Koreans no choice but to bark back, "Please leave then. We can defend ourselves. Incidentally, the American commander will be replaced by a Korean commander." As Rumsfeld continued to repeat his plans for relocating and reducing U.S. forces in a threatening tone, Roh's entourage insisted on self-reliant defense and independence from the United States. As one senior White House official later stated, "Hardliners in the U.S. government and those on the left-wing in South Korea formed strange bedfellows—or unholy bedfellows."[74]

On one hand, some messages that Rumsfeld sent to the Roh government aroused South Koreans' fear of being abandoned:

> Now that South Korea has become so powerful, it should take care of its own national defense. If South Koreans hate the U.S. forces stationed in South Korea so much, we are prepared to withdraw them any time. In particular, the 2nd Division is now needed to enhance stability in Iraq and other parts of the world.

On the other hand, he sent messages that raised the fear of being entrapped:

> If the United States instead of North Korea is seen to impose threats on South Korea, we are ready to remove American soldiers stationed along the DMZ. To begin with, we should not allow this tripwire arrangement, which

de facto makes American soldiers hostages. If we remove the tripwire, it becomes much easier to carry out a preemptive attack on North Korea. If the situation turns around, we can mobilize the force thus relieved to deter any Chinese invasion of Taiwan, too.

As Jonathan Pollack and Mitchell Reiss, both scholars of international relations and experts on nonproliferation (Reiss later became director of the State Department's Policy Planning Staff in the Bush administration), pointed out, the United States "accomplished the seemingly impossible feat of raising Seoul's fears of abandonment and entrapment simultaneously" with Rumsfeld's proposals to restructure U.S. forces in South Korea.[75]

"One or Two Trivial Problems"

The U.S.–South Korea alliance is a coalition for cooperation to counter any possible threat from North Korea. The two countries have shared a military operations plan, Operation Plan 5027, to be implemented if and when North Korea violates the 1953 Korean War Armistice Agreement and attacks South Korea. The armistice was concluded by the commander in chief of the UN Command and the supreme commander of the Korean People's Army (who also commanded the Chinese People's Volunteers), ending the Korean War. U.S. Lieutenant General William K. Harrison, U.S. Army senior delegate of the UN Command delegation, and General Nam Il of the Korean People's Army, signed the agreement.[76] South Korea was not a signatory because its president, Rhee Syngman, opposed the armistice.

It was in July 1950, immediately after the eruption of the Korean War, that command of South Korea's troops was handed to the United States. Rhee Syngman told General Douglas MacArthur, commander of the U.S. troops, that South Korea would give the United States total command of South Korea's troops as long as the military operations continued. In 1994, peacetime command was returned to the South Koreans, while wartime command remains in the hands of the commander of the UN forces stationed in South Korea.[77]

U.S. and South Korean military authorities have also shared a contingency plan that prepares for the collapse of the current North Korean regime; the plan is under the command of the U.S. forces in South Korea. In the latter half of the 1990s, during the Clinton administration, the U.S. military constructed a variety of scenarios that might follow regime collapse in North Korea, in part because of the worsening of the famine there. What should the United States and South Korea do if the North Korean regime were to collapse? What if Kim Jong-il were to be assassinated? What if a general uprising were to erupt all over North Korea? What if armed conflicts were to begin? What if armed conflicts developed into a general civil war? What if massacres were to occur? What role should the UN forces and the South Korean troops play? How could proliferation of North Korean weapons of mass destruction be prevented? What if there was a massive exodus of refugees from North Korea?

In 1999, U.S. and South Korean military authorities drew up an operations plan to respond to the above scenarios and named it Plan 5029-99. A division of labor was agreed on under which the primary role of the U.S. troops would be to restrain North Korean threats and the primary mission of the South Korean troops would be to enter North Korea. When Rumsfeld took over the Department of Defense in the Bush administration, he attempted to revise the plan. "Why can't U.S. forces enter North Korea?" he demanded. "Why wouldn't we go in and try to get rid of the regime? Isn't a good offense the best defense?" North Korea's enhanced WMD capabilities, including nuclear arms, as well as its missile capabilities led to a stronger U.S. inclination toward making a preemptive attack on North Korea or a decisive first strike.[78] National defense authorities in the United States and South Korea agreed to revise Plan 5029-99, which was a CONPLAN (conceptual operation plan), and construct a more detailed plan based on 5029-99.

Toward the end of 2004, the Roh government received a report from the Combined Forces Command (CFC) that it would complete the revised plan, Contingency Operational Plan 5029-05, within 2005. But in January 2005 Korea's National Security Council instructed the CFC to nullify the plan and reported its action to the United States, saying that "the plan could be a serious obstacle to exercising Korea's sovereignty."[79] The Roh government was worried in particular that hasty, unilateral U.S. military action could trigger a full-scale Korean Peninsula war in which South Korea would be entangled.[80]

But from the U.S. perspective, the contingency plan for the Korean Peninsula would directly affect the national interest and security of the United States. At any given time, Korea hosts about 100,000 American civilians, whom the United States would have to evacuate in case of a crisis involving North Korea. The United States also would have to protect its armed forces stationed in South Korea. In addition, it would have to restrain the proliferation of North Korean weapons of mass destruction.[81]

In the process of rejecting the 5029-99, the South Koreans took the following positions:

—They refused to use the phrase "instability of North Korea" in describing the scenario itself, demanding that "instability" be replaced by "situation of sudden change."

—They suggested a division of labor by which the U.S. troops would control the plutonium nuclear facilities in Yongbyon while South Korea would attend to the highly unstable civilian sector.

—They demanded to know why the contingency operation plan had to be changed abruptly from a CONPLAN to an OP-PLAN (operation plan). [82]

The United States was bewildered. Normally, this kind of operation planning would be done between the countries' military authorities; it was not something in which the KNSC, an arm of the Blue House, should intervene. But the KNSC not only rejected the plan but also attempted to negate its very raison d'etre by criticizing it as an "obstacle to exercising sovereignty," which was very strong language. The U.S. Department of Defense became increasingly distrustful of the South Korean government, which seemed "eager to throw eggs at the U.S. face."[83]

The trouble did not stop there. When the issue became politicized by the United States and South Korea, the Blue House claimed that "it became a problem because it was an OP-PLAN. If it is changed to a CONPLAN as it should be, we have no problem." The new South Korean position was conveyed to the United States when Lee Jong-seok visited the United States in late April 2005.[84] In response, the U.S. Department of Defense tried to explain to Lee that both a CONPLAN and an OP-PLAN are plans and that the department had already stopped distinguishing between the two; that an OP-PLAN is inoperative unless further revisions are made; and that plans are just starting points—political leaders decide whether to use them or not. But Lee was not convinced. "If the two are the same plan, why demarcate?" he demanded to know. "Why do they have to have two different names?" He added:

> 5029 is not merely a military issue. Politics and diplomacy are deeply involved in this issue and, therefore, this is not an issue that can be discussed only between the military authorities of the two countries.

Lee insisted that the plan would not be acceptable to South Korea until it was converted into a CONPLAN. Lee seemed to distinguish a CONPLAN, a plan that South Korea was not obliged to implement, from an OP-PLAN, which South Korea would be obliged to carry out, although the United States argued that the two must not be divided along that line. Regarding this exchange, one Pentagon official later said, indignantly:

> The South Koreans are afraid to . . . authorize their side to start planning again, because it would be leaked. And when it is leaked . . . the guys in Pyongyang are going to get angry. That's what they're worried about. . . . It's the politics of North-South discussions.[85]

A White House official found the South Korean position to be "too nationalistic and full of wishful thinking" and found it "highly doubtful [that the plan] is functional as an operation plan."[86]

But South Korea's concerns were not confined to "North-South discussions." The Roh administration had to take all kinds of factors into consideration, including North Korea's reaction and South Korea's sovereignty as well as the possible Chinese response. A senior South Korean government official later emphasized the depth of the issue:

> If the U.S. troops should enter North Korea, China would not remain a silent bystander and it would further complicate the situation. If the United States should intervene in South Korea's leadership role, it would violate South Korea's sovereignty.[87]

This issue is one that South Korea has to tackle as a long-term, strategic challenge pertaining to its harmonious coexistence with China and to the future of the Korean Peninsula.

The most sensitive, hidden point of the argument between the United States and South Korea regarding Plan 5029 concerned the U.S. refusal to allow South Korea to take possession of North Korea's weapons of mass destruction, including nuclear arms, if and when North Korea collapsed. To paraphrase a former official at the Pentagon, the ultimate concern of the United States was to prevent South Korea from obtaining them: "South Korea will claim the North Korean nuclear weapons as 'uri (our)' weapons. So we must tell the South Koreans that we will manage and dispose of those nuclear weapons. Once the South Koreans grab those weapons, they will never let them go."[88] A current Pentagon official, however, offered a different view: "If South Korea were to hang on to the nuclear weapons, neither Japan, the United States, nor China would assist in reconstruction of the former North Korea after it is reunified with the South. Therefore, South Korea will not hold on to the nuclear weapons."[89]

In addition, there was an issue related to strategic flexibility. The United States had a plan to modify the mission of its forces stationed in South Korea from one of ensuring peace and stability on the Korean Peninsula alone to one of ensuring the stability of Northeast Asia as a whole. A former Department of Defense official had the following to say regarding the modification:

> Well, after September 11, things changed. Now, not only has the Army undergone a 'strategic flexibility.' [The 2nd] division, which is now a brigade along the DMZ, can fight anywhere. They could fight the North Koreans. They could fight the Iraqis. They could fight in Africa. The same with the 7th Air Force: The 7th Air Force doesn't have to just fight on the Korean Peninsula. They can fight anywhere. If there is another contingency that U.S. military forces must meet somewhere in Asia, troops could be pulled out of Korea to meet that contingency. If that place is China, South Korea is saying "we don't want that to happen," [but] there

is no way the United States government is ever going to offer them that guarantee.[90]

However, the South Koreans strongly opposed expanding the geographical scope of the mission of the U.S. forces in South Korea from the Korean Peninsula to a larger theater. As a part of the global reorganization of U.S. forces, the United States started preparations to convert its forces in South Korea into a mobile force, evoking North Korea's adamant opposition. South Korea had to take that into consideration.

A much larger concern was relations with China. In case of an international crisis in the Taiwan Strait, the U.S. forces in South Korea might be mobilized. If that were to happen, South Korea likely would become involved in a military conflict between the United States and China. In order to avoid at any cost involvement in any such war, South Korea strongly resisted the U.S. notion of strategic flexibility of the U.S. forces in South Korea. South Korea was more concerned about the reactions of North Korea and China if it were to accept the U.S. proposal than about U.S. displeasure if it were to reject it. Although the defense authorities of the United States and South Korea "once again affirmed the continuing importance of the strategic flexibility of U.S. forces in the ROK," the Blue House was more inclined to restrict their flexibility.[91]

In their June 2005 summit in Washington, President Bush and President Roh discussed the issue of the handling of North Korea's weapons of mass destruction as well as the issue of U.S. unilateral military action in Northeast Asia. Or perhaps it is more accurate to say that Bush brought them up abruptly and Roh responded. Next to Bush were Secretary of State Condoleezza Rice and Defense Secretary Donald Rumsfeld. Originally, Rumsfeld was not going to attend because of other engagements, but he decided to join the group at the last minute. Everyone present sensed that Bush's questions were based on a memorandum that Rumsfeld had submitted to him. Roh made the following comments:

—In case of a crisis in North Korea, easy resort to military actions could ignite an all-out war. It would be only natural for South Korea to take the initial action. Only when it became beyond South Korea's capacity would it request the assistance of the United States. With regard to the handling of North Korea's WMDs, South Korea recognizes the special role that U.S. forces would play.

—As a sovereign nation, South Korea cannot allow foreign troops stationed in its territory to make a unilateral move without its knowledge and, as a consequence, let itself be entangled in a regional conflict, however exceptional the case might be. South Korea retains the right to express its views on this issue. South Korea must be consulted before any action is taken.[92]

In short, South Korea asked to be consulted concerning the transfer of the U.S. forces in South Korea on the principle of strategic flexibility and Bush refrained from pursuing the issue further. After the summit, Bush remarked to Rumsfeld that "Roh was reasonable and he made his point rather well," but Rumsfeld looked dissatisfied.[93] But that did not mean that the two leaders came to any agreement on the two issues. According to one senior U.S. administration official, President Bush and President Roh agreed that they needed "at least [to] have a process whereby [they could] try to close the gaps," but that did not mean that the United States agreed with South Korea's requests.[94]

After the summit, Lee Jong-seok said that "one or two minor disagreements" remained unresolved. What he was referring to were differences in the two nations' stand on Plan 5029 and the U.S. concept of strategic flexibility for its forces.[95] One senior U.S. administration official later remarked:

> The toughest talks I had ever with Lee Jong-seok was on this. "We can take care of it. If we need you, we'll call you." That's what he said. I said "You're gonna need us," and then I listed all the reasons. It was tough.[96]

The United States never made any concessions with regard to strategic flexibility, which enabled the prompt dispatch of its troops, particularly the Army, to anywhere in the world.

Later, Lee Jong-seok was criticized at the National Assembly by a government party member for "promoting pro-American policies without even consulting with the president when documents were received from the U.S. government." That allegation resulted in an investigation of Lee by Roh's close aide, Moon Jae-in, and Unification Minister Chung Dong-young. It was Lee Jong-hun, the "*nosamo*" diplomat, and Kwon Kae-hyun, another "*nosamo*" diplomat and a key player in the campaign against Lee Jong-seok, who leaked the information to ruling party members, reportedly because of Lee's "pro-American" posture. Lee Jong-hun and Kwon Kae-hyun had been criticizing Lee Jong-seok since they were transferred from the Foreign Ministry's Treaties Bureau to the Blue House, after they helped oust Yoon Young-kwan. According to them, "although Lee Jong-seok advocates self-reliance and independence in front of the president, he turns to a pro-American advocate in internal meetings."

Lee Jong-hun was suspended for three months on the charge of violating the rule obliging public servants to keep state secrets. Kwon Kae-hyun also was spotted, as he was with Lee Jong-hun when Lee leaked the information, but Kwon was not punished, because he had left the civil service several months before.[97] Lee Jong-seok denied the accusation, declaring that he had reported each and every development to the president.

The Balancer Controversy

In the spring of 2005, President Roh Moo-hyun started advocating a new concept: that of South Korea as "balancer." For example, in his address on the 86th

March 1st Independence Movement Day, he declared that "we are now beefing up national power, enabling us to play a balancing role in Northeast Asia."[98] Further, in his commencement speech at the Korea Third Military Academy on March 22, Roh said:

> We are more qualified to talk about peace than anyone else [in Northeast Asia]. . . . We should play a balancing role not only on the Korean Peninsula but also for the peace and prosperity of Northeast Asia.[99]

On the same occasion, he added that "the power equation in Northeast Asia will change depending on the choices we make."

The balancer theory was loudly advertised as the Roh Moo-hyun Doctrine. One senior official of South Korea's NSC has explained it as follows:

> The order in which Korea plays one leg of the three-way alliance with the United States and Japan was a product of the Cold War. . . . Korea wants to extract itself from a stand-off centered on the peninsula between a "Southern alliance" of South Korea, the U.S., and Japan . . . and a "Northern alliance" of North Korea, China, and Russia.[100]

The concept of South Korea as the balancer was formulated by Roh's inner-circle advisers, not Korea's NSC. According to one KNSC staff member, "All of a sudden we were ordered by our superiors to substantiate this strategic concept and to draft a concept paper. That made KNSC look like a subcontractor receiving an OEM [original equipment manufacturer] order from the parent company."[101] Roh, in his above-mentioned speech on March 1, nevertheless used a draft that was totally different from the one that the KNSC had prepared, shocking the KNSC staff immensely.[102] In any case, the concept envisioned South Korea in the role of balancer between the United States and China, on one hand, and between the U.S.-Japan alliance and China on the other, working to prevent conflicts from arising among the parties.

The balancer concept contained several elements. First, it reflected a subtle shift in South Korea away from the United States and more toward China in anticipation of an enormous historic transition: the rise of China. One South Korean diplomat who supported the six-party talks remarked:

> Whether the term "balancer" was appropriate or not, I can understand what President Roh tried to set out. In a nutshell, it was new thinking, about graduating from dependence on the United States. South Korea had to think of its foreign policy and security based on the premise of the rise of China. After all, the United States would not stay in South Korea forever.[103]

From the Pentagon's perspective, Roh Moo-hyun's security policy had two fundamental problems: its willingness to compromise the alliance to accommodate

North Korea and its tendency to see the alliance in opposition to national sovereignty.[104] There also was South Korea's aspiration to self-reliant defense. The Roh government had publicly announced that it would aim to "retrieve" wartime command from the United States and develop the South Korean military into a self-reliant force. Those objectives were based not only on the passive wish not to be involved in any possible U.S.-China or Japan-China conflict but also on a more proactive desire to affect the behavior of neighboring countries, which, in Roh's view, South Korea was capable of doing. One veteran South Korean diplomat offered the following analysis:

> [At the base of the balancer concept] was the conviction that South Korea had become powerful enough to position itself between Japan and China and between the United States and China and to influence the behavior of those countries. It was more akin to an aspiration for total independence. And it was totally different from simply staying neutral and withdrawn so as not to be entangled.[105]

At a meeting of the Roh government's subcommittee on unification, foreign, and security policies, Lee Jong-seok and Suh Dong-man expressed a vision of a South Korean position that was somewhat similar to that of neutral states such as Austria or Switzerland, a position that Yoon Young-kwan strongly opposed.[106] Whatever it might be, the balancer concept definitely did not advocate neutrality; it was an argument for self-reliance if not total independence.

Reactions to the concept within South Korea were ambivalent. The daily *Chosun Ilbo* presented the following criticisms:

> Playing a stabilizing role in Northeast Asia between the U.S.-Japan camp and the North Korea–China-Russia camp is a pipe dream far above the reality of international politics.
>
> The government's idea . . . is bound to result in isolation, because it will not win the trust of either camp.
>
> Washington and Tokyo might review [their] respective strategies now that South Korea might ally with the opponent side and become an imaginary enemy."[107]

Park Geun-hye, chairwoman of the opposition Grand National Party, also criticized the balancer concept:

> At present, China, Japan, and Russia, as well as North Korea, do not recognize South Korea as a balancer in the region. Under the circumstances, any more isolation outside the framework of the Korea-U.S. alliance would not serve Korea's interests.[108]

On the other hand, one opinion poll showed that 68 percent of responding South Koreans supported or sympathized with the concept.[109] In the poll, "balancer" was translated into a Korean word that could also mean "moderator" or "middle of the roader," which has a positive Confucian connotation; the translation might have altered the traditional European power politics connotation, pushing up the number of sympathizers. But presidential press secretary Cho Ki-suk attributed the high support rate to the appeal among Korean citizens of the "diplomacy of [a] one-on-one battle with the United States." She was of the view that the balancer concept also touched the hearts of Koreans because it advocated maintaining the proper degree of distance from the United States.[110]

In the United States, however, the reactions to the balancer theory were cool. One senior White House official brushed it off:

It is basically an attempt to shift the "main enemy" from being North Korea to being Japan, and that is a very poisonous proposition. South Korea is not yet capable of playing a balancer role and it is hard to imagine that this kind of argument will take root as a strategy.[111]

The harshest criticisms of the concept came from the Pentagon. Prior to President Roh's visit to the United States in June 2005, Deputy Under Secretary of Defense Richard Lawless told Hong Seok-hyun, South Korea's ambassador to the United States, that "Korea's Northeast Asia balancer role is a concept that cannot coexist with the Korea-U.S. alliance. If you'd like to change the alliance, say so anytime. We'll do as you like."[112] A Pentagon official concerned with East Asian affairs also criticized the concept as follows:

A fulcrum is necessary for a balancing scale. Isn't the U.S.–South Korean alliance this fulcrum? The United States would not allow South Korea to use this alliance for the purpose of balancing Japan, another ally of the United States. South Korea can get on China's bandwagon, but it cannot balance Japan. The U.S. presence in South Korea might be a stabilizing force, but it is not a balancing force."[113]

The Roh government initially had intended to use the balancer concept to extract itself from a "Southern triangle alliance" in Northeast Asia—one involving South Korea, the United States, and Japan—and eventually to function as a balancer between Japan, the United States, and China. However, faced with harsh criticism from the United States, the Roh government downgraded the concept to one of balancer between China and Japan. But there remained an undercurrent of the South Korean sentiment that Japan was a potential enemy. For South Korea, although Japan was not a strategic enemy, it was an enemy in the emotional realm.

In order to develop a common perception of future security issues in East Asia, the U.S. and South Korean defense authorities decided to produce a classified Comprehensive Security Assessment (CSA). In the process, the two nations had a head-on collision over Japan and China. The South Koreans would not accept the U.S. draft, which discussed security challenges that China was likely to present in the future. The United States would not accept the South Korean draft, which touched on future instability that Japan might create. The South Korean draft classified Japan as a "potential threat." The United States responded, "You must understand that, out of sensitivity to the fact that China is your neighbor, we've removed wording that you've objected to about China. But out of sensitivity to the fact that Japan is our ally, you must realize that in a combined document, we are not going to say negative things about Japan."[114] One senior Department of Defense official who has been involved in the CSA later clarified the issue:

> [People at the South Korean defense authority] are not "pro-China" . . . they do recognize that long-term China is a security concern. . . . When the Minister for Defense came here two years ago, he wanted a briefing on China. National assemblymen come visit, they want to talk about China. They don't ask us about Japan. They ask us about China. They complain to us about Japan. They try to lecture us about Japan. . . . But they ask about China."[115]

Regarding South Korea's role as balancer vis-à-vis China, one veteran U.S. diplomat who has long been associated with U.S. Far Eastern policy offered the following assessment:

> President Roh suspects that China has been maneuvering North Korea so that it can exercise political influence on Pyongyang. If this is indeed the case, South Korea will have to confront China. Roh is more terrified of China than he is of the "normal country Japan." Roh's balancer theory is, in essence, derived from his anxiety over China.[116]

Some observers have referred to Roh's remarks at the U.S.–South Korea summit of June 2005 as an example of the severity of his perception of China. During the summit, Roh told Bush that South Korea had been the victim of foreign invasions more than 1,000 times, of which one-third were by Japan and two-thirds were by China and barbarians from the north, Manchuria and Mongolia. Bush listened intently.[117] However, one senior official of South Korea's Foreign Ministry commented that Roh deliberately included mention of invasions by China only to appease Bush, who would have been displeased if Roh had made clear his true intention, which was to criticize Japan. "To Roh, it is now too risky to allow anti-American nationalism to be fanned further and it is expedient to vent it on Japan." That was, according to this official, another "balancer performance" by Roh.[118]

Roh's "balancer performance" ended up creating more questions about the dilemma with respect to South Korea's security than it answered:

Does the Roh government think that South Korea has enough power to play the role of balancer? Or does it aspire to obtain that power in the future? Is it prepared, if need be, to dissolve the U.S.–South Korea alliance and become totally independent?

Why should the Roh government publicly declare a strategic scheme based on the premise of an armed conflict (between the United States and China or between Japan and China or both) at this particular point, when there is no such conflict? Although South Korea must maintain and develop good relations with neighboring countries and all other countries concerned in order to function as a balancer, it has actually worsened its relations with both the United States and Japan. How does the Roh government explain that discrepancy?

Of all the numerous criticisms of the balancer theory, the severest and the most penetrating came from former president Kim Dae-jung:

Basically, South Korean foreign relations work most effectively within three frameworks: solid South Korea–U.S. relations; the triple entente among Japan, the U.S., and South Korea; and collaboration among four major powers in the region. This is not a choice, but a position that we have to accept fatalistically. This is our destiny.[119]

The balancer concept might have been a psychological device by which South Korea hoped to escape from new geopolitical pressures, but it never took root as a strategic concept for coping with those pressures. It had lacked the geopolitical realism from the beginning. By the time of the U.S.–South Korea summit in June, even Roh ceased to refer to it. Announced, with a flourish, as a "new doctrine" in March, it did not last three months.

False Dawn: Unification Minister Visits Pyongyang

After the Roh Moo-hyun government came into power, some in the Roh entourage envisioned holding a second ROK-DPRK summit in order to take the initiative concerning the future of U.S.-DPRK relations. However, although South Korea conveyed its intentions to North Korea through several channels, the North Koreans paid no attention. On the contrary, on the very day that the South Korean delegation was to depart for a ministerial meeting between North and South Korea scheduled for April 2003, the North Koreans canceled. Relations between the two Koreas were strained further when the Roh government appointed a special prosecutor to investigate allegations of the illegal transfer of money to North Korea by a right-hand man of former president Kim Dae-jung who had been in charge of the summit between Kim Dae-jung and Kim Jong-il. The investigation resulted in the arrest and indictment of a former chief aide of Kim's, actions that North Korea harshly criticized.

Toward the end of April 2003, on the eve of the three-party talks among North Korea, China, and the United States, the Blue House received a message from a certain channel that North Korea would accept the Blue House's special envoy. The message seemed to imply that a Roh-Kim summit might be possible. In fact, when Lim Dong-won had visited Pyongyang in late January 2003, Kim Yong-soon told Lim something along the lines of "the Dear General will meet your special envoy when the time is ripe," raising Lim's expectations.

The question was whether the time was ripe or not. Judging that the time was not yet ripe, Roh decided against sending an envoy. Roh must have concluded that it was highly unlikely that Kim Jong-il could take a flexible stance on the nuclear issue on the eve of the three-party consultations.[120] One of Roh's cabinet members later reminisced, "Roh thought it would not make sense to have a summit with Kim Jong-il before North Korea made a big decision about the nuclear issue. Roh had been consistent on this point."[121]

Roh was repeatedly heard to say that "we don't need to have a summit for the sake of having a summit. It's the substance that matters."[122] That did not necessarily mean that the Roh government had refused to have a summit with Kim Jong-il. In fact, when Foreign Minister Ban Ki-moon met Paek Nam-sun at the ASEAN regional forums in 2004 and 2005, he raised the possibility, and on neither occasion did the North Koreans reject it outright.[123]

When national security adviser Condoleezza Rice visited Seoul in the summer of 2004, she raised the question directly with Roh. "Although the mass media speculate that I am going to North Korea, I have no intention of doing so now," he replied. "I have no intention of having a talk just for the sake of a talk. I want a serious talk with substance."[124] The South Korean media reported that during their conversation Rice asked Roh not to go to Pyongyang, but that was not true. Ban Ki-moon later remarked, "Rice said no such thing. The U.S. government has never expressed concern about a North-South summit."[125]

As a matter of fact, Lee Jong-seok had secretly explored the idea of a visit to Pyongyang at the time of the transition team's "Operation Personal Letter." Lee visited Washington in November 2004, just after the U.S. presidential election, and had lunch with Stephen Hadley, deputy national security adviser, at the Hay Adams Hotel, across the street from the White House. Lee confided his cherished idea of sending a special envoy to Pyongyang and having him carry the U.S. president's personal letter to Kim Jong-il. Lee added that who would go to

Pyongyang, Chung Dong-young or himself, would depend on the situation. Hadley showed interest and urged Lee to keep him posted. Lee was encouraged. However, there was no follow up from Lee on the matter.

Three months later, Lee had lunch in Seoul with Michael Green, senior director of East Asian Affairs at the NSC, and presented a proposal:

Lee: I'm going to Pyongyang; why don't we go to Pyongyang together? You can go as an observer. You could bring a personal letter from President Bush with you. Maybe the letter could say that President Bush would be willing to go to a six-party meeting of heads of state at APEC.

Green: I just don't think it's very likely.

Lee: What about you going to Pyongyang?

Green: I can ask Hadley, and Secretary Rice. . . . It's an interesting idea, but they may be skeptical. But I'll ask.

Back in Washington, Green repeated the conversation to Hadley and Rice. "The advantage of this is that they're 'in the lead' and that they accept that North-South dialogue and the U.S.-ROK alliance are not inseparable, and that's very advantageous." Neither of them was interested.[126]

Lee Jong-seok's idea was designed to have a U.S. special envoy go to Pyongyang in the hope that U.S.–North Korea bilateral consultations would resume.[127] However, the idea went nowhere.

In June 2005, the Roh government had direct negotiations with Kim Jong-il on various issues, including nuclear development. On June 17, a South Korean delegation led by Unification Minister Chung Dong-young had a two-and-a-half-hour talk with Kim Jong-il at the Taedonggang Guest House in Pyongyang. The delegation consisted of forty government officials and 300 representatives of the private sector. Among them were Lim Dong-won and Choi Sung-hong, former cabinet members of the Kim Dae-jung government, who were present primarily to attend the June 15 ceremony to celebrate the first North-South summit, which had been held on June 15, 2000.

In the evening of June 16, it was suddenly announced that Kim Jong-il would meet Chung Dong-young. When they met, Kim Jong-il was in a talkative mood. Regarding the nuclear issue, he said, "Because the other party looked down on us, we had no choice but to develop our own for self-defense." Although Kim denied the existence of the uranium enrichment program, he told Chung that North Korea was prepared to respond to U.S. concerns. Prior to this meeting, Roh, immediately after talking with President Bush in Washington, had appealed to North Korea to make a "strategic decision to abandon nuclear arms." Kim Jong-il told Chung that North Korea would have no reason to possess nuclear arms if the security of his regime was guaranteed; in fact, he said, Kim Il-sung's dying instructions were that North Korea was not to possess nuclear arms. He also affirmed that the 1992 North-South Joint Declaration on Denuclearization of the Korean Peninsula was still valid.

Chung urged Kim Jong-il to resume the six-party talks. "If North Korea does not come back to the table for the six-party talks," he said, "North-South relations will not improve, either." Kim remarked that North Korea had not rejected or abandoned the six-party talks, hinting that he intended to revive the multilateral framework if certain conditions were met. However, he added that "the United States' stance seems to remain fluid, to buy time," implying that whether North Korea would do so would depend on how the United States behaved.[128]

At the end of the talk, Chung proposed a second summit between Kim Jong-il and Roh Moo-hyun. Kim Jong-il responded, "That will be realized when the proper time comes."[129] More than three years had passed since Lim Dong-won visited Pyongyang in April 2002, but Chung succeeded in having Kim Jong-il suggest his intention to resume the six-party talks. One veteran South Korean diplomat later praised Chung's success, saying, "Chung Dong-young's visit to Pyongyang might not have been decisive, but it certainly was significant. That visit promoted revitalization of the six-party talks process."[130]

Chung himself attributes the success solely to good timing. One year had passed since the previous six-party talks in June 2004, and international pressure on North Korea to come back had been increasing. Chung believes that Kim Jong-il was looking for an exit. In addition, Kim might have been favorably impressed because the Roh government, which had been rather cool about the North-South summit anniversary on June 15, 2005, changed its attitude and celebrated the day as a national event, including the dispatch of a delegation to North Korea.[131]

THE ROOSEVELT ROOM

After Chung Dong-young came back from Pyongyang, he visited the United States. In part because Chung was rumored to be the most likely presidential candidate of the Uri Party in 2008, he was able to see Stephen Hadley, the national security adviser, at the White House. Chung was taken to the Roosevelt Room, which is across the corridor from the Oval Office and is often used as a conference room.

When Roh Moo-hyun visited the United States in June 2005, he was taken to the Roosevelt Room first, before joining President Bush in the Oval Office. Some in the Blue House found that outrageous. Information had been received that the Roosevelt Room contained, along with portraits of Theodore Roosevelt (twenty-sixth president of the United States) and William Taft (twenty-seventh president), a portrait of a smiling samurai. To Koreans, the Treaty of Portsmouth (1905), which Theodore Roosevelt had mediated, and the Taft-Katsura Agreement, a secret agreement between then Secretary of War William H. Taft and Prime Minister Taro Katsura of Japan, were the loathsome results of backroom deals made by Japan and the United States to deprive the Korean nation of the right to control its own foreign policy and to promote Japan's annexation of the Korean Peninsula.

Blue House staff, angry also because South Korea's diplomats did nothing to stop this insult to their president, initiated an investigation of what had really happened, including a probe concerning the responsibility of the Foreign Ministry.

In the Roosevelt Room, Chung found only a portrait of Theodore Roosevelt in uniform and mounted on a horse, along with a copy of the Nobel Peace Prize certificate that Roosevelt had been awarded in 1906 for his role in bringing about the Portsmouth Treaty. The attending White House staff person had taken Chung to the room in order to show what was on display there. "No portrait of President Taft here, only President Roosevelt," he said. "These are American soldiers, and this is San Juan Hill," he added, pointing at the portrait of Lieutenant Colonel Theodore Roosevelt leading the "Rough Riders" in the Battle of San Juan Hill, one of the bloodiest battles of the Spanish-American War. Somewhat embarrassed, Chung responded, saying, "I see. Please don't bother yourself any more."[132] Needless to say, the South Korean embassy in Washington later sent a telegram to the Foreign Ministry in Seoul (as well as the Blue House, surely) to report on Chung's visit, adding "There was no samurai in the Roosevelt Room."[133]

Since the spring of 2005, Roh had frequently raised with the U.S. government the significance of certain historical issues in Northeast Asia. When in March 2005 Condoleezza Rice visited Seoul for the first time as the U.S. secretary of state, Roh called her attention to Prime Minister Junichiro Koizumi's visit to the Yasukuni Shrine and the Japanese history textbook issue, stressing the danger of Japan's possible remilitarization. Roh told Rice that Japan's refusal to squarely face the past had harmed that nation's relations with both South Korea and China.[134]

Forty-five minutes of the eighty-minute talk were devoted to the Japan problem. During the U.S.–South Korea summit in June, Roh also criticized Japan for not accepting the view that the Pacific War was a conflict between democracy and fascism and consequently failing to educate its people properly.[135] South Korea's ambassador to Japan, Ra Jong-yil, had the idea of suggesting that Roh, when he met Bush for the summit, raise the issue of the insensitivity of current Japanese leaders regarding the nature of the Pacific War.[136] Although Bush nodded when Roh referred to "democracy and fascism," he had no intention of putting pressure on Japan. Bush was even suspicious of the motivation behind Roh's criticism of Japan. According to a senior U.S. administration official, Bush thought that because Roh's anti-U.S. diplomacy had arrived at a deadlock and because Roh could not find a way to directly express his anti-American sentiment adequately, he did so vicariously by turning his aggression toward Japan.[137]

CHAPTER EIGHT

Hu Jintao's "New Thinking" Diplomacy

Saturday, March 8, 2003, was a cloudless, sunny day in Pyongyang. Early in the morning, a Chinese government–chartered plane touched down at Sunan International Airport. About one week earlier, in international waters off the eastern coast of the Korean Peninsula, a North Korean jet fighter had come very close to a U.S. reconnaissance airplane, and the U.S. crew reported the incident as a near collision. That was one of the reasons why the atmosphere was tense that morning.

The Chinese government plane soon took off; one and a half hours later, it landed at Samjiyon Airport at the foot of Baekdusan Mountain.[1] Because the runway was rough, the airplane shook violently when it touched down. One of the Chinese crew complained, "I've never seen an airport as bad as this before. Land and take off here three times, and your plane is gone."[2] In and around the airport, cliffs of piled-up snow could be seen.

Samjiyon is believed to be the site of a battle in the well-known anti-Japanese military struggle led by Kim Il-sung. In May 1979, a monument was erected, reportedly at Kim Il-sung's initiative, along Lake Samjiyon to commemorate the fortieth anniversary of the Koreans' victory. A bronze statue of Kim Il-sung stands in the center, flanked by groups of statues of soldiers and peasants on both sides; a fifty-meter-high beacon tower stands to the right of the statues.

After disembarking, the passengers headed for the guest house. Some of the Chinese visitors had heard a rumor that the guest house was hidden inside a cave, which turned out not to be the case. Over their heads was an infinite expanse of clear blue sky. One member of the party marveled at the sky. "Whenever I come to this country, the sky is always blue," he thought. "Why is North Korea so full of blue sky? China used to have blue skies like this when I was a kid. How long has it been since we had blue skies?"[3]

The location was very close to the China–North Korea border. It was said that Chairman Kim Jong-il had secluded himself there since February 2003. Although the United States was preparing itself for war with Iraq, North Korea strongly suspected that the United States might attack North Korea on the pretext of attacking Iraq. CNN reported that the U.S. Air Force had begun to position long-range strategic bombers—a dozen B-1 bombers and a dozen B-52 bombers—at Anderson Air Force Base on Guam.[4]

The Chinese party included its leader, Vice Premier Qian Qichen (the former foreign minister); Vice Foreign Minister Wang Yi; Fu Ying, the director general of the Foreign Ministry's Department of Asian Affairs; and some others. The purpose of Qian Qichen's visit was to consult with the North Koreans on ways to settle the North Korean nuclear crisis and, in particular, to encourage North Korea to participate in the multilateral consultation proposed by the United States.

Kim Jong-il was at the state guest house to welcome the party, and the discussion began immediately. He was accompanied by First Deputy Foreign Minister Kang Sok-ju. Qian Qichen, while stressing that the Chinese government strongly hoped for the denuclearization of the Korean Peninsula, conveyed to Kim Jong-il the Chinese government's intention to pursue a peaceful settlement.[5] Qian talked about the history of China's reforms and opening up. "Through reform and opening up, the living standards of the Chinese people improved greatly," he said. "It should be noted also that a peaceful international environment had been an indispensable precondition for our success." He added, "We have no intention of imposing our methods on you. But we do wish to share our experiences with you." Although Qian did not quote Deng Xiaoping, what he said was the same thing that Deng Xiaoping had once said to Kim Il-sung. Kim Jong-il replied:

> The conditions that North Korea faces are totally different from the Chinese case. North Korea is a tiny, backward country, and it is not a great power like China. Economic reform may have worked well in China, but it does not necessarily mean the Chinese method will work for us. I agree that a peaceful international environment is an essential condition for economic development. But the United States has consistently adopted hostile policies toward us, and we have never been provided with a peaceful environment. It is the United States, not us, that should be blamed for the absence of a peaceful environment on the Korean Peninsula.[6]

Kim Jong-il repeatedly stressed that North Korea's nuclear development program was a countermeasure to hostile U.S. policies toward North Korea, and that the issue therefore was a strategic issue between the United States and North Korea. Qian listened with a calm smile to what Kim Jong-il had to say.

The discussion then turned to the nuclear issue itself, particularly with respect to North Korea's development of highly enriched uranium (HEU). Kang Sok-ju, who had attended the meeting at the request of Kim Jong-il, provided the Chinese guests with a detailed briefing on his exchange with U.S. Assistant Secretary of State James Kelly, including the atmosphere at the meeting, when Kelly visited Pyongyang in October 2002. Wang Yi asked a few questions about the HEU issue.[7] Kang adamantly denied the existence of the HEU program. "The United States didn't show any evidence," he declared. "They one-sidedly accused us without showing any evidence."[8]

After that exchange, the main topics of discussion were introduced. Qian proposed the launching of trilateral consultations among the United States, North Korea, and China. Worried that the nuclear crisis might deepen, China wished to act as intermediary, convening the consultations in Beijing. China very much hoped that North Korea would participate in such a meeting.[9] When Kim Jong-il showed disapproval of his proposition, Qian continued to attempt to convince him:

> Even though it will be a trilateral consultation, the main actors would be North Korea and the United States. China would merely be a catalyst, a host country. North Korea can talk freely with the United States, and we will just listen to the discussion quietly. . . . It really doesn't matter whether China is present or not. What is important is for the United States and North Korea to meet and to talk to each other. It should be pointed out, though, that the United States has been quite particular about the format of a multilateral meeting, and we must respect this.[10]

Kim wanted to be reassured. "Do you guarantee that U.S.–North Korean bilateral consultations will be held?" he asked. Qian replied that he would see to it that they were set up. "Then we will participate in the trilateral meeting," Kim said.[11]

After the meeting, Kim Jong-il hosted a luncheon. It was a lavish affair, including an abundance of fresh fish, even though the guest house was located deep in snowy mountains near the China–North Korea border. Kim Jong-il played the role of charming host.[12]

This was Qian's first visit to North Korea since 1992, when he had been entrusted with an important mission. In September 1992, China normalized its diplomatic relations with South Korea, thereby shaking the very foundation of the relations between China and North Korea, which had fought side by side in the Korean War. For North Korea, China's action was nothing short of betrayal. Earlier, in April 1992, China had sent President Yang Shangkun to Pyongyang as an envoy to participate in the celebration of Kim Il-sung's eightieth birthday and to try to obtain North Korea's approval of China's normalization of relations with South Korea. North Korea had been utterly unaware of the movement to normalize relations. Yang made not an a priori request for a consultation but an after-the-fact unilateral announcement of what was virtually a fait accompli. One North Korean diplomat later reminisced:

> When Kim Il-sung heard from Yang Shangkun of the plan for China–South Korea normalization, he completely ignored it. He didn't utter a word. Although Yang was China's president, in terms of the ranking in the East Asian history of communist revolutionaries, Yang was much lower than Kim. When Yang Shangkun arrived at Pyongyang airport [before the meeting], a big crowd of North Korean VIPs was there to welcome him. But when he departed Pyongyang, nobody was at the airport to see him off."[13]

Yang had visited North Korea previously, in May 1984, accompanying Chairman Hu Yaobang, the Chinese Communist Party's general secretary. Yang went to Pyongyang again in 1988, after he became president of China. It was believed that he was close to Kim Il-sung. Of all the Chinese leaders in those days, Yang was the one who was most outspoken in his support of North Korea, and when the Chinese leadership was debating diplomatic normalization with South Korea, Yang opposed it, going head to head with such normalization advocates as Premier Li Peng and Communist Party general secretary Jiang Zemin.[14] Nevertheless, Kim Il-sung let Yang leave as if he were brushing Yang off.

In July 1992, Jiang Zemin, sensing that it was urgent to secure Kim Il-sung's approval quickly, had dispatched Qian Qichen, who was then the foreign minister, to Pyongyang. In the past Qian had always been met with a big welcome at Pyongyang Airport, but this time Qian's plane was directed to the most remote berth at Sunan Airport. Kim Yong-nam, North Korea's foreign minister, was the only one to welcome Qian. At the airport, Qian and Kim boarded a helicopter, where they were seated at a tiny table across from each other. Inside the cabin, the heat generated by the engine intensified the mid-summer heat, and it was unbearably hot. Soon a large lake appeared below, and the helicopter started to descend. After landing, Qian was taken to a state guest house, where a meeting between the two men took place. Qian conveyed the following message from Jiang Zemin:

> China wishes to continue to develop the traditions and friendship that our two communist parties and countries have shared over a period of prolonged struggle, to support the growth of socialism and the peaceful unification of the Korean Peninsula, to help reduce tensions on the peninsula, and to contribute to the improvement and development of U.S.–North Korean and Japan–North Korean relations.

Kim Il-sung remained in deep thought for a while. "General Secretary Jiang Zemin's message is very clear," he finally said. "We understand that China has made a decision about its foreign policy based on the principles of China's independence, self-determination, and equality. We, too, will continue to pursue the strengthening of friendship with China. We shall overcome all obstacles."

At the end of their brief meeting, Kim Il-sung asked Qian to convey his best wishes to Deng Xiaoping and other leaders of the Chinese Communist Party. Kim thanked Qian for the carved jade and lychees that Qian had brought as gifts; he then left the room. As far as Qian Qichen could remember, "that was the briefest meeting that Chairman Kim Il-sung had had with a foreign delegation. We were not invited to the customary reception after the meeting, either."[15]

Lee Jong-soek, a research fellow at Sejong Institute, Seoul, who later became foreign and security policy adviser to President Roh Moo-hyun, analyzed China's motive for normalizing diplomatic relations with South Korea as follows: "In a sense, diplomatic normalization with South Korea can be interpreted as a demonstration of China's intention to, if need be, force North Korea to pursue international settlement of its nuclear issue, including ceasing its development of nuclear weapons, which China has opposed."[16]

Kim Il-sung must have suspected the Chinese government's hidden agenda. His displeasure at the message, however, was converted into displeasure with the messenger, and Qian Qichen was the unfortunate one who had to play that role. Qian recalled in 2003 that it had been ten years since that ordeal with Kim Il-sung, and he again was in the state guest house at Samjiyon. But this time he was able to go home light-hearted. After lunch, Qian and his party got on the government plane and took off for Beijing.

Qian's visit would prove to be decisive in that it marked "a total change in China's manner of dealing with the North Korean nuclear issue," as one senior Chinese diplomat put it. "By the time of the visit, China worried that the escalation of the crisis could go out of control, then, determined to change its previous manner [it took a direct hand in the nuclear issue].... China's diplomacy on the North Korean nuclear issue entered a new phase ... starting with Qian's visit, the trilateral meeting [in April 2003] and the launch of the six-party talks [in August 2003]."[17]

JIANG ZEMIN'S "EGO"

In a sense, the six-party talks originated in a phone call that Jiang Zemin made to Bush late one night. When the 9/11 attacks occurred, Jiang Zemin saw the news on Phoenix TV, a Hong Kong–based cable news network—"for the Chinese community all over the world"—that tens of millions of mainland Chinese are said to watch every day. CCTV, China's national television network, was deliberately not running the story.

Jiang immediately called Foreign Minister Li Zhaoxing. The following exchange is believed to have taken place between the two:

Jiang: What are you doing right now?

Li: I've been reading.

Jiang: Turn on the TV right now. To Phoenix TV.[18]

Two hours later, Jiang telephoned Bush to express his condolences and to communicate China's determination to fight terrorism together with the United States. Assistant Secretary of State James Kelly later recalled:

> The very first strong message of sympathy that came to President Bush was from China. So, they were immediately on board with the war on terror, and that just shredded the agenda of anybody who wanted to get going with the new cold war.[19]

Looking at it from a somewhat different angle, one senior U.S. administration official stressed the importance of Jiang Zemin himself as a factor: "Jiang Zemin has a big ego and that makes him different from Hu Jintao. It was his ego that made issues out of EP-3, Falun Gong, and Taiwan. But it is also true that U.S.-China relations became easier to manage because of his ego."[20]

The official was referring to China's high-handed stance at the time of the forced landing of the U.S. EP-3 reconnaissance airplane that had been on a mission near Hainan Island; to China's equally hard-line posture concerning domestic peace and order manifested in its oppression of the religious group Falun Gong; and to Jiang's almost personal hatred of Taiwan's president, Lee Teng-hui. While those issues may have become more serious because of Jiang Zemin's personality and personal ambition, it can also be said that Jiang's ego made the U.S.-China summit talk in Crawford, Texas, possible. Jiang wanted to show off to the world how close he was to Bush, and Bush treated Jiang accordingly. Jiang wished to establish broader U.S.-China relations, allowing the two countries to discuss various issues in Asia and the Pacific, and Bush responded positively. Jiang's wish can also be regarded as the wish to be a "concerned country" or even a "major actor" in regional affairs in the Asia Pacific region.

The U.S.-China summit talk at President Bush's ranch in Crawford on October 26, 2002, lasted four hours, becoming a "strategy session on how to deal with a nuclear crisis on the Korean peninsula and the disarming of President Saddam Hussein of Iraq."[21] On the previous day, a spokesman for North Korea's Foreign Ministry had released a statement claiming that when James Kelly visited Pyongyang, Kelly had "asserted, producing no evidence, that DPRK has been actively engaging in the enriched uranium program in pursuit of possessing nuclear weapons in violation of the DPRK-U.S. Agreed Framework," and the spokesman strongly criticized the U.S. attitude in the consultation as "one-sided and highhanded."[22] The target of his remarks obviously was the China-U.S. summit talk, which was scheduled for the following day.

During the U.S.-China summit talk, Jiang Zemin repeatedly emphasized that "the Korean Peninsula must remain denuclearized." Jiang shared with Bush what he had told North Korea's leaders some ten years earlier: "If a war were to break out as a result of North Korean mismanagement of its nuclear issues, we would simply continue on our path toward national development. I need your understanding on this point."[23] Jiang's message was crystal clear: China would not allow North Korea to possess nuclear arms, and China would not support North Korea if a war broke out as a result of North Korea's nuclear activities. Jiang did not forget to mention another fundamental position of China—that the North Korean nuclear issue was a bilateral concern of the United States and North Korea. In effect, he reminded Bush that Bush would be barking up the wrong tree if he expected China to play some special role regarding the issue. With respect to the news that North Korea had admitted the existence of its HEU program, Jiang told reporters that "China had no knowledge of it."[24] Although that probably was true initially, Jiang's comment might also have been aimed at reining in any excessive expectations regarding China's role concerning the matter.

In 1990, Jiang Zemin visited North Korea for the first time as the general secretary of the Chinese Communist Party. He had been scheduled to visit the Soviet Union, but the Gorbachev government's "New Thinking" foreign policy and the dramatic changes in eastern Europe required a last-minute change of destination. Kim Il-sung belonged to the first-generation of revolutionaries, along with Mao Zedong, Zhou Enlai, and Deng Xiaoping, and he boasted of his role in writing the history of the communist movement in East Asia in the twentieth century. He might not have felt much affinity with Jiang Zemin, who was a third-generation party apparatchik and technocrat.

It is possible that Jiang Zemin felt the same way toward Kim Il-sung. Former South Korean president Kim Young-sam once said that when he met Jiang Zemin, he sensed that Jiang's attitude toward Kim Il-sung was less than favorable. Kim Young-sam had had breakfast with Jiang Zemin one day in November 1995, when Jiang was visiting South Korea for the first time as the president of China and the first Chinese head of state to visit South Korea.[25] When Kim tried to initiate a tête-à-tête discussion of the North Korean issue, Jiang was very evasive, claiming, "I know nothing of North Korea." Recalling the conversation, Kim Young-sam said, "I think Jiang secretly despised Kim Il-sung. When Kim Jong-il succeeded Kim Il-sung, Jiang was inwardly displeased by Kim Jong-il's arbitrary behavior."[26]

During the Jiang Zemin era in the 1990s, China was hesitant to take a clear-cut position one way or the other vis-à-vis the North Korean nuclear issue. However, China presented the following three principles for dealing with the first North Korean nuclear crisis:

—denuclearization of the Korean Peninsula

—settlement between the parties directly concerned: North Korea, the United States, and the International Atomic Energy Agency (IAEA)

—avoidance of sanctions against North Korea.[27]

In other words, during the first nuclear crisis China took the position that it was not one of the parties directly concerned. In February 1993, China abstained from voting on an IAEA Board of Governors resolution to denounce North Korea. Because China had been believed to be opposed to the resolution, the United States was so encouraged by China's abstention that it asked China to help persuade North Korea to take "responsible action." However, when a diplomat from the U.S. embassy in Beijing visited China's Foreign Ministry, the official in charge of North Korean affairs handed the American a poem by Lu You, a famous poet of the southern Song Dynasty, that roughly translates as follows: "Nobody knows where the mountains and trees will go in the end. And yet, all of a sudden, people will find a new village where willows bend to the wind and flowers flourish."[28] In China, the poem has often been presented to diplomats as a thought to keep in mind—that is, that an opportunity might present itself at the very moment that you seem to be at the end of your rope.[29]

China was not a party to the 1994 Agreed Framework, which settled the first North Korean nuclear crisis, nor did it join the resulting Korean Peninsula Energy Development Organization (KEDO). At the time of the first nuclear crisis, China's relations with North Korea were much worse than they had been some years before because China had normalized diplomatic relations with South Korea. China's usefulness as leverage therefore was limited.

However, at the time of the second nuclear crisis, ten years later, conditions were totally different. Jiang Zemin visited Pyongyang in September 2001 and reached an agreement with Kim Jong-il that could be summarized by sixteen Chinese characters that can be translated into English as "continuation of tradition," "future orientation," "good neighborliness," and "cooperation and collaboration." That agreement, coupled with Kim Jong-il's visits to Beijing in May 2000 and January 2001, seemed to establish at last a foundation for the normalization of the relationship between China and North Korea. Moreover, China obtained a foothold from which it could affect both Koreas. In addition, China's relationship with the Bush administration, which had been sluggish at the beginning, took a turn for the better after the 9/11 terrorist attacks in the United States. Ten years after the U.S. embassy received the puzzling poetic message mentioned above, China resorted to modern e-mail exchanges, instead of ancient Chinese poetry, to present its views to the United States.

China has consistently advocated the denuclearization of the Korean Peninsula. But Jiang Zemin, faced with the second nuclear crisis, reaffirmed that principle in clearer terms and even in public—to the extent that Jiang chided Foreign Ministry spokeswoman Zhang Qiyue for not having been clear enough about it at a press briefing.[30]

In December 2002, Jiang had a summit talk with Russia's president, Vladimir Putin, in Beijing. During the talk, Jiang made explicit his intention to ask North Korea to abandon its nuclear program. In the joint statement issued after the summit, the presidents of China and Russia pointed out that "it is crucial to peace and security in Northeast Asia to maintain a nuclear-free status of the Korean peninsula" and called for the DPRK and the United States to abide by the Agreed Framework and to normalize their relations.[31] On January 10, 2003, North Korea announced that it would withdraw from the Nuclear Non-Proliferation Treaty (NPT). Hearing the announcement, Bush phoned Jiang Zemin and said, "This binds us in common purposes."[32] Jiang made it very clear that he did not agree with North Korea's decision. Subsequently, when Russia abstained from voting for the aforementioned IAEA resolution to denounce North Korea, China voted for the resolution. China was shifting from its united front with Russia to a united front with the United States.[33]

An integral part of China's new foreign policy was cooperation with the United States toward denuclearization of the Korean Peninsula, a position that the United States praised highly.[34] At the U.S.-Japan Strategy Dialogue held in Washington in February 2003, the U.S. representative, Richard Armitage, deputy secretary of state, said the following to the Japanese representative, Yukio Takeuchi, vice minister for foreign affairs:

> China has just made a major decision concerning its new foreign policy. It will no longer confront the United States, and it will collaborate with the United States in carrying out policies toward North Korea. It is determined to settle the North Korean nuclear issue, even if that calls for pressure on North Korea. This is a major change.[35]

Armitage was referring to the deepening of a shared U.S.-China view, triggered by the Crawford summit, regarding the North Korean nuclear issue. The elation of the U.S. administration after the Crawford summit was so remarkable that it made a veteran Japanese diplomat who had long experience with the United States wonder whether the United States was not "overestimating China in relation to the North Korean issue."[36]

In the midst of the second nuclear crisis, Chinese diplomacy was carried out in a hop-step-and-jump fashion until China came up with the multilateral consultation framework. The summit talk with Bush in Crawford, Texas, in October 2002 was the hop; the Jiang Zemin–Colin Powell talk in Beijing in February 2003 was the step; and Qian Qichen's visit to North Korea in March 2003 was the jump. Behind the process was China's deep concern about the new U.S. strategic thinking after 9/11, particularly the argument for preemptive attack.

At the time, the United States was preparing for military action to prevent the proliferation of Iraqi weapons of mass destruction, and it had not denied the possibility of an attack on North Korea, which had been identified as part of an axis of evil, along with Iraq and Iran. If a crisis on the Korean Peninsula were to erupt, everything was liable to blow up in the air, including the stable international environment and South Korea's economy. That had to be prevented at any cost. While Bush made it publicly known that the United States would pursue a multilateral approach to the North Korean nuclear issue, he kept announcing that "all options are on the table," implying that he had not excluded the option of attacking North Korea militarily.

China deeply feared a U.S. military attack on North Korea. It was worried not only about the possibility of the United States performing military "surgery" on North Korea's nuclear facilities but also about the danger of a military confrontation between the United States and North Korea caused by eccentric behavior on the part of the latter. In early March 2003, a North Korean MiG intercepted an RC-135 U.S. reconnaissance plane above the Sea of Japan/East Sea, causing a big stir in the region. China took the incident quite seriously.[37] The greatest risk for China in the short term was a military confrontation between the United States and North Korea. One senior U.S. administration official later reminisced, "In those days, the United States was acting tough. We attacked Saddam Hussein's army and annihilated it like nothing. China was very fearful of the United States." He added:

> They didn't want to get involved, but they were afraid we would use force. And there were subtle hints from the president and others, that we would. ... In 1991, something like 5 percent of the bombs were smart bombs. The Chinese knew that in 2003, 90 percent of the bombs dropped were precision Smart Bombs. So the Chinese, at that point, in March and in most of 2003, I think, were very afraid of us, and very responsive to us. .... I think it was Iraq. Because by 2004 it was obvious we were in trouble in Iraq. .... So we became "less frightening" because of Iraq, and North Korea became more frightening, became more difficult. My impression was that the Chinese ... after the North Koreans announced that they had a nuclear deterrent, the Chinese, I think they just became discouraged.[38]

COLIN POWELL VISITS CHINA

Colin Powell was convinced that the North Korean nuclear issue had to be settled mainly between the United States and North Korea. He had played a critical role in bringing back to normalcy U.S.-China relations, which had been strained by the forced landing by a Chinese fighter of a U.S. reconnaissance airplane flying over the sea near Hainan Island in April 2001. Powell gradually developed personal relations with Foreign Minister Tang Jiaxuan and his successor, Li Zhaoxing, which allowed Powell to discuss matters with them over the phone. On those occasions, Powell openly shared his expectations concerning China's exercise of its influence on North Korea. "About one-half of China's foreign assistance goes to North Korea, and some 80 percent of the energy and economic assistance that North Korea receives is provided by China," he pointed out in an interview in February 2003. "China has a role to play. I hope China plays this role."[39] While Powell noted that "China has considerable influence" on North Korea, one senior Department of State official added, "They can do more."[40]

Powell was scheduled to attend the inauguration ceremony of President Roh Moo-hyun toward the end of February. He decided to visit Japan and China beforehand in order to consolidate the framework of the multilateral consultations for settling the North Korean nuclear crisis. In Japan, Powell talked with Foreign Minister Yoriko Kawaguchi, who was accompanied by Mitoji Yabunaka, the Japan Foreign Ministry's director general for Asian and Oceanian affairs. Powell introduced a ten-party talk scheme, which the U.S. government, particularly the Department of State, had thoroughly studied, that would involve the five permanent members of the UN Security Council plus South Korea, North Korea, Japan, Australia, and the European Union.[41]

Kawaguchi was new to the job. "Well, I don't know," she said. "Maybe ten is too many?" It was an unimposing comment, but the message was very clear. She continued:

> The Japanese government believes consultation among five parties, including North Korea, will be a good arrangement. We can consider Russia's participation at a later stage. For the time being we believe that consultation among five countries will be appropriate. The Japanese government wishes to propose five-party talks. But the crucial thing is to include China among the parties concerned. For this reason we believe it is a good idea to ask China to host the consultation.

Her comments were followed up by Yabunaka, who said, "If five-party talks are proposed by Japan, we are afraid China will oppose them. Why don't you suggest this to China as a U.S. proposal?" Kawaguchi immediately agreed. "Yes," she said. "It works better if you propose the five-party talks and persuade China and South Korea to agree to this."[42]

Powell nodded at the suggestion and said, "This is great. I am going to Beijing next, and I'll talk to them."[43] During this exchange, the Japanese picked up on the fact that the White House was cool to the idea of ten-party talks.[44] When Powell introduced the scheme, he was aware that Bush was less than enthusiastic about it. One of the main reasons for Bush's hesitation was the number of participants—too many countries would be involved. Besides, North Korea itself remained negative to Powell's proposal, which was conveyed to its leaders on January 22 through what they called the "New York channel"—that is, from the U.S. Department of State to North Korea's permanent mission at the UN to Pyongyang. Indeed, three days later North Korea rejected the proposal, stating that multilateral consultations would not be appropriate for discussing a "U.S.–North Korea nuclear issue."[45] Consequently, Powell decided to propose five-party talks to China instead.[46]

On February 24 in Beijing, Powell had a series of talks with Foreign Minister Tang Jiaxuan, Vice President Hu Jintao, and President Jiang Zemin, one after another.[47] At every meeting, the Taiwan issue and the Korean Peninsula issue were the two main topics. Hu Jintao stressed the following Chinese position vis-à-vis the Korean Peninsula issue, almost reading from the prepared talking points:

—China insists that the Korean Peninsula be denuclearized and that peace and security on the peninsula be guaranteed.

—The North Korean nuclear issue can be settled properly only through dialogue and consultation.

—China hopes that the United States and North Korea will engage in direct dialogue.[48]

In Powell's subsequent talk with Jiang Zemin, the same points were repeated. In addition, Jiang emphatically stated that escalation of the nuclear crisis must be prevented.[49] In response, Powell asked China to host a multilateral forum to settle the North Korean nuclear issue. When Powell suggested a five-country forum among the two Koreas, the United States, "China, and Japan, Jiang was skeptical. "This is an issue that needs to be settled by the United States and North Korea," he said.

"Our president is fully determined to address this issue through multilateral consultations," Powell responded. "All the other options are simply too gloomy."

"But this is an issue that the United States and North Korea must settle between themselves," Jiang insisted. "China has nothing to do with the North Korean nuclear issue."

Powell repeated, "Our president does not think it is a bilateral issue. He believes it is an issue that has to be settled multilaterally."

After both sides had reiterated the same views three times, the atmosphere became rather tense. Then, all of a sudden, Jiang Zemin announced, "I understand the U.S. position. Let us think it over for a while."[50]

On the same day, Hu Jintao convened a high-level meeting to discuss how to respond to Powell's proposal. As a result, it was decided to convene what later became known as the "trilateral meeting," which included the United States and

North Korea. "Although the United States insists on multilateral consultations, North Korea demands bilateral negotiation with the United States," Hu said. "China needs to satisfy these two requests, which is a tall order. Let us therefore convene a minimally multilateral consultation among three countries." Hu reported the outcome of the meeting to Jiang, who approved of it.[51]

The next day, Fu Ying, the director general of Asian Affairs at the Chinese Foreign Ministry, called Michael W. Marine, deputy chief of mission at the U.S. Embassy in Beijing, to let him know that "China will start preparations to invite North Korea to a multilateral consultation meeting."[52]

After Qian Qichen visited North Korea and brought back Kim Jong-il's agreement to participate in trilateral consultations, China immediately dispatched Vice Foreign Minister Wang Yi to the United States to convey North Korea's response to Colin Powell. Although China reported that "the North Koreans were hesitant to include Japan and South Korea in the consultations," the United States initially suspected that it was China, not North Korea, that was hesitant.[53] But Powell was determined that multilateral consultations had to begin with the three-party talks.

When Powell reported the outcome to Bush, the president's mood immediately turned sour. "That would be U.S.–North Korea bilateral negotiations, with China acting as a broker, rather than multilateral consultations," he complained. There was another reason that Bush was not happy—the exclusion of Japan and South Korea from the forum. "I'm not going to do that to Koizumi," Bush said. However, when Powell explained that he had already asked China to host multilateral consultations along the agreed line, Bush said, "All right, I'm going to let you do it this one time," endorsing the trilateral meeting.[54]

Bush then said to Powell, "I'm going to call Koizumi and Roh to apologize." Bush called Junichiro Koizumi and Roh Moo-hyun in late March and early April, respectively; he expressed his gratitude to both for their country's support and contributions to the Iraq war, then touched on the North Korean nuclear issue and asked for their understanding with regard to the trilateral meeting, while expressing his remorse for the arrangement.[55]

Koizumi, thanking Bush for giving him a direct phone call concerning these matters, expressed Japan's wish to participate in future multilateral consultations. Roh, in contrast, told Bush that the important thing was to have a dialogue on the nuclear issue no matter what the format might be, and he thanked Bush for his consideration.[56] In addition to the telephone calls, Howard Baker, the U.S. ambassador to Japan, met Foreign Minister Yoriko Kawaguchi at the ministry's Azabu annex and informed her of the directive that he had received from the U.S. government. "China replied it would host a meeting on the North Korean nuclear issue if it is going to be a trilateral talk," he said. "What will be

Japan's reaction regarding this arrangement?" It was obvious that "Japan did not have the option of saying 'no.'"[57]

Although North Korea agreed to participate in the trilateral meeting, it maintained its position that the nuclear issue was a bilateral issue between the United States and North Korea. It continued to request, through its permanent mission at the United Nations, bilateral consultations. China, however, requested U.S. confirmation that, as far as the trilateral meeting was concerned, China would be the only official channel of communication with North Korea, and the United States agreed to restrain contact with the North Korean officials in New York. From that point on, whenever North Korea sent comments and questions through its permanent mission at the UN, the United States responded to them via China. By the second week of April, the problem of double channels of communication was resolved, and the United States and North Korea finally agreed to a trilateral meeting, which would be held in Beijing toward the end of April.[58]

HU JINTAO'S "NEW THINKING" DIPLOMACY

Of course, Jiang Zemin's ego was not the only factor underlying China's new approach. Hu Jintao had been involved from the very beginning, as was obvious from the fact that it was his decision to convene the trilateral meeting. The sixty-year-old Hu Jintao was elected general secretary of the Central Committee in 2002 at the Sixteenth National Congress of the Chinese Communist Party. In March 2003, at the first session of the Tenth National People's Congress, he was elected to succeed Jiang Zemin, who was seventy-six years old, as president of China. That marked China's shift from third-generation to fourth-generation leadership; the first generation was led by Mao Zedong. The *Economist* wrote that "such simplicity from a leader strikes many in China as a refreshing change from the pomposity of Mr. Jiang who, it was clear to see, enjoyed all the ceremony. Nor can the more subdued Mr. Hu be expected to indulge in the sort of showmanship favored by his predecessor, whose singing and poetry recitals looked to many Chinese, and perhaps to his hosts as well, suspiciously like so much buffoonery."[59]

The first diplomatic challenges that Hu Jintao had to face were the crises concerning North Korea and Iraq. The leaders of the Chinese Communist Party had received numerous reports and proposals regarding policy toward North Korea; however, in the end a policy proposal drafted by Vice Foreign Minister Wang Yi was adopted almost in its entirety. Wang's proposal stressed the importance of changing China's North Korea policy to one more oriented toward China's national interests, which North Korea's nuclear development might greatly harm.

At the same time, the proposal recognized the need for peace and stability on the Korean Peninsula, and it stressed the need to peacefully settle the dispute.[60]

In the face of the second North Korean nuclear crisis, the Chinese government adopted three principles:

—denuclearization of the Korean Peninsula
—maintenance of peace and stability in Northeast Asia
—settlement through dialogue and negotiation.

The question of whether China was a concerned party with regard to the North Korean nuclear issue, about which China had been very nervous at the time of the first North Korean nuclear crisis, did not affect the new policy.[61]

In 1993, Hu Jintao led the Chinese delegation to Pyongyang to attend the fortieth anniversary of the Korean War Armistice Agreement (known in North Korea as the Victory in the Homeland Liberation War). At the time, he was a member of the standing committee of the Politburo of the Central Committee. Kim Il-sung held a huge banquet, but the only other foreign VIPs present were Prince Norodom Sihanouk from Cambodia and Yasser Arafat of the Palestine Liberation Organization.[62] While Jiang Zemin's first overseas trip as president was to North Korea, the first overseas trip for Hu Jintao was his visit to Europe in June 2003 as a representative of developing countries at the G-8 Evian summit.

On March 16, 2003, for the first time since he became president of China, Hu telephoned George Bush. Hu reassured Bush that China would cooperate with the United States to settle the North Korean nuclear issue and, at the same time, he urged the United States to engage in dialogue with North Korea, "as soon as possible." The very fact that Hu himself telephoned Bush to talk about the North Korean nuclear issue indicated China's positive stance on the matter.[63]

In April 2003, Hu talked with Jo Myong-rok, first deputy chairman of North Korea's National Defense Commission, who visited China around the time of the trilateral meeting. Although Jo described China–North Korea relations as those of "blood and bullets," Hu used the more moderate "traditional friendship."[64] Between the lines one could read Hu's anxiousness to move beyond "blood-bound China–North Korea relations."

In early February 2005, Hu Jintao met with two staffers of the White House National Security Council, Michael Green and William Tobey, who had been dispatched to China by President Bush. North Korea had invited Hu Jintao to Pyongyang before the visit by Green and Tobey, but the Chinese had not yet confirmed that Hu would go. North Korea must have found it troubling that at that particular stage Hu decided to hear a briefing on the new intelligence about North Korea's nuclear development activities from mid-level staffers of the White House.[65] Hu Jintao seemed to be deliberately sending a message to North Korea.

It was in October 2005 that Hu Jintao first visited North Korea as China's president. He was scheduled to participate in the APEC summit to be held in

Busan, South Korea, in November 2005, so by visiting North Korea before the meeting in Busan, he enabled North Korea to save face. Although Hu Jintao keeps a poker face most of the time, his expression occasionally turns sour when talking about North Korea and Kim Jong-il; reportedly, in "private meetings with U.S. officials, Hu makes clear his impatience for Kim and frustration with the North's self-defeating policies."[66]

In his meeting with Bush and senior U.S. officials, Hu had to acknowledge the existence of North Korea's enriched uranium program. He called the North Korean nuclear issue a "headache" and even used the expression "serious trouble." When Bush criticized North Korea's violation of human rights, Hu did not defend North Korea; Hu also implied that it was hard to understand how Kim Jong-il could be so insensitive to the suffering of his own people. When Bush asked if he thought that North Korea's economic reforms would succeed, Hu simply said, "I just don't know. But we have decided to keep giving them economic aid because it's the best bet we have."[67]

The second North Korean nuclear crisis erupted at the very time of the transition of power from Jiang Zemin to Hu Jintao. China's responses vis-à-vis the nuclear crisis, particularly the decision to convert the trilateral meeting to six-party talks, were decided by Hu Jintao. However, one veteran Chinese diplomat who has had long experience with Japan later described the proposal for six-party talks as "a joint product of Jiang Zemin and Hu Jintao,"[68] a view that was backed by a former Chinese diplomat who said that "the idea of six-party talks was seeded during the Jiang Zemin era, and it put forth buds in the Hu Jintao era."[69] While both statements seem to reflect political rhetoric, the six-party talks might appear to be a joint product because the idea for the talks arose when leadership of the government was being transferred from Jiang Zemin to Hu Jintao.

It should be noted, however, that there were differences of nuance in the two leaders' approaches to North Korea. Hu Jintao has attempted to convert China–North Korea relations into "more normal relations"; he also has taken a more severe stance toward the North Korean nuclear issue. While Jiang Zemin maintained that the North Korean nuclear issue was essentially a U.S.–North Korea bilateral issue that did not concern China, Hu made it clear that it did.

Regarding the difference between the two Chinese leaders, one senior South Korean government official concerned with the six-party talks said, "Jiang Zemin still believes in party-to-party relations and feels sympathy for North Korea. In contrast, Hu has no sympathy for North Korea and has a businesslike attitude toward the country." He added, "Jiang Zemin is still dragged by the past. Hu Jintao always demands preconditions when he deals with North Korea. Hu also intends to extend China's influence on the North Korean economy."[70]

One senior China-watcher in the U.S. administration observed another difference: "While the extrovert Jiang Zemin dared to enter the global geopolitical game, the introvert Hu Jintao makes much of the social stability and harmony within China. For Hu, North Korea is a possible source of disturbance to this stability and harmony. It is, to Hu, a liability."[71]

DAI BINGGUO'S SHUTTLE DIPLOMACY

It was Chinese diplomats who steadily helped to effect, in terms of administrative steps, the transformation of Chinese diplomacy from the trilateral meeting to the six-party talks. Particularly remarkable was the role played by Deputy Foreign Minister Dai Bingguo. Dai is a member of the Central Committee and, like Hu Jintao, a fourth-generation apparatchik. Born in 1941 to a peasant family in Guizhou Province, Dai is of Tujia ethnicity. The Tujia are a minority group that lives in the mountains of China's Hunan and Hubei Provinces. (It is a Tujia tradition to perform Maogusi, a dance and recital of an oral epic recounting the creation of the world, at the time of the Chinese New Year.)

After studying Russian at the Foreign Affairs College in Beijing, Dai was for a long time concerned with China's relations with the Soviet Union/Russia; he also served as China's ambassador to Hungary. He became assistant minister for foreign affairs in 1992, deputy head of the Chinese Communist Party's International Liaison Department in 1995, and head of the department in 1997. As department head, Dai submitted to party leaders several excellent analyses of subjects such as the collapse of the Communist Party in the Soviet Union and new politicians in Japan.[72] During his nearly seven-year tenure as head of the department, Dai frequently visited North Korea and built close relations with Kim Yang-gon, director of the International Department of the Workers' Party of Korea, the ruling party of the DPRK. In March 2000, Dai visited North Korea and met with Kim Jong-il at the Chinese embassy in Pyongyang to pave the way for Kim's visit to China in May 2000. Dai also escorted Kim Jong-il aboard his special train throughout Kim's visits in May 2000 and January 2001, and Kim has been favorably disposed toward Dai since then. In April 2003, Dai was appointed deputy foreign minister, a cabinet-level ministerial post. As a result, Dai wore three leadership caps, the other two being those of Communist Party secretary of the Foreign Ministry and head of the party's International Department until he was replaced at the International Department by Wang Jiarui in April 2003.

Dai once confessed to a Japanese guest, "Originally I planned to work at the Foreign Ministry in the morning and at the Zhongnanhai [a complex of buildings in Beijing that houses China's main party and government offices] in the afternoon, but it has become difficult to maintain that schedule because of the series of guests I must receive at the Foreign Ministry."[73]

During foreign policy consultations among Japan, China, and South Korea, it is not unusual for participants to enjoy *karaoke* at night, and the participants in the China-Japan Senior Officials Dialogue, which began in May 2005, were no exception. After a full-day meeting, Dai took Shotaro Yachi, Japan's vice minister for foreign affairs, to his hometown, Gui Yang, in Guizhou Province, for more leisurely policy consultations. (In similar fashion, Yachi took Dai to his hometown in Niigata the following year.) After dinner, diplomats from both nations competed in singing *karaoke*. On such occasions, Dai resonantly recites Mao Zedong's poems a cappella.[74]

What Dai pays special attention to and engages in personally as deputy foreign minister is China's relations with the United States, Japan, the Korean Peninsula, India, and Russia.[75] When the second North Korean nuclear crisis erupted, Dai still was head of the International Department. In January 2003, he flew to Pyongyang and had a five-hour exchange of views with Kang Sok-ju in which he aimed to convey China's concern about the nuclear crisis and to ascertain North Korea's "true intentions." Dai was alarmed when he sensed that North Korea's intention was to pursue its nuclear options.[76]

A former senior White House official saw that incident as a decisive factor in China's decision to act on North Korea. "It sent them [the Chinese] through the roof ... they were deeply concerned that it could have resulted in U.S. military action."[77] Another factor that alarmed China was a mid-air confrontation between the United States and North Korea (see chapter 3).[78] China admonished the North Koreans not to provoke the U.S. military again but assured Pyongyang that "we will protect you diplomatically." In other words, that incident also led to China's fuller commitment to settling the North Korean nuclear crisis. And here, Dai was China's point man.[79]

When Dai visited Pyongyang again in July 2003, he was deputy foreign minister. In the course of his four-day stay, Dai had a four-hour consultation with Kang Sok-ju, who reported on the talk to Kim Jong-il. Even though Dai was not able to secure North Korea's agreement to participate in the six-party talks, he succeeded in making North Korea "consider such participation positively."[80]

When China faces such critical situations, it is always Dai who is asked to deal with them. When Dai visits North Korea on a mission, he arrives as the special envoy of the government of China, and he customarily meets with Kim Jong-il.[81] It is said, however, that the Chinese never request a meeting with Kim Jong-il; they would rather make the North Korean government acknowledge the significance of Dai's visit.[82]

Before visiting Pyongyang, Dai visited Moscow in early July 2003 to meet with Foreign Minister Igor Ivanov to establish the groundwork for the six-party talks and to secure Russia's participation. At the same time, Vice Foreign Minister Wang Yi flew to Washington, also to handle groundwork for the six-party talks. Immediately after Dai came back from Pyongyang in mid-July, he himself flew to Washington, raising the curtain on China's shuttle diplomacy for the six-party talks.

On Friday, July 18, 2003, on the seventh floor of the U.S. Department of State building in Washington, the U.S. flag and the Chinese flag stood next to each other in the circular Treaty Room, the floor of which was covered with a Persian carpet. The United States gave Dai the treatment it accords a member of the cabinet. Powell expressed his gratitude for "the tremendous effort China has put into this matter [the North Korean nuclear issue]."[83] But Dai started his talk with an explanation of China's position vis-à-vis Taiwan and began what soon seemed like an endless monologue, occasionally referring to specific talking points: Taiwan is an integral part of China; assistance to secessionists in Taiwan is unforgivable; the United States should not sell arms to Taiwan; and so on and so forth. Powell put up with it for quite some time, but at last he interrupted Dai, saying, "You are testing my patience."[84] Looking back on the incident, Powell said:

> There have been three or four occasions in my career as secretary of state where I didn't feel like hearing any more . . . and I had to revert to my first profession, which is soldier, and say "Wait a minute." You know, particularly when they start to get offensive toward my government, then I have to respond. . . . It was necessary for me to say "Enough. I've heard you. You don't have to keep going on. Now let me tell you what I think." But it's like a summer storm. It comes and goes.[85]

Powell had set aside thirty minutes for his talk with Dai, but it lasted two hours and fifteen minutes.[86] Dai asked Powell to hold another trilateral meeting. In response, Powell reminded Dai that the United States had participated in the trilateral meeting only because that meeting was to be followed by a meeting that would involve more nations. Powell strongly insisted on including Japan and South Korea in the future multilateral talks. Although Dai continued to refer to the trilateral meeting for some time, at one point he ceased to mention it. The change was so quick that it made James Kelly ask himself, "So, did he do what he was supposed to do? There might be some domestic reason that he had to refer over and over to the trilateral meeting." Toward the end, Dai made some positive remark about a multilateral talk involving more countries, which could have been interpreted as his tacit approval of the participation of Japan and South Korea. Furthermore, Dai suggested that Russia, too, should be included, which was agreeable to Powell.[87]

The question was whether the United States would agree to having a bilateral talk with North Korea during the multilateral talks. Because one of the major causes of the failure of the trilateral meeting in April was that it had been held without confirming the willingness of the United States to engage in bilateral negotiations with North Korea, China found the question to be crucial.

By that time, Powell had obtained Bush's approval to mention that the U.S. delegation could have direct contact with the North Korean delegation during the six-party talks, and Powell used that as a bargaining card in dealing with Dai.[88] The Chinese had already informed the United States that it would be difficult for China to host six-party talks unless the United States committed itself beforehand to holding bilateral negotiations with North Korea. One of the reasons that Dai had failed to persuade North Korea to participate in six-party talks when he visited Pyongyang before he came to Washington was that he could not assure the North Koreans that bilateral negotiations between North Korea and the United States would take place. This time, Dai was able to secure Powell's commitment to holding the negotiations, and that would be an important card that Dai could use in dealing with North Korea.

During their talk, Powell had said to Dai, "You've met Kim Jong-il several times. By now you must be able to see through him and read his real intentions. Do you think we can trust him?"

"It's interesting that you say that," Dai responded. "Kim Jong-il said the same thing: 'Do you think we can trust the United States?'"[89]

Two-, Three-, Four-, Five-, Six-Party Talks

As noted, China had considered the North Korean nuclear issue to be basically an issue between the United States and North Korea. North Korea also had regarded the issue (which it calls the "Korea-U.S. nuclear issue") to be a concern of North Korea and the United States. At the same time, China has had to be extra careful to avoid seeming to be at least partially responsible for the North Korean nuclear issue. Although North Korea was driven to develop its own nuclear arms by its belief that the United States was a threat, it is undeniable that North Korea's sense of isolation and its feeling of having been abandoned and betrayed by China were factors as well. China's strategic adjustments following the end of the cold war, in particular the normalization of diplomatic relations with South Korea, were difficult for North Korea to accept. China is aware of this aspect of North Korea's psychology. That is why it has repeatedly insisted that the nuclear issue is basically a bilateral issue between the United States and North Korea.

At the same time, although North Korea regards the United States as its greatest threat, it aims to establish bilateral relations with the United States. That is to say, North Korea wishes to normalize diplomatic relations with the United States, and as the Chinese influence on North Korea increased after 2000, North Korea has aspired all the more for normalization. North Korea's overblown expectations of James Kelly's visit in 2002 revealed that wish clearly. One U.S. Department of State official concerned with Korean Peninsula affairs analyzed the situation as follows: "Chinese influence is growing, and at some point in time the Chinese are not going to need Kim Jong-il. There are a lot of reasons why Kim Jong-il should try to seek a relationship with the United States. The problem is he's not able to do so in a consistent sort of way."[90]

The United States, however, continued to refuse bilateral talks with North Korea and requested China's cooperation in launching multilateral consultations. In the end, it agreed to start with a trilateral meeting, and China tried to restrict its role in that meeting to that of an intermediary. Indeed, according to one Chinese diplomat, China's role in the trilateral meeting was to be confined "to providing a venue."[91]

It should be noted, however, that China was not satisfied with only providing a venue for the meeting; China intended to steer it in a direction beneficial to its own national interest. From that angle, the trilateral meeting was a convenient forum. Aside from imposing on China the relatively light burden of being a broker between the United States and North Korea, a burden that did not demand too much of a commitment from China, it allowed China, to use the expression of a senior official in the U.S. administration, to "project an image of U.S.-China bipolar domination of East Asia."[92]

China initially intended to institutionalize the trilateral meeting. After the first round of the meeting in April 2003, however, North Korea was very displeased with the format and threatened to boycott any future trilateral meetings. China nevertheless persisted in trying to convene the second round. The United States showed no interest at all. In fact, in May 2003 Bush had promised Prime Minister Koizumi and President Roh that the trilateral meeting would be replaced by multilateral consultations that would include Japan and South Korea. In the end, China had to give up the idea of additional trilateral meetings. One Chinese diplomat later confessed:

> Having played the role of a broker in the trilateral meeting, we found it was too much of a burden. We might be able to do that for another two or three occasions, but we had to admit that it is not sustainable for the long term. That is why China decided to head for the six-party talks.[93]

From the very beginning, China had been very cautious about five- or six-party talks. Some in the Communist Party and the government leadership insisted on excluding Japan from the multilateral forum;[94] others insisted on continuing the trilateral meeting as long as possible and, should that prove too difficult, to convert it to a four-party talk including South Korea. Although South Korea had not been enthusiastic about multilateral consultations before the trilateral meeting, it changed its attitude afterward and started to lobby China for multilateral consultations that would include South Korea. One Chinese official involved with the six-party talks later said, "We have always kept in mind that we need to respect South Korea's will."[95] That was based on the judgment that peace on the Korean Peninsula would be inconceivable without South Korea's involvement.

The four-party talks were proposed by the United States and South Korea in the 1996–97 period as a multilateral mechanism involving the two Koreas, the United States, and China in an effort to "achieve a permanent peace" on the Korean Peninsula.[96] In the beginning, North Korea resisted the inclusion of China. Instead, it proposed a two-step formula—a three-plus-one approach—suggesting that North and South Korea and the United States meet first, with China coming in at a second stage. At the time, China–North Korea relations were bumpy, and North Korea did not like to sit at the same table with China. But a more fundamental reason for the rejection of China was North Korea's basic position: that the United States and North Korea must be the core of peace building on the Korean Peninsula.[97] But South Korea opposed the exclusion of China, and China ended up participating in the four-party talks. China, however, opposed the U.S. suggestion to include Japan and Russia. China took the view that Japan and Russia could be included in a separate six-country consultation to be convened later.[98]

As far as a multilateral framework in Northeast Asia was concerned, China tended to envision a trilateral scheme involving the United States, China, and North Korea or perhaps a quadrilateral scheme with South Korea on the periphery. While promoting the trilateral meeting, China at one point justified itself to the United States by saying that "North Korea does not like five- or six-party talks." But actually North Korea had suggested, after the trilateral meeting in April 2003, that a multilateral forum should include Japan and Russia.

In the course of the negotiations for normalizing diplomatic relations between Japan and North Korea, which culminated in Koizumi's historic visit to Pyongyang in the autumn of 2002, Hitoshi Tanaka, director general of the Ministry of Foreign Affairs' Bureau of Asian and Oceanian affairs, and X, his North Korean counterpart, also talked about launching a consultation among six countries. From spring through summer of 2003, X would say that "the launching of six-party consultations is getting closer." At least at that point, North Korea strongly hoped to advance normalization of its relations with Japan, and it showed no interest in the multilateral consultation minus Japan that China aspired to.[99] China had been hesitant to participate in a multilateral framework that would include Japan and Russia, probably because China feared that its control over North Korea (and the Korean Peninsula) might be diluted. In particular, China has had a sense of rivalry with Japan that is rooted in the history of the two nations. One senior White House official later said, "If the United States did not strongly demand the inclusion of Japan and South Korea, China would have started the talks without these two countries."[100] But James Kelly is of a different view. Recalling Powell's spring 2003 trip to Japan, China, and South Korea, on which he accompanied Powell, Kelly remarked:

> When Powell presented the idea of a six-party [five-party at that time] consultation, China seemed to be reluctant to include Japan. But they did not resist for long. We made it clear that the United States would include Japan, which China was well aware of. Koizumi had already visited Pyongyang and signed the Pyongyang Declaration.[101]

On this particular point, one Chinese diplomat who was involved with the six-party talks later said, "China had been convinced since the time of the trilateral meeting that Japan and South Korea had to be included, because sooner or later the settlement of the North Korean issue would require economic power. Therefore, there were major roles for Japan and South Korea to play."[102]

Although that might have been the judgment of a working-level Chinese diplomat, party and government leaders seemed to have had a somewhat different view. Initially China had also intended to exclude Russia from the multilateral scheme. But a mid-level Chinese diplomat later acknowledged, "While some suggested launching a five-party consultation and inviting Russia at a later stage, we insisted on launching it with all the members if we later would have to include Russia anyway."[103] Underlying that attitude was the Chinese conclusion that in the case of four-party talks, a two-versus-two rivalry (China and North Korea versus the United States and South Korea) might cause negotiations to stagnate, while the inclusion of Russia might tip the balance in favor of the China–North Korea side. In a nutshell, the game plan that China had pursued at the beginning consisted of the following points:

—The trilateral meeting would be the core of the multilateral scheme.

—Japan would not be included.

—If one other country must be included, it would be South Korea.

—To avoid a two-versus-two stalemate, Russia should be invited to form a China–North Korea–Russia coalition.

To make the trilateral meeting the core of the scheme was a decision made by Chinese President Hu Jintao; therefore, the Chinese diplomats pursued that possibility until one month before the convening of the first round of the six-party talks. It was decided to exclude Japan because, according to one senior member of a Chinese government organization, "There was almost no one among the party and government leaders who supported Japan's participation."[104]

The countries to be included and excluded were subsequently changed as the circumstances changed. Among the countries concerned, however, China was most strongly opposed to holding a five-party meeting from which North Korea would be excluded. As mentioned earlier, when the United States first envisioned a framework for dealing with the North Korean nuclear issue, the White House was thinking of something along the lines of a multilateral "contact group," such as the one formed during the peace process in Yugoslavia, to put pressure on a "rogue state." China opposed that idea, believing that "it would make North Korea feel more isolated and psychologically cornered."[105]

The United States was highly dissatisfied with China's rejection of five-party talks excluding North Korea. U.S. Deputy Secretary of State Richard Armitage, having pointed out that the weakness of the six-party talks lies in the absence of consultation among the five (without North Korea being present), later described the current six-party talks as "not five versus one, but five and one or five plus one," emphasizing the benefits of a consultation among the five nations. China, however, would not listen to any proposal for five-nation consultations.[106] James Foster, of the U.S. Department of State's Korea desk, at one time attempted to organize regular luncheons in Washington among the representatives of the five countries' missions, but he had to abandon the plan because China refused to participate.[107]

WANG YI AND WU DAWEI

In addition to Dai Bingguo, the following Chinese diplomats handled the North Korean issue: Tang Jiaxuan, state councilor and former foreign minister; Li Zhaoxing, foreign minister; Wang Yi, vice foreign minister; Wu Dawei, vice foreign minister; Fu Ying, director general of the Asian Affairs Department, Ministry of Foreign Affairs; Cui Tiankai, director general of Policy Research (subsequently director general of the Asian Affairs Department), Ministry of Foreign Affairs; Ning Fukui, newly established ambassador in charge of North Korean talks; Li Bin, successor to Ning Fukui; Yang Xiyu, general office director, Office of the Ambassador in Charge of North Korean Talks; and Yang Jian, successor to Yang Xiyu.

When Li Zhaoxiang was a student at Beijing University in the 1960s, he shared a dormitory room with a North Korean student. The North Korean student slept on the upper bunk and Li on the lower bunk. The North Korean student was Kang Sok-ju, who later became a leading North Korean diplomat, the same diplomat who confronted James Kelly in their fateful encounter of October 2002. Whenever a Chinese delegation is to meet with Kang Sok-ju, Li has the delegation bring some *maotai* (a Chinese liquor made from fermented sorghum) for Kang. And whenever a North Korean diplomatic delegation is to visit China, Kang entrusts it with some Korean distilled spirits for Li. Although they have had a close relationship, it has rarely led to a breakthrough in the nuclear issue.[108]

Wang Yi was the head of the Chinese delegation at the six-party talks, and he chaired all the sessions during the talks. Helped no doubt by his good looks, Wang Yi's debut at the six-party talks impressed the world with the rise of China and its entry on the international stage. Wang Yi was born in Beijing. He was in his teens during the Great Cultural Revolution and was sent to a rural farming village in Heilongjiang Province for almost eight years to farm. In winter, the temperature there drops to minus 22 degrees Fahrenheit—sometimes to minus 40 degrees—and Wang and others kept warm by drinking cheap local distilled spirits. After having served as director of the Japan Division in the Ministry of Foreign Affairs, as counselor at the Chinese embassy in Japan, and as director general of the Asian Affairs Department of the Ministry of Foreign Affairs, Wang was appointed vice minister for foreign affairs in 2001. Wang, as the foremost Japan expert in China's Foreign Ministry, is regarded as a potential successor (along with Wu Dawei) to Tang Jiaxuan, state councilor and former foreign minister.

As the rivalry between China and Japan intensified in the mid-1990s, however, Japan-related posts within the Chinese Foreign Ministry became tricky assignments. Jiang Zemin's visit to Japan in 1998, which turned out to be a failure and strained the relationship between the two countries, was decisive. Ever since Prime Minister Koizumi's visit to the Yasukuni Shrine in 2001, officials in the Japan-related sections at the Chinese Foreign Ministry must be feeling as if they are treading on a field full of land mines.

In 1994, which was a trying time for China–North Korea relations, Wang Yi first visited North Korea; at the time, he was deputy director general of the Asian Affairs Department. The main purpose of his visit was to exchange views on the first nuclear issue. Subsequently, Wang participated in the four-party talks in Geneva, and since then he has been consistently involved in North Korean affairs. After the start of the six-party talks in 2003, Wang started visiting Pyongyang two or three times a year.[109] Wang's achievements as vice foreign minister have included successful border negotiations with Vietnam and stronger relations with India.

At the time of the first round of the six-party talks, James Kelly asked a Chinese diplomat where he might find Wang Yi. The diplomat replied that "Wang Yi has been talking for a long time on his cell phone. He is talking to the sea." Kelly thought, "Talking to the sea? What on earth does that mean?" The Chinese diplomat had translated the Chinese expressions "people in the sea" and "place a phone call to the sea" literally, and the resulting English was confusing. "People in the sea" refers to the inhabitants of the Mid-South Sea (Zhongnanhai)—that is, the top leaders of the Communist Party and the Chinese government. Thus, the diplomat meant to say that Wang was talking on his cell phone to some top leader in Zhongnanhai.[110]

In February 2003, in the middle of the second North Korean nuclear crisis, Wang Yi talked with North Korea's foreign minister, Paek Nam-sun, who was visiting Beijing. On the previous day, the Panmunjeom representative of the North Korean People's Army announced that the "KPA side will be left with no option but to take a decisive step to abandon its commitment to implement the Armistice Agreement as a signatory to it."[111] The armistice was signed on July 27, 1953, but even today, the resulting ceasefire is a delicate one, formally supported only by the agreement. Because of a continuing chain of North Korean acts of brinkmanship, Wang Yi warned Paek that "renewed provocations by the North toward the United States could strain Chinese–North Korean relations."[112]

Among friends, Wang Yi is described as being like a violin's G-string. Because of his appearance, his pickiness about his hairdo, his pride, his forcefulness and concentration, his grasp of all the details of a matter, and his logical presentations, the description may imply that Wang is constantly in a state of high tension, like a high-tone violin string.[113]

Wu Dawei, in contrast, can be likened to a low-tone contrabass. Although he has his tense moments, he generally manifests an air of Oriental magnanimity. Wu was born in Heilongjiang Province in Northeast China. People from Northeast China are believed to be talkative, and Wu Dawei is no exception. Legend has it that during the Great Cultural Revolution, Wu, representing a group of young radicals at the Foreign Ministry, had heated discussions with Zhou Enlai and on one occasion argued with Zhou for three hours, learning Zhou's knack for managing relations with Japan.[114]

In 2004, immediately after Wu became vice foreign minister, the historic Goguryeo incident occurred between China and South Korea. When the two nations' bilateral relations became strained over the history of the ancient Goguryeo kingdom—that is, over whether it was a local regime within Chinese territory or an independent state of Korean nationals—and over the boundary of modern Goguryeo, Wu succeeded in persuading South Korea to leave the issues to be settled through academic studies and negotiation. His ability to settle such a thorny issue was highly praised.[115]

Having served as the Chinese ambassador to South Korea and Japan, Wu developed an extensive network of acquaintances in both countries. His greatest achievement was the joint statement after the fourth round of the six-party talks in September 2005 when, with the help of the head delegates of Japan and South Korea, he took the lead in persuading the United States to agree at the last minute to the inclusion in the statement of its commitment to provide light-water reactors to North Korea.

Still, Wu might doubt his ability to negotiate effectively with the United States. Even after he was put in charge of the six-party talks, he did not visit the United States, even once, before or during the fourth round of the talks. (He might have thought that he had "outsourced" that function to Japan and South Korea.) One Japanese diplomat related the following episode, which might explain Wu's attitude toward the United States: "He once said during lunch that if he got drunk, we should drop all formalities. Although this is more or less permissible in an

Asian context, the Americans seriously doubted his sincerity."[116] Similarly, one U.S. diplomat who has been a regular participant in the six-party talks once said, noting the Chinese fables and anecdotes that Wu habitually quotes, "Wu Dawei talks in proverbs: The Donkey and the Tiger. I suspect those things work very well in China but it doesn't translate internationally."[117]

But to the United States, the biggest question mark concerning Wu arises from the suspicion that "what he tells North Korea is different from what he tells the United States."[118] To be sure, that suspicion has not been confined to Wu alone. In fact, the United States had made the same complaint regarding Wang Yi. It should be noted, however, that both of these Chinese diplomats also have been suspected by North Korea of being "running dogs of the United States" and "Japan lovers."[119]

In September 2004, Li Changchun, a member of the standing committee of the Politburo of the Chinese Communist Party, visited Pyongyang, accompanied by Wu, who had just been appointed vice foreign minister. But Wu was not called into the discussion between Li and Kim Jong-il. During the visit, Wu requested a meeting with Kim Gye-gwan, deputy minister for foreign affairs and head of North Korea's delegation to the six-party talks, but Kim did not agree to the meeting until 10:00 p.m. of the night before the delegation was to return to Beijing.[120]

At the time, North Korea was critical of "China's unfriendly attitude" toward North Korea, China's actions regarding such matters as the Goguryeo issue, the treatment of defectors from North Korea, and the military training exercises of the People's Liberation Army near the China–North Korea border. North Korea also was upset at a Chinese magazine, *Zhanlue Yu Guanli* (*Strategy and Management*), that was critical of North Korea, in particular because of an article by Wang Zhongwen that it had published.[121] At the same time, the North Koreans were aware that Wu Dawei was a straight talker. When Wu visited Pyongyang in August 2005, he raised a very blunt question: "Whenever you open your mouth, you stress the importance of bilateral relations with the United States and Japan. And yet at the last minute you let go the best chances to improve bilateral relations with these countries. What's going on? Can someone tell me what's happening?"[122]

His comment about the best chance to improve bilateral relations with the United States was a reference to the heightened momentum toward normalization that culminated in Secretary of State Madeleine Albright's visit to Pyongyang in the fall of 2000; in the case of Japan, it was in reference to the full-fledged drive toward normalization after Prime Minister Koizumi's visit to Pyongyang.

Fu Ying, like Wang Yi and Wu Dawei, built her career in the Asian Affairs Department of the Ministry of Foreign Affairs, but she also had studied at Kent State University, Ohio, for one year, in 1985–86. She was a member of the Chinese delegation to the peace negotiations in Cambodia in the early 1990s. Richard

Solomon, then assistant secretary of state for East Asia and the Pacific and a U.S. negotiator on the Cambodian peace talks, remembers that he was impressed by this international-minded and flexible female diplomat.[123]

After serving as Chinese ambassador to the Philippines in 1998–2000, Fu Ying was appointed director of the Asian Affairs Department. She was the Chinese representative at the trilateral meeting in Beijing in April 2003, and the United States was encouraged when during the meeting Fu Ying took a clear stance in favor of denuclearization in front of the North Korean delegation. One U.S. administration official involved in the trilateral meeting later recalled, "The United States and China tuned in with each other the best while Fu Ying was active on the Chinese side."[124]

After Fu Ying was appointed Chinese ambassador to Australia in 2004, Cui Tiankai succeeded her as director general of the Asian Affairs Department. A senior U.S. administration official once described Cui as having the "style and sophistication . . . of a vice president of a Wall Street investment bank."[125] After serving as an interpreter for China's permanent mission to the United Nations, Cui was appointed director of the Department of International Organizations and Conferences at the Ministry of Foreign Affairs; deputy director of the Information Department of the Ministry of Foreign Affairs; counselor of the permanent mission to the UN; deputy director and subsequently director of the Policy Research Office of the Ministry of Foreign Affairs; and director general of the Asian Affairs Department of the Ministry of Foreign Affairs. Cui was promoted to assistant deputy foreign minister in 2006.

In the early 1990s, Cui was a member of the Chinese delegation to negotiate with the host country, South Korea, concerning China's participation in the APEC meetings there. His South Korean counterpart during the negotiations was Chun Young-woo, who later became the head of the South Korean delegation to the six-party talks. Cui's knowledge and insight in policy matters is among the best in the Chinese Foreign Ministry. Members of the U.S. Department of State Policy Planning Staff were so impressed with Cui's independent thinking, his logical and well-structured presentations, and his gentle manner (when he was still at the Policy Research Department) that they sensed the "emergence of a new type of Chinese diplomat with wider vision."[126] In the fourth round of the six-party talks, Cui, then director general of the Asian Affairs Department, was put in charge of drafting the joint statement, and he played a major role in achieving agreement among the participating parties.[127]

In December 2003, the Chinese Ministry of Foreign Affairs established a new post, that of ambassador in charge of North Korean talks. Ning Fukui, a North Korea specialist who studied at Kim Il-sung University in Pyongyang and also served as Chinese ambassador to Cambodia, was the first ambassador to the talks. In the four-party talks (among the two Koreas, the United States, and

China), Ning was deputy head of the Chinese delegation. After Ning became ambassador to South Korea, Li Bin succeeded Ning as ambassador in charge of North Korean talks. Li, like his predecessor, had studied at Kim Il-sung University and speaks fluent Korean.

In order to support the ambassador in charge of North Korean talks and to help plan policies concerning the North Korean nuclear issue, the General Office of North Korean Talks was established within the Asian Affairs Department in anticipation of the institutionalization of the six-party talks. Because the North Korean nuclear issue is intertwined with China's relations with the United States and its nonproliferation policy, the General Office is charged with coordinating China's policies regarding those matters. The first director of the General Office was Yang Xiyu, who also had experience in helping to coordinate the four-party talks. After Yang Xiyu went to the United States to conduct research at Stanford University, he was succeeded by Yang Jian, who had been counselor at the Chinese embassy in Washington. While Ning and Li were old Korea hands who had specialized in Korean affairs throughout their careers, Yang Xiyu and Yang Jian had long been posted in the United States, and their attitudes toward North Korea and the United States were equally businesslike.

The Department of North American and Oceanian Affairs of China's Foreign Ministry also has had a major say in the North Korean nuclear issue, and its director general, He Yafei, has been deeply involved. To begin with, within the Foreign Ministry, the Department of North American and Oceanian Affairs has consistently had greater influence than the Department of Asian Affairs since the normalization of diplomatic ties between China and the United States.[128] In addition, the Chinese bureaucracy suffers from the idiosyncrasy of intraministry factions or "schools." According to a Chinese diplomat specializing in U.S. affairs, once a bureaucrat becomes a member of one faction or school, he or she cannot break free; in addition, each school treats all nonmembers as outsiders and offers no support or assistance to any nonmember.[129] One senior officer of a different department within the Foreign Ministry who attended the six-party talks several times had the following to say about the feuds between factions at the time that the Chinese delegation to the six-party talks was being organized:

> In the beginning, there was a lot of noise about which department should be in charge of the six-party talks and who should be the head delegate. It was the same type of bureaucratic politics you can find anywhere in the world. At first, representatives of both the Asian Affairs Department and the North American and Oceanian Affairs Department were equal deputy delegates, but, after a while, the influence of the Asian Affairs Department became overwhelming.[130]

Some in the U.S. government have had doubts about how much influence the Chinese Ministry of Foreign Affairs actually has concerning China's policies toward North Korea. One North Korea watcher in the Pentagon analyzed the situation as follows:

> To begin with, China realized the seriousness of the North Korean nuclear issue too late. In the past forty years, the Chinese Foreign Ministry has never taken leadership in diplomacy vis-à-vis North Korea. That had always been handled by the Chinese Communist Party and the People's Liberation Army. The Foreign Ministry just drops in toward the end of the party."[131]

Although official visits between China and North Korea had declined significantly within a few years after Kim Il-sung's death, there were still fifteen state visits by military personnel of the two nations (eight Chinese delegations and seven North Korean delegations) during the 1994–98 period.[132] But the military attaché posted in the Chinese embassy in Pyongyang is not allowed to meet any member of the North Korean military one to one. The North Korean is obliged to be accompanied by two civilian officials of the North Korean defense agencies. That is because North Korea is wary of the Chinese military. "Mil-mil" exchanges deserve that name when the two sides train and exercise together, but that has never been the case with China and North Korea. Some Chinese diplomats say that the nature of China–North Korea military exchanges has been changing into something more ceremonial and symbolic.[133]

At present, the nine members of the standing committee of the Politburo of the Chinese Communist Party do not include a single member of the military. The North Korean military would interpret that as evidence that reform and opening would reduce the authority and prestige of the military. One Chinese diplomat who has extensive knowledge of the North Korean situation pointed out, "The North Korean military basically is opposed to reform and opening up. That is particularly true among young, upcoming officers who are greedy for power. They tend to look down on China as a bad example."[134]

Although it is uncertain to what extent China's People's Liberation Army (PLA) has its own view of and policy toward North Korea, it is believed that the predominant view within the PLA makes much of the strategic value of the Korean Peninsula both as a buffer state between China and the United States and as an area that is "interlocked" with Taiwan. Some in the PLA advocate reinforcement of the North Korean regime and China–North Korea relations in order to block adverse effects, such as encouraging Taiwan's quest for independence, if and when North Korea is toppled by the United States.[135] It also is believed that the older generation within the PLA is more sympathetic toward North Korea than the younger officers, who tend to be critical.[136] It is highly likely that future military exchanges between China and North Korea will be further subdued.

In the summer of 2003, at Dandong Station on the China–North Korea border, China's public security authorities confiscated a shipment of tributyl phosphate (TBP) that was on a train bound for Pyongyang. TBP is a liquid substance that is used as a catalyst in extracting weapons-grade plutonium. The U.S. Central Intelligence Agency had already obtained information about the transport of TBP to North Korea as early as the end of 2002. The purchaser was identified as an agent of a North Korean intelligence agency, and the amount to be transported was determined to be twenty tons. The shipper was a company based in Dalian, China. Even though the U.S. government knew the details, it could not prevent the transaction. When that was found out, there were strong suspicions within the U.S. administration that "the Chinese government would not cooperate" with the United States in investigating the case.[137]

By the summer of 2003, the situation had changed. As the second North Korean nuclear crisis deepened, relations between the United States and China tipped toward mutual cooperation and the six-party talks. Again a debate arose within the Bush administration over whether it should ask for Chinese cooperation regarding the matter. Although Under Secretary of State John Bolton opposed the idea on the grounds that it would increase the risk of exposure of the source of the intelligence, Secretary of State Colin Powell decided to go ahead, a decision that was endorsed by President Bush. This time the U.S. government notified the Chinese government of the transaction and asked the Chinese government to block it.[138]

However, there also were debates within the Chinese government over whether to collaborate with the United States on the matter. The Foreign Ministry and Ministry of Public Security insisted on collaborating with the United States, while the People's Liberation Army was opposed, because, it said, North Korea should not be made to feel isolated. It was said that in the end, President Hu Jintao himself made the decision to collaborate with the United States.[139]

THE INTERNATIONAL DEPARTMENT

In addition to the Foreign Ministry and the PLA, China has yet another channel of communication with North Korea: the International Department of the Central Committee of the Chinese Communist Party (CCP/ID). It is also known as the International Liaison Department (ILD), its name prior to 1995.[140] This 100-member office in the Communist Party has used its own information to cultivate a deep relationship with North Korea for its own purposes. An important mission of the department has been to maintain good relations with the Workers' Party of Korea, which has long been a friend of the Chinese Communist

Party. Coordination of exchanges between top leaders of the two countries is an important function of the CCP/ID, in cooperation with the International Department of the Workers' Party of Korea.

The International Liaison Department was established in 1951 as an instrument of China's ideological diplomacy to promote exchanges with communist parties, socialist parties, and nationalist parties across the world—and with other political parties and groups believed to be progressive—and to advance the cause of "anti-imperialism, anti-colonialism, and anti-hegemonism." The ILD changed its English name to International Department in 1995, although its Chinese name, *Zhongyang Duiwai Lianluo Bu,* remained the same.[141] As the Chinese discarded traditional ideological diplomacy and adopted a more pragmatic approach, the International Department began to promote exchanges with the political parties of all countries. Nevertheless, in the case of countries such as North Korea, Vietnam, and Cuba, China has pursued its traditional special relations with their respective communist parties or workers' parties. Of particular importance for China is its relationship with the Workers' Party of Korea. Restoration of relations between China and North Korea since 1999–2000 owes much to the efforts of the CCP/ID, and particularly to Dai Bingguo, its director at the time. Dai was succeeded by Wang Jiarui, a party bureaucrat who had served in various posts, including as mayor of Qingdao City, Shandong Province. He was appointed deputy director of the CCP/ID in 2000 and director in April 2003.

It is not easy for outsiders to grasp the role and function of the CCP/ID in China's overall policy toward North Korea. Many in the Chinese Foreign Ministry would say that "the CCP/ID's major task is essentially to take care of protocol."[142] That view is widely shared by people who support the emergence of the "New Thinking" diplomacy in China. Some hold an even harsher view:

> The ILD's clientele is limited to North Korea, Vietnam, and Cuba. It has a small staff of a little more than 100. They talk about "party-to-party" relations, but their talk has no substance. Like the Chinese Academy of Social Sciences, it has nothing except vested interests from the old days. It might not be dead yet, but it is dying."[143]

Nevertheless, when it comes to relations with North Korea, the CCP/ID remains a channel of communication that cannot be ignored. One of the reasons for its prominence is that the North Koreans are convinced that the CCP/ID is the most important organization in China. A North Korean diplomat once said, "If something urgent happens in North Korea, what is needed is the ID, not the Foreign Ministry."[144] That conviction is rooted in the fact that the CCP/ID and the Workers' Party of Korea take the lead in managing summit diplomacy, on which North Korea's national strategy relies for the maintenance and development of China–North Korea relations. When the media ask for confirmation of a visit to

China by Kim Jong-il, for example, the Foreign Ministry's spokesperson often tells them to "ask the ILD." That clearly shows which office is really in charge, at least as far as Kim Jong-il's visits are concerned.[145]

It was the director of the CCP/ID, Wang Jiarui, whom China dispatched to Pyongyang to persuade North Korea to come back to the six-party talks in February 2005, immediately after North Korea announced that it possessed nuclear arms.[146] Wang Jiarui's visit to Pyongyang had long been scheduled, originally to lay the groundwork for Hu Jintao's scheduled visit to North Korea. However, after North Korea's announcement, the Chinese government decided to use the visit to discuss the nuclear issue and sent Ning Fukui along to accompany Wang.[147] Nevertheless, the negotiations for the visit still remained the job of the CCP/ID, and the Foreign Ministry could only ask the CCP/ID to make the necessary arrangements with North Korea. It was said that on that particular occasion state councilor Tang Jiaxuan personally asked for the assistance of the CCP/ID and succeeded in having Wu Dawai accompany the delegation.[148]

Because there are constant and countless contacts and exchanges between the CCP/ID and the Workers' Party of Korea, the network of contacts can be converted at any time to a channel for diplomatic negotiations in case of an emergency. That flexibility has been one strength of China's diplomacy toward North Korea. In February 2003, immediately after the eruption of the second nuclear crisis, a South Korean delegation that included Lee Jong-seok, a member of the transition team for the Roh Moo-hyun government, visited Beijing and met senior officials of the CCP/ID. During the meeting, the CCP/ID officials related that since October 2002, when James Kelly had visited North Korea, China had been making efforts to prevent a second nuclear crisis through more than fifty mutual-exchange programs with North Korea.[149]

However, throughout the 1990s, North Korea's nuclear activity was a sensitive issue that no one at the Foreign Ministry wanted to touch.[150] Nonetheless, one Chinese diplomat later said, "If not for the nuclear issue, relations with North Korea would be small enough that an assistant division director, not even a division director, could handle them."[151]

The first North Korean nuclear crisis erupted at the beginning of the 1990s. It had the potential to seriously affect China's national interest and security, through potential reactions such as a U.S. military attack on North Korea, the UN Security Council's adoption of sanctions against North Korea, revision of Japan's self-defense policy, enhancement of the U.S.-Japan security pact, changes in Russia's Far East policy, and economic repercussions in South Korea. Another nuclear crisis erupted in the fall of 2002, resulting in the possibility of adverse effects on China's economic development, the status and perception of China by the international community, the direction of China-U.S. relations, Japan's nuclear policy, the future of the Korean Peninsula, and the direction of nationalist movements in Northeast Asia. The North Korean issue thus became an issue that the president of China himself had to handle, whether or not he wanted to.

A STRATEGIC LIABILITY AND A STRATEGIC ASSET

It was on October 6, 1949, five days after the birth of the People's Republic of China, that China and North Korea established diplomatic relations. Six months later, the Korean War erupted. China sent 2 million volunteer troops, saving North Korea from annihilation. When the armistice agreement was signed in July 1953, the war—which had lasted more than two years and required some 575 meetings for negotiations between the delegates of the United States, North Korea, and China—ended. The process that led to the agreement was itself an extension of the bloody war, colored by hatred and mutual distrust, and the negotiations were later called "the longest armistice negotiations in history."[152]

Although China suffered tremendous damage and human loss in the war, it entered the center stage of international politics and established itself as a leader of the third world. For China, therefore, North Korea became a strategic liability and, at the same time, a strategic asset. Since then, the China–North Korea relationship has been called one of "teeth and lips," with North Korea being the lips and China being the teeth. Without lips, teeth are exposed to damage, but without teeth, lips cannot keep their shape; therefore, they are mutually dependent.

In 1961, China and the DPRK entered into the Treaty of Friendship, Cooperation, and Mutual Assistance, giving birth to a military alliance based on their responsibility to defend one another. As time went on, the cold war ended, China and South Korea normalized diplomatic relations, and the international environment surrounding the China–North Korea relationship changed dramatically. Consequently, relations between China and North Korea became more bumpy, and they were further aggravated by the death of Kim Il-sung in 1994. In March 1996, Foreign Minister Gong Ro-myung of South Korea met with China's minister of foreign affairs, Qian Qichen, in Beijing. It was reported that during their talk, Qian noted that "after Kim Jong-il took over from Kim Il-sung, relations with North Korea became more difficult. It is now difficult for us to even meet Kim Jong-il."[153] At the time, the exchange of high-ranking officials between the two countries was practically nonexistent.

In 1996, China announced that it was considering reducing its food aid to North Korea, to which North Korea responded by threatening to open economic relations with Taiwan, as it did when China and South Korea normalized diplomatic relations. Hastily, China offered a comprehensive assistance package to North Korea. Then, in 1997, a group of Chinese agricultural experts visited North Korea under the United Nations Development Programme (UNDP) and recommended the introduction there of Chinese-style agricultural reform.

North Korea started a campaign to label Deng Xiaoping a traitor to socialism for his recommendation to implement agricultural reforms. China retaliated with a threat to reduce food aid to North Korea, in response to which North Korea immediately started negotiating with Taiwan regarding the opening of an air route between the two. Taiwan hinted at the possibility of providing 5 million tons of food aid to North Korea. China terminated its food-aid reduction plan, and North Korea terminated negotiations with Taiwan.[154]

In 1997, Hwang Jang-yop, a former president of Kim Il-sung University and a theorist of the *juche* (national self-reliance) philosophy that was the core of Kim Il-sung's ideology, sought political asylum in the South Korean embassy in Beijing. The incident symbolized the collapse of the *juche* philosophy. North Korea even sent an armed squad across the border to Beijing to kill Hwang, which made China extremely angry. Although North Korea immediately demanded that China transfer Hwang into North Korean custody, China "expelled" Hwang, who entered South Korea via the Philippines. South Korea granted Hwang political asylum.[155]

In August 1998, North Korea launched a test of its Taepodong missile without giving prior notice to China. When questioned by China, North Korea "rudely" said that such an action was the "prerogative of a sovereign state."[156]

In China, meanwhile, calls grew stronger for China to revise it relations with North Korea to reflect China's national interests and strategy instead of tradition or sentiment.[157] Three primary arguments were made:

—China's main goals are to promote domestic economic development and unification with Taiwan, and care must be taken so that those goals are not obstructed by North Korea's conduct. The risks of strengthening relations with North Korea must be minimized.

—Because China's air force and navy play a larger role in the nation's defense than does the army, the strategic value of the Korean Peninsula as a buffer has declined. Indeed, China should be careful to avoid involvement in any military conflict provoked by North Korea.

—Because South Korea has pursued the sunshine policy, China does not have to choose between South Korea or North Korea. That provides China with greater freedom of action, including keeping North Korea at arm's length.

It was absolutely necessary for China to keep North Korea in its camp during the cold war in order to rival the Soviet Union. However, after China's relations with the Soviet Union were normalized and the Soviet Union eventually collapsed in 1989, North Korea lost its strategic value to China.

There was even a debate within China over whether to maintain the 1961 China-DPRK Treaty of Friendship, Cooperation, and Mutual Assistance, whose second article provides that

The Contracting Parties undertake jointly to adopt all measures to prevent aggression against either of the Contracting Parties by any state. In the event of one of the Contracting Parties being subjected to the armed attack by any state or several states jointly and thus being involved in a state of war, the other Contracting Party shall immediately render military and other assistance by all means at its disposal."[158]

The right of collective defense may be exercised only if the partner country is attacked by another country, not if the partner country attacks another country. Therefore, in 1997, as Tang Jiaxuan, who was then foreign minister, made clear, the Chinese government considered the military assistance clause in the treaty to be "a remnant of cold war era thinking and no longer relevant to the current situation."[159] According to a retired high-ranking Chinese army officer, China was disgusted to hear North Korea argue that it had been and remained a frontline defense against U.S. hostilities. "They are saying, in effect, that they are defending and protecting us from the U.S. That argument is unacceptable to us," he said.[160] Those in China who insisted on revising the China-DPRK Treaty of Friendship, Cooperation, and Mutual Assistance demanded inclusion of the above arguments along with a provision that China would not assist North Korea if the latter violated international laws or agreements. Shen Jiru justified China's position as follows:

—If a North Korea–U.S. war were to break out over the North Korean nuclear issue, China would not be obliged to send its troops to fight in such a war, a war that it does not believe in. Therefore, the treaty should be revised.

—By making China's intention to revise the treaty clear and by letting the world know of China's position regarding the issue, China will be able to convert China's mode of involvement in a possible U.S.–North Korea war from a passive one to a more proactive one.

—That way, if North Korea envisions a war with the United States, then China, by discouraging any North Korean expectation that China will be obliged to join the war, can deter North Korea from rushing into conflict with the United States.[161]

On the other hand, those who defended the treaty argued that China would lose leverage over North Korea if the alliance were dissolved by abolishing the treaty:

—China should use the alliance to restrain North Korea by making it known that China will not assist North Korea if the latter mishandles a situation. That could also restrain South Korean conduct.

—The treaty should be maintained as a deterrent both to North Korea's nuclearization and to a U.S. preemptive attack against North Korea.

—In other words, on one hand China should threaten to abolish the treaty in order to restrain North Korea from joining the world's nuclear nations, and, on the other hand, it should tell the United States that China would honor its responsibility to defend North Korea in order to dissuade the U.S. from a pre-emptive attack against North Korea.[162]

In the spring of 2003, the Chinese government and Communist Party leaders decided to continue the half-century-old treaty. The decision was based on the belief that the treaty would serve to deter a military attack on North Korea by the United States and South Korea as well as North Korean adventurism. However, a Chinese diplomat later confessed that China was not anxious to prolong the life of the treaty but that rather than terminate it, China would simply wait for it to die a natural death. And yet China succeeded in making North Korea agree that it would abide by the armistice agreement, which would remain valid until a new peace regime was established.[163] That had the effect of constraining North Korea from even dreaming about attacking South Korea.

The present China–North Korea alliance has been described as "neither allied abandonment nor allied entrapment."[164] The alliance is, so to speak, "blighted but still standing." China has no intention of using the alliance as a military alliance, and North Korea is aware of that. It should be noted, however, that China's view on North Korea is complicated by diverse factors. China might be said to feel a complicated "sentimental bond" with North Korea. First, the Chinese soldiers who fought in the Korean War (and their families and descendants) do not want to abandon North Korea. Then, the old-time leftist intellectuals and workers feel sympathy toward the "underdog" North Korea and antipathy toward the United States. That sympathy is also seen among the younger generation, a side effect of their antipathy toward the United States. In addition, there are ethnic Korean minorities in China, who are hypersensitive to China's slighting and ditching of North Korea. According to field research conducted by the International Crisis Group, a Brussels-based international NGO, elders in China still have strong feelings of nostalgia with respect to the Korean War—in which China fought heroically, directly engaging "American imperialists"—as well as a feeling of intimacy toward their war-comrade, North Korea.[165]

However, many among the elite in China feel that North Korea is harming both China's national interest and its image in the international community. The middle-class citizens of the coastal cities hold an especially severe view of North Korea, at least in part because they have been exposed to foreign media.[166]

On the strategic and policy levels, advocates of the "New Thinking" diplomacy—a new diplomacy based on the redefinition of China's national interest and strategy as a world power—propose keeping a "distance from North Korea." For example, Shi Yinhong, a professor at Renmin University of China, asserting that "Chinese participation in the Korean War was clearly a mistake," said that in coming to North Korea's aid, "China missed the chance to unify Taiwan and, instead, obtained a troublesome neighbor"; he also maintained that "if North

Korea's nuclear development causes a war on the Korean Peninsula, China should not intervene."[167]

Shi's view that China's participation in the Korean War was a mistake is based on a new historical perception that China was tricked into entering the Korean War by Stalin.

Wang Zhongwen, an economist at the Center for Overseas Economic Research of the Tianjin Academy of Social Sciences, has severely criticized the hereditary system of succession and political oppression in North Korea:

> Kim Jong-il [is] practicing ultra-leftist politics and political persecution in order to maintain dynastic rule. . . .
>
> North Korea has long made light of good neighborly relations with China and never repaid its debt of goodwill when China needed it. . . .
>
> North Korea's irresponsible conduct often stagnates China-U.S. relations. Moreover, North Korea oftentimes causes conflicts between China and the United States.[168]

Wang's major point was that North Korea's policies and conduct have greatly harmed China's national interests. The article in which Wang made his remarks was distributed through the Internet and caught the attention of the South Korean media and of North Korea, which, as described earlier, severely criticized the article and the bimonthly, *Zhanlue Yu Guanli*, in which it was published. *Zhanlue Yu Guanli* was forced to cease publication by Chinese authorities.[169]

There are those who claim that Wang and his associates are saying things that the new leadership of the Chinese government and the Chinese Communist Party believe but cannot say publicly. China's desire for the return of Taiwan, domestic economic development, major power status, China-U.S. strategic cooperation, nationalism, and so on supports the "New Thinking" diplomacy both logically and emotionally. To them, North Korea is nothing but a negative legacy of the past.

CHAPTER NINE

THE RISE OF CHINA

During the second Korean nuclear crisis, China insisted on denuclearization of the Korean Peninsula, as it had done during the first. Although the amount of highly enriched uranium (HEU) possessed by North Korea remained uncertain, China had no doubt that North Korea intended to develop nuclear arms. China's distrust of and apprehension toward North Korea deepened. China was not happy that North Korea had secretly advanced its uranium enrichment program, but it was more displeased by North Korea's cunning. North Korea had used the uranium enrichment issue as if it were a new bargaining card but had neither acknowledged nor denied the existence of the uranium enrichment program to U.S. special envoy James Kelly; then, after Kelly's departure, Pyongyang had acted as if North Korea were a full-fledged nuclear power. Regarding North Korea's behavior, one veteran Chinese diplomat, a long-time Asia watcher, later remarked:

> The biggest mistake that North Korea made was admitting that it had that [uranium enrichment program]. That turned the situation around. Had it not admitted that, North Korea could have been able to play a different game. As it turned out, that gave hard-liners in the Bush administration a great excuse to attack North Korea.
>
> That admission de facto killed the Agreed Framework, which had been most beneficial for North Korea. It also killed the momentum toward diplomatic normalization with Japan, too. . . . What's puzzling me is why in North Korea nobody is taking responsibility for one of the greatest diplomatic errors in history. Is it because it was a decision personally made by Kim Jong-il? This is a serious matter.[1]

That same diplomat added that the denuclearization of the Korean Peninsula had consistently been China's position, even during the 1960s, when it was pursuing its ideological foreign diplomacy: "Even during the Mao Zedong era, China never provided North Korea with even a tiny bit of material for use in North Korea's nuclear or missile programs. That was a decision made for China's own national interest and security. And that has not changed even now." [2]

China was already bordered by three nuclear powers: Russia, India, and Pakistan. However, how seriously China felt that its security was directly threatened by the nuclearization of North Korea was questionable. In fact, "China did not think that North Korea possessed nuclear deterrent power."[3]

Although North Korea might not be a direct threat to China, it could be an indirect threat. For one thing, there is the danger that the United States might destroy North Korea's nuclear facilities. In fact, the United States had considered a military attack on North Korea's nuclear facilities in the early 1990s, during the George H. W. Bush administration, and in the mid-1990s, during the Clinton administration.[4] When the Clinton administration advanced its preparations to attack North Korea's nuclear facilities in Yongbyon in 1994, China formulated plans to support North Korea by sending between 50,000 to 75,000 ground troops as well as approximately 10,000 rapid deployment troops along the China–North Korea border. China was preparing for a worst-case scenario.[5]

What China now needs most is economic development, and that requires a peaceful international environment. If a war breaks out on the Korean Peninsula, a massive number of refugees might rush across the border into China; even armed North Korean troops might cross into Chinese territory. If the United States were to bomb North Korean facilities where weapons of mass destruction are stored—facilities that are concentrated in the China–North Korea border region—China might not remain damage free. In that case, China might get entrapped in the conflict, thereby interfering with its own economic miracle. That must be avoided at any cost.

Another danger or indirect threat to China is that North Korean nuclearization might induce Japan, South Korea, and even Taiwan to develop their own nuclear arms. China has not forgotten that in the past South Korea and Taiwan both have attempted to develop nuclear weapons. Also, although Japan has consistently taken a non-nuclear policy stance, if it were to go nuclear, that could drastically change the international environment in East Asia. Even without any additional provocation, calls have been getting louder in Japan for the government to upgrade its defense in order to counter North Korea's missile threat. To avoid giving Japan an excuse to do that, North Korea must not be allowed to possess nuclear weapons. Moreover, China is worried that even if Japan would not go so far as to develop its own nuclear weapons, Japan might use the existence of North Korean nuclear weapons as an excuse to expand its own conventional military capability. One Chinese diplomat remarked, "At present, China does not believe that Japan will go nuclear, but it is apprehensive about Japan expanding its military readiness by taking advantage of North Korea's nuclear capability."[6]

Such arguments against the nuclearization of the Korean Peninsula take a longer-term, strategic perspective. China is aware that a heightened sense of national isolation in North Korea might hasten the collapse of the current regime if North Korea receives too much pressure from outside. A variety of post-collapse scenarios, from insurgencies to all-out civil war, are possible; therefore, North Korea must not be cornered. China is also apprehensive about possible turmoil in North Korea adversely influencing the socioeconomic development and stability of China's northeastern region.

Since the second Korean nuclear crisis, China has decided to aim at further stabilizing the Korean Peninsula by expediting the denuclearization of the peninsula, which will make it possible to prevent a war and the collapse of the regime in North Korea. In other words, China aims to simultaneously achieve both denuclearization and the stability of the Korean Peninsula.

Among the strategic risks that China faces, the one that it most fears is that of Japan going nuclear. However, some think that "China is in the process of reviewing the logic that nuclearization of North Korea will automatically make Japan and Taiwan develop their own nuclear weapons." One observer said:

> After the Iraq War, . . . if the United States perceives the nuclearization of Japan and Taiwan as opposed to U.S. interests, the United States will not let that happen. . . . What China worries about most is that the United States will help Japan and Taiwan to build up theatre missile-defense systems using the North Korean nuclear threat as an excuse.[7]

Which does China fear most: Japan's development of nuclear weapons or a Japan-U.S.-Taiwan missile-defense system? Probably it fears both equally. The Chinese diplomat in charge of the six-party talks referred to "two rumors about Japan" heard in the "corridors" at the six-party talks:

> One [rumor] is that the abduction issue has been overblown by some Japanese politicians who do not want the North Korean nuclear issue settled. Their ultimate aim is to make it easier for Japan to possess nuclear arms by heightening tensions with North Korea, using the abduction issue and publicizing the horror of a nuclearized North Korea. The other one is that, even though Japan has claimed that settlement of the abduction issue is a precondition for diplomatic normalization, it will not actually normalize ties with North Korea even after the issue is settled. Japan will next promise normalization after the settlement of the nuclear issue, which has been premeditated from the beginning.[8]

THE RISE OF CHINA / 303

The source of these rumors must be someone in the "corridors" of China. Reportedly some in the Bush administration at the time, notably Vice President Dick Cheney and Under Secretary of State John Bolton, considered stimulating China's fear of Japan's nuclearization to make China take a larger role in settling the North Korean nuclear issue. When Dick Cheney appeared on NBC's *Meet the Press* on March 16, 2003, he was confronted with the following question: "If nothing is done to stop it, North Korea will possess six nuclear weapons by June. Do we have any other choice than having a one-to-one dialogue with North Korea or to launch a preemptive attack on them?" Cheney replied:

> [Our friends in the region]—Japan, South Korea, and especially China— are far more directly affected than we are. . . . [T]he idea of a nuclear- armed North Korea with ballistic missiles to deliver those weapons will, I think, probably set off an arms race in that part of the world, and other nations, perhaps Japan, for example, may be forced to consider whether they want to readdress the nuclear question. That's not in China's interest.[9]

That interview took place two days before the U.S. attack on Iraq, at a time when he and the administration were preoccupied with Iraq. John Bolton made a sim- ilar statement in testimony on June 4, 2003, before the U.S. House Committee on International Relations:

> A nuclear-capable North Korea may not be a direct threat to China as such. . . . I think the balance of opinion of those who have looked at the region carefully is that a nuclear-capable North Korea could well produce a deci- sion in Japan to seek a nuclear weapons capability. And a nuclear-capable Japan would fundamentally alter the calculus in Northeast Asia, and that does get China's attention. . . . I am not sure how the Chinese resolve that dilemma. I do not think it is really for us to be that concerned about, frankly.[10]

Both Cheney and Bolton are saying the same thing: China must exert more pres- sure on North Korea to dissuade the latter's nuclear development activities, because China, due to its rivalry with Japan, might be most adversely affected if Japan decided to go nuclear. Voices were heard among the neocons pointing out that it was odd that China had not spoken out about the danger of Japan's nuclear armament. One powerful neocon has said, "Although the United States can tolerate a nuclear power, Japan, if it has to, that would be a crucial develop- ment for China. Why, then, doesn't China say anything about it?"[11]

The Japanese government was perplexed. Having experienced the atomic bombing of Hiroshima and Nagasaki, the Japanese government has consistently stuck to three non-nuclear principles: Japan shall neither possess nor manufacture nuclear weapons, nor shall it permit their introduction into Japanese territory.

These three principles have had the full support of the Japanese people since they were first articulated by Prime Minister Eisaku Sato in 1967, and since then Japan has ratified the Nuclear Non-Proliferation Treaty and accepted International Atomic Energy Agency inspections of its nuclear power facilities. Japan's security policy has been formulated on the basis of its alliance with the United States and on U.S. extended deterrence (that is, a nuclear umbrella). Japan believes that it is protected by this formula, and it has never felt the necessity to develop its own nuclear arms. It was therefore beyond its comprehension when the United States publicly warned of the danger of Japan's possible nuclear armament and directed that warning to China in particular. When the U.S.-Japan Strategy Dialogue was convened in Tokyo in June 2003, Yukio Takeuchi, Japan's vice foreign minister, requested Deputy Secretary of State Richard Armitage to control such tactless remarks by senior U.S. administration officials. Takeuchi's question was blunt: "How will the U.S. take responsibility for its Japan nuclear domino theory if it will alarm and propel China to push for its nuclear arms buildup?"[12] Armitage became furious when he heard what Takeuchi said. "Who said that? Who said that?" he said angrily. "If I find out who said it, I'm going to drop a f***ing safe on their head!" During the coffee break, Armitage asked Michael Green, the director of East Asian Affairs for the National Security Council, "Who said that?" Green said, "Rich, it was the vice president." Armitage barked out, "God damn it, f***ing idiot."[13]

Around the same time, Deputy Defense Secretary Paul Wolfowitz also insisted that pressure be applied on China under this "nuclear domino" theory. NSC's Stephen Hadley and Michael Green were quoted as noting that that tactic could backfire:

> The problem is if we say to the Chinese "We don't trust Japan," then we open a gap between the U.S. and Japan that will encourage the Chinese to drive a wedge [between the United States and Japan].[14]

The Chinese government, for its part, never mentioned the "nuclear domino" theory. It never referred to the possibility that North Korea's nuclearization might induce Japan to nuclearize itself. One senior U.S. administration official said, "The Chinese don't like to talk about it. That's our talking point, and why they should get more involved. And, you know, our side raises the nuclear domino theory frequently."[15] China, however, has to be constantly on guard concerning the negative aspects of exerting too much pressure on North Korea.

Moreover, China also must keep in mind the danger of critically worsening China-Japan relations if China openly emphasized, in conjunction with the North Korean nuclear crisis, the possibility of Japan's arming itself with nuclear weapons. If that were to happen, Japan would accuse China of transforming the

North Korean nuclear issue into the issue of Japan's nonexistent nuclear aspirations in order to avoid responsibility for not dealing with North Korea. That would make the situation in Northeast Asia even more difficult.

As pointed out earlier, China's two major objectives are the real and total denuclearization of North Korea and maintenance of peace and stability in Northeast Asia. According to one Chinese diplomat, "These two objectives are not two sides of a coin from which one is to be chosen."[16] Therefore, if the denuclearization of the Korean Peninsula were to harm the peace and stability of Northeast Asia, China would not hesitate to postpone the settlement of the North Korean nuclear issue. It was exactly that point that Robert Zoellick, U.S. deputy secretary of state, asked Dai Bingguo, China's deputy foreign minister, to clarify:

> China's fear of collapse of the North Korean regime overrides its concern about the North Korean nuclear weapons. It must be because regime collapse is a more imminent danger. But I am afraid it will be difficult to maintain a balance between these two concerns for long. The North Korean regime itself manages to survive by conducting criminal activities.[17]

One senior U.S. administration official who had been engaged in policy dialogue with China remarked, "Rather than opting for the collapse of [the North Korean] regime, China will choose to live with ambiguity. A less-obvious nuclear weapon is something China might be compelled to live with."[18]

OUTSOURCING DIPLOMACY TO CHINA

From the beginning, the North Korean nuclear issue has also been a matter of China's policy concerning the United States. When China decided to host multilateral consultations to settle the issue, coordination and control of its relationship with the United States was a major factor behind the decision—that is, China hoped that the multilateral process would help improve and stabilize its relations with the United States.

When the Bush administration praised itself by announcing that "the six-party talks are really a bright spot in China-U.S. relations,"[19] it was partly because the United States was convinced that to China, the North Korean issue was "the variable" in its relations with the United States, "one of the levers that allows us [the U.S.] to improve U.S.-China relations." It was from that angle that the United States welcomed the Chinese approach to the North Korean issue.[20]

It actually was a little puzzling that the United States decided to leave to China most of the responsibility for promoting peace on the Korean Peninsula, particularly the settling of the North Korean nuclear issue. The Korean Peninsula is, after all, a strategically critical region for the United States. It was all the more puzzling when one considers that the key posts in the Bush administration were dominated by Pentagon hawks and neocons who were deeply suspicious of China. Moreover, it was during the peak period of neocon domination of U.S. politics that the Bush administration decided to have China play a major role.

Some in the administration were worried that by hosting the six-party talks China might become more influential in East Asia, including the Korean Peninsula. But the advocates of a realistic foreign policy rationalized the arrangement:

> We knew from the beginning that the United States is paying a political cost [by having China host the six-party talks], but it will be more than compensated for if North Korea abandons its nuclear program. We don't know what will be the real cost and what will be the benefit until the very end.[21]

Given the lack of better ideas, it was realistic to let China play that role. Assistant Secretary of State James Kelly later said, regarding the suppression of opposition from the neocons, "It was because the president had strongly supported the six-party talks. As long as he did, even the neocons had to give way. Besides, anti-China elements in the administration were concentrated in the somewhat lower echelon, not at the top level."[22] But some in Washington were not very happy with having China play such a major role. Lawrence Wilkerson remarked, "I am convinced that many of them thought that China was going to fail and that would make their job easier. 'Just stand back boys. We'll watch China, and China won't ever deliver. And therefore, as I told you, China's untrustworthy.'"[23]

However, although China welcomed the persistent U.S. requests that China help the United States launch multilateral consultations, it was convinced that the United States did so only because it had no other choice. It was a temporary measure, not a longer-term, strategic measure. One veteran Chinese diplomat offered this analysis of the situation:

> The priority issues for the United States are Iraq, the Middle East, and the war against terrorism. These already are a handful for the United States, and it cannot handle other issues. The United States does not wish to distract its focus from its top priorities because of the North Korean nuclear issue. It wishes to buy time. And that's why it decided to use China, to outsource it to China, so to speak. And China accepted the order. While China is busy setting up the multilateral forum, the United States can just hide behind the curtain. If we succeed, the United States takes the bow, and if we fail, China takes the blame. We in China are aware that this is what the United States has in mind.[24]

After the 9/11 terrorist attacks, the United States and China shared a deepened sense of the threat posed by radical Islamic terrorists. In Washington, the threat posed by radical Islamic terrorism replaced the perception, which had been spreading, of the threat posed by China. Nevertheless, the root of the tension between the United States and China remained. China was apprehensive after 9/11 that the U.S. inclination toward unilateral action in general—and toward regime change and military action vis-à-vis terrorism and weapons of mass destruction in particular—would strengthen. Buried yet deeper are issues relating to U.S.-China competition, including the rise and fall of power; ideology; the Taiwan issue; economic interests; regional-order schemes; alliances versus regionalism; and multilateral versus unilateral approaches to solving problems. China has been coolly observing how those issues evolve. For example, Qian Qichen, China's vice premier, said in a speech in September 2002 marking the one-year anniversary of the 9/11 attacks that "generally speaking, Sino-U.S. relations are developing forward, but there are also many frictions and struggles. . . .There is no change in the basic contradictions between China and the United States."[25]

For its part, the United States has projected onto its policies its perception of China—a perception that includes fundamental contradictions. The 2001 issue of the *Quadrennial Defense Review Report (QDR)* of the U.S. Department of Defense touched on "the possibility . . . that a military competitor with a formidable resource base will emerge in the region" and stressed that among America's "enduring national interests" is "precluding hostile domination of critical areas, particularly Europe, Northeast Asia, the East Asian littoral . . . defined as the region stretching from south of Japan through Australia and into the Bay of Bengal."[26] Five years later, the 2006 *QDR* described China as a country with "the greatest potential to compete militarily with the United States," more explicitly expressing alarm regarding an arms race.[27]

The Korean Peninsula and Northeast Asia in general are the areas where the strategic "contradictions" between the United States and China are most extreme. The six-party talks can be regarded as China's new response to those contradictions. China's ambition has been to transfigure, in the long run, the U.S.-centered defense structure in the region, which is based on the hub-and-spoke network that the United States created during the cold war. Piao Jianyi, an expert on Korean Peninsula issues at the Institute of Asia-Pacific Studies, Chinese Academy of Social Sciences, has expressed his hopes concerning the six-party talks: "China will use the six-party talks effectively to take in the old security regimes of the U.S.-Japan and U.S.–South Korea alliances, to establish a new security regime in the region, and to solve contradictions between China and the United States."[28]

One Japanese diplomat who specializes in China offered a similar assessment of China's goals:

China aims to reduce the U.S. presence in this region in general and to promote a reduction of United States military forces. If China brings these up directly with the United States, their bilateral relations might become awkward. Therefore, China intends to advance slowly toward these goals within the framework of the six-party talks.[29]

What significance will the unification of the Korean Peninsula have in China's game plan? If eliminating the U.S. military presence in the region is desirable to China, unifying the Korean Peninsula is highly desirable. If the peninsula is unified, U.S. troops in South Korea will have no reason to stay there. Short of that, if cooperation and reconciliation between North Korea and South Korea deepen through South Korea's sunshine policy and its peace and prosperity policy, the need for and legitimacy of the U.S. military presence in South Korea will decrease. The nuclear crisis has been an obstacle to that, but the obstacle can be eliminated by settling the North Korean nuclear issue. Many in China insist that "that is why the United States does not wish to settle this issue. Once it is settled, the raison d'etre for the U.S. troops remaining in South Korea will be gone."[30]

However, others in China view the U.S. military presence in the Asia Pacific region as a stabilizing force. That strategic perception has been passed on from one leader to another in China since the time of Mao Zedong. Henry Kissinger once observed, "China tacitly encouraged our presence in the Philippines and Thailand and, while it followed Pyongyang's basic line, it never really pressed us to remove our forces from Korea. It correctly judged that the visible presence of American power was crucial for maintaining a balance of power in Asia and Europe."[31]

At the policy-planning level on the occasion of the 2002 policy dialogue between China and the United States, the Chinese announced that "China does not feel that the U.S. troops stationed in South Korea pose a threat to China."[32] China has indirectly expressed concern about the implications of the "strategic flexibility" that the United States has demanded on South Korea, but, instead of raising the issue head-on, it decided to have its ambassador to South Korea, Ning Fukui, give a tacit warning to the United States.[33]

It should be noted, however, that the direction of the reorganization of the U.S. military remains uncertain, given the uncertainty of the relative positions of the "long war" with Islamic terrorists and the presence of U.S. troops in South Korea. Although the Chinese do not oppose the continued presence of U.S. troops on the Korean Peninsula after reunification of the two Koreas, there are strong voices in the Chinese government opposing the prospect of U.S. troops advancing into and staying in the territory of the former North Korea afterward. There seems to be strong resistance within the Chinese government against U.S. troops advancing into North Korea in case—and just in case—the North Korean regime collapses.[34]

During the U.S.-China Senior Dialogue, Robert Zoellick confronted Dai Bing-guo regarding the Chinese "traditional view" that the reunification of the Korean Peninsula is not desirable because it will invite deployment along North Korea's border with China of the U.S. troops currently in South Korea.

> Get real! If Korea unifies, we're not going to have big military forces any-where in the country. We probably would agree with Japan and China and South Korea. You probably want the United States to keep a relationship with South Korea because of the uncertainty that South Korea has with Japan and China. But it would probably [be] air and naval assets in the South. Okay?"[35]

One Chinese diplomat in charge of East Asian affairs noted that "China will not oppose continuation of the U.S.–South Korea alliance and the U.S.-Japan alliance as long as the United States does not obstruct Taiwan's return to China."[36] From a different angle, it can be said that the sounding out regarding a mutually acceptable format for the presence of U.S. troops on the unified Korean Penin-sula had already begun. It should be noted that China appreciates the U.S. mili-tary presence "to a certain extent" because, on the flip side of the coin, China is strongly suspicious of Japan's remilitarization. Although China opposes the pres-ence of foreign military bases in East Asia, China secretly wishes that the United States would hold Japan by the neck indefinitely. This ambivalence might well be reflected in China's traditional attitude to "accept the U.S.-Japan pact even though China does not welcome it." Furthermore, China's true wish might not be for the withdrawal of U.S. troops from the Korean Peninsula but for the con-tinued presence of U.S. troops in Japan. Robert Scalapino, a leading U.S. scholar of Asia, wrote, "If U.S. troops still remain on the Korean Peninsula after reunifi-cation, it is very unlikely that China would accept willingly an American military presence on its border. After nearly fifty years, the Korean War would have been lost."[37] China might have such a perception, depending on the future develop-ment of China-U.S. relations.

But, as Scalapino also pointed out, it is equally possible that the withdrawal of U.S. troops from the Korean Peninsula or "an adjustment of this nature would likely cause complications with the PRC."[38] Signs of such an adjustment already have appeared, in the form of the reduction of the number of U.S. troops in South Korea, the weakening of the U.S.–South Korea alliance, and the strength-ening of the U.S.-Japan alliance. Although the tighter alliance between the United States and Japan has been triggered by the worldwide threat of terrorism as well as by the heightened threat of North Korean nuclear arms and missiles, with-drawal of U.S. troops could promote further tightening of the alliance, depend-ing on the scale and speed of U.S. withdrawal from South Korea as well as on the future development of the U.S.–South Korea alliance. If a latent, structural conflict between the U.S.-Japan alliance and China underlies the strengthening of the U.S.-Japan alliance, China cannot expect the U.S.-Japan alliance and the U.S. military presence in East Asia to function only as a cork to contain Japan. Besides, China has to take into consideration such risks as the rise of nationalism on the Korean Peninsula and growing instability along the China-Korea border arising from Korean nationalism.

One senior member of a Chinese government organization who has long been involved with Korean affairs confessed that China had been displeased by Kim Jong-il's remark that "we will tolerate the presence of U.S. troops as a peace-keeping force even after unification," which he made after the North-South summit talk in June 2000. The Chinese official observed, "That remark was Kim Jong-il's expression of distrust of China. In short, he intends to restrain China using the United States. In both North and South Korea, Korean nationalism has been on the rise, and his remarks also reflected this trend."[39]

Another senior staffer of a Chinese government organization who frequently visits North Korea had this to say about China's perception of the rise of Korean nationalism:

> This time, the North Korean delegation to South Korea paid a visit to the national cemetery, which includes graveyards of the victims of the Korean War. This goes to show that North Korea has also started using this kind of Korean-nationalism card. We must pay close attention to these changes on the Korean Peninsula.[40]

His comment was in reference to the visit of a North Korean delegation to the Seoul National Cemetery on August 15, 2005, on the occasion of the sixtieth anniversary of Korean national independence. It is interesting, however, that South Korea interprets North Korea's conduct as an expression of North Korea's wish that when the next South Korean delegation goes to Pyongyang, it will, in return, visit Kumsusan Memorial Palace, where the remains of Kim Il-sung lie in state.

TAIWAN AND NORTH KOREA

Soon after becoming president, Bush said that he would do "whatever it took to help Taiwan defend herself."[41] And some among the neocons in the Bush administration were sympathetic to Taiwan's aspiration for independence. China accordingly suspected that the Bush administration might revise its traditional "one China" policy and support Taiwanese independence behind the scenes. In May 2002, Hu Jintao, then the vice president of China, visited Washington and met with President Bush, Vice President Cheney, Defense Secretary Rumsfeld, and a few others. The primary purpose of Hu's visit was to ask the United States to confirm that it would adhere to the one-China principle and refrain from sending any inappropriate signals to advocates of Taiwanese independence. Both Bush and Cheney clearly announced that they supported the traditional principle of one China.[42] After the talk with Bush, Hu was in such high spirits that he said to reporters, in English, "It was a very good talk."[43] When James Kelly escorted Hu to the airport, Hu wore a big smile. Shaking Kelly's hand, he said, "I have enjoyed this visit to Washington so much. Please pass this on to the president and vice-president and secretary." Hu held Kelly's hand for more than thirty seconds, as if he would never let it go. Behind Hu were "nine happy Chinese senior officials with big smiles and grins."[44]

Nevertheless, China continued to be nervous about the Bush administration's Taiwan policy. However, during Prime Minister Wen Jiabao's visit of December 2003 to the United States, Bush reaffirmed the one-China policy. At the joint press conference after his talk with Wen, Bush announced in an unusually strong tone, "Comments and actions made by the leader of Taiwan indicate that he may be willing to make decisions unilaterally to change the status quo, which we oppose," restraining the movement toward Taiwanese independence.[45] At the time, the Chen Shui-bian government of Taiwan was pushing the movement toward Taiwanese independence, including by holding a national referendum on the issue.

Some in the United States suspected that China might demand that the United States support China regarding the Taiwan issue in return for contributing to the denuclearization of the Korean Peninsula by hosting the six party talks. It was even reported that some American diplomats in the U.S. embassy in Beijing had been secretly undertaking such a "linkage operation."[46] Wang Yiwei, a young, up-and-coming Chinese scholar of international politics, has explained the "linkage operation" as follows:

> Many ordinary Chinese accept the view that if China helps the United States in dealing with the North Korean nuclear issue, the United States should return the favor by helping to settle the Taiwan issue through cooperation between China and the United States. . . . [The government of] China will not have such unrealistic, extravagant hopes, of course. . . . Still, public opinion does influence the Chinese government . . . the Chinese government does need to achieve a balance between the North Korean nuclear issue and the Taiwan issue.[47]

However, an official of the Bush administration and self-proclaimed "neocon" later remarked, "China has flown trial balloons several times in an attempt to link the North Korean issue with other issues, such as Taiwan, human rights, and nonproliferation. We immediately shot them down every time, though."[48]

During the second round of six-party talks, in February 2004, China took a much more critical position toward the U.S. North Korea policy. Some in the

Bush administration suspected that China had deliberately linked the Taiwan issue with the North Korean issue. One U.S. participant in the talks later raised the following question:

> China thinks the denuclearization of North Korea is necessary to improve its own security. But China calculates what it will do in the North Korean case if the United States makes a certain contribution to the Taiwan issue. Therefore, if it judges that the United States has not sufficiently followed the "correct attitude" toward the Taiwan issue that the United States had indicated in the U.S.-China summit talk last December, China could reverse its attitude toward the North Korean issue and start saying that it would be sufficient for North Korea to freeze its nuclear development program instead of abandoning it, or that peaceful use of nuclear power is tolerable.[49]

That particular remark might have reflected a touch of paranoia. One senior White House official offered a different view: "Both the United States and China know what is important to them—the pursuit of which has inadvertently resulted in a linkage between the Taiwan and North Korean issues. And in my experience the Chinese government never linked them, never even implicitly linked them."[50] James Kelly also echoed that view: "We were constantly accused that the Chinese were saying they would do more on North Korea if we do more on Taiwan. The woods were full of Chinese academics that would throw that stuff around. Never, ever hear that from— Chinese are way too smart."[51]

When Dai Bingguo visited the United States in December 2004, he talked with Stephen Hadley, the deputy national security adviser, for nearly two hours, 75 percent of which was devoted to the Taiwan issue and 25 percent to North Korea. Dai regarded as a "new policy" the December 13, 2003, statement by Bush that the United States opposed any Taiwanese unilateral decision to change the status quo. Using that statement as a "new baseline for U.S. policy," Dai criticized the United States, saying that it had fallen back since that statement was made. In response, Hadley tried to make it clear to the Chinese that the "the president opposes unilateral changes to the status quo by either side . . . that we stand by the Taiwan Relations Act." Hadley brushed off the Chinese accusation by saying that the Chinese labeling of Bush's remark as a "new policy" was the result of their over-interpretation of Bush's words.[52] As is evident in the talk between Dai Bingguo and Hadley, which was monopolized by the issues of Taiwan and North Korea, the conduct of the United States or China concerning either issue inevitably and automatically affects the conduct of the other country.

China has a tendency to view both the Taiwan and the Korean Peninsula issues as belonging to the same geopolitical theater; they also belong to the same historical theater and theater of memory. Some in China caution that there is "a strategic pitfall" waiting for China if it intervenes in Korean Peninsula affairs:

> China fought Japan over the Korean Peninsula in the Sino-Japan War and consequently lost Taiwan. China fought the United States over the same peninsula in the Korean War and missed the opportunity to liberate Taiwan. If a war breaks out one more time over the Korean Peninsula, it might give Taiwan a chance to become independent.[53]

The priority for China, therefore, is to prevent turmoil—to promote peace and stability—on the Korean Peninsula in order not to lose Taiwan again. If North Korea will collapse no matter what China does, China hopes that it will crumble peacefully. China pays full attention to peace and stability on the peninsula, and it watches closely how the United States behaves regarding the Taiwan issue. According to one Chinese diplomat who has long been involved with Asian affairs, China "hopes that the improvement of both China-U.S. relations and the international environment in Northeast Asia through the six-party talks will contribute to the settlement of the Taiwan issue, and China is attempting to facilitate such improvements." Yet, at the same time, China has been careful to avoid linking the China-U.S. issue to the six-party talks. The diplomat quoted above also said, "We have never linked these two issues technically."[54] China does not wish to make the Taiwan issue a multilateral issue, nor does it wish to create a connection between North Korea and Taiwan.

The United States has taken every opportunity to appreciate and praise China's painstaking efforts to facilitate the six-party talks. For example, in testimony before the U.S. House Foreign Relations Committee in June 2004, James Kelly evaluated China's role as follows: "In the key area of security, by being a strong and reliable partner on the counterterrorism front and an active participant in the Six-Party Talks, China has proven that where its interests coincide with ours, it can be extraordinarily helpful in enhancing regional stability. It also shows promise that it is prepared to take on global responsibilities."[55]

But the United States remains cautious about China interpreting what it has done for the six-party talks as a favor to the United States and about China feeling that the United States owes China a favor in return. The United States is of the view that China should contribute to denuclearization of the Korean Peninsula for the sake of China's own national interest and security, not for the benefit of the United States. One veteran Asia watcher, journalist Richard Halloran, believes that "the Chinese argument for linkage between the North Korean and Taiwan issues is fundamentally flawed," and, he points out, "China no more wants North Korean nuclear missiles on its border in Manchuria than Washington wants them pointed at U.S. forces in Asia or at Alaska and Hawaii."[56]

That perception is widely shared within the Bush administration, as the congressional testimony of John Bolton quoted earlier—"I am sure how the Chinese resolve that dilemma. I do not think it is really for us to be that concerned about, frankly."—clearly reveals. And that view is not confined to the neocons. Deputy Secretary of State Richard Armitage has also been heard to say that "we don't want China to feel that we owe it for the denuclearization of North Korea. This is not the issue."[57]

A RESPONSIBLE STAKEHOLDER

The first term of the Bush administration started with confrontation between the United States and China and ended in their bilateral cooperation. Immediately after Bush's first inauguration, the Chinese forced the landing of a U.S. reconnaissance plane off Hainan Island; during the incident, the leaders of the Chinese government and the Chinese Communist Party even refused to answer phone calls from President Bush and Secretary of State Powell. It was Powell who somehow managed to settle the issue diplomatically. In the process, however, Powell was struck by a feeling of indefinable irritation toward China. Some time after the incident, Powell lectured Vice Premier Qian Qichen: "Don't you have crisis management in China? To begin with, you wouldn't even answer the phone in an emergency. How can you fill the responsibility of a major power of the region and the world? How are you going to stabilize and manage relations with the United States?" He then added:

> Please do not hesitate to call me any time. In return, please make it possible for me to call you any time. In these phone calls, let us skip the niceties and go directly into the main topic. Let us converse in a "There is a situation here," and "What can we do to help you?"–style. Isn't that like a responsible power of the world?[58]

After 9/11, however, relations between the United States and China were stabilized through the formation by the two countries of a joint antiterrorist front—a foundation that made it possible to launch the six-party talks.

At the U.S.-China summit talk during the APEC summit conference in Santiago, Chile, in the autumn of 2004, the parties agreed to launch a "Senior Dialogue"—what the Chinese call a "strategic dialogue"—among high-ranking U.S. and Chinese officials. The first meeting was held in Beijing in August 2005, at the same time as the fourth round of the six-party talks, between Dai Bingguo, China's deputy minister of foreign affairs, and Robert Zoellick, who had become deputy secretary of state in the spring of 2005, during the second term of the Bush administration, when Condoleezza Rice became secretary of state. Zoellick lived in Hong Kong in 1980, and during the year he visited China for the first time. He told Dai how much he was impressed by China's remarkable development since then. In those twenty years, China had begun to participate in the international system and to develop its economy. But Zoellick emphasized, "[A]s China's influence grows, it will be important for China to also try to work with us as a stakeholder in that system."[59] When Zoellick gave a talk before the National Committee on United States–China Relations in New York on September 21, 2005, he further elaborated on the idea of China as a responsible stakeholder. After praising the U.S. policy of engaging China, which he said must have helped China to decide to join the international system and contributed to China's remarkable development, Zoellick emphasized that

> China needs to recognize how its actions are perceived by others.... Uncertainties about how China will use its power will lead the United States—and others as well—to hedge relations with China. Many countries hope China will pursue a "peaceful rise" but will not bet their future on it.[60]

The "peaceful rise" concept was first advocated by Zheng Bijian, chairman of the China Reform Forum, who is believed to be a member of Hu Jintao's brain trust. To summarize Zheng's concept, the recent rise of China is an extension of a long-term historic trend since 1979 and as such is irreversible and uncontainable; it will never disrupt the existing international order, from which China has benefited greatly and which it considers in its own national interest to maintain; China needs to cooperate with the international community, including the United States, and it has made cooperation a cornerstone of its national strategy; and the rise of China is a "peaceful rise," in contrast to the hegemonic rises that Germany and Japan pursued from the late nineteenth century to the mid twentieth century and that the Soviet Union pursued in the latter half of the twentieth century.[61]

The "peaceful rise" argument somehow has the flavor of the determinism of the Marxist view of history, which is one reason why it arouses some people's suspicions. Nevertheless, China did in fact develop peacefully during the 1980s and 1990s. That was partly attributable to the principle of "low-profile diplomacy," a faithful embodiment of Deng Xiaoping's teaching of *"Tao guang yang hui"* ("Hide one's capabilities and bide one's time"), which had been applied since 1989. It also reflected other principles that Deng Xiaoping adopted as the basis for Chinese diplomacy in the midst of the great backlash against China after the Tiananmen Square incident, such as "Observe calmly," "Consolidate one's foothold," and "Respond with composure."

The greatest achievement of the principle of low-profile diplomacy has been the settlement of numerous border issues. In the 1990s, China succeeded in settling seventeen of the twenty-three border disputes that it had been engaged in previously. China wished to develop its economy, which called for a peaceful

environment in the neighboring region, which in turn called for settling outstanding border issues and signing agreements. As one senior Chinese government official said, "China has borders with twenty-three countries either on land
or on the sea. In contrast, the United States has borders with only two countries,
Canada and Mexico. Therefore, Chinese diplomacy is much more complex and
requires much more prudence. And North Korea is one of those twenty-three."[62]

However, since the late 1990s Chinese diplomatic initiatives to break the status quo have become conspicuous, particularly in connection with natural
resources, including initiatives to acquire oil and natural gas concessions; to
deepen relations with failed states, such as Sudan, that have oil; and to challenge
neighboring countries regarding maritime resources, particularly Japan over
East China Sea oil and gas fields.

What Zoellick asked of China by calling it a "responsible stakeholder" was for
China to prove that it is pursuing a peaceful rise not so much in language as in
actions. "The most pressing opportunity [for China to prove itself] is North
Korea," Zoellick said. He continued:

> Since hosting the Six-Party Talks at their inception in 2003, China has
> played a constructive role. This week we achieved a Joint Statement of
> Principles, with an agreement on the goal of "verifiable denuclearization of
> the Korean Peninsula in a peaceful manner." But the hard work of imple-
> mentation lies ahead, and China should share our interest in effective and
> comprehensive compliance.[63]

The entire text of Zoellick's speech was uploaded to the web page of the U.S.
Department of State, but it immediately became impossible to access the page
from China.[64] Access was restored after the U.S. embassy in Beijing protested to
the Chinese Foreign Ministry. It was believed that the Chinese government might
have been bewildered by several severe criticisms of China that were included in
Zoellick's speech, including China's lack of transparency regarding its military
and its involvement in Iranian nuclear development activities.[65]

In December 2005, Zoellick and Dai met in Washington for the second round
of the Senior Dialogue, where they engaged in a heated discussion over the definition of a "responsible stakeholder." According to one senior U.S. administration official, the exchange occasionally took on the "appearance of a Scholastic
discussion."[66]

Dai: "What is a stakeholder? Is it the same as a shareholder?"

Zoellick: "No, it is not. A shareholder invests and receives a dividend. A
stakeholder is different from a shareholder. . . .Tony Blair said 'Let's create
a stakeholder society.' This is the stakeholder concept I am talking about. It's
a concept that entails not only benefits but also inherent responsibilities."

Dai: "We have no Chinese word that accurately describes this concept. Can we interpret it as a strategic partnership?"

Zoellick: "No, it is not the same as a strategic partnership."

Dai: "China believes that to play a responsible role and to interact in the United Nations is to be a stakeholder, because a responsible role in the international community should be played in the United Nations. To begin with, who is going to judge if one country is fulfilling its responsibilities as a stakeholder? Why does it have to be the United States? To accept the United States' judgment means to accept U.S. hegemony in the world, doesn't it?"

Zoellick: "It won't only be the United States. There will be others in the process, and they can have influence. Everyone is making the rules. The rules of the international community are not those of a hierarchical system. It is true, though, that the United States has played a special role and has had special responsibilities in creating the international rules. The same thing can be said about globalization. As Mr. Zheng Bijian wrote in his *Foreign Affairs* essay, Chinese leaders had made a significant strategic choice "to embrace economic globalization rather than to detach themselves from it." No other country in the world has benefited from globalization as much as China has. And fundamentally, it was the United States that created this globalization. To protect globalization is in the national interest of China. To protect globalization—the status quo—is in the national interest of China."[67]

The Zoellick-Dai discussion covered a wide range of issues. Dai obviously had not prepared any talking points beforehand; he only occasionally referred to something that he had scribbled on a yellow pad in his hands. The only exception was when the two discussed the North Korean issue, at which time Dai read aloud specific talking points. The United States was reminded once again that the North Korean issue was a sensitive issue for China.[68]

The third round of the Senior Dialogue took place in Beijing in January 2006. The term "stakeholder" had been translated into Chinese as *"liyi xiangguan zhe,"* which had already been widely used by the Chinese media before the third round. The Chinese, however, often tended to omit "responsible" from "responsible stakeholder."[69]

One of the issues covered in the third round was relations between China and Japan, particularly with regard to their perceptions of history. During the dialogue, Zoellick proposed a meeting among historians from China, Japan, and the United States to help overcome the history issues, but China did not respond positively to his proposition. In the press conference after the meeting, Kong

Quan, a Chinese Foreign Ministry spokesman, said, "There is a peculiarity in the history of Northeast Asia. Only China, South Korea, and Japan are directly related to this historic peculiarity."[70] One senior U.S. administration official later said, "China didn't like Zoellick treating Japan and China as equals in the history issue. China denounced as moral relativism what Zoellick had done."[71]

Being a "responsible stakeholder" is to fulfill "the responsibility of a major power." The George W. Bush administration has been closely observing and evaluating whether China is willing to accept that responsibility and whether it deserves to be treated as a major power. The United States decided to use China's handling of the North Korean nuclear issue, particularly in the forum of the six-party talks, as the "touchstone" for evaluating answers to those questions.

MULTILATERAL DIPLOMACY

In addition to the role that China has played in advancing U.S.-China relations, China also has pursued a role that would increase its presence and influence in East Asia. Behind those roles was regret that China had been compelled to put up with playing a passive role at the time of the first North Korean nuclear crisis in the 1990s. The United States and North Korea settled the first crisis through a bilateral process, typically represented by the Agreed Framework of 1994. China did not take part in the process—not even in the Korean Peninsula Energy Development Organization (KEDO)—significantly limiting its influence.

The four-party talks among the two Koreas, the United States, and China, which began in 1997 in order to promote long-lasting peace on the Korean Peninsula, also were an agonizing experience for China. Although China did participate, the process was basically driven, again, by the United States and North Korea, leaving China only a marginal role.[72] Those experiences were behind China's more proactive and more vigorous engagement in resolving the second Korean nuclear crisis.

China also was confident that it could engage in the issue a little more effectively than before. China's diplomatic assets increased after it restored its relations with North Korea after 2000 and increased its assistance to North Korea. Time seemed to be on China's side. The United States was too preoccupied with Iraq to handle the North Korean nuclear issue, and South Korea, fearful of North Korean provocations and renewed tension on the Korean Peninsula, hoped that China could stabilize North Korea. Japan, having stumbled in the process toward diplomatic normalization with North Korea because of the abduction issue, was not in a position to readily take the initiative in this case. The situation was evolving in such a way that, depending on China's actions, North Korea could once again become a strategic asset for China.

In addition, China has been pursuing a regional strategy by which it hopes to enhance its national interests by advancing regional cooperation with neighboring countries and, eventually, by developing East Asian regionalism through such forums as ASEAN Plus 3 and the East Asian Summit. In order to do that, China needs multilateral consultations and multilateral diplomacy. In fact, some in China have suggested that the six-party talks, which were designed to achieve the denuclearization of North Korea, should be reevaluated in that context. The most vocal advocate of this view has been the Department of Policy Planning at China's Foreign Ministry, which has been emphasizing the importance of multilateral diplomacy for China since about 1997. Initially, resistance within the ministry was quite strong, citing the danger of China's sovereignty being violated; that view, however, started to change around 2000.[73]

China joined the World Trade Organization (WTO) in December 2001 and, at the same time, started negotiations toward a free trade agreement (FTA) with individual members of the Association of Southeast Asian Nations (ASEAN). In the course of the ASEAN negotiations, it became necessary to engage in direct dialogue, and because ASEAN is a multilateral consultative organization, that automatically called for multilateral diplomacy on China's part. China signed the Treaty of Amity and Cooperation (TAC) with ASEAN in 2003. The ASEAN Plus 3 (Japan, China, and South Korea), which was established in the aftermath of the 1997–98 Asian economic crisis, gave rise to the nucleus of regionalism in East Asia. The United States was not included in that meeting. In Shanghai in June 2001, under a huge map that did not include the Americas, China launched the Shanghai Cooperation Organization (SCO) with the signing of the Declaration of Shanghai Cooperation Organization by the heads of state of China, Russia, Kazakhstan, Kyrgyzstan, Uzbekistan, and Tajikistan. China offered its representative to the SCO to serve as secretary general and financed the organization's administrative and operational costs.[74] Now China finds itself in the advantageous position of being at the center of two regional-cooperation arrangements that, when combined, can be visualized as forming the shape of a fan: the six-country Shanghai Cooperation Organization and the six-party talks, based in Beijing. One Chinese Foreign Ministry official who was in charge of designing China's multilateral diplomacy at the time later said:

> By the summer of 2002, we were quite ready to lay out the direction of our multilateral diplomacy, when the plan for multilateral diplomacy to settle the North Korean nuclear issue evolved. There was no longer a sense of China being a misfit. And as we went along, we were able to consolidate ideas and concepts. It was not like deciding a major strategy.[75]

A meeting between the directors of policy planning of the United States and China was held in Beijing in the summer of 2002. At the meeting, the United

States was strongly impressed by the great advances that China had made toward multilateral diplomacy.[76] China had abandoned its traditional passive role, characterized by its victim mentality and lack of self confidence, for a positive role as a self-confident, major world power.[77] Hu Jintao's "New Thinking" diplomacy was created by projecting China's new self-image onto the nation's foreign policy. That approach entails redefining the national interest and strategy of China as a regional and global power and developing a new line of diplomacy based on the redefinition. China's North Korea policy is an extension of this new foreign policy posture.

"What Do You Think I Was Doing in Pyongyang? Having a Picnic?"

One major difference between China's responses to the first and second North Korean nuclear crises was China's economic power, which had grown remarkably in the preceding ten years. China's economic influence on North Korea also increased tremendously in the same period. Today, the value of China–North Korea trade amounts to US$2 billion, or 40 percent of North Korea's total trade.[78] It is twice as large as North Korea–South Korea trade and six times as large as Japan–North Korea trade. China also is the largest supplier of food and oil to North Korea. China has regularly monitored the food supply in North Korea to determine whether the latter can maintain a minimum basic supply. Although China supplied a total of 500,000 tons of food to North Korea in 2005, monitoring by the UN Food Programme has not been able to confirm that the food provided was distributed to ordinary households. It is beyond doubt, however, that China has provided a significant amount of food aid to North Korea.[79] China also provides North Korea with 300,000 to 1 million tons of heavy oil every year through a pipeline from the Daqing Oil Field, 800 kilometers north of the China–North Korea border.[80] China has also started providing North Korea with other types of free, large-scale assistance.

Since the first round of the six-party talks was convened in August 2003, North Korea has taken a critical stance toward the talks and has made remarks hinting at its intention to boycott the next round. In October 2003, Wu Bangguo, chairman of the standing committee of the National People's Congress, visited Pyongyang, accompanied by Wang Yi, China's vice foreign minister, who had chaired the first round of the six-party talks. When Wu met Kim Jong-il, he gave Kim a jade tablet on which Kim's name was inscribed in Chinese characters. The Chinese also brought another gift—a promise to construct a glass factory worth RMB200 million (US$25 million), free of charge.[81] As evidenced by the fact that plastic instead of glass is used for the windows of most of the houses in North Korea's rural areas, the country had been suffering from a serious shortage of glass. Construction was completed within two years after the Wu-Kim talk, and the inauguration ceremony was attended by a Chinese delegation headed by Vice Premier Wu Yi, who is a member of the Politburo, and 7,500 North Koreans, including Kim Jong-il and a number of central and local government leaders. One member of the Chinese delegation had this to say regarding the gift of the factory:

> Although the gift of the glass factory was a carrot to lure North Korea to continue to participate in the six-party talks, it also had a longer-term objective. We had to stabilize the North Korean economy. [Construction of the glass factory] is a boost to Kim Jong-il's reputation and Kim's status there.[82]

As China had hoped, North Korea agreed to continue the six-party talks in order to pursue a peaceful settlement of the "Korea-U.S. nuclear issue."

In January 2004, it was reported that China offered North Korea an additional US$50 million in free economic assistance, again to secure the latter's participation in the six-party talks.[83] In September 2004, Li Changchun, a member of the standing committee of the Politburo of the Chinese Communist Party, visited North Korea to induce Pyongyang to end its self-imposed isolation, which had been in effect since the third round of the six-party talks in June 2004. On February 19, 2005, after North Korea's February 10 declaration that it possessed nuclear arms, another emissary, Wang Jiarui, head of the International Department of the party's Central Committee (CCP/ID), visited North Korea to try to prevent a recurrence of the nuclear crisis and to bring North Korea back to the six-party talks. During his visit, Wang announced that China was prepared to expand its supply of energy to North Korea.[84] In October 2005, President Hu Jintao also visited Pyongyang, and it was reported that Hu promised an additional US$2 billion (some say US$3 billion) in economic assistance.[85]

Although the Chinese government denied the report of US$2 billion in economic assistance, the economic aid could not have been small. A large number of business deals were negotiated and signed, including one regarding the Maoshin iron mine, which will produce 10 million tons of iron ore to be shipped to China. Because that will reduce China's reliance on Australian iron ore, suspicions are that the Chinese are behind the project.[86]

China's free economic assistance has encouraged private investment in North Korea, which has accelerated since 2004. China's direct investment in North Korea in 2004 amounted to US$200 million, a sharp increase from the US$1.3 million of previous years. China also has expanded its technical cooperation with North Korea; for example, China currently is training a few hundred North Korean engineers at facilities in Beijing and Shenyang to help them obtain employment in China's information technology industry.

In the northern part of North Korea, China's currency, *renminbi* (RMB), is in daily use. China is, in a way, launching "RMB diplomacy" with respect to North Korea, so much so that some in South Korea have begun to worry about North Korea shortly becoming the fourth province of China's northeast.[87]

However, as China–North Korea trade flourishes, there is an increasing danger that technology, parts, and materials relating to nuclear weapons and missiles will flow out of China into North Korea. Now that many of the chemical corporations in China are privately owned, it has become difficult for the Chinese government to supervise them. The government therefore has established among the relevant government ministries a committee to control the export of products to North Korea that have both peaceful and military applications (dual-use products). One senior official of a Chinese government organization remarked, "Every time an export is restricted by this committee, we hear complaints and demands from Pyongyang. The busier trade with North Korea becomes, the more complicated bilateral relations will be."[88]

In any case, China is being transformed from a patron of North Korea to its lifeline, which should make it easy for China to exert pressure on North Korea. But China insists that there is a limit to its influence on North Korea. One Japanese diplomat recalled that in the spring of 2003, immediately before the trilateral meeting, a tremendous amount of disinformation about North Korea flowed out from China:

> China was deliberately spreading information such as that relations between China and North had cooled off; China had not been informed by North Korea of Prime Minister Koizumi's visit to Pyongyang; China had not been informed of the special economic zone in Sinuiju; North Korea had not informed China of its intention to withdraw from the NPT, etc.[89]

By spreading such "disinformation," China must have been warning the other countries concerned against building up their expectations concerning China's role vis-à-vis North Korea. On one occasion the Chinese government also declared that it would refuse to use its shipments of oil and food to North Korea as a tool for exerting pressure, the logic being that ordinary trade with a neighboring country should be separated from the nuclear issue.[90] At one point, a South Korean diplomat involved in the six-party talks asked one of the Chinese diplomats why China would not exert more pressure on North Korea. The Chinese diplomat's reply, in which he quoted a Chinese saying, *"Yizhen Jianxie"* (roughly, "The prick of a needle is followed by a drop of blood"), can be interpreted as saying that too much direct pressure is rather counterproductive vis-à-vis North Korea.[91]

One U.S. administration official involved in the six-party talks pointed out that since China hosted the six-party talks, it not only has applied more pressure on North Korea but also has begun to do so in cooperation with the United

States. However, he cautions, with that being the case, that China must be all the more careful not to seem to be putting pressure on North Korea in response to a request from the United States. In the summer of 2005, one North Korea watcher in a U.S. intelligence agency analyzed the situation as follows:

> The more the United States insists that China must exert pressure on North Korea, the less North Korea is likely to give in because of its apprehension about being looked at as a puppet of China. Instead, North Korea might venture to engage in more-eccentric activities, such as launching missiles and conducting nuclear tests, just to prove that it is not a puppet.[92]

Just one year after that prediction, North Korea conducted a missile launch. Its admission, on February 10, 2005, that it possesses nuclear weapons also is an example of the behavioral pattern described above. North Korea did not give prior notice of its announcement to China, which, as a result, lost face in the world.

One senior U.S. administration official has remarked that "it has always been amazing how frightened the Chinese are of North Korea."[93] In North Korea, rumors have been going around to the effect that Kim Jong-il is looking for a place in China to seek political asylum and that more than 100 North Korean military officers already have defected to China. North Korean authorities have become hypersensitive to such "information," originating in China. Some observers have commented that the "North Koreans have a gnawing suspicion that the United States buys off Chinese to spread these rumors in order to expedite the collapse of the North Korean regime."[94]

China, however, uses a stick against North Korea when it must. During the first nuclear crisis, China hinted to North Korea that it would not use its power to veto any UN Security Council resolution to impose economic sanctions on North Korea, even though China was opposed to sanctions. That suggestion might have played some role in persuading North Korea to conclude the Agreed Framework with the United States.[95] During the second nuclear crisis, "China warned North Korea in private that if North Korea were to abstain indefinitely from negotiating, China would not oppose the United States' bid to hand over the North Korean nuclear issue to the U.N. Security Council and that China would abstain from voting when the UN would consider imposing sanctions against North Korea."[96]

In the spring of 2003, China stopped supplying heavy oil to North Korea for three days. The Chinese attributed the interruption to technical problems and the need for repairs. In September of the same year, James Kelly, testifying before the U.S. Senate Foreign Relations Committee, said:

> It was last February or March, and it was around the time that the then Vice-Premier Qian Qichen . . . traveled to Pyongyang and prompted the

first occasion of North Korea coming to the table [for the trilateral meeting]. . . . I am skeptical . . . of the official explanation [of the cause of the sudden cut-off of oil] of some technical failure.[97]

It was speculated that China cut off the oil supply as a warning to North Korea to stop its provocations, including its restarting of experimental reactors in the nuclear facility near Yongbyong, but Kelly has said that in his view it was a Chinese sign to impress on North Korea the importance of its participation in the trilateral meeting. Earlier, in November 2002, China had stopped the operation of the China-Mongolia railway for two days, citing a technical failure.[98] A Chinese diplomat pointed to the following considerations in stressing that the stoppage had not been designed to exert pressure on North Korea:

> That could have damaged the pipeline. We were fully aware of that danger. We had been severely criticized for a similar measure we had taken against Mongolia, which made the measure dysfunctional. Therefore, we learned to be cautious about applying that kind of pressure.[99]

Regardless, it is highly likely that North Korea regarded the stoppage as pressure.

When does North Korea listen to China? One senior Chinese government official said, "First, send the right person to North Korea. Second, meet the right person in North Korea. Speak the truth, even if they don't want to hear it." He pointed to the visit of Deputy Foreign Minister Dai Bingguo to North Korea in July 2003 as the best example of that approach.[100]

Of course, there is a limit to China's ability to exert pressure on North Korea. Although it might be easier, and perhaps more effective, to put pressure on North Korea to participate in a trilateral meeting or the six-party talks, pressure might not work on such sensitive issues as the abandonment of nuclear weapons or the imposition of financial sanctions.

What does China wish to accomplish by putting pressure on North Korea? That is the question that has been of most concern to the United States. In testimony at a U.S. Senate hearing on September 11, 2003, Assistant Secretary of State James Kelly remarked that "China has been making an effort to make North Korea participate in the conference through China's sustained exercise of influence. It has overall been positive pressure, but it has not been decisive."[101] Joseph DeTrani, special envoy for the six-party talks, later said at a U.S. Senate hearing on March 15, 2005, "We believe that China can do even more to bring its full influence, not just to persuade North Korea to return to the talks as soon as possible, but to commit to comprehensive denuclearization."[102] Others in the United States have demanded that China put more pressure on North Korea. One Chinese diplomat involved with the six-party talks responded to such U.S. demands by saying, "China would have put much more pressure on North Korea long before if that alone would settle the nuclear issue. But because we know that won't solve the problem, China is trying to settle this issue through the six-party talks in cooperation with the United States and others."[103]

China's pressure on North Korea could take additional forms, such as "abolition or review of the China-DPRK Treaty of Friendship, Cooperation, and Mutual Assistance" and a blockade of the China–North Korea border. After North Korea launched missiles in the summer of 2006, a "review of traditional policies toward North Korea" was debated within the Chinese government, and the UN Security Council resolution condemning North Korea's missile tests, which China approved, turned out to be much more severe than the traditional Chinese stance toward North Korea. Nevertheless, China still remains cautious with respect to exercising pressure on North Korea.[104] One Chinese diplomat who has long been involved with Asian affairs has said, laughing, "At the outset of the six-party talks process, we were determined to use a carrot, not a stick, unless it became absolutely necessary to do so. The United States would be there to use the stick, and China had no reason to get in the way."[105]

It is difficult to estimate how much pressure China is actually putting on North Korea. In March 2005, Ning Fukui, China's ambassador in charge of talks with North Korea, visited the United States to exchange views with his U.S. counterparts regarding North Korea's announcement the preceding month of its possession of nuclear weapons. All Ning said was that North Korea hoped for denuclearization of the Korean Peninsula and continuation of the six-party talks. The United States was disappointed with Ning, who was essentially repeating what North Korea had said. When the National Security Council's Michael Green (in charge of East Asian affairs) and John Rood (in charge of nonproliferation of weapons of mass destruction) asked Ning whether China had really put pressure on North Korea—and, if so, when and what kind of pressure— Ning adamantly refused to answer.[106] When Green and Rood persevered, Ning cut them short. "What do you think I was doing in Pyongyang?" he snapped. "Having a picnic?"[107] The talk ended in acrid silence.

THE STATUS QUO FOREVER

China has remained a reluctant host of the six-party talks. A senior official of the U.S. administration noted that "China has been hesitant about hosting the six-party talks. If we were to tell China that we would be the host because it would be inappropriate to ask China to keep on hosting, China surely would say 'Please.' China has taken on that responsibility, and it is a hard job."[108] However, a Japanese government official had a different take:

Once during Japan-China bilateral consultations, the Chinese declared that they would stop hosting the six-party talks after two more rounds [that is, after the first round]. But they said nothing this time [the second round]. In its heart of hearts, China probably wants to remain the host. But it wants to be asked by other members to remain the host.[109]

A Chinese diplomat once described China's attitude and posture toward the hosting of the six-party talks as *"bantui banjiu,"* an expression used in China to describe a person who acts wishy-washy even though he or she is more or less determined to do a task. Perhaps, although China is good at constructing clear scenarios concerning what it does not wish to take place (what China opposes), it might not be very good at envisioning what it wishes to happen (what China favors).

One can envision numerous scenarios for Northeast Asia that China wishes to avoid, including a nuclear North Korea, a nuclear arms race in Northeast Asia, a U.S. military attack on North Korea, a U.S.-China military conflict, the collapse of North Korea, and disorder along the China–North Korean border. For China, therefore, the six-party talks might be a crisis-management tool to preclude such nightmarish scenarios.

Other participants in the six-party talks often wonder what China's true intentions are in participating in the talks. One senior U.S. administration official observed that "China finds it to its own advantage to continuously test the United States, using the six-party talks. China knows that the United States is immobilized now by the Iraqi issue, and it tries to sell its services to the United States for as high a price as possible."[110] Others claim that China is not enthusiastic about settling the North Korean nuclear issue or even that it is not interested in doing so.

Although Chinese diplomats who have dealt directly with North Korean nuclear issues strongly reject that kind of view, a senior member of a Chinese government organization made the following observation:

> What China has to do is keep the six-party talks rolling. It should not bend over backward to settle the issue. Anyway, it is not easy to settle this issue. If this issue is settled, China will be faced with newer, more difficult challenges. Keeping the status quo is the best option.[111]

What, then, is the "status quo"? It probably means that China wants the two Koreas to be divided as long as possible, because a unified Korea could radically change the status quo. In early 2006, a North Korean diplomat said:

> China is not so sure of the direction of a unified Korea in fear of it being much influenced by the U.S. The U.S. is not so sure of [a unified Korea] for its concern about Chinese influence. That is the scenario we envision in the foreseeable future.[112]

U.S. policies toward China are the most important factor in China's view of the status quo; China, therefore, has to make appropriate efforts to stabilize and consolidate its relations with the United States. In other words, the United States and China should have consultations that serve to maintain a multilateral framework whose aim is to bring peace and stability to Northeast Asia. During the six-party talks, the United States and China should maintain good communications and should encourage each other to become more engaged so that together they can quietly apply pressure on North Korea to restrain itself.

China has the idea that the six-party talks, if institutionalized, might also prevent a U.S. military attack on North Korea. From the Chinese perspective, the talks can be likened to tying down Gulliver—the United States—in cooperation with the five other participants. If the United States changes its posture and thereby poses a greater threat to China, the Chinese perception of the status quo would change, too. Wang Yiwei wrote:

> If the Bush administration is carrying out a so-called "hedge strategy" . . .
> playing the card of Taiwan independence . . . and forming a U.S.-Japan bloc
> against China, . . . China will change its strategy regarding the North
> Korean nuclear issue. In this regard, South Korea's choices will be very
> important.[113]

Wang proposes China–South Korea cooperation against the United States. On the other hand, the U.S. perception of the status quo will change if China challenges the U.S. presence in East Asia. The prospect of China–South Korea cooperation might be one of those challenges to the United States. However, that proposition lies well outside the realm of Chinese mainstream thinking and government policymaking.

In reference to community building in East Asian, Zheng Bijian wrote, "It would not be in China's interest to exclude the United States from the process. In fact, Beijing wants Washington to play a positive role in the region's security as well as in its economic affairs."[114] It is significant that this kind of view is emerging in China. It must have been one of the most important factors in China's decision to launch the six-party talks in cooperation with the United States and other countries. Although the talks are a consultative mechanism to tackle the North Korean nuclear issue, the talks could not proceed without U.S. participation. China's involvement in the talks is in itself a departure from any notion of excluding the United States from East Asian affairs. It remains uncertain, however, how firmly established China's more inclusive view has been in Chinese diplomacy overall, because at present the status quo seems to be the best scenario for China in Korea, East Asia, Asia Pacific, and the world as a whole.

One veteran Russian diplomat who graduated from Kim Il-sung University in Pyongyang summarized the essence of China's North Korea policy as "status quo forever."[115] But will North Korea allow China to maintain the status quo? Won't the status quo that China is said to aspire to in North Korea actually crumble?

Isn't North Korea's nuclear deterrence a symptom of that danger? A veteran Chinese diplomat argues that maintaining the status quo is not what China wants to achieve through the six-party talks:

> A strong consensus on the two points exists among Chinese officials. But the different views revolved around this question: Can China, as well as the international community, achieve both lasting peace/stability and denuclearization, or can they realistically achieve only one of them? If the answer goes to the latter, then the debate changes to this question: should China give top priority to peace/stability, rather than denuclearization, or vice versa?[116]

Richard Armitage said that he came out with one strong impression from his own meeting with Dai Bingguo in December 2004: he sensed in Dai's remarks the Chinese conviction that North Korea will not abandon its nuclear arms.[117] Dai might have gotten the same feeling from Armitage with respect to the view of the United States. One Chinese diplomat who was present at the Armitage-Dai talk had this impression:

> We sensed that the United States was convinced that North Korea would not give away its nuclear-deterrence capability. The United States knows that this issue cannot be settled via the six-party talks. And yet, it keeps on playing a game that is based on the assumption that it can.[118]

CHAPTER TEN

THE LAUNCHING OF THE SIX-PARTY TALKS

At 9:00 a.m. on April 23, 2003, the trilateral meeting of the United States, North Korea, and China was convened in one of the nineteen buildings of the Diaoyutai State Guest House in Beijing. Wang Yi, China's vice foreign minister, announced the opening of the meeting, which was to be chaired by Fu Ying, director general of the Asian Affairs Bureau of China's Foreign Ministry. Opening remarks were made by Li Gun, deputy director general of the North American Affairs Bureau of North Korea's Foreign Ministry; James Kelly, U.S. assistant secretary of state; and Fu Ying, in that order. Five delegates from each of the three countries were seated on each side of a triangular table.[1]

Li Gun is known as North Korea's old hand at diplomatic maneuvering vis-à-vis the United States, having once served as the deputy permanent representative for North Korea at the United Nations in New York. He also participated in the 1997–99 four-party talks in Geneva on peace on the Korean Peninsula. "The cause of the current nuclear issue is the United States' hostile policies toward our republic—policies that threaten our right to survive," he said in his opening statement. He claimed that North Korea was prepared to "eliminate the United States' concerns if the United States would drop its hostile policies." Li demanded once again that the United States enter into a mutual nonaggression treaty with North Korea, as North Korea had repeatedly requested, as evidence of the U.S. commitment to dialogue with North Korea.

Li Gun also gave the United States a warning: North Korea was serious. "As we communicated to the United States in New York three weeks ago, we have already finished reprocessing 8,000 spent nuclear-fuel rods," he said. "We were forced to do so by the United States' suppressive policies toward our republic."[2]

James Kelly asked North Korea to "abolish comprehensively and permanently all of its nuclear development activities, including secret development using HEU [highly enriched uranium] and the development of plutonium." He demanded that North Korea also present concrete means for verification of compliance with that request.

Then it was Fu Ying's turn. Her opening statement seemed to the members of the American delegation to fulfill China's assurances that China would act as a full participant in the meeting, not merely as host or convener. Fu Ying emphasized the critical importance of denuclearization of the Korean Peninsula. She referred to and praised the 1992 Joint Declaration between North and South Korea, which prohibited nuclear reprocessing and enrichment.[3] She stated also that nuclear weapons in North Korea would "bring chaos" to the Korean Peninsula, making it clear that China would not allow North Korea to possess nuclear weapons.[4]

The conference room was filled with a heavy silence. When Kelly said, "We have to negotiate, but it's not our only option," the atmosphere became even more tense. Then, suddenly, a ring tone to the tune of "Happy Birthday to You" was heard. It was Li Gun's cell phone. Everyone in the conference room burst into laughter as Li briskly walked out of the room. One member of the U.S. delegation wondered whether the purpose of the phone call was to give Li instructions from an assistant of Jo Myong-rok, first vice chairman of the National Defense Commission, who happened to be visiting Beijing at that time and who had talked with Hu Jintao the day before.[5] It was obvious that at the trilateral meeting North Korea intended to boast that China–North Korea relations were as close as "teeth and lips"; the U.S. delegation wondered whether by doing so the North Koreans wanted to demonstrate China's support for North Korea's position to the United States.[6] One of the U.S. delegation suspected that China might have promised Jo to provide oil to North Korea.[7]

Throughout the meeting, Li Gun looked fidgety and repeatedly made hard-line statements.

The plenary meeting took the whole morning. Afterward, the Chinese suggested that the U.S. team have a bilateral talk with the North Korean team, a proposal that the United States turned down. During the lunch break that followed, the Chinese provided a buffet in the courtyard. When Michael Green, director of East Asian affairs at the National Security Council (NSC), and David Straub, country director at the Korea desk at the Department of State, went to the courtyard, they found a few members of the North Korean delegation eating lunch together in a corner. When the two asked whether they could join the North Korean group, one of the North Koreans said, "We are sorry, but we are not allowed to eat lunch with members of the U.S. delegation."

The meeting guidelines that the U.S. team had received from Washington stipulated that the main role of the U.S. delegation was to participate in the multilateral conference and that the U.S. delegation was not allowed to have formal bilateral contact with the North Koreans, although informal contact was permissible. Although formal dialogue had to be carried out multilaterally—among the United States, China, and North Korea—Green and Straub thought that eating lunch with the North Koreans constituted only informal contact.

However, the instructions that the North Korean delegation had received from Pyongyang were the opposite of those that the U.S. delegation had received from Washington. The main role of the North Korean delegation during the trilateral meeting was to engage in bilateral negotiations with the United States. The delegates, therefore, could meet bilaterally with the Americans only in formal meetings; they were not allowed to have informal contact. The North Koreans must have regarded Green and Straub's request to join them for lunch as informal contact and so refused it.[8]

In the evening, a reception was held for the participants in the meeting. When Green and Straub arrived at the reception, the Chinese and other U.S. participants and the two nations' staff were there, but the North Koreans had not yet arrived. Green and Straub had a chat with Fu Ying, who asked the two why the United States would not engage in bilateral negotiations with North Korea.

Green: Ambassador Fu, Washington told us that we can talk with the North Koreans, and, in fact, we were encouraged to—but only in a multilateral setting. We won't engage in bilateral negotiations with North Korea, as we did in the late 1990s. This issue affects all of Northeast Asia, and it has to be settled multilaterally in the region. But we have no intention of refusing bilateral talks. As a matter of fact, we approached the North Korea delegation to have lunch together, but we were rejected.

Fu: Please have a bilateral talk with the North Koreans—you can have a group-to-group talk in a separate room.

Green: But you know that we're under instructions from Dr. Rice to have formal negotiations with North Korea only in a multilateral setting.

Fu: It'll be a disaster if you don't engage in bilateral negotiations.

Green: Why?

Fu: We'll be in big trouble, because to get the North Koreans to come here we promised them that you would. . . . Some people on your side signaled that it would be possible.

Green: Well, they steered you wrong. We never promised bilateral negotiations with North Korea. That would be against policy."[9]

The rivalry within the Bush administration over North Korea policy had continued, forcing Kelly to talk and move exactly according to the script prepared and agreed on by all the U.S. departments and agencies involved. Although there were people in the Department of State, including Charles "Jack" Pritchard, who stressed the importance of bilateral negotiations with North Korea if the United States wanted to achieve a breakthrough, the Pentagon, the White House—particularly NSC staff concerned with the nonproliferation of weapons of mass destruction—and Vice President Cheney's office remained cautious about bilateral negotiations with North Korea. There already had been a showdown between the two camps, with Defense Secretary Donald Rumsfeld suggesting that Under Secretary of State John Bolton replace James Kelly as the head delegate, a proposal that Secretary of State Colin Powell rejected.[10] A member of the U.S. delegation suspected that "it was probably somebody in State or in the embassy who told the Chinese that U.S.–North Korean talks would be possible in Beijing. But the Chinese also selectively hear what they want to hear."[11]

THE TRILATERAL MEETING

When Kelly and the U.S. delegation arrived at the conference room on April 24, 2003, the second day of the trilateral meeting, no one from China or North Korea was there. The U.S. team waited a while for the other delegations to arrive, but no one appeared. Kelly used his cell phone to call Mitoji Yabunaka, director general of the Asian and Oceanian Affairs Bureau of Japan's Ministry of Foreign Affairs, in Tokyo. "Mitoji, how are you?" Kelly asked. Then, laughing, he said, "I'm in the middle of a conference in Beijing. It's a unilateral session."[12] Kelly had promised the Japanese that he would promptly inform them of the outcome of the trilateral meeting.

In the afternoon, China had bilateral consultations with North Korea and then with the United States, but the United States refused to have bilateral consultations with North Korea. Li Zhaoxing, China's foreign minister, escorted Li Gun to the conference room, but Li Gun refused to attend the trilateral meeting, demanding bilateral negotiations with the United States instead. Around the same time, China's ambassador to the United States phoned national security adviser Condoleezza Rice to try to persuade her that the United States should have bilateral consultations with North Korea, a request that Rice rejected.[13]

In the evening, the delegates attended a dinner hosted by Wang Yi, China's vice foreign minister. In the middle of dinner, both Wang Yi, who was at the head table, and Fu Ying disappeared. They had excused themselves to go to the restroom, but they did not come back for quite some time. Meanwhile, the other Chinese participants also disappeared, unnoticed, from the other tables. The Chinese had discreetly removed themselves from the scene to induce de facto bilateral consultations then and there by leaving only the U.S. and North Korean delegations in the banquet room. The buffet lunch on the previous day also had been strange. When the Americans returned to their tables after serving themselves, they found no Chinese members sitting there. They had all gone out to the courtyard, leaving only Americans and North Koreans at the table.

Later that day, during dinner, Kelly and Li Gun chatted over Japan–North Korea relations, U.S. politics, and the history of the Agreed Framework, but they never touched on the key issue of North Korea's nuclear weapons. That was the situation at the other tables, too. Even so, one member of the U.S. delegation later remembered how startled he was to hear very candid comments from a North Korean member who was seated next to him. "We, the Foreign Ministry, are always under pressure from the military," the North Korean said. "Even the talking points our head delegate has to follow were prepared and written by the military. The Foreign Ministry has no control over the talking points."[14] It should be noted, however, that Kelly is of the view that even those "candid confessions" had been carefully pre-orchestrated by North Korea; the penalty for departing from the script is so severe that no independent remarks can be expected from North Korean diplomats.[15]

At the dinner, Wang Yi and Fu Ying came back to the table about the time that dessert was being served. Someone on the Chinese side must have been observing the situation in the banquet room and have alerted them that the trick to induce a U.S.–North Korea bilateral consultation had failed.[16]

After the dinner was over, Choi Son-hui, Li Gun's English interpreter, who was seated at the far side of the large banquet room, looked sharply at Li Gun. Li Gun stopped Kelly, who was preparing to leave, saying that he had something to tell Kelly. Confirming that most of the guests and the hosts had already left the room, Li said to Kelly, in English, "I have three things to tell you. First, our republic has nuclear capability." Kelly instructed his interpreter, Tong Kim, to ask Li Gun to repeat, in Korean, what Li had just said. His words were interpreted by Choi as follows:

> Is the United States aware that we have nuclear capability? We had already informed the U.S. of our nuclear weapons in 1994. You should have paid closer attention to that information. Second, we can produce more and demonstrate it physically. Third, we can transfer our capability abroad. What we do with that depends solely on the conduct of the United States.[17]

Kang Sok-ju once told a Chinese diplomat that in negotiations with the United States, he had Li Gun play the bad guy, because Li was perfect for the job.[18] (However, an American diplomat who had negotiated with both Kang Sok-ju and Li Gun opined that of the two, Kang would make a far better attack dog.)[19] On that day in the banquet room, Li performed perfectly. It was obvious that he had been instructed by Pyongyang to inform the U.S. team of North Korea's nuclear capability during bilateral consultations, but he must have decided to make the announcement at the dinner table, because if he missed that opportunity, he would not have another chance.[20] That night, Kelly reported Li Gun's remarks to Wang Yi. A Chinese government official who was involved in the trilateral meeting later remarked:

> We immediately heard from the United States side what Li Gun had said about a nuclear test and the transfer of nuclear arms. As displeased and disappointed as we were, we decided against overreacting to that. Li Gun was too low in ranking to be taken seriously, and we judged that he had said those things as a tactic to draw the United States into bilateral negotiations. We thought that the United States delegation was thinking along a similar line.[21]

But China took Li Gun's remark about a possible nuclear test and overseas transfer of nuclear weapons extremely seriously. During subsequent bilateral consultations with North Korea, the Chinese tried to intimidate the North Koreans, demanding to know whether they wanted "to commit suicide." One Chinese diplomat has described the Chinese stance toward North Korea and the United States during the six-party talks as *"bankou banxia,"* or half-coaxing and half-threatening. At that particular point, China took a threatening posture.[22]

On April 25, the last day of the trilateral meeting, China repeatedly attempted to hold a plenary meeting of the three participating countries, but Li Gun adamantly refused to join; Li Zhaoxing therefore invited Li Gun to a China–North Korea consultation instead. The Chinese foreign minister had a TV camera and crew standing by outside the conference room where the China–North Korea talk was being held. He also had his aides hold the U.S. delegation at the entrance hall of the villa rather than escort them to another room, as usual, so that the Americans would be blocking the path that the North Korean delegation had to use to depart. Soon Li Zhaoxing and Li Gun came walking out of the conference room, and Li Zhaoxing announced to the TV camera, "We will now convene the trilateral meeting." With a big smile on his face, Li Zhaoxing shook hands with Kelly and Li Gun, cameras flashing all around. Li Gun looked bewildered and at the same time horrified at having walked into the trap.[23]

Within hours there were significant public leaks in Washington of Li Gun's remarks about nuclear testing and the transfer of nuclear arms, which were included in the then-classified report that Kelly filed almost immediately at the end of the meeting. President Bush, in response to a question from NBC on April 24, said that North Korea seemed to have returned to its old game of blackmail but that the United States would not be intimidated, an obvious reference to Li Gun's statement.[24] On April 25, a spokesman for North Korea's Foreign

Ministry made the following announcement, blaming the United States for the failure of the trilateral meeting:

> Although North Korea made a bold proposal to overcome the concerns of both North Korea and the United States over the nuclear issue on the Korean Peninsula, the United States did not make any new proposal and merely continued to repeat the trite request that North Korea must abandon its nuclear programs before the United States will engage in dialogue.[25]

While the trilateral meeting was being held, severe acute respiratory syndrome (SARS) broke out all across China. People were seen walking in front of the Diaoyutai State Guest House wearing face masks to protect themselves against infection. Members of the U.S. delegation to the trilateral meeting who flew back to Washington via a Chinese airline were served by Chinese flight attendants wearing vinyl gloves and face masks. Michael Green had to see a doctor immediately on arrival in Washington to secure a health clearance before being allowed to meet with President Bush and national security adviser Rice on the outcome of the trilateral meeting. As soon as Green and Rice entered the Oval Office, Bush asked Green whether he had SARS. Green assured Bush that he had been cleared by the doctor, but Bush, looking at his watch, joked, "Mike, I want you to stand over there for a while." Upon hearing Green's report, Bush said, "We'll have to include Japan and South Korea on the next occasion."[26]

After Kelly returned to Washington from Beijing, he had people go through the notes and records of Li Gun's remarks, but no one found any specific disclosure by North Korea of its nuclear weapons in 1994.[27]

The United States was particularly apprehensive about Li Gun's reference to "overseas transfers." As discussed earlier in this book, the Bush administration has not clarified what constitutes the "red line" that North Korea must not cross; in contrast, the Clinton administration made it clear that the red line was nuclear fuel reprocessing. However, after 9/11 the Bush administration became very concerned about the prospect of nuclear weapons reaching the hands of terrorists, and Li Gun's reference to "overseas transfer" of the DPRK's nuclear weapons therefore touched an especially raw nerve. That experience may have taught the North Koreans that the transfer of nuclear weapons was a serious red line for the United States, perhaps even more serious than a nuclear test would be. North Korea has never referred to any possible transfers since then.

When the U.S. journalist Selig Harrison visited Pyongyang in May 2004, Kim Yong-nam, chairman of the Presidium of the Supreme People's Assembly, referred to Dick Cheney's warning, made immediately before Harrison's visit, that Pyongyang might sell nuclear materials to al-Qaeda. "We're entitled to sell missiles to earn foreign currency," Kim had said, but he insisted that "in regard to nuclear materials, our policy—past, present, and future—is that we would never allow such transfers to al-Qaeda or anyone else. Never."[28]

Intelligence agencies of both the United States and South Korea soon confirmed that North Korea had begun reprocessing nuclear fuel. Then, in early May of 2004, Pyongyang announced that it had completed the reprocessing and that it would take the measures necessary to bolster its nuclear arsenal for defensive purposes.[29]

Everyone thought that the trilateral meeting was a big disappointment. Department of State advocates of U.S.–North Korea bilateral consultations insisted that a multilateral approach would not work if the United States continued to refuse bilateral negotiations. Jack Pritchard, a representative figure of that school of thought remarked that "in the end, what Beijing had hoped for did not come about. The meeting was a failure."[30] The criticisms of the neocons were even louder:

North Korea threatens to transfer. I had to listen to EAP [East Asia and Pacific Affairs Bureau of the Department of State] argue about what is the distinction in the English language between *transfer* and *export*. And I said, "I don't really care." If you want to get into a semantic debate about what the literal distinction is between *transfer* and *export*, the American public will laugh at you.[31]

Advocates of the multilateral approach also used the failure of the trilateral meeting as leverage to move the United States toward five- or six-party talks.

China's assessment of the trilateral meeting was similar to that of the United States. One Chinese diplomat had the following to say:

We wish no more trilateral meetings. China will be bashed from both sides no matter what. We have an old saying in China, we are always expected to give them [North Korea] things with *haokan haochi* [with both good looks and good taste]. North Korea would be unhappy if both the appearance and the substance were not satisfactory. We have had enough. One cause of the failure might be that we had forcefully pulled a reluctant North Korea to the meeting.[32]

North Korea indeed had been reluctant. The fact that it dispatched Li Gun—who was deputy director general of the North American Affairs Bureau and lower in status than Kelly, an assistant secretary of state—clearly betrayed that reluctance.[33] The trilateral meeting is remembered only as a Chinese diplomatic circus. It should be noted, however, that the trilateral meeting did reveal one truth: that of the ultimate mutual distrust between North Korea, which demanded bilateral negotiations with the United States, and the United States, which abhorred the idea of bilateral negotiations with North Korea.

Six-Party Talks, First Round

In front of the conference room in Fangfeiyuan, one of the buildings of the Diaoyutai State Guest House complex, was a spacious courtyard. Green grass was shining under the morning sun. There was a single pine tree in the middle of the yard, its branches extended in perfect balance to the left and right. Here and there what looked like magpies danced up and down.

Fangfeiyuan is the newest, grandest building in the complex, and the signing of the 1992 agreement normalizing diplomatic relations between China and South Korea took place in the grandest conference room in the building. The thick rug covering the floor of the conference room was a signature product of Yunnan Province; woven with threads the color of Tang tricolor pottery, the rug's wavy pattern symbolized the energy of China and its rise. The balustrades surrounding the room were made of copper, as were the knobs of the heavy wooden doors; the ceiling was gilded with gold leaf, shining in the morning sun. When the building was refurbished in 2001, it was decorated in a modernized Tang style. It reflects the Chinese people's admiration of the glory of the Tang dynasty, which has gained in popularity as China's recent rise has continued.

In the middle of the conference room was a gigantic hexagonal table, at which the first round of the six-party talks was about to be convened. The Chinese delegation, the host of the talks, was seated nearest the door, with the door at its back. The other delegations were seated clockwise in alphabetical order according to their country's formal name, starting with the Democratic People's Republic of Korea, which was followed by Japan, the People's Republic of China, the Republic of Korea, the Russian Federation, and the United States of America. Thus, the North Korean delegation was seated between the United States and Japan. The immediate neighbor of any member of the former capitalist camp (Japan, South Korea, or the United States) was a member of the former socialist camp (China, North Korea, or Russia). Although the order was strictly alphabetical, the seating arrangement was intriguing. Initially China's name had been given as *China,* but that would have positioned China between the United States and North Korea, and China wanted them to be seated next to each other. *People's Republic of China* therefore was adopted instead, enabling China to position itself between Japan and South Korea.

The main table in the conference room could seat eighteen delegates, with three from each country on each side of its six sides. One member of the Chinese delegation had attended the 1997–99 four-party talks held in Geneva among the two Koreas, China, and the United States. When he presented the seating arrangement for those talks to North Korea, he explained that "because North Korea and South Korea are the major parties, they should face each other. The United States and China will be treated as outsiders." The diplomat remembered that the arrangement was severely criticized by the North Koreans, who insisted that "all the parties are on equal footing; therefore, all the parties are major parties. The seating arrangement is highly sensitive politically, and we shouldn't introduce such political sensitivity into the matter."[34] From the North Korean standpoint, sitting on par among the other five parties to the six-party talks meant that it and the United States had to be treated as equals.

The Chinese hosts had placed sofas and easy chairs in the four corners of the conference room and positioned leafy plants in such a way that the corners seemed secluded, hoping to create a relaxed environment in which the U.S. and North Korean delegations could talk together. In doing so, the Chinese had been mindful of the U.S. delegation's strict instructions from Washington:

—Kelly was allowed to talk with the North Korean delegation, but such talk could not take the form or appearance of a bilateral negotiation.

—The U.S. delegation was allowed to chat with the North Korean delegation during coffee breaks and buffet meals, either standing or seated on sofas.

—The U.S. delegation was allowed to enter with the North Korean delegation into a room equipped only with chairs or sofas, but it was not allowed to enter a room having a table.

—All the U.S.–North Korea consultations must be conducted within a multilateral framework.

—If for some reason the U.S. delegation had to use a separate room with the North Korean delegation, it first had to request permission from the Secretary of State.[35]

The participants in the plenary conference made their remarks in alphabetical order according to country name. However, in this instance, China was called China and so was entitled to make the first remarks. Chinese diplomacy here was as protean as the Chinese monkey king's magic.[36] The head delegates of the six countries were as follows:

—China: Wang Yi, vice minister of foreign affairs

—North Korea: Kim Yong-il, deputy minister of foreign affairs

—Japan: Mitoji Yabunaka, director general of the Asian and Oceanian Affairs Bureau, Ministry of Foreign Affairs

—South Korea: Lee Soo-hyuk, deputy minister of foreign affairs and trade

—Russia: Alexander Losyukov, deputy minister of foreign affairs

—United States: James Kelly, assistant secretary of state for East Asian and Pacific affairs.

Kim Yong-il had long been involved with African affairs in North Korea's Foreign Ministry, and he had once served as the ambassador to Libya, but it seemed that around 2002 he had been placed in charge of Asian affairs. Mitoji Yabunaka had long been involved with economic and American affairs, having served as director of MOFA's Second North American Division and as Japan's consul general in Chicago; he also served as a negotiator at the GATT Uruguay rounds. In addition, he had written a book on frictions during international economic negotiations.[37] Lee Soo-hyuk had served as the ROK's director general of the European Affairs Bureau and as ambassador to Yugoslavia before being promoted to deputy minister for foreign affairs and trade at the start of the Roh Moo-hyun government. Toward the end of the 1990s, he had participated in the four-party talks while he was minister counselor at the Korean embassy in Washington. Lee had long been involved with the North Korean nuclear issue. Deciding how to describe the rank of each country's head delegate was a challenge for China. The Chinese originally had considered referring to the delegates as being at the deputy foreign minister level, which was North Korea's preference. The United States interpreted that as China's and North Korea's wish to have Hitoshi Tanaka participate in the six-party talks. Tanaka, who had played a major role behind the scenes in realizing Prime Minister Koizumi's visit to North Korea and the signing of the Japan-DPRK Pyongyang Declaration, had been promoted from director general of the Asian and Oceanian Affairs Bureau to deputy foreign minister for foreign affairs in December 2002.[38] In fact, during one of Chief Cabinet Secretary Yasuo Fukuda's visits to Beijing, Wang Yi had sounded out Fukuda as to whether the Japanese government would dispatch Tanaka to the talks. But when Fukuda asked Tanaka what he wanted to do, Tanaka asked him to dispatch Mitoji Yabunaka, Tanaka's successor as director general of the Asian and Oceanian Affairs Bureau.[39]

The North Korean issues, particularly the nuclear issue, had up to then been pursued by the Trilateral Coordination and Oversight Group (TCOG), consisting of Japan, South Korea, and the United States. Building the six-party talks on the achievements of the TCOG would be desirable, and that would also make it natural to dispatch the TCOG head delegates to the talks. At the TCOG, the United States was represented by James Kelly and Japan by Yabunaka. If the United States decided to dispatch Kelly, Tanaka pointed out, then Japan should dispatch Yabunaka.[40]

If the ranking of the head delegates had been upgraded to the deputy minister level, as originally envisioned by the Chinese, North Korea might have dispatched Kang Sok-ju, the first deputy foreign minister, and the United States might have sent Richard Armitage, deputy secretary of state.[41] In fact, Armitage would not have been dispatched. In the first place, he did not wish to participate in the six-party talks, and even if he did, that would have been vetoed by Defense Secretary Donald Rumsfeld, who had recommended that Under Secretary of State John Bolton or Under Secretary of Defense Douglas Feith be sent. But Bolton did not show any sign of interest in the task, having been skeptical and critical of the talks from the beginning.[42]

It was equally uncertain whether Kang Sok-ju would actually attend the six-party talks. On every occasion, whether the trilateral meeting or the six-party talks, North Korea had tested the waters before deciding on its delegates, and it spared Kang, its ace diplomat.[43]

Although the first round of the six-party talks was hosted by China, the participating countries had different views on whether China should continue to host the talks from the next round on. Suggestions were made to convene the subsequent round in Seoul, Pyongyang, and Moscow. The United States considered the possibility of the host role being rotated among the participating countries. China had once complained about the tediousness of the preparations and logistics as well as the considerable financial burden of hosting the talks.[44] In fact, in the second round of the six-party talks, Wang Yi dared to propose that another member country host the following meeting, but none expressed interest.[45] Some in the U.S. administration suggested that Russia should be made to host a round, with the aim of inducing Russia to put more pressure on North Korea. But that suggestion was turned down by James Moriarty, NSC's senior director of Asian affairs. "We should have China host the six-party talks for a while," he said. "Then we can put more pressure on China. Besides, China is proud to host this meeting, and we shouldn't harm its pride." In the end, Moriarty's view was adopted.[46]

All the participating countries were keenly aware of the difficulties in dealing with North Korea. A country that did not have a North Korean embassy or at least a North Korean consulate could not host the talks, because the North Korean delegation was obliged to use the wiretap-free communications line installed in the DPRK's facilities overseas. In the end, China became the permanent host country. Powell was convinced that North Korea would not participate in the six-party talks if it were hosted by any other country;[47] besides, China itself had begun to appreciate the role of host country and the prestige that came with it.[48]

The first round of the six-party talks therefore was convened in Beijing, on August 27, 2003. In his opening remarks to the plenary conference, Wang Yi, China's vice foreign minister, stressed the importance of denuclearization of the Korean Peninsula, elimination of North Korea's concerns about its security, and peaceful settlement of the North Korean nuclear issue through dialogue.

North Korea's deputy foreign minister, Kim Yong-il, was next to speak. He emphasized that the DPRK's ultimate goal was denuclearization of the Korean Peninsula, not possession of nuclear arms. Kim stated that North Korea would abolish its nuclear programs if the United States would cease its hostile policies toward North Korea. He also said that the termination of hostile policies had to include a legally binding mutual nonaggression treaty, normalization of diplomatic relations between the United States and North Korea, and termination of U.S. obstruction of economic cooperation between North Korea, Japan, and South Korea. In addition, Kim expressed North Korea's desire for a package settlement of the nuclear issue, including compensation for the DPRK's loss of electric power due to the U.S. delay in providing light-water reactors.[49]

Mitoji Yabunaka, director general of the Asian and Oceanian Affairs Bureau of Japan's Ministry of Foreign Affairs, declared that North Korea must immediately dismantle all of its nuclear weapons development programs in a complete, irreversible, and verifiable manner. At the same time, Yabunaka stated that it would be possible to deepen the discussion about energy support for North Korea if Pyongyang took concrete steps toward dismantling its nuclear programs. Yabunaka was cautious to say only that it would be possible to deepen the discussion; he did not commit Japan to providing actual assistance. Finally, Yabunaka added that there was no change in Japan's basic position with regard to settling outstanding issues of concern based on the Japan–North Korea Pyongyang Declaration or normalizing relations in a manner that would contribute to the peace and stability of the Northeast Asian region.

Lee Soo-hyuk, South Korea's deputy foreign minister, stressed the importance of peacefully settling the North Korean nuclear issue, continuing humanitarian economic aid to North Korea, and achieving a comprehensive settlement of the nuclear issue. In referring to a "comprehensive settlement," Lee requested the United States to "positively consider providing its assurance of security" to North Korea.[50]

Alexander Losyukov, Russia's deputy foreign minister, stated that denuclearization of the Korean Peninsula could be achieved only through negotiations, and he maintained that the interests of the countries in the region, including North Korea, would be guaranteed.

Last, James Kelly, U.S. assistant secretary of state, emphasized that the United States had no intention of threatening or invading North Korea or of demanding regime change. He also stated that in the next round of talks the United States would be prepared to discuss such issues as North Korea's concern about its security—if North Korea would dismantle its nuclear programs in a verifiable and irreversible manner. After announcing that the United States would not pursue bilateral negotiations with North Korea to settle the nuclear issue, Kelly referred to the possibility of bilateral consultations—ultimately aiming at diplomatic normalization—on a variety of issues, including missiles, conventional arms, counterfeiting of U.S. money, narcotics, terrorism, and abductions. Again, talks would be possible only after North Korea had dismantled all its nuclear weapons.[51] At that point, the United States had already initiated the Illicit Activities Initiative (IAI) to deal with North Korean counterfeiting of U.S. currency, money laundering, smuggling, and narcotics.[52]

In the afternoon, after the end of the plenary session, Kim Yong-il and James Kelly, facing each other on sofas near a window in the conference hall, began the first U.S.–North Korea consultation of the six-party talks:

Kim: What will the United States do for us if we dismantle our nuclear arms?

Kelly: Please carefully read my opening remarks at the plenary session.

Kim: Will the United States raise issues of conventional arms, missiles, narcotics, and human rights even if we dismantle our nuclear arms?

Kelly: Let's work on diplomatic normalization after all the outstanding issues are settled step by step.

Kim: Doesn't the United States have any intention of concluding a mutual nonaggression treaty?

Kelly: The United States has no nonaggression treaty with any country in the world. But we can commit to providing North Korea with security assurances in cooperation with other countries.

Kim: Do you oppose a package settlement?

Kelly: Please read my opening remarks.

Up to that point Kim had been calm, but his attitude changed drastically after he heard Kelly's last response. Apparently displeased by being repeatedly told to read Kelly's opening remarks, he declared, loudly and sharply, that "the United States has not changed at all. We find it impossible to negotiate with the United States." Reading aloud from a memo that he held in his hand, he informed Kelly, "We are prepared to conduct a physical test of our nuclear deterrent and its delivery device." Kelly responded, "I intend to report what I have just heard from you to the other members in the plenary session tomorrow." That was the end of the first U.S.–North Korea bilateral consultation.[53]

On August 28, the second day of the first round of the six-party talks, the chairman's remarks were followed by remarks of the Japanese, South Korean, Russian, and American delegates, in that order. When his turn came, Alexander Losyukov said, as if trying to patiently persuade the North Koreans, "As President Bush said earlier, the United States has no intention of invading North Korea. The United States does not intend to obstruct North Korea's economic activities with other countries, either."

Suddenly, Kim Yong-il's loud voice echoed throughout the conference hall. "You liar! You are a dirty liar, just taking orders from Americans. In Asia, a man's value is judged by whether he is a liar or not."[54]

Losyukov turned around to face his cortege and said bitterly, "Look what happened when I followed your advice."[55]

As if to enlighten Losyukov, Kim started enumerating instances, one after another, of U.S. efforts to obstruct North Korea's economic exchanges with other countries.[56] It should be noted, however, that Kim might have had another reason to explode at the Russians. Immediately before the talks, Russia had participated in a joint naval exercise with Japan and South Korea in the Sea of Japan/East Sea, within sight of North Korea. The joint exercise was conducted to prepare for an emergency humanitarian rescue of a massive outflow of refugees from North Korea, and it was the first time that the navies of the three countries had participated in such an exercise. Russia had invited North Korean officers to observe, but North Korea protested the exercise and refused to send observers.[57]

Kim also barked at the plenary session remarks of Mitoji Yabunaka. Kim seemed to have been angered by Yabunaka's remark that the United States was not trying to come between Japan and North Korea. "Japan is an order-taker for the United States," he said, his hostility obvious. "Are you aware how brutal Japan was in the past?"[58]

When James Kelly's turn came, he disclosed that on the previous day Kim Yong-il had threatened the United States, saying that North Korea was prepared to conduct a physical test of its nuclear deterrent and its delivery devices. Kim Yong-il, following Kelly, made further threatening remarks, declaring, "Our republic has no choice but to expand our nuclear deterrence, proclaim to the world that we possess nuclear capabilities, and prove that we do have those capabilities." Hearing Kim's monologue, Losyukov murmured to his subordinates, "The country you are dealing with [North Korea] is crazy." However, he failed to notice that he had not turned off his microphone, and his comment was heard by everyone in the conference room. One of his subordinates rushed to cup the microphone with his hands, but too late.[59] The atmosphere at the plenary session was far from harmonious. After the session was over, Losyukov half-jokingly said to Kelly, "So much for a special relationship," shrugging his shoulders.[60]

That afternoon, working-level representatives of the six countries got together in a separate room to start working on a draft of the joint statement that would be announced the following day. The group was coordinated by Fu Ying, director general of the Asian Affairs Bureau of China's Foreign Ministry, and it included Li Gun, deputy director general of the North American Affairs Bureau of North Korea's Foreign Ministry; Michael Green, director of East Asian affairs at the NSC; Wi Sung-lac, director general of the North American Affairs Bureau at South Korea's Ministry of Foreign Affairs and Trade; and Koji Tsuruoka, deputy director general of the Foreign Policy Bureau at Japan's Ministry of Foreign Affairs.

The point of greatest contention was how to relate the timing of North Korea's dismantlement of its nuclear weapons to the timing of implementation of various measures to induce dismantlement. China proposed simultaneous implementation of the two. That was close to the simultaneous commitment of "action for action" demanded by North Korea. Each time that North Korea moved toward freezing its nuclear program, it would simultaneously be compensated. The United States proposed "step-by-step, sequential" implementation, implying that Pyongyang had to commit to dismantle its nuclear weapons before anything would be done to benefit North Korea. The idea was "promise for promise" and "action for action." Japan proposed "parallel" implementation, calling for flexible implementation instead of rigid sequencing. The drafting group could not find any point of agreement, and it was facing an impasse when China submitted a compromise proposal for "synchronized" implementation.

In the end, the members of the group managed to come up with a draft sentence—"The participants in the Six-Party Talks agreed to seek a fair and realistic resolution in a manner that is phrased and synchronized or parallel in implementation"—which incorporated various contending views. But Li Gun would not move an inch from his demand that the United States first indicate what it intended to offer. Green rejected Li's demand, saying, "We are currently engaged in six-party talks and not U.S.–North Korea negotiations. This is not about what the United States would do first." Li Gun appeared ill at ease with the task of drafting directly in English in a multilateral setting. In fact, at first he had refused to participate in the drafting of the statement; he eventually joined the group, persuaded by Fu Ying, one hour after the beginning of the meeting.

Another point of contention during the talks was a provision concerning "not taking actions that could escalate the situation." The United States intended by that clause to deter North Korean brinksmanship, and it expected North Korea to use it to deter a U.S. military attack. As soon as the discussion started, however, Li Gun ceased to say anything and, after a while, left the room with his interpreter, Choi Son-hui. When they came back to the room some time later, it was Choi who did all the talking. She kept on insisting that North Korea opposed the distribution of a joint statement and that further discussion of the statement would be meaningless. Fu Ying then persuaded Li Gun to consult with Pyongyang about the compromise proposal.[61]

It was planned that the same members of the drafting group would get together again on August 29, one hour before the start of the closing session, to finalize a joint statement. But Li Gun did not appear. Fu Ying, who arrived late, reported to the rest of the group that the North Korean delegation had not yet received a directive from Pyongyang on the wording. However, it was quite likely that that was China's polite cover-up of what actually happened. It was later revealed that Li Gun had received a directive from Pyongyang to the effect that "a joint statement before the United States changes from its hardliner stance would mean our surrender. Do not give in."[62]

Li Gun's absence offered a rare opportunity for the five other countries to discuss the North Korean nuclear issue without a North Korean representative present. Michael Green took the opportunity to talk about the DPRK's missile preparations, insisting that there would be "provocations," which nobody wanted. He also urged the Chinese and Russians to use their "good offices and their influence to stop North Korea from blowing up these talks." For Green, "That was the most satisfying moment in the six-party talks."[63]

Eventually, China gave up the idea of releasing a joint statement and decided to have the chairman deliver an oral summary of the "common understandings" of the participants during the closing session, whether North Korea agreed or not. But they could not agree on the date of the next round of the talks either. Although China Central Television (CCTV) reported on the afternoon of August 29 that the participants had agreed to convene a second round of talks within two months, North Korea did not even take part in the discussion of the schedule.[64] Toward the end of the closing session, Kim Yong-il read aloud the talking points from a paper in his hand, as if to deliver a parting shot: "This meeting is useless, and we have no interest in this. We will not participate in this kind of meeting any longer." Wang Yi, completely ignoring Kim's remark, began to read the host country summary:

> The participants in the Six-Party Talks called for a nuclear-free Korean Peninsula and shared the view that North Korea's reasonable concerns over its security must be considered and resolved.
>
> The participants in the Six-Party Talks agreed to seek a fair and realistic resolution in a manner that is phased and synchronized or parallel in implementation.
>
> The participants in the Six-Party Talks agreed not to take actions that could escalate the situation during the process of resolving the issue peacefully.

Wang concluded by saying, "The participants in the Six-Party Talks agreed to continue the process of the Six-Party Talks and to decide as soon as possible through diplomatic routes the place and time of the next meeting."[65]

When Wang Yi said "agreed to continue," the head delegates from participating countries, including Kim Yong-il, applauded.[66] But on August 30, the same Kim Yong-il who had clapped in approval of those words made the following statement to the press corps at Beijing International Airport before he departed for Pyongyang: "The six-party talks was nothing but talk. We have no interest in or expectations of this kind of talk, which does no good and a lot of harm."[67] Throughout the talks, Kim had looked horrified to be given this very public responsibility and possibly fearful of what might happen to him if his performance was seen by Pyongyang as weak.[68]

It was an exhausting experience for China to come to the table as scheduled.

And Foreign Minister Li Zhaoxing was unable to convene a late meeting with Kim Yong-il on the evening before the last session, because, as James Kelly heard the story, when Kim finally arrived, "Li was totally inebriated and barely able to sit for the meeting."[69]

During completion of the first round of the six-party talks, the United States learned from satellite photos that North Korea was preparing to deploy a newly developed mid-range missile. It also received intelligence that North Korea was preparing to show off its new weapon at the military parade during the celebration of the fifty-fifth anniversary of the founding of the DPRK on September 9. The United States conveyed to China and Russia its view that if North Korea deployed the new missile and carried out a military parade, it would violate the host country summary, in which "the participants in the six-party talks agreed not to take actions that could escalate the situation during the process of resolving the issue peacefully." Thus, discussion commenced on what constituted "actions that could escalate the situation," with the United States insisting that the participants in the talks agree on a shared definition of the phrase.[70] China was of the view that a common definition was unnecessary and that interpretation should be left to each country's discretion. China also took a cautious stance, stating that the six-party talks were essential for settling the North Korean nuclear issue and that therefore they should not address the missile issue anew.[71] Despite China's expressed reservations, the United States later learned from the British embassy in Pyongyang that both China and Russia had conveyed their concerns about the missile to North Korea.[72] During the September 2003 North Korean anniversary parade of 10,000 troops and civilians in Pyongyang, the missiles were conspicuous in their absence.[73]

By the summer of 2003, what most worried China was not North Korea's missiles but its nuclear test and possible U.S. military action against North Korea. Before China agreed to host the six-party talks, it had obtained a U.S. pledge that the United States would not seek a UN Security Council resolution approving economic sanctions against North Korea as long as "the process of resolving the issue peacefully" continued.[74] In July 2006, when North Korea launched its missiles, China decided to include such launches in its definition of "actions that could escalate the situation," and on July 15, 2006, it joined the rest of the Security Council's members in voting to penalize North Korea under Resolution 1695. China concluded that "the process of resolving the issue peacefully" had been destroyed by North Korea's launching of missiles on July 5.

SIX-PARTY TALKS, SECOND ROUND

Immediately after completion of the first round of six-party talks, the Chinese government started moving toward hosting the second round. Since the end of the first round, North Korea had been sending a variety of signals that it was no longer interested in the talks and that it found participation in such meetings meaningless. China, therefore, had to create a "turning point" (to use the expression of a Chinese diplomat involved with the six-party talks) in order to secure North Korea's participation in the second round. In October 2003, the Chinese government dispatched Wu Bangguo, chairman of the Standing Committee of the National People's Congress, to Pyongyang. Wang Yi accompanied Wu on his visit, during which he talked with Kang Sok-ju about the next round of six-party talks. In a "political push to bring about a turning point," Wu Bangguo pledged to Kim Jong-il that China would give North Korea free assistance for the construction of a glass factory. Wang Yi and Kang Sok-ju worked out the details.

Another matter that China had to work on was persuading the United States to take a more flexible stance toward North Korea; the Chinese thought it would be difficult for the six-party talks to accomplish much unless the United States loosened up. After the end of the first round, for example, Wang Yi had complained that "America's policy toward the DPRK—that is the main problem we are facing."[75] China also had to find out what the "bottom lines" of the United States and North Korea were, and it had to make the two comply with the basic rules.[76] For that purpose, a joint statement had to be compiled.

China accordingly dispatched Fu Ying to Washington in December 2003. Fu Ying presented a draft of the joint statement that China wished to publish at the end of the next round of the six-party talks, and she exchanged views on the draft with James Kelly and Deputy Secretary of State Richard Armitage. The main point of the Chinese proposal was that while retaining the ultimate goal of getting North Korea to abandon its nuclear programs, the six-party talks should set an interim goal of getting North Korea to agree to freeze the programs. The other members of the talks would be obliged to take certain "corresponding measures"—that is, to offer compensation if and when North Korea actually complied with its agreement.

The United States was not very enthusiastic about the proposal, indicating that it was not interested in freezing for the sake of freezing.[77] A similar proposal was communicated to President Bush when Premier Wen Jiabao of China visited the United States one week after Fu Ying's visit. Bush, believing that "freezing was Clinton language," gave the proposal the cold shoulder.[78] The goal of the United States was not freezing but the complete abandonment of all of North Korea's nuclear programs. Besides, the United States did not find it important to work on a draft joint statement at that stage; it was more concerned about consolidating the six-party talks process and firmly establishing the multilateral approach to the North Korean issue.[79]

The convening of the second round of the talks, which had originally been scheduled for mid-December 2003, was delayed. On December 25–27, Vice

Foreign Minister Wang Yi visited Pyongyang, and North Korea agreed that the second round would be held early in 2004.[80]

In mid-January 2004, North Korea invited a group of U.S. experts, including Siegfried Hecker, the former director of Los Alamos National Laboratory—the central institution for U.S. nuclear arms development—and staff members of the U.S. Senate Foreign Relations Committee to visit Yongbyon, where they could observe graphite-moderated nuclear reactors, storage for spent nuclear fuel rods, and the reprocessing facilities. During the visit, the North Koreans showed their visitors a piece of metal and a green-colored powdery substance that the North Koreans said was plutonium recently reprocessed at the Yongbyon facility, explaining that the items were components of North Korea's nuclear deterrent. There were no spent fuel rods in storage, proving the truth of the DPRK announcement in October 2003 that it had completed the reprocessing of some 8,000 spent rods. Throughout the site visit, North Korea emphasized that while it actually possessed weapons-grade plutonium, it did not have the enriched uranium program that it had been accused of having. At the same time, the North Koreans also communicated to Hecker and others that they were prepared to freeze their nuclear development programs.[81]

The United States interpreted that message as a North Korean attempt to shake up the members of the six-party talks in preparation for the next round.[82] In response, the United States took the counteroffensive. On January 31, 2004, the government of Pakistan dismissed A. Q. Khan from his position as chairman of Khan Research Laboratories and formally admitted that in exchange for monetary compensation he had transferred to foreign countries blueprints and technologies relating to Pakistan's nuclear arms.[83] Meanwhile, the United States loudly praised Libya's decision to dismantle its nuclear arms in order to normalize diplomatic relations with the United States and other nations, labeling its action the "Libyan model." On the eve of the second round of the six-party talks, a senior White House official said, "If they say we have no HEU or . . . if they try to hide large parts of the program that we know are there, that's a bad sign. That's like Saddam Hussein. We want them to be more like Qaddafi [of Libya]."[84]

On February 24, one day before the start of the second round, George Tenet, director of the Central Intelligence Agency, testified before the U.S. Senate Intelligence Committee, warning that "we also believe Pyongyang is pursuing a production-scale uranium enrichment program based on technology provided by A. Q. Khan, which would give North Korea an alternative route to nuclear weapons."[85]

The second round of the talks was held February 25–28, 2004, at the Diaoyutai State Guest House in Beijing, where the first round had been held. This time, North Korea sent Kim Gye-gwan, its deputy foreign minister, as head delegate, in place of Kim Yong-il. At the time of the first nuclear crisis, in 1993–94, Kim Gye-gwan, then a deputy to Kang Sok-ju, had been in charge of the negotiations for the Agreed Framework, and at the four-party talks in Geneva in 1997–99, he was North Korea's head delegate. At the peak period of Eurocommunism in the 1970s, Kim was posted in Europe, and he visited many areas of the continent. Diplomats of other countries suggested that Kim must have obtained his air of sophistication during those European days.[86]

At the trilateral meeting, North Korea's head delegate was Li Gun, who was nothing but a loudspeaker for North Korea. Kim Yong-il was sent to the first round of the six-party talks, betraying North Korea's less-than-earnest commitment to the multilateral framework. By sending Kim Gye-gwan to the second round, however, North Korea gave the other delegations reason to believe that Pyongyang had finally gotten serious.[87]

On February 25, the first day of the talks, the plenary session started with opening remarks by the head delegate of each of the six countries. Kim Gye-gwan, in turn, proposed a "comprehensive nuclear cessation plan" by which the United States would be required to provide North Korea with a security assurance and economic assistance and, in return, North Korea would take the interim step of freezing its nuclear program overall. However, North Korea would not be obliged to completely dismantle all of its nuclear weapons or abandon all of its nuclear programs. In response, James Kelly announced that if North Korea implemented "complete, verifiable, and irreversible dismantlement of all of its nuclear programs," the United States was "prepared to join with other parties in providing a security assurance" to North Korea. At the same time, Kelly announced that "President Bush has also made clear that the United States has no intention of invading or attacking the DPRK. This remains the policy of the United States."[88]

Lee Soo-hyuk of South Korea said that North Korea's freeze of nuclear programs had to meet three conditions: all of its nuclear facilities and nuclear materials must be dismantled; North Korea must accept inspections by a neutral authority; and the transition to total dismantlement must be completed as quickly as possible. Lee then proposed the following three-step plan:

Step 1: A "nuclear dismantlement proclamation" by North Korea, followed by an oral commitment from the United States and its allies to providing a "security assurance"

Step 2: A North Korean freeze of its nuclear programs, followed by the presentation of "corresponding measures" to be taken by the five other participants in the six-party talks

Step 3: North Korea's dismantlement of all of its nuclear weapons and abandonment of all of its nuclear programs in a verifiable and irreversible manner, followed by implementation of the above-mentioned "corresponding measures."[89]

Lee also suggested that in order to institutionalize the six-party talks, the participants should meet every other month and hold working-level conferences during the intervals.[90]

At a reception on February 24, Kelly met Kim Gye-gwan for the first time since their last meeting, when Kelly visited Pyongyang in October 2002. As soon as the two started chatting, there was a sort of natural herd reaction among not only the Chinese hosts but all the people present, who responded with relieved nods of their heads. It did not matter if the two diplomats were talking of nothing but the weather.[91]

On the evening of February 25, the United States and North Korea had a one-hour bilateral consultation at the guest house. Kelly was able to carry on a more businesslike talk with Kim Gye-gwan than had been possible with Kim Yong-il during the first round, but the exchange occasionally became tempestuous. At the dinner that evening, the head delegates of the United States and North Korea were seated next to each other, as on the previous evening. It appeared to Kelly, however, that the Chinese, who had so rigorously encouraged him and Kim Gye-gwan to talk together the night before, were anxious for him and Kim to speak with their other dinner companions, as if to minimize the conversation between them. "The Chinese, of course, had the room wired," Kelly had chuckled to himself. "Reading the transcript of our conversation, they must have decided to separate me and Kim Gye-gwan. They must be worried that if the two of us talk only with each other, we'll start to argue."[92] Before the plenary session the following morning, the U.S. delegation shared the content of the U.S.–North Korea bilateral consultation with the other delegations, saying that it believed that "transparency is an important part of the six-party talks, and essential to its core premises."[93]

Although the talks were supposed to be among the six nations, the attention of all of the delegations was concentrated on the contact between the United States and North Korea. The United States, however, summarized the second round as a farewell to bilateral negotiations with North Korea. During their informal bilateral consultations, Kelly had sensed that the North Koreans felt "a kind of a nostalgia"; it was as if they wanted to ask, "Can't we just go back to when you Americans would come and we wouldn't have to worry about the Chinese and Japanese and South Koreans, and we could make beautiful music together?" But Kelly approached all bilateral talks with North Korea with the conviction that North Korea should know that "that tune is gone forever."[94] He was determined to make transparent all of North Korea's words and conduct at the six-party talks, thereby stripping North Korea of its favorite attire—its veil of mystique.

Prior to the second round, North Korea had announced that it was completing the reprocessing of its nuclear fuel, as if to remind the others that "we'll participate in the second round, but don't forget that our volume of plutonium is constantly increasing."[95] In the negotiations for dismantling its nuclear programs, North Korea had been demanding that the United States first make a down payment for North Korea's interim measure of freezing its nuclear programs, instead of making a full payment later for complete abandonment of the programs. And North Korea kept on producing plutonium, possibly to jack up the price of compensation.

The second plenary session was held on the morning of February 26. North Korea insisted that the target of dismantlement should be limited to its nuclear weapons program, not to peaceful uses of nuclear energy. As in the first round of the six-party talks, North Korea denied that it had highly enriched uranium. On the evening of February 26, a member of the North Korean delegation announced to the press corps in front of the North Korean embassy in Beijing that the target of the dismantlement would be limited to nuclear development for military use. But Kelly brushed that off, saying, "The problem is I'm not aware of any peaceful nuclear programs in the DPRK."[96] The United States believed that if peaceful uses were approved, the "denuclearization of the Korean Peninsula" could be diluted to a "Korean Peninsula without nuclear weapons." If that were to happen, North Korea could declare that it had an HEU-production program "for peaceful use" and then play its new nuclear card in future negotiations.

When North Korea introduced the "nuclear freeze first" idea the previous day, it justified the freeze as a first step toward complete nuclear dismantlement, hoping perhaps to secure the support of the participants. In response, the United States resorted to an "ultimate settlement" logic—because all the nuclear programs would ultimately be dismantled, it did not matter whether some were for peaceful use or whether they were frozen in an interim step.[97]

The scope of dismantlement, the peaceful use of nuclear energy, and a nuclear freeze and appropriate "corresponding measures" (that is, compensation) have remained issues of contention throughout the six-party talks. Along the way, those issues have shaken the collaboration among Japan, South Korea, and the United States. Although Japan and the United States remained cautious about providing North Korea with compensation, South Korea insisted that economic assistance should be extended if North Korea froze its nuclear programs in a verifiable manner.[98] South Korea questioned the U.S. attitude regarding the freeze. "If you're driving and you want to put the car into reverse, you have to stop the car first," it pointed out. "How do you expect total dismantling to take place without an interim step of freezing?"[99] The United States failed to provide a clear-cut answer to the question. However, the United States did explain that although it could not commit itself to doing so, it would "understand and support" South Korea and the other participants in the six-party talks if they were to provide North Korea with energy cooperation when the latter froze its nuclear programs.[100]

February 28 was scheduled to be the last day of the second round of the talks. The drafting of the joint statement turned out to be a bumpy process that went on until midnight of the day before, but in the end, the drafting committee had somehow reached agreement on the wording. However, when the statement was ready to be distributed at the closing session, Kim Gye-gwan proposed a revision: "while differences remained" should be inserted after the comma in the clause "Through the talks, the Parties enhanced their understanding of each other's positions." Kim looked highly agitated, and the other participants wondered whether he might have been severely reprimanded by Pyongyang. "Then we have to do it all over again," Kelly said in a loud voice. "We don't have time for that."[101]

The previous evening, the U.S. delegation had decided not to include "CVID" in the joint statement so that it would be more easily endorsed by the participants. "CVID" stands for "complete, verifiable, and irreversible dismantlement." Some in Washington had been adamant that the term be included in the joint statement. Although most members of the U.S. delegation were worried that the White House would not endorse a statement that did not include "CVID," Kelly communicated the situation to Colin Powell who, in turn, worked to secure President Bush's approval.[102] The draft statement was a product of such an agonizing process that Kelly lost his temper at Kim's last-minute proposal.

The closing session was temporarily interrupted. Foreign Minister Li Zhaoxing met Kim Gye-gwan alone outside the conference room and tried to dissuade Kim, who would not listen, citing the directive from Pyongyang. If he gave in, Kim told Li, he would not be allowed to fly back to Pyongyang. Kim looked pathetic when he said that he would have to go back by car.[103]

In the end, time ran out. The document, which had been designed to be a joint statement, had to be downgraded to a chairman's statement. Li Zhaoxing set up a joint press conference, inviting the head delegates of the six countries. Kim Gye-gwan did not show up until the last minute, making the Chinese hosts panicky.[104] The chairman's statement reads in part as follows:

> The Parties agreed that the second round of the Six-Party Talks had launched a discussion on substantive issues, which was beneficial and positive, and that in the discussion the attitudes of all parties were serious. Through the talks, although differences remained, the Parties enhanced their understanding of each other's positions.
>
> The Parties expressed their commitment to a nuclear-weapons-free Korean Peninsula, and to resolving the nuclear issue peacefully through dialogue in a spirit of mutual respect and consultations on an equal basis, so as to maintain peace and stability on the Korean Peninsula and the region at large.

The Parties expressed their willingness to coexist peacefully. They agreed to take coordinated steps to address the nuclear issue and address the related concerns.[105]

The statement included the "nuclear-weapons-free Korean Peninsula" advocated by North Korea instead of the "all of the nuclear programs" wording on which Japan, South Korea, and the United States had insisted. Wang Yi stressed that it was significant that, for the first time, a formal document had been adopted.[106] This time, unlike at the first round, it was agreed that the next round would be convened toward the end of June 2004 and that a working group would be launched to prepare for the third round. Thus, in the end, Kim Gye-gwan was able to fly home safely.[107]

Kelly also was relieved. In fact, ever since Kelly requested instructions from Powell concerning the chairman's statement, the Bush administration had been divided between Powell and Armitage, who supported the decision made by the U.S. delegation to endorse the chairman's statement, and Cheney and Rumsfeld, who opposed it. When North Korea requested insertion of "while differences remained" in the statement, Kelly turned down the request, claiming that he could not request instructions from Washington again. In fact, if Kelly had asked for Washington's instructions, it was highly likely that the answer would have been no. Thus, in Kelly's view, the United States was saved by North Korea's last-minute act of defiance—it masked the inconsistencies between Washington and the U.S. delegation.[108]

Mantras: CVID, the Libyan Model, and HEU

The United States insisted that North Korea's dismantlement of its nuclear program be a "complete, verifiable, and irreversible dismantlement," introducing the acronym CVID into the six-party talks. In response, North Korea refused to refer to CVID, a term that it said was used only to refer to a defeated nation.[109] During the press briefing after the closing session, a member of the U.S. delegation remarked, "CVID . . . it's not our mantra anymore. It's the ROK's, Chinese, and Japanese determination as well, and we think that's a pretty solid accomplishment."[110] Nevertheless, it was a mantra that only the United States used. Hearing Kelly repeat "CVID" close to twenty times during his remarks at the plenary session, Lee Soo-hyuk advised him not to repeat it any more. Kelly remained silent. Later, South Korea formally requested that the U.S. side refrain from overusing the term.[111]

In fact, many of the members of the U.S. delegation, including Kelly himself, became secretly doubtful about its usefulness. The idea behind CVID "was and is U.S. Policy," but the words represented by the acronym "suggested the kind of preemptive surrender that North Korea was unlikely to negotiate for." In the process of finalizing the joint statement, Kelly, in fact, decided to eliminate "CVID" from the draft, in favor of "less loaded" words.[112] But "the counterproliferationists" at the White House, such as Robert Joseph, strongly insisted on inclusion of the term.[113]

A Department of State official seated behind Kelly overheard him when he murmured to Joseph DeTrani, the State Department's special envoy for the six-party talks, "I see both people [Cheney and Joseph] got to the president," a reference to the fact that the recommendation that "CVID" not be used had been turned down by the White House leadership.[114] Nevertheless, Secretary of State Powell allowed the U.S. delegation to take the term out of the draft joint statement, and Kelly was able to endorse it.[115]

It was only after the third round of the six-party talks that the U.S. delegation was released from using the acronym. One member of the U.S. delegation later recalled that "the neocons insisted on 'irreversible,' but the president didn't pay any particular attention to this word. In fact, he didn't even mention this word. And that's why we didn't have to use this slogan."[116]

But around the time of the second round of the six-party talks, CVID advocates were full of big talk, riding the tailwind of the "Libyan model." On December 19, 2003, Libya, which the United States had labeled a rogue state and a sponsor of terrorism, announced that it would completely dismantle its weapons of mass destruction. In an official statement, Libya's Foreign Ministry announced that "[Libya] wants all countries to follow its steps, starting with the Middle East, without any exception or double standards."[117] On the same day, leaders of the United States and the United Kingdom released the following statement praising Qaddafi's decision: "Should Libya pursue internal reform, America will be ready to help its people to build a more free and prosperous country. . . . And I hope that other leaders will find an example in Libya's announcement today."[118]

The United States called this pattern of nuclear dismantlement the "Libyan model" and, hoping for an easy second win, insisted that North Korea adopt it. But North Korea rejected the Libyan model, which it interpreted as proof of Libya's defeat by the United States, and further intensified its attacks on the United States, calling the United States "foolish enough to calculate that such a model, imposed upon Libya, would be accepted by the DPRK, too."[119] North Korea rationalized its rejection of the Libyan model using its often-quoted rhetoric: "When both sides are leveling guns at each other, how can the DPRK trust the United States and drop its gun? What we want is for both sides to drop their guns at the same time."[120]

The "Libyan model" became another mantra, along with "CVID," for hardliners on North Korea. John Bolton and Robert Joseph were most vocal in claiming that the Libyan model was a model of success; because of that, the term began to take on a "neocon" connotation, making Kelly and others averse to using it. During the third round of the six-party talks, the neocons tried to incorporate "the Libyan model" in Kelly's opening statement, but Kelly and others deleted many of the references.[121]

Although the United States and Japan strongly advocated the Libyan model, China, Russia, and South Korea did not seem to be very enthusiastic about it. Some observers believed that those three countries plus North Korea might have had the Ukrainian model in mind instead.[122] In 1994, Ukraine had issued a joint statement with the United States and Russia concerning the disposal of nuclear warheads that the Soviet Union left behind in Ukraine. The permanent members of the UN Security Council later signed a memorandum of understanding regarding the joint statement, which referred to Ukraine's declaration to sign the Nuclear Non-Proliferation Treaty (NPT); the movement of nuclear warheads to Russia; "security assurance," including respect for Ukraine's sovereignty; and energy cooperation, including U.S. and Russian provision of uranium for nuclear reactors.[123]

However, South Korea's view on the Libyan model was more nuanced. One senior Blue House official later said that "when the United States started pushing the Libyan model on North Korea, we all applauded."[124] South Korea saw the Libyan model as a case in which both parties had made a strategic decision in favor of nuclear dismantlement and diplomatic normalization, and Seoul very much wished that both the United States and North Korea would learn from that example. The Blue House official had the following to say:

> The United Kingdom played an important role behind the success of the Libyan case. The United Kingdom had quietly negotiated with Libya behind the United States' back. It was a victory of quiet diplomacy. It goes to show how important it is to quietly discuss what can be done with an adversary and this should be the lesson from the Libyan model. In the case of North Korea, only Japan and South Korea can play the role that the United Kingdom had played, and we requested the United States to give that serious consideration."[125]

Some in Japan's Foreign Ministry believed that Japan should play a role similar to that played by the United Kingdom in the Libyan settlement.[126] But the United States remained hesitant. A senior U.S. administration official later said, "I don't think people were frankly comfortable having Hitoshi Tanaka [Japan's chief negotiator with North Korea during the first Japan–North Korea summit] play the role of the British, and by the way, it wasn't the British Foreign Ministry, it was the MI6, it was intelligence people working with the CIA. So people didn't think Tanaka was the right role model for that."[127] In any case, a senior Blue House official later noted, "Although the United States repeatedly referred to the Libyan model, it never attempted to discuss the matter directly with North Korea."[128]

The third mantra was "HEU." The United States claimed that the Pakistani government's admission in early 2004 of the transfer of nuclear technology by A. Q. Khan endorsed the U.S. allegations about North Korea's development of highly enriched uranium. The United States subsequently tried to instill a common perception of the HEU issue among the five participants, excluding North Korea, in the six-party talks. In the U.S.–North Korea bilateral consultation during the second round of the talks, Kelly attempted to corner North Korea on the HEU issue, saying, "You know, we know, and other countries know."[129] But that failed to change North Korea's stance of outright denial. After the second round of the talks, Kim Gye-gwan made the following announcement to the press corps:

I hereby clarify that there are no enriched uranium, no HEU facilities, no HEU scientists.[130]

We have had mutual dealings with Pakistan and earned hard currency by selling missiles to Pakistan. . . . However, we have no relationship with Pakistan regarding highly enriched uranium.[131]

Lee Soo-hyuk, South Korea's head delegate, maintained throughout the second round that South Korea could not fully endorse the U.S. position, a stance that was described by one member of the U.S. delegation as an "ambiguous posture." Lee Soo-hyuk was of the view that even if A. Q. Khan had sold North Korea blueprints and technology relating to HEU production, including centrifuges, that did not necessarily mean that North Korea had advanced enough to produce weapons-scale enriched uranium. Lee Soo-hyuk was not the only one to hold that view; other nations, including China, Russia, and Japan, did too. During the second round, South Korea proposed that the wording "uranium enrichment program" (UEP) should be used in place of "HEU." Both Japan and the United States accepted the proposal, and since the third round of the talks, "HEU" has been replaced by "UEP."[132] China had also urged the United States to change the wording. A Chinese diplomat in charge of the six-party talks questioned a U.S. counterpart, asking "if the U.S. had evidence indicating the North had enriched the uranium up to 80 percent, or even higher, of the density?" The U.S. official demurred. According to the Chinese diplomat, "Since then, the U.S. side quietly changed the term from 'HEU' to 'UEP.'"[133]

A member of the U.S. delegation later acknowledged, "That was a fig leaf to try to make it a little bit easier to put it [the UEP issue] on the table."[134] Japan and the United States, by making it possible for North Korea to save face even if it had to admit the existence of the uranium enrichment program, hoped to induce North Korea to admit it. At the same time, with the introduction of the UEP issue, it became possible to include all uranium, whether for military or civilian use, in the nuclear dismantlement target. It was a policy that combined both a hard and a soft approach.[135]

As it turned out, the fig leaf did not produce the intended effect. Whether in the form of HEU or UEP, China did not put the uranium enrichment issue on the table at the six-party talks.

SIX-PARTY TALKS, ROUND THREE

The third round of the six-party talks was convened on Wednesday, June 23, 2004. In his opening remarks, Wang Yi, chairman of the talks, announced:

> This round of talks will discuss in depth two substantial topics.
> One is how to realize a nuclear weapon-free Korean Peninsula, including ways to abandon nuclear programmes and solve the concerns of all parties.
> The second is how to take the first step towards the nuclear weapon-free goal, including freezing of nuclear facilities.[136]

After Wang spoke, North Korea's head delegate, Kim Gye-gwan, slowly took off his glasses and started to read his opening remarks, saying, in part, that North Korea "will put forward concrete plans on freezing nuclear programmes if the U.S. party withdraws its demand for complete, verifiable and irreversible dismantlement and accepted the 'freeze for compensation' programme."[137]

James Kelly, the U.S. head delegate, stated, in turn, "The United States is prepared to have sincere consultations, and we have brought with us a new proposal." The "new proposal," a seven-page English document, was presented the following day. It encompassed the following steps. First, North Korea was to declare that it would dismantle its nuclear weapons and programs. That declaration would be followed by the denuclearization process, which would begin with the provision of heavy oil to North Korea by concerned countries other than the United States. Next, within three months, the actual dismantling of the nuclear facilities would begin, including dismantling of the plutonium nuclear development facility in Yongbyon and the uranium enrichment program. Once it was verified that the process had started, interim provision of a multilateral "security assurance" would be initiated, and the provision of long-term energy aid and the lifting of economic sanctions would be considered.[138]

On the morning of June 24, the United States and North Korea had a bilateral consultation that lasted for two hours and twenty minutes, focusing mainly on the new U.S. proposal. Although Kim Gye-gwan evaluated the proposal rather positively, calling it "constructive," he seemed to sense that the United States was not yet deeply committed to a policy of engagement with North Korea, its hesitation revealed by the fact that "security assurance" was to be provided only at the last stage. Although Kim raised various questions about the U.S. proposal, Kelly understood his main concern to be the true position of the United States regarding the issue of compensation for North Korea's freezing of the graphite-moderated nuclear reactors in Yongbyon. Kelly interpreted Kim Gye-gwan's remarks as an indication that North Korea might not yet have made a final decision concerning abandonment of its nuclear programs.[139]

In the middle of their talk, Kim Gye-gwan referred to a "very powerful sector" within the North Korean government. Kim spoke for well over thirty minutes, saying that this powerful sector controlled North Korea's nuclear capability, that this sector zealously aspired to conduct a nuclear test so that it could boast of North Korea's capability, and that the possibility of a nuclear test increased as the negotiations continued without the United States abandoning its hostile policies toward North Korea. It was not hard to imagine that this "very powerful sector" was the military. Kim Gye-gwan concluded his monologue by saying, "I am not threatening you."[140] In fact, Kim was polite during the consultation, and he remained calm when he talked. He did not show any sign of the hostility demonstrated by his predecessors—Li Gun, during the trilateral meeting, and Kim Yong-il, during the first round of the six-party talks.

On June 25, in order to find out the true intentions behind Kim Gye-gwan's reference to a possible nuclear test, the U.S. delegation proposed to the North Korean delegation that they have another bilateral consultation. That was a highly unusual move for the United States, which up to then had avoided bilateral consultations with North Korea. But this time North Korea rejected the proposal. In the past, whenever North Korea made a hard-line remark on the nuclear issue, the subject of the sentence always was "we." But this time Kim Gye-gwan had specified a certain sector in the government. Could he be trying to convey that some drastic change was taking place in Pyongyang—for example, the downfall of technocrats like Kim himself and the rise of the hardliners? Or, noting that the United States had indicated for the first time that it might accept the idea of compensation for a freeze, was he trying to raise the price of compensation by referring to the possibility of a nuclear test?

Kelly tried in every possible way to decipher Kim's remarks, but Kim's true intentions remained obscure. It was clear, however, that Kim Gye-gwan had been acting on instructions from Pyongyang. Kim Gye-gwan had attempted to revise Li Gun's remark in April 2003 that North Korea was capable of transferring nuclear weapons abroad, saying, "No, you didn't get that right, that's not what he said." All the North Korean delegation members seated at the back, including Han Song-ryol, deputy permanent representative to the UN, immediately put fake grins on their faces. Kelly felt that they might have rehearsed their performance beforehand.[141]

After the meeting, Kelly made the following comments:

Kim Gye-gwan must have been trying to inform us that hardliners in the North Korean government are dreaming of obtaining the status of a nuclear power. North Korea must be dying to be treated like Israel, Pakistan, and India. But North Korea will never be like that.

Kim Gye-gwan's remark was a foolish one. First of all, the countries that will be most furious if North Korea conducts a nuclear test are Japan, South Korea, and China. The United States will not be directly affected by the test. Second, he is minimizing his own power as a negotiator. If the opinions of the hardliners are so important, we are inclined to think that it is a waste of time to have discussions with the likes of Kim Gye-gwan.[142]

However, Kelly sensed that something in the North Korean attitude was in the process of changing. It might have had something to do with Pyongyang's discovery of the value of the six-party talks as an arena in which North Korea could enjoy the attention of the world's major powers, including the United States. Or, the talks might have convinced North Korea that it could attract the attention of those countries only if it possessed nuclear arms. That might have been behind what seemed to be an obsession on the part of North Korea to boast and brag about its nuclear deterrence.[143]

On Friday, June 25, the North Korean delegation presented its own proposal, the gist of which it announced on the same day to the press corps in front of the North Korean embassy in Beijing. The proposal consisted of the following elements:

—Freezing would be the first step toward dismantlement, and it would be implemented in a verifiable manner.

—North Korea would freeze its nuclear programs only after the United States retracted its request concerning CVID and agreed to provide compensation.

—The target of the freeze would encompass all of the DPRK's facilities relating to nuclear weapons and products whose use had been changed through reprocessing as well as other nuclear activities that the DPRK had engaged in since its withdrawal from the NPT, and nuclear weapons would no longer be produced, transferred, or tested.

—Freezing would be implemented when compensation was provided.

—Compensation would include the provision by the United States and other countries of 2 million watts of energy assistance to North Korea, removal of North Korea from the U.S. list of terrorist states, and suspension of economic sanctions and blockades against North Korea.[144]

On Saturday, June 26, Chairman Wang Yi read the chairman's statement and pronounced the end of the third round of the six-party talks. The statement included the following points:

[The Parties] ... reaffirmed their commitments to the goal of denuclearization of the Korean Peninsula and stressed the need to take first steps toward that goal as soon as possible.

The Parties stressed the need for a step-by-step process of "words for words" and "action for action" in search for a peaceful solution to the nuclear issue.

The Parties agreed in principle to hold the Fourth Round of the Six-Party Talks in Beijing by the end of September 2004.[145]

In the press conference after the end of the third round, Wang Yi remarked, "That the stances of the United States and North Korea were getting closer was easily visible during the current round," and he proudly enumerated a number of developments that had occurred "for the first time" during the third round:

—For the first time, North Korea clearly stated that "a freeze would be the first step toward nuclear dismantlement." North Korea, also for the first time, had referred specifically to "nuclear facilities in operation," including its graphite-moderated reactors in Yongbyon, as among the targets of a freeze.

—For the first time, the United States referred to offering compensation to North Korea for freezing its nuclear programs.

—For the first time, Japan announced that it was prepared to join in providing energy aid to North Korea in return for a freeze. Japan also made it clear that it would pursue "nuclear settlement in the six-party talks and the abduction issue in bilateral negotiations," based on the partial progress toward the settlement of the abduction issue by Prime Minister Koizumi during his second visit to Pyongyang one month earlier.

The third round of the six-party talks was able to achieve an agreement among the participants specifying that North Korea would freeze its nuclear programs as the first step toward ultimate denuclearization. That in turn enabled discussion of the real subject of the talks, denuclearization, which was by far the largest accomplishment of the third round. At the same time, Wang Yi also pointed out two "major difficulties": the scope and method of nuclear dismantlement and the scope of both a nuclear freeze and appropriate corresponding measures.

As for the scope of the nuclear freeze, the United States asked that it include not only the existing nuclear facilities but all nuclear weapons and programs, including those for the development of peaceful uses of nuclear energy. In contrast, North Korea insisted on limiting the target to "nuclear facilities currently in operation," such as the graphite-moderated reactors in Yongbyon, but included reprocessed plutonium. North Korea again denied the existence of any uranium enrichment program.

Wang Yi announced that the six-party talks process was an "irreversible and historical trend." At the same time, he added, "We are not a major party to a nuclear settlement. We objectively recognize that China does not hold the key for a successful settlement, and we have taken care to not to go beyond our position and role." By that statement, Wang Yi warned against excessive expectations of China's role.[146]

On June 28, a spokesman for North Korea's Foreign Ministry issued a statement in which he said, "An agreement was reached on such issues as simultaneously taking action on the principle of 'words for words' and 'action for action,' and mainly discussing the issue of 'reward for freeze.' This was positive progress made at the talks." The spokesman pointed out that "it was fortunate that the U.S. did not use the expression of CVID," but he added that "scrutiny of the United States' proposal suggests that, to our regret, it only mentioned phased demands for disarming the DPRK. Therefore, "the talks could not make a decisive breakthrough."[147]

THE U.S. PROPOSAL

The proposal that the United States submitted at the third round of the six-party talks was produced over two days in June 2004 at a hotel in Washington in a joint initiative of the White House and the Blue House. The individuals involved in drafting the proposal included Kwon Chin-ho, head of the National Security Council at the Blue House, and senior policy coordinator Wi Sung-lac and Park Sun-won, both also of the Blue House NSC; Michael Green, director of East Asian affairs for the National Security Council at the White House; and William Tobey, director of counterproliferation at the White House NSC. Kwon Chin-ho, holding the position formerly held by Ra Jong-il, was an army lieutenant general, and he had once led the South Korean Army's intelligence command. He also was a veteran of the Vietnam War.

South Korea had proposed the joint drafting. The Roh Moo-hyun government welcomed the middle-of-the-road, pro-engagement posture represented by Secretary of State Colin Powell and Assistant Secretary of State James Kelly; however, because those "middle-of-the-road, pro-engagement" people were so helpless vis-à-vis the neocons, Lee Jong-seok, deputy secretary of the Blue House NSC, was urged to work directly with White House officials in order to influence U.S. policy toward North Korea.[148] The Blue House decided to pursue the new route, even though it might strain U.S.–South Korea relations, which traditionally had been managed by the U.S. Department of State and South Korea's Ministry of Foreign Affairs and Trade. U.S. national security adviser Condoleezza Rice was very receptive to the idea. She had wanted to reinvigorate the six-party talks, which had been launched at the initiative of the White House.

The purpose of the joint exercise was to draw a roadmap for the denuclearization of North Korea. Since the beginning of the Roh Moo-hyun government, the differences between the U.S. and the South Korean approach to North Korea had widened. Among the differences were the following:

—Although South Korea believed that both the carrot and the stick were necessary to induce North Korea to dismantle its nuclear programs, the United States believed in applying the stick before giving the carrot.

—Although South Korea was convinced that ultimately U.S.–North Korea bilateral negotiations would be necessary if the North Korean nuclear issue was to be settled, the United States took the position that the issue was essentially a regional one and that settlement called for a multilateral approach.

—Although South Korea believed that an interim freeze of North Korea's nuclear programs was necessary before complete dismantlement was done, the United States disagreed, demanding immediate dismantlement.

During the Japan–South Korea–U.S. consultations prior to the first round of the six-party talks, South Korea presented a roadmap to denuclearization that included North Korea's abolition of its nuclear programs, U.S. commitment to a security guarantee for North Korea, and efforts to normalize U.S.–North Korea diplomatic relations. But the United States was not very receptive. To begin with, the United States insisted that North Korea commit itself to nuclear dismantlement; the United States would not commit itself to a security assurance; and the United States envisioned normalization of diplomatic relations with North Korea as a process that would take place only in the distant future.[149]

South Korea and the United States nevertheless continued their policy consultations in order to develop a common position, and they were able to agree on the following basic principles:

—Both dialogue and pressure would be necessary to advance negotiations with North Korea toward the dismantlement of its nuclear programs.

—Although underlying the nuclear crisis was the disagreement and tension between the United States and North Korea, a regionwide, multilateral approach was important, and South Korea had to play a positive role in this approach.

—Although the ultimate goal of the talks remained the complete dismantlement of North Korea's nuclear programs, some interim step such as "a halt of the nuclear program" or "cessation of the nuclear program would be necessary."[150]

On the eve of the third round of the six-party talks, South Korea decided to prepare a U.S.–South Korea joint proposal to be submitted during the third round. Before beginning, the White House NSC contacted the Japanese government to ask for its reaction to the idea. Mitoji Yabunaka, director general of the Asian and Oceanian Affairs Bureau of the Foreign Ministry, welcomed the initiative. "If you're working with the Koreans, that's good for Japan," he said. "We're not worried that you and Korea are going to come up with something that's bad for us. You know, if it was just Korea we would be nervous. If it was just you, we'd be nervous." Following that response, the esteem in which the NSC held Yabunaka soared, and he became regarded as someone who would think strategically in order to manage the alliance.[151]

By the time the preliminary draft of the U.S. proposal prepared by the Department of State had been delivered to the White House, officials at the White House and the Blue House had discussed the draft and agreed on the complete dismantlement of North Korea's nuclear programs, the provision of a security assurance to North Korea as a reward, and provision of energy assistance to North Korea. South Korea remained skeptical that North Korea had highly enriched uranium, but it agreed to include "uranium enrichment program" as one target of dismantlement. As for the time allowed for complete dismantlement, South Korea insisted on one year, while the United States demanded six months.

Predominant in the Bush administration was the dispassionate stance that the United States would do nothing until North Korea abolished its nuclear weapons and programs. Behind that stance was the belief that North Korea, because it alone had caused the current crisis by secretly developing highly enriched uranium in violation of the Agreed Framework, should not be rewarded at all until it repented of its past sins and completely dismantled its nuclear programs. Robert Joseph was a representative figure of that school, which, in a nutshell, declared that the United States would not agree to negotiate with North Korea unless and until the latter agreed to complete, verifiable, and irreversible dismantlement. That was, in effect, an ultimatum demanding North Korea's unconditional surrender. However, one NSC official was apprehensive about the negative impact of this view. "If we put that idea forward in the talks," he said, "I personally believe that Korea and Japan will openly split with us, and it will be devastating."[152] That comment expressed, in short, "apprehension from the perspective of alliance management."[153] That apprehension was shared by Condoleezza Rice, who explored a new approach: to set up—between the initial action of "resumption of operation of existing nuclear facilities" and the final goal of "complete dismantlement"—an interim stage of "disabling all nuclear facilities." Rice proposed that approach to Bush, who gave his approval. During the drafting of the joint proposal, the United States side advocated this three-step approach, which ended up in the final proposal.[154] Blue House officials were elated at having had such intensive policy consultations with White House officials for the first time since the launching of the six-party talks process and, moreover, at having succeeded in producing a joint proposal.

However, diplomats in both countries were not especially happy with the draft because they had not been involved in its production. The secret consultations between the White House and the Blue House were timed to occur three days before the U.S.–Japan–South Korea trilateral meeting in Washington, at which the draft was to be presented. The draft was handed over to Kelly and Lee. Although Kelly accepted the draft, Lee was less than enthusiastic about using a draft that bore no trace of his fingerprints as a foundation for the trilateral consultation. However, there soon arose a more serious obstacle.[155]

As soon as the South Korean delegation left Washington, the draft joint proposal became the target of a severe backlash within the administration. The most notable manifestation was Vice President Dick Cheney's opposition to inserting a "freeze" step in the dismantlement process, no matter what terminology was used to describe that step. He was, therefore, opposed to the three-step approach. Cheney instructed Victoria Nuland, his principal deputy national security adviser, and Stephen Hadley, assistant to the president for national security affairs, to consult together regarding the joint proposal. Nuland's position was that the fundamental error of the Clinton administration's Agreed Framework was that it had allowed North Korea to freeze its nuclear programs instead of abolish them and thereby allowed Pyongyang to buy time. The United States had been set up by North Korea, which had never had any intention of abolishing its nuclear programs. Agreeing with a freeze as the first step in the joint U.S.–South Korea proposal—and in the Agreed Framework—was the fundamental mistake.[156] In the end, the White House took a step back, deciding not to accept a "freeze" stage or even the term *freeze*. Accordingly all references to a freeze were removed from the U.S.–South Korea joint proposal.[157]

But that was not the end of it. Secretary of Defense Donald Rumsfeld concluded that the transition period of six months—in which preparations were to be made for dismantling North Korea's nuclear weapons and removing them from the country—was too long, and he insisted on three months instead. That condition, too, was adopted by the U.S. leadership, and the joint proposal was revised accordingly. When James Kelly departed for the third round of the six-party talks, the White House gave him a revised version of the joint proposal incorporating the new provisions.[158]

Meanwhile, South Korean officials concerned with the six-party talks had been irritated by the lack of response from the United States. Even on the eve of the third round, the United States still had not sent South Korea the final version of the joint proposal. Agitated, South Korea hinted that it might consider submitting its own proposal unilaterally at the third round if the United States did not release the joint proposal.

On June 22, one day before the start of the third round of the six-party talks, the U.S. delegation invited the head delegates of the other five participating countries to a meeting at the U.S. embassy in Beijing for a briefing on the U.S. proposal. The draft circulated at the time was dated "as of the morning of Monday, June 21." In other words, it was not a clean copy, revealing that even at the last minute there was an struggle within the Bush administration over the proposal.[159] On reading the draft, one senior official at the Blue House called the White House and yelled over the phone, "Fifty percent of what we had agreed to incorporate in the joint proposal has been changed. We can't call this a joint proposal any longer." The "joint proposal" was to be downgraded to a "coordinated proposal."[160] That same Blue House official later remarked:

I strongly protested to the United States. The document that I saw might have had the same skeleton [as our draft], but the flesh was totally different. We thought that the joint proposal that we had spent one full day to prepare was a finished product, but obviously the United States didn't think so. . . .

The United States proposal narrowed the entry gate for North Korea to denuclearize itself. It had the effect of dampening North Korea's appetite for denuclearizing itself. Besides, it was utterly unrealistic to request North Korea to dismantle and remove from itself all of its nuclear weapons, including nuclear warheads, within three months.[161]

In the briefing for other delegations at the U.S. embassy in Beijing, the United States had announced that it would provide its own reward (more concretely, "security assurance") if North Korea would officially declare that it would abolish its nuclear weapons and programs, clearing the first stage. But the following day, Kelly announced, as mentioned earlier, that during the first stage the United States would support only the provision of heavy oil to North Korea by the other countries and that a security assurance would be provided at a later stage. The United States did not provide Japan and South Korea with any prior explanation concerning the change of policy, and the members of the Japanese and South Korean delegations could only vent their frustration at the division within the Bush administration.

Although the United States removed from the proposal all references to a freeze, the concept persisted. The chairman's statement for the third round of the six-party talks stressed "the need to take a first step toward that goal [denuclearization of the Korean Peninsula] as soon as possible." During the press conference after the third round, Wang Yi, the chairman of the third round, identified that "first step" as a "freeze." The first step was, in effect, a synonym for *freeze*. And yet, there remained a number of unresolved issues. First, what should North Korea freeze? During the third round, North Korea announced that it was prepared to include in the freeze all of its nuclear-related facilities, as well as all nuclear materials produced by reprocessing after it withdrew from the NPT in the spring of 2003. In addition, North Korea pledged that it would no longer produce, transfer, or test nuclear weapons. Because the extent of the freeze was connected to the amount of compensation that North Korea would receive, it seemed that North Korea was attempting to maximize its compensation by the announcements and pledges it made. The United States became thoroughly disgusted and angry. The administration maintained the position expressed by Secretary of

State Colin Powell, as noted by Department of State spokesman Richard Boucher: "We don't have any intention of rewarding North Korea for things it never should have done to begin with."[162]

Second, what should be the time frame for the freeze? North Korea offered to implement a freeze when compensation was provided, but the prospect of providing compensation at the freeze stage was hard for the United States to swallow. However, the process toward denuclearization could not even be started without at least simultaneous implementation of a freeze and provision of compensation.

Thus, in the third round of the six-party talks, the participants agreed on the necessity of an interim "first step," but they failed to agree about how a freeze should be connected to a reward/compensation and whether the freeze and compensation should occur simultaneously.

In the end, the plan to produce a joint United States–South Korea proposal was crippled at the last stage and left unrealized. A veteran South Korean diplomat who was involved in the six-party talks later said that "the failure was attributable to our lack of understanding concerning the inflexibility of the U.S. vis-à-vis the freeze."[163] But, at the same time, it was beyond doubt that South Korea's efforts had a part in bringing the United States to a more pragmatic, give-and-take approach to the negotiations. As mentioned earlier, underlying the U.S. transformation was the NSC's concern with regard to maintaining the U.S.–South Korean alliance. South Korea's head delegate, Lee Soo-hyuk, made the following comment praising the South Korean initiative:

> We explained the South Korean proposal [which was more flexible than the U.S. proposal] to the U.S. team and contributed to the drafting of the United States' own proposal. It was in response to our request that North Korea also presented a concrete proposal. South Korea prided itself on having influenced both the United States and North Korea.[164]

To be sure, it was not only South Korea's efforts and the NSC's concern over alliance management that brought the United States back to a more pragmatic approach. The campaign for the U.S. presidential election of November 2004 was another element. The Democratic candidate, John Kerry, proposed that the issue be settled through U.S.–North Korea bilateral negotiations, and he criticized Bush for not negotiating with North Korea. Faced with that challenge, Bush and his White House team were under pressure from the "political side," and they did not want North Korea "to be an issue."[165] Certainly, there was a well-defined "firewall" between the National Security Council and the domestic political operatives. Accordingly, NSC staff were informally advised that it would be sufficient if a multilateral approach in the form of the six-party talks at least seemed to be restricting North Korea's behavior. It was crucially important for the six-party talks to produce some concrete proposal. In short, Bush and his White House team had to set up an alibi for their inability to denuclearize North Korea, and they had to make some small concessions to the pragmatic school in order to do so.

At the same time, North Korea also may have been paying close attention to the U.S. presidential election campaign.[166] Because Bush might be reelected, North Korea was obliged to go along with the general thrust of the six-party talks to a certain extent. But, given the possibility that Kerry could win the race, North Korea would not join hands with Bush. South Korea, for its part, tried to persuade the North Koreans that making a deal was a great chance to make Bush feel indebted to North Korea. Lee Soo-hyuk warned Li Gun, who attended a track-two conference[167] on North Korea in New York, that "he [Bush] is a crazy man. You have to strike a deal with him now. Otherwise you'll be in big trouble after he is reelected."[168] Although the fourth round of the six-party talks had originally been scheduled for September 2004, nobody moved on it. North Korea seemed to have decided to watch the U.S. presidential race, which in November ended in a victory for Bush.

NEGOTIATING STYLE

The U.S. delegation to the talks included representatives of the White House, the Department of State, and the U.S. military, but all of the delegations of the five other countries were composed mainly of diplomats. Among those diplomats were officers concerned with Korean Peninsula affairs, nonproliferation of weapons of mass destruction, and U.S. affairs. Japan, China, and South Korea had come to the six-party talks after deciding on the direction that they wanted to take given their respective policies toward North Korea (and toward South Korea, in the case of Japan and China), denuclearization, and U.S.-related affairs. None of the three had had much experience with multilateral diplomacy, which was not yet developed in Northeast Asia, so the six-party talks process was a new challenge for them. For instance, when the chairman called for a draft of a statement, they had to promptly prepare a draft in English, a task that was more difficult than preparing one in their respective native languages.

The six-party talks process subtly affected Northeast Asian regional policies and negotiation styles. One Chinese diplomat described this development simply: "Secret diplomacy is becoming increasingly difficult."[169] Because the process was multilateral, all of the participating countries had to compare notes on information and assessments of each other's intentions and initiatives, increasing the transparency of the process. The United States, for instance, disclosed to the other participating countries the content of the U.S.–North Korea bilateral negotiations immediately after each meeting.

The new process was challenging for the host country, China. It constantly had to help the other participants understand its intentions and the direction of its policies and persuade them to have confidence in those policies. In light of the depth of the mutual distrust between the United States and North Korea, that was not an easy task. It required China to change its previous secretive style of diplomacy toward North Korea, which had been controlled by the Communist Party's International Department. For the Chinese Foreign Ministry, the six-party talks became a venue in which it could negotiate directly with North Korea, giving the Foreign Ministry and China itself a chance to depart from their cold war orientation and enter into "new thinking" diplomacy. Against that backdrop, the delegates of the other countries were amazed to witness the emergence of Chinese diplomats who had a new style. Among them was Fu Ying, director general of China's Asian Affairs Bureau. James Kelly later recalled:

> While I was in Beijing for the six-party talks, finalizing a statement with my counterparts, Washington instructed me to request revision of some wording. I think probably at around 10 o'clock at night I called Fu Ying, who had given me her cell phone number, which itself was exceptional in the Chinese system, and I said we had a statement. I apologized for calling at night, but we had about one hour to get this thing cleared and to find out if there were any serious Chinese objections, and so I read her the statement. She called me back in five minutes and said, "Yes, we think that statement is just fine. It's better than what we're doing, [and so] we've taken a couple of lines [from yours] and put them into ours." But this decisiveness and ability to get things done . . . is completely opposite to all the experiences I had previously had with China.[170]

It might have been difficult, however, for the Chinese diplomats who had been in charge of North Korean affairs, such as Ning Fukui, to adjust to the new environment. Ning, as the ambassador in charge of North Korean talks, visited the United States several times, but the U.S. view of him became increasingly critical with each new visit. One U.S. official who had negotiated with Ning later recalled:

> Ning Fukui is very, very tactical, extremely tactical. We wanted to have a candid exchange of views on the situation in North Korea, but he was far from candid. He always tried to hide what the North Koreans had in mind or what they had told the Chinese. He tried to push us to see what rhetorical device or gimmick he could use to take back to Pyongyang to declare progress. . . . [H]e treated us like we were a variable or a tool that he needed to somehow wield to get North Korea to change.[171]

In terms of personal discretion and freedom of negotiation, the North Korean delegates must have been under the tightest restrictions. One member of the

U.S. delegation characterized it as "99 percent talking-points-recital diplomacy."[172] Even during bilateral negotiations, only the head delegate spoke. It was extremely difficult for diplomats from other countries to build relationships of mutual trust with the North Korean diplomats. Whenever members of the North Korean delegation saw Kelly at one of the cocktail parties, which were held often, they kept a respectful distance from him; Kelly had the impression that they were extremely fearful of having to engage in "small talk" with him.[173] Jack Pritchard, who once served the Bush administration as special envoy for negotiations with North Korea, made the following observations:

> I have been able to cut off an opening monologue and to tell my North Korea counterpart to just pretend that he had given the [required] speech and I would pretend that I had listened, and then we could get down to business. That is possible only after developing a personal relationship that comes with extended contact. Having a forty-minute encounter in a corner of a room will not do it. My first serious exposure to bilateral talks with North Korea lasted eleven hours, and that was only the first day.[174]

It is uncertain how much the North Korean diplomats were influenced by multilateral diplomacy through the six-party talks. For diplomats from a country that operates under quasi-wartime conditions, in an eat-or-be-eaten environment, individual initiatives, transparent discussions, joint drafting of statements in English, and quiet diplomacy remained too alien. Besides, the communications between the North Korean delegation and Pyongyang seemed to be extremely ossified. Although the Chinese occasionally asked the North Korean delegation to urgently telephone Pyongyang to consult with the leadership there, the North Koreans would never agree. The delegation was under strict orders not to use a telephone, which might have been tapped by the enemy, and it insisted instead on contacting Pyongyang through wiretap-free lines.[175]

It was South Korea that carefully explained the North Korean situation to the other delegations and provided the North Korean delegation with friendly advice. It must have helped that Lee Soo-hyuk and Kim Gye-gwan had known each other since the four-party talks in the late 1990s and had developed an amicable relationship. Lee reportedly once gave Kim the following advice:

> You guys are not familiar with the American mentality. You should not lie to Americans. In the United States, they dislike lying so much that elementary school teachers summon the parents of a kid who tells lies, and they suggest that the child be transferred to another school. In your case, it too often happens that you first deny something only to admit it later. Why does this happen? I think it is because you apply different ethics in the

private versus public realms. In the private realm, you teach your children not to tell a lie. But in the public realm, a totally different ethical principle is applied.[176]

The North Korean just listened quietly to Lee's advice.

For the U.S. delegation, one American diplomat said, "the time difference was an enemy."[177] The U.S. delegation had to contact Washington, which is twelve or thirteen hours behind Beijing, to receive instructions, report on the consequences of following instructions, and receive subsequent instructions. The fourth round of the six-party talks in July 2005 turned out to be a marathon of negotiations. According to one member of the U.S. delegation, a typical day in Beijing began with a team meeting at 7:00 a.m. at the U.S. embassy to review the strategy for that day's negotiations. After the meeting, the delegates went to the Diaoyutai State Guest House, where they would be locked inside until around 7:00 p.m. Often bilateral negotiations took place at 9:00 p.m. or even 11:00 p.m. After they were over, the delegation headed back to the hotel and sent telegrams and e-mail messages to Washington. It was usually around midnight or even after 1:00 a.m. before they could finally go to bed. Some of the delegates were almost religious about going to the gym in the morning; they woke up between 5:00 a.m. and 5:30 a.m.[178]

If the U.S. delegation had been allowed a little more discretion, it would not have had to contact Washington so often for instructions. But more often than not, Washington sent detailed instructions based on interdepartmental consultations and asked that they be followed religiously. The greater the interdepartmental or interfactional conflict of views, the stricter the directives from Washington. During the fourth round, Washington designated Victor Cha and William Tobey as disciplinarians so that Christopher Hill, the head delegate, would not—in his zeal to pursue agreements among participants—deviate from the directives.[179]

It seems undeniable that ideological conflicts and infighting within the Bush administration regarding policies obstructed policy development and policy coordination with the other participants in the six-party talks. A Chinese diplomat involved with the talks later confessed, "It was difficult to evaluate the U.S. position positively. It was even more difficult to predict the United States' next step. In fact, the United States was more difficult than North Korea. As a moderator, I had a hard time with the United States."[180]

One Chinese official involved with the talks pointed out that although Japan, China, and South Korea occasionally chose to settle issues without clarifying certain ambiguities, the United States always applied a very legalistic approach, causing some cultural friction with the other participants.[181] Some observers also pointed out that Condoleezza Rice's diplomatic style was not always compatible with Asian political and diplomatic culture. One veteran Asia hand in the Department of State remarked:

> Rice thought she could move the Chinese by her direct and personal inter-
> vention. But she just was getting nowhere with them. . . . "You've got to do
> this, you've got to do that". . . they would say all the right things but they
> wouldn't do anything.[182]

China has been criticized, if not publicly, by the other participants for its sometimes clumsy and unequal treatment of the participating countries. Such remarks
were heard particularly in the earlier stages of the six-party talks. A Japanese
diplomat pointed out China's lack of experience in multilateral diplomacy:

> First, as an honest broker, China should have distributed the draft simul-
> taneously. However, China showed the draft first to the North Koreans, giv-
> ing it a de facto veto on the wording. Second, China played the tune to
> North Korea and the U.S. that they wanted to hear. North Korea checked
> with the U.S. to validate it and found some differences. Hence both deval-
> ued China's sincerity.[183]

Nonetheless, such maneuvering might have been necessary to keep the six-party
talks rolling, given the extremely difficult task of getting North Korea on board.

One of the greatest effects of the six-party talks process on Northeast Asian
diplomatic culture and negotiating style was the introduction of the idea of a
"chairperson." At first, China appointed itself as a mediator between the United
States and North Korea. Fu Ying once described the Chinese diplomacy at the six-
party talks as "a diplomacy of equidistance" between Washington and
Pyongyang.[184] China has maintained that the United States and North Korea
are the two main actors, while China is not. But its role gradually evolved from
that of facilitator, to moderator, and then to chairperson.[185] From the U.S. viewpoint, however, it was by no means a straightforward, linear evolution. In fact,
China even appeared to regress on occasion, side-stepping to become a moderator. Sometimes it appeared as if China chose the role most appropriate to the
situation.

NORTH KOREA ANNOUNCES ITS NUCLEAR CAPABILITY

In the 2004 presidential election, Bush won a solid victory. Although many of
the Japanese and South Korean officials involved in the six-party talks were
convinced that the Bush administration would review its North Korea policy at
the beginning of its second term, there was no policy review and only some personnel were changed. But those personnel changes made a great difference.
National security adviser Condoleezza Rice was appointed secretary of state, and

Christopher Hill, the U.S. ambassador to South Korea, became assistant secretary of state in charge of East Asian and Pacific affairs.

At the beginning of his second term, President Bush announced that the central pillar of his administration in the war on terror, after Iraq, would be the democratization of autocratic and tyrannical states. At his second inaugural speech, Bush declared that "it is the policy of the United States to seek and support the growth of democratic movements and institutions in every nation and culture, with the ultimate goal of ending tyranny in our world."[186] The Bush administration's "democracy promotion diplomacy" was set in motion. Among the oppressive states to be reformed was North Korea. In a congressional hearing on January 8, 2005, concerning the nomination of Condoleezza Rice as secretary of state, Rice harshly criticized North Korea in her written statement, calling it an "outpost of tyranny."[187] In his State of the Union address on February 2, 2005, President Bush repeated the word *tyranny* five times, without identifying a country, and he declared that "America will stand with the allies of freedom to support democratic movements in the Middle East and beyond, with the ultimate goal of ending tyranny in our world."[188]

Early in February 2005, the Bush administration dispatched White House NSC staff members Michael Green, senior director of Asian affairs, and William Tobey, director of nonproliferation, to Japan, China, and South Korea to explain the administration's North Korea policy, which included the following objectives:

—To continue to pursue the peaceful settlement of outstanding issues through the six-party talks

—To present and share new intelligence and the U.S. evaluation of the North Korean enriched uranium program

—To seek other countries' cooperation in promoting the nonproliferation of weapons of mass destruction.

In their background briefing to Japan, China, and South Korea concerning North Korea's uranium enrichment activities, Green and Tobey revealed that North Korea had exported uranium hexafluoride to Libya. The cooperation that the United States asked for in order to prevent proliferation of weapons of mass destruction included activities related to what later became labeled as "defensive measures," such as detection of money laundering.[189]

On February 10, North Korea's Foreign Ministry released a statement accusing the Bush administration of maintaining its intention to stifle North Korea and declaring that North Korea therefore was compelled to suspend its participation in the six-party talks for an indefinite period. It also publicly announced that North Korea had "manufactured nukes for self-defence." Although in the past North Korea had repeatedly hinted that it had produced and possessed nuclear arms, that was the first time that the government officially acknowledged, in the form of a Foreign Ministry statement, that it did in fact possess nuclear weapons.[190]

The United States responded calmly to the statement. Richard Boucher, the Department of State's spokesman, announced that the Department of State would ignore the statement, saying, "Yesterday they said they were suspending indefinitely; today they said they will come back under certain conditions. I don't want to try to parse this rhetoric too much."[191] Joseph DeTrani, the U.S. special envoy for six-party talks, said that "we have long believed that North Korea has the capability to produce nuclear weapons. The DPRK's February 10 Foreign Ministry statement . . . doesn't change our perception of North Korea's capability, but it deepens our concern about the [DPRK's] potential to transfer nuclear materials and technology."[192] The basic stance of the United States was that it would refuse to treat North Korea as a nuclear power and enter into bilateral negotiations with North Korea under such a fabricated threat.

In Japan, although voices demanding economic sanctions against North Korea erupted within both the Liberal Democratic Party and the Democratic Party of Japan, the Japanese government remained cautious. Prime Minister Koizumi said that "the window for negotiations will be kept open," referring to both the six-party talks and Japan–North Korea negotiations.[193]

South Korea was in such a state of shock that the nation's unification minister, Chung Dong-young, seriously considered resigning.[194] If North Korea were to proceed from possessing nuclear arms to conducting nuclear tests, the very foundation of the Roh Moo-hyun government's policies for peace and prosperity might collapse; nonetheless, the Roh government tried all the more to seem calm. South Korea's National Intelligence Service announced that in its view, North Korea did not have the capability to produce either enriched uranium or a nuclear warhead.[195] The basic position of the South Korean government was that the true intention of North Korea's statement was not so much to boast of its nuclear capability as to force the United States to change its hostile policies toward North Korea. The South Korean government therefore believed that the U.S. government should do so.[196]

Perhaps it was China, which had been chairing the six-party talks, that was most affected by North Korea's statement, which Pyongyang had issued without giving China prior notice. "With that statement, North Korea stepped onto the threshold of nuclear states," a Chinese diplomat who was involved in the six-party talks later said. "It had a profound meaning that we received seriously." Continuing, he said, "Perhaps more than its message, the timing of the announcement, only two days before the Chinese New Year, made us angry in China. We replied to North Korea with full sarcasm, saying 'Thank you very much for picking such perfect timing.'" China concluded that by issuing the statement, North Korea aimed to "market its own importance to the United States." The same diplomat observed that "North Korea's suggestion that the six-party talks should be converted to an arms-control conference among the nuclear-deterrent countries, or something like that, was a comment that should be understood in the context of this 'marketing.'"[197]

In fact, Wang Jiarui, the head of the Chinese Communist Party's International Department, was scheduled to visit North Korea immediately after North Korea issued the statement. The Chinese diplomat quoted above later said that "North Korea must have carefully timed the announcement. It probably wished to give the world an image of China rushing to North Korea immediately after the announcement. At the same time, North Korea might have hoped to use Wang's visit as some kind of shock absorber."[198] Wang visited Pyongyang as scheduled and had a talk with Kim Jong-il. Wang requested denuclearization of the Korean Peninsula and encouraged North Korea to return to the six-party talks, and he was reported to have told Pyongyang of China's difficulty in continuing its energy aid to North Korea if North Korea developed nuclear weapons—a clear indication of China using its economic leverage.[199]

Why did North Korea choose that particular time to issue such a statement? Before the announcement was made, the United States found out that North Korea had been exporting uranium hexafluoride to Libya, and it dispatched Michael Green and William Tobey to Japan, China, and South Korea to give a briefing on the incident. Jack Pritchard conjectured that given that fact, North Korea had attempted to postpone its participation in the six-party talks, suspecting that the United States was planning to bring the issue up and put North Korea on the defensive.[200] But North Korea's harrumphing over hard-line remarks by Bush and Rice, including Rice's comment about the DPRK being an "outpost of tyranny," should be regarded basically as just another act of brinksmanship intended to lure the Unites States into bilateral negotiations.[201]

Other North Korea watchers in the administration interpreted the statement as a North Korean tactic to gradually increase exposure of its nuclear arms. Following its declaration of nuclear capability in February, North Korea disclosed in May that it had completed extracting 8,000 nuclear fuel rods from the graphite-moderated nuclear reactors in Yongbyon. It also announced that it was taking the measures necessary to increase its nuclear storage capacity and that it was resuming construction on 50,000-kilowatt and 200,000-kilowatt nuclear reactors that had been frozen.[202]

At the time, quite a number of North Korea observers predicted North Korea would hold nuclear tests. On May 15, 2005, national security adviser Stephen Hadley said in an interview with CNN that "if that [nuclear test] is really launched, the United States must take action." That comment was a warning to North Korea, and it also was interpreted as implying that the U.S. government regarded North Korea's conducting of a nuclear test as crossing a "red line."[203] A senior U.S. administration official shared his apprehension, saying, "What worries us most is that there has been a progression of openness among the North Koreans about their nuclear capabilities." Although North Korea traditionally had relied on "obscure tactics"—keeping its nuclear capability obscure—after the February statement it switched to "exposure tactics," boasting of the destructive power of its nuclear weapons.[204]

Toward the end of May 2005, the U.S. government announced that it had transferred fifteen Stealth bombers to South Korea.[205] At the same time, as the new team for the second-term Bush administration was completed, the U.S. government started its quest to resume the six-party talks. Behind the move were Secretary of State Rice, Assistant Secretary of State Christopher Hill, and Joseph DeTrani, special envoy to the six-party talks. Also that May, the New York channel of communication with North Korea, which had been the Department of State's point of contact with North Korea but had been closed since the February 10 statement, showed signs of activity. In a press conference on March 31, President Bush referred to North Korea's leader as "*Mr. Kim Jong-il.*" North Korea's reaction was prompt. The Foreign Ministry's spokesman announced on June 3 that the North Korean government "took note" of Bush's reference to "Mr. Kim Jong-il," and it said that "if Bush's remarks put an end to the scramble between the hawkish group and the moderate group in the United States, which has thrown the Korean policies into a state of confusion, that would help create an atmosphere for the Six-Party Talks." North Korea translated "mister" into the Korean word for "master."[206]

The U.S. government subsequently stressed repeatedly to North Korea, through the New York channel, that it had no intention of attacking or invading North Korea, that it was prepared to provide energy aid in exchange for North Korean's abandonment of its nuclear weapons, and that it would promote normalization of diplomatic relations with North Korea. Those assurances were essentially based on the comprehensive approach that the United States had proposed in the third round of the six-party talks in June 2004.

In mid-June, Chung Dong-young, South Korea's unification minister, visited Pyongyang and succeeded in drawing a positive response from Kim Jong-il regarding North Korea's return to the six-party talks. Now all that North Korea required was a final push. On July 1, Li Gun, director general of the North American Affairs Bureau of North Korea's Foreign Ministry, was attending a track-two seminar in New York concerning the North Korean nuclear issue. Taking advantage of the occasion, Joseph DeTrani, the U.S. special envoy for six-party talks; Victor Cha, NSC's director of East Asian affairs; and James Foster of the Korea desk at the Department of State had an informal discussion with Li Gun and other North Korean participants at the conference. Li Gun declared that "the only way for North Korea to return to the Six-Party Talks is for the United States to formally retract Secretary Rice's description of North Korea as an 'outpost of tyranny,'" and he asked whether the United States would retract it.

When the Americans refused, Li Gun said, "How should we interpret her comment? Can we interpret it as her personal opinion?" Cha responded, "Interpret it as you wish." At that point, Choi Son-hui, a North Korean Foreign Ministry researcher who was sitting next to Li Gun, said, poking Li's arm with her own, "The U.S. officials won't give us a satisfactory answer if you push them. You have done enough. Why don't we leave the rest to the natural flow of things." Verbally stating that "North Korea recognized the Rice comment as her personal opinion," Li Gun wrote something in his notebook.[207]

The United States, judging from those exchanges that North Korea was looking for an excuse to return to the six-party talks, accordingly prepared a suitable carrot as an appetizer. It was a promise that Christopher Hill, the U.S. head delegate to the six-party talks, would invite Kim Gye-gwan to dinner on the night before the talks.[208]

On July 9, while Hill was in Beijing as a member of the advance team for Secretary of State Rice's visit to China, he invited Kim Gye-gwan, who also was in Beijing at that time, to lunch, where they decided that the six-party talks would resume the last week of July. On July 10, the Korean Central News Agency, reporting on the talk between Hill and Kim Gye-gwan, announced that the United States had recognized North Korea as a sovereign state, had no intention of invading North Korea, and had formally announced that it would have bilateral talks with North Korea within the framework of the six-party talks. The news agency also reported that North Korea, interpreting these remarks by the United States as a retraction of Rice's previous reference to the DPRK as an "outpost of tyranny," decided to participate in the six-party talks, which the participants agreed to convene the week of July 26.[209]

CHAPTER ELEVEN

SIX-PARTY TALKS ADRIFT

It was Sunday, July 24, 2005, at the St. Regis Hotel in Beijing. As soon as U.S. Assistant Secretary of State Christopher Hill arrived, he was swarmed by reporters. In speaking with them, Hill remarked, "I did pack a few extra shirts," a comment that was interpreted as a sign of his resolve that the fourth round of the six-party talks would not be a carbon copy of the previous three rounds.[1] While previous rounds were over in two or three days and produced nothing more than an oral summary by the chairman (the first round) or a chairman's statement (the second and third rounds), Hill was prepared for a long battle, even if it lasted one week, two weeks, or more, and he was determined to end the fourth round with a joint statement. In contrast to his predecessor, James Kelly, who immediately before getting in the car said nothing more than "Good morning, everybody" to the press corps, Hill stood in the hotel lobby to answer questions from reporters, without any prepared documents, twice a day, once in the morning and once in the evening, almost every day during the fourth round.

In the evening, Hill and Deputy Foreign Minister Kim Gye-gwan of North Korea had a talk over dinner at a Korean restaurant in Beijing. According to a member of the South Korean media, that was "the first prior consultation between the United States and North Korea in the history of the six-party talks." Hill described the talk with Kim Gye-gwan as "businesslike."[2]

In the fourth round of the six-party talks, the North Koreans insisted, in reference to the U.S. proposal submitted at the third round, that it would not be fair for North Korea alone to be obliged to yield before any other party.[3] North Korea made an issue of the sequencing of activities. Which should occur first: North Korea's elimination of its nuclear weapons or the other nations' provision of energy assistance to North Korea? The United States took the position that if

North Korea would dispose of its nuclear weapons first, the United States would guarantee North Korea's security, ensure that energy was supplied to North Korea, and engage in negotiations to normalize diplomatic relations. North Korea insisted that its elimination of nuclear arms and the implementation of all of the measures proposed by the United States should be carried out simultaneously. In addition, North Korea continued to strongly insist on the adoption of a step-by-step approach, particularly one that included compensation for a North Korean nuclear freeze.

On Monday, July 25, China's foreign minister, Li Zhaoxing, hosted a banquet to welcome the participants.

Tuesday, July 26

The fourth round of the six-party talks began on July 26 at the Diaoyutai State Guest House in Beijing. The head delegates of the six participating countries were Wu Dawei, vice minister for foreign affairs, China; Kim Gye-gwan, deputy minister of foreign affairs, North Korea; Christopher Hill, assistant secretary of state, the United States; Alexander Alexeyev, deputy minister of foreign affairs, Russia; Song Min-soon, deputy minister of foreign affairs and trade, South Korea; and Kenichiro Sasae, director general of the Asian and Oceanian Affairs Bureau of the Ministry of Foreign Affairs, Japan.

Song Min-soon, before assuming his current position, had served in South Korea's Ministry of Foreign Affairs and Trade as director of the North American Affairs Division and director general of the North American Affairs Bureau. He had impressed his American counterparts as a tough negotiator during talks to revise the Status of Forces Agreement regarding U.S. troops in South Korea. Song had become close to Christopher Hill, a former U.S. ambassador to Poland, while Song was South Korea's ambassador to Poland.

Alexander Alexeyev had served in Russia's Foreign Ministry as director general of the Third Asian Affairs Bureau, as ambassador to Pakistan, and as Russia's permanent representative to the Organization for Security Cooperation in Europe (OSCE). He speaks fluent Hindi.

Kenichiro Sasae had served in Japan's Foreign Ministry as director of the Second North American Affairs Division and as director of the Northeast Asian Affairs Division; he also had been personal assistant to Prime Minister Yoshiro Mori and director general of the Economic Affairs Bureau. He has long been involved with Japan's policy toward the Korean Peninsula, and he is known as one of the toughest negotiators in the Foreign Ministry.

Perhaps the most critical difference between the third and fourth round of talks was that the United States dispatched a new team headed by Ambassador Christopher Hill. The team also included Joseph DeTrani, special envoy for the six-party talks; National Security Council staffers Victor Cha and William Tobey;

Richard Lawless, deputy under secretary of defense; and James Foster, director of the Korea desk at the Department of State. DeTrani and Foster served as Hill's implementers, supporting his efforts "even when he appeared to go beyond his instructions."[4] Cha and Tobey were the enforcers—that is, they tried to keep the U.S. negotiating position within the bounds of the instructions from Washington as much as possible. They would report back to national security adviser Stephen Hadley at the White House, through Michael Green and John Rood, and sometimes brought back new instructions in the morning, a practice that "was often seen by Hill . . . as trying to undermine his negotiating position."[5] Lawless worked largely with Cha and Tobey, but he had other responsibilities at the talks, including the negotiations on the Defense Posture Review Initiative (DPRI) force realignment, which were, at that time, at a delicate stage.[6]

In the fourth round, as in the past, the opening remarks were delivered in alphabetical order by country name, although the opening statements at the plenary meeting were made in the reverse order. In his opening remarks, North Korean representative Kim Gye-gwan said:

> Those directly involved should make a political and strategic decision to rid the threat of war from the Korean Peninsula, and we are ready to do so. . . . I hope the U.S. and other nations are ready to do the same.[7]

When it was Hill's turn to speak, he said:

> All the parties have made clear that we are prepared to address the [Democratic People's Republic of Korea's] security concerns. We have made clear we are prepared to address the DPRK's energy needs. . . . [T]he U. S. has absolutely no intention to invade or attack the DPRK, and we remain prepared to speak with the DPRK bilaterally in the context of the talks.[8]

Friday, July 29

The United States and North Korea had a bilateral talk almost every day, and the morning of July 29 was no exception. The greatest points of contention were the scope of denuclearization—which of its nuclear programs North Korea had to abandon—and whether North Korea's peaceful use of nuclear energy would be tolerated. North Korea denied the very existence of a uranium enrichment program within its borders, but the United States insisted on including any uranium enrichment program (UEP) within the scope of denuclearization. Although North Korea emphasized that the peaceful use of atomic energy is a privilege of any sovereign nation, the United States pointed out that discussions concerning the peaceful use of nuclear power should await North Korea's elimination of its nuclear weapons, its reaffirmation of the Nuclear Non-Proliferation Treaty (NPT), and its acceptance of inspections by the International Atomic Energy Agency (IAEA).

At the "Hill Briefing" that evening, Christopher Hill made the following remarks to reporters:

> One of the tough questions is in fact the uranium enrichment program. [Another is the] peaceful use of nuclear power. . . . [W]e don't challenge the fact that North Korea has rights under the treaty to do this. But we would challenge whether North Korea should be exercising these rights.[9]

Saturday, July 30

The Chinese delegation circulated among the delegations the first draft of the joint statement of the fourth round.

Sunday, July 31

The United States and South Korea held a bilateral consultation. In the plenary meeting, South Korea proposed that 2 million kilowatts of electric power be provided to North Korea, and the United States agreed. North Korea, however, neither accepted nor rejected the proposal. At that evening's "Hill Briefing" in the lobby of the St. Regis Hotel, Hill said:

> The offer of electricity [from South Korea] is of course in the draft agreement . . . and I can be pretty certain that it'll be in the final draft as well. . . . This is a supply of conventional electric power and the U.S. government formally supports this proposal. . . . I believe that the DPRK should cooperate with South Korea in developing conventional electric power instead of atomic energy.

Hill added, "I just sent eight shirts out to be cleaned today."[10] Late that night, the Chinese circulated the second draft of the joint statement.

Monday, August 1

In the middle of the U.S.–North Korea bilateral consultation that afternoon, Kim Gye-gwan left the table, saying, "I have to answer a phone call from Pyongyang." He soon returned to the table and announced that "as long as the U.S. threat exists, we cannot eliminate our nuclear weapons." Hill, surprised by the abrupt change of attitude—it was hard to believe that the announcement had come from the same person who had just left the room—proposed a temporary halt to negotiations. Regarding the sudden telephone call, the delegates of the other countries made a wild guess that the North Korean military must have expressed strong opposition to the direction that the negotiations had taken during the past week.[11]

North Korea brought up the issue of light-water reactors almost at the very outset of all the U.S.–North Korea bilateral negotiations during the fourth round of the six-party talks, and it did so again this afternoon. The North Koreans seemed to be testing the reaction of the United States by repeatedly bringing up and retracting the light-water reactor issue, assuming that North Korea would obtain what had been promised by the Agreed Framework, plus something else.

Throughout the day, the drafting committee, which was made up of representatives from the six participating countries, discussed the second draft of the joint statement. The main members of the drafting committee were Cui Tiankai, director general of the Department of Asian Affairs of the Ministry of Foreign Affairs, China; Joseph DeTrani, special envoy for the six-party talks, the United States; Cho Tae-yong, director general of the task force on the North Korean nuclear issue, Ministry of Foreign Affairs and Trade, South Korea; and Akitaka Saiki, deputy director general of the Asian and Oceanian Affairs Bureau of the Ministry of Foreign Affairs, Japan.

Of the six countries, only China and the United States had prepared their own preliminary draft of a joint statement. The United States had submitted its draft—which was based on the "core principles" for a joint statement that had been produced by the head delegates of the United States, Japan, and South Korea in a secret meeting in Seoul in February 2005—to the Chinese prior to the August 1 meeting.[12] By presenting its draft before the first meeting of the drafting committee, the United States hoped to influence the Chinese draft and to participate in the meeting in an advantageous position. Its concerns about "missiles, human rights, humanitarian issues, terrorism, and criminal conduct" were, however, cleanly erased from the Chinese draft. The U.S. proposal's particular reference to the human rights provisions in the UN charter was completely ignored.[13] It was a long day for the committee, which was locked up in a room for close to twelve hours.

Tuesday, August 2

In the morning, the Chinese circulated the third draft of the joint statement, which was followed by a fourth draft, distributed that evening. The fourth draft, which reflected the absorbing, editing, revising, and integration of the contents of the consultations concerning the previous three drafts, was much more solid. On reading the fourth draft, one member of the U.S. delegation felt that China had transformed itself from being a mediator to being the chairman.[14]

Wednesday, August 3

Throughout the day the delegates discussed the fourth draft. Among the remarks that Hill made during his routine "Hill Briefing" were the following:

> [W]e have really worked very hard with the Chinese on their drafts. We've shown a lot of flexibility. . . . The United States, we're essentially on board with the Chinese draft. The Russians are essentially on board. Japan is

essentially on board. South Korea is essentially on board. So, let's see where the DPRK is. Again, I don't want to pressure them. . . .

[The DPRK] is a country suffering from a profound number of problems and . . . none of those problems can be solved with nuclear weapons. Nuclear weapons are not going to pave the roads. They're not going to build health care. They're not going to build schools. Nuclear weapons can do very little for the top 1,000 problems that the DPRK suffers from.[15]

Thursday, August 4

It was the tenth day of the fourth round. The Chinese delegation had a series of bilateral consultations with other delegations.

In the fourth draft of the joint statement, the scope of denuclearization was defined as "all the nuclear weapons programs." That wording had been revised from "all nuclear weapons and related programs" (first draft), "all nuclear weapons and nuclear programs" (second draft), and "all nuclear weapons and programs" (third draft).[16] In regard to "all nuclear weapons and related programs," the delegates discussed what exactly "related programs" meant and whether they were related to nuclear weapons or to nuclear power. The positions of the United States and North Korea remained far apart on the issue of a uranium enrichment program and the question of whether programs for the peaceful use of atomic energy should be abolished. The United States and Japan wanted North Korea to abandon not only "all the nuclear weapons programs" but also "all the nuclear programs."

The head delegates from the six countries met together at a little after 9:00 p.m. for half an hour to discuss whether to continue the fourth round or not. Christopher Hill brought up the the Dayton Agreement (the General Framework Agreement for Peace in Bosnia and Herzegovina of 1995), which he had helped to draft and which had required twenty-two consecutive days of negotiations before it was finalized and signed. Pointing out that only ten days had passed since the start of the fourth round, he indicated the willingness of the United States to continue.[17] While the Dayton negotiations had taken place during a closed-door meeting inside a U.S. Air Force base in Dayton, Ohio, with the press shut out, Christopher Hill volunteered to be the unofficial spokesman for the fourth-round participants as a whole. That evening, in the St. Regis Hotel lobby, Hill said, "I suspect we really are getting toward the last couple of days of this. . . . There are differences. There are differences between the DPRK on the one hand and the other participants on the other."[18]

Friday, August 5

The following exchange took place during the "Hill Briefing" in the evening:

Question: South Korea's chief negotiator mentioned creative ambiguity in addressing the dispute. . . .

Hill: ... [C]reative ambiguity works in a lot of things. But, I'm a little reluctant to have them in nuclear weapons negotiations. . . . I think we need some real clarity ... clarity of thought ."

Question: Tomorrow is going to be the 60th anniversary of Hiroshima. Does that in any way influence the fact that we're dealing with nuclear weapons here?

Hill: I'm working on a text . . . . Obviously I have some personal thoughts about any time you think about the use of nuclear weapons, but I'd rather kind of stick to what I have to do.[19]

The same evening, after praising the United States highly for having had more than eight bilateral talks with North Korea, a senior Chinese government official murmured, "Since yesterday, the wind turned a little to a bad direction." He was referring to the fallout from Hill's remark to the effect that every country except North Korea agreed to the draft statement. According to the official,

Hill put too much emphasis on the five in agreement. If the formula of five versus one becomes too obvious, North Korea will stiffen its attitude. And, although Hill said he would not challenge the fact that North Korea had rights to peaceful nuclear development, do the White House and the Pentagon also agree with that? Is Hill influential enough to get their agreement?[20]

Sunday, August 7

The plenary meeting was convened at 8:30 a.m. to decide on a temporary recess until the week of August 29. In the end, the issue of the provision of light-water reactors became the stumbling block. Some time later that morning, Kim Gye-gwan held a press conference inside the North Korean embassy in which he characterized the provision of light-water reactors as "physical proof of confidence-building." In the afternoon, Hill had the following to say in the St. Regis Hotel lobby:

[I]n the last few days, it began to emerge that the problem with reaching an agreement was not just the issue of their desire to retain the right to develop ... so-called peaceful energy, but also they began to insist on light-water reactors, and indeed wanted to have their desire for light-water reactors included in the agreement. . . .

[I]f the DPRK is interested in light-water reactors not because of energy, or not because of electricity or the need for electricity, but rather for something else, well, we'd better know what this is. . . .

[W]e're going to focus on the so-called fourth draft—I guess that's an unlucky number in Chinese terms—but we're going to focus on that fourth draft.[21]

Hill admired China's excellence as a host, and he said, "I think we really see eye to eye on this [North Korean nuclear issue], and we really have the same interests on this. I would say our relationship with China is better as a result of the six-party talks process."[22] Most of the delegations left Beijing for home later in the day.

A "NONSTARTER"

The fourth round of the six-party talks resumed Tuesday, September 13. At Pyongyang Airport, before departing for Beijing, Kim Gye-gwan had set off a diplomatic offensive by announcing that "the light-water reactor issue is the key to success. The light-water reactor issue is about whether the other countries concerned are trustworthy."[23] In contrast, Hill had warned North Korea by announcing to the press before the beginning of the six-party talks that "the idea of providing North Korea with a reactor before disarmament would be a nonstarter."[24] "Nonstarter" was an expression that President Bush had used during his talk with President Hu Jintao of China in New York on September 13.[25] Bush, reminding Hu that North Korea had continued to develop enriched uranium and in so doing violated the Agreed Framework, which promised that North Korea would be provided with light-water reactors in return for eliminating its nuclear programs, announced that it would be a nonstarter if North Korea brought up the topic of light-water reactors again. Because Bush's comment was rather abrupt, Hu had no reaction. Hill merely repeated it.[26]

Thursday, September 15
At the meeting of the head delegates, Kim Gye-gwan gave a fifteen-minute oration, saying in part that "North Korea possesses a graphite-moderated nuclear reactor, and it is currently in operation. If it is feared that its by-products will be made into arms, provide us with a light-water reactor." Kim added, "I am not threatening you. I am just relating a fact."

North Korea was in effect reviving the bargain that had been incorporated in the Agreed Framework of 1994. North Korea started taking a high-handed attitude. Moreover, during the morning U.S.–North Korea bilateral consultation, Kim announced that "if we stop the graphite-moderated nuclear reactor, we will have a problem of how to employ 200,000 workers currently working at the nuclear powerhouse," hinting at the need for compensation for the workers.[27]

After the meeting of the head delegates ended, the North Korean and Japanese head delegates remained in the room to chat at the North Korean table. The entire North Korean delegation listened attentively to what the Japanese head delegate, Kenichiro Sasae, said about the position of the United States. Witnessing the scene, one member of the Japanese delegation sensed that the North Koreans really wanted to reach an agreement.[28]

Late at night, in the China World Hotel lobby, Hill said, "They [the North Korean delegates] want a light-water reactor provided. . . . [N]o delegation is prepared to offer North Korea a light-water reactor. That has to do with the fact that North Korea is not in the NPT at this time."[29]

From September 15 on, North Korea mounted a campaign of public diplomacy to achieve agreement regarding the provision of light-water reactors. On the same day, Hyon Hak-bong, a member of the North Korean delegation and a researcher at the Ministry of Foreign Affairs, held a press conference at which he announced that North Korea had "consistently raised the issue of light-water reactors since the early stage of the current nuclear issue" and that it was an issue that was "related to the political will of the United States to drop its hostile policies and pursue peaceful coexistence."[30]

Friday, September 16

The Chinese delegation presented the fifth draft of the joint statement. It differed from the fourth draft with respect to two points. First, the target of elimination was changed to "all nuclear weapons and existing nuclear programs" by inserting "existing" before "nuclear programs," as requested by North Korea. North Korea wanted to keep the right to develop a nuclear program in the future if it abandoned its current programs.[31] Second, a new provision was added that stated that "the DPRK stated that it has the right to peaceful uses of nuclear energy. The other parties expressed their respect and agreed to discuss, at an appropriate time, the subject of the provision of light-water reactor to the Democratic People's Republic of Korea." Thus, "light-water reactor" made its appearance, although Hill had said that he did not want to see "any mention of light-water reactor" in the draft.[32] Also, the United States balked at the use of the vague term "appropriate." The U.S. position was that if it ever agreed to discuss provision of light-water reactors to North Korea, it would do so only after North Korea had abandoned all of its nuclear programs, rejoined the NPT, and accepted inspections by the IAEA.

This time, China's zeal to produce a joint statement was quite awesome. In order to accomplish the task, China adopted a "take it or leave it" attitude. A member of the South Korean delegation remarked, "The Chinese draft [the fifth draft] was de facto a North Korean draft. Ignoring the United States' needs, it tried to fulfill North Korea's needs. Frankly, we thought it was a little too imposing."[33] China, South Korea, and Russia endorsed the fifth draft.

Like that of the United States, Japan's position was that provision of light-water reactors should not be mentioned in the draft statement. From the Japanese viewpoint, the fourth draft, which the top Japanese leadership in Tokyo thought provided a good framework for addressing the North Korean nuclear issue and other North Korea–related concerns, was the best one. But the Japanese delegation in

Beijing was of the view that it should endorse the fifth draft. Even the controversial provision concerning light-water reactors was covered with layers of disclaimers, making it practically impossible for the provision to cause any harm. The Japanese delegation, considering all the negative effects that would result if the fifth draft were not adopted, concluded that it should endorse the fifth draft, which might not be the best but was better than the other options. Accordingly, that is what it recommended to Tokyo.[34]

The real question was whether North Korea would endorse the fifth draft. The Japanese delegation, assuming that China could persuade North Korea to do so, conveyed to the Chinese its support of the fifth draft. However, although that was the position of the Foreign Ministry and the delegation in Beijing, opposition to the inclusion of the light-water reactor provision remained within the prime minister's office and the Liberal Democratic Party. The White House National Security Council therefore received, one after another, two Japanese opinions, both coming from the heart of the Japanese government: first, from the Japanese delegation, that Japan had no choice but to endorse the Chinese draft, and second, from Tokyo, that the draft should not be endorsed.[35]

Meanwhile, what was China's move? After the end of the first session of the fourth round, Wu Dawei flew to Pyongyang to talk with Kim Gye-gwan. During their talk, Wu was made to realize that North Korea would not agree with any statement unless the Chinese characters for *light-water reactors* and *provision* were incorporated. Wu thought that the North Koreans, sensing the heightened possibility of agreement concerning a joint statement after going through four drafts, were ready to mount another offensive. Accordingly, Wu, while promising to include "provision of light-water reactors" in the joint statement, asked Kim Gye-gwan to leave the exact wording and the timing of the insertion to the Chinese. Kim agreed, and the result was the fifth draft.[36]

Saturday, September 17

Saturday night was the eve of the Mid-Autumn Festival. There was a full moon that night, and Dai Bingguo, China's deputy foreign minister, hosted a moon-viewing dinner party. Moonlight shone through the glass windows of the reception hall, wrapping itself around the participants. A Chinese diplomat recited a line from a famous poem by Li Po: "Lifting my head; I watch the bright moon; lowering my head; I dream that I'm home."[37] Dai Bingguo spoke to all the participants:

> The moon of mid-autumn is the roundest of all. In China, that is a season for families to get together, and it is also a season for good harvests. Although we are here from different countries, we are all dwellers on the same Earth, enjoying the same bright moon together.[38]

Dai Bingguo praised the fifth draft as "the most realistic—an excellent product of collaboration that will be most beneficial to all the countries concerned," and he asked all the parties to endorse it. The cell phones of Hill and Sasae, who were seated at the head table, kept on ringing, forcing them to leave the table each time. Watching the two come and go, Dai observed, "Everyone seems to be busy tonight," a satisfied look on his face.[39]

After the dinner, the participants went out and sat at tables placed in the yard, enjoying conversation. Wu, Hill, Sasae, and Kim shared a table. Everyone was trying to find how far the United States and North Korea would be willing to go to arrive at a compromise. And everyone, including Hill and Kim, sensed in the air some kind of magnetic force pulling the parties into an agreement. By the evening, the members of the U.S. delegation, including Richard Lawless, deputy under secretary of defense for Asian and Pacific affairs, had reached the consensus that they had to accept the fifth draft.

Hill had sent an official telegram to Secretary of State Rice, informing her that the delegation had concluded that "the deal is possible."[40] Within the Bush administration, however, there was strong opposition, most notably from Under Secretary of State Robert Joseph, to the vague expression "at an appropriate date," and some demanded a more precise definition. Rice, galvanized by the official telegram from Beijing calling the deal "possible," took the position that the wording was acceptable as long as the provision of light-water reactors would be discussed only after North Korea completely eliminated its nuclear weapons.[41] She instructed Hill to make that explicit,[42] and the U.S. delegation immediately presented a counterproposal that did so.

But the Chinese response was cool at best. In fact, it was revealed later that the Chinese had been determined from the beginning to avoid the "sequencing issue" during the negotiations concerning the joint statement. One Chinese official involved in the six-party talks later disclosed, "We left this issue in order to discuss more substantive issues. We left this sequencing issue for the future."[43] Over the weekend, the Chinese increased pressure on the United States to sign the joint statement or take responsibility for the breakdown of the talks. At one point, the Chinese told the United States that it was totally isolated with respect to the sequencing issue and that the Chinese would go to the media and explain that the United States had sunk the accord.[44]

At that point, the U.S. delegation came up with an idea to arrange for the United States, Japan, and South Korea to circulate separate statements at the closing session that expressed their common understanding that the light-water reactor issue would be discussed after North Korea had completely eliminated its nuclear program, so that that understanding would go on the record.[45]

It so happened that at the time, the foreign ministers of both Japan and South Korea were in New York attending a meeting of the U.N. General Assembly.

Taking advantage of the opportunity, Secretary of State Rice held meetings with each foreign minister individually and then with both at the same time on the afternoon of September 17 (early morning of September 18, Beijing time). Immediately before the meetings Japan's foreign minister, Nobutaka Machimura, received a phone call from Kenichiro Sasae in Beijing. Sasae told Machimura that it would be impossible at that stage to specify the sequence of actions in the joint statement, and in an attempt to get all five countries on board, he asked Machimura to persuade Rice to agree orally to inclusion of the "abolition of nuclear weapons and programs first" sequencing in the closing statement of each participating nation, to be made prior to the announcement of the joint statement. Hearing that, Machimura felt that Christopher Hill must be behind Sasae's request. Machimura suspected that Hill was having a hard time persuading Rice and therefore was trying to persuade her by using Japan as leverage.[46] But, as it happened, Machimura did not have to persuade Rice, since she herself had brought up the idea.

During the meeting of the foreign ministers of Japan, the United States, and South Korea, Rice stressed that it was important that, at the time of the closing statements, the three countries take a unified stance regarding the primacy of North Korea's abolition of its nuclear weapons and programs. She said:

> At this point, it might be difficult to revise the draft joint statement. In that case, we need to keep it clearly on the record that discussion concerning the provision of light-water reactors would have to be off the table until North Korea completely abolishes all of its nuclear weapons and programs.[47]

Rice elaborated on her idea of "on-the-record statements from each nation's head delegate during the closing statements," explaining that it was her own idea and that it had not been endorsed by President Bush. The statements would confirm on the record that Japan, the United States, and South Korea commonly interpreted "an appropriate time" to mean "after North Korea's elimination of its nuclear weapons and programs has been verified."

Although South Korea's foreign minister, Ban Ki-moon, stated that the issue really should be settled in the fifth draft, he supported Rice's "personal idea." The question was whether North Korea would endorse the fifth draft. If it would not, then the whole idea of including a special reference to the sequencing of actions in the three nations' separate closing statements would be irrelevant. But Ban sounded very confident when he said that "after Ambassador Song Min-soon had a talk with Kim Gye-gwan, he was convinced that the probability was 90 percent or even 98 percent that North Korea will endorse the fifth draft." In the meeting with Rice it was also agreed that Japan, the United States, and South Korea should persuade the Chinese and Russian governments to prepare similar wording for their closing statements.[48]

All through the meetings, Rice had John Bolton, the U.S. ambassador to the UN, accompany her. This was an attempt both to silence Bolton—who had been critical about the inclusion of a reference to light-water reactors in the joint statement, no matter what—and, at the same time, to contain Bolton so that he wouldn't torpedo the joint statement.[49] Rice instructed Hill to persuade China and Russia to include similar wording in their closing remarks. Accordingly, Hill contacted Wu Dawei and Alexander Alexeyev and requested the inclusion of "abolition of North Korea's nuclear programs first" in their respective closing remarks. But China resisted and never committed itself to complying with his request.

Hours later, Hill received a phone call from Rice, who told him that President Bush had endorsed the idea of including the above-mentioned special wording in the closing statements.[50]

Sunday, September 18

In the morning, China gathered all the head delegates in a room and in that secluded environment made a last-minute attempt to reach an agreement on the joint statement. Wu Dawei asked Hill whether he would call Washington and thereby contribute to achieving an agreement that morning. "It's already too late in Washington," Hill responded. "Neither the president nor the secretary of state is available now. Please give it one more day. Here's where we just have to be patient." Wu Dawei, who is not a person to wait patiently in silence, retorted, "But Mr. Hill, you have called your secretary of state every night. Why can't you call them today?" Hill responded, "Our Chinese friends seem to know the times of our phone calls much better than we ourselves do." Wu Dawei looked genuinely embarrassed by Hill's comment, which insinuated that the U.S. delegation was aware of China's wire-tapping.[51]

The U.S. delegation drafted the U.S. statement at the closing session, comparing it with the draft statements of the Japanese and South Korean delegations, and then sent them to Washington as a telegram. Hill did not seem very enthusiastic about comparing the U.S. draft statement with those of Japan and South Korea, but he had been instructed to do so by the White House NSC. However, the greatest challenge turned out to be how to achieve consensus within the Bush administration on the closing remarks.

Due to the U.S. delay in achieving a consensus, China had to revise its initial plan to bring down the curtain on the fourth round of the six-party talks on Sunday, September 18, after adoption of a joint statement. The end of the round was postponed until September 19.

Monday, September 19

At 6:30 a.m., Washington sent back a significant revision of the U.S. delegation's draft statement in which it enumerated all of North Korea's vices, including its violation of human rights, its biological weapons program, its ballistic missiles program, its missile proliferation activities, its involvement in terrorist activities, and the various criminal activities of the North Korean government. Although William Tobey, who was in charge of issues concerning weapons of mass destruction, insisted that Hill read the Washington version word for word, some in the U.S. delegation, particularly James Foster, called for prudence, recommending that Hill not read all of the Washington revisions when making his closing remarks.[52]

At 8:00 a.m., Christopher Hill got into his car, telling the reporters in the hotel lobby, "I really think we're at the end game this morning."[53] The plenary meeting began at 9:00 a.m., with some 200 delegation members from the six countries participating. Wu Dawei had been scheduled to accompany Vice Premier Wu Yi on an overseas visit on the same day. He sounded out the other delegations on the possibility of starting the closing session at 4:30 a.m., but none responded favorably. Someone even said, "Our six-party talks must be conducted in a fair-and-square manner. It is not proper to end the talks in such a clandestine manner in the dark."[54]

Accordingly, it was reconfirmed that the closing session would begin at 9:00 a.m. Although the joint statement was expected to receive unanimous agreement, Hill proposed a revision, asking for replacement of the term "peaceful coexistence," which was used in the sentence that defined the relations between the United States and North Korea.

Hill had received a phone call from Rice just before the plenary meeting. She told Hill that "peaceful coexistence" was an expression that had been used in the Soviet Union's peaceful offensive during the cold war and that therefore it was not desirable to use it. In fact, Rice said, the United States itself never used the term in those days. Some in the U.S. delegation, including Victor Cha and William Tobey, had been against using "peaceful coexistence" in the joint statement. They claimed that the term had been used in North Korean propaganda for decades only to advertise an image of North Korea–initiated unification, including the withdrawal of the U.S. troops in South Korea and cancellation of the U.S.–South Korean alliance. They also insisted that the wording could even affect the security of the United States and Japan. Their case was taken up in Washington by Michael Green and John Rood, who agreed and took the issue to Stephen Hadley at the White House and J. D. Crouch at the Pentagon. On the other hand, James Foster and lawyers at the Department of State did not see the term "peaceful coexistence" as being problematic because legally it did not carry such long-term connotations or place any new obligations on the United States.[55]

Despite these comments, Hill did not ask to have the expression deleted. At the last minute, however, Rice demanded that he do so. In the end, Rice had to consult directly with Wu Dawei over the phone about revising the wording, but Wu did not concede. Rice then asked to talk directly with China's foreign minister,

Li Zhaoxing, who happened to be in New York. A three-way conference call among Rice, Li, and Wu ensued, during which the delegates from the six countries stood by in the lounge outside the conference room. Following the call, Rice and Li first agreed to change "peaceful coexistence" in the English draft to "live peacefully together."[56] Some joked that the new phrase sounded as if John Lennon had written it. Whether that had any influence or not, in the end "exist peacefully together" was adopted instead of "peaceful coexistence." Wu returned to the lounge, flushed with excitement. Murmuring to Sasae, "It's OK. It's OK," Wu rushed to Kim Gye-gwan, who nodded upon hearing what Wu had to say.

Thus commenced the closing session. Wu, after announcing that a portion of the English version had been revised, proclaimed that the delegates at the fourth round of the six-party talks had adopted the joint statement. All the head delegates stood up and applauded, and the TV and press reporters were allowed to cover the scene.

After the press left the room, the representatives of the six participating countries made their respective closing remarks, starting with Song Min-soon of South Korea. When Hill's turn came, he whispered, half-audibly, to the members of the U.S. delegation sitting on either side of him, Joseph DeTrani and Victor Cha, "How can you say this? This is horrible!" Then he gave his closing remarks:[57]

> [T]he 'appropriate time' [in the joint statement] will come only when the DPRK has promptly eliminated all nuclear weapons and all nuclear programs and this has been verified to the satisfaction of all the parties . . . and when the DPRK has come into full compliance with the NPT and IAEA safeguards. . . .
>
> The United States wishes to have it noted that it will take concrete actions necessary to defend itself and its allies against any criminal activities and proliferation attempts by North Korea. . . .
>
> The United States intends to take up during discussions toward the diplomatic normalization between our two countries such issues as violation of human rights, biological weapons programs, ballistic-missiles programs and the proliferation of such missiles, terrorism, and any other criminal acts by North Korea.

Hill added, "The U.S. acceptance of the Joint Statement should in no way be interpreted as meaning we accept all aspects of the DPRK's system, human rights situation, or treatment of its people."[58]

Hearing Hill's statement, members of the North Korean, South Korean, and Chinese delegations grimaced.[59] In particular, his reference to not accepting the DPRK system in its entirety could be interpreted as a sign that the United States intended to promote regime change in North Korea. The word *system* had not been in the U.S. draft statement earlier, when the United States, Japan, and South

Korea had compared their respective drafts; it was inserted at the very last minute on instructions from Washington.

As Kim Gye-gwan listened to what Hill had to say, his anger showed in his entire body. He pushed back into his briefcase the statement that the North Korean delegation had prepared for his closing remarks. After Hill, it was Kim's turn to speak, but he did not read his statement. Instead, he spoke spontaneously, saying, "I see that we've climbed one mountain only to find that there's a higher mountain behind it."[60]

What happened to the "on-the-record" statements about the "appropriate time" to discuss light-water reactors? Japan and the United States used the same expression—"after North Korea abolishes its nuclear weapons and programs in a verifiable fashion and after it returns to the Treaty on the Non-Proliferation of Nuclear Weapons and accepts IAEA safeguards." South Korea also made a statement stressing the need for North Korea to verifiably eliminate its nuclear weapons and programs and to return to the NPT and accept IAEA safeguards. But, with respect to the "appropriate time" to discuss the provision of light-water reactors, South Korea chose to say "when it comes," as if it would come naturally, like one of the four seasons. The Russian statement was, according to a U.S. diplomat, too ambiguous to understand. China did not even touch on it.[61]

After the session, the delegates of the six countries paid a twenty-minute courtesy visit to Chinese State Councilor Tang Jiaxuan inside the Diaoyutai State Guest House. It was the twentieth working day since the fourth round had started in July.

The Joint Statement

The joint statement, reaffirming that "the goal of the Six-Party Talks is the verifiable denuclearization of the Korean Peninsula in a peaceful manner," provides that "The DPRK committed to abandoning all nuclear weapons and existing nuclear programs and returning, at an early date, to the Treaty of the Non-Proliferation of Nuclear Weapons and to IAEA safeguards."[62] The greatest achievement of the joint statement was that it recorded in a formal document that North Korea officially accepted and committed itself to verifiable denuclearization. Moreover, the denuclearization must be achieved in a peaceful manner.

The Chinese chose to use in the draft statement the term "denuclearization" instead of "nonnuclearization." The choice of the former word was based not so much on the North Korean announcement of its nuclear deterrence capability as on the assumption that "North Korea possesses six to eight nuclear weapons."[63] What, then, does "denuclearize" mean? The statement is very explicit in that respect: it means "abandoning all nuclear weapons and existing nuclear programs," including past nuclear weapons that were not dealt with at the time that the Agreed Framework was formulated.

The six countries had to negotiate a long and winding road to agree on that expression. The provision thereby targets basically all nuclear programs, whether for military or peaceful use. It also encompasses the HEU issue, which had triggered the second North Korean nuclear crisis. Throughout the previous rounds of the six-party talks, North Korea consistently had denied that it possessed highly enriched uranium. In the working group session in Beijing in May 2004, prior to the third round of the talks, the United States had handed a list of detailed inquiries about HEU to North Korea and asked that it answer each of them. North Korea simply ignored it.[64]

In the fourth round of the talks, North Korea continued to deny that it had highly enriched uranium. The South Koreans whispered to the North Koreans that North Korea should acknowledge the existence of a uranium enrichment program (UEP) instead of an HEU program because the former could be regarded as a permissible peaceful use, but the North Koreans did not take their advice.[65] As long as North Korea adamantly denied the existence of an HEU program, confronting North Korea over its existence and including it for elimination would not work. In fact, China informed the United States that North Korea would not sign the joint statement if HEU was mentioned.[66]

The United States, therefore, undertook a "stealth operation" that upheld its intention to target the HEU program but hid that intention behind something else. The United States interpreted the phrase "existing nuclear programs" to include the DPRK's HEU program. One member of the U.S. delegation explained the tactic as "using a 'staged approach'" to pursue denuclearization.[67] The first stage would deal with plutonium, and the second stage would deal with uranium. Hill was pressured by the hardliners in Washington, who said that the fourth round would be a failure if the joint statement did not mention highly enriched uranium, but he had no choice but to paper over the issue.

However, the North Koreans undertook their own "stealth operation." Their concern was that the term "all nuclear programs" would cover any that they might develop in the future. They therefore requested that "existing" be inserted before "nuclear programs," expecting that the new wording would protect their right to future programs.[68]

China shared with the United States a strong wish for denuclearization, including elimination of the HEU program. The Chinese version of a "stealth operation" was to hide behind the 1992 Joint Declaration on the Denuclearization of the Korean Peninsula, in which the two Koreas committed themselves to not pursuing plutonium reprocessing or uranium enrichment. The joint statement draft prepared by the Chinese cited the declaration twice. First, regarding the scope of denuclearization, the Chinese draft stated, "North Korea should abandon all of its nuclear weapons and all the nuclear programs prohibited by the 1992 Joint Declaration," ensuring that both plutonium and uranium would be included in the nuclear programs to be abandoned. Second, the draft stated, "The 1992 Joint Declaration on the Denuclearization of the Korean Peninsula must be complied with and realized." North Korea responded that it would accept these two conditions.

The United States was hesitant, however, because from the U.S. perspective, "prohibited by the 1992 Joint Declaration" would not cover all of its concerns about the transfer and proliferation of nuclear materials. One member of the Chinese delegation who was bewildered by the U.S. attitude said, "Have they really read the Joint Declaration? In the Joint Declaration there were seven *no*'s." He was referring to the first article of the declaration, which states, "South and North Korea shall not test, manufacture, produce, receive, possess, store, deploy or use nuclear weapons."[69] The same official said that "all activities regarding nuclear weapons have been prohibited by the Joint Declaration. That's why I firmly insist on introducing the Joint Declaration. Theoretically, and practically, we cannot prohibit North Korea from 'peaceful use.'"[70] Although the joint statement of the fourth round did not include those seven *no*'s as specific targets of denuclearization, it retained to the end the sentence incorporated in the first draft that states "The 1992 Joint Declaration of the Denuclearization of the Korean Peninsula should be observed and implemented."

Some in the U.S. administration were critical of referring to the 1992 Joint Declaration in the fourth round joint statement. North Korea had violated the 1992 Joint Declaration, which it had signed with South Korea, just as it violated the 1994 U.S.-DPRK Agreed Framework. It would be absurd, the critics said, to refer in a solemn way to that "damaged document" and to expect that doing so would actually have some positive effect.[71] Although their point was well taken, the United States eventually agreed on inclusion of the reference in the joint statement.

From the beginning, the United States had used the expression "to dismantle the North Korean nuclear weapons and programs." When the six-party talks started, it even used the expression "CVID" (complete, verifiable, and irreversible dismantlement). The first Chinese draft used "abandon," which was changed in the second draft, at the request of the United States, to the stronger word "eliminate." However, "abandoning" appeared in the third draft, at the request of North Korea, which preferred a somewhat looser term than "dismantling." North Korea wished to stress that it was not a defeated country and that it would act to eliminate its nuclear weapons and programs on its own initiative, and it felt that "abandon" conveyed that idea.[72]

The next provision in the joint statement relates to the security assurance to be provided to North Korea, expressed as follows: "The United States affirmed that it has no nuclear weapons on the Korean Peninsula and has no intention to attack or invade the DPRK with nuclear or conventional weapons." This type of "security assurance" is a "negative security assurance" (NSA)—a pledge by nuclear members of the NPT not to use nuclear weapons against non-nuclear members. North Korea had long demanded, as a prerequisite for denuclearization, that the United States cease its hostile policies toward North Korea and explicitly announce that it would not attack or invade North Korea. North Korea had consistently insisted that without such a security assurance by the United States, it could not guarantee its own denuclearization. The Chinese draft included this "security assurance."

However, Robert Joseph remained cautious about granting any "security assurance" to North Korea, and some in the Pentagon also were uneasy about it. The United States will not affirm that it will not resort to a preemptive nuclear attack, convinced that any such affirmation would reduce the nation's nuclear deterrent capability. Although the United States endorses "negative security assurances," it makes some exceptions. For instance, if a non-nuclear state, in cooperation with a nuclear state, were to attack or invade the United States or one of its allies, the United States would not be bound by any negative security assurance. The United States also takes the position that it would not hesitate to retaliate with nuclear weapons if attacked with biological weapons.

In the case of North Korea, all of the considerations above must be taken into account. North Korea does in fact possess biological weapons, and the United States has warned North Korea that it is prepared to retaliate with nuclear weapons if North Korea uses its biological weapons. Such possibilities underlie the U.S. resistance to the requests of non-nuclear states to make negative security assurances legally binding. The Japanese government supports the idea of making negative security assurances legally binding, but it takes the position that it would not prohibit retaliation with nuclear weapons against an attacker using biological weapons. Obviously, that position reflects consideration of the situation with respect to North Korea. Those in the U.S. administration who were cautious about endorsing the joint statement noted all the points above.

However, legal counsel at both the Department of State and the White House concluded that the joint statement neither declared a U.S. no-first-use policy nor weakened the U.S. nuclear deterrence strategy. They underscored that the joint statement would be only a "political statement" of the U.S. commitment to nonaggression with no legally binding force. In their judgment, no problem would result if the United States were to sign the joint statement.[73]

In the end, President Bush's past remarks were the decisive factor in the U.S. position. Ever since Bush declared, on visiting South Korea in February 2002, that the United States has no intention to invade or attack North Korea, he has repeatedly used that expression. Those in the U.S. administration who advocated accepting the joint statement quoted the president's remarks to persuade the skeptics. When the drafting committee of the fourth round of the six-party talks discussed the issue in Beijing, one Chinese member jokingly said to the U.S. member, "This was a remark made by your president, wasn't it? If you oppose that, it means that you oppose your president, who was elected by your people, and that means that you oppose your people."[74] But the Bush administration was by no means in unison with Christopher Hill on the matter.

In the end, the United States accepted the provision. When the Russian representative to the drafting committee, Minister Counselor Sergey Goncharov of the Russian embassy in Beijing, heard about the U.S. decision, he said in a strong voice, "This is an extremely important decision. I admire your resolve to compromise that much," and he volunteered to make sure that the North Koreans understood the significance of the U.S. decision. And in fact, the Russian delegation subsequently contacted the North Korean delegation to make sure that they did.[75]

Once both "denuclearization" and "security assurance" were incorporated in unambiguous forms in the draft, the backbone of the joint statement was complete. One of the Chinese drafters commented:

> Frankly speaking, when I introduced the "negative security assurance" wording into the document, I was extremely uncertain whether or not we'd be able to keep this wording in the final draft. But, anyway, I think at least we can put everything in the document. . . . That term makes North Korea sincerely consider whether or not they should accept the document.[76]

In the next sentence of the joint statement, South Korea reaffirmed its commitment, in accordance with the 1992 Joint Declaration of the Denuclearization of the Korean Peninsula, not to receive or deploy nuclear weapons and affirmed that no nuclear weapons existed within its territory. North Korea demanded a guarantee that no nuclear weapons would be introduced on the Korean Peninsula. It emphasized the need to inspect U.S. military bases and warships stationed in and around the Korean Peninsula and demanded all of the data concerning the movement of U.S. nuclear weapons into and out of South Korea for the entire post–World War II period. The U.S. simply disregarded this request, snapping, "They're just trying to buy time."

The North Koreans conducted the negotiations as a country that had nuclear deterrent capability, on equal footing with the United States and China. It insisted that if it was forced to eliminate its nuclear deterrent capability, South Korea had to do the same; if North Korea's elimination of its nuclear weapons had to be verified, so did South Korea's; and if the United States and South Korea were to inspect North Korea's nuclear facilities, North Korea was to be able to inspect those in South Korea. The United States brushed aside the North Korean argument, stressing that the denuclearization of both South Korea and North Korea should be carried out as provided for in the Joint Declaration on the Denuclearization of the Korean Peninsula of 1992. The United States took the position that the six-party talks was not a proper forum for discussing the issue of the extended nuclear deterrence that the United States provides for South Korea (the so-called nuclear umbrella).

On the other hand, the United States demanded that North Korea cease operating its nuclear reactors as well as cease testing missiles and their carrying devices. The North Koreans brushed aside that demand. "We can't talk about those matters," they said. "Those are North Korean military matters." They added, "Those matters are not 'principles'. Those matters are 'actions' that we're going to take and are 'actions' for which you need to compensate us."[77]

Two other provisions in the joint statement merit special attention:

The DPRK and the United States undertook to respect each other's sovereignty, exist peacefully together, and take steps to normalize their relations subject to their respective bilateral policies.

The DPRK and Japan undertook to take steps to normalize their relations in accordance with the Pyongyang Declaration, on the basis of the settlement of unfortunate past and the outstanding issues of concern.

These two provisions explicitly indicate that normalization of diplomatic relations with the United States and with Japan constitute for North Korea compensation that it would expect to receive for contributing to the creation of a framework for achieving a comprehensive settlement of the nuclear issue, which was the ultimate aim of the joint statement of the six-party talks. At the request of the United States and Japan, those two sentences had been included in the statement since its first draft.

Although North Korea agreed that diplomatic normalization with Japan and the United States was desirable, it concluded that the insertion of the two sentences, particularly the second one concerning North Korea–Japan relations, was politically motivated. North Korea therefore repeatedly attempted to delete them. The United States insisted on the settlement of human rights and criminal activity issues, while Japan insisted on settlement of the abduction and missile issues, as "measures required for diplomatic normalization." Japan used the more focused expression "steps . . . [for settling] outstanding issues of concern." However, North Korea feared that if the abduction and missile test issues were inserted in the joint statement, they might be interpreted as its endorsement of Japan's demands to settle the abduction issue. At the closing ceremony of the first session of the fourth round of the six-party talks on August 7, Kim Gye-gwan announced that the reference to North Korea–Japan relations was unacceptable to North Korea and demanded its deletion. South Korea also was reluctant to include the North Korea–Japan provision, in fear that it might agitate North Korea. On this point, China supported the requests from the United States and Japan and persuaded North Korea to accept them.[78]

PEACEFUL USE OF ATOMIC POWER AND
PROVISION OF LIGHT-WATER REACTORS

North Korea never compromised on its position that the peaceful use of atomic energy is an unalienable right of a sovereign nation. At an ad hoc press interview on August 4 in front of the North Korean embassy in Beijing, Kim Gye-gwan said, "All the countries in the world are entitled to their own development of nuclear power for peaceful purposes. North Korea didn't lose any war nor has it committed any sin. Why isn't North Korea allowed to pursue its own peaceful use of atomic energy?" One Chinese diplomat, elaborating on the North Korean position, had this to say:

> To North Koreans, the logic that it has the right to the peaceful use of nuclear energy but that it is not allowed to exercise that right is utterly unacceptable. It especially won't accept the logic that North Korea is denied the same right that India is allowed to exercise and that Japan is allowed to exercise. Why is Japan, which had been defeated in World War II, allowed that when North Korea, which had not been defeated in any war, is not? This is totally unacceptable to them.[79]

Although China took a firm stance vis-à-vis the denuclearization of North Korea, it also took the position that it could not deny North Korea the right to the peaceful use of nuclear energy, which is an inherent right of a sovereign state, guaranteed by Article 4 of the Nuclear Non-Proliferation Treaty.

The joint statement stipulates the elimination of *existing* nuclear programs and not nuclear programs that might exist in the future. In this way North Korea would be allowed to pursue the peaceful use of nuclear energy if and when it returned to the NPT, accepted the IAEA safeguards, and abandoned "all nuclear weapons and existing nuclear programs."

As mentioned earlier in this chapter, Hill once said regarding North Korea's peaceful use of atomic energy that "we don't challenge the fact that North Korea has rights under the treaty to this. But we would challenge whether North Korea should be exercising these rights."[80] But the Bush administration was by no means unanimous in agreeing with Hill on the matter. A White House official, brushing off the argument of the rights of a sovereign nation, insisted, "We should not discuss the North Korean peaceful use of nuclear power from the purely legalistic viewpoint when North Korea keeps on ignoring laws and rules. This is a political issue."[81] Bush himself expressed the view that North Korea did not need that kind of right. In a press conference at the Bush ranch in Crawford, Texas, on August 9, 2005, Bush said, "The international community is willing to accept a civilian nuclear program in Iran, but not in North Korea because . . . South Korea is willing to provide electricity to North Korea."[82]

Nevertheless, Hill was able to leave North Korea a small space for the right to protect its future freeom of action, but a space so small that, to paraphrase the Bible, it would be about as easy to exercise that right as it would be for a camel to go through the eye of a needle. Hence, the final provision in the joint statement reads as follows: "The Democratic People's Republic of Korea stated that it has the right to peaceful uses of nuclear energy. The other parties expressed their respect and agreed to discuss, at an appropriate time, the subject of the provision of light-water reactor to the Democratic People's Republic of Korea."

The participants in the six-party talks thus respected North Korea's assertion of its right to peaceful uses of nuclear energy but refrained from expressing either approval or rejection of that right. However, North Korea had to agree to scrap its existing nuclear programs in order to get that right mentioned in the joint statement. Thus, although North Korea could claim at any time its right to the peaceful use of nuclear energy, the document clearly stated that it was not allowed to exercise that right at that point in time.

But it was not to assert its sovereignty that North Korea was so adamant about its right to the peaceful use of nuclear energy. It is highly likely that North Korea was driven by two underlying motives: to establish a foothold for a future enriched uranium program and to justify its demand for light-water reactors. First, North Korea needed to back up its argument that its enriched uranium program was a low-enrichment program intended for generating electric power, not for producing highly enriched uranium for weapons use, as the United States had charged. In addition, North Korea needed to establish its right to peaceful use in order to demand the provision of light-water reactors, which it insisted would be used for peaceful purposes.[83]

During the U.S.–North Korea and Japan–North Korea bilateral consultations, Kim Gye-gwan cited two reasons why North Korea was requesting the light-water reactors: to solve the nation's energy shortage, and to deter attacks on the country from outside. [84] Both Japan and the United States brushed aside that reasoning as too unconvincing to be accepted at face value. Hill later said:

> [T]heir national grid has essentially broken down . . . mainly because of transmission and distribution problems. But again, they are not interested in distribution or transit problems for electricity. They are interested in a light-water reactor. In short, one gets the impression that this is not so much an economic development issue or an energy issue but rather a political issue and an issue relating to the idea that they want to have a sort of trophy project.[85]

During one of the U.S.–North Korean bilateral consultations, Kim Gye-gwan referred to the need to satisfy the North Korean military, saying that "the only way that the army will accept an agreement in this round is if it contains light-water reactors." Hill immediately responded, "So you need a peaceful light-water reactor and the institution that wants it is the army?"[86]

In contrast, one senior Chinese government official expressed the view that North Korea had been insistent about the light-water reactor basically because of its energy situation. "They need energy to survive," he said. "It is an issue of their grand national strategy and their national development strategy. It is not merely a bargaining chip. It is their real intention to obtain light-water reactors." However, the same Chinese official severely criticized the other reason that North Korea had presented—constructing light-water reactors to deter attacks from the outside:

> Two light-water reactors as a shield against outside attack? Security assurance? I don't buy this argument at all. But I think this is how the North Koreans see the benefit of obtaining light-water reactors. They believe that the United States wouldn't dare to attack North Korea because it might destroy nuclear reactors in North Korea [causing nuclear fallout elsewhere]. To have a thought like this is extremely dangerous.[87]

Nevertheless, at the last minute, China squeezed into the draft of the joint statement the sentence about the provision of light-water reactors to North Korea. However, five of the six countries participating in the talks accordingly attached three safety provisions to the joint statement: the parties to the six-party talks were committed to a future *discussion* of the subject of the provision of light-water reactors, not to the future *provision* of reactors; the joint statement did not specify when such a discussion would be held; and the five parties other than North Korea would decide on whether to provide light-water reactors.

In the English version of the joint statement the singular "light-water reactor" was used instead of the plural "light-water reactors," and the definite article *the* did not precede "light-water reactor"—that is, the wording was "the subject of the provision of light water reactor to the DPRK." The use of the singular form and the non-use of the definite article *the* was intended to imply that the light-water reactor to be provided was not either of the two unfinished reactors to be constructed under the auspices of KEDO.[88] But in the Chinese, Korean, and Japanese versions, one could not tell the difference.

Why was North Korea so insistent about obtaining light-water reactors? Was it because, as Hill concluded, North Korea wanted a trophy? North Korea claimed that the provision of light-water reactors was necessary as "a physical groundwork for building bilateral confidence."[89] During the first nuclear crisis, when North Korea presented its demand—in effect, a demand to be given a new nuke to eliminate an existing nuke—U.S. chief negotiator Robert Gallucci, in response to the almost surreal absurdity of the proposal, "laughed aloud as if it were a joke."[90] But, in the end, it became the "physical groundwork" of the Agreed

Framework, a political connection between the United States and North Korea, and a gigantic project worth US$4.6 billion.[91]

There is another possible answer to the question of why North Korea was so insistent about obtaining light-water reactors. To North Korea, the reactors represented the achievement of dialogue and negotiations between the DPRK and the United States and the starting point of mutual confidence-building, a process that North Korea wants to resume. It also was an undertaking that Kim Jong-il started and completed. For North Korea, if the United States would again agree to commit itself to the idea of provision of light-water reactors to North Korea, it would symbolize that the United States had returned to its commitment under the Agreed Framework. And that would allow North Korea to save face.[92]

Another possible answer is that North Korea needed to have that clause included in the joint statement to hide its diplomatic defeat in having been forced to agree to extremely restrictive wording requiring it to eliminate its nuclear weapons and programs. The North Koreans may have been anxious to include the provision concerning light-water reactors in order to make the joint statement look like the Agreed Framework, so that "they could claim that they had not suffered a defeat."[93]

Yet another answer is possible. By incorporating in the joint statement wording concerning the provision of light-water reactors, the North Korean diplomats could claim that not only did they push the United States into bilateral consultations with North Korea, they also succeeded in "converting" the United States into accepting more engagement with North Korea.[94]

The United States, for its part, suspected that North Korea had no intention of agreeing at the six-party talks to abandon its nuclear weapons and programs and that North Korea raised the light-water reactors issue only to wreck the joint statement. One member of the U.S. delegation later said:

> North Korea's military had not expected that the United States would compromise as much as it did in the fourth round. Thus, it raised the light-water reactor issue, which the United States would never approve, in order to torpedo the joint statement. That was a poison pill.[95]

What does "appropriate time" mean in "to discuss at an appropriate time the subject of the provision of light water reactor"? One Department of State official later remarked, "In actuality, it means 'never' to us and 'tomorrow' to the North Koreans. The compromise idea that the Chinese side offered was this 'appropriate time.'"[96]

But North Korea attacked the ambiguity of the phrase. This time, ten years after North Korea first introduced the "absurd" idea of a trade-off between nuclear development and light-water reactors, nobody laughed. The United States was faced with a nightmare, and the North Korean nuclear issue returned to its original status. Everyone present was struck with a sense of déjà vu and a feeling of futility.

In July 2005, before the fourth round, South Korea reconfirmed its proposal to provide North Korea with 2 million kilowatts of free electricity. However, the inclusion in the joint statement of the wording concerning the provision of light-water reactors invalidated the South Korean offer, which had been made as a surrogate for a commitment to provide the reactors. When South Korean unification minister Chung Dong-young proposed this on July 12, the ROK Ministry of Foreign Affairs and Trade had not been informed of it, nor had the United States been consulted beforehand. The United States supported the proposal, however, hoping that it would help induce North Korea to give up the light-water reactors.[97]

But North Korea turned a cold shoulder to the South Korean offer. At the U.S.–North Korean bilateral consultations in Beijing during the six-party talks, North Korea informed the United States that the proposal had been made unilaterally by South Korea without prior consultation with North Korea and that it was by no means the product of an agreement between North Korea and South Korea.[98] One U.S. Department of State official reached the following conclusion about what had happened:

> North Korea didn't like the political dynamics of being "assisted" by South Korea. Moreover, cables extending from South Korea could be cut by South Korea in case of emergency. North Korea did not like to be under the control of South Korea. Also, the South Koreans must not have sufficiently studied the situation regarding electric wires and cables in North Korea. If that much volume of electricity were to be transmitted to the North, its wires and cables would be overloaded. It is technically infeasible.[99]

One of the members of the U.S. delegation who was present at these U.S.–North Korea negotiations later revealed that, in the end, South Korea had to ask for North Korea's approval to include the offer in the joint statement. North Korea ignored the request.[100] The South Korean proposal therefore was put in limbo.

THE ESSENCE OF FAILURE: "ACTION FOR ACTION"

The six-party talks were created as a forum to settle the North Korean nuclear issue, but from the very moment that the talks were conceived, they were overburdened with the excessive expectation that they should lead to the creation of a consultative body on peace and stability in the Northeast Asia region. That expectation betrayed the fact that Northeast Asia had no multilateral regional institution for consultation on matters of security. The region is characterized by deep mutual distrust among its neighbors; it is strategically naked, with a fragile structure, and lacks any regional security framework.

The six-party talks constituted the first multilateral forum for security consultations in the region. The joint statement includes a provision stating, "The Six Parties committed to joint efforts for lasting peace and stability in Northeast Asia." China inserted the provision in the hope that the talks might be made into a "peace mechanism," to use the expression of a Chinese official, for settling a variety of security issues in Northeast Asia as a whole after settling the North Korean nuclear issue.[101] All the other countries supported the Chinese initiative, and Hill told reporters that the six-party talks had the potential to develop into an embryonic form of a Northeast Asian regional organization.[102] But in the end, the above-quoted provision remained little more than an abstract expression. The delegations that gathered in Beijing that summer could not afford to go any further.

In the joint statement, that provision is followed by the following sentence: "The directly related parties will negotiate a permanent peace regime on the Korean Peninsula at an appropriate separate forum." That sentence was not in China's first draft; South Korea proposed including it in the second draft, and the Chinese inserted it.[103] When the Chinese presented it to the North Koreans, they immediately endorsed it. The North Koreans had stressed—throughout the earlier U.S.–North Korea bilateral consultations, including those through the "New York channel"—the need to upgrade the Korean War armistice agreement to a peace treaty.[104]

During the drafting of the joint statement, although the United States proposed including the term "peace mechanism" instead of "peace regime," both North Korea and South Korea insisted on "peace regime."[105] Some in the U.S. administration suspected that China had made South Korea propose the provision,[106] and others believed that it had been a North Korean proposal reflecting Pyongyang's wish to generate a U.S.–North Korean initiative in the process,[107] but the Chinese denied both views. The Chinese diplomat who actually negotiated with the Koreas on the issue later said that "they were in perfect unison about discussing, in a forum separate from the six-party talks, a peace regime to replace the current armistice agreement."[108] The phrases "the directly related parties" and "an appropriate separate forum" were left undefined and ambiguous, but one could easily read between lines the intention and emotion behind those phrases. One senior Department of State official later said, "That provision aimed at two objectives. One was to indicate to North Korea that regime change was not being called for. The other was to eliminate Japan and Russia from the process of building the peace regime."[109]

It was probably because of the potential for lessening Japan's influence on the Korean Peninsula more than anything else that both North and South Korea agreed on the "peace regime."[110] In a press briefing held on September 19, Unification Minister Chung Dong-young explained: "Three or four countries will participate in it. They will be either North and South Korea and the United States or these three countries plus China, because it will handle replacing the armistice agreement with a peace accord.[111]

What China paid the most attention to was the North Korean response. North Korea had traditionally taken the position that a peace treaty was a matter for U.S.–North Korea negotiation. In order to have a formal reason for excluding South Korea from negotiations, North Korea cited the fact that South Korea had not signed the armistice agreement. But China recognized a certain change in the North Korean attitude. As one Chinese diplomat said:

> It had been the North Korean strategy to claim that the major actors on the Korean Peninsula issue were North Korea and the United States. But gradually it became obvious to the North Koreans that this strategy wouldn't work. North Korea now needs South Korean assistance to manage North Korea's relations with the United States. A triangle relationship among North Korea, South Korea, and the United States is now emerging. It was South Korean nationalism that brought about this relationship.[112]

The Chinese sensed that although it was highly likely that "an appropriate separate forum" would take the form of four-party talks among the United States, China, and the two Koreas, the emotional basis of this formulation was the nationalism of the two Koreas, which demanded negotiations involving three (the two Koreas and the United States), plus one (China).

The joint statement next states, "The Six Parties agreed to take coordinated steps to implement the aforementioned consensus in a phased manner in line with the principle of 'commitment for commitment, action for action.'" That principle has consistently guided negotiations throughout the five rounds of the six-party talks, although the original phrasing was "word for word, action for action." It was originally a North Korean proposal, one that represents a behavioral pattern in which North Korea asks its negotiating partner to take a comparable action for each and every one of its own actions and reciprocates only after the other party has done so. That way there will be compensation at every stage of negotiations. Thus, "freezing of nuclear facilities requires compensation," and "the act of freezing should always be accompanied by an act of compensation." The United States proposed replacing "word for word" with "commitment for commitment," and the Chinese side was pleased that the United States responded. As one Chinese official who was involved later said, "We zealously welcomed this U.S. counterproposal. This statement thus became a joint product between the United States and North Korea."[113] The United States intended to prevent futile wars over the "word for word" idea—for example, when the

United States referred to Kim Jong-il as either Chairman Kim or Mr. Kim, North Korea would reciprocate by using an honorific title, and when the United States did not, North Korea would demonstrate similar disrespect.

Throughout the fourth round of the six-party talks, the United States asked North Korea to terminate the operation of its nuclear reactors during the negotiations. In other words, the United States asked North Korea to freeze its nuclear operations but refused to include freezing as one of the items for negotiation. The United States was tired of North Korea's demands for compensation for freezing operations, and it wanted to prevent the start of a downward spiral based on the "action for action" idea. The United States therefore concentrated on North Korea's abandonment of its nuclear programs instead, hoping to persuade the North Koreans that the result would be the same because the programs eventually would have to be abandoned. During the six-party talks, North Korea continued its nuclear development activities and continued to store plutonium. The more nuclear weapons that North Korea possesses, the greater the risk of their being transferred to some other country. The six-party talks process thus produced a situation similar to one in which choking someone else's neck results in one's own neck being choked.

Philip D. Zelikow, counselor to the Department of State, observed that "you had a diplomatic process of trying to ameliorate conflict with North Korea through tit-for-tat exchanges of favors . . . [that] played into the North Korean style and in a way did not help the North Koreans make fundamental choices about their future, because it fit so easily into their existing routine and diplomatic style."[114] Those "tit-for-tat" exchanges revealed how deep the distrust between the two nations was. During the U.S.–North Korea bilateral negotiations, Kim Gye-gwan announced that North Korea needed compensation for giving up nuclear tests and not transferring nuclear capabilities or devices. "You can't make that statement," Hill replied, a displeased expression on his face. "If you test or transfer weapons, that's the end of everything. We're not having a negotiation anymore."[115]

As soon as the U.S. delegation returned to Washington, the North Korean Foreign Ministry announced that the "provision of light-water reactors [must come] first." On September 20, a ministry spokesman released an announcement stating that "the United States should not even dream of the issue of the Democratic People's Republic of Korea's dismantling its nuclear deterrent capability before providing light-water reactors, which is a physical guarantee for confidence building."[116]

The United States downplayed the significance of the statement. At that time, Secretary of State Condoleezza Rice was attending a meeting of the UN General Assembly, and at a post-meeting joint press conference with Russia's foreign minister, Sergei Lavrov, she said, "I think we will not get hung up on this statement. . . . We will stick to the text of the Beijing statement." Her comments were followed up by Lavrov, who, brushing off the North Korean Foreign Ministry announcement, said, "We shouldn't rely on oral statements."[117] However, the Chinese complained to the United States that its closing remarks triggered the North Korean announcement.

Some members of the U.S. delegation voiced strong criticisms and complaints about the U.S. closing statement. "It hurt that at the last minute Rice made us waste three hours on the semantics of 'peaceful coexistence,'" one official said. "She should have used the time instead to maneuver in Washington so that that kind of statement would not have been sent to us."[118]

Yet another member of the U.S. delegation did not find it fair to blame the U.S. closing statement, as if it were the source of all evils:

> We adopted in the joint statement all of North Korea's demands. The closing remarks constitute an opportunity for each delegation to express its respective position, and one of the intended audiences is the delegation's domestic audience. The United States also had things that it had to say to North Korea in front of the American audience. In our closing remarks, we just did that.[119]

South Korea interpreted North Korea's announcement as an attempt to put its position vis-à-vis the issue on the record, especially because Kim Gye-gwan's closing remarks had been gravely inadequate.[120] But the announcement served to confirm the U.S. view that, from the very beginning, North Korea had no intention to commit itself to the joint statement. One senior U.S. Department of State official who was involved with the talks remarked:

> From the beginning, the North Koreans had no intention of signing a joint statement. But because the United States very flexibly made concessions, they eventually had to sign the document. Thus they decided to later release such an announcement from the Foreign Ministry, taking advantage of its own inadequate closing remarks, in order to invalidate the joint statement.[121]

Another Department of State official who was a member of the U.S. delegation saw the matter from a somewhat different angle:

> Perhaps North Korea did not expect that China would force North Korea to promise denuclearization to that extent and to strip North Korea to the skin. When North Korea was prodded into signing the joint statement, the North Koreans must have felt serious fear. They did not know what China would do to them in planning the implementation specifics. This might be in the background of North Korea's abruptly bringing up the issue of light-water reactors and reacting so acridly and unilaterally announcing its requirement regarding the timing of the provision of light-water reactors.[122]

HILL'S UNREALIZED VISIT TO NORTH KOREA

During the fourth round of the six-party talks, the United States and North Korea had had more bilateral consultations than ever before. However, on those occasions Kim Gye-gwan hardly revealed any new information or gave any hints or clues as to the next step that North Korea would take. Through the six-party talks process, the United States came to realize how little discretion the North Korean Foreign Ministry was given. Many in the U.S. delegation felt that Kim Gye-gwan kept repeating the same thing over and over, like a broken record, no matter how long they talked with him. But in late July, soon after the fourth round of the talks started, Hill confided a secret plan to Kim:

> If we can agree on North Korean denuclearization and agree on a joint statement for the six-party talks, I would be prepared to visit Pyongyang anytime. I will go to Pyongyang then and talk with your leadership about how we can accomplish this [agreement reached at the fourth round] and also talk about what the prospects are for a better relationship with the United States.
>
> But I can't go if the nuclear reactors in Yongbyon are still operating. I'll visit Pyongyang on the condition that you'll stop them.[123]

Although Hill was speaking in general terms, Kim Gye-gwan extended an invitation then and there. When Hill added, "If it is at all possible, I hope Jay Lefkowitz can come with me," Kim responded, "We would welcome the visit of Ambassador Lefkowitz."[124]

In the fall of 2004, when the U.S. North Korean Human Rights Act was enacted, the Bush administration established the new post of special envoy on human rights in North Korea and appointed Jay Lefkowitz to the post. Lefkowitz had long been involved with human rights issues, including as a member of the U.S. delegation to the UN Human Rights Commission. The United States was a little surprised at the unexpectedly positive response to the proposed visit, especially that of the special envoy on human rights.

Hill had held on to the idea of such a visit since he became an assistant secretary of state, hoping to deal directly with the real decisionmakers behind Kim Gye-gwan. The North Korean counterparts to James Kelly (Hill's predecessor at the six party-talks) and Joseph DeTrani (special envoy for the talks) had always been either Kim Gye-gwan or Li Gun. The United States was dissatisfied with the situation because "neither Kim Gye-gwan nor Li Gun has any flexibility, and they are not granted any discretion in negotiations."[125] Even if Hill were to fly to Pyongyang, he might not be able to see the real—and sole—decisionmaker in North Korea, Kim Jong-il. But Hill at least might be able to see First Deputy Foreign Minister Kang Sok-ju, whom Kim Jong-il trusted. If Hill could talk with

Kang, Kim Jong-il might hear a recording of the talk, or he might even peek in at the talk.[126]

Hill was confident of his negotiating skills. He had fought through the Yugoslavian peace negotiations with Slobodan Milosevic, and as deputy to Richard Holbrooke, the chief U.S. negotiator, he had helped bring about the Dayton Agreement. But North Korea was not a war-defeated country like Serbia was, and it would be impossible to draw Kim Jong-il to the negotiating table. Thus the circumstances of the negotiations with North Korea were quite different from those of the Yugoslavian negotiations. Nonetheless, the State Department officials in charge of Korean affairs also were confident of Hill's skills as a negotiator, which had led to his appointment as assistant secretary of state in charge of East Asia and the Pacific after only one year as U.S. ambassador to South Korea. The State Department officials in charge of Korean affairs also had high expectations of Hill as a negotiator. Hill was a stark contrast to his predecessor, James Kelly. A career diplomat who knew both men observed:

> Chris might not know everyone in the region, and he might not be a deep thinker. That's his major difference from Jim. Jim Kelly is a great strategist and he understands the region very well. But he's not a negotiator. Chris Hill is a negotiator . . . [H]e could sell you a used car, and he's pretty good at that.”[127]

In March 2005, when Hill's appointment was approved by the U.S. Senate Foreign Relations Committee, he quietly sounded out the White House NSC staff about a possible visit to North Korea. “What are you going to negotiate in Pyongyang?” an official asked. “While they're still producing plutonium, what is there to negotiate about?” The office of Vice President Cheney took the position that termination of the operation of the nuclear reactors in Yongbyon was a prerequisite for doing anything, and Hill was challenged to clarify what he could bring back from North Korea in return for his visit to Pyongyang.[128] Hill was then told by NSC officials that the following three preconditions had to be met before he could visit Pyongyang:

—North Korea must return to the six-party talks (following its withdrawal after the Banco Delta Asia issue erupted).

—North Korea must acknowledge the existence of its highly enriched uranium program.

—North Korea must stop operating the nuclear reactors in Yongbyon.[129]

Department of State officials in charge of Korean affairs had high expectations of Hill's proposed visit to North Korea. They were concerned about the lack of bilateral consultations between North Korea and the United States, which they believed had adversely affected the six-party talks process; moreover, they were aware that North Korea wanted to expand its contacts with the United States, being wary of China's continuing economic advances into North Korea.[130] But deeper down, those officials must have been driven by passion to negotiate with North Korea and to restore the relevance of diplomacy vis-à-vis U.S.–North Korea relations. One senior official quoted Hill as saying that "every other member of the six-party talks has a secret pipeline to North Korea and a line of communication with Kim Jong-il. The United States is the only exception."[131]

If Hill could actually visit Pyongyang, what should he attempt to accomplish there? Of course, he had been told by White House staff that North Korea had to stop operating its nuclear reactors in Yongbyon before he could go. But Hill hoped that if North Korea were willing to do that so that he could visit North Korea, while in Pyongyang he would work first to restore U.S.–North Korea relations to their state before the second nuclear crisis, which had been triggered by the U.S. intelligence concerning the HEU program. He also envisioned the subsequent establishment in Pyongyang of a liaison office that would allow U.S. government officials posted there to contact and initiate exchanges with a wider range of North Koreans than the officials of the Foreign Ministry, who the United States had learned were kept on a very short leash.[132] That kind of scenario was envisioned by both Hill and Korean affairs specialists in the Department of State.[133]

During the fourth round of the talks, Hill repeated his plan to Rice for a secret visit to North Korea. If there were any major breakthroughs, he hoped to go to Pyongyang in the first or second week of October.

After the fourth round of the six-party talks was over, North Korea contacted the United States to say that North Korea would welcome Hill's visit to Pyongyang. At the time of the UN General Assembly meeting toward the end of September 2005, North Korea's deputy foreign minister, Choe Su-hon, announced that "North Korea would welcome a visit by U.S. negotiator Christopher Hill if he came with the intention of resolving the nuclear issue."[134]

In light of those developments, Hill once again discussed with White House NSC staff his proposal and the conditions that the United States would demand of North Korea in exchange for his visit. One of the previous three conditions was revised, although the other two remained intact—North Korea had to return to the six-party talks and it had to stop operating the nuclear reactors in Yongbyon. But instead of requiring North Korea to acknowledge the existence of its HEU program, the third condition stated that "North Korea must resume a moratorium on missile launching."[135]

Nevertheless, the White House remained reluctant to endorse Hill's visit. Although it was whispered within the Department of State that Hill's initiative was killed by Cheney's office, reluctance on the part of Rice, Hill's boss, was the biggest factor.[136] Rice relayed the verdict to Hill during the fourth round of the talks, when an upbeat Hill told her his idea. "No," she said. "It's not the right time. You're being silly because you're selling yourself cheap. Don't sell yourself cheap."[137] On the next day, after the signing of the joint statement of the fourth round on September 19, 2005, North Korea had to spoil everything by releasing the Foreign Ministry announcement mentioned above, which was followed by loud publicity about its invitation to Hill to visit Pyongyang. As a result, Rice became deeply convinced that it would be a waste of time to negotiate with North Korea.[138]

At the same time, Rice was considering a totally different approach. Having found the six-party talks of limited utility, she commissioned Philip D. Zelikow, counselor of the U.S. Department of State, to formulate a grand design to settle the North Korean nuclear issue. It had to be a strategy that would allow a dash to the goal instead of the slow step-by-step march down the field required by the "commitment for commitment, action for action" concept. In short, it had to be a vision for creating a peace regime on the Korean Peninsula.

Hill had not been consulted beforehand, and the new arrangement made his relations with Zelikow awkward, so much so that Deputy Secretary of State Robert Zoellick had to interfere and demarcate their roles: Zelikow would formulate strategy and Hill would handle negotiations. Zoellick was skeptical about Hill's plan to visit North Korea. Zoellick was convinced that it would take someone in a position at least as high as his, if not higher, for the proposed trip to work. He suspected that the North Koreans would not respond seriously to anyone lower in rank.[139]

One senior Department of State official pointed out that Hill was at least partly responsible for the impasse because he had failed to clarify his intentions and agenda sufficiently:

> Chris's approach made people uncomfortable, too. It was like saying "never mind the instructions, just let me do it." And the Pentagon and Cheney's office began to be suspicious about his motive. We were not saying he shouldn't visit Pyongyang no matter what. But we thought that should be the move of last resort instead of the first step. To begin with, it wasn't clear at all what he intended to do.[140]

North Korea never responded to the U.S. questions about North Korea's reason for the invitation and the agenda items that would be discussed during Hill's visit.[141] The New York channel also remained silent. By mid-October, according to one Department of State official, "most of the air went out of our tires" as far as Hill's visit to North Korea was concerned.[142]

Banco Delta Asia

On August 25, 2005, some time after the fourth round of the six-party talks was temporarily disrupted, United Press International dispatched the following article from Macau:

Two Asian men accused of smuggling weapons and counterfeit bills into the United States laundered $1.15 million in Macau bank accounts, U.S. investigators said.

Co Khanh Tang and Jyimin Horng are among eighty-seven alleged members of a criminal syndicate accused by the U.S. government of smuggling weapons, counterfeit money, drugs, and fake cigarettes into the country, the *South China Morning Post* reported Thursday.

Agents arrested fifty-nine people last weekend, most of them in a New Jersey sting operation that lured suspects to a mock wedding party aboard a luxury yacht.

Tang and Horng reportedly received $1.15 million from undercover law enforcement agents in exchange for $3.35 million of high-quality counterfeit dollars.

The men also received a $50,000 deposit toward a $1 million shipment of arms, including seventy-five anti-tank missiles, fifty rocket-propelled grenade launchers, 1,200 AK-47 assault rifles, and various other firearms, the newspaper said. Horng allegedly planned to smuggle the weapons into the United States with the help of two military generals in two unnamed countries.

Tang and Horng had payments deposited into a Bank of China account in Macau and an International Bank of Taipei account in Taiwan, the report said. Spokesmen at both banks declined to say whether the accounts had been frozen.[143]

The sting operation was carefully engineered: the criminal syndicate tycoon involved—who thought that he was going to his wedding aboard a luxury yacht, the *Royal Charm*, just off Atlantic City, New Jersey—did not know that the woman that he was supposed to be marrying was an undercover agent. Many of his men, from various locations in East Asia as well as from the U.S. West Coast, rode in limousines to the port, dressed for the occasion in tuxedoes. All were taken into custody—a wholesale arrest, indeed. One of the "unnamed countries" mentioned in the report was North Korea.

Then, on September 9, 2005, the *Wall Street Journal* carried the following article:

The Bank of China and two banks based in Macau are under U.S. scrutiny for possible connections to North Korea's sprawling, illicit fund-raising network, which U.S. officials believe finances Pyongyang's nuclear program.... The operation comes as delicate multilateral negotiations aimed at dismantling North Korea's nuclear-weapons program are set to resume next week, with China playing a key role. It also comes amid plans for an initial public offering next year by Bank of China, which recently hired

Goldman Sachs Group Inc., of New York, to prepare the move. . . . The FBI and Justice Department haven't publicly acknowledged that the operation is aimed at North Korea. Law-enforcement officials say they believe this silence is tied to the Department of State's concern that the crackdown could undercut attempts to disarm Pyongyang.[144]

The immediate target of the U.S. government's scrutiny was Banco Delta Asia, also headquartered in Macau and located next to a casino owned and managed by casino mogul Stanley Ho. It became the object of inquiry in the mid-1990s, when it was suspected of attempting to pass a large number of counterfeit U.S. bills. Since then, U.S. investigative agencies have kept a close watch on the bank. More than fifty North Korean corporations have conducted money laundering through the bank, and some 40 percent of its business has been North Korea–related. It also has been discovered that North Korean corporations have used several other banks in China and Macau, including the Bank of China, for money laundering.[145]

The banks were used for channeling a portion of the US$500 million in illicit payments that the government of South Korea had made to North Korea as "compensation for contacts." On June 12, three days before the North-South summit talk, the South Korean intelligence agency reportedly intercepted a message from the head of North Korea's Jokwang Trading Company in Macau (a known front for Bureau 39) to Workers' Party officials in Pyongyang saying that illicit secret payments made by the South Korean Hyundai Group had been received.[146] (It was said that Kim Jong-il initially had demanded US$1 billion from South Korea.)[147] In short, both South Korea and North Korea and even China had long been aware of the hidden function of the banks, including the Bank of China.

At the fifth round of the six-party talks, held November 9–11, 2005, the biggest issue was money laundering through Banco Delta Asia in Macau. Kim Gye-gwan criticized the United States, saying, "The United States raided the Banco Delta Asia after the announcement of the joint statement of the fourth round."[148] Kim also compared financial flows to blood circulation in the body—if clogged, it would stop the heart. One member of the Japanese delegation who was there when Kim spoke later said, "It sounded like a cry squeezed out from deep inside his body. I thought that was the first occasion that North Korea allowed itself to expose its true weakness."[149] Kim criticized the United States, too, during the U.S.–North Korea bilateral consultations. "We want you to return the US$24 million that is frozen due to the financial sanctions," he said repeatedly. "If you don't return the money, we won't participate in the six-party talks any longer."[150]

In response to that ultimatum, Hill had this to say:

Article 311 of the Patriot Act aims at protecting the U.S. financial sector, not at prosecuting illegal financial deals. In applying this article, the

United States has not targeted North Korea and, in fact, this article has been applied to financial institutions in the Middle East. This is a part of the war with terrorists and a part of U.S. defensive measures. What the United States did was merely to identify Banco Delta Asia as a money-laundering institution. The United States merely requested financial institutions in the United States to freeze transactions with this bank. It was the financial authority in Macau, not the U.S. authorities, that froze the North Korean accounts. To begin with, this was a financial regulatory action and not a subject appropriate for discussion at the Six-Party Talks that are being held for consultations on the North Korean nuclear issue. I am not in a position to control the U.S. investigative authorities. The U.S. government, however, can provide to the North Korean government a briefing on this issue.[151]

In 2003 the Bush administration decided to launch the Illicit Activities Initiative (IAI) in order to develop a government-wide response to North Korea's illegal activities and to set up a special task force to implement this initiative, which encompasses fourteen departments and agencies, including the State, Treasury, Justice, Homeland Security, and Defense departments and the Federal Bureau of Investigation. David Asher, senior counselor to the East Asia and Pacific Affairs Bureau of the Department of State, was appointed the head of the task force.

The United States, believing that North Korea's illegal activities—such as manufacturing and smuggling counterfeit bills, cigarettes, machine guns, and Viagra—were not limited to those that violated U.S. domestic laws but also included activities, such as procurement of parts and materials for weapons of mass destruction, that were related to international terrorism, aimed to prepare appropriate policy measures in response. The U.S. government estimated that such activities earn North Korea an average of US$500 million per year, which constitutes 35 percent to 40 percent of the amount North Korea earns each year through foreign trade.[152]

In the beginning, neither the CIA nor the Treasury Department was enthusiastic about dealing with North Korea's illegal activities this way. James Kelly explained:

> When the CIA analyzes the North Korean economy, it customarily includes, in the category of "errors and omissions," income from illegal activities. We had to persuade the CIA people that these "errors and omissions" have profound significance in the North Korean economy. We also explained to officials of the U.S. Treasury that Taiwan was so infested with counterfeit US$100 bills that, for some months, a $100 bill was not accepted there, which caught the attention of the Treasury Department's leadership.[153]

The Illicit Activities Initiative was intended to promote the denuclearization of North Korea as well as to control illegal activities. David Asher defined the IAI as "aggressive law enforcement to support the goal of influencing the North Korean leadership to make a positive strategic choice by making its current criminal framework unsustainable." Underlying that approach was the judgment that genuine reform and opening would be impossible and diplomatic progress unlikely if North Korea's incentive structure did not change.[154]

The United States suspected that North Korea's illegal financial activities, starting with money laundering, must be deeply related to North Korea's nuclear development activities. It was discovered that donations from the Hyundai Group and the transfer of US$500 million in illicit funds to North Korea at the time of the North-South summit talks in 1999 through 2001 roughly coincided with the aggressive procurement by the North Korean government of components for producing highly enriched uranium. Moreover, procurement of the nuclear materials was conducted by Bureau 39 of the Korean Workers' Party, which also was engaged in money laundering.[155]

The United States repeatedly warned North Korea that the production of counterfeit dollar bills was an act of war against the United States. In December 2005, President Bush stated that "North Korea is a country that has declared boldly they're got nuclear weapons, they counterfeit our money, and they've starving their people to death," stressing the graveness of the situation.[156] Moreover, Sheena Chestnut, a researcher concerned with North Korea's criminal activities, concluded that counterfeiting the dollar bills "could be justified [by North Korea] under the *juche* ideology and allowed the regime to advertise its anti-capitalist, anti-American credentials."[157] Thus, the issues of money laundering and counterfeiting dollar bills became new areas of "unarmed" conflict between the United States and North Korea.

During its intensified investigation of North Korean money laundering, the United States attempted to collect evidence to put pressure on China; Chinese banks, after all, had been involved in North Korea's money-laundering scheme. The U.S. government decided that it had to inform the Chinese authorities of the DPRK's shady transactions and ask the Chinese government to take firm measures against North Korea. Accordingly, James Kelly, assistant secretary of state; David Asher, senior counselor for East Asian and Pacific Affairs at the Department of State; and Michael Green, director of East Asian Affairs for the NSC, brought up the subject of North Korea's money laundering vis-à-vis China for the first time in August 2003, at the time of the first round of the six-party talks.[158]

Because Macau is supported solely by casinos and the financial industry, the investigation might well have shaken up its entire economy. Moreover, if the involvement of the Bank of China, one of four major commercial banks in

China, was exposed openly, it could raise the question of the credibility of China's financial system. And it so happened that the Bank of China had been preparing to list its stock on the New York Stock Exchange.[159]

When Kelly visited China in August 2003, he pointed out that the transfer of centrifugal separators to North Korea by A. Q. Khan had gone through Chinese territory and that North Korea's export of missiles to Iran also had gone through China and that both of those events were directly related to the nuclear and missile issues. In addition, Kelly repeatedly called China's attention to North Korea's criminal activities, such as counterfeiting money and cigarettes and laundering money, as well as the relation between the nuclear and missile issues and those criminal activities.

In the summer of 2004, the United States began to talk with China about fake US$100 notes that the Americans called "supernotes," as well as related illegal financial activities such as money laundering.[160] At first Kelly was not satisfied with the Chinese reaction. But as the United States repeatedly briefed the Chinese on the details of North Korea's activities, China came to realize the seriousness of the situation. Kelly later said:

> At one time I think we were told that they had apprehended a great deal of counterfeit American bills, and the indication was that they were going to share them with us. . . . They indicated that they were going to let our law enforcement people look at what they had captured.[161]

As it turned out, actual cooperation between China and the United States regarding counterfeit money never materialized while Kelly was in office. It was only after 2005 that the Chinese government, particularly the Foreign Ministry and the People's Bank of China, China's central bank, started taking the matter seriously. According to one senior U.S. Treasury Department official, China's financial authorities sent a warning to the three northeastern Chinese provinces that border North Korea Jilin, Liaoning, and Heilongjiang provinces—about the inflow of counterfeit U.S. currency.[162]

Following its own independent investigation of Banco Delta Asia, the Chinese government also became convinced that the bank had been used in North Korean money-laundering operations.[163] In December 2005, China's vice foreign minister, Wu Dawei, visited Shenyang to meet secretly with North Korea's deputy foreign minister, Kim Gye-gwan. Wu intended to consult with Kim concerning the money-laundering and counterfeiting issues, and he was accompanied by personnel from the People's Bank of China and other specialists. In the meeting, Kim repeated that North Korea would not participate in the six-party talks unless the financial sanctions against North Korea were lifted, but he indicated that if the U.S. evidence of counterfeiting and money laundering issues was indisputable, it might be possible to investigate the implicated North Koreans and take "certain measures." Kim's remark was interpreted to mean that although North Korea would never acknowledge that the state had been involved in illegal activities, it might acknowledge the wrong-doings of individual North Koreans.[164] In March 2006, the Bank of China circulated a warning to other banks in China that a massive number of counterfeit U.S. one-hundred-dollar bills had come into China from overseas.[165]

Following the fifth round of talks, North Korea requested bilateral consultations with the United States in order to discuss the money-laundering issue. In March 2006 in New York, the U.S. government provided North Korea with briefings by officers from the U.S. Treasury Department and other agencies, and Li Gun, director general of the North American Affairs Bureau of North Korea's Foreign Ministry, attended a briefing session. North Korea had requested a one-to-one consultation with a U.S. official, but the United States refused the request on the grounds that it involved a "law enforcement matter."

Li Gun said, "Yes, counterfeiting is happening, and we condemn this counterfeiting. But it's happening because the U.S. won't allow North Korea to have bank accounts, so we have to use cash. So if the DPRK has to keep using cash, we can't control this counterfeiting." He continued, "We want to cooperate with you to stop this counterfeiting, so if you give us the highest-technology machines to catch counterfeit hundred dollar bills, we can use them." The United States was not interested in such "cooperation," anticipating that North Korea would only learn how to make better hundred-dollar bills.[166]

North Korea subsequently made repeated requests for bilateral consultations with the United States on the money-laundering issue; the United States in turn repeated that it would agree to bilateral consultations only if North Korea committed itself to return to the six-party talks. North Korea replied that it would return to the talks only if the United States agreed to bilateral consultations, leading to a prolonged stalemate.[167]

Thus, the issues of money laundering and financing of criminal activities became a new element of U.S. policy concerning North Korea. The financing issue became a new battle zone in the "long war" against terrorism and weapons of mass destruction, and it invited the participation of a powerful bureaucracy, the U.S. Department of the Treasury.

During the time between the adoption of the USA Patriot Act in October 2001 and the measures implemented in late 2004 and early 2005 to strengthen intelligence and organizational capabilities with respect to weapons of mass destruction, the U.S. Department of the Treasury greatly expanded the targets of its surveillance and restriction of money-laundering activities—from terrorist-related monetary and financial transactions to transactions that were suspected of being related to weapons of mass destruction as a whole.[168] The Treasury Department thus became a financial sheriff, so to speak, whose duty is to monitor, track, and investigate financial flows relating to rogue states, international terrorist groups, money laundering by criminal organizations, counterfeiting, fundraising related to WMDs, payments for purchases of WMDs, and payment for missile exports. One senior Treasury Department official observed that "in the case of North Korea, it is highly likely that counterfeit money will be spread around where its embassies and consulates are located. But they attempt to distribute it globally and not just locally, requiring us to chase it globally, too."[169]

Robert Kimmitt, the deputy secretary of the treasury, noted that tackling money laundering and the financing of criminal activities was a new frontline in the war against terrorism, quoting Gordon Brown, Britian's chancellor of the exchequer, who said, "The Treasury itself had to become a department for security."[170] Kimmitt has claimed that eliminating North Korea's money-laundering activities would contribute greatly to crippling North Korea's development of weapons of mass destruction and severing the country's relations with international terrorist groups. Thus, in terms of its policy toward North Korea, the United States has come to police financial transactions as well as the proliferation of weapons of mass destruction. The Treasury Department, as financial sheriff, had an important part in including the "money laundering must be stopped" wording in UN Security Council Resolution 1695, which was passed against North Korea after it launched missiles in July 2006. Kimmitt has claimed that this resolution is a historic document.[171]

As mentioned earlier, during the fourth round of the six-party talks, the United States raised the money-laundering and human rights issues. Although China first took them into account in drafting the joint statement, they subsequently were dropped.[172] U.S. hardliners vis-à-vis North Korea, including Robert Joseph, were strongly dissatisfied with both the absence of the money-laundering issue in the joint statement and the inclusion of the wording regarding light-water reactors.[173] The Bush administration emphasized that pursuit of the money laundering issue was by no means intended to facilitate regime change in North Korea, either explicitly or implicitly. But one Department of State official involved with the six-party talks believed that accommodating North Korea, as exemplified in the joint statement, ended up reinforcing the argument for North Korean regime change, which once again had gathered momentum within the Bush administration. He went on to say:

> Long knives again came out after the agreement. I don't know if Cheney himself moved or not. Cheney doesn't need a long knife because he could just whisper into the president's ear. But Rice did not take any effective action against Bob Joseph's office's rollback operation. We should have consolidated a firm regime not to allow division within the government over the North Korean policy, but we failed to do so.[174]

After the fifth round of the six-party talks, Kim Gye-gwan repeatedly criticized the United States for imposing financial sanctions on North Korea following the announcement of the joint statement of the fourth round, calling it a new U.S. conspiracy to topple the North Korean regime. The view that the sanctions were a backdoor attempt to strangle North Korea improvised by the United States as a substitute for military action was not confined to the North Koreans; it was shared by many in China and South Korea. A senior Treasury Department official declared that the investigation of North Korean money-laundering and counterfeiting activities, including those of Banco Delta Asia, had nothing to do with the six-party talks process, denying the allegation of a connection between the bank issue and supporting the joint statement. He said, in part:

> We are tired of hearing all kinds of conspiracy theories. This particular timing might mean something from the perspective of those who have been watching North Korea in conjunction with the six-party talks process, but from our viewpoint, after watching the financial flow for years in the past, the incident just surfaced when it should.[175]

The true picture was as follows: The decision to take action on Banco Delta Asia had been on the table since the summer of 2005, but it had been put on hold to avoid having a negative impact on the six-party talks. Some thought that the action against Banco Delta Asia was insignificant and would go unnoticed; others believed that it could have the broad impact that it did. At a meeting co-chaired by Joseph DeTrani, James Foster, and Victor Cha, it was decided to delay making a decision on what to do until after the fourth round of the talks. After the first session of the fourth round, the group met again to deliberate. At that meeting, the Department of State wanted to continue delaying, while the vice president's office, the Department of the Treasury, and the Department of Defense complained to National Security Council staff that the delay could not continue. The Department of State was overruled, and the committee decided to take action. The fact that the decision came so close behind the joint statement was purely coincidental.[176]

A Chinese official involved with the six-party talks offered the following analysis of North Korea's psychology:

> If North Korea comes back to the negotiation table when the United States is applying pressure concerning the money-laundering issue, people would think that North Korea has very deep financial problems. This is what the North Koreans fear, and that's why they can't come back to the six-party talks. It is about losing face.[177]

One senior Chinese government official conjectured that the U.S. government decided to make a frontal attack on Banco Delta Asia mainly because it felt that it had conceded too much to North Korea in agreeing to the joint statement of the fourth round of the six-party talks. He added that North Korea's missile launching in July 2006 was motivated chiefly by Pyongyang's determination to take a strong stance on the Banco Delta Asia issue vis-à-vis the United States.[178]

FROM ARMISTICE AGREEMENT TO PEACE TREATY

After the release of the joint statement on September 19, 2005, the Bush administration started to explore two new initiatives vis-à-vis the Korean Peninsula. One was the aforementioned plan for Christopher Hill to visit North Korea, but Secretary of State Rice showed no interest in that idea, and in the end it was abandoned. The other initiative, proposed by Philip D. Zelikow and endorsed by Rice and Robert Zoellick, was to pursue a lasting peace regime on the Korean Peninsula. The pillar of that vision is the conversion of the current Korean War armistice agreement into a peace treaty.

Officials at the State Department's Bureau of East Asian and Pacific Affairs felt betrayed by "Rice's change of heart." In their eyes, Rice seemed to have lost interest in the six-party talks and to have jumped at a fantasy proposed by a scholar of West European international politics who had no insight into the reality of Asia. It seemed that Rice, hearing North Korea's criticism of the joint statement immediately after the end of the fourth round of talks, had decided that the "tit-for-tat" style of the diplomatic negotiations with North Korea would never succeed.[179] She was searching for a new mode of approaching North Korea.

The United States and North Korea have been in a state of truce since the armistice agreement ending the Korean War was signed in 1953. The armistice agreement has managed to prevent the eruption of war on the peninsula until now, but it has done nothing more than maintain a state of non-war. It was Zelikow who began to ask whether the agreement could be converted into a peace treaty in order to establish a permanent peace regime.

Zelikow is a scholar of international politics, specializing in European politics. He served as the executive director of the National Commission on Terrorist Attacks upon the United States, better known as the 9/11 Commission, and he is well known for the commission's report, which is regarded as the most authoritative narrative and analysis of the 9/11 terrorist attacks. During the George H. W. Bush administration, Zelikow was in the White House NSC and contributed to the formulation of the administration's European policy during such historical transitions as the end of the cold war, the reunification of Germany, and the integration of Europe. He coauthored *Germany Unified and Europe Transformed* with Condoleezza Rice, his colleague at the NSC at that time.

Zelikow has explored the possibility of applying to the Korean Peninsula, another divided state, strategic leverage similar to that applied in the case of

Germany. He wondered whether, as the first step, the current armistice agreement could be converted into a permanent peace treaty that, if the Korean Peninsula could be unified, eventually would enable the creation of a new multilateral framework for peace and stability in Northeast Asia, thereby allowing the United States to secure a new role and presence in the region. He formulated a bold strategic vision, regarding which he has said, in part:

> We should discuss not only the North Korean nuclear issue but, more important, whether we should further continue the Korean War.
>
> What is the best way to approach the future of the Korean Peninsula? The most important feature of the future of Northeast Asia is not the future of North Korea, it's the future of China and Japan and the Korean Peninsula between them as always. But above all, the future of China and Japan.
>
> Along the way, we need South Koreans to understand that the United States does not oppose the future reunification of the Korean Peninsula. We will have to "free up" a Korean relationship with America instead of [keeping South Korea in a position of] grudging dependence on the United States.[180]

Zelikow has been interested in this concept since the spring of 2005, and he discussed it with Rice, who sounded out the idea with the leaders of China, Japan, and South Korea when she visited those countries in July 2005. When she met Foreign Minister Ban Ki-moon in South Korea, Ban was fascinated by the idea. China's foreign minister, Li Zhaoxing, simply registered what Rice had to say. Rice's last stop was Japan, and a senior U.S. administration official who accompanied Rice on her trip remarked, "Although Koizumi said Japan could play some role, MOFA showed no interest whatsoever."[181]

Zelikow was not the first U.S. government official to propose the establishment of a permanent peace regime by converting the armistice agreement into a peace treaty. During the four-party talks in the late 1990s, Ambassador Charles Kartman, U.S. special envoy for the Korean peace talks, made a similar proposal. Although Kartman's proposal envisioned the future signing of a peace treaty, its major thrusts were to mitigate tension and to promote confidence-building measures. North Korea showed interest in the possibility of a peace treaty between North Korea and the United States, but it went no further. From the very beginning, North Korea had been suspicious regarding the United States' true intentions.[182]

But this time, both North Korea and South Korea were advocating the plan, and the United States had already secured China's support, a great change from the previous occasion. Nevertheless, Zelikow's proposal became the target of severe criticism from within the Bush administration. Various objections were raised:

—It is inconceivable to conclude a peace treaty with North Korea with no conditions.[183]

—The North Koreans are armed with nuclear weapons, and they deploy 1 million troops along the North-South border. They have 200 Rodong missiles aimed at Japan.[184] North Korea is a dangerous country that has launched a Taepodong missile at the United States. There will be no peace treaty unless we eliminate this threat and create peace. Where there is no peace, there is no peace treaty.[185]

—If a peace treaty is concluded, everything will have to be reviewed, including the current U.S.–South Korea alliance, the command system and chain of command, the U.S. military bases in South Korea, the U.S.-Japan alliance, and the new structure of current alliance relations. There would be the danger that the U.S.–South Korean command system might be unraveled. The vision is too big and too complicated. It is unrealistic.[186]

—"Yes" to a peace mechanism to create a framework for peace and stability in Northeast Asia based on the six-party talks. But "no" to a peace treaty with North Korea.[187]

Zelikow attempted to promote his proposal in a capacity that was largely independent of the State Department's Bureau of East Asian and Pacific Affairs. Rice also acted to support the scheme and directly introduced it at cabinet-level meetings. Although Vice President Cheney and Defense Secretary Rumsfeld did not oppose Zelikow's vision, they raised a lot of questions, including "Wouldn't it further encourage North Korea's whiny attitude to present such a vision at this stage?"[188] Although Zelikow persisted in promoting the idea, the White House, the Pentagon, and the Bureau of East Asian and Pacific Affairs continued to give it the cold shoulder. To them, Zelikow "simply did not understand the complexities of East Asian international politics."[189]

In fact, internal papers had been written on the idea by the Department of State and the National Security Council. Many different National Security Council staff members, such as Michael Green, John Rood, Robert Joseph, William Tobey, and Victor Cha, had written such papers at the request of both Rice and Stephen Hadley when each was national security adviser. Zelikow's draft actually drew on the previous internal papers, but it eventually was redrafted at a writing session chaired by J. D. Crouch and attended by Zelikow, Richard Lawless, Green, Cha, and Tobey.[190]

Among those who were against the idea of a peace treaty was Vice President Cheney's chief of staff, Lewis "Scooter" Libby, who held a very harsh view of the proposal. Libby is an old Japan hand, and he once lived in Kanazawa, a city in central Japan, when he was young. In 1999 he published *The Apprentice,* a thriller set in Japan toward the end of the Edo period.[191] Libby has defined his role in the Bush administration as a quiet anchor of the U.S.-Japan alliance. "What good does a piece of paper like a peace treaty do?" he said. "The most urgent thing now is to strengthen the U.S.-Japan alliance and maintain deterrence toward North Korea."[192]

In the end, because of Libby's comments, Zelikow's proposal was shelved;[193] the cabinet-level meeting on the peace treaty issue scheduled for November 2005 never took place. Nevertheless, Rice remained interested in the idea, and Rice, together with Zelikow and Zoellick, started to mold Zelikow's vision into a policy. In the spring of 2006, Rice and Zoellick presented President Bush with a strategic concept paper on the scheme, in the form of a plan for creating a peace regime based on the conclusion of a peace treaty on the Korean Peninsula. Initially Bush was a little reluctant, but in the end he endorsed the concept paper. "It's worth trying," he said. "Let's move it around."

It was decided to sound out the Chinese about the plan and get their feedback rather than propose it to them outright and request a consultation. As it happened, President Hu Jintao was scheduled to visit the United States in April 2006. Rice and Zoellick devised a game plan: to have Bush talk to Hu Jintao about the plan and ask Hu to convey it to Kim Jong-il.[194]

On April 20, 2006, Bush met and talked with Hu Jintao, mainly about the North Korean nuclear issue and Iran's nuclear development activities. The talk included, as expected, a Chinese request that the United States show more "flexibility" vis-à-vis the North Korean nuclear issue and a U.S. request that China exercise its "considerable influence" on North Korea.[195]

During the lunch, which was hosted by President and Mrs. Bush, President Bush moved his chair next to Hu Jintao's seat to have a deep discussion with Hu about North Korea, ignoring the first ladies. Bush said, "Look. Deng Xiaoping had the courage to sort of open up the economy and to start to change the economy in the 1980s. What about Kim Jong-il?" Hu answered:

> Well, one of the differences, however, was that in the 1980s Deng Xiaoping knew that he didn't face a security threat, so he could take risks internally, and the external environment was not a threat. Kim Jong-il feels he's got a security threat with the United States. That's why he has to be cautious toward opening up and reform.

Then Bush said, "Well, if he's willing to work for a peace treaty, we're willing to do that. Tell him that!"[196]

On April 27, Hu Jintao dispatched State Councilor Tang Jiaxuan and Vice Foreign Minister Wu Dawei to North Korea to convey Bush's message to Kim Jong-il. They flew in a government-chartered airplane to North Korea, where they changed planes and then flew northeast to an airport on the east coast, near the location of a North Korean missile base. They met Kim Jong-il at a nearby guest house. That could have meant that North Korea had started missile-launching preparations by that time. When Tang conveyed Bush's message, Kim replied, in part: "It was we who first proposed a peace treaty. . . . The United States decided to send such an important message not directly but through China. What was its intention in doing that? . . .

The United States speaks of a peace treaty, but what about the nuclear issue?"[197]

The response that the United States received was ambiguous, neither negative nor positive. Zhou Wenzhong, China's ambassador to the United States, went to the Department of State to convey the North Korean response:

—Before anything, the United States must suspend financial sanctions against North Korea.

—The United States must give North Korea tangible compensation [for its cooperation] instead of merely proposing a concept as abstract as the signing of a peace treaty.

Hearing that response, Zoellick thought that North Korea might not trust China.[198] Watching the Chinese diplomacy in this case, which amounted to nothing more than sending a "messenger boy" (as described by a State Department official), the United States wondered how serious China had been. One Department of State official had the following to say:

> President Bush even said we could discuss this between the United States and North Korea. That's why we wanted China to handle this issue more carefully. If the Chinese had known that North Korea would say no to this, we wish they would not have brought it up with the North Koreans. I can't help but think that the Chinese did it knowing full well what the North Korean reaction would be. And probably it was more convenient for China if North Korea said no. This way, the Chinese can say that the United States should take a more flexible stance toward North Korea.[199]

Some indicators suggest that China might have been concerned that this peace treaty scheme might become a Northeast Asian version of the Helsinki Accord of 1975. The Helsinki Accord is perceived to have facilitated mutual contact and exchange in the areas of security, economic reform, and human rights/culture; to have promoted confidence building; to have lowered the barriers between different regimes; and eventually to have created a peace regime. To the Chinese the peace treaty scheme might have appeared to be a means for *heping yanbian*. Although this Chinese expression translates literally as "peaceful evolution," it carries the connotation of using nonviolent means to transform another society for the purpose of extending one's own influence.

The North Koreans might have been even more suspicious of the scheme. They might have interpreted the idea of economic reform as a tool for *heping yanbian* and regarded the idea of advancing human rights as an instrument for regime change. But Zelikow maintained that his idea was "not really some great wicked scheme to try to knock over the North Korean regime. It really gives the North Korean regime a chance to answer for themselves the question, 'What do you wish to become?'"[200]

It was quite possible that North Korea also interpreted the U.S. proposal as an attempt to revise the joint statement of the fourth round of the six-party talks.[201] While the North Koreans speak openly of the need for a comprehensive settlement, they actually show no interest in anything other than deals involving "commitment for commitment, action for action."[202] In a general atmosphere of distrust, the six-party talks was about the only framework left in which they could negotiate with others. Besides, North Korea would probably attempt to normalize diplomatic relations with the United States and Japan before agreeing to a peace treaty, in which case the United States would have to take into consideration how Japan, which would not be a signatory to the peace treaty, would react.[203]

The U.S. proposal, therefore, would have to cope with a highly complicated structure. To begin with, because the United States had not given a proper explanation to the Chinese, the Chinese were not able to give North Korea a satisfactory answer to the question of how the United States related the peace treaty and the nuclear issue. It must have been difficult for China to do anything more than act like an ill-informed messenger. If China had praised the U.S. scheme in order to sell it to North Korea or had tried to persuade North Korea to accept it, Pyongyang would have suspected that China was conspiring with the United States. In fact, during the U.S.-China senior officials meeting in January 2006, the Chinese had frankly acknowledged the difficulty of talking to the North Koreans about this specific issue.[204] A Chinese diplomat confided later that "Bush's message was too vague to be doable."[205]

The South Koreans, in contrast, were very enthusiastic about the peace treaty scheme. In fact, a senior South Korean government official seemed to believe that their input had influenced Zelikow's concept.[206] During the U.S.–South Korea summit talk on the occasion of the November 2005 APEC summit in Kyongju, Blue House staff had argued strongly for a "permanent peace regime," and they attempted to elaborate on it in the U.S.–South Korean joint statement. But the White House was reluctant to discuss the regime further, because the North Korean nuclear issue had not been settled.

In the end, the joint statement specified that the two leaders agreed to establish a forum regarding a "durable peace regime" among the concerned countries, separate from the six-party talks. It also states that it is hoped that discussions in the new forum and discussions at the six-party talks will be mutually reinforcing.[207] It should be noted, however, that even though South Korea carries the idea of a permanent peace regime high as a political symbol of its desire for regional peace and prosperity, it has not shown any inclination to transform the idea into policy. A senior South Korean government official once said to his U.S. counterpart, "It is more urgent to create a state of peace. A 'peace treaty' is something for the year 2015 or way in the future."[208]

Although during the six-party talks both North Korea and China supported the idea of establishing a permanent peace regime, they remained skeptical about the peace treaty idea that the United States had abruptly proposed. For example, South Korea's unification minister, Lee Jong-seok, said, "Would North Korea take seriously the United States' proposition for the peace treaty even though the United States maintains hostile policies toward North Korea on everything else, including the money-laundering investigation?"[209]

The Bush administration did not attempt to inject Zelikow's plan into the six-party talks or to take the policy initiative there. The State Department's Bureau of East Asian and Pacific Affairs, the National Security Council, and the Department of Defense remained cool toward what they regarded as an attempt by the European school (Rice, Zelikow, and Zoellick) to mechanically apply the European model to Northeast Asia. The division of labor between "Zelikow for strategy and Hill for negotiation," after all, remained a mere division. A senior U.S. administration official said later that "the idea of a peace treaty separate from a larger peace mechanism process is dead. . . . Zelikow pushed the idea of a standalone peace treaty, which did die, but the overall peace mechanism idea is clearly spelled out in various U.S.-ROK and six-party joint statements."[210]

COLLAPSE OF THE JAPAN-U.S.–SOUTH KOREA CONSENSUS

Throughout the six-party talks, it had been customary for Japan, the United States, and South Korea to have consultations among themselves prior to the discussions among the six countries. At the fourth round, however, that procedure failed to work as intended. Although Japan and the United States attempted to hold the customary consultation among the three countries, the South Korean delegation refused to sit at the same table with the Japanese delegation.[211] In fact, when the heads of the three delegations—Christopher Hill, U.S. assistant secretary of state; Kenichiro Sasae, director general of the Asian and Oceania Affairs Bureau of Japan's Ministry of Foreign Affairs; and Song Min-soon, deputy minister of South Korea's Ministry of Foreign Affairs and Trade—had lunch together, the television reports showed only Hill and Sasae coming and going. Song Min-soon used the back door of the restaurant, claiming that as the South Korean head delegate, he could not be shown on TV with the other two. One State Department official even referred to that time as the "collapse of the Japan-U.S.–South Korean consensus."[212]

Japan–South Korea relations had become tense because of a territorial dispute that erupted in the spring of 2005 over Takeshima/Dokdo Island. Behind it, of course, was the history issue between the two countries. In his opening remarks, Song Min-soon criticized the speech by Kenichiro Sasae. While Sasae raised the abduction and missile issues up front, Song maintained that the fourth round of the talks should focus first on settling the nuclear issue. Song is known for his tough, nationalistic character, and some in the Japanese delegation suspected that he might harbor some anti-Japanese feeling.[213] Similarly, some at the Blue House were not favorably disposed toward Sasae, who had once preached endlessly to Lee Jong-seok, deputy chief of the Blue House NSC, about the importance of the abduction issue.[214]

During the first stage of the fourth round (July–August 2005), Japan and South Korea had only one bilateral consultation, and that one took place because the United States had pushed the South Korean delegation into accepting Japan's invitation. Learning that South Korea had been refusing bilateral consultations with Japan, the White House complained directly to the Blue House.[215] Victor Cha and Richard Lawless were strong advocates of trilateral consultations, and they were "astounded that Hill was so apathetic about this." As one of the U.S. delegation members said later, "trilateral coordination with allies in Seoul and Tokyo was a no-brainer, but for Hill, because of his close relationship with Song, who did not want to do these for political reasons, he did not want to do these."[216]

South Korea was proud that it had succeeded in making North Korea come back to the six-party talks by proposing to supply free electric power to North Korea and by dispatching Unification Minister Chung Dong-young to Pyongyang. From South Korea's point of view, Japan inflated the importance of the abduction and missile issues and occasionally took a hard-line stance vis-à-vis North Korea, sometimes a much harder stance than the United States did; as a result, Japan-U.S.–South Korea consultations often were divided into two camps—the Japan-U.S. team versus South Korea. It was that "dynamic the Koreans didn't like because they thought it was disadvantageous, because the U.S. and Japan were containing South Korea."[217]

Because South Korea felt increasingly obliged to consider North Korea's sensitivities, it may have concluded that it would do more harm than good to have trilateral consultations with the United States and Japan, and that may have been one of the reasons that South Korea refused trilateral consultations in the fourth round. After Christopher Hill, a former U.S. ambassador to South Korea, was appointed the U.S. head delegate, South Korea seemed to have decided to cut off Japan and concentrate on coordinating with Hill. From that angle, the Japan-U.S.–South Korea consultation was of no use.

The United States, sandwiched between two allies who were spitting at each other, had a tough time coordinating its efforts relating to the two. One member of the U.S. delegation later recalled the situation:

When we had a bilateral consultation with South Korea, we had to brief the Japanese delegation about its content. When we had a U.S.-Japan consultation, we had to inform South Korea on what we had talked about. Why couldn't we just have had a U.S.-Japan–South Korea consultation instead? We were struck by a sense of futility at that time.[218]

One senior U.S. administration official remarked that Japan, South Korea, and the United States "sang the same song" until the third round of the six-party talks. "Because it was a consultation among six different countries, we should not project a united front among the three, but the three sang the same song," he said. "The same song but with different melodies."[219] In the fourth round of talks, however, Japan and the United States sang the same song, with the same melody, and South Korea, although it may have sung the same song, sang it with a different melody and even with some different lyrics.

It was not only between Japan and South Korea that tension was heightened. On occasion, relations between the United States and South Korea also became tense—for example, in their discussions of whether North Korea was to be allowed the peaceful use of nuclear energy and how to express that in the draft joint statement. At one point, Song threatened Hill, saying, "If the United States cannot accommodate its policy towards North Korea in line with the one suggested by its alliance partner, the viability of the alliance will be endangered."[220] That remark was immediately reported to Washington, causing sharp displeasure within the U.S. administration; one official described it as "unacceptable."[221] One senior official spat out, "When, where, and how did Song ever work for strengthening the U.S.–South Korean alliance?"[222]

Some in Japan and the United States were concerned that the six-party talks might end up eroding the cooperation that until then had existed among Japan, South Korea, and the United States. In fact, that had been a concern since the launching of the first round. When Arata Fujii, at the time the director of the Northeast Asian Affairs Division of the Ministry of Foreign Affairs, saw that the seating arrangement in the conference room at Diaoyutai State Guest House separated the three allies, he wondered whether China intended to dissolve the cooperative relationship among them, "like soap in water."[223]

As far as the six-party talks were concerned, the United States had decided to talk with Japan first; then seek a consensus among Japan, the United States, and South Korea; and finally present China with their consensus view. However, according to one senior U.S. administration official, China had approached the United States with the proposition that "the United States and China should consult together first." In these multilateral settings, the U.S. government's orientation often has been divided between the Department of State, which customarily and reflexively chooses to settle down with China, and the White House, which chooses to meet with China after first consulting with Japan and then with Japan and South Korea.[224] Although China had been concerned that the United States, Japan, and South Korea might present a joint proposal, they never presented a joint proposal throughout the six-party talks.

China had not launched the talks in order to cause the Japan-U.S.–South Korea consensus to collapse, but even if it had, there was no need to do so; the trilateral consensus was already falling apart under its own weight. It should be noted, however, that the collapse of the Japan-U.S.–South Korea consensus did not begin at the fourth round of the talks. The moment the six-party talks process began, differences in the three nations' approaches toward North Korea became evident. The differences had become more visible since the second round of the talks, particularly between the United States and South Korea, over such issues as North Korea's possession of highly enriched uranium, the freezing of North Korea's nuclear programs, and CVID (complete, verifiable, and irreversible dismantlement). To the Japanese and the U.S. delegations, it appeared that South Korea was basing its positions on a sole criterion: that they not provoke North Korea.

The United States and Japan suspected that South Korea, walking away from its previous trilateral relationship, might even ally itself more closely with China. Prior to the fourth round of the six-party talks, Japan, the United States, and South Korea got together to draft a statement of their "core principles" regarding the content of the joint statement to be issued at the end of the fourth round. But the United States, finding out that South Korea occasionally sat down with China to go over the draft, was displeased.[225]

Behind the collapse of the consensus among Japan, the United States, and South Korea were changes in domestic politics in both Japan and South Korea. Even earlier than that, one could have seen symptoms of the future collapse in the proceedings of the Trilateral Coordination and Oversight Group (TCOG), which preceded the six-party talks. The TCOG, a Japan-U.S.–South Korea consultative group on North Korean issues, was launched during the Clinton administration in the aftermath of the first nuclear crisis and the missile crisis of 1998, but it began to decline after the onset of the Bush administration. James Kelly explained that the Bush administration found the necessity of compiling statements every time that the TCOG met to be distracting and so decided to change the procedure:

> The TCOG required a statement at the end of each meeting, and this was a huge distraction. . . . We wanted it to be a forum where the three countries could meet and discuss more freely. . . . To have to have the damn statement just got in the way of our coordination. So we would call [it] an informal trilateral meeting—sort of the same thing—but we didn't have to waste time on the statement.[226]

At the time of the second nuclear crisis in 2002, the TCOG was divided between the Japan–South Korea camp and the United States over the treatment of the Agreed Framework and the Korean Peninsula Energy Development Organization (KEDO), as was dramatically revealed in the clash between Hitoshi Tanaka and Lee Tae-sik on one side and James Kelly on the other (see chapter 3). The last meeting of the TCOG took place in Honolulu in June 2003; two months after that meeting, the six-party talks were launched. It should be recognized that the demise of the TCOG and the Japan-U.S.–South Korea working-level informal consultations was due to differences among the three countries in their perception of the threat posed by North Korea and in their approaches to North Korea as well as to the tensions between and among the three themselves.

The schism among the three countries became even more pronounced during the 2003–04 period with the birth of the Roh Moo-hyun government in South Korea and the heightened tension between South Korea and the United States. A major turning point was the trilateral consultation meeting—the first meeting of new delegates from the three countries—in Seoul in February 2005, which was affected by the state of South Korea–Japan relations around that time.

The position of the South Korean government had become increasingly difficult in the midst of various events that had taken place, including the U.S. comment about North Korea being an "outpost of tyranny," North Korea's February 10 proclamation of its nuclear capability, and Japan's adoption of a more hardline position vis-à-vis the abduction and missile issues. In the spring of 2005, as Japan–South Korea relations deteriorated due to the eruption of territorial and history issues, one senior White House official lamented, "Japan-U.S.–South Korea consultation became impossible because of the Takeshima/Dokdo Island and Yasukuni Shrine issues."[227]

South Korea already was more interested in consultations among South Korea, North Korea, and the United States than in consultations among South Korea, the United States, and Japan. From the viewpoint of South Korea, the six-party talks functioned also as an opportunity to facilitate North-South dialogue and mutual confidence building. One senior South Korean government official once proudly remarked that it was from North Korea, not the United States or China, that South Korea first learned of the launching of the six-party talks.[228]

Direct consultations between South Korea and North Korea materialized during the first round of the talk. After the welcome dinner, China's head delegate, Wang Yi, whispered to South Korea's head delegate, Lee Soo-hyuk, that the head delegates of South Korea and North Korea should have a direct talk, adding that North Korea's deputy head delegate, Li Gun, was very much interested. When Lee turned to look at Li, Li signaled OK with his fingers. The bilateral talk between North and South Korea took place immediately in a room that Wang Yi had prepared for that purpose. Lee Soo-hyuk calmly and earnestly told Kim

Yong-il, North Korea's head delegate, that the U.S. Congress would never ratify the kind of nonaggression treaty that North Korea was demanding from the United States. He even referred to the history of the U.S. Senate, which had not approved U.S. membership in the League of Nations even though its creation had been advocated by President Woodrow Wilson just after World War I.[229]

In the North-South bilateral consultations during the third round of the six-party talks, Lee Soo-hyuk offered the following advice to Kim Gye-gwan: "You might have originally started up the five-megawatt nuclear reactor for experimental purposes, but its use was subsequently changed. You had better not use the expression 'peaceful use.'"

Lee was inclined to "advise, not persuade" the North Koreans. He had participated in the earlier four-party talks, in which the North Korean delegation had taken a very condescending attitude toward the South Koreans. This time, the North Koreans listened very attentively to what Lee had to say and vigorously took notes. Also during the third round, Kim Gye-gwan proposed "national cooperation." "Let our two delegations harmonize our steps following the hope of all Korean nationals," he said. "Let us defend the common interests of the Korean nation." In response, Lee Soo-hyuk softly admonished Kim, "That is correct thinking. But maybe you had better not use that expression here."[230] One South Korean diplomat who attended the meeting later recalled, "It was like a talk between two brothers."[231] A White House official quipped that South Korea was like North Korea's lawyer.[232]

During the fourth round of the six-party talks, the United States and North Korea had bilateral consultations twice, but toward the last stage of finalizing the joint statement, the United States refused to negotiate directly with North Korea. Even though Wu Dawei tried to persuade Hill to resume U.S.–North Korea bilateral consultations, Hill would not. Song Min-soon then invited Hill and Kim Gye-gwan, the North Korean head delegate, to sit together on a sofa in a corner of the conference room in an attempt to encourage dialogue between the two, and they accepted his invitation.

According to one senior South Korean government official, the trilateral consultations among South Korea, North Korea, and the United States "revived and reopened the door for Washington-Pyongyang dialogue."[233] But on that occasion both the conversation and the body language were awkward, and from the U.S. point of view, there was "hardly any conversation with substance."[234] At the outset, Kim Gye-gwan said to Hill, "I'm sorry that we need to meet with three parties and that just the two of us can't meet," and then he added, "I'm sorry that we need to meet like this with a mediator again." The latter statement was a reference to the first trilateral consultation in April 2003, when China had served as the intermediary. In short, Kim Gye-gwan was treating South Korea only as an intermediary. Unable to control himself, Song Min-soon abruptly interrupted, yelling at Kim Gye-gwan in Korean. Hill was simply taken back, not knowing what to do. In his fury, Song said, "Wait a second! Wait a second! South Korea is not just a mediator. We are a party to these talks, and you should not treat us like this. We give you so much food aid. We give you a lot of stuff."[235]

That evening, Wu Dawei, China's head delegate, called an urgent meeting of the head delegates. During the meeting, Wu said, "You [the head delegates] can continue your endeavors. Or you can adjourn the meeting if you wish. " That was an expression of Chinese displeasure with South Korea's conduct, which China regarded as usurping China's role as host and chairperson of the talks.[236] China had previously invited the U.S. and North Korean delegations to sit together to work on the draft joint statement, but that did not work out. Therefore, when South Korea easily arranged for a U.S.–North Korea meeting, China felt that it had lost face.

Besides, China still remembered that once toward the end of the 1990s, it had been added on to participate in what originally had been envisioned as a North Korea–South Korea–U.S. trilateral meeting, the four-party talks. (However, Lee Jong-seok, South Korea's unification minister, later said in bewilderment, "We had given prior notice to the Chinese about the South Korea–North Korea–U.S. consultations." South Korea was of the view that it was not for China to say anything about the consultations.)[237]

Meanwhile, South Korea totally rejected Japan. During the first stage of the fourth round of the six-party talks, Japan was also totally rejected by North Korea. A bilateral consultation between North Korea and Japan took place only once, on August 7, the last day of the first stage of the fourth round. It was engineered, at Japan's request, by Wu Dawei, China's head delegate, who had encouraged Kim Gye-gwan behind the scenes to have a bilateral talk with the Japanese. Kim was reluctant, on the grounds that he would not be able to secure Pyongyang's approval. Wu pleaded with Kim to accept the proposal. "I am the one who said that such a meeting could be held," he said. "Help me save face." The Japan–North Korea bilateral consultation finally materialized after the end of the first session.[238] The North Koreans stressed that the meeting was a part of the informal contacts held during the recess. The two head delegates did not even shake hands.

But at the second stage in September, the bilateral consultations between North Korea and Japan were transformed into something more substantive. At North Korea's request, the two delegations started discussing not only issues directly related to the two countries themselves but also broader issues facing the six-party talks. North Korea's motive might have been to use Japan's connections with the United States and China, but the landslide victory of the Liberal Democratic Party under the leadership of Prime Minister Koizumi in the September general election might have been a greater factor. North Korea probably expected Koizumi to once again take a strong leadership role in promoting the normalization of diplomatic relations between Japan and North Korea.

CHAPTER TWELVE

KIM JONG-IL VISITS CHINA

It was still dark at 6:30 a.m. on Tuesday, January 10, 2006, and an icy wind was blowing over the surface of the frozen Yalu. Above the river, on the bridge connecting Sinuiju City, in North Korea, with Dandong City, in China, the train carrying Kim Jong-il slowed down as it made its way to the other side, where the Chinese flag was flying. Just downstream was another bridge, which extended from the Chinese side to a little beyond the midpoint of the river, where it ended. Both bridges had been built by the Japanese before World War II, and after the war they were shared by China and North Korea. When the Korean War erupted in 1950, China sent its People's Volunteer Forces en masse to North Korea, for the most part over the two bridges. In November 1950, the U.S. Air Force bombed the bridges, destroying both, and after the war, only one was reconstructed.

In 1990, the rebuilt bridge was named the China-DPRK Friendship Bridge, in commemoration of the fortieth anniversary of China's participation in the Korean War. Kim Jong-il has visited China four times since 2000, each time traveling over the Friendship Bridge on his special train, which consists of twenty-three cars painted in a dark-green camouflage pattern.[1]

On this trip, Kim's train stopped briefly in Dandong, where the platform had been covered with a red carpet in his honor. Several senior members of the International Department of the Central Committee of the Chinese Communist Party (CCP) had come from Beijing to welcome Kim, and after talking with them for about fifteen minutes in the station's VIP room, Kim and his group headed for Shenyang.[2] Outside, freshly fallen snow covered everything; even the air seemed to be white. Underneath the snow was a vast expanse of now barren cornfields, but at the time of Kim's visit in April 2004, the green expanse of the fields had been impressive. Corn was planted even in small spaces beside rice paddies. Between the cornfields, rows and rows of plastic greenhouses were lined up neatly.

South Korea's Yonhap News Agency released the first report of the passage of Kim's train through Dandong Station.[3] The international media had been chasing news about Kim's movements, but only scraps of information were available. Reuters reported on January 10 that General Secretary Kim appeared to head for Russia via China;[4] Yonhap News Agency reported from a "well-informed source" that Kim had arrived in Shanghai by air;[5] and *Ming Pao,* a Chinese-language daily in Hong Kong, reported that Jiang Zemin, China's former president, had accompanied Kim as he traveled on his special train from Shanghai to Guangzhou.[6]

Some of the conflicting news reports might have been the result of a diversionary campaign launched by the Chinese authorities to keep the media confused about Kim's actual whereabouts. In fact, the Chinese government did not even confirm that Kim Jong-il was visiting China when he allegedly was. When reporters asked about Kim Jong-il's visit, a Chinese Foreign Ministry spokesman, Kong Quan, evaded the question, referring them to the International Department of the Central Committee. However, all department personnel concerned with North Korean affairs had turned off their cell phones and cut communications with the outside.[7]

When Kim visited China in May 2000, he had told his Chinese hosts that, with regard to visits to China, he wished to follow the example of his late father, visiting China when the need arose and paying no heed to formalities. The Chinese welcomed his comment.[8] And while the Chinese made only two visits to North Korea—Jiang Zemin's visit in September 2001 and Hu Jintao's visit in October 2005—to Kim's four visits to China, the imbalance can be attributed to Kim Jong-il's decision to travel whenever he feels the need to.[9]

When President Hu visited Pyongyang in October 2005, all the top leaders of the North Korean government welcomed him at the airport and the streets from the airport to the guest house were lined with hundreds of thousands of cheering citizens. During his visit, Hu invited Kim Jong-il to come to China anytime, and as soon as Hu returned to Beijing, he instructed the International Department to begin preparing for a visit immediately.[10]

However, the Chinese had informed the North Korean government that because China had already ceased calling for such old-style mass congregations of citizens, it could not reciprocate with a grand welcome for Kim Jong-il, and the North Koreans understood.[11] Nevertheless, the Chinese made certain that all nine members of the standing committee of the Politburo of the Chinese Communist Party would see Kim while he was in China. Prior to Kim's visit, the North Koreans had dispatched an advance team led by Prime Minister Pak Pong-ju to Shenyang, Shanghai, and some other cities for site visits to state enterprises, special economic zones, electric power facilities, information technology centers, educational institutions, and agricultural areas. It was decided on the basis of the advance team's reports that this time Kim would visit Wuhan, Yichang, Guangzhou, Zhuhai, Shenzhen, and Beijing.

From Shenyang, Kim's train raced to Wuhan, without stopping in Beijing, and arrived at Hankou Station on Wednesday, January 11. Waiting there to welcome Kim were Vice Premier Huang Ju; Wang Jiarui, chief of the International Department; and Yu Zhengsheng, party secretary of Hubei Province. Kim and his entourage stayed at the Donghu Hotel, on the eastern bank of the Yangtze River. On the hotel's premises there used to be a summer villa belonging to Mao Zedong, where Mao once planted a tree with Kim Il-sung.

Early in the morning of Thursday, January 12, Kim's group left Wuchang by car for a four-hour drive to the Three Gorges Dam, which is scheduled to be completed and fully operational in 2009. It is expected that when completed, the dam will generate 104.2 billion kilowatts of power, to be transmitted throughout China. Power has already been distributed to eleven provinces and cities, including Guandong and Sichuan Provinces; after 2009 it will be distributed to other areas, such as Heilongjian and Jilin Provinces. North Korea has hoped that it will receive some of the power to be distributed to Jilin Province. Although there are five power plants in China along the China–North Korea border, only three are in operation.

Kim Jong-il praised the Three Gorges Dam, saying that it was "a gigantic structure, to be recorded in Chinese history."[12] On January 12, Kim's party stayed overnight in Yichang. Looking out from the top of the hotel, Kim saw the city lights glittering below. "I thought Yichang was just a provincial town," he said. "I didn't expect such a big city."[13] Yichang has a population of 1 million.

On the morning of Friday, January 13, Kim's party arrived in Guangzhou. Li Changchun, a member of the Politburo's standing committee, and Zhang Dejiang, party secretary for Guangdong Province, welcomed Kim and his entourage. Zhang is fluent in Korean, and he escorted Kim Jong-il throughout his stay in Guangdong. Zhang had studied at the Faculty of Economics at Kim Il-sung University in the late 1970s, and he also was very knowledgeable about northeast China, having served as party secretary in Jilin Province. It is believed that Zhang escorted Deng Xiaoping to Kim Il-sung University when Deng visited North Korea in 1978. Having Zhang as his escort, Kim Jong-il was very relaxed.[14]

In the afternoon, Kim and his party paid a visit to Zhongshan (Sun Yat-sen) University, Kim's first visit to a university in China. This university is a representative institution of higher education in southern China, having thirty faculties, including faculties of Chinese literature, history, mathematics, and computer science, and twenty-two research institutions. Zhongshan University, with more than 41,000 students, is now one of the largest universities in China, and it enrolls about 700 students from North Korea. That afternoon, Kim Jong-il announced that a university was under construction in Pyongyang (probably a reference to Pyongyang Science and Technology University), and he strongly urged enterprises in Guangdong to invest in North Korea.[15] In the evening, Zhang hosted a reception for Kim and his entourage on a boat on the Pearl River. As the boat moved along the river, Kim and his group enjoyed the view of Guangzhou at night.

On Saturday, January 14, the party visited the Industrial and Commercial Bank of China in Zhuhai to observe its computer system. In the afternoon, they departed for Shenzhen, briefly stopping at Dongsheng Farm Company along the way. The company was started by entrepreneurs in Hong Kong, and it has become well-known for its production of organic vegetables and high-quality fruits.

Kim's last stop was Shenzhen, where on Sunday morning, January 15, Kim visited Yantian Port to observe its container terminal. Yantian has become the world's fourth-largest container terminal; only those in Hong Kong, Singapore, and Shanghai are larger.

No other city in China has developed as much as Shenzhen in the past twenty-five years. When it was designated a special economic zone, Shenzhen was an agricultural city with a population of 300,000. Now, twenty-five years later, its population is 10 million. Under the slogan "Time is money and efficiency is life," it has achieved an average growth rate of 30 percent a year. At present, Shenzhen's GDP is the fourth-highest in China, less than that of only Shanghai, Beijing, and Guangzhou, while its GDP per capita, at US$8,000–$9,000 a year, is China's highest.

In September 2005, during the twenty-fifth anniversary of the establishment of the Shenzhen special economic zone, Premier Wen Jiabao said, "Shenzhen's development has [served to demonstrate and promote] reform, opening up, and economic development of the whole country, and has made important contributions to the smooth reversion of and maintenance of prosperity and stability in Hong Kong and Macao."[16] In many ways, Shenzhen resembles California at the time of the white settlement of the American West. Virtually all the workers in Shenzhen are guest laborers, who account for 80 percent of the entire population. On weekends, large numbers of people from Hong Kong rush into Shenzhen, where, because the price of real estate is astoundingly less than in Hong Kong, some of them have built a house or a second house. On the observation deck on top of Shenzhen's tallest (sixty-nine-story) building are wax statues of Deng Xiaoping and Margaret Thatcher, made after the negotiations between the two concerning the reversion of Hong Kong to the People's Republic of China in 1982. Deng Xiaoping is regarded as the founding father of Shenzhen.

In Shenzhen, Kim Jong-il stayed in the presidential suite at Wuzhou Guest House, a government-owned hotel frequented by foreign VIPs that has a French restaurant, an indoor swimming pool on the ninth floor, and a golf course in front of the hotel. Kim's room, on the eight floor, commands a full view of the golf course, beyond which lies Hong Kong. The two days while Kim was there were fine, cloudless days.

At 10:30 p.m. on January 15, Kim's party left the hotel for Shenzhen's railroad station, the southernmost station on the Jingjiu line and the last station before entering the Hong Kong Special Administrative Region. It has two interconnected sections: one for trains to and from Hong Kong, and the other for trains to and from Guangzhou. It is a spacious, newly renovated structure, somehow resembling a round-the-clock airport. Kim's train quietly started moving, passing through a forest of tall buildings and flying past numerous neon signs, including those of the International Friendship Shop, the Export-Import Bank of China, the China Construction Bank, discount store KTV, and on and on. The train soon entered a canyon of apartment buildings whose windows, shining brightly in the dark night, made them look like the walls of a gigantic honeycomb. Soon enough, the train passed the first station in Dongguan.

Rapid train service covers the distance between Shenzhen and Guangzhou in two hours and between Guangzhou and Beijing in twenty-two hours. But Kim Jong-il's train is heavily armored, and it cannot travel fast.[17] At its speed of 80 kilometers, about 50 miles, per hour, it would take thirty-three hours for Kim's train to arrive in Beijing.

Every detail of Kim Jong-il's activities in Shenzhen was reported, minute by minute, to the top officials at China's Foreign Ministry in Beijing, including such tidbits of information as

> It was clear and sunny in Shenzhen. It is reported that the Chairman of the National Defense Commission looked in the direction of Hong Kong from the top of Wuzhou Guest House. He may have seen the skyscrapers of Hong Kong.[18]

At 8:00 a.m. on Tuesday, January 17, Kim's train arrived at the Fengtai railway station, which is located in a suburb of Beijing. From there the party proceeded through an underground passage to Diaoyutai State Guest House, where they were to stay. Rumor has it that more than ten underground passages connect the guest house with the Fengtai railway station, Beijing airport, and the Zhongnanhai building complex, the party leadership's headquarters. In the morning, Kim had a talk with President Hu Jintao, followed by a luncheon hosted by Prime Minister Wen Jiabao. In the afternoon, Hu Jintao escorted Kim on a visit to the Institute of Crop Research of the Chinese Academy of Agricultural Sciences in Beijing. The academy had cultivated a portion of farmland in North Korea to develop an "organic agricultural production base," and at present, some ten Chinese agricultural engineers from the academy are stationed in North Korea to offer technical advice. (On January 18, the Chinese media reported on this visit as a major event.) In the evening, Hu Jintao hosted a reception in honor of Kim Jong-il, after which Kim and his party left to return to North Korea.[19]

The Chinese stressed that all the visits were arranged at the request of the guest. (However, it is worth noting that a North Korean diplomat later said, "Inasmuch as there were sites that the Chinese wanted us to see and visit, it would have been impolite not to have visited them."[20] Probably he was subtly trying to imply that the Chinese had "suggested" what and when to visit.) However, there were some sites of interest to the North Koreans that they did not visit. For example, the Chinese could not arrange a visit to the border trade area between China and Vietnam, although they did arrange a visit later for another North Korean mission that included Jang Song-thaek, first deputy director of the Metropolitan Construction Division of the Korean Workers' Party, and Foreign Minster Paek Nam-sun.[21] One senior Chinese government official explained why that site was important: "Because North Korea borders China, Russia, and South Korea, it seems beneficial for North Korea to develop border trade."[22] Also not visited was the part of northeast China that borders North Korea. The Chinese explained that because North Korea's premier, Pak Pong-ju, had rigorously observed state enterprises and other facilities in that area, it made sense to have Kim Jong-il concentrate on southern China.[23] However, that area might have been skipped because it was politically too sensitive to invite the supreme leader of North Korea to northeast China, which is home to not only ethnic Koreans but also numerous defectors from North Korea.

SOUTHERN TOUR Á LA DENG ZIAOPING

The Chinese had suggested that Kim visit southern China since the time of Jiang Zemin's visit to Pyongyang in September 2001,[24] and it was reported that President Hu Jintao had also suggested the visit to Kim Jong-il personally when Hu visited Pyongyang in October 2005.[25] The point might have been to capitalize on Deng Xiaoping's tour of the southern cities in 1992, which he had undertaken to accelerate reform and opening after the Tiananmen Square incident, and the resulting Nanxun (Southern Tour) Legacy.

By following in the footsteps of Deng Xiaoping, Kim Jong-il could demonstrate clearly that he was prepared to accept the Chinese arguments for reform and opening. One can speculate that Kim might have intended to communicate to China's leaders that he had been facing resistance from the conservative elements in Pyongyang similar to that faced by Deng from conservatives in Beijing years before.[26]

In the talk between Kim Jong-il and Hu Jintao, Kim praised China's rapid development, saying, "Under the leadership of the Communist Party of China, the People's Republic of China has achieved great successes in the socialist modernization drive with Chinese characteristics."[27] In fact, during his visit to China, Kim repeatedly praised China's development.

Kim Jong-il was accompanied on his visit by five top North Korean leaders: Premier Pak Pong-ju; Kang Sok-ju, the first deputy minister of foreign affairs; Pak Nam-gi, director of the Department of Planning and Finance of the Korean Workers' Party; Ri Kwang-ho, director of the WPK's Department of Science and Education; and Ro Tu-chol, vice-premier for China-DPRK economic relations. The Chinese believed that WPK department directors were higher ranked than cabinet members. Considering that North Korea, as indicated by the members of the North Korean entourage, was interested not only in economic development but also in intellectual development—including education, particularly higher education, and scientific research—the Chinese were pleased with the inclusion of WPK department directors, and they expected North Korea to begin to work seriously to promote its own reform.[28]

Another fact that the Chinese took special notice of was that no military leader accompanied Kim, a fact that they also viewed as "evidence that North Korea is seriously tackling economic reform."[29] In previous visits, Kim had been accompanied by quite a number of military personnel. In January 2001, for instance, Kim was accompanied by some 100 top leaders of various sectors, of whom close to 40 percent were members of the military.[30] In the past he had been accompanied in particular by North Korea's top military leaders, including Jo Myong-rok, first vice-chairman of the National Defense Commission (Kim's first visit); Kim Yong-chun, chief of the general staff of the Korean People's Army (his first, second, and third visits); and Yon Hyong-muk, vice-chairman of the National Defense Commission (his second and third visits).

But in January 2006, not even the shadow of a member of the military could be seen. Standing next to Kim Jong-il was always Premier Pak Pong-ju, who was accompanied in turn by Kang Sok-ju. One might read in this arrangement a message—perhaps that North Korea would advance its efforts toward economic reform and opening and that tensions with other countries would be settled through diplomacy.

It is almost needless to say that the Chinese urged Kim Jong-il to have North Korea return to the six-party talks. The top leaders of China and North Korea had agreed to "consistently maintain the stand of seeking a negotiated peaceful solution to the [nuclear] issue" and to "push forward through sustained joint efforts the process of the six-party talks so as to contribute to the eventual and peaceful settlement of the nuclear issue on the Korean Peninsula." However, Kim Jong-il spoke of "the difficulties lying in the process of the six-party talks," although he also noted that there had been "no change in the DPRK's basic stand of maintaining the goal of denuclearizing the Korean Peninsula, implementing the joint statement issued at the fourth round of the six-party talks, and pursuing a nego-tiated peaceful settlement."[31]

In preparing for Kim's visit in January 2006, North Korea told China that it wished to explore the following three subjects during the visit:

—how to normalize diplomatic relations with the United States, and how to cope with the United States in general

—how to keep out bad external influences while opening up the country

—how the Communist Party should function in an economy in which private enterprises are the main players.

With respect to the third question, a senior member of the Communist Party of Guangdong Province reportedly told Kim:

> In China today, private entrepreneurs are allowed to be members of the Communist Party. When an entrepreneur joins the party, he can secure the trust and confidence of the government and the party, upgrading the value of his business. I recommend this method to you. Even in foreign-capital companies, the Communist Party is very active. A branch of the party is usually the most influential body in a private corporation.

When Kim asked what would happen if a labor union was organized, the cadre replied, "The Communist Party will not allow such a thing."[32]

After Kim's visit to China in January 2006, Chinese leaders shared the impression that Kim Jong-il seemed to be determined at last to tackle the issue of reform in earnest. There was even a rumor going around that Kim was so overwhelmed by China's achievements that he could not sleep and woke up in the middle of the night and asked his Chinese escorts how North Korea could carry out reform like China's.[33]

Kim Jong-il's January 2006 visit to China was his fifth. He went to China for the first time in 1983, accompanying his late father, Kim Il-sung, at the invitation of General Secretary Hu Yaobang. At the time, three or four years had passed since China started on the path to reform and opening, and Kim Jong-il had just turned forty years old. The two Kims used a special train, but the visit was declared to be *neibu fanwen,* an internal and informal affair, and it was not made public. In Beijing, Kim Jong-il had a talk with Hu Yaobang. Kim Jong-il also went to Shanghai and Shenzhen, and in Shanghai he visited the Baoshan steel mill, guided by Hu Yaobang. The trip to Shenzhen was made at Deng Xiaoping's suggestion.[34] But the real reason for the visit was to secure recognition among the Chinese leadership of Kim Jong-il as Kim Il-sung's successor.[35]

However, upon returning to North Korea, Kim Jong-il criticized China's policy of reform and opening up, reportedly infuriating Deng Xiaoping. Added to that was North Korea's involvement in a 1987 terrorist attack in Rangoon, Burma (now Myanmar). The Chinese evaluation of Kim Jong-il, therefore, had been unfavorable for a long time.

THE DECADE WHEN NORTH KOREA LOST EVERYTHING

For North Korea, the 1990s was a lost decade; even more, it was a decade in which North Korea lost everything. In a matter of two or three years, a chain of cataclysmic events took place, one after another: the Tiananmen Square mass protest and crackdown, the end of the cold war, the normalization of diplomatic relations between South Korea and the Soviet Union, and the collapse of the Soviet Union.

Of those incidents, the Tiananmen Square protest and the demise of the Soviet Union were unspeakably shocking to first-generation socialist revolutionaries such as Deng Xiaoping and Kim Il-sung. At that historical juncture, Deng Xiaoping stressed the following principles, which he expressed in a maxim of four lines of four Chinese characters:
—To observe calmly
—To consolidate one's foothold
—To respond with composure
—To hide one's capabilities and bide one's time.
In 1991, Kim Il-sung took a two-week tour of China on his special train. During his visit, Deng Xiaoping shared the above four principles with him, but, according to one Chinese diplomat, Kim Il-sung was no good at following any of them.[36] During the trip he visited Qufu, the birth place of Confucius, as well as Jiangsu Province, the home of Jiang Zemin. This trip to China, which was Kim Il-sung's thirty-ninth, turned out to be his last.[37]

The series of what were for North Korea unexpected, negative events continued with the normalization of diplomatic relations between China and South Korea, the death of Kim Il-sung, and large-scale natural calamities and famine in North Korea. In September 1992, the Korean Central News Agency criticized China as "a defector/traitor that bowed down to imperialism," clearly reflecting North Korea's strong antipathy toward the normalization of diplomatic relations between China and South Korea. In 1994, Kim Jong-il stated, in his paper entitled "Socialism Is Science," "Today traitors to socialism harbor illusions about capitalism and raise their hopes high for economic assistance from imperialists," an obvious jab at China's policy of reform and opening.[38]

After Kim Jong-il succeeded Kim Il-sung, who passed away in 1994, North Korea–China relations became strained even further. One Chinese diplomat explained the difficulty that Kim Jong-il posed for North Korea–China bilateral relations as follows:

Although Kim Il-sung remained culturally connected with China, being able to speak the Chinese language and memorizing a few Chinese poems, Kim Jong-il has no such cultural ties with China. On the contrary, he is deeply suspicious of China. In addition, he is paranoid about losing his power base if economic reforms advance.[39]

Not surprisingly, then, in 1995 there were only three instances of official visits by one side or the other between the two countries, all involving military personnel. One Chinese diplomat said that it had not been unusual for visits to exceed 120 a year during Kim Il-sung's time.[40]

Of all that North Korea lost in the 1990s, perhaps most tragic was the loss of between 600,000 and 1 million people to a famine caused by misplaced policy and ideology.[41] The famine was due more to structural than to environmental reasons. The public distribution system virtually collapsed.[42] People were abandoned. Survival of the fittest, the politically connected, was ruthlessly pursued.

Throughout the 1990s, the economy continued to stagnate, and the growth rate was negative for nine years straight. Over the decade the North Korean economy confronted "four difficulties and four stagnations": a food shortage, an energy shortage, a raw materials shortage, and a foreign currency shortage, plus a low company operating rate, low labor productivity, low technological capacity, and low commodity supply capacity.[43]

It was only after Kim Yong-nam, president of the Presidium of the Supreme People's Assembly, visited China in 1999 that bilateral relations between the two countries started to show signs of improvement. In March 2000, Kim Jong-il suddenly visited the Chinese embassy in Pyongyang to meet the Chinese government's special envoy Dai Bingguo, the head of the International Department of the CCP. The meeting was regarded as groundwork to prepare for Kim's visit to China in May 2000,[44] and it also marked the beginning of a series of North Korean diplomatic initiatives, including efforts to normalize diplomatic relations with European countries and Australia, a summit talk with South Korea, and visits by President Vladimir Putin of Russia, Secretary of State Madeleine Albright of the United States, and Prime Minister Junichiro Koizumi of Japan.

Kim Jong-il's May 2000 visit to China was his first trip overseas since becoming the chairman of the National Defense Commission, and some seventeen years had passed since his last visit to China. When Kim was escorted to Tiananmen Tower by Jia Qinglin, a member of the Politburo and Communist Party secretary of Beijing Municipality, Kim reportedly was so impressed by how the city had changed that he said, "The only thing that has not changed is Tiananmen."[45] Kim also visited the IT industrial complex in Zhongguancun, where he observed a computer factory of the Legend Computers Group (Lianxiang Jituan). It was after this visit that North Korea started emphasizing the IT industry as the center of its economic policies. During Kim Jong-il's talk with President Jiang Zemin, Kim praised the achievements of China's reform and opening policies.[46]

The highlight of Kim's January 2001 trip was his visit to Shanghai. Kim saw evidence of the remarkable development of Pudong District from the top of the Oriental Pearl Tower, which is located in the Pudong New Area special economic zone and at that time was said to be the tallest in Asia. Kim also visited joint ventures of NEC and GM with Chinese firms, as well as a steel mill belonging to Shanghai Baogang Steel Group (formerly the Baoshan steel mill). It should be noted that Kim visited the Shanghai Stock Exchange twice. This time Kim said, "The only thing [in Shanghai] that has not changed is the water of the Huangpu River."[47] He also said, "We will establish special economic zones like that of Shanghai and will induce investments from the South [Korea]."[48] Kim stayed at the Xijiao State Guest House, where VIPs from both within and outside China, including Mao Zedong, Deng Xiaoping, and Queen Elizabeth II, had stayed.

When Kim visited China in April 2004, he visited the model farming villages at Han Cun He in Beijing's Fang Shan District. In a meeting with Kim Jong-il, President Hu Jintao proposed "boosting economic and trade cooperation between the two countries," and Premier Wen Jiabao promised that the "Chinese side would encourage the Chinese enterprises to have mutually beneficial cooperation of different forms with the DPRK side." In other words, China indicated that it would do a great deal more to assist reform in North Korea than it had before.[49]

THE "SOLEMNITY, SENSITIVITY, AND STRATEGIC NATURE" OF THE CHINA–NORTH KOREA BORDER

Of all Kim Jong-il's visits to China, his stay in Shanghai in January 2001 must have had the greatest impact on him. Following that visit, Kim Jong-il decided to launch a full-fledged special economic zone in North Korea. After crossing the Yalu River back into North Korea, Kim Jong-il suddenly decided to get off the train in Sinuiju City and visit a factory there, although it was quite late at night, perhaps because he was thinking of designating Sinuiju City a special economic zone.[50] He went to the top of a high-rise building, enjoying the view of the glittering lights of Dandong, across the river in China. He turned around and gazed momentarily at the North Korea side, which was shrouded in jet-black darkness. Kim Jong-il kept staring into the darkness without saying a word.[51]

During his stay in Shanghai, Kim Jong-il had visited a farm managed by a Chinese-Dutch businessman named Yang Bin. Yang Bin, who was thirty-nine years old at the time, ran a real estate business and frequently commuted between Europe and China on his private jet. In 2002, he occupied the number-two position on *Forbes* magazine's list of China's richest people.[52] He had a replica of the Dutch royal palace in his office in Shenyang. After Kim visited Yang's farm, Yang started to visit Pyongyang frequently. In February 2002, Kim took Yang Bin to Sinuiju City and later decided to put him in charge of developing a special economic zone there. It is said that the decisive factors in Kim's decision were that Yang Bin promised to invest a huge amount of money in the development of the zone and to donate fresh flowers every day to Kumsusan Memorial Palace in Pyongyang, where the remains of Kim Il-sung lay in state.[53]

Instead of a simple special economic zone, Yang Bin proposed creating in Sinuiju City a special administrative district like those of Hong Kong and Macau and giving full legislative, administrative, and judicial powers to its chief executive for fifty years. The North Korean government was not to interfere at all except to handle foreign relations and defense. Yang proposed separating the zone from the rest of the country by a wall, although no visa would be required to enter the zone. The U.S. dollar and Chinese yuan were to be used as currency, and the establishment of casinos would not be prohibited. In other words, the zone would be, to quote Yang, "totally capitalist." And Yang would be the zone's first chief executive.[54]

In September 2002, the North Korean government announced a plan to create such a special economic zone, without having engaged in any prior consultations with China. A week after the announcement, Yang Bin was arrested in China on suspicion of illegal business practices, and in 2003, the Shenyang Intermediate People's Court (the equivalent of a U.S. district court) sentenced Yang Bin to eighteen years in prison. Beijing was concerned about large-scale illegal activities such as "huang, du, du" (prostitution, casinos, and heroin) in the zone.[55] The Chinese were apprehensive about provoking nationalism among ethnic Koreans living in China near the border and having to deal with the corruption and decadence that would be associated with the casinos that Yang was planning to establish.[56] What made China most furious was that the North Korean government had ignored the grave importance of the 1,300-kilometer-long border that it shares with China. To use the expression of a Chinese diplomat, North Korea "did not respect fully the solemnity, sensitivity, and the strategic importance of the China–North Korea border."[57]

In addition to economic issues, the subject of peace and stability on the Korean Peninsula arose during all four of Kim Jong-il's visits to China since 2000. Kim's visit in May 2000 was deliberately set for the eve of the North-South summit talk, probably because Kim Jong-il wished to improve China–North Korean relations in order to improve his foothold and his bargaining position vis-à-vis Kim Dae-jung before the talk.

An underlying factor might have been the threat that North Korea had felt from the United States following the U.S.-led NATO air raid on Belgrade in 1999, during which China's embassy was bombed. Kim Jong-il must have taken into consideration Chinese anger over the bombing.[58]

Kim's visit to China in January 2001 took place just before President George W. Bush was sworn in as president of the United States. Both China and North Korea must have felt uncomfortable about Bush, who advocated a missile-defense system and criticized the Clinton government's policies toward China and North Korea as having been too soft. It was not hard to imagine that by undertaking this visit, Kim Jong-il intended to show off the invincibility of the relations between China and North Korea.

One of the purposes of Kim's April 2004 visit was to celebrate the advent of China's new Hu Jintao government and to consolidate the friendship and cooperation between the two countries with the new leadership in China. After the previous visit, the secret uranium enrichment program in North Korea had been disclosed, triggering the second Korean nuclear crisis. To resolve the crisis, the six-party talks process was initiated, with China to serve as the host; for that reason, Kang Sok-ju began to accompany Kim Jong-il on Kim's visits to China beginning in 2004.

Kim's visit in 2004 took place immediately after U.S. Vice President Dick Cheney's visit to China. Cheney, emphasizing that "time is ticking away" regarding the North Korean nuclear issue, asked China to increase pressure on North Korea. Hu Jintao, after briefing Kim Jong-il about Hu's talk with Cheney, urged Kim to help advance the six-party talks. For his part, Kim Jong-il assured China's leaders that "North Korea will take an active part in the six-party talks with patience and flexibility and make contributions to the progress of the talks"; he also said that "we emphasized the importance of peaceful settlement of the nuclear issue with a final target of denuclearization."[59] According to the English-language version of a Xinhua News Agency report, Kim referred specifically to a "Korean Peninsula ultimately free of nuclear arms" and not to "a nuclear-free Korean Peninsula." That implies that while Kim Jong-il might have made concessions about nuclear arms, he would not give up North Korea's right to develop the nonmilitary use of nuclear power. It also implies that China endorsed Kim's determination in that regard.[60]

The hidden agenda of Kim's January 2006 visit was to discuss the heightened tension between the United States and North Korea regarding money laundering through Banco Delta Asia in Macau and the counterfeiting of money as well as to talk about resuming the six-party talks. Kim's government, interpreting the U.S. investigation and exposure of the money-laundering scheme as a way to facilitate regime change in North Korea, reacted violently to the U.S. investigation. North Korea chose to hide behind China to protect itself from the United States while demonstrating to China that it was determined to launch full-fledged reform and opening.[61] (See chapter 11 of this volume.)

Nevertheless, China's leaders were not fully convinced of Kim Jong-il's resolve. One senior Chinese government official expressed suspicion about North Korea's true intentions, pointing out that after Kim Jong-il came back from China, the North Korean media ceased to refer to reform and opening.[62] Chinese leaders also were told that although Kim Jong-il repeatedly praised China's reform throughout his stay, he almost never discussed any details of the means for reform or asked questions about specific policies.[63]

When Dai Bingguo, China's deputy minister of foreign affairs, met Robert Zoellick, U.S. deputy secretary of state, in Beijing for policy consultations toward the end of January 2006, Dai told Zoellick that Kim Jong-il had led a new delegation to China and that he had asked many questions. But Dai had a cool view on the effect of the visit, saying, "I wonder how much of what he learned here would be really followed up." Dai summarized Kim Jong-il's expressions of interest in reform and opening as being "nothing more than anecdotal expressions"[64]—for example, this utterance attributed to Kim: "I thought that China is a socialist country. But it is full of capitalism all over."[65] The United States heard a hint of Chinese disappointment in North Korea, because, in the words of Philip Zelikow, the counselor of the Department of State who attended the meeting, "they haven't seen the sparks of apparent interest, and all these ideas have not grown into a little fire."[66]

At the same time, though, the Chinese might have felt a sense of déjà vu. It was reported that at the reception hosted by the city of Shanghai in January 2001, Kim Jong-il remarked, "You must be cautious when you revise prices, so that your boat is not overturned."[67] Kim might have sensed that, of all the components of economic reform, the reform of price controls would pose the toughest challenge. During his April 2004 visit to China, Kim never used the term "reform" on formal occasions, although he did not hesitate to use it during informal talks with his Chinese hosts.[68] (A Chinese government official in charge of North Korean affairs later observed that while North Koreans are now allowed to use "reform" in informal discussions, they cannot yet use "market.")[69]

Also during this visit, it was reported that there were "some arguments" between Kim Jong-il, who was enthusiastic about reform, and North Korea's military leaders, who remained negative.[70] That might have been one of the reasons that Kim did not bring along any military leaders when he visited China in January 2006. Reform and opening under a dictatorship was not easy, even for Kim Jong-il, the dictator himself.

NO INTEREST IN THE CHINESE MODEL

Kim Jong-il has refrained from publicly denouncing China's reform and opening since his visit to China in 2000. One senior Chinese Foreign Ministry official later said, "In the 2000–01 period, there emerged in North Korea a tendency to look at China as a model, but a change started to emerge in the North Korean economy beginning in the 2003–04 period."[71] Accordingly, China started to pay more attention to the reform and opening drive in North Korea. Policymakers in China were heard comparing North Korean reform to China's "adjustment" period after the Great Chinese Famine (1959–61) resulting from the failure of the Great Leap Forward policy or to the dawn of China's own reform, when Deng Xiaoping, after having been purged during the Great Cultural Revolution, reemerged toward the end of the 1970s.

In August 2005, Vice Foreign Minister Wu Dawei took a six-hour drive with his staff from Pyongyang to Dandong, China, via Sinuiju. In Pyongyang, they saw privately owned restaurants and markets in which all types of goods were freely exchanged. Wu wondered whether what he was seeing was similar to conditions in China during the "adjustment" period in the early 1960s or to those at the beginning of reform and opening in the late 1970s. He came to feel that the North Korean situation was more comparable to the latter.

In 1993 Wu had accompanied Vice Foreign Minister Tang Jiaxuan when Tang traveled from Pyongyang to Dandong by car, together with Sha Zukang, who later became Chinese ambassador to Switzerland, and Li Bing, who later became ambassador to South Korea. Throughout the trip, they never saw even the shadow of a dog, a fact that they attributed to the severity of the food shortage in North Korea; in contrast, during Wu's 2005 trip, numerous dogs appeared along the way. At about the midpoint of the trip, Wu found a market and got out of the car to walk around. He noticed a girl eight or nine years old and a boy of five or six eating what appeared to be box lunches. After Wu had a stroll through the market, he saw that the box lunches that the girl and boy had disposed of still had some food left in them. Impressed, Wu and the party talked among themselves, "Maybe the food supply has improved a little bit?"[72]

Another thing that caught Wu's attention during the drive to Dandong was the presence of seemingly idle uniformed soldiers everywhere he went, and he wondered whether that was a result of North Korea's "military first" policy. Some members of the Chinese delegation remembered a similar phenomenon in China during the Great Cultural Revolution. When public order was in flux, the government used the military as a last resort to maintain stability, a formula that apparently was being applied in North Korea. The soldiers might therefore be serving more as deterrents to internal turmoil than to threats from outside the country.

When Chinese people consider present-day North Korea, they have a tendency to view the country in terms of how China was and how it is now. Whenever Hu Jintao introduces Kim Jong-il to other Chinese leaders, he calls Kim "comrade," and the Chinese media often show Hu and Kim in a somewhat theatrical embrace.

As one Chinese think tank researcher said, such scenes make the Chinese "look back to their own past, as if through a time capsule" and "compare present-day North Korea with China in those days." The researcher continued:

> When we think of the Great Leap Forward, severe famine, the Great Cultural Revolution, and "Down to the Countryside," we are struck with how we could survive those times, which shifts to the self-imposed question of how we could come this far despite those obstacles, which in turn slides to the question whether North Korea can manage and advance reform as well as we have.[73]

Regarding that question, Chinese officials who have been involved with Asian affairs, particularly Korean Peninsula affairs, including those at the Foreign Ministry, have replied, as if in a chorus:

—The problem of the North Koreans is that they cannot do reform and opening simultaneously in North Korea's existing difficult external situation. But a reform-only strategy will kill rather than revive the North Korean economy. Possessing nuclear weapons makes it more dangerous rather than safer for the North Koreans because it isolates them from external markets and resources.[74]

—The younger generation in North Korea may be different, but the mid-level bureaucrats there are not committed to or capable of playing a central role in economic reform. The organizational and bureaucratic obstacles are horrendous. In addition, it will be difficult to promote reform unless Kim overcomes the danger of sabotage by the military. Deng Xiaoping was smart to get full control of the military and to force the old members to retire.[75]

—China was desperate to start it all over again to avoid repeating the tragedy of the Great Cultural Revolution. In fact, if the dismantling of the people's communes is taken into consideration, the reform and opening in the late 1970s constituted de facto regime change. But North Korea does not appear to be prepared to face comparable regime change.[76]

—If the leader who is to promote reform does not have legitimacy, the people will not support reform. Because Deng Xiaoping suffered persecution for his opposition to the Great Cultural Revolution, he gained the trust of the people, who decided to support his reforms, albeit uneasily. But the only source of legitimacy for Kim Jong-il is his late father. It would be extremely difficult to change the regime by criticizing his own father in a heavily Confucian society like North Korea.[77]

—It depends on whether Kim Jong-il is artful enough to do what Deng Xiaoping did in terms of his [post-mortem] evaluation of Mao Zedong. Deng's summary of Mao was that although Mao had been 30 percent wrong, he had been 70 percent right. Can North Korea adopt this method and evaluate only 70 percent of the nation's past achievements as positive?[78]

—Because North Korea had received economic assistance from the Soviet Union, its economy faced tremendous hardship when the Soviet Union collapsed. In the case of China, Soviet assistance had been cut off at a much earlier stage and China had no choice but to be self-reliant.[79]

—In the case of China, overseas Chinese have played a great role, particularly through their investments. North Korea does not have an equivalent source of overseas investment.[80]

Kim Jong-il himself frequently commented on which developmental model would be most appropriate for North Korea. In their fall 2000 meeting in Pyongyang, Kim and U.S. Secretary of State Madeleine Albright had a few exchanges about the term "opening." Kim Jong-il was heard to say that "opening means different things to different countries. We do not accept the Western meaning of opening. Opening should not harm our traditions." Kim continued to say he was not interested in the Chinese model of mixing free markets and socialism but that he was intrigued by the Swedish model. When Albright asked about other models, Kim said, "Thailand maintains a strong traditional royal system . . . and yet has a market economy. I am also interested in the Thai model."[81]

Kim's remarks regarding Sweden and Thailand can be viewed as a sideshow act. The important message was that he was not interested in the Chinese model. But realistically speaking, the only model that North Korea can emulate, aside from the South Korean model, which is politically incorrect, is the Chinese model. In fact, North Korea must be anxious to learn "reform and opening" from China, and yet it is difficult for North Korea to admit that outright. After all, it has advocated the ideology of *juche* (self-reliance), and it is understandably reluctant to be viewed as a copy of a foreign country. A North Korean diplomat remarked:

> Although we wish to learn from China's experiences, we are not interested in the Chinese model. China itself did not adopt some other country's model in its entirety. Reform in China advanced with different regions emulating different models—that is, Guangdong from Hong Kong, Fujian from Taiwan, Shanghai from Singapore, Shandong from South Korea, and Liaoning from Japan.[82]

The worsening of China–North Korea relations during the late 1980s and early 1990s also must underlie North Korea's hesitation to subscribe to the Chinese model of reform and opening. The Tiananmen Square incident in 1989 brought home to the North Koreans the peril inherent in the Chinese model, and the incident further deepened North Koreans' initial inclination to reject it. Moreover, China's normalization of diplomatic relations with South Korea in 1992 left the North Koreans with a sense of having been betrayed, further strengthening their antipathy toward China. Those events are definitely among the reasons why North Korea prefers to use the terms *adjustment* and *improvement* instead of *reform*.

Despite repeated visits to China by Kim Jong-il, the conservative elements in North Korea, particularly the military, do not hide their aversion to the Chinese model. In May 2005, the *Rodong Sinmun* (Workers' Daily) carried a commentary warning of the danger of introducing the Chinese model: "A cat cannot catch mice after knowing the taste of beef, and a revolutionary cannot engage in revolution after knowing the taste of money."[83]

A Peaceful Environment

Perhaps the largest difference between North Korea's movement toward reform and opening and that of China lies in their respective environments at the time that reform was undertaken, as President Hu Jintao told President Bush during their summit talk in April 2006. When China pursued reform and opening in the late 1970s, it had already improved its relations in general and expanded its economic exchanges, particularly with the United States and Japan, and it was preparing its infrastructure to receive economic assistance (yen loans) from Japan. Motivated in part by its need to counteract the Soviet Union's invasion of Afghanistan, the United States supported China's reform and opening and opened up its own markets for Chinese products in order to pursue strategic cooperation with China. The United States, however, would not provide North Korea with the same privileges.

Moreover, North Korea must constantly be on the alert to threats from the United States. As a result, the North Korean economy is somewhat similar to a wartime economy. North Korea spends close to 30 percent of its national budget on building up its military; that 30 percent has been dominated by the Second Economic Committee (SEC), under the National Defense Commission, which has turned into a dinosaur-like entity. Together with the underground economy, the SEC has worn out the North Korean economy. When Kim Jong-il admitted that it had cost North Korea tens of millions of dollars to carry out the Taepodong missile test, he said:

> Although I was fully aware that our people were not eating properly or living comfortably, I had to allow the funds to be used for the Taepodong test in order to protect the integrity and fate of our country and people and for us to eventually realize our goal of a being "a wealthy nation having a strong army."[84]

Therefore, even if Kim Jong-il truly wishes to advance reform, he will be constantly restricted in that pursuit by the sacred "military first" policy. But where there is no reform, there is no modernization of the military. However, the military fears that if the country proceeds with reform, the military will lose control; therefore, the military will tend to sabotage efforts at reform.

One veteran Chinese diplomat who has long been involved with Korean Peninsula affairs at the Foreign Ministry remarked that "even the North Korean leaders are aware how important a peaceful environment is for economic development. They also are aware of the importance of opening. That is why they so badly wish to normalize diplomatic relations with the United States."[85] Without diplomatic normalization with the United States, there will be no peaceful environment. No peaceful environment, no reform. But a huge barrier has to be overcome first— the nuclear issue.

Perhaps the Chinese senior official who is most trusted by the North Koreans is Dai Bingguo, the deputy minister of foreign affairs. Another Chinese government official related the following attempt by Dai to persuade the North Koreans to give up nuclear weapons:

> Can you survive if you have nuclear arms? The answer must be no. Look at the Soviet Union. So many nuclear arsenals, but it collapsed. In contrast, look at Cuba. It does not have any nuclear arms, but even the United States has given up trying to topple the Castro regime. The United States only waits for Castro to be called by God.[86]

The same government official added that "the best insurance policy for North Korea to maintain its regime is economic development and economic integration with South Korea. If this happens, even the United States cannot take any military action against North Korea." North Korea, however, has its own take on the "logic for denuclearization." As one North Korean diplomat said:

> If China likes denuclearization so much, why did it develop nuclear arms in the first place? Would China say it had to have nuclear arms to develop itself because it had special conditions? Maybe China did not need nuclear arms to develop, either. Why is North Korea different from China? This is what I want to know.[87]

A peaceful environment first, or reform and opening first? Kim Jong-il once commented to Madeleine Albright (as noted in chapter 3) on the path taken in the 1970s by Deng Xiaoping, who, unfettered by fears of external security threats, had been able to "refocus [China's] resources on economic development." Kim maintained that given the proper security assurances from the United States, he would be free to pursue a similar focus, having satisfied North Korea's military that the United States no longer posed a threat. [88]

However, it simply is not true to argue that China had no external threats, because it faced a constant threat from both the United States, until the late 1960s, and the Soviet Union, until the late 1980s. Nonetheless, Kim's remarks revealed the role of politics, particularly bureaucratic politics, which are always at work, even in a totalitarian state.

Bureaucrats struggle to expand their share of the budget and their staff regardless of the political regime. In addition, North Korea operates under special conditions, including its "military first" ideology and the war-readiness that it had been forced to maintain since the Korean War. In fact, within North Korea there has been a conflict between pro-reform technocrats and the conservatives, particularly the military, concerning a peaceful environment and reform and opening.

Technocrats have expected a great deal from the Economic Management Improvement Measures (the so-called July 1 Measures) that were implemented on July 1, 2002. When James Hoare, who was then the British chargé d'affaires to North Korea, heard one of the deputy directors general of the North Korean Foreign Ministry describe the measures as "the most important reform since the birth of the DPRK in 1948," Hoare was impressed by the historic significance attached to the measures. The Foreign Ministry gave the foreign diplomatic corps posted in Pyongyang a briefing about the significance of the measures, a highly unusual occurrence.[89] The Foreign Ministry obviously supported the reform and opening policies.

North Korea was very much looking forward to the visit of U.S. Assistant Secretary of State James Kelly in July 2002, a fact that should be interpreted as a sign of North Korea's wish to link normalization of relations with the United States with the drive toward internal reform and opening. North Korea's resumption of the temporarily interrupted secret negotiations with Japan regarding Prime Minister Junichiro Koizumi's visit to North Korea must have been motivated by the same wish with respect to relations with Japan. The Yellow Sea Incident toward the end of June, however, forced the postponement of Kelly's visit until October. Nevertheless, the North Korean government announced the July 1 Measures as originally planned.[90]

But the July 1 Measures, by raising only prices when there was a shortage of commodities as well as deficiencies in the nation's infrastructure, triggered hyperinflation in North Korea. The boat did not overturn, as Kim Jong-il had feared, but it took on a lot of water. The reform advocates were cornered. To make the situation even worse for the reformers, Kelly's visit in October turned out to involve nothing but tit-for-tat arguments concerning the HEU issue. Kelly's visit, instead of advancing the prospect for normal diplomatic relations between the United States and North Korea, triggered the second nuclear crisis. For the reform advocates, everything went wrong.

Moreover, by August the conservative camp in North Korea had already started, in the newspaper *Rodong Sinmun*, a campaign against those who "hold out their hand for outside help" on the pretext of adapting to a new environment.

It is obvious that they were apprehensive about the advancement of normaliza-tion of relations between Japan and North Korea and economic assistance from Japan.[91] The conservatives likely launched a counteroffensive against the reform advocates after Kelly's visit. What was unforgivable for the conservatives was that even though the reform advocates still subscribed to the "military first" philos-ophy, in their arguments for reform they pointed out the military's lack of eco-nomic productivity and they placed a new emphasis on striking a balance between the military budget/defense industry and the civilian economy. Prior to Kelly's visit, the conservatives clearly had been on the defensive. The reversal of positions after Kelly's visit was, to the conservatives, like manna from heaven.[92]

The reform advocates, of course, fought back. On October 5, 2002, the last day of Kelly's visit, the North Korean media continued to carry commentaries by reform advocates. The *Rodong Sinmun* carried an article that emphasized the need to "carry out economic work in a creative manner in accordance with the changed environment and realistic conditions"; the article made no reference to "military first" ideas.[93] In the latter half of October, a North Korean Foreign Ministry spokesman made the following announcement:

> The Democratic People's Republic of Korea has taken a series of new steps in economic management and has adopted one measure after another to reenergize the economy . . . [T]hese developments contribute in practical ways to peace in Asia and the world, and . . . almost all countries except for the United States have welcomed and hailed them, which is a great encour-agement to the Democratic People's Republic of Korea.[94]

Even so, the conservatives continued their unrelenting attacks on the reform advocates, attacks in which they occasionally became so fierce that they called their opponents "the enemy of the proletariat." An article in the *Rodong Sinmun* in May 2003 stated that at the time of "the 1962 Cuban missile crisis, which . . . serves as a reminder of the 'traitors to the revolution' in the Soviet Union," North Korea decided to "boost military spending in order to develop an independent defense capability." The article tacitly implied that those who insisted on the reduction of the military budget also were "traitors to the revolution."[95]

The North Korean military refers to officials of the Foreign Ministry as "those necktie fellows," as if diplomats were one rank below themselves.[96] On the other hand, Foreign Ministry officials have occasionally called the attention of their for-eign counterparts to the ominous presence of "hardliners" in North Korea, a term that does not require much imagination to define. Sometimes North Korean diplomats even referred to this "ominous presence" in order to gain leverage dur-ing international negotiations. One South Korean diplomat disclosed that he had heard that "twice during bilateral consultation with North Korea at the six-party talks the 'hardliners' within North Korea would not listen to the diplomats."[97]

In a nutshell, how does North Korea perceive a peaceful environment, economic development, and, in particular, the relations between nuclear weapons and reform?

—Does North Korea believe that nuclear weapons will become unnecessary when reform advances?

—Does it intend to abandon nuclear weapons if the United States revises its hostile policies toward North Korea?

—Is talk about reform only lip service? Does North Korea have no real intention of giving up its nuclear program?

—Are the references to the hostile policies of the United States only a pretext? Does North Korea view nuclear weapons as a means to consolidate Kim Jong-il's authority and the power base of the military?

—Does North Korea desire both nuclear weapons and reform?

—Does North Korea intend its nuclear arms to be a deterrent not only to the United States and Japan but also to China and South Korea?

Those are not necessarily "either/or" questions, and the option of pursuing both nuclear development and reform indicates that the respective interests and hidden agendas of the advocates of the two goals partially overlap. For example, the military, too, no doubt finds the economic development of North Korea desirable because economic power is the base of military power. If economic development requires reform, even the military cannot deny outright the need for reform.

Kangsong Taeguk (a powerful and prosperous nation), Kim Jong-il's vision for a future North Korea, identifies economic development as the most important element for realizing such a nation. Kim has said, "When economic might joins with our politico-philosophical power and military might, North Korea can become a powerful and prosperous nation both in name and in substance."[98] The reform advocates also subscribe to the national goal of *Kangsong Taeguk* and stress the importance of developing North Korea's economic power and production capacity as well as adopting reforms that can promote such improvements.

However, now that North Korea's economic power has rapidly deteriorated and intersectoral competition for economic resources has become much more severe, North Korea's leaders are obliged to establish a more clear-cut ordering of priorities in regard to the allocation of resources. It is highly likely that the military is convinced that the only way to guarantee North Korea's survival is to have nuclear arms, a conviction based on their confidence that North Korea can maintain a position of advantage in the nuclear arms race. Moreover, if the reform advocates hope to advance economic reform, it is imperative that they reduce conventional forces. Thus, even they might begin to think that nuclear weapons are a better choice if they cost less than conventional arms. However, a Chinese diplomat long engaged in Asian affairs was highly skeptical of that possibility:

There is no controversy in North Korea over which is more desirable, nuclear weapons or conventional weapons. Its military is convinced that it needs both and that both are essential. As a matter of fact, nuclear development has been a great waste of resources for North Korea. It is not true that nuclear weapons are more cost-effective than conventional arms.[99]

If the threats perceived by North Korea are not confined to a military threat from the United States and also include those of "being economically swallowed by China" and "being merged into South Korea," North Korean nuclear arms might be used as a political weapon against China and South Korea. However, as long as Pyongyang continues its nuclear development activity, there will be a limit to the international community's engagement with North Korea and its isolation will continue.

Reform and opening in North Korea will not necessarily lead to abandonment of its development of nuclear arms, but possession of nuclear arms will certainly obstruct North Korea's reform and opening. One senior Chinese government official who has been deeply involved in the six-party talks process has expressed a note of cautious pessimism in that regard. "As to whether North Korea is prepared to advance economic reform and regime reform or even to abandon its nuclear development program," he said, "I do not think it has made its mind up yet."[100] Similarly, another Chinese diplomat reflected, almost as if to himself:

> I am sure the North Koreans are aware that without denuclearization there will be no normalization of relations with Japan or the United States. Some say that does not matter to those to whom nuclear power is all that matters. They might be correct, but then what will happen to economic reform and sustainable economic growth? If they continue their nuclear arms development program, economic development will be almost impossible. What are they going to do about that?[101]

External Threats, Internal Threats

During the second nuclear crisis, North Korea engaged in some highly complicated behavior. Internally, while reform and opening was being promoted, some factions sabotaged the process, creating chaotic conditions, such as hyperinflation and massive migration, in the nation's economy and society. Externally, the country played hardball and, when rejected, resorted to brinkmanship diplomacy in order to bring the other parties into negotiations. Such conduct clearly reflected the North Koreans' fundamental sense of insecurity. Nuclear weapons are the physical crystallization of their fear and sense of being menaced; moreover, the crystallization process has been underway for more than forty years. In examining diplomatic documents relating to North Korea from Soviet-camp countries during the 1962–86 period, historian Kathryn Weathersby learned that North Korea launched nuclear development activities in 1963.[102] One North Korean engineer from the Mining Institute in Pyongyang boasted to a Soviet specialist, "If we tell our workers . . . that we are taking up such a task [building an atomic bomb], they will agree to work free of charge for several years."[103] In 1967, Kim Il-sung secretly visited Moscow to request Soviet cooperation in the DPRK's nuclear development program, but he was turned down.[104] Weathersby concluded that the fundamental reasons why Kim Il-sung moved toward nuclear development were fear of nuclear attack by the United States and distrust of North Korea's allies, China and the Soviet Union, which he feared might betray North Korea.[105] A senior Chinese Foreign Ministry official in charge of the six-party talks made the following observations concerning the dangers felt by North Korea:

> North Korea is facing two threats. The larger of the two is the military threat from the United States. Although the United States openly says that it has no intention of invading North Korea, it keeps on badmouthing North Korea, including its political leaders. For the North Koreans, the military threat from the United States is real. . . .
>
> The second, smaller threat is the economy. It threatens the country's survival. In the short term, this threat is the much more urgent one. The effects of a military threat can be delayed, but that cannot be done with regard to an economic threat. Inflation does not wait for anyone. The nature and the scope of North Korea's opening will be decided on the basis of which threat seems more urgent.[106]

Fear of the United States became a genetic trait that has been passed on in North Korea since the Korean War. One North Korean diplomat commented:

> The biggest problem for our republic is our relationship with the United States. If we can have stable relations with the United States, we will not need a one-million-strong military force or nuclear weapons. We will have no justification for maintaining them. But, unfortunately, the United States does not want this to happen, because it needs a justification for maintaining its troops in South Korea. In short, the United States wants tension with North Korea.[107]

Initially, North Korea requested the United States to sign a nonaggression treaty but soon learned that that was infeasible; the United States has no intention of abandoning its duty to defend Japan and South Korea in order to enter into a nonaggression treaty with North Korea.[108] North Korea changed its target accordingly, asking instead for a security assurance from the United States. In response, the Bush administration has repeatedly declared since the spring of

2002 that it has no intention of invading North Korea. In fact, as described in chapter 5, during the U.S.–South Korea summit talk in Bangkok in October 2003, President Bush publicly announced that the United States was prepared to provide North Korea with the desired security assurance. However, as James Kelly noted, "after the presidential announcement in Bangkok, the North Koreans almost stopped referring to security assurance. Stashing what they wanted into their pocket, they make light of a security assurance, as if to say the United States now can't and won't attack North Korea."[109] Similarly, one South Korean government official commented, "The North Korean media ignored President Bush's remarks. What was the fuss all about? We were all so disappointed."[110]

As a veteran South Korean diplomat said, "What country in the world, including the United States, wants to invade and occupy North Korea, knowing that it will have to feed 22 million starving people?"[111] But North Korea still suspects that the United States is just hiding its intention to attack North Korea militarily and that the United States has not given up its plan to topple the North Korean regime.

It should be noted that what the senior Chinese official quoted above called "the second threat"—the economic threat—comes mainly from China. The single-lane China–North Korea Friendship Bridge over the Yalu River, used for both trains and motor vehicles, might embody North Korea's sense of threat from China in that regard. Every hour, vehicles departing from the Chinese side and vehicles departing from the North Korean side take turns crossing the bridge. There are few vehicles going from North Korea into China, and almost all the trucks from North Korea have no cargo. In contrast, on the Chinese side a long line of vehicles waits to cross the bridge. Only one vehicle goes over the bridge every minute, reflecting North Korea's reluctance to open its society to China.[112] At present, 80 percent of the trade between China and North Korea is conducted over this bridge.[113] On the Chinese side, facing the mouth of the Yalu, is Dandong (previously Ang dong), the largest of all the border cities in China. Dandong, which has a population of 2.4 million, is a prosperous city, having textile, chemical, and food industries, and it is a key point of traffic between the two nations. The Dandong–Sinuiju area is the most active of the nine border trade centers that China has created. The Dandong side of the Yalu is lined with high-rise buildings, similar to the Bund in Shanghai, and it is full of tourists.

In 2003, the Chinese government began to develop a program to revitalize the old industrial base in the northeastern region, which was a major industrial center during the 1950s and 1960s but had since turned into a rust belt. As outlined by Wen Jiabao in March 2004, the goals of the reform program included restructuring state-owned firms; promoting the private sector; optimizing the industrial mix; and increasing domestic and overseas investment.[114] To further those goals, the Chinese government plans to construct transportation infrastructure, and its plans include providing assistance for modernization of North Korea's portion of the Seoul-Sinuiju Line and resumption of the maritime route between Dandong and Nampo in North Korea.[115]

China's offer of assistance for Sinuiju's development is an extension of China's plan for development for its northeast region. Economic integration between northeast China and the northern part of the Korean Peninsula, which led Imperial Japan in the 1930s to observe that "Manchu and Korea [are] like one entity," is today taking the form of "China and North Korea are like one entity." One after another, general merchandise manufacturers in Dandong have invested in Sinuiju, and, as a result, the latter is quickly becoming a production center for subcontractors. In Dandong, people in Sinuiju are called "*tongsan*-ists." "Tong" stands for money, and "san" stands for people. Put together, the two words convey the idea that people in Sinuiju do anything for money.[116]

With its single lane, the Friendship Bridge seems too narrow for this booming economic center and the region as a whole. As reported in the *People's Daily*, "the proposal on the new bridge over Yalu was first made in 2000 at an annual session of the Ninth National People's Congress, China's top legislature, and the message was then conveyed to the DPRK side through relevant Chinese departments."[117] But North Korea's response was lukewarm. With a grin on his face, one North Korean diplomat offered the following explanation: "We have an ancient legend in Korea that it is bad luck to build a new bridge where an old bridge was." Nor is North Korea very enthusiastic about China's offer to assist in the construction of a highway between Pyongyang and Sinuiju.[118] As one North Korea watcher in the U.S. administration observed, "You can lead a horse to water, but you can't make it drink."[119] North Korea seems to be apprehensive about the difficulty that might result in maintaining the regime. Normally, a threat is perceived as something that comes from the outside. However, the North Korea watcher remarked that in the case of North Korea, what might go on inside is perceived as a more serious threat:

> Insecurity caused by something that goes outside is much more serious than insecurity caused by something that comes inside. In other words, the threat of public order insecurity is more significant than a military threat. In North Korea, the public order authorities might have more say about the construction of a bridge than the military authorities do.[120]

One senior South Korean government official expressed a similar view: "The substance of North Korean insecurity is derived more from its own people than from foreign countries. The North Korean government keeps on stressing the security threat from the United States in order to justify the maintenance of the current regime."[121]

ARMS DO NOT BETRAY

If one were to strip North Korea of its layer upon layer of psychological defenses, one would find at its core the kind of insecurity that is inherent in a dictator and a dictatorship. On April 22, 2004, eight or nine hours after Kim Jong-il's train crossed the Yalu River into North Korea, a huge explosion took place at Ryong-chon station, in North Pyongan Province, destroying trains and killing a large number of people. Located about nine miles (fifteen kilometers) south of the China–North Korea border, Ryongchon is a station on the Pyongyang-Sinuiju Line as well as the terminal of a branch line. The North Korean government issued a statement saying that "an explosion occurred at Ryongchon Railway Station in North Pyongan Province on April 22 due to electrical contact caused by carelessness during the shunting of wagons loaded with ammonium nitrate fertilizer and tank wagons."[122]

However, rumors spread immediately that the blast was an attempt to assassinate Kim Jong-il.[123] Chinese President Hu Jintao was in Boao on Hainan Island to participate in the Boao Forum when the incident occurred, but many of the senior officials of the Communist Party and government who were with Hu immediately rushed back to Beijing. It was said that they returned to Beijing to prepare for possible political upheaval in Pyongyang.[124] The Chinese must have recalled that Kim's visit to China originally had been scheduled for April 28, but on April 18 the Chinese government suddenly received an announcement that Kim would visit China on that very day, causing a stir on the Chinese side.[125]

It is said that Kim Jong-il inspects the North Korean troops some sixty times a year in order to demonstrate his perfect control of the military, but he may do it in order to reassure himself as well.[126] It also is said that when Kim Jong-il inspects troops, the soldiers are ordered to unload their guns.[127] In North Korea, nobody trusts anybody.

When Hwang Jang-yop, former president of Kim Il-sung University and the theoretician of the *juche* philosophy, sought political asylum in South Korea in 1997, Kim Jong-il was heard to say, at a meeting of senior officials of the Korean Workers' Party, "Man betrays man. But arms do not betray man."[128] Kim Hee-sang, who once was a military adviser to President Roh Moo-hyun, recalled that around 1992 he was approached by a senior North Korean military officer with whom Kim Hee-sang had become acquainted through the newly started inter-Korean military talks. In a hushed voice and with a serious expression, the officer told Kim, "I have a proposition to make in case the peninsula is unified, no matter in what form. If North Korea swallows up the South, I will look after your family. If, on the other hand, the South swallows up the North, you will look after my family."[129] That episode implies that even military officers, the very backbone of the North Korean regime, had started worrying about the collapse of the current regime. It had been more than ten years since that conversation took place when Kim Hee-sang recounted it. That makes one wonder whether now Kim Jong-il might regard nuclear arms as the ultimate weapons that would not betray a man—that would not betray *him* in particular—and that would ensure that the military would not betray him.

Kim Jong-il is insecure for another reason—the potentially disruptive issue of someday passing on his power to one of his sons. It is by no means certain that a hereditary system can be maintained. The eldest son of Kim Jong-il is Kim Jong-nam, born to Song Hye-rim, a former actress, in 1971. Kim Jong-nam, having studied in an international school in Geneva and a French school in Moscow in the early 1980s, was expected to become the general manager of the Pyongyang Informational Center after he returned to North Korea in 1989. More details have emerged lately about his lavish life in Macau since his Tokyo Disneyland escapade in 2001 (see chapter 2). In addition to Jong-nam, Kim Jong-il has two other sons, both born to the late Ko Young-hee, a former dancer: Kim Jong-chul (born in 1980), and Kim Jong-woon (born in 1984). Both are still in their twenties.

In 2004 a South Korean diplomat related a rumor that was circulating among the residents of Pyongyang, after first emphasizing that it was only a rumor:

> Recently, a North Korean military leader hesitantly advised Kim Jong-il that it might not be wise to automatically pass his power to one of his sons. He said, "We will protect your family and descendants forever. But your son is very young, and he might have a hard time managing the country. Collective leadership might be the only alternative." In response, Kim Jong-il said, "I do not subscribe to the hereditary system. But what do you think of making my son some kind of a symbol of the nation, like the Japanese emperor?"[130]

If Kim Jong-il wishes to maintain a hereditary system, his position vis-à-vis the military will necessarily be weaker, because he will need the military's endorsement. Moreover, the closer the time gets to the passing of power, the less effective Kim might become in terms of controlling the military. That process might well have started already.

When Kim Jong-il visited China in January 2006, he took his eldest son, Jong-nam, with him.[131] It has been said that Kim Jong-il was also accompanied by another son, Kim Jong-chul.[132] The Chinese, remembering that in 1983 Kim Il-sung took Kim Jong-il on his special train to visit China, tried to see some sign of Jong-nam's future succession in the 2006 visit; in the end, however, they concluded that Jong-nam's presence had nothing to do with the successor issue.[133] A Chinese diplomat observed that "Kim Jong-il has been troubled over the successor issue."[134]

Around the time of Kim Jong-il's train trip to China in January 2006, it was reported that South Korea's former president, Kim Dae-jung, planned to take a train trip to Pyongyang. In fact, Kim Dae-jung had been entertaining the train trip idea for quite some time. He had a dream of reconnecting the railway between North and South Korea and then connecting it to the Siberian Railway in order to create a Eurasian "Iron Silk Road." The first concrete step toward realizing that dream would be to reconnect the 499-kilometer Gyeongui Line between Seoul and Sinuiju, which originally was constructed by Imperial Japan during the Russo-Japanese War to transport procurements from Keijo (now Seoul) to Sinuiju. In 1908, the express train Yun Hee began service between Busan and Sinuiju. After the Yalu bridge was constructed on the Dandong-Sinuiju Line in 1911, the railway company started selling tickets for a Keijo-London trip in 1913 via the Gyeongui Line, the South Manchurian Railway, and the Siberian Railway. But, of course, that was during the Japanese occupation.

Kim Dae-jung envisions a new trans-Korea railway in anticipation of the eventual reunification of the country. When reconnection of the Gyeongui Line was agreed on during the June 2000 North-South summit talk, the first step was taken toward realization of Kim's vision. Construction to reconnect the line was started in September 2002. In September 2003, it was agreed at North-South working-level consultations between military officials of the two nations that a trial reconnection of the main roads should be launched.

While reconnecting the severed railroads has obvious symbolic meaning, Kim Dae-jung's train visit to Pyongyang, if realized, would have political implications. Han Wan-sang, president of the South Korean Red Cross, told reporters, "Ultimately, Kim Dae-jung seems to be saying to Kim Jong-il, 'The railway that I'm coming through on is safe, and you can make a return visit using the same route,'" implying not only the safety of the route, but also political safety.[135]

Kim Dae-jung was determined to persuade Kim Jong-il to accept his plan, saying, "North Korea has no choice other than to live in the international community, abiding by the rules and etiquette of the international community. Even if I am hated for that, there is nobody else but me to say this."[136] There was another matter that Kim Dae-jung wanted to discuss quietly and at length with Kim Jong-il: China. Now, only China shelters North Korea; China is the only country powerful enough to do that. North Korea therefore has no choice but to be embraced by China, but that might not be the wish of North Korea. How did Kim Jong-il envision North Korea's relations with China?[137]

In February 2006, Lee Chul, president of the Korea Railroad Corporation, visited Pyongyang to negotiate with North Korea to expedite the reconnection of the railway between North and South Korea, regarding which progress had been slow. The North Korean response was unfavorable. Lee Chul concluded that

"President Kim Dae-jung's train visit to Pyongyang is technically feasible at any time," but after he returned to Seoul he reported that

> North Korea's railroads are in need of repair and so trains can only run at an average speed of sixty kilometers (thirty-seven miles) per hour on the Gyeongui line and about forty kilometers an hour between Kaesong and Pyongyang. . . . Since the North's Kim Il Sung said in 1994 that the inter-Korean railroad project would bring about $1.5 billion in economic benefits to the North, North Koreans have been paying special attention to it. . . . But the North's military, fearing the country's collapse, is acting negatively.[138]

It is said that North Korea, on hearing Kim Dae-jung's idea to visit Pyongyang by train, suggested that he come directly to Pyongyang by plane. It was rumored that the military was behind the counterproposal.[139]

It had been agreed that the first test run of the reconnection of the main railroads would be held on May 25, 2006. But on May 24, North Korea unilaterally announced its cancellation of the test. North Korea had started preparing to launch missiles instead, and on July 4 it actually launched seven. With that, Kim Dae-jung's dream of making a railway trip on the line between the two Koreas evaporated.

Hong Kong Is In Sight

Kim Jong-il's train trip in January 2006 lasted ten days, and the scenario was virtually the same at every place that Kim's party stayed overnight. Each hotel at which Kim stayed shut out all general guests, and the area around the hotel was made off limits to other people. The hotel's restaurant was forced to close down for the day, and all parties or other events scheduled for the night of Kim's stay were canceled. Fifty automobiles with curtained windows pulled up alongside the hotel. Kim Jong-il, wearing sunglasses and a moss-green jacket, walked briskly into the hotel. Inside the hotel, Kim, surrounded by rings of security guards, headed for the elevator, clapping his hands lightly to acknowledge well-wishers. Outside the special suite where Kim stayed, two North Korean security guards stood on constant alert, and they would not allow any Chinese into the suite. While Kim Jong-il stayed in the hotel, all of its security cameras were covered. Meals were prepared by Kim's own cook, whom he brought along from Pyongyang, and served by three young North Korean women. Kim never went out of his suite except for scheduled formal events. Kim's escorts did not say anything more than the minimum necessary, and they spoke no English. The cameras used by what appeared to be the North Korean press crew were old and extremely large. One witness said, "They were like forty-year-old cameras."[140]

On the evening of January 17, President Hu Jintao hosted a reception welcoming Kim Jong-il at the Great Hall of the People in Beijing. In his address, Kim Jong-il said:

Our long-cherished hope to visit the southern part of the Chinese land has come true at last thanks to your proposal and particular care. . . . Warm hospitality accorded to us by Chinese comrades in Wuhan, Guangzhou, Zhuhai, Shenzhen, and every other place we went and the warm southern climate pleased us, away from intense cold of mid-winter though for a short time.[141]

After the reception, Kim Jong-il and his party headed for the Beijing railway station. The party was seen off by various Chinese officials, including Jia Qinglin, chairman of the Chinese People's Political Consultative Conference. Kim Jong-il had to return to the severe coldness of mid-winter in North Korea. On January 18, Kim's special train crossed the Yalu from Dandong and entered Sinuiju.

Two days later, a senior Chinese government official told a foreign guest, "We were worried about the arrangements for Chairman Kim, because his visit was so close to the Chinese New Year. If we had to adjust the train schedules to accommodate Kim's special train, people might have complained and criticized their leaders. We are so relieved that nothing bad happened." He then added, "As a matter of fact, we thought of taking Chairman Kim to Hong Kong, too. Well, that has to wait for the next time, doesn't it?"[142]

CHAPTER THIRTEEN

THE PENINSULA QUESTION

On October 9, 2006, at 10:36 a.m. local time, the South Korean Ministry of Defense and the National Intelligence Service recorded a 3.58 to 3.7 magnitude explosion in northeastern North Korea. A more detailed analysis by the U.S. National Geological Survey raised the estimate of magnitude to 4.2 on the Richter scale and placed the explosion forty-two kilometers (twenty-six miles) northwest of Kilchu in Hamgyong Province, a remote area approximately 385 kilometers (240 miles) northeast of Pyongyang.[1] The Korean Central News Agency reported that the DPRK had "successfully conducted an underground nuclear test ... at a stirring time when all the people of the country are making a great leap forward in the building of a great prosperous powerful socialist nation."[2]

Before the test, North Korean officials had notified their Chinese counterparts that a test was imminent. The Chinese in turn notified the United States through the U.S. embassy in Beijing. President Bush was informed by Stephen Hadley, the national security adviser, that a test was imminent "shortly after 10:00 p.m.," or about thirty minutes after the test had taken place.[3] The following morning, President Bush said in a speech to the nation, "Last night the government of North Korea proclaimed to the world that it had conducted a nuclear test. We're working to confirm North Korea's claim. Nonetheless, such a claim itself constitutes a threat to international peace and security. The United States condemns this provocative act. Once again North Korea has defied the will of the international community, and the international community will respond."[4]

Shortly after Bush's speech, the UN Security Council met to consider action against North Korea.[5] The United States proposed action under chapter 7 of the UN charter, which allows for military action by the council to "restore international peace and security."[6] John Bolton, the U.S. permanent representative to the

UN, noted the unanimity of the meeting that morning: "The entire discussion
. . . took only 30 minutes. . . . No one defended it; no one even came close to
defending it."[7]

On October 3, 2006, a week before the test, North Korea had announced that
it would "in the future conduct a nuclear test."[8] International condemnation
came quickly. On the same day that North Korea made its announcement, Japan's
prime minister, Shinzo Abe, said, "A nuclear test would be unforgivable for Japan
and for the international community."[9] Ambassador Christopher Hill warned,
"We are not going to live with a nuclear North Korea."[10] The United States and
Japan agreed to seek a statement from the UN Security Council condemning
North Korea for its announcement.

On October 4, the following day, the Security Council urged in a presidential
statement, which is nonbinding, that "the Security Council deems that, should
the DPRK carry out its threat of a nuclear weapon test, it would jeopardize peace,
stability and security in the region and beyond."[11]

While China's rebuke of North Korea was stronger than usual, calling the test
"flagrant," they still rejected the U.S. call for tough action against North Korea.[12]
In the midst of the negotiations in New York, China sent Tang Jiaxuan, a state
councilor and former foreign minister, to the White House in an attempt to
soften the U.S. approach.[13] Amendments proposed by Japan prohibiting North
Korean ships and planes from entering any ports were dropped, but the Japanese later enacted tough unilateral sanctions against North Korea.[14] Both the Chinese and the Russians were sensitive to U.S. proposals for inspections at sea
and at North Korea's borders because the first plan would require U.S. Navy
operations very near Chinese and Russian waters, while the latter would include
checks on their shared borders with North Korea.[15] Despite their restraint,
this time both conceded to invoking chapter 7 of the UN Charter, although they
had refused to do so under Resolution 1695, regarding North Korea's July 2006
missile test.

On October 14, the Security Council unanimously adopted Resolution 1718,
which demands that North Korea refrain from further tests, abandon its ballistic missile programs, and terminate its nuclear programs in a "complete, verifiable, and irreversible manner."[16] Negotiations took only six days, representing the
council's stronger consensus on this resolution than on Resolution 1695.

The following week, the United States dispatched Secretary of State Condoleezza Rice to Northeast Asia to help diffuse rising tensions and bring North
Korea back to the six-party talks.[17] China, for its part, dispatched a delegation led
by Tang Jiaxuan to Pyongyang on October 19. The delegation met with Kim
Jong-il—his first meeting with foreigners after the test—and "conveyed to Kim
Jong Il a personal message from Hu Jintao."[18] Kim reassured Tang that, despite
rumors, North Korea was not preparing for a second nuclear test.[19]

Nearly two weeks after the test and a day after Tang's visit, on October 20, North Korea celebrated its nuclear test, holding a rally in Kim Il-sung Square, with "a hundred thousand servicepersons and citizens from all walks of life."[20]

The six-party talks had failed. It was clear now that the new process had not prevented North Korea from developing a nuclear weapon; even worse, the talks may have inadvertently helped North Korea accelerate its pitch.

"A Great Leap Forward"

The nuclear test followed North Korea's missile test three months earlier. The missile test was a harbinger of the nuclear test—in a way, a dress rehearsal. At 3:32 a.m. on July 5, 2006, North Korea had launched a ballistic missile over the Sea of Japan/East Sea. It launched six more missiles later that morning and another one at 5:22 p.m. North Korea had been preparing for the launchings for about a month. Near the end of June, China's premier, Wen Jiabao, had requested self-restraint on the part of North Korea, announcing that "China expects North Korea to refrain from taking measures that would worsen the situation." Behind the scenes, Vice Foreign Minister Wu Dawei summoned Choe Jin Su, North Korea's ambassador to Beijing, three times to communicate "China's position, stance, and views," but North Korea avoided giving a solid reply. On July 6, a North Korean Foreign Ministry spokesman announced the launching of the missiles. It was only one hour before the public announcement that the North Korean ambassador notified Wu Dawei of the launching—in another attempt by North Korea to "humiliate" China. China requested an explanation from North Korea, but Pyongyang remained silent.[21]

In the announcement by the Foreign Ministry spokesman, North Korea described the launching as "part of the routine military exercises staged by the KPA to increase the nation's military capacity for self-defence."[22] North Korea claimed that therefore the launchings were not subject to restrictions under any international agreements, including the Japan-DPRK Pyongyang Declaration, which provided for a moratorium on missile launchings. Furthermore, North Korea warned the international community that it would continue its missile-launching exercises in the future and that any attempt to force North Korea to cease its launchings would be answered with stronger measures.[23] Japan proposed issuing a UN Security Council resolution that included sanctions against North Korea in accordance with chapter 7 of the UN charter. The United States endorsed the Japanese proposal, but China, South Korea, and Russia did not, although both China and South Korea expressed strong regret about the launchings.[24]

But both China and South Korea found it more problematic that some Japanese members of the Diet referred to the need to make a preemptive military strike against the North Korean missile base. Jiang Yu, a spokesperson for the

Chinese Foreign Ministry, strongly criticized their comments, calling them "extremely irresponsible."[25] And when U.S. Assistant Secretary of State Christopher Hill flew to Beijing twice to consult with the Chinese government immediately after the missile launching, he realized that "China was more alarmed by the developments in Japan than by the North Korean missile launching itself."[26]

On July 9, South Korea's Office of the President posted this statement on its website: "No defense authority in the region announced a state of emergency, because the missiles were aimed at no particular country. There is no reason to fuss over this from the break of dawn like Japan is doing."[27]

On July 11, the Blue House issued the following statement criticizing the Japanese arguments for a preemptive strike: "They reveal the militant nature of Japan, which warrants our intense vigilance . . . these grave and threatening statements endanger peace in Northeast Asia. [Japan is trying to] justify the militarization of Japan."[28] South Korea was strongly opposed to the UN Security Council resolution that Japan and the United States were promoting to impose sanctions against North Korea, insisting that the effectiveness of any such sanctions would be doubtful;[29] accordingly, South Korea lobbied the members of the Security Council to vote against the resolution.[30]

The North Korean missile launchings became a test of China's diplomacy with respect to North Korea. China had been the host of the six-party talks, and when North Korea launched the missiles, China was engaged in groundwork to convene an informal meeting of participants in the talks in Shenyang, in northeastern China. It so happened that Vice Premier Hui Liangyu, a member of the Politburo of the Chinese Communist Party, was scheduled to visit North Korea on July 11 to celebrate the forty-fifth anniversary of the 1961 China-DPRK Treaty of Friendship, Cooperation, and Mutual Assistance, and the Chinese government immediately decided to have Wu Dawei accompany Hui. Wu stood by in Pyongyang for two days, hoping to have a talk with Chairman Kim Jong-il, but the talk never materialized.

It was rumored in Beijing that the North Korean government implied that Wu might be able to see Kim Jong-il if the Chinese monetary authorities would return the North Korean funds that China had confiscated in response to the earlier money laundering incident.[31] China suspected that the missile launching itself was connected to the money laundering incident. A Chinese diplomat later said:

> First, the missile launchings were a clear assertion of North Korea's protest against the U.S. countermeasures to the money laundering. Second, the launchings reflect the fact that the North Korean military could no longer endure waiting. The DPRK military thinks that it has already waited for seven long years (since the Taepodong launch in 1998), and it must have

decided that the current North Korea–U.S. confrontation provided an ideal opportunity to test launch its missiles.[32]

When Wu Dawei met Kim Gye-gwan during his visit to Pyongyang, Wu once again communicated China's "grave concern" about the North Korean missile launchings and asked North Korea to commit itself to abstaining from further missile launching tests; returning to the six-party talks; and abiding by the joint statement of the fourth round of the six-party talks in September 2005. But North Korea did not make its position clear.[33] At times the conversation between Wu Dawei and Kim Gye-gwan grew highly tense:

Wu: This kind of conduct goes against the long friendship between North Korea and China.

Kim: We base every action on the principle of our being a sovereign state. As a sovereign state, we are allowed to develop and test missiles. Friendship has nothing to do with that principle.

Wu: Friendship is a very basic principle. It is an important principle agreed upon by Chairman Mao Zedong and Chairman Kim Il Sung. You have no right to change this principle unilaterally.

Kim: China should go its own way. We will go our own way. Still, we will survive.

After hearing Kim's last comment, Wu realized that it would be a waste of time for him to stay in Pyongyang any longer.[34] He departed for China in the evening of July 14, one day earlier than originally planned, leaving Hui Liangyu behind. While Wu was in Pyongyang, the Chinese government had been toying with a scenario that involved postponing the vote on the Security Council resolution proposed by Japan and others and diluting the resolution into a nonbinding "chairman's statement," using what Wu would bring back from Pyongyang as leverage. However, that scenario had to be abandoned when Wu brought back nothing from Pyongyang.[35]

The North Korean missile launchings betrayed the limit of China's influence on North Korea. When Guo Boxiong, vice chairman of China's Central Military Commission, visited the United States in late July, he disclosed that "there has been no military-to-military communication between China and North Korea since around the time of the missile launchings. The North Koreans will not even answer our phone calls."[36] At a U.S. Senate Foreign Relations Committee hearing held at around the same time, the chairman, Richard Lugar (R–Ind.), made the following comments:

The North Korean missile tests demonstrated that China's influence over its ally is limited. China had appealed directly to the North Korean government to suspend the missile tests, but Kim Jong-il's regime disregarded these appeals. Now, the missile launches underscored that North Korea has its own agenda, distinct from Beijing's long-term interests.[37]

Moreover, inasmuch as a key assumption of the six-party talks was that China had significant influence on North Korea, the North Korean missile launchings adversely affected the prospects for the success of the talks.

In South Korea, the launchings shook the very foundation of the Roh Moo-hyun government, which had promoted a policy of peace and prosperity with regard to North Korea. ROK Unification Minister Lee Jong-seok declared that "the United States made the greatest number of mistakes," as if to accuse the United States of having cornered North Korea into launching the missiles. When Lee's comment was criticized by the opposition parties and the press, President Roh instructed his cabinet members to reply by asking whether their critics were convinced of the infallibility of the United States.[38] But Yoon Young-kwan, a former minister of foreign affairs and trade, broke his silence for the first time since his resignation to criticize the North Korea policies of both the United States and the Roh government. Yoon said that it was former West German chancellor Helmut Kohl, who had achieved the unification of Germany, who represented the spirit of genuine independence:

> Through close diplomatic ties with the United States, Germany achieved unification by overcoming fears of a united Germany in neighboring countries or former enemies like France, the Soviet Union, Britain, and Poland. [In contrast, selling out our independence] is what our leadership and its activist henchmen do by embracing, at the dawn of the 21st century, the outmoded perception that independence means freeing ourselves from the clutches of big powers. . . . Seoul's North Korea policy must be in line with international currents. Otherwise, both South and North Korea may get lost and become orphans in the international community.[39]

In Japan, the Koizumi government's diplomatic initiative toward normalization of relations with North Korea experienced a further setback. Because North Korea had failed to honor its commitment to "maintain the moratorium on missile launching in and after 2003," the initiative was completely derailed. Koizumi was to step down from his position as prime minister on September 26, and the missile launchings were like an early "salute" to Koizumi by North Korean guns. Immediately before the launchings, the Japanese government had tried—through Mr. X—to dissuade North Korea from launching the missiles. But while the Japanese were imploring, "If the missiles are launched, the Japan-DPRK Pyongyang Declaration will be just a piece of paper," all X could do was sigh.[40]

Koizumi had just visited Washington as a state guest, and during his summit talk with George Bush, Koizumi asked the United States to conduct high-level bilateral talks directly with North Korea. "North Korea is anxious to have a dialogue with the United States," he said. "For a country like North Korea, it is only a direct dialogue between leaders that can move things." Coming from Koizumi, who had visited Pyongyang twice and had succeeded in retrieving the surviving abduction victims, those words were filled with obvious sincerity.

Koizumi continued, "It is the United States, not China, that can settle the North Korean issue. . . . Although China might have some influence on North Korea, we should not forget that the United States does, too. Besides, the relationship between North Korea and China is highly complicated."[41] But Bush remained adamant in his refusal to have a direct dialogue with North Korea. "If we accept a direct dialogue, we will fall into a North Korean trap," he said.[42] "And if the direct dialogue does not work, what are we going to do? We can't think of a good way out."[43] He then added, "We don't want to repeat the mistake of the Clinton government."[44]

During Koizumi's visit, it was speculated that North Korea would launch missiles at any time. Although Koizumi stated his conviction that North Korea would not launch the missiles, Bush was convinced that North Korea would.[45] Koizumi continued to try to persuade Bush to talk with the North Koreans, even while they were aboard Air Force One, on their way to visit Graceland, Elvis Presley's former home. "It took Nixon to visit China and it takes you to have a dialogue with North Korea," Koizumi said.[46] But Bush would not change his mind.

On the morning of the missile launchings, Koizumi, looking a little embarrassed, asked a visitor in his office at the prime minister's residence, "The North launched missiles, didn't they?"[47] He probably ridiculed himself not only for having failed to persuade Bush but also for having remained a spectator of the end of his North Korean initiative, including the move toward normalization of diplomatic relations between North Korea and Japan.

LOST OPPORTUNITIES

The second Korean nuclear crisis was marked by a series of lost opportunities. The greatest lost opportunity for the Bush administration during its first term involved James Kelly's visit to North Korea in October 2002. The administration could have refrained from having Kelly read the talking points on the highly enriched uranium (HEU) issue as if he were delivering an ultimatum and instead have lured North Korea into diplomatic negotiations toward dismantling "all the nuclear weapons and existing nuclear programs," which would have included HEU. In fact, in preparing the joint statement of the fourth round of the six-party talks in September 2005, the United States did not pursue a confrontation on the HEU issue, instead taking the position that the agreements recorded in the joint statement encompassed HEU.

In 2005, the Bush administration decided to apply a more realistic, two-step approach—to have North Korea first give up its plutonium, followed by its uranium. It had taken the administration three years to make that decision. Even before that, the Bush administration should have taken a more pragmatic approach and attempted to amend and supplement the Agreed Framework, instead of just discarding it. The Bush administration's failure to develop the earlier North Korean policy promoted by the Powell-Armitage alliance was a major mistake.

The greatest lost opportunity in the Bush administration's second term was the failure to uphold the joint statement of the fourth round of the six-party talks in September 2005. The United States failed to back the diplomatic expression "to discuss the issue of light-water reactors at a suitable time" with political will. And it was a mistake to include wording in the U.S. closing statement that North Korea could use to its own advantage. Above all, the Bush administration should have been more aware that the joint statement was as fragile as a house of cards.

The Bush administration's North Korea policy, and its foreign policy in general, has been characterized by a pessimism that focuses on the past—that is, it has been a reactive policy rather than one based on future-oriented optimism. Moreover, it has often wobbled. The most typical manifestation of the latter characteristic has been Dick Cheney's "passive-aggressive" politics. Even with respect to such a future-oriented and positive initiative as the six-party talks, the U.S. pursued a regressive approach based on rejection of the bilateral negotiations with North Korea that the Clinton administration had undertaken. Moreover, with respect to the six-party talks, the United States tossed virtually all the responsibility to China.

In the first two years (2005–06) of Bush's second term, none of the State Department's initiatives materialized, including Christopher Hill's plan to visit North Korea and the Korean Peninsula peace-treaty scheme. The prospect of a peace treaty had excited only some senior members of the department before it dwindled away. Meanwhile, any efforts to apply an organized and flexible diplomacy toward North Korea, one suited to the idiosyncrasies of the region, fizzled out. In lieu of diplomacy, the administration pursed only anti–criminal conduct initiatives concerned with preventing the proliferation of weapons of mass destruction and preventing illegal financial transactions.[48]

Powell once described Bush as the "mother of the six-party talks" and his own role as that of "midwife."[49] But the Bush administration has failed to make full use of the strategic opportunities presented by the six-party talks, particularly during Powell's time at the State Department, which were the product of great effort on the part of various parties. In the process of promoting the denuclearization of North Korea, the Bush administration has lacked the pragmatism, imagination, and political flexibility necessary to widen and deepen the links between the alliance structure of the United States and the multilateral framework in Northeast Asia.

Accordingly, the strategic issue of how, in a multifaceted way, to consolidate the U.S. commitment to, and presence for, maintaining the peace and stability of the region has been left in limbo. It should be recognized that strengthening the links between the alliance structure of the United States and the multilateral framework in Northeast Asia would create the environment most conducive to promoting and, if necessary, forcing, the denuclearization of North Korea. It appears that the United States has lost an important part of the reputation and respect—the most important diplomatic assets for any country—that it earned in East Asia in past decades.

At the same time, South Korea, in its quest to pursue too many opportunities at once, seems to have failed to use the opportunities right in front of it. Preoccupied with its own dreams and challenges, the Roh Moo-hyun government has oftentimes lost sight of its foothold—its alliance with the United States and the trilateral cooperation and coordination among itself, Japan, and the United States. Nonetheless, the Roh government has rigorously pursued an active role in order to settle the nuclear crisis. Its pursuit of that role, including its engagement policy vis-à-vis North Korea, will be a positive element in the establishment of peace in Northeast Asia in the future.

It should be remembered that South Korea played a major role in convincing the Bush administration to provide North Korea with a security assurance in the fall of 2003. It was, therefore, ironic and tragic that the Roh government aroused the distrust of the United States and, as a result, damaged U.S.–South Korea relations, despite the great efforts made to strengthen and reorganize the U.S.–South Korea alliance by the dispatch of South Korean forces to Iraq, the relocation of the Yongsan U.S. military base, the downsizing and consolidation of U.S. military bases in South Korea, and the transfer of wartime command authority from the United States to South Korea. Although the United States shares the blame for the deterioration of bilateral relations (because of the words and deeds of Donald Rumsfeld in particular), it must be said that the Roh government has been too opportunistic, as exemplified by its one-time inclination toward the "balancer theory," which was nothing more than a feel-good model of foreign policy based on nationalistic sentiment and wishful thinking.

The Roh government, while declaring that it was continuing President Kim Dae-jung's sunshine policy, in fact destabilized what had been the sunshine policy's very foundation: good relations with neighboring countries and other concerned parties. All the countries involved with the North Korean nuclear issue have been watching South Korea's approach closely to get an indication of the nature of a post-unification Korean Peninsula, the peninsula's future strategic direction, and the future of the peninsula as a whole. South Korea has failed to convince neighboring countries and other concerned parties that South Korea is willing and able to raise, tackle, and overcome the "Peninsula question." South Korea leaves a lot of issues to be dealt with later as "homework," and that inclination might have caused South Korea's greatest loss of opportunities.

Japan also has lost a great opportunity. Prime Minister Junichiro Koizumi failed to consolidate within Japan's political agenda his dramatic initiative toward normalizing Japan–North Korea diplomatic relations. Japan's policy toward North Korea has begun to show schizophrenic tendencies. By working to normalize relations with North Korea, the Koizumi government intended to apply the finishing touch to the process of normalizing relations with other Asian countries that Japan had vigorously pursued during the post–World War II era. What Koizumi had pursued—described as "great peace" by Hitoshi Tanaka when he was director general of the Asian and Oceanian Affairs Bureau at the Ministry of Foreign Affairs and as a "cause" by Teijiro Furukawa, former deputy chief cabinet secretary—was a way for Japan to overcome its own past, to reconcile and live in harmony with its Asian neighbors, and to construct a framework for peace in Northeast Asia.

Unfortunately, however, North Korea's admission of its past abduction of Japanese nationals and its launching of missiles in 2006 led to a backlash in Japan. The Japanese began both to demand greater economic sanctions against North Korea and to expect regime change in North Korea, widening the gap between Japan's approach toward North Korea and that of China and South Korea.[50] The drive to overcome the negative legacy of Japan's pre–World War II days has unintentionally paved the way for a drive to simply reject that legacy. Japan's attempt to "enter Asia" has unintentionally led to a drive to "depart from Asia."

The politics of pursuing Japan's identity (or the politics of restoring Japan to its standing as a "normal country"), seen in the massive backlash after North Korea admitted to the abductions, has also found expression in the prime minister's visits to Yasukuni Shrine and in twisted efforts among some conservative politicians to deny Japan's past. Whatever the personal intentions, conscience, or sincerity of Koizumi as a person, it is beyond doubt that his conduct hurt the national sentiments of Japan's neighbors, particularly China and South Korea. It is equally undeniable that Prime Minister Koizumi's visits to Yasukuni heavily damaged Japan's Asia policy in general.[51]

Japan may have lost many more opportunities than it appeared to lose through its approach to North Korea. Considering that the history of Japan has been gravely influenced by geopolitics on the Korean Peninsula, it will be crucial, in strategic terms, for Japan to reflect on and define what it really has lost.

In contrast, China, perhaps more than any other party, has tried to seize the opportunities that it has been given. Faced with the second Korean nuclear crisis—and in a major shift from its stance at the time of the first—China directly engaged itself in the issue. In contrast to Bush, Roh, and Koizumi, whose increasingly ideological foreign policies have often obstructed efforts to find pragmatic solutions to problems, China's leaders adopted less ideological and more practical policies. When the United States became shaken after the 9/11 terrorist attacks and the Iraq war, its allies began to explore new roles in the "long war" against terrorism and the proliferation of weapons of mass destruction, and a realignment of the U.S.-centered alliance structure began to take place. China, for example, has succeeded in performing, to a certain extent, the stabilizing function in Northeast Asia that the United States performed previously but more recently had given only lax attention. That was the structural factor behind the "outsourcing" to China of primary responsibility for holding the six-party talks. But it remains to be seen whether China can maintain its new role as a stabilizer and, in particular, whether the six-party talks can be firmly institutionalized. China's tacit understanding with the United States that the latter would not bring any new problems to the UN Security Council while the six-party talks process continued has already been broken by North Korea's missile launchings and nuclear test. China had no choice but to endorse the Security Council resolution condemning North Korea.[52]

Moreover, it is still uncertain whether North Korea will dismantle its nuclear weapons and programs. That will depend both on what the United States does and on the domestic political conditions in North Korea. Has North Korea come closer to dismantling its nuclear weapons and programs since China first hosted the six-party talks? Is it possible that North Korea is now even more motivated to develop nuclear weapons because it feels threatened not only by the United States but also by China? Those are questions that China must deal with.

In addition, China's policy toward North Korea has been essentially ambiguous. As Robert Zoellick pointed out, the equilibrium that would enable "status quo forever" on the Korean Peninsula—a balance between concern about North Korea's nuclear weapons on one hand and concern about the collapse of the North Korean regime on the other—cannot last long. Nor can North Korea be freely converted from a strategic asset to a strategic liability and back again as long as need be. Because China's calculated strategic decision to host the six-party talks came after China took into account a number of variables—including the nuclear domino phenomenon, its relations with the United States, its own predominance in Northeast Asia, and the future of the Korean Peninsula—China has to promote its policy toward denuclearization of North Korea while simultaneously paying attention to many other factors. Such strategic ambiguity gives rise to the potential danger of causing the other countries concerned to become suspicious of China's intentions. A nuclearized North Korea would negate both the above-mentioned equilibrium and the strategic ambiguity that China favors. North Korea's nuclear test on October 9 is truly a testing ground for China. China has won a battle but not yet won the war.

A MULTILAYERED CRISIS

Of all the countries that have lost opportunities, North Korea has lost the most. Earlier in this book, I noted that the 1990s was a decade in which North Korea lost everything, but it kept losing opportunities even after the turn of the century. North Korea failed to keep the momentum going on normalization of diplomatic relations with Japan, which it had patiently taken a number of extraordinary steps to achieve, including signing the Japan-DPRK Pyongyang Declaration and even admitting and apologizing for its abduction of Japanese citizens. In the end, even the Pyongyang Declaration was gravely damaged by North Korea's missile launchings.

At the six-party talks, even though the joint statement after the fourth round gave North Korea almost everything that it requested, Pyongyang immediately brought everything back to square one through a Foreign Ministry statement that was highly critical of the United States.

Why did North Korea launch its missiles? When asked for his view at a U.S. Senate hearing, Assistant Secretary of State Christopher Hill gave the following possible reasons:

—to force the United States into serious engagement with North Korea (in order to make the United States lift the financial sanctions against North Korea and resume bilateral negotiations)

—to divert Chinese pressure on North Korea (to prevent economic domination by China and a China-U.S. coalition)

—to be treated as a nuclear power (to demonstrate its nuclear deterrence by showing off its delivery capability)

—to appease the North Korean military, whose influence is growing (an indication of Kim Jong-il's reduced control of the military, due to the prospective father-to-son transfer of power).

In addition to those reasons, Hill referred to the trauma that North Korea has suffered: "History's already happened. It's over. And you can imagine if there's a trauma there. I mean, you can imagine how they feel about that, and so how do they catch up? They catch up with a sort of super weapon."[53] The subsequent nuclear test reveals perhaps even more poignantly this kind of reasoning.

Thus, the North Korean nuclear crisis is an expression of a deep identity crisis on the part of North Korea—which has been left behind by the world, by the times, by history itself—as well as a regime crisis. That might be what Yoon Young-kwan meant when he described North Korea as an orphan. What is alarming is that North Korea has chosen to express its sense of loss and alienation by obtaining nuclear weapons. What is even more alarming is that North Korea appears to be convinced of its own comparative advantage in the "race of terror"; that is how strong its fetish for nuclear weapons has become. But, in fact, the world's other nuclear powers, such as the United States, China, and Russia, are no different from North Korea in terms of their obsession with nuclear capability. And the more the United States and others emphasize the virtues of the Libyan model, the more North Korea will stick to the Pakistani model.

In chapter 10 I referred to a track-two conference held in New York in 2005 on the North Korean nuclear issue—a conference that proved to be the turning point in efforts to convene the fourth round of the six-party talks. When a U.S. administration official who participated in the conference saw more than 100 journalists waiting for the arrival of Li Gun, director general of the American Affairs Bureau of North Korea's Foreign Ministry, at a reception hosted by Henry Kissinger at the exclusive 21 Club in Manhattan, he became convinced that North Korea would never abandon its nuclear weapons or programs. "Does Kissinger invite Li Gun to a reception if North Korea does not possess nuclear weapons?" he asked. "And who would want to report on the arrival of Li Gun at the reception site?"[54]

The same thing can be said about the six-party talks. As James Kelly observed in a Beijing hotel room after the third round of the six-party talks, the multilateral process might have been a double-edged sword. It might have given a sense of empowerment to North Korea, leading it to believe that it was because of its nuclear capability that the other participants in the talks paid North Korea so much attention.[55] The existence of the six-party talks has come to be a safety net for North Korea and its brinkmanship diplomacy—something North Korea does not want to destroy. Accordingly, North Korea will be less inclined to dismantle its nuclear programs, because to do so will deprive it of the six-party talks.

Nuclear proliferation has caused a tectonic change in international politics, where nuclear capability has been the ultimate symbol of power, and that is one source of the recent wobbling and turbulence in the orientation of U.S. foreign policy. To blame only the incompetence and ideological fixation of the Bush administration for the instability is not justified, although those definitely are contributing factors. After the 9/11 attacks, a new element of the war on terror—the connection between terrorists and nuclear arms—emerged in international politics. The North Korean nuclear crisis is, therefore, also a manifestation of the crisis in the nuclear situation of the United States and of the world as a whole.

The second Korean nuclear crisis is a strange crisis. Although no one, including the United States, openly declares that there is a crisis, all the countries concerned have contributed to deepening it. The reason that the United States has avoided acknowledging that a crisis exists is its fear of being trapped by North Korean brinkmanship. South Korea has not done so because of its fear of being criticized for the failure of its policy to bring peace and prosperity to the Korean Peninsula. In the case of China, it has loathed being asked to put more pressure on North Korea. While all of these countries have tried to avoid openly recognizing the existence of the crisis, North Korea has used the crisis to its advantage.

Once the six-party talks were instituted to address the crisis, North Korea created another crisis, on the very stage set by the six-party talks. During the five rounds of the talks, however, the five other countries never, not even once, took a concerted step toward settling the North Korean nuclear issue. We have already observed how Japan, South Korea, and the United States are losing their sense of commonality and solidarity.

Hence the six-party talks have drifted. Meanwhile, the international environment surrounding Northeast Asia has experienced a historic transformation involving many factors: the rise of China, rapprochement between South Korea and North Korea and the rise of Korean nationalism, Japan's aspiration to become a "normal country," and the U.S. preference for an "alliance of the willing" to settle and manage conflicts (the regionalization and multinationalization of conflict management).

It is essential to construct a regional, multilateral framework for peace and stability in order to prevent Northeast Asia from becoming polarized. The six-party talks process has the potential to become the foundation of such a framework. The joint statement of the fourth round of the six-party talks includes the declaration "The Six Parties committed to joint efforts for lasting peace and stability in Northeast Asia" because, no matter how crude and unrefined that goal might be, it is still the hope and expectation of all the neighboring countries and other countries concerned. Nevertheless, the six participating countries have not been able to take pragmatic steps toward attaining that goal. Particularly serious among the problems that the six-party talks process has failed to address is the structure of the crisis, at the bottom of which lies a profound mutual distrust that is deeply embedded among the nations of Northeast Asia.

Located between a continent and an ocean, the Korean Peninsula has always suffered from the geopolitical liability of its exposure to pressures from neighboring countries. Unable to dispose of the remnants and relics of the cold war and the "hot war" associated with it—the Korean War—it is still permeated by the rule of the jungle. The people of North and South Korea have confronted each other for more than half a century, figuratively dying to be unified but scared to death of being unified. Although the histories of Japan, China, and Korea are highly interwoven and to a large extent inseparable, the countries themselves do not share a vision of peace and order in Northeast Asia, either in their past or for their future. Japan, China, and Korea have been viewing their own histories separately. And when they view the past from their own perspective, the past is even more unpredictable than the future.

The second Korean nuclear crisis is a multilayered affair, one composed of North Korea's identity crisis coupled with a regime crisis, a worldwide crisis with respect to nuclear proliferation, and a crisis of trust among the nations of Northeast Asia, which has become like a cold Balkan Peninsula.

CHRONOLOGY

December 1985: North Korea signs the Nuclear Non-Proliferation Treaty (NPT).

December 1988: First official U.S.–North Korean contacts in Beijing.

September 1990: Formal diplomatic relations between the Soviet Union and South Korea are established.

May 1991: North Korea joins the United Nations (UN).

December 1991: North Korea and South Korea finalize nonaggression agreement and North-South Denuclearization Declaration.

April 10, 1992: North Korea Supreme People's Assembly ratifies International Atomic Energy Agency (IAEA) safeguards agreement.

May 4, 1992: North Korea submits initial inventory of nuclear materials to the IAEA.

August 24, 1992: Formal diplomatic relations between China and South Korea are established.

March 1993: North Korea declares its intent to withdraw from the Nuclear Non-Proliferation Treaty. After eighty-nine days pass, North Korea suspends its withdrawal. (The NPT requires ninety-day notice before a country can withdraw.)

July 8, 1994: Kim Il-sung dies and is succeeded by his son Kim Jong-il.

April 19, 1994: Pyongyang notifies the IAEA that it will de-fuel its reactor at Yongbyan and reprocess the spent fuel into plutonium for weapons.

June 16, 1994: Former U.S. President Jimmy Carter visits North Korea on a private trip to diffuse the mounting nuclear crisis.

October 21, 1994: The Agreed Framework between the United States of America and the Democratic People's Republic of Korea is signed.

February 25, 1998: Kim Dae-jung is elected president of South Korea and initiates his "Sunshine Policy" toward North Korea.

August 31, 1998: North Korea launches a Taepodong missile over the Sea of Japan/East Sea into the Pacific Ocean. The United States initiates a policy review on North Korea.

October 23, 2000: Secretary of State Madeleine Albright visits Pyongyang, becoming the highest-ranking U.S. government official to visit since the Korean War.

January 20, 2001: George W. Bush is inaugurated president of the United States.

March 7, 2001: President Kim Dae-jung visits President George W. Bush at the White House.

March 13, 2001: North Korea cancels ministerial-level talks with Seoul.

June 13, 2001: U.S. special envoy Charles "Jack" Pritchard meets in New York with the North Korean representative to the UN, Hyong-chol Yi, to make arrangements for bilateral talks.

July 6, 2001: Deputy Secretary of State Richard Armitage confirms that North Korea tested a rocket in late June.

August 4, 2001: During a meeting in Moscow with President Vladimir Putin, Kim Jong-il reaffirms his pledge to maintain a moratorium on ballistic missile tests until 2003.

August 13, 2001: Japanese Prime Minister Junichiro Koizumi visits the Yasukuni Shrine in Tokyo.

November 17, 2001: Hitoshi Tanaka, director general of the Asian and Oceanian Affairs Bureau of Japan's Ministry of Foreign Affairs (MOFA), meets secretly with "Mr. X" of North Korea.

February 2002: President Bush visits South Korea.

April 1, 2002: President Bush refuses to certify North Korea's compliance with the Agreed Framework but waives U.S. law prohibiting the United States from funding Korean Peninsula Energy Development Corporation (KEDO).

June 29, 2002: A naval clash between North and South Korea leads to the death of four South Korean sailors and the sinking of a North Korean vessel.

July 2, 2002: The United States cancels a planned visit to North Korea.

July 31, 2002: The U.S.-Japan foreign ministers meeting takes place on the occasion of the ASEAN Regional Forum (ARF) in Brunei.

August 7, 2002: Charles Pritchard, ambassador and special envoy for negotiations with the DPRK and the U.S. representative to KEDO, visits North Korea.

September 17, 2002: Prime Minister Junichiro Koizumi of Japan visits Pyongyang. Japan and North Korea sign the Pyongyang Declaration.

October 3–5, 2002: James Kelly, assistant secretary of state for East Asian and Pacific affairs, visits Pyongyang.

October 16, 2002: Bush signs the Authorization for Use of Military Force against Iraq Resolution of 2002, laying the legal groundwork for an invasion of Iraq.

October 26, 2002: Chinese President Hu Jintao visits President George Bush at his ranch in Texas.

November 8–9, 2002: Trilateral Coordination and Oversight Group (TCOG) meeting takes place in Tokyo.

November 14, 2002: The executive board of KEDO announces the suspension of heavy fuel oil deliveries to North Korea.

November 29, 2002: The IAEA adopts a resolution calling on North Korea to "clarify" its "reported uranium enrichment program." North Korea rejects the resolution.

December 12, 2002: North Korea unfreezes its operation and construction of nuclear facilities.

December 21, 2002: North Korea removes all IAEA surveillance cameras and seals at its nuclear facilities.

December 31, 2002: North Korea expels IAEA inspectors.

January 6, 2003: The IAEA Board of Governors adopts a resolution condemning North Korea's decision to restart its nuclear reactor and resume operation of its related facilities.

January 10, 2003: North Korea announces its withdrawal from the Nuclear Non-Proliferation Treaty, effective January 11.

January 18–21, 2003: Alexander P. Losyukov, deputy foreign minister of Russia, visits Pyongyang.

January 27, 2003: Lim Dong-won, South Korean president Kim Dae-jung's special adviser for foreign, security, and unification policies, visits Pyongyang.

February 5, 2003: North Korea says that it has reactivated its nuclear power facilities.

February 12, 2003: The IAEA finds North Korea in breach of nuclear safeguards and refers the matter to the UN Security Council.

February 24, 2003: North Korea test fires a land-to-ship missile into the Sea of Japan/East Sea.

February 25, 2003: Roh Moo-hyun is sworn in as South Korea's president.

March 2, 2003: Four armed North Korean jets intercept a U.S. Air Force reconnaissance aircraft over the Sea of Japan/East Sea.

March 8, 2003: Vice Premier Qian Qichen of China (former foreign minister); Vice Foreign Minister Wang Yi; Fu Ying, director general of the Foreign Ministry's Department of Asian Affairs; and some others visit Pyongyang.

March 10, 2003: North Korea test fires another surface-to-vessel, anti-ship missile into the Sea of Japan/East Sea.

March 31, 2003: Han Song-ryol, North Korean deputy permanent representative to the United Nations, tells Charles Pritchard and David Straub that North Korea has restarted reprocessing fuel rods.

May 13, 2003: South Korea's president, Roh Moo-hyun, visits Washington, D.C.

April 9, 2003: The UN Security Council expresses concern about North Korea's nuclear program but fails to condemn Pyongyang for pulling out of the Nuclear Non-Proliferation Treaty.

April 23–25, 2003: The United States, North Korea, and China hold trilateral talks in Beijing.

August 27–29, 2003: The first round of six-party talks is held.

October 2, 2003: North Korea announces that it has reprocessed its spent fuel rods.

December 2003: Libya abandons its nuclear program.

February 25-28, 2004: The second round of six-party talks is held.

May 22, 2004: Prime Minister Junichiro Koizumi again visits Pyongyang.

June 23–25, 2004: The third round of six-party talks is held.

July 2, 2004: U.S. Secretary of State Colin Powell meets North Korea's foreign minister, Paek Nam-su.

July 18, 2004: Charles Jenkins arrives in Japan via Indonesia and later reports to a U.S. military installation to face charges.

September 28, 2004: North Korea says that it has turned plutonium from 8,000 spent fuel rods into nuclear weapons.

January 19, 2005: President George W. Bush is inaugurated president for his second term. Condoleezza Rice is nominated secretary of state.

February 10, 2005: North Korea admits that it has nuclear weapons.

February 19, 2005: Wang Jiarui, head of the International Department of the Central Committee of the Communist Party of China, visits North Korea.

April 18, 2005: South Korea says that North Korea has shut down its Yongbyon reactor.

May 1, 2005: North Korea fires a short-range missile into the Sea of Japan/East Sea.

May 11, 2005: North Korea says that it has completed extraction of spent fuel rods from Yongbyon.

May 16, 2005: North and South Korea hold their first talks in ten months.

May 25, 2005: The United States suspends efforts to recover the remains of missing U.S. servicemen in North Korea.

June 22, 2005: North Korea requests more food aid from South Korea.

July 9, 2005: North Korea says that it will rejoin nuclear talks.

July 9, 2005: U.S. Secretary of State Condoleezza Rice begins a tour of the region.

July 26–August 7, 2005: The first session of the fourth round of the six-party talks is held.

September 13–19, 2005: The second session of the fourth round of the six-party talks is held.

November 9–1, 2005: The first session of the fifth round of the six-party talks is held.

January 10–20, 2006: Kim Jong-il visits China.

July 4, 2006: North Korea test fires at least six missiles, including a long-range Taepodong-2. A seventh missile follows the next day.

July 15, 2006: The UN Security Council passes Resolution 1695.

October 3, 2006: North Korea announces that it intends to carry out a nuclear test.

October 9, 2006: North Korea conducts an underground nuclear test.

October 14, 2006: The UN Security Council passes Resolution 1718.

October 16, 2006: North Korea's nuclear test is confirmed by U.S. intelligence officials.

December 18–22, 2006: The second session of the fifth round of the six-party talks is held.

February 8–13, 2007: The third session of the fifth round of the six-party talks is held.

March 19–22, 2007: The sixth round of the six-party talks is held.

Notes

Preface

1. George A. Lensen, *Balance of Intrigue: International Rivalry in Korea and Manchuria, 1884–1899* (Tallahassee: University Presses of Florida, 1982).

2. Joel Wit, Daniel Poneman, and Robert Galluci, *Going Critical: The First North Korean Nuclear Crisis* (Brookings, 2004).

3. "North Korea: Denuclearization Action Plan," U.S. State Department, February 13, 2007 (www.state.gov/r/pa/prs/ps/2007/february/80479.htm).

Chapter One

1. Verbal exchanges in the anteroom at the Paekhwawon Guest House have been reconstructed based on interviews with Junichiro Koizumi in Tokyo (December 20, 2002; October 5, 2005; January 27, 2006; and May 10, 2006), with Shinzo Abe in Tokyo (November 15, 2002, and December 6, 2002), and with other high-ranking government officials who were present, in several locations: Tokyo (September 4, 2002; December 19, 2002; October 27, 2003; September 28, 2004; February 23, 2005; September 6, 2005; October 4, 2005; October 7, 2005; July 22, 2005; April 15, 2006; and October 4, 2006), London (February 7, 2006), and Berlin (February 9, 2006). Also see Hitoshi Tanaka and Soichiro Tahara, *Kokka to Gaiko* (*State and Diplomacy*) (Tokyo: Kodansha, 2005), pp. 51, 53–54.

2. Shinzo Abe, interview, Tokyo, November 15, 2002.

3. Interview with a high-ranking Japanese government official, Tokyo, December 19, 2002, and September 6, 2005; interview with a senior U.S. administration official, Washington, March 13, 2006.

4. Junichiro Koizumi, interview, Tokyo, January 27, 2006.

5. Voice of Korea, formerly known as Radio Pyongyang, is the North Korean international broadcasting service. It broadcasts on shortwave in several languages, including Korean, Chinese, Spanish, German, English, French, Russian, Japanese, and Arabic.

6. Interview with a senior Japanese government official, Tokyo, May 17, 2004.

7. Son Bonson, *Kin Shonichi Tettei Kenkyu* (*A Thorough Study of Kim Jong Il*) (Tokyo: Sakuhin-sha, 2005), pp. 173–74.

8. "Niccho Kaidan no Yaritori" ("Exchanges of the Japan-DPRK Summit"), *Asahi Shimbun,* September 18, 2002.

9. Shinzo Abe, interview, Tokyo, October 31, 2002.

10. Interview with a senior Japanese government official, Tokyo, September 28, 2004.

11. "Niccho Kaidan no Yaritori" ("Exchanges of the Japan-DPRK Summit"), *Asahi Shimbun,* September 18, 2002.

12. Junichiro Koizumi, interview, Tokyo, January 27, 2006.

13. "Niccho Kaidan no Yaritori" ("Exchanges of the Japan-DPRK Summit"), *Asahi Shimbun,* September 18, 2002.

14. Isao Iijima, interview, Tokyo, April 15, 2006.

15. Interview with a Japanese diplomat, Tokyo, October 4, 2005.

16. For a more detailed analysis of the abduction issue, see "Japan and North Korea: Bones of Contention," *International Crisis Group Asia Report 100* (Brussels: International Crisis Group, June 27, 2005).

17. Visits by a prime minister to the Yasukuni Shrine are controversial primarily because of Japan's constitutional separation of religion and state and because the shrine honors fourteen Class A war criminals from World War II who were enshrined in 1978.

18. Masahide Moriyama, "Koizumi Shusho Rokokyo Shisatsu" ("Prime Minister Koizumi Visited Marco Polo Bridge"), *Sankei Shimbun,* October 9, 2001.

19. "Mori Shusho ni mo Hocho Dashin Atta" ("Prime Minister Mori Also Received a Feeler to be Invited to North Korea"), *Asahi Shimbun,* September 1, 2002; "Kitachosen Sakunen Ichigatsu ni wa Junan Shisei" ("North Korea Showed a Flexible Stance Last January"), *Asahi Shimbun* (evening edition), October 12, 2002; Yoshiro Mori, interview, Tokyo, October 5, 2005.

20. Yoshiro Mori and Shigezo Hayasaka, "Mori no Seidan" ("Mori's Frank Talk"), *Shokun* (monthly magazine), December 2002; Yoshiro Mori, interview, Tokyo, October 5, 2005.

21. The "Japanese wives" refers to the 1,861 Japanese women who married Korean men who immigrated to or were brought to Japan before the end of World War II. The women went to North Korea with their spouses from 1959 to 1982.

22. "Kisha no Me: Sugata Kieta Kou Jiseki Daihyo" ("Reporter's Eye: Hwang Chul, Deputy Representative, Disappeared"), *Tokyo Shimbun,* November 1, 2000; "Niccho Kaidan, Kita no Shikake Nin" ("Japan-DPRK Talks: Point Man from the North"), *Sankei Shimbun,* May 16, 2003.

23. Interview with a MOFA official, Tokyo, April 21, 2006; "Niccho Kaidan, Kita no Shikake Nin" ("Japan-DPRK Talks: Point Man from the North"), *Sankei Shimbun,* May 16, 2003.

24. The dialogue between Hitoshi Tanaka and X was reconstructed on the basis of interviews with government officials, including those who were present, in Tokyo (September 9, 2005; January 26, 2006; April 21, 2006; February 7, 2006; April 15, 2006; September 4, 2002; December 19, 2002; October 27, 2003; March 18, 2004; May 17, 2004; July 16, 2004; September 28, 2004; February 23, 2005; October 1, 2005; July 22, 2005; September 6, 2005; September 9, 2005; January 26, 2006; and April 21, 2006) and in London (February 7, 2006; March 30, 2004; and February 5, 2006). Also see "Kensho Koizumi Hocho 1" ("Survey: Koizumis's Visit to North Korea 1"), *Asahi Shimbun,* September 19, 2002, and "Seiji no Genba: Koizumi Gaiko" ("Politics on the Scene: Koizumi's Foreign Policy") a series of twenty-five articles published November 18 to December 24, 2004, in *Yomiuri Shimbun.*

25. Interview with a Japanese diplomat who has long been involved in Japan–North Korea negotiations, Tokyo, April 15, 2006.

26. Interview with a senior Japanese government official, London, March 30, 2004.

27. "Japan Urged to Apologize for Sugishima's Espionage," *Korean Central News Agency,* March 13, 2000.

28. Analysis of a MOFA official who was in charge of Northeast Asian affairs at the time, Tokyo, April 21, 2006.

29. "Arimoto Keiko, 'Kitachosen ni Rachi,' Yodogo Menba Moto Tsuma Kyojutsu" ("'Keiko Akimoto Was Abducted to North Korea,' Testified a Former Wife of a Yodo-go Hijacker"), *Asahi Shimbun,* March 12, 2002.

30. As of the writing of this book, three of the nine hijackers had died, two had returned to Japan to be arrested, and five—Takahiro Konishi, Shiro Akagi, Kimihiro Uomoto (former surname Abe), Moriaki Wakabayashi, and Takeshi Okamoto—are still believed by the Japanese National Police Agency to be in North Korea (although one of them is suspected to have died). The hijackers were members of the "Kyosanto Sekigunha," or the Red Army faction of the Communist League. The goals of the Japanese Red Army are to overthrow the Japanese government and create world anarchy. "Movements of the Japanese Red Army and the 'Yodo-go' Group," in *The Oncoming Threat of Terrorism: The Growing Severity of the International Terrorism Situation* (Toyoko: National Police Agency, 2005) (www.npa.go.jp/keibi/kokutero1/english/0302.html [May 23, 2007]).

31. "Rachi Mondai wa Tanaagesezu" ("I Will Not Shelve the Abduction Issue"), *Asahi Shimbun,* March 13, 2002.

32. "DPRK Ready to Hold Talks with Japan Red Cross Society," *Korean Central News Agency,* March 22, 2002.

33. Hitoshi Tanaka and Soichiro Tahara, *Kokka to Gaiko* (*State and Diplomacy*) (Tokyo: Kodansha, 2005), p. 33; Takashi Kokubu, "Who's Going to Open the Door of North Korea? A Lesson from Koizumi's Visit to Pyongyang," paper presented at the Paul H. Nitze School of Advanced International Studies, Washington, March 9, 2005.

34. For example, according to Professor Ken'ichi Nukaya of Tokyo's Hitotsubashi University, "The total number of laborers forcefully transported to Japan between 1939 and 1945 is estimated to be more than one million." See Yukio Takeda, ed., *Chosen-shi* (*History of Korea*) (Tokyo: Yamakawa Shuppan-sha, 2000), p. 318; *Chosun Ilbo* reported that the estimate was 1,032,684, with 930,081 survivors, 77,603 dead, and 25,000 wounded. See "Seoul Demanded $364 Million for Japan's Victims," *Chosun Ilbo,* January 17, 2005. According to a list presented to the ROK government by the Japanese government after diplomatic relations between the two countries were normalized, the number of Korean military and paramilitary personnel and civilians drafted from the Korean peninsula totaled 480,000.

35. "Hachi Okuen Ouryo Yogi de Chosen Soren Moto Kyokucho Ra Taiho" ("Former Chosen Soren Officials Were Arrested on Suspicion of Embezzlement of ¥800 million"), *Asahi Shimbun,* November 29, 2001; "Shinso: Chogin Jiken" ("True Picture of the Chogin case"), *Sankei Shimbun,* December 20, 2001.

36. Hitoshi Tanaka, "Niccho Kaidan wo Jitsugenshita Otoko no Hatsushuki" ("The First Account of the Person Who Made the Japan-DPRK Summit Happen") *Ronza* (monthly magazine), November 2005.

37. Junichiro Koizumi, interview, Tokyo, January 27, 2006.

38. Interview with a senior Japanese government official, Tokyo, September 28, 2004.

39. Shin Kanemaru, an LDP strongman, led the first trip seeking rapprochement with North Korea in 1990. He was rumored to have told Kim Il-sung that Japan would offer compensation of $8 to $8.5 billion for North Korea. He was severely criticized both in Japan and South Korea. Interview with a senior Japanese government official, Tokyo, November 22, 2005; "Japan and North Korea: Bones of Contention," *International Crisis Group Asia Report 100* (Brussels: International Crisis Group, June 27, 2005), p. 3.

40. Junichiro Koizumi, interview, Tokyo, December 20, 2002.

41. The Japanese government decided to salvage the boat on June 21, and the salvage operation determined that the boat was heavily armed. According to the *New York Times*, "Disguised as a fishing boat, the North Korean vessel carried an impressive arsenal: 2 rocket launchers, 12 rockets, a recoilless rifle, 2 light machine guns, 3 automatic rifles and 6 six grenades. Divers also found an antiaircraft gun and two antiaircraft missile launchers." James Brooke, "Japan Says North Korea Boat in Sea Battle Was a Spy Ship," *New York Times,* October 5, 2002.

42. "Joint Press Release on talks between FMs of DPRK and Japan," *Korean Central News Agency,* July 31, 2002.

43. "Rachi Mondai Kin Soshoki no Ketsudan Unagasu" ("Japan Urged General Secretary Kim to Make Up His Mind on Abduction Issue"), *Nihon Keizai Shimbun,* August 27, 2002.

44. Interview with a senior Japanese government official, Tokyo, September 4, 2002.

45. "Koizumi Shusho Raigetsu Hocho" ("Prime Minister Koizumi Will Visit North Korea Next Month"), *Kobe Shimbun* (evening edition), August 30, 2002; interview with a senior Japanese government official, October 7, 2005.

46. Hitoshi Tanaka, interview, Tokyo, March 18, 2004.

47. "Niigata he Ryoko? Nazono Hitokoto" ("Trip to Niigata? A Mysterious Word"), *Asahi Shimbun,* September 25, 2002.

48. Hitoshi Tanaka and Soichiro Tahara, *Kokka to Gaiko* (*State and Diplomacy*) (Tokyo: Kodansha, 2005), p. 19.

49. The Peace, Friendship, and Exchange Initiative is a government-sponsored program "for the purpose of looking squarely at the past together with various exchange programs geared toward the strengthening of mutual understanding with neighboring Asian nations." See "Outline of the 'Peace, Friendship, and Exchange Initiative,'" Ministry of Foreign Affairs of Japan (www.mofa.go.jp/policy/postwar/outline.html [May 17, 2007]). The Asian Women's Fund is a private-public foundation established in order "to make atonement from the Japanese people to the former 'Comfort Women,' and to try to solve today's problems regarding women's honor and dignity." See "Purpose of Establishment," Asian Women's Fund (www.awf.or.jp/english/about/establish.html [May 17, 2007]). The Asian Women's Fund's mandate expired in March 2007. See "Asian Women's Fund to Be Disbanded amid Sex Slave Debate," *Kyodo,* March 6, 2007.

50. Hitoshi Tanaka, interview, Tokyo, October 27, 2004.

51. Interview with senior Japanese government officials, London, March 30, 2004, and February 6, 2006.

52. Furukawa resigned in September 2003, after serving in that post for eight years and seven months.

53. Yasuo Fukuda, interview, Tokyo, January 30, 2006.

54. Teijiro Furukawa, interview, Tokyo, October 24, 2002.

55. Teijiro Furukawa, *Kasumigaseki Han-Seiki* (*Half a Century at Kasumigaseki*) (Saga: Saga Shimbun-sha, 2005), p. 223; Teijiro Furukawa, interview, Tokyo, April 20, 2006.

56. Teijiro Furukawa, interview, Tokyo, April 20, 2006.

57. Interview with a senior Japanese government official, London, March 30, 2004. The pied piper of Hamelin is a German folk character who, by playing his pied pipe, successfully lured all the rats of the village of Hamelin to a river, where they drowned. Then, angered by the villagers' stinginess in paying him as agreed, he lured all the village's children away.

58. Interview with participants in a meeting at a MOFA vice minister's office, Tokyo, October 24, 2002; April 13, 2006; April 20, 2006; and April 21, 2006.

59. Interviews with senior MOFA officials, Tokyo, April 13 and 20, 2006.

60. Yasuo Fukuda, interview, Tokyo, January 30, 2006.

61. Statement by Prime Minister Tomiichi Murayama, "On the Occasion of the Fiftieth Anniversary of the War's End," Ministry of Foreign Affairs of Japan, August 15, 1995 (www.mofa.go.jp/announce/press/pm/murayama/9508.html [May 17, 2007]).

62. Interview with a senior Japanese government official, Tokyo, July 22, 2004.

63. Interview with a senior MOFA official, Tokyo, November 22, 2005.

64. Soji Takasaki, *Kensho Niccho Kosho* (*A Survey of Japan-DPRK Negotiations*) (Tokyo: Heibon-sha, 2004), p. 175.

65. Interview with a senior Japanese government official, Tokyo, July 22, 2004.

66. Masahiko Komura, interview, Tokyo, April, 21, 2006.

67. Yasuo Fukuda, interview, Tokyo, January 30, 2006.

68. Yasuo Fukuda, interview, Tokyo, July 15, 2004.

69. Interview with a senior Japanese government official, Tokyo, November 22, 2005.

70. Soji Takasaki, *Kensho Niccho Kosho* (*A Survey of Japan-DPRK Negotiations*) (Tokyo: Heibon-sha, 2004), p. 46.

71. Interview with a senior MOFA official, Tokyo, November 22, 2005.

72. Interview with a MOFA official, Washington, May 5, 2006.

73. Interview with a senior Japanese government official, Tokyo, September 28, 2004.

74. Interview with a senior MOFA official, Tokyo, July 22 and September 28, 2004.

75. Tomiichi Murayama, interview, October 27, 2004.

76. Interview with a senior MOFA official, Tokyo, September 9, 2005.

77. James Kelly, interview, Seattle, October 18, 2005; interview with a senior Japanese government official, Tokyo, October 7, 2005.

78. Interview with a Japanese diplomat, Beijing, November 15, 2005.

79. James Kelly, interview, Washington, September 23, 2005.

80. Interview with a senior Japanese government official, Tokyo, July 22 and September 28, 2004.

81. Interview with a senior Japanese government official, Tokyo, January 24, 2006.

82. Interview with a senior Japanese government official, Tokyo, October 7, 2005.

83. Junichiro Koizumi, interview, Tokyo, January 27, 2006.

84. Interview with a MOFA official, London, February 7, 2006.

85. Interview with a senior Japanese government official, Tokyo, March 18, 2004.

86. "Tenken Pyon'yan Sengen II" ("Inspection of the Pyongyang Declaration II"), *Nihon Keizai Shimbun*, September 29, 2002; interview with a MOFA official, Washington, August 1, 2006.

87. Interviews with senior MOFA officials, Tokyo, September 26, 2004, and November 22, 2005.

88. Interview with a senior MOFA official, Washington, October 26, 2005.

89. *Korea Encyclopedia* (Juche 93 [2004]) (Pyongyang: Korea Science and Encyclopedia Publishing House, 2004).

90. Interview with a senior MOFA official, London, February 7, 2006.

91. Interview with a senior Japanese government official, Tokyo, July 22 and September 28, 2004.

92. Junichiro Koizumi, interview, Tokyo, January 27, 2006.

93. Interview with a senior Japanese government official, Tokyo, December 19, 2002, and September 6, 2006.

94. Interview with a senior Japanese government official, Tokyo, September 5, 2005.

95. Interview with a senior Japanese government official, Tokyo, January 23, 2004.

96. Interview with a senior Japanese government official, Tokyo, September 5, 2005.

97. Japan House of Representatives Budget Committee, Record of Proceedings, vol. 10, 155th Ordinary Diet Session, October 24, 2002, p. 27.

98. Interview with a senior Japanese government official, Tokyo, December 19, 2002.

99. Yasuo Fukuda, interview, Tokyo, November 24, 2005.

100. Interview with a senior Japanese government official, Tokyo, July 22, 2005.

101. "Rachi Kaito Tsukon no Seika" ("North Korea's Bitter Response to the Abduction Issue"), *Asahi Shimbun,* September 18, 2002.

102. *Sukuu Kai Zenkoku Kyogikai News* (*Newsletter of the National Association for the Rescue of Japanese Kidnapped by North Korea*), September 20, 2002 (www.sukuukai. jp/houkoku/log/200209/02-09-20-1.htm).

103. For suspicions concerning the list of survivors and MOFA, see Katsuei Hirasawa, "Kokuzoku Tanaka Hitoshi no Boso" ("Uncontrollable Behavior of the Traitor Hitoshi Tanaka"), *Shokun* (monthly magazine), November 2002. Comments regarding the release of Hitomi Soga are from an interview with a senior MOFA official, Tokyo, December 14, 2004.

104. "Tanaka Kyokucho Namida no Toben" ("General Director Tanaka Answered the Questions with Tears"), *Asahi Shimbun* (evening edition), September 26, 2002.

105. "Niccho Kokko Kosho Nijukunichi Saikai" ("Japan-DPRK Talks Will Start on 29th"), *Asahi Shimbun,* October 10, 2002.

106. Yasuo Fukuda, interview, Tokyo, April 19, 2006.

107. "Seiji no Genba: Koizumi Gaiko" ("Politics on the Scene: Koizumi's Foreign Policy"), *Yomiuri Shimbun,* November 27, 2004.

108. Yasuo Fukuda, interview, Tokyo, January 30, 2006.

109. Shinzo Abe, interview, Tokyo, December 26, 2002.

110. Sumio Yamagiwa, *Abe Shinzo Monogatari* (*The Shinzo Abe Story*) (Tokyo: Kodansha, 2003), p. 160.

111. Junichiro Koizumi, interview, May 10, 2006.

112. Interviews with Teijiro Furukawa, Tokyo, April 20, 2006, and a senior government official seconded to the prime minister's office, Tokyo, August 10, 2004.

113. Hitoshi Tanaka and Soichiro Tahara, *Kokka to Gaiko* (*State and Diplomacy*) (Tokyo: Kodansha, 2005), p. 62.

114. Interview with a senior Japanese government official, Tokyo, April 13, 2006.

115. Interview with a U.S. administration official, Washington, April 3, 2006; interview with a senior Japanese government official, Tokyo, January 30, 2006.

116. "Niccho Shonichi wa Heikosen" ("Gap Was Not Narrowed on the First Day of the Japan-DPRK Talks"), *Asahi Shimbun,* October 30, 2002.

117. The dialogue between Tanaka and X was reconstructed on the basis of interviews with senior government officials in Tokyo (May 17, 2004; July 16, 2004; October 7, 2005; and December 14, 2004) and in Beijing (November 15, 2005).

118. Junichiro Koizumi, interview, Tokyo, October 5, 2005.

119. Interview with a senior government official, Tokyo, May 17, 2004.

120. Junichiro Koizumi, interview, Tokyo, October 5, 2005; "Niccho no Mizo, Hiroku Fukaku" ("Gap between Japan and North Korea Remains Wide and Deep"), *Asahi Shimbun,* February 15, 2004.

121. Yasuo Fukuda, interview, Tokyo, January 30, 2006.

122. The second round of six-party talks was held in February 2004.

123. Interview with a MOFA official, Washington, March 13, 2006.

124. Hiroshi Samejima, "Koizumi Shusho ga Tanaka Hitoshi wo Kirenai Riyu" ("Why Can Prime Minister Koizumi Not Dismiss Hitoshi Tanaka?"), *Shukan Asahi* (weekly), March 12, 2004; "Foreign Ministry Spokesman on DPRK Visit of Japanese F.M. Delegation," *Korean Central News Agency,* February 14, 2004.

125. Interview with a senior Japanese government official, Tokyo, September 12, 2005.

126. Interview with a senior Japanese government official, Tokyo, January 26, 2006.

127. Ibid.

128. Interview with a senior MOFA official, Tokyo, September 12, 2005.

129. Interview with a MOFA official, Washington, February 17, 2006.

130. Interview with a senior MOFA official, Tokyo, January 26, 2006.

131. "Kensho: Niccho Rachi Kyogi" ("Survey: Japanese–North Korean Negotiations on the Abduction Issue"), *Mainichi Shimbun,* February 16, 2004.

132. Interview with a senior Japanese government official, Tokyo, February 17, 2004, and October 7, 2005.

133. Jasper Becker, *Rogue Regime: Kim Jong Il and the Looming Threat of North Korea* (Oxford University Press, 2005), p. 141.

134. Junichiro Koizumi, interview, Tokyo, October 5, 2005.

135. The exchanges in the prime minister's office on April 28 were reconstructed on the basis of comments by Koizumi, Fukuda, and others who were present. Junichiro Koizumi, Tokyo (October 5, 2005, May 10, 2006, and January 27, 2006); Yasuo Fukuda, Tokyo (July 15, 2004, November 24, 2005, January 30, 2006, April 19, 2006, July 3, 2006, and July 5, 2006); and others, Tokyo (May 17, 2004, July 16, 2004, and January 24, 2006).

136. Yasuo Fukuda, interview, Tokyo, July 5, 2006.

137. Ibid.

138. Junichiro Koizumi, interview, Tokyo, January 27, 2006.

139. Interviews with Junichiro Koizumi, Tokyo, January 27, 2006, and a senior Japanese government official, Tokyo, May 17, 2004, and July 16, 2006.

140. Interview with a Japanese MOFA official, Washington, March 13, 2006.

141. "Seiji no Genba: Koizumi Gaiko" ("Politics on the Scene: Koizumi's Foreign Policy"), *Yomiuri Shimbun,* December 4, 2004.

142. "Report on Meeting and Talks between Kim Jong Il and Koizumi," *Korean Central News Agency,* May 22, 2004.

143. Interview with a high-ranking Japanese government official, Tokyo, April 13, 2006.

CHAPTER TWO

1. Conversations during the summit meeting have been reconstructed on the basis of interviews with Junichiro Koizumi in Tokyo (May 10, 2006) and several other Japanese participants in Tokyo (February 23, 2005; October 7, 2005; September 6, 2006; December 14, 2004; June 21, 2004; and September 11, 2006), Beijing (July 14, 2006), and Washington (March 13, 2006). Also see "Seiji no Genba Koizumi Gaiko," ("Politics on the Scene: Koizumi Foreign Policy"), *Yomiuri Shimbun,* December 7, 2004; Yoichi Funabashi, "Koizumi Gaiko no Nimensei Mita" ("Two Opposite Directions of Koizumi Diplomacy Revealed"), *Asahi Shimbun,* May 24, 2004.

2. Interview with a senior Japanese government official, Tokyo, April 13, 2006.

3. Kim Chin-kyung, president of Yanbian University of Science and Technology, the first university in China funded and staffed by foreigners, told the author in Yanji, China, on May 18, 2004, that a visitor from North Korea had told him that Koizumi was coming to North Korea to apologize for Japan's past colonization of Korea. President Kim shared his conjecture that people in Pyongyang had heard a rumor to that effect.

4. The World Food Program reported that "in January 2005 there was a declared reduction in rations to an average of 250 grams per person per day—some 40 percent of the internationally recommended minimum calorie intake—from 300 grams. An ostensible revitalisation of the PDS [Public Distribution System] last October to provide an average of 500 grams a day appears to have had very limited success. It coincided with the

imposition of a ban on private trading in cereals that remains in place." See "World Hunger," World Food Program (2007) at www.wfp.org/country_brief/indexcountry.asp? country=408 [May 23, 2007].

5. Regarding Koizumi's food assistance to North Korea and its complications, see Stephan Haggard and Marcus Noland, *Famine in North Korea: Markets, Aid, and Reform* (Columbia University Press, 2007), pp. 139–40.

6. "Kensho 5/22 Niccho Shuno Kaidan" ("An Examination of the May 22 Japan-DPRK Summit Talk"), *Asahi Shimbun,* June 4, 2004.

7. This refers to the "Yodo-go incident," the March 1970 hijacking of Japan Airlines flight 351 from Tokyo to Fukuoka, by the Red Army Faction of the Communist League, as described in chapter 1.

8. Interview with a senior Japanese government official, Tokyo, April 13, 2006.

9. Prime Minister Koizumi briefed President Bush on his conversation with Kim Jong-il during their meeting at the APEC Summit in Santiago, Chile, in November 2004. See "Japan-US Summit Meeting (Summary)" (www.mofa.go.jp/policy/economy/apec/2004/us.html [May 23, 2007]).

10. Interview with a senior Japanese government official, Tokyo, April 25, 2006.

11. "Kurosuappu (Closeup) 2004: Rokkakoku Kyogi Beicho Bimyona Henka" ("Subtle Changes Have Emerged in the U.S.-DPRK Atmosphere in the Six-Party Talks"), *Mainichi Shimbun,* June 24, 2004; interview with a Japanese diplomat, Beijing, November 15, 2005.

12. Interview with a senior Japanese official, Tokyo, April 13, 2006.

13. Charles R. Jenkins, *Kokuhaku* (*Confession*), trans. Makoto Ito (Tokyo: Kadokawa Shoten, 2005), p. 204.

14. Interview with a senior Japanese government official, Tokyo, May 11, 2006.

15. "Soga Hitomi San no Otto Jenkinsu-sanga 'Pekin Saikai' wo Teian" ("Hitomi Soga's Husband Mr. Jenkins Proposed a 'Reunion in Beijing'"), *Asahi Shimbun,* May 25, 2004.

16. Junichiro Koizumi, interview, Tokyo, October 5, 2005.

17. Charles R. Jenkins, *Kokuhaku* (*Confession*), trans. Makoto Ito (Tokyo: Kadokawa Shoten, 2005), pp. 200–01; Jeremy Kirk, "Exclusive Interview: Four Decades in North Korea," *Far Eastern Economic Review,* September 9, 2004.

18. Junichiro Koizumi, interview, Tokyo, January 27, 2006.

19. Mitoji Yabunaka, interview, Tokyo, April 13, 2006.

20. "Kensho 5/22 Niccho Shuno Kaidan" ("An Examination of the May 22 Japan-DPRK Summit Talk"), *Asahi Shimbun,* June 4, 2004.

21. Junichiro Koizumi, interview, Tokyo, January 27, 2006; Hiroyuki Hosoda, interview, Tokyo, November 24, 2005; Ichiro Aizawa, interview, Tokyo, September 28, 2006.

22. Nikazoku Saikai Yorokobi Hikaeme" ("Two Families Reunite with Restrained Joy"), *Asahi Shimbun,* May 23, 2004.

23. "Hatsugen Hihan ni Taishi Rachi Higaisha Kazoku kai ga Kenkaian" ("Association of the Families of Victims Kidnapped by North Korea Issues Its Statement on the Criticisms of Its Remarks"), *Asahi Shimbun* (evening edition), May 25, 2004.

24. "Koizumi Shusho no Hocho wo Shichiwari Hyoka ni Seifu Ando" ("Government Relieved with 70 Percent Public Approval Rate for Prime Minister Koizumi's Visit to North Korea"), *Asahi Shimbun,* May 24, 2004; "Koizumi Shusho Saihocho Hyoka Suru, Rokujuni pasento" ("Public Approval Rate for Prime Minister Koizumi's Second Visit to North Korea Reached 62 Percent"), *Mainichi Shimbun,* May 24, 2004.

25. Junichiro Koizumi, interview, Tokyo, January 27, 2006.

26. Interview with a senior MOFA official, Tokyo, June 21, 2004.

27. Interview with a senior Japanese government official, Tokyo, July 16, 2004; "Seiji no Genba Koizumi Gaiko" ("Politics on the Scene: Koizumi Foreign Policy"), *Yomiuri Shimbun,* December 4, 2004.

28. Interview with a senior MOFA official, Washington, March 13, 2006.

29. Yasuo Fukuda, interview, Tokyo, July 15, 2004.

30. The conversation on board the government plane was reconstructed on the basis of interviews with Koizumi in Tokyo (May 10, 2006), Abe in Tokyo (June 17, 2003), and a few others who knew of the content of the conversation, in Tokyo (September 28, 2004 and January 24, 2006). Also see "Seiji no Genba Koizumi Gaiko" ("Politics on the Scene: Koizumi Foreign Policy"), *Yomiuri Shimbun,* November 30, 2004.

31. Interview with a senior Japanese government official, Tokyo, January 24, 2006.

32. Charles Jenkins and his two daughters went to Japan via Jakarta in July 2004. Jenkins subsequently reported to a U.S. military base in Japan to be court-martialed for desertion and conduct benefiting the enemy. He was found guilty and sentenced to thirty days of confinement in a military jail. Jeremy Kirk, "Exclusive Interview: Four Decades in North Korea," *Far Eastern Economic Review,* September 9, 2004, p. 20; Jim Frederick, "The Long Mistake," *Time,* December 6, 2004.

33. "Kitachosen 'Yokota-san no Ikotsu'" ("North Korea Alleges 'They Are Miss Yokota's Remains'"), *Asahi Shimbun,* November 16, 2004.

34. "Kitachosen Gawa no Setsumei 'Urazuke Kaimu'" ("The North Korean Explanation 'Utterly Groundless'"), *Asahi Shimbun,* December 25, 2004.

35. Nobutaka Machimura, interview, Tokyo, May 10, 2006.

36. Ibid.

37. Junichiro Koizumi, interview, Tokyo, May 10, 2006; "Seifu, Keizai Seisai Ron he no Taisho ni Kuryo" ("Government Faces Difficulties of Dealing with the Economic Sanctions Arguments"), *Asahi Shimbun,* December 11, 2004.

38. Junichiro Koizumi, interview, Tokyo, May 10, 2006.

39. Austin Ramzy, "In Search of Lil' Kim," *Time,* February 8, 2007.

40. Yasuo Fukuda, interview, Tokyo, July 5, 2006.

41. Nobutaka Machimura, interview, Tokyo, September 7, 2006; interviews with senior Japanese government officials, Tokyo, April 14, 2006.

42. Yasuo Fukuda, interview, Tokyo, July 5, 2006.

43. "Tanaka Gaisho Onmitsuri no Taikyo Shiji" ("Foreign Minister Tanaka Recommended Secret Deportation"), *Mainichi Shimbun,* May 24, 2001.

44. Yasuo Fukuda, interview, Tokyo, July 5, 2006.

45. Ibid.

46. Junichiro Koizumi, interview, Tokyo, May 10, 2006.

47. "Tanaka Gaisho Onmitsuri no Taikyo Shiji" ("Foreign Minister Tanaka Recommended Secret Deportation"), *Mainichi Shimbun,* May 24, 2001.

48. Nobutaka Michimura, interview, Tokyo, May 10, 2006. The Japanese government decided to cut its 250,000 tons of grain by half in response to North Korea's "rupture of trust." Interview with a senior Japanese government official, Tokyo, January 26, 2006.

49. See "Famous Japanese Abductee 'Married South Korean,'" *Chosun Ilbo* (English) (http://english.chosun.com/w21data/html/news/200604/200604070024.html). The National Research Institute of Police Science in Tokyo, which failed to extract any DNA from the five samples of remains from North Korea, conducted the initial analysis. However, Professor Tomio Yoshii at Teikyo University tested an additional five samples using a different process. He announced that the samples did not match the DNA of Megumi

Yokota. Later, the British journal *Nature* revealed in an interview with Yoshii that the samples had become contaminated during testing. Later, Yoshii was named head of the Tokyo metropolitan police department. He has refused to speak with reporters, and his position has shielded him from testifying at the Diet. In an editorial, *Nature* was later critical of the handling of the case by the Japanese government, concluding that "Dealing with North Korea is no fun, but it doesn't justify breaking the rules of separation of science and politics." Charges by North Korea that the DNA tests were intended by hardline elements in Japan to derail moves toward improved relations, originally dismissed, have been given credibility by these actions. "Japan and North Korea: Bones of Contention," *International Crisis Group Asia Report 100* (Brussels: International Crisis Group, June 27, 2005).

50. "Seifu Hyoka ni Anshin-kan" ("Government Expressed Its Relief with Public Approval"), *Asahi Shimbun,* September 19, 2002.

51. "Niccho Kosho no Kongetsu Saikai, Sanpi Nibun" ("The Japanese Public Is Split over the Resumption of Japan-DPRK Talks This Month"), *Asahi Shimbun,* October 7, 2002.

52. "Koizumi Shusho Hocho 'Hyoka' Rokujushichi Pasento" ("67 Percent Positive in Prime Minister's Visit to North Korea"), *Asahi Shimbun,* May 24, 2004.

53. Diet of Japan, *Proceedings of 155th Lower House Plenary Session,* as found in *Asahi Shimbun* (evening edition), October 18, 2002.

54. "Niccho Pyonyan Sengen, 'Anzen Hosho' ni Hadoru" ("The Pyongyang Declaration Is Weak on the 'National Security Side'") *Asahi Shimbun,* September 19, 2002.

55. Interview with a North Korean diplomat, April 16, 2006.

56. Interview with a senior Japanese government official, Tokyo, April 21, 2006.

57. Teijiro Furukawa, interview, Tokyo, April 20, 2006.

58. Yasuo Fukuda, interview, Tokyo, November 24, 2005.

59. "Obuchi Shusho Kaiken: Nichibei Shuno Kaidan: Yoshi" ("Gist of Prime Minister Obuchi's Press Conference after the U.S.-Japan Summit"), *Asahi Shimbun,* September 24, 1998; Takaaki Mizuno, "Beikoku ga Iradatsu 'Musenryaku' Nippon" ("Japan without a Strategy: An Irritant to the United States"), *AERA* (weekly), October 26, 1998.

60. Hitoshi Tanaka, interview, Tokyo, September 6, 2006.

61. Yasuo Fukuda, interview, Tokyo, November 24, 2005.

62. Kenji Hiramatsu, "Sori Hocho to Niccho Pyon'yan Sengen Shomei heno Michi" ("The Road Leading to the Prime Minister's Visit to Pyongyang and the Signing of the Japan-DPRK Pyongyang Declaration"), *Gaiko Foramu* (monthly), December 2002.

63. Interview with a senior MOFA official, Tokyo, January 26, 2006.

64. Interview with a senior Japanese government official, Tokyo, July 22, 2005; interview with a senior MOFA official, London, February 7, 2006.

65. James Kelly, e-mail interview, January 4, 2007.

66. Yasuo Fukuda, interview, Tokyo, July 15, 2005, and November 24, 2005.

67. Interview with a senior Japanese government official, Tokyo, October 7, 2005.

68. Chiharu Mori, *Chosen Hanto ha Toitsu Dekiruka (Can the Korean Peninsula Be Unified?)* (Tokyo: Bungei Shunju-sha, 2003), p. 140.

69. Hitoshi Tanaka, interview, Tokyo, October 7, 2005.

70. Interview with a senior Japanese government official, Tokyo, July 16, 2004.

71. Yasuo Fukuda, interview, Tokyo, November 24, 2005.

72. Interview with a MOFA official, Tokyo, September 9, 2005.

73. Interview with a senior Japanese government official, Tokyo, October 7, 2005.

74. Interview with Japanese and U.S. government officials, Tokyo, October 7, 2005.

75. Yasuo Fukuda, interview, Tokyo, November 24, 2005.

76. Yoriko Kawaguchi, interview, Tokyo, November 25, 2005.

77. Junichiro Koizumi, interview, Tokyo, December 20, 2002.

78. Interview with a senior MOFA official, Tokyo, April 12, 2006.

79. Junichiro Koizumi, interview, Tokyo, December 20, 2002.

80. Interview with a senior Japanese government official, Tokyo, October 7, 2005.

81. "Kensho: Koizumi Hocho 2" ("Survey: Koizumi's Visit to North Korea 2"), *Asahi Shimbun,* September 20, 2002.

82. Interview with a senior MOFA official, London, February 7, 2006.

83. Hitoshi Tanaka and Soichiro Tahara, *Kokka to Gaiko (State and Diplomacy)* (Tokyo: Kodansha, 2005), p. 58.

84. Richard Armitage, interview, Washington, January 4, 2006.

85. Ibid.

86. Ibid.; quote as found in John 14:2, English Standard Bible.

87. Interview with a senior Japanese government official, Washington, October 25, 2005.

88. Yoriko Kawaguchi, interview, Tokyo, November 25, 2005.

89. Interview with a senior Japanese government official, Tokyo, March 25, 2003.

90. Interview with a U.S. intelligence officer, Washington, December 12, 2005.

91. Interview with a senior U.S. administration official, Washington, August 17, 2005.

92. Ryozo Kato, interview, Washington, December 9, 2005.

93. Interview with a senior MOFA official, Washington, December 9, 2005.

94. Arata Fujii, interview, Tokyo, August 8, 2003. (Fujii passed away in January 2004.)

95. Robert A. Wampler, ed., *North Korea and Nuclear Weapons: The Declassified U.S. Record* (National Security Archive Electronic Briefing Book 87, April 25, 2003); Department of State, telegram from Secretary Baker to Secretary Cheney (E. O. 12356 Subject: Dealing with the North Korean Nuclear Problem: Impressions from My Asia Trip). Available at http://www.gwu.edu/~nsarchiv/NSAEBB/NSAEBB87/nk16.pdf.

96. Interview with a senior Japanese government official, Tokyo, December 19, 2002; *Sankei Shimbun,* October 2, 1998; Bill Gertz, "Pyongyang Working to Make Fuel for Nukes," *Washington Times,* March 11, 1999.

97. Benjamin A. Gilman. "Gilman Releases North Korea Report," press release, November 3, 1999 (www.nautilus.org/archives/pub/ftp/napsnet/special_reports/NKAG_Report.txt [May 30, 2007]); Randeep Ramesh, "The Two Faces of Rumsfeld," *Guardian,* May 9, 2003; David E. Sanger, "After-Effects: Nuclear Standoff; Administration Divided over North Korea," *New York Times,* April 21, 2003.

98. Interview with a senior Japanese government official, Tokyo, September 6, 2006.

99. Yoichi Nishimura, Washington, "Bei Seikennai Kyokoha Taiwaha no Semegiai" ("The Struggle between Hardliners and Engagers in the U.S. Administration"), *Asahi Shimbun,* September 19, 2002; Conversation with a U.S. Department of Defense official, Washington, July 19, 2005.

100. "DoD News Briefing: Secretary Rumsfeld and Gen. Pace," news transcript, U.S. Department of Defense, September 16, 2002 (www.defenselink.mil/transcripts/2002/t09162002_t0916sd.html [May 30, 2007]).

101. Rumsfeld's memo arguing for regime change in North Korea, with the cooperation of China, was leaked in April 2003. Also see chapter 4 of this volume. Sanger, "After-Effects: Nuclear Standoff."

102. Interview with a U.S. Department of Defense official, Washington, December 22, 2005.

103. Interview with a senior Japanese government official, Washington, August 30, 2004. Also see "Press Conference 24 September 2002," Ministry of Foreign Affairs of Japan, September 24, 2002 (www.mofa.go.jp/announce/press/2002/9/0924.html [May 30, 2007]).

104. Interview with a senior U.S. administration official, Washington, December 27, 2005.

105. Colin Powell, interview, Washington, March 31, 2006; interview with a senior MOFA official, Tokyo, September 9, 2005.

106. Yoriko Kawaguchi, interview, Tokyo, January 30, 2006.

107. Colin Powell, interview, Washington, March 31, 2006.

108. "The United States and Japan: Advancing toward a Mature Partnership," *Institute for National Strategic Studies Special Report,* October 11, 2000 (www.ndu.edu/inss/strforum/ SR_01/SFJAPAN.pdf [May 30, 2007]).

109. Interview with a senor U.S. administration official, Washington, September 23, 2005.

110. James Kelly, interview, Washington, September 23, 2005.

111. Interview with a MOFA official, Washington, January 6, 2006; interview with a U.S. Department of State official, New York, January 9, 2006.

112. Interview with a U.S. administration official, New York, January 9, 2006.

113. Interview with a U.S. intelligence officer, Washington, December 12, 2005.

114. Interview with a U.S. intelligence officer, Washington, December 12, 2005.

115. Interview with a senior U.S. administration official, Washington, December 22, 2005.

116. Interview with a U.S. Department of State official, Washington, December 27, 2005.

117. Interview with a senior Japanese government official, Tokyo, January 24, 2006.

118. Interview with a senior Japanese government official, Washington, August 30, 2004; Conversation with a senior ROK government official, Washington, December 7, 2005.

119. Interview with a senior Japanese government official, Tokyo, December 19, 2002.

120. Lawrence Wilkerson, interview, Washington, September 19, 2005.

121. Stephen Yates, interview, Washington, March 30, 2006.

122. Interview with a U.S. Department of State official, New York, January 9, 2006.

123. Interview with a senior U.S. administration official, Seoul, November 14, 2002.

124. Richard Armitage, interview, Washington, January 4, 2006.

125. James Kelly, interview, Washington, September 23, 2005.

126. Lawrence Wilkerson, interview, Washington, September 19, 2005.

127. Conversation with a senior Japanese government official, Tokyo, February 23, 2005.

128. Hiroshi Hoshi, "Gaiatsu Danomi Mo Furui (Yomitoku Seiji)" ("To Rely on Foreign Pressure Is Obsolete: Anatomy of Politics"), *Asahi Shimbun,* August 21, 2004.

129. Richard Armitage, interview, Washington, January 4, 2006.

130. Interview with a senior Japanese government official, Tokyo, January 23, 2004.

131. Interview with a senior Japanese government official, Tokyo, October 27, 2003.

132. Interview with a senior Japanese government official, Tokyo, January 24, 2006.

133. Interview with a senior U.S. administration official, Washington, August 17, 2005.

134. Interview with a senior Japanese government official, Tokyo, January 24, 2006.

135. Interviews with senior Japanese and U.S. administration officials, Tokyo, January 24, 2006, and Washington, March 13, 2006.

136. Interview with a senior U.S. administration official, Washington, March 13, 2006.

137. Interview with a senior Japanese government official, Tokyo, April 23, 2004.

138. Conversation with a senior Japanese government official, Tokyo, April 24, 2004.

139. Interview with a senior U.S. administration official, Washington, December 12, 2005.

140. Interview with a senior U.S. administration official, Washington, August 22, 2003.

141. Interview with a senior Japanese government official, Tokyo, July 22, 2005.

142. Hitoshi Tanaka and Soichiro Tahara, *Kokka to Gaiko* (*State and Diplomacy*) (Tokyo: Kodansha, 2005), p. 17; Hitoshi Tanaka, interview, Tokyo, December 19, 2003.

143. Yoshihiro Makino and Nobuyoshi Sakajiri, "Kitachosen no Meiro" ("North Korea's Labyrinth"), *Asahi Shimbun,* June 9, 2005; interview with a senior MOFA official, Washington, November 22, 2005.

144. Interview with a senior Japanese government official, Tokyo, December 19, 2003.

145. Interview with a senior Japanese government official, Tokyo, September 4, 2002.

146. Interview with multiple participants, Washington, June 5, 2003, and Tokyo, November 25, 2005.

147. Interview with a senior U.S. government official, Washington, February 24, 2006.

148. Michael Green, interview, Washington, June 5, 2003.

CHAPTER THREE

1. In describing the circumstances surrounding Kelly's group and the North Korean side as well as the U.S. delegates' impressions of the meetings, the author has relied on interviews with James Kelly, Michael Dunn, and other members of the U.S. delegation in Washington on February 24, 2006; May 5, 2006; August 10, 2006; December 27, 2005; March 10, 2004; November 2, 2005; and September 30, 2005.

2. Michael R. Gordon, "Nuclear Arms: For Deterrence or Fighting?" *New York Times,* March 11, 2002.

3. Charles L. Pritchard, *Failed Diplomacy* (Brookings, 2007), p. 38.

4. Article III, section 1 of the Agreed Framework between the United States and the Democratic People's Republic of Korea states, "The U.S. will provide formal assurances to the DPRK, against the threat or use of nuclear weapons by the U.S."

5. Nobuyoshi Sakajiri, "'Noshuku Keikaku Mitometa no ha Yosogai,' Kerii Zen Kokumujikanho Kaiken Yoshi" ("'I Did Not Expect Them to Acknowledge a Uranium Enrichment Program': Excerpts of the Interview with Former Assistant Secretary Kelly"), *Asahi Shimbun,* June 18, 2005.

6. James Kelly, interview, Washington, September 23, 2005.

7. James Kelly, "Mounting Tensions in Northeast Asia: What Are the Deeper Causes?" *Pacnet 23B,* June 10, 2005.

8. James Kelly, "United States to North Korea: We Now Have a Pre-Condition," *Yale Global Online,* December 12, 2002 (http://yaleglobal.yale.edu/display.article?id=566 [June 1, 2007]).

9. "Bei 'Shogekiteki na Kaimonoda'" ("The U.S. Regards It as a 'Shocking Shopping List'"), *Asahi Shimbun,* June 5, 2005.

10. Interview with a senior U.S. administration official, Washington, February 24, 2006.

11. Conversation with a U.S. administration official, Washington, March 10, 2004.

12. Interview with a senior U.S. administration official, Washington, August 10, 2006.

13. Ibid.

14. Interview with a senior U.S. administration official, Washington, March 1, 2006.

15. Michael R. Gordon, "U.S. Concern Rises over North Korea Atom Plant," *New York Times,* October 25, 1989; Joel S. Wit, Daniel B. Poneman, and Robert L. Gallucci, *Going Critical: The First North Korean Nuclear Crisis* (Brookings, 2004), p. 6.

16. Michael Dunn, interview, Washington, March 2, 2006.

17. Interview with a member of the delegation, Washington, February 24, 2006.

18. James Kelly, interview, Washington, May 20, 2006.

19. James Kelly, interview, Washington, May 20, 2006.

20. Interview with a member of the delegation, Washington, November 2, 2005.

21. James Hoare, interview, London, February 6, 2006.

22. James Kelly, interview, Washington, May 20, 2006.

23. James Kelly, U.S. Senate Committee on Foreign Relations, *The North Korean Nuclear Calculus: Beyond the Six Power Talks: Hearing before the Committee on Foreign Relations,* 108th Cong., 2nd sess., March 2, 2004; Kelly, "United States to North Korea: We Now Have a Pre-Condition."

24. James Kelly, interview, Washington, September 23, 2005.

25. Michael Dunn, interview, Washington, March 2, 2006.

26. Don Oberdorfer, "My Private Seat at Pyongyang's Table," *Washington Post,* November 10, 2002. A little later Kim Gye-gwan told Oberdorfer, who was visiting Pyongyang, that he had consulted with top leaders during the coffee break and that they had held an emergency meeting in order to prepare their responses.

27. Interview with a member of the delegation, Washington, April 3, 2006; Kelly, "United States to North Korea: We Now Have a Pre-Condition."

28. Charles L. Pritchard, "A Guarantee to Bring Kim into Line," *Financial Times,* October 10, 2003; interview with a member of the delegation, Washington, November 2, 2005.

29. *North Korea's Weapons Programmes: A Net Assessment* (London: International Institute of Strategic Studies, 2004), p. 14.

30. Youichi Shimada, *Amerika Kitachosen Kososhi* (*History of the Struggle between the U.S. and DPRK*) (Tokyo: Bunshun Shinsho, 2003), p. 105.

31. The full text of the original is as follows:
   III. Both sides will work together for peace and security on a nuclear-free Korean Peninsula.
      1. The U.S. will provide formal assurances to the DPRK, against the threat or use of nuclear weapons by the U.S.
      2. The DPRK will consistently take steps to implement the North-South Joint Declaration on the Denuclearization of the Korean Peninsula.
      3. The DPRK will engage in North-South dialogue, as this Agreed Framework will help create an atmosphere that promotes such dialogue.

32. Interview with a member of the delegation, Washington, September 30, 2005.

33. Interview with a member of the delegation, Washington, March 13, 2006; James Kelly, interview, Tokyo, February 8, 2007.

34. James Kelly, U.S. Senate Committee on Foreign Relations, *The North Korean Nuclear Calculus: Beyond the Six Power Talks: Hearing before the Committee on Foreign Relations,* 108th Cong., 2nd sess., March 2, 2004.

35. Michael Dunn, interview, Washington, March 2, 2006; Charles Pritchard, interview, Washington, August 10, 2005.

36. Michael Dunn, interview, Washington, March 2, 2006.

37. Pritchard, *Failed Diplomacy,* p. 34; Michael Dunn, interview, Washington, March 2, 2006.

38. James Kelly, interview, Washington, May 20, 2006.

39. Charles Pritchard, e-mail interview, May 22, 2007.

40. Interview with a senior administration official, Washington, September 22, 2006.

41. Michael Dunn, interview, Washington, March 2, 2006.

42. James Kelly, interview, Washington, September 23, 2005.

43. Ibid.

44. Interview with a member of the delegation, Washington, August 10, 2006.

45. Interview with a member of the delegation, Washington, August 10, 2006; for an example, see "Chinese Detain Boss of North Korea's Sinuiju," *JoongAng Daily,* October 5, 2002.

46. Interview with a member of the delegation, Washington, August 10, 2006.

47. Interview with a member of the delegation, Washington, February 24, 2006.

48. Interview with a senior South Korean government official, Seoul, October 11, 2005.

49. Interview with a senior South Korean government official, Seoul, October 11, 2005.

50. Interview with a former senior Blue House official, Seoul, October 11, 2005.

51. "U.S. President's Special Envoy Arrives," *Korean Central News Agency,* October 3, 2002.

52. Koichi Kosuge, "Bei Tokushidan Pyon'yan ni Tochaku" ("The U.S. Special Delegation Arrived at Pyongyang"), *Asahi Shimbun,* October 4, 2002.

53. James Hoare, interview, London, February 6, 2006.

54. "Spokesman for DPRK FM on DPRK Visit of Special Envoy of U.S. President," *Korean Central News Agency,* October 7, 2002.

55. Interview with a U.S. Department of State official, Washington, December 19, 2005.

56. James Kelly, interview, Washington, May 20, 2006.

57. Conversation with a U.S. Department of State official who attended the briefing, New York, June 5, 2006.

58. Colin Powell, interview, Washington, March 31, 2006.

59. Interview with a senior U.S. administration official, Washington, March 13, 2006.

60. Interview with a senior U.S. administration official, Washington, May 5, 2006.

61. Barbara Slavin, "N. Korea Admits Nuclear Program," *USA Today,* October 17, 2002.

62. "North Korean Nuclear Program," press statement, U.S. Department of State, October 16, 2002 (www.state.gov/r/pa/prs/ps/2002/14432.htm [June 4, 2007]).

63. "Conclusion of Non Aggression Treaty between DPRK and U.S. Called For," *Korean Central News Agency,* October 25, 2002.

64. "KEDO Executive Board Meeting Concludes–November 14, 2002," Korean Peninsula Energy Development Organization (www.kedo.org/news_detail.asp?NewsID=23 [June 4, 2007]).

65. Conversation with Charles Pritchard, Seoul, November 3, 2005.

66. Conversation with Joel Wit, Washington, February 28, 2004.

67. James Kelly, interview, Washington, September 23, 2005. Choi was the North Korean interpreter during the six-party talks, but her title was researcher, Ministry of Foreign Affairs. It is believed that a researcher is on the level of the director of a division.

68. Interview with a U.S. Department of State official, Washington, September 30, 2005.

69. Kim Hak-joon, *North and South Korea: Internal Politics and External Relations since 1988* (Seoul: Society for Korean and Related Studies, 2006), p. 284.

70. Colin Powell, interview, Washington, March 31, 2006.

71. Interview with a senior U.S. administration official, Washington, February 24, 2006.

72. Michael Dunn, interview, Washington, March 2, 2006.

73. Ibid.

74. Interview with a senior U.S. administration official, Washington, August 10, 2006.

75. Interview with a member of the delegation, Washington, September 30, 2005.

76. Interview with a senior U.S. Department of State official, Washington, April 26, 2006.

77. Interview with a U.S. Department of State official, Washington, September 30, 2005.

78. Colin Powell, interview, Washington, March 31, 2006.

79. Interview with a senior Blue House official, May 24, 2006.

80. Michael Dunn, interview, Washington, March 2, 2006.

81. Pritchard, *Failed Diplomacy*, p. 38.

82. Don Oberdorfer, "My Private Seat at Pyongyang's Table," *Washington Post*, November 10, 2002.

83. James A. Kelly, "Ensuring a Korean Peninsula Free of Nuclear Weapons: Remarks at the Research Conference 'North Korea: Towards a New International Engagement Framework,'" Washington, February 13, 2004 (www.state.gov/p/eap/rls/rm/2004/29396. htm [June 4, 2007]).

84. Interview with a senior U.S. administration official, Washington, February 12, 2003.

85. Kelly, "Ensuring a Korean Peninsula Free of Nuclear Weapons."

86. Interview with a Russian diplomat, Seoul, July 11, 2006.

87. "Press Availability with Her Excellency Anna Lindh, Minister of Foreign Affairs of Sweden," March 6, 2001, U.S. Department of State (www.state.gov/secretary/former/ powell/remarks/2001/1116.htm [June 4, 2007]).

88. James Mann, *Rise of the Vulcans* (New York: Viking, 2004), p. 277–78.

89. Kim Dae-jung, interview, Seoul, March 24, 2006.

90. "Remarks by President Bush and President Kim Dae-Jung of South Korea," March 7, 2001, White House (www.whitehouse.gov/news/releases/2001/03/20010307-6.html [June 4, 2007]).

91. Kim, *North and South Korea: Internal Politics and External Relations since 1988*, p. 223.

92. "Joint Statement between the United States of America and the Republic of Korea," March 7, 2001, White House (www.whitehouse.gov/news/releases/2001/03/ 20010307-2.html [June 4, 2007]).

93. Thomas Hubbard, interview, Washington, February 14, 2006.

94. Interview with a senior U.S. administration official, Washington, June 2, 2006; Mann, *Rise of the Vulcans*, p. 279.

95. Interview with a senior U.S. administration official, Washington, May 31, 2006.

96. "Secretary of State Colin Powell Discusses International Affairs," *CNN Live Event/Special* (transcript), aired May 14, 2001, 09:45ET (http://transcripts.cnn.com/ TRANSCRIPTS/0105/14/se.01.html [June 4, 2007]).

97. Charles Pritchard, interview, Seoul, December 1, 2005.

98. Quoted in David Rothkopf, *Running the World: The Inside Story of the National Security Council and the Architects of American Power* (New York: Public Affairs, 2005), pp. 403–04.

99. "Statement by the President," June 13, 2001, White House (www.whitehouse. gov/news/releases/2001/06/20010611-4.html [June 4, 2007]).

100. "Kim's Nuclear Gamble: Thomas Hubbard, Interview," *Frontline*, April 10, 2003 (www.pbs.org/wgbh/pages/frontline/shows/kim/interviews/hubbard.html [June 4, 2007]).

101. Thomas Hubbard, interview, Washington, February 14, 2006.

102. Ibid.

103. Michael Gordon, "Nuclear Arms: For Deterrence or Fighting?" *New York Times*, March 11, 2002.

104. National Security Strategy of the United States, White House, September 17, 2002, p. 14–15 (www.whitehouse.gov/nsc/nss.html [June 4, 2007]).

105. Interview with a senior South Korean government official, May 24, 2006.

106. Kim Dae-jung, interview, Seoul, March 24, 2006; interview with a senior U.S. administration official, Washington, September 21, 2006.

107. Interview with a White House official, Washington, June 2, 2006.

108. "President Bush and President Kim Dae-Jung Meet in Seoul," February 20, 2002, White House (www.whitehouse.gov/news/releases/2002/02/20020220-1.html [June 4, 2007]).

109. Elisabeth Bumiller, "Bush Says the U.S. Plans No Attack on North Korea," *New York Times,* February 20, 2002.

110. "President Bush Visits Demilitarized Zone," February 20, 2002, White House (www.whitehouse.gov/news/releases/2002/02/20020220-2.html [June 4, 2007]).

111. Remarks at the Brandenburg Gate, West Berlin, Germany, June 12, 1987 (www.reaganfoundation.org/reagan/speeches/wall.asp [June 4, 2007]).

112. Interview with a senior U.S. administration official, Washington, March 1, 2006.

113. Interview with a senior U.S. administration official, Washington, September 22, 2006.

114. Interview with a senior U.S. administration official, Washington, June 27, 2006.

115. Interview with a U.S. Department of State official, Washington, September 30, 2005.

116. Interview with a senior U.S. administration official, Washington, July 21, 2006.

117. Interview with a senior U.S. administration official, Washington, February 24, 2006.

118. James Kelly, interview, Washington, September 19, 2006.

119. "Daily Press Briefing," July 2, 2002, U.S. Department of State (www.state.gov/r/pa/prs/dpb/2002/11620.htm [June 4, 2007]).

120. "North Is Ready for Resumed Ministerial Talks: Hot-Line Message," *People's Korea,* July 27, 2002.

121. "Foreign Ministry Spokesman on DPRK-U.S. Dialogue," *Korean Central News Agency,* July 26, 2002.

122. Interview with a U.S. Department of State official, New York, January 9, 2006.

123. "Powell Meets N.K. Foreign Minister," *Korea Herald,* August 1, 2002.

124. James Kelly, interview, Washington, September 23, 2005; conversation with a U.S. administration official, Washington, March 10, 2004.

125. Colin Powell, interview, Washington, March 31, 2006.

126. James Kelly, interview, Tokyo, February 8, 2007.

127. Interview with a U.S. Department of State official, New York, January 9, 2006.

128. Ibid.

129. Interview with a senior U.S. administration official, Washington, February 24, 2006.

130. Interview with a U.S. Department of State official, Washington, September 30, 2005.

131. James Kelly, interview, Tokyo, February 8, 2007.

132. David Sanger and Eric Schmitt, "Satellites Said to See Activity at North Korean Nuclear Site," *New York Times,* January 31, 2003.

133. The RC-135, also known as the "Rivet Joint," is used for on-scene intelligence collection, analysis, and dissemination. More technical information is available at www.af.mil/factsheets.

134. "N. Korean Jets Intercept U.S. plane," *CNN.com,* March 4, 2003.

135. Hiroyuki Akita, "Kitachosen Sentoki, Bei Teisatsuki ni Sekkin" ("North Korean Jet Fighters Came Close to the U.S. Reconnaissance Plane"), *Nihon Keizai Shimbun,* March 5, 2003.

136. The USS *Pueblo* was boarded and seized by a small number of North Korean forces in 1968, after North Korea claimed that the boat had strayed into its territorial waters. One American was killed, three were injured, and the remainder of the crew was detained in North Korea for eleven months. The *Pueblo* remains in Pyongyang today. In order to secure the release of the detained crew, the U.S. government signed an apology admitting that the *Pueblo* had been operating in North Korean territorial waters, but

immediately after their release the United States contended that the *Pueblo* had been operating within international waters. A year later, in 1969, a U.S. EC-121 long-range early-warning reconnaissance aircraft was shot down over the Sea of Japan/East Sea by a North Korean fighter, killing all thirty-one crew members. The North Korean government announced that it had shot down a U.S. reconnaissance aircraft deep in its territorial airspace, and it denounced the United States for the intrusion. For more information on the USS *Pueblo* incident, see Mitchell B. Lerner, *The Pueblo Incident: A Spy Ship and the Failure of American Foreign Policy* (University Press of Kansas, 2002) and the USS Pueblo Veteran's Association homepage, www.usspueblo.org. For more on the EC-121 incident, see Joseph G. Bermudez, *North Korean Special Forces* (London: Jane's Publishing, 1988), p. 34.

137. While similar to the RC-135 "Rivet Joint," the KC-135 "Stratotanker" is a midair refueling aircraft. More technical information is available at www.af.mil/factsheets.

138. "U.S. Commits Aerial Espionage on DPRK," *Korean Central News Agency,* February 25, 2003.

139. Takashi Uemura, "Bei no Kanshi Kyoka Kensei ka" ("Has North Korea Increased Its Surveillance of U.S. Intelligence?"), *Asahi Shimbun,* March 5, 2003.

140. Bradley Graham and Glenn Kessler, "North Korean Jets Intercept U.S. Plane over Sea of Japan/East Sea," *Washington Post,* March 4, 2003.

141. Interview with a U.S. Department of Defense official, Washington, May 3, 2006. While similar to both the RC-135 "Rivet Joint" and the KC-135 "Stratotanker," the WC-135, also known as the "Constant Phoenix," is an atmospheric data collection aircraft used to detect radioactive material. The WC-135 was deployed to verify whether the Test Ban Treaty of 1963 was being complied with. It had previously been sent on reconnaissance missions at the time of the Chernobyl incident, China's nuclear tests in the 1990s, and the nuclear tests by India and Pakistan in 1998 in order to collect samples of radioactive particles generated by those events. More technical information is available at www.af.mil/factsheets.

142. Interview with a U.S. Department of Defense official, Washington, August 24, 2006.

143. Interview with a senior U.S. Department of Defense official, Washington, May 3, 2006.

144. Interview with a senior U.S. administration official, Washington, June 2, 2006.

145. Interview with a senior U.S. administration official, Washington, March 13 and June 2, 2006.

146. Interview with a senior White House official, Washington, March 13, 2006.

147. Interview with a senior U.S Department of Defense official, Washington, May 3, 2006.

148. Ryu Jin, "Roh Tells Bush 'Don't Go Too Far,'" *Korea Times,* March 5, 2003.

149. Choi Sung-hong, interview, Seoul, May 9, 2006.

150. Interview with a senior South Korean government official, Seoul, October 11, 2005; interview with a U.S. intelligence analyst, Washington, April 27, 2006.

151. Interview with a senior South Korean government official, Seoul, May 9, 2006.

152. David E. Sanger, "In North Korea and Pakistan, Deep Roots of Nuclear Barter," *New York Times,* November 24, 2002.

153. Eishiro Takeishi, London, "Kitachosen kara Misairu Gijutsu Donyu Pakisutan Moto Shusho Shogen" ("Former President of Pakistan Testified She Had Introduced Missile Technology from North Korea"), *Asahi Shimbun,* July 18, 2004.

154. Interview with a U.S. administration official who was briefed by Benazir Bhutto, Washington, May 30, 2006.

155. Regarding the Pakistan–North Korea connection, see David E. Sanger and James Dao, "U.S. Says Pakistan Gave Technology to North Korea," *New York Times,* October 17,

2002; Sanger, "In North Korea and Pakistan, Deep Roots of Nuclear Barter"; Seymour Hersh, "The Cold Test," *New Yorker,* January 27, 2003; Walter Pincus, "North Korea's Nuclear Plans Were No Secret," *Washington Post,* February 1, 2003; and Gaurav Kampani, "Second-Tier Proliferation: The Case of Pakistan and North Korea," *Nonproliferation Review* 9, no. 3 (2002): 107–16. President Pervez Musharraf, in an exclusive interview by Japan's Kyodo Press, August 25, 2005, said that Khan had been "providing North Korea with finished centrifugal separators, parts thereof, and assembly plans therefore since the beginning of the 1990s," but he denied the allegation that Pakistan had received North Korean missile technology in return for providing nuclear technology. "Pakistan Daito-ryo, 'Kitachosen ni Gijutsu Iten' Kan Shi Kanyo Hajimete Meigen" ("President of Pakistan Admitted for the First Time that Khan Had Transferred Technology to North Korea"), *Hokkaido Shimbun,* August 25, 2005.

156. Kim Min-cheol, "Hwang Tells of Secret Nuke Program," *Chosun Ilbo,* July 4, 2003 (http://english.chosun.com/w21data/html/news/200307/200307040016.html [June 4, 2007]).

157. Interview with a senior U.S. administration official, Washington, September 23, 2005. A different high-ranking U.S. administration official informed the author that North Korea had obtained between twenty-five and forty-five of two types of already assembled centrifugal separators. Interview with a high-ranking U.S. administration official, Washington, September 30, 2005.

158. Jeremy Bernstein, "The Secrets of the Bomb," *New York Review of Books* 53, no. 9 (2006). The above-mentioned official's testimony very much agrees with reports regarding the nature and development of exchanges between Pakistan and Libya regarding centrifugal separators that were disclosed at a later time. In the case of Libya, although twenty prototype separators were supplied, two of the L-2 units (equivalent to the North Korean P2) were inoperative. Also, 10,000 of the L-2 units were missing key parts. Moreover, some parts that were necessary in order to assemble L-2 units were defective and hence unusable. Wyn Q. Bowen, "Libya and Nuclear Proliferation," Adelphi Paper 380 (May 2006), p. 45.

159. "Germans Shipping Nuke Parts to N. Korea?" *WorldNet Daily,* August 19, 2003.

160. Mitchell B. Reiss and Robert L. Gallucci, "Red-Handed," *Foreign Affairs* 84, no. 2 (2005): 142–48; Junichi Furuyama, "Kitachosen Moto Gaikokan Hacchu ka Doitsu kara no Arumikan Mitsuyu" ("A Former North Korean Diplomat Suspected of Smuggling Aluminum Tubes from Germany"), *Asahi Shimbun,* September 21, 2003.

161. Interview with a senior U.S. administration official, Washington, April 3, 2006.

162. Interview with a senior U.S. administration official, Washington, March 1, 2006.

163. Interview with a senior U.S. administration official, Washington, February 24, 2006.

164. As quoted by James Kelly, U.S. Senate Committee on Foreign Relations, *A Report on Latest Round of Six-Way Talks Regarding Nuclear Weapons in North Korea: Hearing before the Committee on Foreign Relations,* 108th Cong., 2nd sess., July 15, 2004.

165. Jonathan D. Pollack, "The United States, North Korea, and the End of the Agreed Framework," *Naval War College Review* 56 no. 3 (2003): p. 111.

166. Samuel Berger, interview, Washington, February 23, 2004.

167. Thomas Hubbard, interview, Washington, February 14, 2006.

168. Richard Armitage, U.S. Senate Committee on Foreign Relations, *WMD Developments on the Korean Peninsula: Hearing before the Committee on Foreign Relations,* 108th Cong., 1st sess., February 4, 2003.

169. Interview with a senior U.S. administration official, Washington, April 26, 2006.

170. Interview with a senior U.S. administration official, Washington, February 24, 2006, and June 2, 2006.

171. Interview with a senior U.S. administration official, Washington, May 30, 2006.

172. Interview with a U.S. Department of State official, New York, January 9, 2006.

173. Interview with a U.S. Department of State official, Washington, March 10, 2004.

174. This list is based on the author's interviews with U.S. administration officials on February 24, 2006; May 5, 2006; June 27, 2006; August 10, 2006; March 10, 2004; November 2, 2005; April 27, 2006; and April 26, 2006.

175. Interview with Stephen Yates, Washington, March 30, 2006. The term "slam dunk" became a decisive key term when Bush decided to start the war with Iraq. When CIA director George Tenet showed Bush what Tenet claimed were satellite photos of Iraqi weapons of mass destruction, Bush, with a dubious look, asked Tenet, "Is this all? Nothing more?" Tenet responded, "It's a slam dunk case that Saddam Hussein has WMDs." Bush later told Bob Woodward of the *Washington Post,* "Slam-dunk is as I interpreted is a sure thing, guaranteed. No possibility it won't go through the hoop." "Woodward Shares War Secrets," *60 Minutes,* April 18, 2004.

176. David E. Sanger and William J. Broad, "Tests Said to Tie Deal on Uranium to North Korea," *New York Times,* February 2, 2005; interview with a senior U.S. administration official, Washington, May 30, 2006.

177. One senior U.S. administration official told the author that "the U.S. has never believed nor had any evidence that North Korea had a capability of making [hexaflouride]." Interview with a U.S. administration official, Washington, May 20, 2006. Dafna Linzer, "U.S. Misled Allies about Nuclear Export," *Washington Post,* March 20, 2005.

178. Interview with a senior U.S. administration official, Washington, May 20, 2006.

179. Selig S. Harrison, "Did North Korea Cheat?" *Foreign Affairs* 84, no. 1 (2005): 99–110.

180. Interview with a U.S. Department of State official, Washington, May 3, 2006.

181. Interview with a senior U.S. administration official, Washington, May 5, 2006.

182. Interview with a senior U.S. administration official, Washington, February 24, 2006.

183. Ibid.

184. Mitchell B. Reiss and Robert L. Gallucci, "Red-Handed," *Foreign Affairs* 84, no. 2 (2005): 142–48.

185. Pervez Musharraf, *In the Line of Fire: A Memoir* (New York: Free Press, 2006), p. 296.

186. Interview with a senior U.S. administration official, May 5, 2006. The question of how much the North Korean uranium enrichment program has produced resurfaced as a critical issue when the six-party talks entered into the initial action stage beginning in February 2007. It has been reported that the Bush administration has softened its position on the issue. David Sanger and William Broad reported that Condoleezza Rice, in a meeting at the CIA in 2004, asked officers there how they knew how quickly the North Koreans could produce weapons-grade uranium. One official was quoted as saying, "No one was sure. It was really a guestimate about timing." David E. Sanger and William J. Broad, "U.S. Concedes Uncertainty on North Korean Uranium Effort," *International Herald Tribune,* February 28, 2007.

187. Interview with a senior U.S. Department of State official, Washington, August 24, 2004. It should be noted, however, that a senior U.S. administration official said that the Bush administration had stopped using the term "HEU" in order to "keep the South Koreans happy," not because the United States became convinced that North Korea was not developing HEU. Interview with a senior U.S. administration official, Washington, May 5, 2006.

188. Joseph S. Bermudez Jr., "Exposing North Korea's Secret Nuclear Infrastructure," *Jane's Intelligence Review* 7, no. 1 (1999): 45.

189. Interview with a U.S. administration intelligence analyst, Washington, April 27, 2006.

190. Interview with a senior U.S. Department of State official, Washington, April 26, 2006.

191. John Lancaster and Kamran Khan, "Pakistan's Nuclear Club? Scientist Says He Aided North Korea with Superiors' Knowledge," *Asian Wall Street Journal,* February 4, 2004.

192. Interview with a U.S. administration intelligence analyst, Washington, April 27, 2006. On this point, Kenneth R. Timmerman quoted in his book a Department of State official's view: "The idea that the North Koreans signed the Agreed Framework [which required them to abandon their plutonium-based facilities] only *after* they had an enrichment program in place to provide an alternative uranium route to the bomb would be in character." Kenneth E. Timmerman, *Countdown to Crisis: The Coming Nuclear Showdown with Iran* (New York: Crown Forum, 2005), p. 126.

193. "Statement of FM Spokesman Blasts UNSC's Discussion of Korean Nuclear Issue," *Korean Central News Agency,* April 6, 2003.

194. Interview with a U.S. Department of State official, Washington, May 3, 2006.

195. Conversation with a North Korean diplomat, Beijing, April 17, 2006.

196. James Kelly, interview, Beijing, June 27, 2004.

197. James Kelly, interview, Washington, September 23, 2005.

198. Kim Yeon-kwang, "Hwang Jang-yeop ui kodokhan wechim/Bangmi dongheng chuijegi" ("'Hwang Jang-yop's Solitary Scream.' I Covered His Trip to the U.S."), *Wolgan Chosun,* December 2003. According to a senior U.S. administration official, when Hwang visited the United States in November 2003 he gave a similar briefing to two White House officials, Robert Joseph and Michael Green. Interview with a senior U.S. administration official, Washington, March 1 and May 30, 2006. It should be added that some Korean scholars question the veracity of Hwang's statements.

199. Interview with a senior U.S. administration official, Washington, May 5, 2006.

200. Chae-Jin Lee, *A Troubled Peace: U.S. Policy and the Two Koreas* (Johns Hopkins University Press, 2006), p. 179.

201. James Kelly, interview, Washington, September 23, 2005.

202. Interview with a senior U.S. administration official, Washington, April 26, 2006.

203. Charles Pritchard, "A Guarantee to Bring Kim into Line," *Financial Times,* October 10, 2003.

204. James Kelly, "Mounting Tensions in Northeast Asia: What Are the Deeper Causes?" *PacNet 23B,* June 10, 2005. As pointed out earlier, however, the INR had raised questions about this point.

205. Charles Pritchard, interview, Washington, June 4, 2003.

206. Interview with a senior U.S. administration official, Washington, June 2, 2006.

207. Ibid.

208. Colin Powell, interview, Washington, March 31, 2006.

209. Interview with a senior U.S. administration official, Washington, March 13, 2006.

210. Interview with a senior Japanese government official, Tokyo, September 6, 2006; interview with a senior South Korean government official, Seoul, October 11, 2005.

211. Interview with a senior U.S. administration official, Washington, March 13 and April 3, 2006.

212. Interview with a senior U.S. Department of State official, Washington, February 15, 2006.

213. Interview with a senior South Korean government official, Washington, December 7, 2005.

214. Don Kirk, "A Conflict of Views Sharpens in Korea," *International Herald Tribune,* June 3, 2003.

215. Jeffrey T. Richelson, *Spying the Bomb: American Nuclear Intelligence from Nazi Germany to Iran and North Korea* (New York: W. W. Norton, 2006), p. 529.

216. Glenn Kessler, "N. Korea Nuclear Estimate to Rise," *Washington Post,* April 28, 2004.

217. Interview with a senior Japanese government official, Tokyo, September 3, 2003.

218. Interview with a senior U.S. administration official, Washington, March 1, 2006.

219. Interview with a senior South Korean government official, Seoul, October 10, 2005.

220. Exchange reconstructed on the basis of a conversation with a senior Chinese government official, Tokyo, May 12, 2006.

221. Kim, *North and South Korea: Internal Politics and External Relations since 1988,* p. 436.

222. However, Yoon regarded the sealing of plutonium production as the most urgent task. He thought that it was "illogical to usher in urgent danger by preventing distant changes." Interview with a senior South Korean government official, Seoul, May 8, 2006.

223. Interview with a senior official of Japan's Ministry of Foreign Affairs, Tokyo, December 21, 2005.

224. Musharraf, *In the Line of Fire: A Memoir,* p. 296.

225. Interview with a senior U.S. administration official, Washington, August 26, 2004.

226. Interview with a senior Chinese government official, Tokyo, May 12, 2006.

227. Ibid.

228. Interview with a Chinese diplomat, Washington, August 24, 2004.

229. Harrison, "Did North Korea Cheat?" pp. 99–110.

230. Interview with a U.S. Department of State official, New York, June 6, 2006.

231. Jim Wolf, "Rumsfeld Clears Musharraf of Nuclear Trafficking," *Yahoo! News,* March 28, 2004.

232. Interview with a U.S. administration official, New York, January 9, 2006.

233. Interview with a U.S. Department of State official, Washington, May 3, 2006.

234. Douglas Jehl, "Tug of War: Intelligence vs. Politics," *New York Times,* May 8, 2005.

235. James Kelly, interview, Washington, May 20, 2006.

236. Interview with a U.S. government intelligence analyst, Washington, April 26, 2006.

Chapter Four

1. James Kelly, interview, Washington, May 20, 2006.

2. Interview with a senior U.S. administration official, Washington, May 5, 2006.

3. Lawrence Wilkerson, interview, Washington, September 19, 2006.

4. Karen DeYoung, "U.S. Might Try to Salvage Part of North Korea Accord," *Washington Post,* October 25, 2002.

5. Mike Allen and Karen DeYoung, "Bush Seeks China's Aid to Oppose North Korea: Jiang's Statement Not as Forceful as U.S. Hoped," *Washington Post,* October 26, 2002.

6. "Joint Statement by the Trilateral Coordination and Oversight Group, Tokyo, November 9, 2002," U.S. Department of State (www.state.gov/r/pa/prs/ps/2002/15037.htm [June 5, 2007]).

7. Robert Carlin, interview, New York, June 5, 2006.

8. Ibid.

9. Ibid.

10. Interview with a senior U.S. administration official, Washington, February 24, 2006.

11. Interview with a senior U.S. administration official, Washington, April 26, 2006.

12. Interview with a senior U.S. administration official, Washington, April 3, 2006.

13. Interview with a senior U.S. administration official, Washington, February 24, 2006.

14. Interview with a senior U.S. administration official, Washington, February 24, and April 3, 2006.

15. Ibid.

16. Michael Gordon, "U.S. Readies Plan to Raise Pressure on North Korea," *New York Times,* December 29, 2002.

17. Interview with a senior U.S. administration official, Washington, April 3, 2006.

18. Ibid.

19. Interview with a senior U.S. Department of State official, Washington, August 23, 2003.

20. Richard L. Armitage, "A Comprehensive Approach to North Korea," DPRK Briefing Book, March 1999, National Defense University, Institute for National Strategic Studies (www.nautilus.org/DPRKBriefingBook/uspolicy/Armitage.html [June 5, 2007]). In chapter 3, I discuss how these proposals were reflected in the Bush administration's June 2001 "review" of U.S. North Korea policy, including the banning of missile exports by North Korea.

21. After serving as special envoy for the six-party talks, DeTrani joined the new Office of the Director of National Intelligence in April 2005 as mission manager for North Korea. "Joseph DeTrani," June 5, 2007, Office of the Director of National Intelligence (www.dni.gov/aboutODNI/bios/detrani_bio.htm [June 5, 2007]).

22. Richard Armitage, interview, Washington, January 4, 2006. There is some debate over who is considered a neocon. Some do not include Rumsfeld himself as a neocon, but many people associated with the Project for the New American Century (PNAC) are considered neocons. Of the twenty-five signatories of the PNAC's Statement of Principles, signed in June 1997, ten went on to serve in the George W. Bush administration, including Dick Cheney, Donald Rumsfeld, and Paul Wolfowitz, among others. "Statement of Principles," *Project for the New American Century,* June 3, 1997 (www.newamericancentury.org/statementofprinciples.htm [June 5, 2007]). For more about the neocon debate, see "Empire Builders: Neoconservatives and Their Blueprint for U.S. Power," *Christian Science Monitor,* June 2005 (www.csmonitor.com/specials/neocon/ [June 5, 2007]); Irving Kristol, "The Neoconservative Persuasion," *Weekly Standard,* August 25, 2003; Max Boot, "What the Heck Is a 'Neocon'?" *Wall Street Journal,* December 30, 2002.

23. David Rothkopf, *Running the World* (New York: Public Affairs, 2005), p. 421.

24. In October 2005, Libby resigned after he was indicted on charges of perjury, making false statements, and obstruction of justice related to statements he made in the course of the investigation into the disclosure of the identity of undercover CIA officer Valerie Plame, whose husband, Ambassador Joseph C. Wilson IV, was sent by the CIA to Africa to investigate reports that Iraq was trying to buy nuclear materials. On March 6, 2007, he was convicted on four of those five charges. On July 2, 2007, President Bush granted Libby clemency, commuting his thirty-month prison sentence. Jim VandeHei and Carol D. Leonnig, "Cheney Aide Libby Is Indicted," *Washington Post,* October 29, 2005; Carol D. Leonnig and Amy Goldstein, "Libby Found Guilty in CIA Leak Case,"

Washington Post, March 7, 2007; "Statement by the President on Executive Clemency for Lewis Libby," July 2, 2007, White House (www.whitehouse.gov/news/releases/2007/07/20070702-3.html [July 11, 2007]).

25. Interview with a senior U.S. administration official, Washington, February 24, 2006.

26. Ibid.

27. James Carney and John F. Dickerson, "'Big Time' Punches In," *Time,* February 12, 2001; Elisabeth Bumiller, "White House Letter: Bush-Cheney Dynamic under Scrutiny Again," *International Herald Tribune,* November 20, 2005.

28. Conversation with a U.S. military commander, Brussels, Belgium, April 9, 2006.

29. Lawrence Wilkerson, interview, Washington, September 19, 2005.

30. Lawrence Wilkerson, "The White House Cabal," *Los Angeles Times,* October 25, 2005.

31. Stephen Yates, interview, Washington, March 30, 2006.

32. Lawrence Wilkerson, interview, Washington, September 19, 2005.

33. Bob Woodward, "Cheney Was Unwavering in Desire to Go to War," *Washington Post,* April 20, 2004.

34. David J. Rothkopf, "Look Who's Running the World Now," *Washington Post,* March 12, 2006.

35. Leon V. Sigal, "An Instinct for the Capillaries," Policy Forum Online 06-36A: May 9th, 2006 (www.nautilus.org/fora/security/0636Sigal.html [June 5, 2007]).

36. "Kim's Nuclear Gamble," transcript, *Frontline,* April 10, 2003 (www.pbs.org/wgbh/pages/frontline/shows/kim/etc/script.html [June 5, 2007]).

37. Interview with a U.S. Department of State official, Washington, December 19, 2005.

38. Speech at "The Third Global Structures Convocation: Human Rights, Global Governance, and Strengthening the United Nations," Washington, February 2–6, 1994 (www.ips-dc.org/comment/bennis/boltontrans.htm [June 27, 2007]).

39. "Background: John Bolton's Nomination to the U.N.," *NPR.org,* June 3, 2005 (www.npr.org/templates/story/story.php?storyId=4648850 [June 5, 2007]).

40. Christopher Marquis, "Absent from the Korea Talks: Bush's Hard-Liner," *New York Times,* September 2, 2003.

41. Interview with a senior U.S. administration official, Washington, August 22, 2006.

42. John R. Bolton, "A Dictatorship at the Crossroads," speech given at the East Asia Institute, July 31, 2003 (www.state.gov/t/us/rm/23028.htm [June 5, 2007]).

43. "Spokesman for DPRK Foreign Ministry Slams U.S. Mandarin's Invective," *Korean Central News Agency,* August 2, 2003.

44. Interview with a U.S. Department of State official, New York, January 9, 2006.

45. Interview with a senior U.S. Department of State official, Washington, September 29, 2005.

46. Interview with a senior U.S. Department of State official, Washington, August 22, 2003.

47. Richard Armitage, interview, Washington, January 9, 2006.

48. Conversation with a U.S. Department of Defense official, Washington, July 19, 2005.

49. James Mann, *Rise of the Vulcans: The History of Bush's War Cabinet* (New York: Viking, 2004), p. 242.

50. David E. Sanger, "After-Effects: Nuclear Standoff: Administration Divided over North Korea," *New York Times,* April 21, 2003.

51. Interview with a senior U.S. Department of Defense official, Washington, May 3, 2006.

52. Interview with a U.S. Department of Defense official, Washington, July 19, 2005.

53. Interview with a senior U.S. Department of Defense official, Washington, September 11, 2004.

54. Jonathan D. Pollack and Mitchell B. Reiss, "South Korea: The Tyranny of Geography and the Vexations of History," in *The Nuclear Tipping Point: Why States Reconsider Their Nuclear Choices,* edited by Kurt M. Campbell, Robert J. Einhorn, and Mitchell B. Reiss (Brookings, 2004), p. 262.

55. Lawrence Wilkerson, interview, Washington, September 19, 2005.

56. Interview with a senior U.S. administration official, Washington, February 24, 2006.

57. Bill Keller, "At the Other End of the Axis: Some F.A.Q's," *New York Times,* January 11, 2003.

58. Charles L. Pritchard, *Failed Diplomacy* (Brookings, 2007), p. 50.

59. Interview with a senior U.S. Department of State official, Washington, September 3, 2004.

60. Richard Armitage, interview, Washington, January 4, 2006.

61. Interview with a U.S. Department of State official, Washington, March 3, 2006.

62. Interview with a senior U.S. administration official, Washington, February 24, 2006; Lawrence F. Kaplan, "Condi Should Tame Foggy Bottom," *New Republic,* December 13, 2004.

63. Interview with a senior U.S. administration official, Washington, February 24, 2006.

64. Interview with a senior U.S. administration official, Washington, May 5, 2006. As described in chapter 10 of this volume, during the DPRK-U.S. negotiations on the occasion of the China-DPRK-U.S. trilateral talks in Beijing in late April 2003, Li Gun told Kelly, "As we warned you earlier in New York, we finished reprocessing." Some of the members of the U.S. delegation were upset to hear that and suspected that the Department of State had withheld the information that North Korea had finished reprocessing. However, David Straub told the author that the North Korean Foreign Ministry spokesman announced that they had finished reprocessing prior to the U.S.-DPRK bilateral meeting in Beijing. On April 18 the Korean Central News Agency reported, quoting a North Korean Foreign Ministry spokesman, "As we have already declared, we are successfully reprocessing more than 8,000 spent fuel rods at the final phase as we sent interim information to the U.S. and other counties concerned." "Spokesman for DPRK Foreign Ministry on Expected DPRK-U.S. Talks," Korean Central News Agency, April 18, 2003. James Kelly refuted the charge that the State Department had withheld information: "I believe this story is a serious exaggeration, and may be completely fictitious. I do not recall (or believe) any such thing from March 2003. At no time was new or vital information from any North Korean withheld from the White House." James Kelly, e-mail interview, January 16, 2007.

65. Ibid.

66. Lawrence Wilkerson, interview, Washington, September 19, 2005.

67. "Dr. Rice Speaks at Vanderbilt," May 17, 2004, White House (www.whitehouse.gov/news/releases/2004/05/20040517.html [June 6, 2007]).

68. Condoleezza Rice, "Promoting the National Interest," *Foreign Affairs* 79, no. 1 (2000): 45–62.

69. Interview with a White House official, Washington, February 24, 2006.

70. Interview with a senior White House official, Washington, November 27, 2002.

71. Interview with a senior White House official, Washington, February 24, 2006.

72. Bob Woodward, "A Course of 'Confident Action,'" *Washington Post,* November 19, 2002.

73. "DPRK Foreign Ministry Spokesman Blasts Bush's Reckless Remarks," *Korean Central News Agency,* August 23, 2004.

74. "North Korea Hurls Taunts at Bush," *International Herald Tribune*, May 11, 2005, quoting from *Rodong Shinmun*, April 29, 2005.

75. Interview with a senior U.S. administration official, Washington, March 13, 2005.

76. Interview with a senior U.S. Department of State official, November 4, 2004.

77. Lawrence Wilkerson, interview, Washington, September 19, 2005.

78. Kim Dae Jung, interview, Seoul, March 24, 2006.

79. Interview with a senior U.S. administration official, Washington, April 26, 2006.

80. Interview with a former senior U.S. administration official, Washington, April 26, 2006.

81. James Kelly, interview, Washington, May 20, 2006.

82. Interview with a U.S. Department of State official, Tokyo, July 14, 2005.

83. Interview with a U.S. Department of State official, Tokyo, February 9, 2004.

84. James Kelly, "Firmness and Realism Needed on North Korea," *PacNet 45*, Center for Strategic and International Studies, November 20, 1998.

85. James Kelly, U.S. House Committee on International Relations, Subcommittee on East Asia and the Pacific, *U.S. Foreign Policy in East Asia and the Pacific: Challenges and Priorities for the Bush Administration*, 107th Cong., 1st sess., June 12, 2001.

86. Scott Snyder, "The Fire Last Time," *Foreign Affairs* 83, no. 4 (2004), p. 448.

87. Colin Powell, interview, Washington, March 31, 2006.

88. Interview with a U.S. Department of State official, New York, January 9, 2006.

89. Ibid.

90. Interview with a senior U.S. Department of State official, Washington, May 3, 2006.

91. "President George Bush Discusses Iraq in National Press Conference," March 6, 2003, White House (www.whitehouse.gov/news/releases/2003/03/20030306-8.html [June 6, 2007]).

92. Samuel Berger, interview, Washington, February 23, 2004.

93. Interview with Tim Russert on NBC's *Meet the Press*, December 29, 2002.

94. Interview with a U.S. Department of State official, New York, January 9, 2006. This official argued that North Korea seemed to be aware of stepping over the line by referring to "transfer," which obviated any U.S. need to define the red line. It should be noted that at the six-party talks in August of that year, the North Korean delegation repeatedly stressed that it would not transfer nuclear technology overseas.

95. Richard Armitage, interview, Washington, January 4, 2006.

96. Bill Gertz, "Hwang Says N. Korea Has Atomic Weapons," *Washington Times*, June 5, 1997.

97. Richard Armitage, interview, Washington, January 4, 2006. Armitage's reasoning proved to be wrong; North Korea conducted a nuclear test on October 9, 2006. Yet South Korea still seems to be willing to maintain good ties with North Korea, and China still keeps giving North Korea food and oil.

98. Interview with a senior U.S. administration official, Washington, February 24, 2006.

99. James Kelly, interview, Washington, May 20, 2006.

100. Bob Woodward, *Bush at War* (New York: Simon and Schuster, 2002), p. 351; "U.S. Seeks Peaceful Resolution of North Korean Nuclear Issue," October 17, 2002, U.S. Department of State (http://seoul.usembassy.gov/17_oct_02_-__.html [July 16, 2007]); "Statement by the President," October 16, 2002, White House (www.whitehouse.gov/news/releases/2002/10/20021016-11.html [June 6, 2007]).

101. For more information on the plan to attack Iraq and the briefing of the president, see "Top Secret Polo Step," National Security Archive Electronic Briefing Book 214, February 14, 2007 (www.gwu.edu/~nsarchiv/NSAEBB/NSAEBB214/index.htm [June 6, 2007]).

102. James Kelly, "Ensuring a Korean Peninsula Free of Nuclear Weapons," February 13, 2004, Department of State (www.state.gov/p/eap/rls/rm/2004/29396.htm [June 6, 2007]); e-mail interview with James Kelly, February 4, 2007.

103. Mann, *Rise of the Vulcans: The History of Bush's War Cabinet,* p. 346.

104. Richard Armitage, interview, Washington, January 4, 2006.

105. Interview with a senior U.S. administration official, Washington, February 24, 2006.

106. Interview with a senior U.S. administration official, Washington, July 21, 2006; Yoo Yong-won, "New Rodong-1 Deployment Confirmed," *Chosun Ilbo,* July 18, 2003; "North Korea's Missile Arsenal," *Reuters,* July 4, 2006.

107. James Dao, "Democrats' Criticism of Bush's Policy on Korea Sharpens," *New York Times,* March 5, 2003.

108. Interview with a senior U.S. administration official, Washington, April 3, 2006.

109. Won Hyuk Lim, *Anatomy of A Failure: The Geneva Agreed Framework of 1994* (Seoul: KDI, January 2004), p. 2 (www.rieti.go.jp/jp/events/04011601/pdf/lim.pdf [June 6, 2007]).

110. Interview with a senior U.S. administration official, Washington, April 3, 2006.

111. Richard Haass, interview, New York, June 5, 2006.

112. Colin Powell, interview, Washington, March 31, 2006.

113. Banbury later became the World Food Program's regional director for Asia, managing the food program and monitoring distribution of aid. Anthony Banbury, "Monitoring UN Aid: North Korea Needs Food," *International Herald Tribune,* January 21, 2004. For more, see Stephen Haggard and Marcus Noland, *Famine in North Korea: Markets, Aid, and Reform* (Columbia University Press, 2007), p. 105.

114. Interview with a senior U.S. administration official, Washington, April 3, 2006.

115. Ibid.

116. Ibid.

117. Snyder, "The Fire Last Time," p. 448.

118. Interview with a senior U.S. Department of State official, Tokyo, February 9, 2004.

119. Interview with a senior U.S. administration official, Washington, April 3, 2006.

120. Interview with a senior U.S. administration official, Washington, August 17, 2005.

121. Interview with a U.S. administration official, Tokyo, February 9, 2004.

122. Interview with a senior U.S. administration official, Washington, April 3, 2006.

123. Interview with a senior U.S. administration official, Washington, May 5, 2006.

124. Interview with one of Kelly's delegation team, Washington, March 15, 2006.

125. Interview with a member of the Kelly delegation, Washington, August 10, 2005.

126. Richard Armitage, interview, Washington, January 4, 2006.

127. Interview with a U.S. Department of State official, New York, January 9, 2006.

128. Richard Armitage, interview, Washington, January 4, 2006.

129. Thomas Hubbard, interview, Washington, February 14, 2006.

130. Interview with a senior U.S. administration official, Washington, February 24, 2006.

131. Interview with a U.S. Department of State official, Washington, March 15, 2006.

132. James Kelly, interview, Washington, May 20, 2006.

133. Mitchell B. Reiss and Robert L. Gallucci, "Red-Handed," *Foreign Affairs* 84, no. 2 (2005): 142–48.

134. Thomas Hubbard, interview, Washington, February 14, 2006.

135. Richard Armitage, U.S. Senate Committee on Foreign Relations, *WMD Developments on the Korean Peninsula: Hearing before the Committee on Foreign Relations,* 108th Cong., 1st sess., February 4, 2003.

136. Nicholas Kristof, "Secret, Scary Plans," *New York Times,* February 28, 2003.

137. Richard Armitage, interview, Washington, January 4, 2006.

138. David Straub, interview, Washington, December 27, 2005.

139. Interview with a U.S. Department of State official, New York, January 9, 2006.

140. David Straub, interview, Washington, December 27, 2005.

Chapter Five

1. Atsushi Ijuin, "Soshoki Beicho Kaizen ni Iyoku" ("General Secretary Kim Eager to Have Better Relations with the U.S."), *Nihon Keizai Shimbun* (evening), October 11, 2000.

2. Izuru Yokomura, "Roshia Tokushi Hocho 'Hokatsu Teian wo Kyogi'" ("Russian Special Envoy Discusses Comprehensive Proposal"), *Asahi Shimbun,* January 20, 2003.

3. Conversations between Losyukov and Kan Sok-ju and Kim Jong-il were reconstructed on the basis of conversations with the Russian participants in the talks, including Losyukov, in Tokyo (January 30 and July 7, 2006), and officials of the Russian Foreign Ministry, in Moscow (June 6, 2006) and Seoul (June 4 and July 11, 2006).

4. "V sviazi s namereniem KNDR vyiti iz Dogovora o nerasproctranenii iadernogo oruzhiia," Zaiavlenie Ministerstva inostrannykh del rossiiskoi federatsii ("In Concern over the Intent of DPRK to Withdraw from the Non-Proliferation Treaty," Statement of the Russian Ministry of Foreign Affairs), January 10, 2003.

5. "Russia Advocates Nuclear-Free Status of Korean Peninsula," *Interfax,* January 10, 2003.

6. "Alexander Losyukov obsudil s posolom Respubliki Koreia rossiiskoe predlozhenie o "paketnom reshenii" koreiskoi problemy" ("Russian Proposal for Package Solution of Korean Problems Discussed"), Itar-Tass World Service, January 14, 2003; Seth Mydans, "U.S. Envoy Starts Discussions in Seoul on North Korea," *New York Times,* January 13, 2003; Alexander P. Losyukov, interview, Tokyo, January 30, 2006.

7. Alexander Samokhotkin, "Novye predlozheniia Moskvy i Vashingtona po koreiskomu krizisu" ("New Proposals from Moscow and Washington about the Korean Crisis"), *Vremya Novostei,* January 20, 2003.

8. Alexander P. Losyukov, interview, Tokyo, January 30, 2006.

9. Georgy Kunadze, interview, Moscow, June 8, 2006.

10. Interview with a senior Russian Foreign Ministry official, Moscow, June 8, 2006.

11. Telephone interview with a senior Russian Foreign Ministry official, June 6, 2006.

12. Alexander P. Losyukov, interview, Tokyo, January 30, 2006.

13. Ibid.

14. Interview with a member of the delegation, Seoul, July 11, 2006.

15. Interview with a senior Russian Foreign Ministry official, Moscow, June 7, 2006. The term "power ministries" began to be used around the time of the Chechen crisis, signifying the beginning of the shift in the balance of power from young reformers to those who believed in power and order. Putin is one of the *siloviki,* former members of the power ministries. *Siloviki* share the conviction that "Russia has been a super power and it will remain a super power." They also share a preference for settling conflicts by force. Hiroshi Kimura, "Puchin Gaiko: Sono Tokushitsu to Tekiyo" ("Putin's Diplomacy: Its Characteristics and Application"), *Kokusai Mondai* (*International Affairs*) 531 (June 2004).

16. James Risen, "Threats and Responses: Weapons Monitoring; Russia Helped U.S. on Nuclear Spying inside North Korea," *New York Times,* January 20, 2003.

17. One isotope of krypton (85KR) is produced by fission of either plutonium or uranium. Sources include nuclear weapons testing, nuclear reactors, and the reprocessing of nuclear fuel rods. For more information see "Human Health Fact Sheet: Krypton,"

Argonne National Laboratory EVS, August 2005 (www.ead.anl.gov/pub/doc/krypton.pdf [June 7, 2007]).

18. Alexander P. Losyukov, interview, Tokyo, July 7, 2006.

19. James Risen, "Threats and Responses: Weapons Monitoring; Russia Helped U.S. on Nuclear Spying inside North Korea," *New York Times,* January 20, 2003.

20. Alexander P. Losyukov, interview, Tokyo, January 30, 2006.

21. Ibid.

22. Ibid.

23. Eduard Shevardnadze (trans. Catherine A. Fitzpatrick), *The Future Belongs to Freedom* (London: Sinclair-Stevenson, 1991), p. 164.

24. Seung-Ho Joo, *Gorbachev's Foreign Policy toward the Korean Peninsula, 1985-1991: Power and Reform* (Lewiston, N.Y.: Edwin Mellen Press, 2000), p. 179.

25. Ibid., p. 170.

26. Ibid., pp. 170–71; "Kitachosen 'Kanso Kokko Juritsu Nara' Kakuno Dokuji Kaihatsu wo Hyomei" ("North Korea Expresses Its Intentions to Develop Nuclear Capabilities Independently 'If the Soviet Union Normalizes Diplomatic Relations with South Korea'"), *Asahi Shimbun,* January 1, 1991.

27. Ibid.

28. Interview with a senior Russian Foreign Ministry official, Moscow, June 8, 2006; Georgy Kunadze, interview, Moscow, June 8, 2006.

29. "Shasetsu: Nijuisseiki he" ("Editorial: Toward the Twenty-First Century"), *Mainichi Shimbun,* January 18, 1999.

30. Georgy Kunadze, interview, June 8, 2006.

31. Interview with a senior Russian Foreign Ministry official, Moscow, June 8, 2006.

32. In the summer of 2006, when nuclear development activities in Iran became a serious matter, Bolton said, "I think there is a real debate inside the Kremlin right now. . . . Washington's job is to do what it can to help those whose views coincide with its own to prevail in those debates" (a comment by Bolton during a Fox news program, June 6, 2006, as quoted in the *Moscow Times,* June 8, 2006.) It is a bit unclear to whom Bolton was referring when he talked about "those whose views coincide with its own." A Japanese diplomat posted in Moscow who is a specialist on Korean affairs noted that there are three groups in Russia with interests in North Korea: a pro–North Korea, anti–United States group; pro-American counterproliferationists; and those with business and natural resource interests in North Korea. This diplomat feels Bolton was referring to the second group, although he notes that many in the Ministry of Defense shifted from being pro–North Korean to counterproliferationists after North Korea's October 2006 nuclear test. E-mail exchange, March 2, 2007, with a Japanese diplomat.

33. Interview with a senior U.S. administration official, Washington, May 30, 2006.

34. Ibid.

35. Interview with a senior Russian Foreign Ministry official, Moscow, June 8, 2006.

36. Japan Association for Trade with Russia and NIS, *Roshia Gijutsu Nyusu Reta (Russian Technology Newsletter),* August 2000.

37. Cristina Chuen, "Russian Responses to the North Korean Crisis," Center for Nonproliferation Studies, January 24, 2003 (http://cns.miis.edu/research/korea/rusdprk.htm[June 7, 2007]); Channel One TV, January 10, 2003, in "Russian Minister Says North Korea '50 Years' away from Creating Nuclear Weapons," Foreign Broadcast Information Service (FBIS) Document CEP20030110000360; German Solomatin, "Russian Atomic Energy Minister: N. Korea Has No Nuclear Weapons Technology," ITAR-TASS, January 13, 2003, in FBIS Document CEP20030113000302.

38. Anatoly Yurkin, "KNDR deklariruyet tol'ko mirnuyu napravlennost' svoyoy yader-noy programmy, zayavil ministr RF po atomnyoy energii," ("DPRK Declared Only the Peace Course of Its Own Nuclear Program, the Russian Federation's Minister of Atomic Energy Claimed), ITAR-TASS, January 13, 2003.

39. Interview with a Russian diplomat, Seoul, May 30, 2004.

40. "U.S. Ambassador Says Russia Is 'In Denial' on North Korean Threat," Associated Press, January 9, 2003.

41. Interview with a senior South Korean government official who was in charge of North Korean nuclear issues.

42. "Under Secretary John R. Bolton's Press Availability," January 22, 2003, U.S. Embassy (Seoul).

43. Alexander P. Losyukov, interview, Tokyo, January 30, 2006.

44. Interview with a Chinese diplomat, Tokyo, September 1, 2006; Chuen, "Russian Responses to the North Korean Crisis."

45. Alexander P. Losyukov, interview, Tokyo, January 30, 2006.

46. Ibid.

47. IAEA Board of Governors, IAEA Media Advisory 2003/48, Resolution on North Korea, February 12, 2003.

48. Russian Foreign Ministry Statement, Document 345-12-02-2003, February 13, 2003.

49. On April 9, 2003, the UN Security Council held an informal meeting regarding the North Korean nuclear issue. After the end of the session, the chairman, UN ambassador Adolfo Aguilar Zinser of Mexico, held a press conference in which he announced that the participating countries had expressed concerns about the issue. But no resolution condemning North Korea was adopted.

50. Alexander P. Losyukov, interview, Tokyo, July 7, 2006.

51. Evgeniy P. Bazhanov "Russian Views of the Agreed Framework and the Four-Party Talks," in *The North Korean Nuclear Program Security, Strategy, and New Perspectives from Russia,* edited by James Clay Moltz and Alexander Y. Mansourov (New York: Routledge, 2000), pp. 223–30.

52. Esook Yoon and Dong Hyung Lee, "Vladimir Putin's Korean Opportunity: Russian Interests in the North Korean Nuclear Crisis," *Comparative Strategy* 24 (2005): 185–201.

53. Nobuo Shimotomai, *Ajia Reisen-shi* (History of the Asian Cold War) (Tokyo: Chuko Shinsho, 2004), p. 184.

54. Interview with a Russian diplomat, Seoul, May 9, 2006.

55. Interview with a senior Russian Foreign Ministry official, Seoul, July 11, 2006.

56. The following month, however, Kim went on to say that his earlier promise to end his country's missile program was only "a joke" made to Putin in passing. Don Oberdorfer, *The Two Koreas: A Contemporary History* (New York: Basic Books, 2001), pp. 438–439.

57. Samuel Berger, interview, Washington, February 23, 2004.

58. Gilbert Rozman, "The Geopolitics of the Korean Nuclear Crisis," in *Strategic Asia 2003–04: Fragility and Crisis,* edited by Richard J. Ellings and Aaron L. Friedberg with Michael Wills (Seattle: National Bureau of Asian Research, 2003), p. 255.

59. Esoon Yoon and Dong Hyung Lee, "A View from Asia: Vladimir Putin's Korean Opportunity: Russian Interests in the Korean Nuclear Crises," *Comparative Strategy* 24, no. 2 (2005): 195.

60. Interview with a senior Japanese government official, Tokyo, March 25, 2003.

61. Konstantin Pulikovsky, *Vostochnyi Ekspress: Po Rossii s Kim Chen Irom* (The Orient Express: Through Russia with Kim Jong-il) (Moscow: Gorodets, 2002), p. 46.

62. Ibid., p. 46.

63. Telephone interview with a Russian diplomat specializing in Korean affairs, June 4, 2006.

64. Vladimir Putin, *First Person: An Astonishingly Frank Self-Portrait* (New York: Public Affairs, 2000), pp. 80–81.

65. Interview with a Russian diplomat, Seoul, November 28, 2005.

66. Sergei Blagov, "Russia's Lost Korean Opportunity," *Asia Times*, June 25, 2003.

67. "President Bush Discusses Top Priorities for the U.S.," July 30, 2003, White House (www.whitehouse.gov/news/releases/2003/07/20030730-1.html).

68. "North Proposed Russia to Hold Six-Way Talks," *Dong-A Ilbo*, September 9, 2003.

69. Blagov, "Russia's Lost Korean Opportunity."

70. Interview with a Russian diplomat, Seoul, May 9, 2006.

71. Andrey Ivanov, "Mirovaya Praktika" ("World Practice"), *Kommersant-Daily*, May 22, 2002.

72. Svetlana Vavaeva, "Chestnye koreiskie brokery" ("Honest Korean Brokers"), *Izvestia*, July 30, 2002.

73. Todd S. Purdum and Don Kirk, "Powell Meets with North Korea Counterpart in Brunei," *New York Times*, July 31, 2002.

74. Interview with a senior South Korean government official, Seoul, May 9, 2006.

75. Ibid.

76. "Japan-Russian Federation Summit Meeting at the G-8 Kananaskis Summit (Outline)," Ministry of Foreign Affairs of Japan, June 27, 2002 (www.mofa.go.jp/policy/economy/summit/2002/meet_russia.html [June 7, 2007]).

77. Interview with a senior Japanese government official, Tokyo, March 25, 2003.

78. Interview with a senior Japanese government official, Tokyo, December 19, 2002.

79. Interview with a senior U.S. administration official, Washington, May 30, 2006; interview with a Russian diplomat, Seoul, July 11, 2006.

80. Vitaly Dymarsky, "Mezhdu dvumia Koreiami" ("Between two Koreas"), *Rossiiskaya Gazeta*, July 30, 2002; Alexander P. Losyukov, interview, Tokyo, January 30, 2006.

81. Interview with a Russian diplomat, Seoul, November 28, 2005.

82. Interview with a senior U.S. administration official, Washington, June 2, 2006.

83. Ibid.

84. James Mann, *Rise of the Vulcans: The History of Bush's War Cabinet* (New York: Viking, 2004), pp. 204–205.

85. Alexander P. Losyukov, interview, Tokyo, July 7, 2006.

86. Gong Ro-myong, interview, Seoul, July 28, 2003.

87. Pulikovsky, *Vostochnyi Ekspress* (The Orient Express), p. 112.

88. "Joint Declaration of the Russian Federation and the People's Republic of China," May 27, 2003, Ministry of Foreign Affairs of the Russian Federation, Information and Press Department, Kremlin, Moscow.

89. "President Bush Meets with Japanese Prime Minister Koizumi," May 23, 2003, White House (www.whitehouse.gov/news/releases/2003/05/print/20030523-4.html).

90. Alexander P. Losyukov, interview, Tokyo, July 7, 2006.

91. "President Bush, Russian President Putin Sign Treaty of Moscow," June 1, 2003, White House (www.whitehouse.gov/news/releases/2003/06/print/2003/0601-2.html).

92. Interview with a senior U.S. administration official, Washington, June 2, 2006.

93. James Kelly, interview, Washington, May 20, 2006.

94. Izuru Yokomura, Moscow, "Roshia, Chiiki Anponi Fuseki" ("Russia Steps Forward on Building Regional Security"), *Asahi Shimbun*, August 17, 2003.

95. Interview with a senior U.S. administration official, Washington, June 2, 2006.

According to the *Asahi Shimbun,* Russia had agreed with the United States to discuss sanctions at the UN Security Council when the six-party talks failed. Nobuyoshi Sakajiri, "Anpori Kyogi Roshia Doi 'Rokusha' Ketsuretsu no Baai" ("Russia Agrees to Bring the [North Korean nuclear] Issue to the U.N. Security Council 'in Case of the Failure of the Six-Party Talks'"), *Asahi Shimbun,* May 1, 2005.

96. Elena Shesternina, "Konsul'tatsii s SShA ni k chemy ne privedut" ("Consultation with USA Will Bring Nothing"), *Nezavisimaya Gazeta,* August 14, 2001.

97. Interview with a Russian diplomat, Seoul, May 9, 2006.

98. Andrey Kolesnikov, "Chattanuga-Chuchkhe" ("Chattanooga-Juche"), *Izvestia,* August 21, 2001.

99. Alexander P. Losyukov, interview, Tokyo, January 30, 2006.

100. Alexander Zhebin, "The Bush Doctrine, Russia, and Korea," in *Confronting the Bush Doctrine,* edited by Mel Gurtov and Peter Van Ness (New York: RoutledgeCurzon, 2005), p. 142.

101. Igor Rogachev, interview, Moscow, June 7, 2006.

102. Chae-Jin Lee, *A Troubled Peace: U.S. Policy and the Two Koreas* (Johns Hopkins University Press, 2006), p. 136.

103. Don Oberdofer, *The Two Koreas: A Contemporary History,* rev. and updated (New York: Basic Books, 2001), p. 432.

104. Georgy Kunadze, interview, Moscow, June 8, 2006.

105. Zhebin, "The Bush Doctrine, Russia, and Korea," pp. 149–50.

106. Herbert Ellison, "Russia, Korea, and Northeast Asia," in *Korea's Future and the Great Powers,* edited by Nicholas Eberstadt and Richard J. Ellings (University of Washington Press, 2001), pp. 165–66, 182.

107. Alexander P. Losyukov, interview, Tokyo, January 30, 2006.

108. Interview with a Russian diplomat, Seoul, November 28, 2005.

109. Georgy Kunadze, interview, Moscow, June 8, 2006.

110. Yuri Vanin, interview, Moscow, November 9, 2005.

111. Interview with a Russian diplomat, Seoul, November 28, 2005.

112. Yoon and Lee, "Vladimir Putin's Korean Opportunity," p. 193.

113. "DPRK to React to Unreasonable 'Countermeasures' with Toughest Stance," Korean Central News Agency, January 19, 2003.

114. Interview with a senior U.S. Department of State official, Washington, June 17, 2006.

115. The author is grateful to Georgy Kunadze for illuminating the various aspects of the security guarantee by sharing his concept paper "Definitions Matter: Reassessing the Prospects of the Six-Party Talks," 2005.

116. Georgy Kunadze, interview, Moscow, June 8, 2005.

117. Ibid.

118. Because the reborn Russia switched its trade with North Korea to a dollar-based system, North Korea's trade with Russia, which centered on the import of crude oil, decreased dramatically, eventually triggering an economic crisis in North Korea.

119. Yoon and Lee, "Vladimir Putin's Korean Opportunity," p. 187.

120. Seung-Ho Joo and Tae-Hwan Kwak, "Military Relations between Russia and North Korea," *Journal of East Asian Affairs* 15, no. 2 (2001): 306–07.

121. Nobuo Shimotomai, *Ajia Reisen-shi* (*History of the Asian Cold War*) (Tokyo: Chuko Shinsho, 2004), p. 185.

122. Conversation with a North Korean diplomat, April 17, 2006.

123. Zhebin, "The Bush Doctrine, Russia, and Korea," p. 150.

124. Georgy Kunadze, interview, Moscow, June 8, 2006.

125. Interview with a Russian diplomat, Seoul, July 11, 2006.

126. James Brooke with Elisabeth Rosenthal, "New Seoul Leader to Press U.S. and North to Yield a Bit," *New York Times*, January 4, 2003.

127. Zhebin, "The Bush Doctrine, Russia, and Korea," p. 149.

128. Alexander P. Losyukov, interview, Tokyo, January 30, 2006.

129. Mitchell B. Reiss, "North Korea's Legacy of Missed Opportunities," remarks to the Heritage Foundation, March 12, 2004 (www.state.gov/s/p/rem/30363.htm).

130. Interview with a senior U.S. Department of State official, August 24, 2004.

131. Interview with a Chinese diplomat, Washington, June 26, 2006.

132. Interview with a senior Russian Foreign Ministry official, Seoul, July 11, 2006.

Chapter Six

1. The following exchange between the South Korean delegation led by Lim Dong-won and the North Korean delegation was reconstructed on the basis of the author's interview with members of the South Korean delegation and senior government officials in Seoul (September 9, 2002, and October 11, 2005); Washington (February 17, 2006); and Seoul (March 23, 2006, and May 8, 2006). Another interview was conducted on May 24, 2006.

2. Choi Won Ki and Jung Chang Hyun, *Chosen Hanto no Ichiban Nagai Hi- Nanboku Shuno Kaidan no Shinjitsu* (*The Longest Day on the Korean Peninsula: The Truth behind the North-South Summit Talk*), trans. Keisuke Fukuda (Tokyo: Toyo Keizai Shimpo-sha, 2002).

3. Kim Yong-sun, member of the Central Committee of the Workers' Party of Korea (WPK), deputy to the Supreme People's Assembly of the Democratic People's Republic of Korea, secretary of the WPK Central Committee, and chairman of the Korean Asia-Pacific Peace Committee, died on October 26, 2003, of complications from a traffic accident on June 16, 2003. ("Kim Yong Sun Dies," *Korean Central News Agency*, October 27, 2003.)

4. Joseph Coleman, "South Korean Envoy Unable to Meet North Korean Leader," Associated Press, January 29, 2003; "KCNA Calls for Proper Understanding of Origin of Nuclear Issue," Korean Central News Agency, January 27, 2003.

5. "Under the Cover of Iraq, the North Moved," *JoongAng Ilbo*, November 1, 2004; Interview with a senior South Korean government official, Seoul, October 11, 2005.

6. Tetsuya Hakoda, "Kakumondai Meguri Gekiron Kankoku Rin Tokushi Hocho-ji" ("South Korean Special Envoy Lim Has Heated Discussions with North Koreans on His Visit to North Korea"), *Asahi Shimbun*, February 14, 2003.

7. Don Kirk, "Kim Jong-il Refuses to See Envoy from Seoul," *International Herald Tribune*, January 30, 2003.

8. It was reported that Chang Song-taek fell from grace in April 2004, only to return to favor in 2006. He was rumored to have been in a car accident in October 2006, and he reportedly traveled to Russia to receive medical treatment for high blood pressure and high cholesterol in March 2007. "North Korean Leader's Brother-in-Law in Russia for Medical Treatment," Yonhap News Agency of Korea, March 9, 2007. He has been considered one of the possible successors to Kim Jong-il. For more on Chang Song-taek, see "North Korea's Secretive 'First Family,'" *BBC News*, February 15, 2007 (http://news.bbc.co.uk/1/hi/world/asia-pacific/3203523.stm).

9. Interview with a senior South Korean government official, Seoul, September 9, 2002.

10. This refers to the March 1970 hijacking of Japan Airlines (JAL) flight 351, or "Yodo-go," by the Japanese Red Army Faction of the Communist League (see chapter 2).

11. Kiyoshi Hasaba, "Kankoku Daitoryo Kin So-Shoki Ugokasu?"("Does the South Korean President Move General Secretary Kim?"), *Asahi Shimbun*, August 31, 2002; interview with a senior South Korean government official, Seoul, October 11, 2005.

12. "Inter-Korean Joint Press Release," Korean Central News Agency, April 6, 2002.

13. Interview with a senior South Korean government official, Seoul, May 9, 2006.

14. After the end of the Korean War, a conference facility was constructed in Panmunjeom within the four-kilometer-wide demilitarized zone (DMZ) that constitutes the ceasefire line. It was decided that the area around the conference site would be guarded jointly by the two Koreas (so constituting a joint security area), and it has been for more than half a century since then.

15. Interview with a senior South Korean government official, Washington, February 17, 2006.

16. Richard Armitage, U.S. Senate Committee on Foreign Relations, *WMD Developments on the Korean Peninsula: Hearing before the Committee on Foreign Relations*, 108th Cong., 1st sess., February 4, 2003 (www.state.gov/s/d/former/armitage/remarks/17170.htm).

17. Interview with a senior South Korean government official, May 24, 2006.

18. Interview with a senior South Korean government official, Seoul, October 11, 2005.

19. Lee Jong-seok, interview, Seoul, March 24, 2006.

20. Lee Jong-seok, interview, Seoul, March 24, 2006; interview with a senior U.S administration official, Washington, February 12, 2003.

21. Mike Chinoy, "The Korean Divide," *CNN International*, January 24, 2003.

22. Interview with a White House official, Washington, February 24, 2006.

23. Lee Jong-seok, interview, Seoul, March 24, 2006.

24. "Another Insult from the North," editorial, *JoongAng Ilbo*, January 29, 2003.

25. Interview with a member of Lim Dong-won's delegation, May 24, 2006.

26. Interview with a senior South Korean government official, Seoul, October 11, 2005.

27. Kim Dae-jung, interview, Seoul, March 24, 2006.

28. Interview with a senior South Korean government official, Washington, February 7, 2006.

29. Interview with a senior South Korean Foreign Ministry official, Seoul, October 10, 2005.

30. Yoon Young-kwan, interview, Seoul, May 8, 2006.

31. Interview with a senior South Korean government official, Seoul, May 8, 2006.

32. Interview with a senior South Korean government official, Seoul, March 23, 2006.

33. Interview with a senior South Korean government official, Seoul, November 29, 2005.

34. Interview with a senior South Korean government official, Seoul, March 23, 2006.

35. Interview with a senior South Korean official, Seoul, November 29, 2005. Also see Kim Hak-joon, *North and South Korea: Internal Politics and External Relations since 1988* (Seoul: Society for Korean and Related Studies, 2006), p. 284.

36. Interviews with members of the subcommittee, Seoul, May 9, 2006.

37. Interviews with members of the subcommittee, Seoul, November 29, 2005.

38. Ashton B. Carter, U.S. Senate Committee on Foreign Relations, *WMD Developments on the Korean Peninsula: Hearing before the Committee on Foreign Relations*, 108th Cong., 1st sess., February 4, 2003.

39. Ashton B. Carter and William Perry, *Preventative Defense: A New Security Strategy for America* (Brookings, 1999), pp. 123–4. Perry told me that in the proposed military action in 1994 the United States did "risk a war" but did not "initiate a war." It was part

of a coercive diplomacy in which the United States would not hesitate to fight a preventative war in the absence of any other rational choice. Perry said that action must have taught North Korea that the United States was serious. Wiliam Perry, interview, Washington, March 22, 2004.

40. Sung Deuk Hahm, *Kim Young-sam Jeongbu-ui Seonggong-gwa Silpae* (*The Kim Young-sam Government: Its Success and Failure*) (Seoul: Nanam, 2001), p. 37.

41. Kim Young Sam, *Gim Geoung Sam Daetongryeong Hoegorog* (*President Kim Young-sam's Memoirs*) (Seoul: Joseon Ilbosa, 2001), p. 316.

42. Kim Young-sam, interview, Seoul, July 3, 2003; "Former S. Korean leader 'Rowed' with Clinton," *BBC News,* January 17, 2003.

43. Interview with a member of the subcommittee, Seoul, May 8, 2006.

44. Remarks by Thomas Hubbard, Seoul-Washington Forum, co-sponsored by the Brookings Institution and the Sejong Institute, Washington, May 1–2, 2006 (www.brookings.edu/comm/events/20060501seoul.htm).

45. Lee Jong-seok, interview, March 24, 2006. Discussions in the subcommittee were reconstructed from interviews with members of the subcommittee, in Seoul (June 1, 2004, and November 29, 2005), Washington (February 17, 2006), and Seoul (March 23 and 24, 2006, and May 8 and 9, 2006).

46. Interview with members of the subcommittee, Seoul, June 1, 2004.

47. Ibid.

48. Interview with a senior South Korean government official, Seoul, November 29, 2005.

49. Interview with a senior South Korean government official, Seoul, March 23, 2006.

50. Lee Jong-seok, interview, Seoul, March 24, 2006; "Seoul to Call on U.S. to Offer N.K. Security Guarantee as compromise," *Korea Herald,* January 4, 2003; James Brooke, "North Korea Issues Warning, and Seoul Seeks Compromise," *New York Times,* January 5, 2003.

51. Chae-Jin Lee, *A Troubled Peace: U.S. Policy and the Two Koreas* (Johns Hopkins University Press, 2006), p. 179.

52. Interview with a senior U.S. administration official, Washington, March 1, 2006.

53. David Sanger, "Bush Says Shift by North Korea Could Bring Aid," *New York Times,* January 15, 2003.

54. James Dao, "Bush Urges Chinese President to Press North Korea on Arms," *New York Times,* February 8, 2003.

55. Vernon Loeb and Peter Slevin, "Overcoming North Korea's 'Tyranny of Proximity,'" *Washington Post,* January 20, 2003.

56. Interview with a senior U.S. administration official, Washington, August 16, 2006.

57. James Dao, "Criticism of Bush's Policy on Korea Sharpens," *New York Times,* March 6, 2003.

58. Thom Shanker, "Lessons from Iraq Include How to Scare Korean Leader," *New York Times,* May 12, 2003.

59. Choi Sung-hong, interview, Seoul, May 9, 2006.

60. Ibid.

61. "President Kim Says Farewell to Nation," *Korea Times,* February 24, 2003.

62. Lee Chul-hee, "Ministry Confirms North's Missile Test," *JoongAng Ilbo,* February 27, 2003.

63. "Nihonseifu ha Reisei na Hanno" ("Government of Japan Responds Coolly"), *Asahi Shimbun* (evening edition), February 25, 2003.

64. Roh Moo-hyun, "Address by President Roh Moo-hyun at the Sixteenth Inaugural Ceremony," Office of the President, February 25, 2003.

65. Kathy Wolfe, "New Korean Leader Calls For Land-Bridge Strategy," *Executive Intelligence Review,* March 14, 2003.

66. Roh Moo-hyun, "Address by President Roh Moo-hyun at the Sixteenth Inaugural Ceremony," Office of the President, February 25, 2003; "North Korea Briefly Reports on Roh's Inauguration," *Korea Times,* February 26, 2003.

67. "North Korea Briefly Reports on Roh's Inauguration," *Korea Times,* February 26, 2003.

68. David I. Steinberg, "The New Political Paradigm in South Korea: Social Change and the Elite Structure," *New Paradigms for Transpacific Collaboration* (monograph), Sixteenth U.S.-Korea Academic Symposium, "New Paradigms for Transpacific Collaboration," University of Washington, Seattle, October 16–19, 2005 (www.keia.org/2-Publications/2-3-Monograph/Monograph2006/06Steinberg.pdf).

69. Kim, *North and South Korea: Internal Politics and External Relations since 1988,* p. 258.

70. Hee Sang Kim, *Korean Security in the 21st Century and Korea-US Relations* (Seoul: Jeonkwang Printing Information, 2001), p. 377.

71. Gallup Korea Survey, December 2002 (sample size, 1,054).

72. Victor Cha, "Anti-Americanism and the U.S. Role in Inter-Korean Relations," in *Korean Attitudes toward the United States: Changing Dynamics,* edited by David I. Steinberg (Armonk, N.Y.: M. E. Sharpe, 2005), p. 128.

73. Chung Min Lee, "Revamping the Korean-American Alliance: New Political Forces, Paradigms, and Roles and Missions," in *Korean Attitudes toward the United States,* edited by Steinberg, p.156.

74. James Brooke, "The World: In Seoul, Longing for the North," *New York Times,* December 22, 2002.

75. Chung-in Moon, "Between Banmi (Anti-Americanism) and Sungmi (Worship of the United States): Dynamic of Changing U.S. Images in South Korea," in *Korean Attitudes toward the United States,* edited by Steinberg, pp.148–49.

76. Kim, *North and South Korea: Internal Politics and External Relations since 1988,* p. 286.

77. Doug Struck, "Alliance Falls Apart on Eve of South Korean Elections," *Washington Post,* December 19, 2002.

78. "No Mu Hyon Kankoku Jiki Daitoryo Kaiken Ichimon Itto" ("Full Text of the Interview with South Korean President-Elect Roh Mu-hyun"), *Asahi Shimbun,* January 24, 2003.

79. Hoon Choi and Shin-hong Park, "Roh Aide Explores the Meaning of Pro-American," *Joong-Ang Ilbo,* April 21, 2005.

80. Kim, *North and South Korea: Internal Politics and External Relations since 1988,* p. 414.

81. James Kelly, interview, Washington, September 23, 2005.

82. Conversation with Yoon Young-kwan, Seoul, June 1, 2004.

83. Conversation with Yoon Young-kwan, New Delhi, India, April 5, 2004.

84. Ibid.

85. Interview with a member of the subcommittee, Seoul, May 8, 2006.

86. Lee Jong-seok, "Achievements and Future Tasks of North-South Summitry," paper presented at the Fourth Sejong National Strategy Forum, June 30, 2000.

87. Thomas Hubbard, interview, Washington, February 14, 2006.

88. Interview with a senior South Korean government official, Tokyo, January 31, 2006.

89. "S. Korea Seeking E.U. Help on N. Korea," *Associated Press,* February 11, 2003.

90. "Foreign Investment in South Korea Falls," *Associated Press,* April 4, 2003.

91. "Minister Kim to Meet Wall Street Investors," *Korea Times,* April 13, 2003.

92. Kim Jin-pyo, "Korea Set to Become One of Top 10 Economic Powers" (full text of speech delivered by the deputy prime minister to the Korea Society in New York), *Korea Times,* April 15, 2003.

93. Interview with a White House official, Washington, March 13, 2006; June 2, 2006; and July 21, 2006.

94. Ibid.

95. Interview with a senior South Korean government official, Seoul, May 9, 2006.

96. Interview with a senior South Korean government official, Tokyo, January 26, 2006.

97. Ban Ki-moon became foreign minister in January 2004 and secretary general of the United Nations in January 2007.

98. Hee-sang Kim, *Korean Security in the 21st Century and Korea-U.S. Relations* (Seoul: Jeonkwang Printing, 2001), pp. 380–81.

99. Interview with a senior South Korean government official, Tokyo, January 26, 2006.

100. Thomas Hubbard, interview, Washington, February 14, 2006.

101. Excerpts from *Roh Moo-hyun Meets Lincoln* (Seoul: Hak-go-jae, 2001), available at www.kois.go.kr/korea/html/B/01/pub_2_excerpt.htm.

102. Ibid.

103. "President and President Roh Discuss Strong U.S.-Korean Alliance," November 17, 2005, White House (www.whitehouse.gov/news/releases/2005/11/20051117.html).

104. David Sanger, "South Korean Leader Wants U.S. Troops to Stay, for Now," *New York Times,* May 13, 2003.

105. Interview with a senior U.S. administration official, Washington, July 21, 2006.

106. Ibid.

107. Interview with a senior South Korean government official, Seoul, May 9, 2006.

108. Interview with a senior U.S. administration official, Washington, July 21, 2006.

109. "Joint Statement between the United States of America and the Republic of Korea: Common Values, Principles, and Strategy," White House, May 14, 2003 (www.whitehouse.gov/news/releases/2003/05/20030514-17.html).

110. Interview with a senior U.S. administration official, Washington, July 21, 2006.

111. "Joint Statement between the United States of America and the Republic of Korea: Common Values, Principles, and Strategy."

112. Interview with a senior South Korean government official, Seoul, May 8, 2006.

113. Interview with a U.S. Department of State official, Washington, November 2, 2005.

114. Interview with a senior South Korean government official, Seoul, May 8, 2006.

CHAPTER SEVEN

1. Interview with a senior South Korean government official, Seoul, March 22, 2006.

2. Hayami Ichikawa, "Bei-Kankoku-Nihon no Iraku Fukkoukouken 'Oie no jijo'" ("The U.S., South Korea, and Japan—Each Has Its Hidden Agenda in the Effort to Rebuild Iraq"), *Asahi Shimbun,* June 15, 2003.

3. Interview with a senior South Korean government official, Tokyo, January 26, 2006.

4. "Bush Vows Efforts for Successful 6-Party Talks," Korean Overseas Information Service (Korea.net), September 5, 2004 (www.globalsecurity.org/wmd/library/news/rok/2003/rok-030905-korea-net02.htm).

5. Michael O'Hanlon and Mike Mochizuki, *Crisis on the Korean Peninsula* (Brookings, 2003). O'Hanlon is a senior fellow in Foreign Policy Studies at the Brookings Institution while Mochizuki holds the Elliot School's endowed chair in Japan-U.S. Relations at George Washington University. Mochizuki formerly was a senior fellow at the Brookings Institution.

6. Interview with a senior South Korean government official in Seoul (May 8, 2006), Washington (April 27, 2006), and Seoul (October 11, 2005); interview with a senior U.S. administration official, Washington, May 3, 2006.

7. Interview with a senior South Korean government official in Seoul (May 8, 2006), Washington (April 27, 2006), and Seoul (October 11, 2005).

8. David Sanger, "Intelligence Puzzle: North Korean Bombs," *New York Times,* October 14, 2003.

9. Colin Powell, interview, Washington, March 31, 2006.

10. "Roh Links Dispatch to security," *JoongAng Daily,* September 26, 2003.

11. Yoo Ihn-tae, interview, Seoul, July 11, 2006.

12. Interview with a senior South Korean government official, Seoul, May 8, 2006.

13. "Seoul Won't Tie Iraq Troop Dispatch to NK Nuclear Talks," *Korea Times,* September 28, 2003.

14. Interview with a senior South Korean government official, Seoul, October 11, 2005; interview with a senior South Korean government official, Washington, April 27, 2006.

15. Colin Powell, interview, Washington, March 31, 2006.

16. Interview with a senior South Korean government official, Seoul, July 11, 2006.

17. Interview with a senior South Korean government official, Seoul, May 8, 2006.

18. Interview with a senior Blue House official, Seoul, November 29, 2005.

19. Yoo Ihn-tae, interview, Seoul, July 11, 2006.

20. Park Sung-hee, "Roh Sent Letter to Bush Reportedly on Iraq," *JoongAng Daily,* October 21, 2003.

21. Oh Young-hwan and Jeong Yong-su, "Korea, U.S. Trade Barbs on Iraq-North Link," *JoongAng Daily,* December 4, 2004.

22. "Roh's Troop Decision Upsets Progressives, Conservatives," *Korea Times,* October 20, 2003.

23. "Over 5000 Troops Eyed for Iraq," *Korea Times,* October 20, 2003.

24. "Roh's Troop Decision Upsets Progressives, Conservatives," *Korea Times,* October 20, 2003.

25. "President Bush Meets with President Roh Moo-hyun," White House, October 20, 2003 (www.whitehouse.gov/news/releases/2003/10/20031020-2.html); "Bush Thanks Roh for Troop Decision," *Korea Times,* October 20, 2003.

26. Interview with a senior White House official, Washington, June 28, 2006.

27. Interview with a senior U.S. Department of State official, Washington, August 24, 2004.

28. Interview with a senior U.S. administration official, Washington, June 2, 2006.

29. Interview with a U.S. Department of Defense official, Washington, August 24, 2006.

30. Interview with a senior U.S. administration official, Washington, June 2, 2006; interview with a senior South Korean government official, Washington, April 27, 2006.

31. Interview with a senior U.S. administration official, Washington, June 27, 2006.

32. Interview with a U.S. Department of Defense official, Washington, August 24, 2006.

33. Interview with a senior U.S. administration official, Washington, June 27, 2006. Lee denied that allegation, saying, "It's nonsense. By that time the figure of 3,000 had already been confirmed within the government." Lee Jong-seok corroborated Lee Soo-hyuk's statement: "In those days, a lot of false information was being passed around in South

Korea and some of the stories were circulated with the political intention of distorting the truth, such as the one that the South Korean government strongly opposed the U.S. government position. The allegation against Lee Soo-hyuk must be one of those." Lee Jong-seok, interview, Seoul, September 4, 2006.

34. Interview with a U.S. Department of Defense official, Washington, August 24, 2006.

35. Interview with a senior U.S. administration official, Washington, June 2, 2006.

36. Interview with a senior South Korean government official, Seoul, July 11, 2006.

37. "Chong Wa Dae Split over Troop Dispatch," *Korea Times,* October 21, 2003.

38. "Roh to Discuss Troop Plan," *Korea Times,* November 11, 2003.

39. "US Requests ROK Troops to Replace 101st Airborne," *Korea Times,* October 2, 2003.

40. Interview with a senior South Korean government official, Seoul, March 22, 2006.

41. Interview with a senior South Korean government official, Seoul, July 11, 2006.

42. "President Roh Gives Guidelines for Forming Korean Military Unit to Be Sent to Iraq." Presidential spokesman Yoon Tai-young, daily press briefing, Cheong Wa Dae Office of the President, November 13, 2003.

43. Korea-U.S. Security Consultative Meeting Joint Communiqué, November 17, 2003 (www.defenselink.mil/releases/2003/nr20031124-0688.html).

44. Interview with a senior South Korean government official, Seoul, March 22, 2006; interview with a senior U.S. administration official, Washington, June 27, 2006.

45. Interview with a senior South Korean government official, Tokyo, January 26, 2006.

46. Lee Jong-seok, interview, Seoul, September 4, 2006.

47. "Korea, U.S. Trade Barbs on Iraq-North Link," *JoongAng Daily,* December 4, 2004.

48. Tadanao Takatsuki, "Kankoku Gaisho, Jijitsu-jono Kotetsu" ("De Facto Removal of South Korean Foreign Minister"), *Asahi Shimbun* (evening edition), January 16, 2004.

49. Interview with a senior South Korean government official, Seoul, July 10, 2006.

50. Seo Soo-min, "Yoon Calls for Balance in Roh's Policy," *Korea Times,* January 15, 2004.

51. Choi Jie-ho, "Foreign Minister Quits under Fire from Blue House," *JoongAng Daily,* January 17, 2004.

52. Interview with a former senior Blue House official, Seoul, October 10, 2006.

53. Interview with a senior South Korean government official, Seoul, May 8, 2006.

54. "Address by President Roh Moo-hyun on the 59th Anniversary of National Liberation," Korean Overseas Information Service (Korea.net), August 15, 2004.

55. Chae-jin Lee, *A Troubled Peace: U.S. Diplomacy and the Two Koreas* (Johns Hopkins University Press, 2006), p. 259; Yoichi Funabashi, *Alliance Adrift* (New York: Council on Foreign Relations, 1999), p. 249.

56. Interview with a senior South Korean government official, Washington, June 23, 2006.

57. Interview with a White House official, Washington, June 27, 2006; Rowan Scarborough, "U.S. Plans to Shift Troops in South Korea," *Washington Times,* March 7, 2003.

58. Interview with a senior U.S. administration official, Washington, June 27 and July 21, 2006.

59. Interview with a senior U.S. administration official, Washington, July 27, 2006.

60. "Joint Statement between the United States of America and the Republic of Korea: Common Values, Principles, and Strategy," White House, May 14, 2003 (www.whitehouse.gov/news/releases/2003/05/20030514-17.html).

61. In June 2003, two schoolgirls were killed when they were hit by an armored personnel carrier on a narrow road near Seoul. Don Kirk, "U.S. Acts to Blunt Protest on Korean Girls' Deaths," *International Herald Tribune,* June 13, 2003.

62. "Soldiers Clamor against Softened Definition of N. Korea as 'Main Enemy,'" *Chosun Ilbo,* November 14, 2004.

63. Interview with a senior South Korean government official, Seoul, October 11, 2005. However, Defense Minister Cho Young-kil told the author that "only the upper echelon of the government changes the view. But down in the military they don't change it." Cho Young-kil, interview, Seoul, March 24, 2006. The phrase "main enemy" formally disappeared from the Defense White Paper 2004, published in February 2005; Kim Hak-joon, *North and South Korea: Internal Politics and External Relations since 1988* (Seoul: Society for Korean and Related Studies, 2006), p. 331.

64. Bruce Bechtol, "The Future of U.S. Airpower on the Korean Peninsula," *Air and Space Power Journal* 29, no. 3 (Fall 2005). Available at www.airpower.maxwell.af.mil/airchronicles/apj/apj05/fal05/bechtol.html.

65. Interview with a senior U.S. administration official, Washington, July 21, 2006.

66. Interview with a senior South Korean government official, Seoul, July 11, 2006.

67. Interview with a senior U.S. administration official, Washington, July 21, 2006.

68. Joint Communiqué: 36th Annual U.S.-ROK Security Consultative Meeting, October 22, 2004 (http://usinfo.state.gov/eap/Archive/2004/Oct/25-900257.html).

69. Interview with a senior U.S. administration official, Washington, July 21, 2006.

70. Interview with a U.S. Department of Defense official, Washington, April 25, 2006.

71. Interview with a senior U.S. Department of Defense official, Washington, August 24, 2006.

72. 37th Security Consultative Meeting Joint Communiqué, October 25, 2005 (www.globalsecurity.org/military/library/news/2005/10/d20051021uskorea1.pdf).

73. Interview with a U.S. Department of Defense official, Washington, April 25, 2006.

74. Interview with a senior White House official, Washington, July 21, 2006.

75. Jonathan D. Pollack and Mitchell B. Reiss, "South Korea: The Tyranny of Geography and the Vexations of History," in *The Nuclear Tipping Point: Why States Reconsider Their Nuclear Choices,* edited by Kurt M. Campbell, Robert Einhorn, and Mitchell Reiss (Brookings, 2004), p. 269.

76. "Text of the Korean War Armistice Agreement," U.S. Department of State, Bureau of Arms Control, July 27, 1953 (www.state.gov/t/ac/rls/or/2004/31006.htm).

77. Chiharu Mori, *Chosen Hanto ha Toitsu Dekirunoka—Kankoku no Shiren* (*Can the Korean Peninsula Be Unified? A Challenge for South Korea*) (Tokyo: Chuo Koron-sha, 2003), pp. 104, 107.

78. Interview with a U.S. Department of Defense official, Washington, August 24, 2006.

79. Yun Sang-ho, "Frictions over Military Plan between South Korea and the U.S.," *Dong-A Ilbo,* April 15, 2005.

80. Jung Sung-ki, "ROK Rebuffs US Contingency Plan on DPRK," *Korea Times,* April 15, 2005.

81. Lawrence Wilkerson, interview, Washington, September 19, 2005; interview with a U.S. Department of State official, Washington, October 14, 2005.

82. Interview with a Department of Defense official, Washington, August 24, 2006; interview with a senior U.S. administration official, Washington, March 1, 2006.

83. Interview with a former U.S. Department of Defense official, Washington, July 25, 2006. Also see Bruce Bechtol, "The ROK-U.S. Alliance During the Bush and Roh Administration: Differing Perspectives and Their Implications for a Changing Strategic Environment," *International Journal of Korean Studies* 20, no. 2 (2005).

84. Kang Chan-ho, "Seoul Proposed Discussing Collapse Plan with U.S.," *JoongAng Ilbo,* May 2, 2005.

85. Interview with a U.S. Department of Defense official, Washington, August 24, 2006.

86. Interview with a White House official, Washington, March 1, 2006.

87. Interview with a senior South Korean government official, Seoul, September 4, 2006.

88. Interview with a former U.S. Department of Defense official, Washington, July 25, 2006.

89. Interview with a senior U.S. Department of Defense official, Washington, August 24, 2006.

90. Interview with a former Department of Defense official, Washington, July 25, 2006.

91. Joint Communiqué: 36th Annual US-ROK Security Consultative Meeting, October 22, 2004 (http://usinfo.state.gov/eap/Archive/2004/Oct/25-900257.html).

92. Interview with a senior U.S. administration official, Washington, August 10, 2006.

93. Interview with a senior South Korean government official, Seoul, July 10, 2006.

94. Interview with a senior U.S. administration official, Washington, March 1, 2006.

95. "Roh and Bush Discussed USFK Flexibility, OP-PLAN," *Chosun Ilbo*, June 14, 2005.

96. Interview with a senior U.S. administration official, Washington, March 1, 2006.

97. Interview with a senior South Korean government official, Washington, April 27, 2006.

98. Roh Moo-hyun, "Address on the 86th March 1st Independence Movement Day," Office of the President, March 1, 2005. Available at http://english.president.go.kr

99. Roh Moo-hyun, "Address at the 40th Commencement and Commissioning Ceremony of the Korea Third Military Academy," Office of the President, March 22, 2005. Available at http://english.president.go.kr

100. "Roh Hints at New East Asian Order," *Chosun Ilbo*, March 22, 2005.

101. Interview with a Blue House official, Seoul, November 30, 2005, and July 10, 2006.

102. Ibid.

103. Interview with a senior South Korean government official, Tokyo, April 17, 2005.

104. Interview with a U.S. Department of Defense official, Washington, April 25, 2006.

105. Interview with a senior South Korean government official, Washington, August 18, 2005.

106. Interview with a senior South Korean government official, Seoul, May 8, 2006.

107. "Korea Wants to Have Its Cake and Eat It, Too," *Chosun Ilbo*, March 31, 2005.

108. Seung-Heon Lee, "GNP Chairman Park Geun-hye's National Assembly Speech," *Dong-A Ilbo*, April 8, 2005.

109. "Majority of Public Back Korea 'Balancer' Role," *Korea Herald*, April 11, 2005.

110. "Who Is Trying to Cash In On Popular Sentiment?" *Chosun Ilbo*, editorial, April 20, 2005.

111. Interview with a senior U.S. administration official, Washington, March 1 and June 2, 2006.

112. "U.S. Keeps Grumbling as Summit Looms," *Chosun Ilbo*, June 9, 2005.

113. Interview with a U.S. Department of Defense official, Washington, April 25, 2006.

114. Interview with a U.S. Department of Defense official, Washington, August 24, 2006.

115. Ibid.

116. Interview with a U.S. Department of State official, Washington, December 27, 2005.

117. Interview with a U.S. administration official, Washington, July 21, 2006; interview with a senior South Korean government official, Seoul, July 10, 2006.

118. Interview with a senior South Korean government official, Seoul, July 11, 2006.

119. "Kim Dae-jung Tells New Uri Leaders to Accept Alliance," *Chosun Ilbo*, April 8, 2005.

120. Interview with a senior Blue House official, Seoul, May 9, 2006.

121. Interview with a cabinet member of the Roh government, Seoul, May 8, 2006.

122. Interview with a senior South Korean government official, Seoul, March 22, 2006.

123. Interview with a senior Blue House official, Seoul, October 10, 2005.

124. Ban Ki-moon, interview, Seoul, March 23, 2006; interview with a senior U.S. administration official, Washington, May 5, 2006.

125. Ibid.

126. Interview with a senior U.S. administration official, Washington, June 2, 2006.

127. Lee Jong-seok, interview, Seoul, September 4, 2006.

128. Tadanao Takatsuki, Seoul, "Kin Soshoki 'Raigetsu Fukki Mo" ("General Secretary Kim Mentions 'Possibility of Returning to Six-Party Talks Next Month'"), *Asahi Shimbun*, June 18, 2005.

129. Ibid.

130. Interview with a senior South Korean government official, Seoul, October 11, 2005.

131. Chung Dong-young, interview, Seoul, March 24, 2006.

132. Interview with a senior U.S. administration official, Washington, June 2, 2006.

133. Interview with a senior South Korean government official, Washington, April 25, 2006.

134. Interview with a senior South Korean government official, Seoul, November 30, 2005.

135. Interview with a senior U.S. administration official, Washington, August 16, 2006; interview with a senior Japanese government official, Tokyo, September 5, 2006.

136. Interview with a senior South Korean government official, Seoul, July 10, 2006.

137. Interview with a senior U.S administration official, Seoul, July 12, 2006.

CHAPTER EIGHT

1. Interview with a senior Chinese government official, Tokyo, May 12, 2006; "Restarting Nuclear Talks, but with Seoul Absent," *JoongAng Daily*, November 18, 2004.

2. Interview with a Chinese diplomat, Tokyo, July 6, 2006.

3. Reconstructed on the basis of a conversation with a senior Chinese government official, May 15, 2006.

4. Barbara Starr, "U.S. Orders 24 Long-Range Bombers to Guam," *CNN.com*, March 5, 2003.

5. Reconstructed on the basis of a conversation with a senior Chinese government official, December 13, 2005.

6. Interview with a Chinese diplomat, December 9, 2005.

7. Reconstructed on the basis of a conversation with a senior Chinese government official, May 12, 2006.

8. Interview with a Chinese diplomat, May 15, 2006.

9. Interview with a Chinese diplomat, September 1, 2006.

10. Reconstructed on the basis of a conversation with a senior Chinese government official, May 12, 2006.

11. Reconstructed on the basis of a conversation with a senior Chinese government official, July 8, 2006.

12. Reconstructed on the basis of a conversation with a senior Chinese government official, May 12, 2006.

13. Reconstructed on the basis of a conversation with a North Korean diplomat, April 16, 2006.

14. Xu Jia-tun, *Xu Jia-tun Xianggang Huiyilu* (*Memoirs of Xu Jiatun*) (Xianggang Lian-hebao), pp. 363–80, 425–56.

15. Qian Qichen, *Waijiao Shi Ji* (*Ten Stories of a Diplomat*) (Beijing: Shijie Zhishi Chuban She, 2003), pp. 157–59.

16. Lee Jong Seok, "Datsu Reisen-ki no Chu-Cho Kankei: Jizokusei to Henka" ("China-North Korea Relations in the Post-Cold War Era: Continuity and Change") in *Kin Shonichi Taisei no Kita Chosen: Seiji, Gaiko, Keizai, Shiso* (*North Korea under the Kim Jong Il Regime: Its Politics, Diplomacy, Economy, and Ideology*), edited by Hajime Izumi and Chang Dal-Joong (Tokyo: Keio University Press, 2004), p. 99. On this point, a senior Chinese official at the Ministry of Foreign Affairs told the author in an e-mail exchange, "China's decision to normalize its relationship with the South contained no element regarding the North's nuclear issue. Actually pressures for normalizing relations with the ROK at that time came [first] from the necessity for further open door policy/domestic economic development, especially from provinces like Shandong and Liaoning. Such needs raised a very sharp and simple question: should China's top priority (economic development) be tied to or abide by another country's top priority? [Second,] the Taiwan issue. Beijing needed normal relations with Seoul to drive out Taiwan's influence in the South, which used to be Taiwan's allied country. [Third,] fundamental changes in international relations surrounding China: the collapse of the Soviet Union and diplomatic relations between Russia and the South; China's need to open new diplomatic frontiers to further break the isolation policy led by the U.S. after the Tian'anmen incident; the South's lobbying for normalization with China, which was mutually beneficial. In short, multiple factors drove the Chinese leadership to make that decision; there was no consideration of the nuclear issue. Beijing had begun to talk about normalization with the ROK before 1992; no one took the nuclear issue into consideration in the decision."

17. Email interview with a senior Chinese diplomat, February 5, 2007.

18. Conversation with Liu Changle, chairman and chief executive officer of Phoenix TV, Beijing, September 25, 2006.

19. James Kelly, interview, Seattle, October 18, 2005.

20. Interview with a senior U.S. administration official, Tokyo, September 2, 2003.

21. David E. Sanger, "Bush and Jiang Vow to Cooperate on North Korea Issues," *New York Times,* October 26, 2002.

22. "Conclusion of Non-Aggression Treaty between DPRK and U.S. Called for," *Korean Central News Agency,* October 25, 2002.

23. Reconstructed on the basis of a conversation with a senior Chinese government official, August 2, 2006; interview with a senior Japanese government official, Tokyo, March 27, 2003.

24. Maura Reynolds, "China's Jiang Vows to Help Stop North Korea's Arms Program. But He's Less Supportive on Iraq," *Los Angeles Times,* October 26, 2002.

25. "Jiang and Kim hold post-summit breakfast meeting," *Agence France-Presse (AFP),* November 15 1995; "China Leader Is in Seoul, A Hint of Warming Ties," *Reuters,* November 14, 1995.

26. Kim Young-sam, interview, Seoul, July 3, 2003.

27. Interview with a Chinese government official, Beijing, March 20, 2006.

28. Joel S. Wit, Daniel B. Poneman, and Robert L.Gallucci, *Going Critical: The First North Korean Nuclear Crisis* (Brookings, 2004), p. 154.

29. Conversation with a Chinese diplomat, September 15, 2006.

30. Reconstructed on the basis of a conversation with a Chinese diplomat, December 9, 2005; interview with a Chinese diplomat, November 25, 2005.

31. "Joint Declaration by the Russian Federation and the People's Republic of China," Russian Embassy, Beijing, December 2, 2002 (www.russia.org.cn/eng/?SID=22&ID=6&print=true).

32. "United States Condemns North Korea's Decision to Quit Nuclear Arms Treaty," Associated Press, January 10, 2003.

33. Russia interpreted China's vote as "a safe move to become tough on North Korea" because "the Chinese knew that we [Russia] would take this position [abstention]." Alexander P. Losyukov, interview, Tokyo, July 7, 2006.

34. James Kelly, interview, Seattle, October 18, 2005.

35. Interview with a senior Japanese government official, Tokyo, February 28, 2003.

36. Interview with a senior MOFA official, Tokyo, June 3, 2003.

37. Jae Ho Chung, "China's Ascendancy and the Korean Peninsula: From Interest Reevaluation to Strategic Realignment?" in *Power Shift*, edited by David Shambaugh (University of California Press, 2005), p. 155.

38. Interview with a senior U.S. administration official, Washington, August 10, 2006.

39. Interview on Fox News Sunday with Tony Snow, U.S. Department of State, February 9, 2003 (www.state.gov/secretary/former/powell/remarks/2003/17499.htm).

40. James Dao, "Powell Seeks China's Help and, at U.N., Its Abstention," *New York Times*, February 24, 2003.

41. Charles L. Pritchard, "The Korean Peninsula and the Role of Multilateral Talks," *Disarmament Forum North East Asian Security* 2 (2005): 27; Nobuyoshi Sakajiri, "'Noshuku Keikaku Mitometa no ha Yosogai': Kerii Zen Kokumujikanho Kaiken Yoshi" ("'I Did Not Expect Them to Acknowledge a Uranium Enrichment Program': Excerpts of the Interview with Former Assistant Secretary Kelly"), *Asahi Shimbun*, June 18, 2005; Dao, "Powell Seeks China's Help and, at U.N., Its Abstention."

42. James Kelly, interview, Seattle, October 18, 2005; Yoriko Kawaguchi, interview, Tokyo, January 30, 2006.

43. Interview with a senior Japanese government official, Tokyo, January 26, 2006.

44. Interview with a senior U.S. administration official, Washington, August 16, 2006.

45. Pritchard, "The Korean Peninsula and the Role of Multilateral Talks," p. 28.

46. Interview with a senior U.S. administration official, Washington, August 10, 2006.

47. "Wrap-Up: Chinese Leaders Meet Powell in Beijing," *Xinhua*, February 24, 2003.

48. "Chinese Vice-President Meets Powell," *Xinhua*, February 24, 2003.

49. Interview with a senior U.S. administration official, Washington, March 13, 2006.

50. Interview with a senior U.S. administration official, Washington, February 24, 2006.

51. Interview with a Chinese diplomat, Beijing, September 25, 2006.

52. Interview with a senior U.S. administration official, Washington, February 24, 2006.

53. Interview with a senior U.S. administration official, Washington, March 13, 2006.

54. Interview with a senior U.S. administration official, Washington, February 24, 2006.

55. "Roh, Bush Confirm Peaceful Resolution of NK Row," Korean Overseas Information Service (Korea.net), April 7, 2003; "Press Conference 21 March 2003," Ministry of Foreign Affairs, March 21, 2003 (www.mofa.go.jp/announce/press/2003/3/0321.html).

56. Interview with a senior U.S. administration official, Washington, March 13, 2006.

57. Interview with a senior Japanese MOFA official, Washington, February 17, 2006.

58. Pritchard, "The Korean Peninsula and the Role of Multilateral Talks," p. 28.

59. "Mr. Hu's Grand Tour," *Economist*, May 31, 2003.

60. Interview with a Chinese diplomat, September 15, 2006.

61. Ibid.

62. "Kim Il-sung Hosts Banquet in War Anniversary Celebrations," BBC Summary of World Broadcasts, July 1993.

63. Interview with a Chinese diplomat, Beijing, January 21, 2006; John Pomfret, "China Urges N. Korea Dialogue," *Washington Post,* April 4, 2003.

64. Jae Ho Chung, "China's Ascendancy and the Korean Peninsula: From Interest Reevaluation to Strategic Realignment?" in *Power Shift,* edited by Shambaugh, p. 166.

65. Interview with a senior U.S. administration official, Washington, December 8, 2005.

66. "China and North Korea: Comrades Forever?" *International Crisis Group Asia Report 112* (Brussels: International Crisis Group, February 1, 2006), p. 6.

67. Interview with a senior U.S. administration official, Washington, March 13 and August 10, 2006.

68. Reconstructed on the basis of a conversation with a senior Chinese government official, May 12, 2006.

69. Reconstructed on the basis of a conversation with a former Chinese diplomat, Shanghai, April 22, 2004.

70. Reconstructed on the basis of a conversation with a senior member of a South Korean government organization, Seoul, November 29, 2005.

71. Interview with a U.S. administration official, Washington, December 8, 2005.

72. Interview with a senior member of a Chinese government organization, Beijing, March 20, 2006.

73. Reconstructed on the basis of a conversation with a Japanese diplomat posted in Beijing, Beijing, August 31, 2005.

74. Reconstructed on the basis of a conversation with a senior Japanese MOFA official, Tokyo, July 5, 2006.

75. Reconstructed on the basis of a conversation with a Chinese diplomat, September 25, 2006.

76. Interview with a senior Chinese government official, Beijing, March 20, 2006.

77. Interview with a senior U.S. administration official, Washington, January 20 and August 21, 2004.

78. Interview with a Chinese diplomat, September 29, 2006.

79. Interview with a senior U.S. administration official, Washington, January 20 and August 21, 2004.

80. Interview with a Chinese foreign ministry official, Beijing, January 20, 2006.

81. Interview with a Chinese foreign ministry official, Beijing, April 17, 2006.

82. Ibid.

83. "China, U.S. hold Korea talks," *CNN.com,* July 17, 2003.

84. Colin Powell, interview, Washington, March 31, 2006; James Kelly, interview, Washington, May 20, 2006.

85. Colin Powell, interview, Washington, March 31, 2006.

86. James Kelly, interview, Washington, September 19, 2006.

87. Ibid.

88. Pritchard, "The Korean Peninsula and the Role of Multilateral Talks," p. 29.

89. Reconstructed on the basis of a conversation with a senior Chinese government official, Beijing, July 13, 2006.

90. Interview with a State Department official, Washington, June 14, 2006.

91. Interview with a Chinese diplomat, Beijing, July 13, 2006.

92. Interview with a senior U.S. administration official, Washington, February 24, 2006.

93. Interview with a Chinese diplomat, December 9, 2005.

94. Conversation with a Chinese diplomat, September 15, 2006.

95. Interview with a Chinese government official, Beijing, July 13, 2006.

96. "Press Event on the Four-Party Talks," *Northeast Asia Peace and Security Network Special Report,* December 11, 1997 (www.nautilus.org/archives/pub/ftp/napsnet/special_reports/Roth_Statement.txt).

97. Robert A. Scalapino, "China and Korean Reunification—A Neighbor's Concerns," in *Korea's Future and the Great Powers,* edited by Nicholas Eberstadt and Richard J. Elling (University of Washington Press, 2001), p. 115.

98. Ibid., p. 116.

99. Interview with a senior Japanese government official, Tokyo, September 10, 2003.

100. Interview with a senior White House official, Washington, April 3, 2006.

101. James Kelly, interview, Seattle, October 18, 2005.

102. Interview with a senior Chinese Foreign Ministry official, Beijing, April 17, 2006.

103. Interview with a Chinese diplomat, Beijing, July 13, 2006.

104. Conversation with a senior member of a Chinese government organization, Beijing, July 13, 2006.

105. Interview with a senior U.S. administration official, Washington, June 2, 2006.

106. Richard Armitage, interview, Washington, August 1, 2006.

107. Interview with a State Department official, Washington, June 26, 2006.

108. A meeting between the two presumably helped China send a high-level delegation headed by Tang Jiaxuan, state councilor, to Pyongyang to meet Kim Jong-il and try to control the damage done by North Korea's nuclear test in October 2006. "China 'Sends Special Envoy to N. Korea,'" *Chosun Ilbo,* October 19, 2006.

109. Interview with a senior Chinese government official, Beijing, August 3, 2004.

110. James Kelly, interview, Washington, May 20, 2006.

111. "Spokesman for Panmunjeom Mission of KPA Issues Statement," Korean Central News Agency, February 18, 2003.

112. John S. Park, "Inside the Multilateralism: The Six-Party Talks," *Washington Quarterly* 28, no. 4 (2005): 83. It was reported that Wang Yi warned North Korea that it should not "play with fire" (*Washington Post,* April 4, 2003), but when I interviewed him in Tokyo, Wang Yi denied making the remark.

113. Conversation with a Chinese diplomat, May 15, 2006.

114. Interview with a Japanese diplomat whom Wu once told about his former "Red Guard" experience, London, February 6, 2006.

115. Interview with a Chinese diplomat, Beijing, August 31, 2005.

116. Interview with a Japanese diplomat who was posted in Beijing, Beijing, November 21, 2005.

117. Interview with a U.S. State Department official, Washington, October 14, 2005.

118. Interview with a senior U.S. administration official, Washington, June 4, 2004; interview with a Chinese diplomat, February 14, 2006.

119. Conversation with a North Korean diplomat, June 5, 2006.

120. Conversation with a senior U.S. administration official, Washington, November 5, 2004.

121. Toshu Noguchi, "Kitahihan Keisai de Haikan Chugoku Dokuritsukei Kakugetsukan Shi" ("Independent Bimonthly Chinese Magazine Forced to Discontinue for Its Criticism of North Korea"), *Sankei Shimbun,* September 21, 2004.

122. Interview with a senior Chinese government official, February 23, 2006.

123. Reconstructed on the basis of a conversation with Richard Solomon, Washington, June 15, 2006.

124. Interview with a U.S. administration official, Washington, March 13, 2006.

125. Interview with a senior U.S. administration official, August 23, 2004.

126. Lawrence Wilkerson, interview, Washington, September 19, 2006.

127. Reconstructed on the basis of a conversation with a Chinese diplomat, February 14, 2006.

128. Interview with a Chinese diplomat, Beijing, July 13, 2006.

129. Ibid.

130. Interview with a Chinese foreign ministry official, February 14, 2006.

131. Interview with a senior U.S. Department of Defense official, Washington, December 22, 2005.

132. Reconstructed on the basis of a conversation with a member of a Chinese government organization, Beijing, January 19, 2006.

133. Conversation with a veteran Chinese diplomat, April 27, 2006.

134. Interview with a Chinese diplomat, Beijing, July 13, 2006.

135. Lin Xixing, "Zhongchao Youyi Suibulao Dan Bukepo" ("Although China–North Korea Friendship Might Not Be Solid, It Should Not Be Broken"), *Yazhou Zhoukan* (Asia Weekly), August 13, 2006.

136. Reconstructed on the basis of a conversation with a senior member of a Chinese government organization, Beijing, March 22, 2006.

137. Bill Gertz, "China Ships North Korea Ingredient for Nuclear Arms," *Washington Times,* December 17, 2002.

138. Interview with a senior U.S. administration official, Washington, August 10, 2006; Nobuyoshi Sakajiri, "Chugoku, Kitachosen Muke Kaku Yobai Oshu" ("China Confiscated a Liquid Substance for Nuclear Development Bound for North Korea"), *Asahi Shimbun,* February 21, 2004.

139. Interview with a senior U.S. administration official, Washington, August 10, 2006.

140. David L. Shambaugh, "China's 'Quiet Diplomacy': The International Department of the Chinese Communist Party," *China: An International Journal* 5, no. 1 (March 2007).

141. Ibid., p. 29.

142. Reconstructed on the basis of a conversation with a Chinese diplomat, April 27, 2006.

143. Conversation with a Chinese diplomat, Beijing, July 11, 2006.

144. Conversation with a North Korean diplomat, June 5, 2006.

145. Nobuyoshi Sakajiri, "Kita no 'Shogun Sama' Wagayo no Haru" ("Dear General of the North 'Enjoyed His Stage and His Season'"), *Asahi Shimbun,* January 23, 2006.

146. "Kim Jong Il Indicates Willingness to Return to Talks," Korean Central News Agency, February 22, 2005; "DPRK Ready to Return to Six-Party Talks If Conditions Met: Kim Jong-il," *People's Daily,* February 17, 2005.

147. Interview with a senior Chinese government official, Beijing, July 13, 2006.

148. Reconstructed on the basis of a conversation with a Chinese diplomat, Beijing, April 17, 2006.

149. Interview with a senior South Korean government official, Seoul, November 29, 2005.

150. Reconstructed based upon a conversation with a Chinese diplomat, December 9, 2005.

151. Reconstructed based upon a conversation with a Chinese diplomat, Beijing, April 17, 2006.

152. John M. Sanford, "The Korean Armistice: Short-Term Truce or Long-Term Peace?" USAWC Strategy Research Project (U.S. Army War College, March 15, 2006),

p. 8; Rosemary Foot, *A Substitute for Victory: The Politics of Peacemaking at the Korean Armistice Talks* (Cornell University Press, 1990), p. ix.

153. Gong Ro-myung, interview, Tokyo, November 3, 2003.

154. Andrew S. Natsios, *The Great North Korean Famine: Politics and Foreign Policy* (Washington: United States Institute of Peace Press, 2002), p. 139.

155. Teresa Poole, "China Rids Itself of Unwelcome Guest," *Independent* (London), March 19, 1997.

156. Robert A. Scalapino, "China and Korean Reunification—A Neighbor's Concerns," in *Korea's Future and the Great Powers,* edited by Nicholas Eberstadt and Richard J. Elling (University of Washington Press, 2001), p. 120.

157. Reconstructed on the basis of a conversation with a member of a Chinese government organization, Beijing, March 20, 2006.

158. "Treaty of Friendship, Cooperation, and Mutual Assistance between the People's Republic of China and the Democratic People's Republic of Korea," *Peking Review* 4 , no. 28 (1967): 5.

159. Yoji Gomi, "Katsute wa 'Chi no Domei Kankei' Chucho Akikaze" ("Relations between China and North Korea Become Frosty: Alliance Based on Bonds of Blood Long Gone"), *Tokyo Shimbun,* September 26, 2003.

160. Interview with a retired high-ranking Chinese army officer, Beijing, August 31, 2005.

161. Shen Jiru, "Weihu Dongbeiya Anquan de Danwu Zhi Ji," ("It Is an Urgent Task to Maintain Northeast Asia's Stability"), *Xijie Jingji Yu Zhengzhi* (*World Economy and Politics*) 9 (2003).

162. Reconstructed on the basis of a conversation with a North Korea expert at a Shanghai think tank, Shanghai, July 31, 2004.

163. James Brooke, "Old Allies Turn Up the Heat on North Korea," *International Herald Tribune,* August 19, 2003.

164. Samuel S. Kim and Tae Hwan Lee, "Chinese-North Korean Relations: Managing Asymmetrical Interdependence," in *North Korea and Northeast Asia,* edited by Samuel Kim and Tae Hwan Lee (Lanham, Md.: Rowman and Littlefield, 2002), p. 117.

165. "China and North Korea: Comrades Forever?" *International Crisis Group Asia Report 112* (Brussels: International Crisis Group, February 1, 2006), p. 7.

166. Wang Yiwei, "China's Role in Dealing with the North Korean Nuclear Issue," *Korea Observer* 36, no. 3 (2005): 473–74.

167. This remark was made by Shi during an Internet debate program in July 2003. Chi Tong-wook, *Chosen Hanto Eisei Churitsuka Ron* (*On Permanent Neutralization on the Korean Peninsula*) (Tokyo: Chuokoron Shinsha, 2004), pp. 225–26.

168. Wang Zhongwen, "Yi Xin Shijiao Shenshi Chaoxian Wenti Yu Dongbeiya Xingshi" ("Examining the DPRK Issue and Northeast Asian Situation from a New Viewpoint"), *Zhanlue Yu Guanli* (*Strategy and Management*) 4 (2004): 92–94.

169. "Article May Signal Shift in China-North Korea Relations," *Epoch Times,* September 18, 2004.

CHAPTER NINE

1. Interview with a senior Chinese government official, March 8, 2006.

2. Ibid.

3. Interview with a Chinese diplomat involved in the six-party talks, March 8, 2006. The official told the author that he strongly supported Siegfried Hecker's argument

regarding the capacity of nuclear deterrence. Siegfried Hecker, a U.S. nuclear physicist who visited North Korea at the beginning of 2004, noted in his testimony before Congress: "I explained that I view a 'deterrent' to have at least three components: 1) The ability to make plutonium metal, 2) the ability to design and build a nuclear device, and 3) the ability to integrate the nuclear device into a delivery system. What we saw at Yongbyon was that they apparently have the capability to do the first. However, I saw nothing and talked to no one that allowed me to assess whether or not they have the ability to design a nuclear device. And, of course, we were not able to assess the integration into a delivery vehicle. Moreover, during additional discussions I cautioned that 'deterrence' might have worked between the United States and the Soviet Union, two equally armed nuclear superpowers, under rather predictable circumstances. The concept of nuclear deterrence may have little meaning for the U.S.–DPRK situation." Siegfried S. Hecker, U.S. Senate Committee on Foreign Relations, *An Update on North Korean Nuclear Developments: Hearing before the Committee on Foreign Relations,* 108th Cong., 2nd sess., January 21, 2004.

4. For exploration of options by the George H. W. Bush administration, see Joel S. Wit, Daniel B. Poneman, and Robert L. Gallucci, *Going Critical: The First North Korean Nuclear Crisis* (Brookings, 2004), pp. 6–15.

5. "North Korean Nuclear Crisis," February 1993-June 1994. Available at: www.globalsecurity.org/military/ops/dprk nuke.htm.

6. Conversation with a Chinese diplomat, September 29, 2006.

7. Wang Yiwei, "China's Role in Dealing with the North Korean Nuclear Issue," *Korea Observer* 36, no. 3 (2005): 471.

8. Interview with a veteran Chinese diplomat, February 23, 2006.

9. Interview with Vice President Dick Cheney, *Meet the Press,* NBC, transcript, March 16, 2003.

10. John R. Bolton, U.S. House Committee on International Relations, *U.S. Nonproliferation Policy after Iraq: Hearing before the Committee on International Relations,* 108th Cong., 1st sess., June 4, 2003.

11. Interview with a senior U.S. administration official, Washington, August 25, 2006.

12. Interview with a senior Japanese government official, Tokyo, September 22, 2004.

13. Interview with a senior U.S. administration official, Washington, March 13, 2006.

14. Interview with a senior U.S. administration official, Washington, March 13, 2006.

15. Ibid.

16. Interview with a senior Chinese government official, December 13, 2005.

17. Interview with a senior U.S. administration official, Washington, August 17, 2006.

18. Interview with a senior U.S. administration official, Washington, May 31, 2006.

19. Christopher Hill, "Remarks on the Six-Party Peace Talks," Asia Society, New York, October 11, 2005. Available at www.asiasociety.org/speeches/hill05.html.

20. Interview with a senior U.S. administration official, Washington, March 13, 2006.

21. Interview with a senior U.S. administration official, Washington, June 7, 2004.

22. James Kelly, interview, Seattle, October 18, 2005.

23. Lawrence Wilkerson's observation. Lawrence Wilkerson, interview, Washington, September 19, 2005.

24. Reconstructed on the basis of a conversation with a Chinese diplomat, August 3, 2006.

25. Bates Gill, "China's Evolving Regional Security Strategy," in *Power Shift: China and Asia's New Dynamics,* edited by David Shambaugh (University of California Press, 2006), p. 262.

26. *Quadrennial Defense Review Report,* Department of Defense, September 30, 2001, pp. 2 and 4 (www.defenselink.mil/pubs/qdr2001.pdf).

27. Ibid., February 6, 2006, p. 29 (www.defenselink.mil/qdr/report/Report20060203.pdf).

28. Piao Jianyi, "Beijing Liufang Huitan Yu Chaoxian He Wenti" ("Six Party Talks and the Korean Nuclear Issue"), *Dandai Yatai (Contemporary Asia-Pacific)* (October 2003), p. 496.

29. Reconstructed on the basis of a conversation with a Japanese diplomat stationed in Beijing, Beijing, August 30, 2005.

30. Wang, "China's Role in Dealing with the North Korean Nuclear Issue," p. 472.

31. Henry Kissinger, *The White House Years* (Boston: Little Brown, 1979), p. 1090.

32. Interview with a senior U.S. administration official, March 1, 2006.

33. Ning Fukui told a Korea Institute for Defense Analysis forum, "The presence of U.S. troops in South Korea is a bilateral system. We can understand if they act in a bilateral framework.... But if it is targeted at a third country, China will have no choice but to shift attention to the matter." Choe Sang-Hun, "Shift GIs in Korea to Taiwan? Never, China Envoy Says," *International Herald Tribune*, March 22, 2006.

34. Interview with a senior Chinese government official, Beijing, April 17, 2006.

35. Interview with a senior U.S. administration official, Washington, August 17, 2006.

36. Interview with a senior Chinese official, February 23, 2006.

37. Robert A. Scalapino, "China and Korean Reunification: A Neighbor's Concerns," in *Korea's Future and the Great Powers,* edited by Nicholas Eberstadt and Richard J. Ellings (University of Washington Press, 2001), p. 120.

38. Ibid.

39. Reconstructed on the basis of a conversation with a senior member of a Chinese government organization, Shanghai, July 30, 2004.

40. Reconstructed on the basis of a conversation with a senior member of a Chinese government organization, Beijing, August 30, 2005.

41. Brian Knowlton, "Bush Pledge: U.S. to Help If Chinese Hit Taiwan," *International Herald Tribune,* April 26, 2001.

42. James Kelly, interview, Washington, May 20, 2006.

43. "Hu Forces White House to Read between China's official lines," *USA Today,* May 2, 2002.

44. James Kelly, interview, Washington, May 20, 2006.

45. "President Bush and Premier Wen Jiabao Remarks to the Press," White House, December 9, 2003 (www.whitehouse.gov/news/releases/2003/12/20031209-2.html).

46. "China Links Taiwan Dispute to North Korea Talks," *Honolulu Advertiser,* February 29, 2004.

47. Wang, "China's Role in Dealing with the North Korean Nuclear Issue," p. 470.

48. Interview with a U.S. Department of State official, New York, January 9, 2006.

49. Ibid.

50. Interview with a senior White House official, Washington, March 13, 2006.

51. James Kelly, interview, Washington, May 20, 2006.

52. Interview with a senior U.S. administration official, Washington, August 10, 2006.

53. Reconstructed on the basis of a conversation with a Chinese government official, Tokyo, November 25, 2004.

54. Interview with a Chinese diplomat, September 29, 2006.

55. James Kelly, U.S. House Committee on International Relations, *U.S. Policy in East Asia and the Pacific: Hearing before the Subcommittee on Asia and the Pacific of the Committee on International Relations,* 108th Cong., 2nd. sess., June 2, 2004 (www.foreignaffairs.house.gov/archives/108/94034.pdf).

56. "China Links Taiwan Dispute to North Korea Talks," *Honolulu Advertiser,* February 29, 2004.

57. Interview with a senior U.S. administration official, Washington, June 7, 2004.

58. Lawrence Wilkerson, interview, Washington, September 19, 2005.

59. "Deputy Secretary Robert Zoellick Press Conference," U.S. Embassy Beijing, August 3, 2005. Available at: http://beijing.usembassy.gov/080205e.html.

60. Robert B. Zoellick, "Whither China: From Membership to Responsibility?" Remarks at the National Committee on United States-China Relations, Gala Dinner, September 21, 2005. Available at: www.ncuscr.org.

61. Zheng Bijian, "China's 'Peaceful Rise' to Great-Power Status," *Foreign Affairs* 84, no. 5 (2005): 18–24.

62. Interview with a senior Chinese government official, Boao, China, April 24, 2004.

63. Robert B. Zoellick, "Whither China: From Membership to Responsibility?" Remarks at the National Committee on United States–China Relations, September 21, 2005 (www.state.gov/s/d/former/zoellick/rem/53682.htm).

64. Ibid.

65. Nobuyoshi Sakajiri and Satoshi Ukai, "Rigai Kyoyu-sha ni Nariuru ka: Bei, 'Sekinin Aru' Taio Yokyu" ("Will China Become a Stakeholder? The U.S. Demands a 'Responsible One'"), *Asahi Shimbun,* April 15, 2006.

66. Interview with a senior U.S. administration official, Washington, December 8, 2005.

67. Interview with a senior U.S. administration official, Washington, December 8, 2005; interview with a U.S. Department of State official, Washington, July 27, 2006.

68. Interview with a U.S. Department of State official, Washington, July 27, 2006.

69. Nobuyoshi Sakajiri and Satoshi Ukai, "Rigai Kyoyu-sha ni Nariuru ka: Bei, 'Sekinin Aru' Taio Yokyu" ("Will China Become a Stakeholder? The U.S. Demands a 'Responsible One'"), *Asahi Shimbun,* April 15, 2006.

70. Nobuyoshi Sakajiri, "Bei Kokumufukuchokan, Nicchu Kaizen ni Kitai" ("U.S. Deputy Secretary of State Hopes for a Better Relationship between Japan and China"), *Asahi Shimbun,* January 25, 2006.

71. Interview with a senior U.S. administration official, Washington, October 19, 2005.

72. Interview with a Chinese diplomat who was involved in the four-party talks, February 23, 2006.

73. Interview with a Chinese Foreign Ministry official, Beijing, July 13, 2006.

74. Hideki Soejima and Koichi Furuya, "Chugoku 'Takyoku-ka' Enshutsu" ("China Dramatizes 'Multipolarity'"), *Asahi Shimbun,* June 16, 2001.

75. Interview with a Chinese Foreign Ministry official, Beijing, July 13, 2006.

76. Lawrence Wilkerson, interview, Washington, September 19, 2005.

77. Evan S. Medeiros and M. Taylor Fravel, "China's New Diplomacy," *Foreign Affairs* 82, no. 6 (2003): 32.

78. "China and North Korea: Comrades Forever?" *International Crisis Group Asia Report 112* (Brussels: International Crisis Group, February 1, 2006), p. i.

79. Ibid., p. 3.

80. Ibid., p. 3.

81. Ibid., p. 3.

82. Interview with a senior Chinese government official, March 8, 2006.

83. Nobuyoshi Sakajiri, "Chugoku Kitachosen ni Mushoenjomo Yakusoku" ("China Promised Free Economic Assistance to North Korea"), *Asahi Shimbun* (evening), January 10, 2004.

84. Toru Shiraishi, "Rokusha Kyogi Kin Soshoki 'Ridatsu Sezu' Hocho no Chugoku

Kokan to Kaidan" ("Kim Jong-il Meets with a High-Ranking Visiting Chinese Official: 'We Will Not Withdraw from the Six-Party Talks'"), *Tokyo Shimbun*, February 23, 2005.

85. You Ji, "Assessing Hu's Visit to North Korea," *China Brief* 5, no. 23 (November 8, 2005): 5. Available at http://jamestown.org/publications_details.php?volume_id=408& issue_id=3519&article_id=2370440.

86. Ibid.

87. "China's Alleged Plot to Annex North Korea," *Chosun Ilbo*, October 19, 2004.

88. Interview with a senior official of a Chinese government organization, Beijing, September 25, 2006.

89. Interview with a senior Japanese government official, Tokyo, March 27, 2003.

90. "China Rules Out Using Sanctions on North Korea," *New York Times*, May 11, 2005.

91. Interview with a senior South Korean government official, Tokyo, April 17, 2005.

92. Interview with a U.S. intelligence officer, Washington, December 12, 2005.

93. Interview with a senior U.S. administration official, Washington, August 10, 2006.

94. Reconstructed on the basis of a conversation with an ethnic Korean-Chinese businessman living in Beijing who has business transactions with North Korea, Beijing, July 13, 2006.

95. Scalapino, "China and Korean Reunification: A Neighbor's Concerns," in *Korea's Future and the Great Powers*, edited by Eberstadt and Ellings, p. 113.

96. Facing the second nuclear crisis, China informally warned North Korea that it would not oppose the U.S. presentation of the issue to the UN Security Council or veto a resolution to impose sanctions on North Korea if Pyongyang boycotted the negotiations. Wang, "China's Role in Dealing with the North Korean Nuclear Issue," p. 485. In the summer of 2006, China actually supported UN Security Council Resolution 1695, joining in the unanimous adoption of the resolution, which condemned and issued sanctions against North Korea after North Korea launched several missiles into the Sea of Japan/East Sea. "Security Council Condemns Democratic People's Republic of Korea's Missile Launches," Security Council 5490th Meeting, July 15, 2006 (www.un.org/News/Press/docs/2006/ sc8778.doc.htm). China also supported UN Security Council Resolution 1718, joining once again in the unanimous adoption of the resolution, which imposed another series of economic and commercial sanctions on North Korea in the aftermath of North Korea's claimed nuclear test of October 9, 2006. "Security Council Condemns Nuclear Test by Democratic People's Republic of Korea," Security Council 551st Meeting, October 14, 2006.

97. James A. Kelly, U.S. Senate Committee on Foreign Relations, *U.S.-China Relations: Hearing before the Committee on Foreign Relations*, 108th Cong., 1st sess., September 11, 2003; "China Seen Toughening Stance against North Korea Nuclear Developments," *Baltimore Sun*, March 28, 2003; Andrew Scobell, "China and North Korea: The Limits of Influence," *Current History* 102, no. 665 (2003): 277.

98. Nobuyoshi Sakajiri, "Tai Kitachosen Chugoku ga Jyuyu Enjo Teishi" ("China Suspends Its Delivery of Heavy Fuel Oil to North Korea"), *Asahi Shimbun*, March 12, 2003.

99. Conversation with a Chinese diplomat, September 29, 2006.

100. Interview with a senior Chinese government official, Tokyo, November 3, 2003.

101. James A. Kelly, U.S. Senate Committee on Foreign Relations, *U.S.-China Relations: Hearing before the Committee on Foreign Relations*, 108th Cong., 1st sess., September 11, 2003.

102. "China Must Help Return North Korea to Talks, Says U.S. Envoy," March 15, 2005 (http://seoul.usembassy.gov/utils/eprintpage.html).

103. Conversation with a Chinese diplomat, Beijing, July 13, 2006.

104. Conversation with a Chinese diplomat, Beijing, July 13, 2006.

105. Conversation with a Chinese diplomat, August 3, 2006.

106. Interview with a senior U.S administration official, Washington, March 13, 2006.

107. Ibid.

108. Interview with a senior White House official, Washington, March 13, 2006.

109. Interview with a senior Japanese government official, Tokyo, March 12, 2004.

110. Interview with a senior U.S. administration official, Washington, June 7, 2004.

111. Reconstructed on the basis of a conversation with a senior member of a Chinese government organization, January 3, 2006.

112. Interview with a North Korean diplomat, April 17, 2006.

113. Wang, "China's Role in Dealing with the North Korean Nuclear Issue."

114. Zheng Bijian, "China's 'Peaceful Rise' to Great-Power Status," *Foreign Affairs* 84, no. 5 (2005): 18–24.

115. Reconstructed on the basis of a conversation with a Russian diplomat posted in Seoul, May 30, 2004.

116. Interview with a veteran Chinese government official, August 2, 2006. North Korea's nuclear test on October 9, 2006, demonstrated in a poignant way the long-term unsustainability of balancing stability and denuclearization. China was forced to give higher priority to denuclearization and take a tougher position on North Korea, and it became impossible for China to "choose to live with ambiguity." In an e-mail interview on February 5, 2007, a Chinese diplomat said that China's unusual statement, as well as its actions in the UNSC, signifies that China has to take a more definite position and policy for denuclearization. Yet, China still seems to hold the view that it can manage to maintain the balance, and the six-party talks help it to do so. Chapter 13 deals with China's dilemma in more detail.

117. Richard Armitage, interview, Washington, August 1, 2006.

118. Reconstructed on the basis of a conversation with a Chinese diplomat, August 2, 2006.

Chapter Ten

1. Reconstructed on the basis of interviews with Chinese participants (May 12, 2006; May 15, 2006; July 6, 2006; and September 1, 2006); with James Kelly in Beijing (June 26, 2004), Washington (May 20, 2005; September 23, 2005; and September 19, 2006), Seattle (October 18, 2005), and Tokyo (February 7, 2007); and with other American participants in Washington (November 2, 2005; December 27, 2005; February 24, 2006; March 13, 2006; August 10, 2006; August 16, 2006; September 11, 2006; and September 22, 2006).

2. James Kelly, e-mail interview, February 26, 2007.

3. James Kelly, e-mail interview, February 26, 2007.

4. Interview with a senior U.S. administration official, Washington, March 13, 2006.

5. Ibid.

6. Ibid.

7. Interview with a member of the U.S delegation, Washington, October 9, 2003.

8. Interview with a U.S. administration official, Washington, March 13 and August 16, 2006.

9. Reconstructed on the basis of an interview with a senior U.S. administration official, Washington, March 13 and June 2, 2006; interview with a Chinese diplomat, May 15, 2006.

10. Glenn Kessler, "State-Defense Policy Rivalry Intensifying; Gingrich to Urge Overhaul of Powell's Department," *Washington Post*, April 22, 2003; James Kelly, interview, Washington, September 19, 2006.

11. Interview with a senior U.S. administration official, Washington, March 13, 2006.

12. Mitoji Yabunaka, interview, Tokyo, September 11, 2006; James Kelly, interview, Washington, September 19, 2006.

13. Glenn Kessler, "U.S. Has Shifting Script on N. Korea; Administration Split as New Talks Near," *Washington Post*, December 7, 2003.

14. Telephone interview with a member of the U.S. delegation, September 11, 2006.

15. James Kelly, interview, Washington, September 19, 2006.

16. Reconstructed on the basis of a conversation with a Chinese diplomat, September 1, 2006.

17. James Kelly, interview, Seattle, October 18, 2005; interview with a U.S. Department of State official, Washington, November 2, 2005.

18. Conversation with a Chinese diplomat, September 1, 2006.

19. Interview with a U.S. diplomat, September 22, 2006.

20. James Kelly, interview, Washington, May 20, 2006.

21. Conversation with a Chinese diplomat, May 15, 2006.

22. Conversation with a Chinese diplomat, September 25, 2006.

23. James Kelly, interview, Seattle, October 18, 2005.

24. David Sanger, "North Korea Says It Now Possesses Nuclear Arsenal," *New York Times*, April 25, 2003.

25. "DPRK Foreign Ministry Spokesman on U.S. Attitude toward DPRK-U.S. Talks," Korean Central News Agency, April 25, 2003.

26. Interview with a U.S. administration official, Washington, August 10, 2006.

27. James Kelly, interview, Washington, September 19, 2006.

28. Selig Harrison, "'Inside North Korea: Leaders Open to Ending Nuclear Crisis," *Financial Times*, May 4, 2004.

29. "Spent Fuel Rods Unloaded from Pilot Nuclear Plant," Korean Central News Agency, May 11, 2003.

30. Charles L. Pritchard, "The Korean Peninsula and the Role of Multilateral Talks," UNIDIR Disarmament Forum (Washington: Center for North East Asian Security, Brookings, 2005).

31. Interview with a U.S. Department of State official, New York, January 9, 2006.

32. Reconstructed on the basis of a conversation with a Chinese diplomat, August 12, 2005.

33. Interview with a senior U.S. Department of State official, Washington, February 24, 2004.

34. Interview with a veteran Chinese diplomat, February 23, 2006.

35. James Kelly, interview, Seattle, October 18, 2005.

36. The "monkey king" is from the classical Chinese text *Xiyouji* (*The Journey West*), written by Wu Ch'eng-en, a Ming dynasty (1368–1644) novelist and poet. It is based on the tale of the pilgrimage of the Buddhist monk Xuanzang (602–664) to India in search of sacred texts. In the folktale, the monkey king wielded magic powers, and through those powers he was able to rule his domain.

37. Mitoji Yabunaka, *Taigai Keizai Kosho: Masatsu no Jitsuzo* (*International Economic Negotiations: The Realities of Economic Friction*) (Tokyo: Simul Shuppan-kai, 1991).

38. Interview with a senior U.S. administration official, Washington, June 2, 2006.

39. Interview with a senior Japanese government official, Tokyo, February 23, 2005.

40. Interview with a senior Japanese government official, Tokyo, September 3, 2003.

41. Interview with a senior Japanese government official, Tokyo, April 27, 2006.

42. Interview with a U.S. Department of State official, New York, January 9, 2006.

43. Interview with a senior Japanese MOFA official, Tokyo, September 11, 2006.

44. Lawrence Wilkerson, interview, Washington, September 19, 2005.

45. Interview with a Chinese diplomat, Tokyo, November 25, 2005.

46. Interview with a U.S. administration official, Washington, March 13, 2006, and August 10, 2006.

47. Colin Powell, interview, Washington, March 31, 2006.

48. As the talks continued, several nonparticipating countries volunteered to act as host, including Switzerland, Canada, and Thailand. Interview with a senior Chinese government official, Boao, China, April 24, 2004; interview with a senior U.S. administration official, Washington, August 10, 2006.

49. "Keynote Speeches Made at Six-way Talks," Korean Central News Agency, August 29, 2003.

50. "Beicho ga Nikokukankyogi, Nichibei Kakuhoki-Rachi ni Genkyu" ("The U.S. and North Korea Have Consultations: Both the U.S. and Japan Refer to Nuclear Dismantlement and Abduction Issues"), *Asahi Shimbun,* August 28, 2003.

51. "Kita-chosen ga Tsutaeta Kakkoku Hatsugen Rokushakyogi 'Yoshi'" ("North Korea Reports Excerpts of Each Representative's Remarks in the Six-Party Talks"), *Asahi Shimbun,* August 30, 2003.

52. Nobuyoshi Sakajiri and Takashi Uemura, "'Shuyaku' Beicho Nikoku, Shonichi Kara Oshu" ("U.S. –North Korea Cross-Fire from Day 1"), *Asahi Shimbun,* August 28, 2003.

53. Interview with a senior U.S. administration official, Washington, May 31, 2006.

54. "Kensho: Hatsuno Rokusha Kyogi" ("A Survey: The First Six-Party Talks"), *Asahi Shimbun,* September 15, 2003.

55. Reconstructed on the basis of a conversation with a member of the Japanese delegation, Moscow, November 9, 2005.

56. Interview with a member of the South Korean delegation, Seoul, November 29, 2005.

57. James Brooke, "North Korea Lashes Out at Neighbors and U.S.," *New York Times,* August 19, 2003; Peter Baker, "Russia Turns from Old Allies to U.S.," *Washington Post,* August 27, 2003.

58. Interview with a senior Japanese government official, Tokyo, September 11, 2006; "Kensho: Hatsuno Rokusha Kyogi" ("A Survey: The First Six-Party Talks"), *Asahi Shimbun,* September 15, 2003.

59. "Kensho: Hatsuno Rokusha Kyogi" ("A Survey: The First Six Party Talks"), *Asahi Shimbun,* September 15, 2003.

60. Interview with a senior U.S. administration official, Washington, May 30 and August 16, 2006.

61. Interview with a member of the U.S. delegation, Washington, September 27, 2006; interview with a member of the Japanese delegation, Tokyo, September 28, 2006.

62. "Kensho: Hatsuno Rokusha Kyogi" ("A Survey: The First Six-Party Talks"), *Asahi Shimbun,* September 15, 2003.

63. Interview with a U.S. participant in the drafting group, Washington, June 2, 2006.

64. Kentaro Kurihara, "Kakumondai Heiwa Kaiketsu de Icchi" ("Peaceful Settlement of Nuclear Issues Agreed On"), *Asahi Shimbun* (evening edition), August 30, 2003.

65. "Host Country Summary by Chinese Vice Foreign Minister Wang Yi," Six-Party Talks on North Korean Issues (Overview and Evaluation), Japanese Ministry of Foreign Affairs, September 2003 (www.mofa.go.jp/region/asia-paci/n_korea/6party0308.html).

66. Arata Fujii, interview, Tokyo, October 2, 2003; "Kensho: Hatsuno Rokusha Kyogi" ("A Survey: The First Six-Party Talks"), *Asahi Shimbun,* September 15, 2003.

67. Kentaro Kurihara, "Kakumondai Heiwa Kaiketsu de Icchi" ("Peaceful Settlement of Nuclear Issues Agreed On"), *Asahi Shimbun* (evening edition), August 30, 2003.

68. James Kelly, interview, Tokyo, February 8, 2007.

69. Ibid.

70. Interview with a senior U.S. administration official, Washington, September 12, 2006.

71. Interview with a senior Chinese government official, September 14, 2006.

72. Interview with a senior U.S. administration official, Washington, September 12, 2006.

73. James Kelly, interview; "North Korea Celebrates Anniversary without Display of Heavy Arms," Associated Press, September 9, 2003.

74. Interview with a Chinese diplomat who was involved in the six-party talks, September 29, 2006.

75. Joseph Kahn, "Chinese Aide Says U.S. Is Obstacle in Korean Talks," New York Times, September 2, 2003.

76. Conversation with a Chinese diplomat, September 28, 2006.

77. Interview with a senior U.S. administration official, Washington, September 12, 2006.

78. That was the expression used by a senior U.S. administration official, Washington, August 10, 2006.

79. James Kelly, interview, Washington, September 19, 2006.

80. Kim Hak-joon, North and South Korea: Internal Politics and External Relations since 1988 (Seoul: Society for Korean and Related Studies, 2006), p. 325.

81. In his testimony before the Senate Committee on Foreign Relations, Sigfried Hecker quoted Kim Gye-gwan as saying that "the U.S. says it will give us a security assurance if we dismantle our nuclear program. We say it differently. The first step would be a freeze of the present [DPRK] nuclear activities. You will see how important a freeze will be when you are at Yongbyon. This means there will be no manufacturing, no testing, and no transferring of nuclear weapons." Sigfried S. Hecker, U.S. Senate Committee on Foreign Relations, An Update on North Korean Nuclear Developments: Hearing before the Committee on Foreign Relations, 108th Cong., 2nd sess., February 24, 2004.

82. Interview with a senior South Korean government official, Seoul, November 29, 2005.

83. John Lancaster and Kamran Khan, "Pakistan Fires Top Nuclear Scientist," Washington Post, February 1, 2004.

84. Background briefing by a senior U.S. administration official at the American Enterprise Institute, February 19, 2004.

85. George J. Tenet, U.S. Senate Select Committee on Intelligence, Current and Projected National Security Threats to the United States: Open Hearing, 108th Cong., 2nd sess., February 24, 2004.

86. Reconstructed on the basis of a conversation with a Japanese diplomat posted in Beijing, Beijing, November 15, 2005.

87. Interview with Charles Pritchard, Washington, February 24, 2004; interview with a senior South Korean government official, Seoul, November 29, 2005; interview with a senior Japanese government official, Tokyo, September 11, 2006.

88. James A. Kelly, "Remarks on Day One of the Second Round of Six-Party Talks," Beijing, China, U.S. Department of State, February 25, 2004 (www.state.gov/p/eap/rls/rm/2004/29861.htm).

89. Kim, North and South Korea: Internal Politics and External Relations since 1988, p. 329.

90. "U.S. Asks NK to Dismantle Nukes," Korea Times, February 26, 2004.

91. Interview with a U.S. Department of State official, Washington, March 10, 2004.

92. James Kelly, interview, Seattle, October 18, 2005.

93. James A. Kelly, U.S. Senate Committee on Foreign Relations, *The North Korean Nuclear Calculus: Beyond the Six Power Talks: Hearing before the Committee on Foreign Relations*, 108th Cong., 2nd sess., March 2, 2004.

94. Transcript of a senior U.S. official speaking about the six-party talks, Press Round-table (background), Beijing, February 28, 2004. The author is grateful to Nobuyoshi Saka-jiri for providing this internal State Department transcript.

95. For example, "DPRK to Continue Increasing Its Nuclear Deterrent Force," Korean Central News Agency, October 2, 2003.

96. Transcript of a senior U.S. official speaking about the six-party talks, Press Round-table (background), Beijing, February 28, 2004.

97. Ibid.

98. Telephone interview with a senior South Korean government official, Seoul, September 8, 2006.

99. Interview with a senior South Korean government official, Seoul, October 10, 2005.

100. Ibid.

101. "Beicho Rongi Dotanba Made" ("U.S.-DPRK Differences Remained until the Last Moment"), *Asahi Shimbun*, February 29, 2004.

102. James Kelly, interview, Washington, September 19, 2006.

103. Interview with a senior Japanese government official, Tokyo, April 13, 2004.

104. Interview with a Chinese diplomat who was involved in the six-party talks, September 1, 2006.

105. "Full Text of Chairman's Statement for Six-Party Talks," *People's Daily Online*, February 28, 2004 (http://english.people.com.cn/200402/28/eng20040228_136102.shtml).

106. "Sagyo Bukai Towareru Yakuwari Rokusha Kyogi ga Heimaku" ("Six Party Talks Ended. How to Define the Role of Working Group Remains to be Seen"), *Asahi Shimbun*, February 29, 2004.

107. Interview with a senior Japanese government official, Tokyo, April 13, 2004.

108. James Kelly, interview, Washington, September 19, 2006.

109. "KCNA Urges U.S. to Accept DPRK's Proposal," Korean Central News Agency, May 22, 2004.

110. Transcript of a senior U.S. official speaking about the six-party talks, Press Round-table (background), Beijing, February 28, 2004.

111. Interview with a senior South Korean government official, Berlin, February 8, 2006.

112. James Kelly, e-mail interview, February 26, 2007.

113. Interview with a member of the U.S. delegation, Washington, September 12, 2006.

114. Interview with a U.S. Department of State official, New York, January 9, 2006.

115. James Kelly, interview, Tokyo, February 8, 2007.

116. Interview with a member of the U.S. delegation, Washington, September 12, 2006.

117. "Libyan WMD: Tripoli's Statement in Full," *BBC News*, December 20, 2003 (http://news.bbc.co.uk/2/hi/africa/3336139.stm).

118. "President Bush: Libya Pledges to Dismantle WMD Programs," White House, December 19, 2003 (www.whitehouse.gov/news/releases/2003/12/20031219-9.html).

119. "DPRK Foreign Ministry Dismisses U.S. Proposal," Korean Central News Agency, July 24, 2004.

120. For example, see: "DPRK Foreign Ministry on Six-Party Talks," Korean Central News Agency, August 30, 2003.

121. Interview with a U.S. Department of State official, New York, January 9, 2006.

122. John S. Park, "Inside Multilateralism: The Six-Party Talks," *Washington Quarterly* 28, no. 4 (2005): 79.

123. "The U.S.-Ukrainian Summit: President Bill Clinton's Visit to Kyyiv," *Ukrainian Weekly*, June 4, 1995.

124. Interview with a senior Blue House official, Seoul, September 4, 2006.

125. Ibid.

126. Interview with a senior Japanese MOFA official, Washington, March 13, 2006.

127. Interview with a senior U.S. administration official, Washington, April 3, 2006.

128. Interview with a senior Blue House official, Seoul, September 4, 2006.

129. Transcript of a senior U.S. official speaking about the six-party talks, Press Roundtable (background), Beijing, February 28, 2004.

130. Joseph Kahn, "U.S. and North Korea Agree to More Talks," *New York Times*, February 29, 2004.

131. Ryu Jin, "Six Nations to Meet Again by June," *Korea Times*, February 29, 2004.

132. Nobuyoshi Sakajiri, Beijing, "Kitachosen no 'Kakujikken' Hatsugen ni Bei Reisei" ("U.S. Cautious on North Korea's Announcement of a Nuclear Test"), *Asahi Shimbun*, June 26, 2004.

133. E-mail interview with a Chinese diplomat in charge of the six-party talks, February 5, 2007.

134. Interview with a senior U.S. administration official, Washington, March 13, 2006.

135. Nobuyoshi Sakajiri, Beijing, "Kitachosen no 'Kakujikken' Hatsugen ni Bei Reisei" ("U.S. Cautious on North Korea's Announcement of a Nuclear Test"), *Asahi Shimbun*, June 26, 2004.

136. Hu Xiao, "DPRK: Concrete Plans Can Help Nuclear Talks," *China Daily*, June 24, 2006 (www.chinadaily.com.cn/english/doc/2004-06/24/content_341944.htm).

137. Ibid.

138. Nobuyoshi Sakajiri, Beijing, "Bei Seifunai, Mikata Mapputatsu Kita-chosen no Kakujikken Hatsugen" ("Two Completely Opposite Views Have Emerged in the U.S. Administration on North Korea's Statement on Nuclear Issue"), *Asahi Shimbun* (evening edition), June 26, 2004; interview with a member of the U.S. delegation, Washington, March 13, 2006.

139. James Kelly, interview, Beijing, June 26, 2004.

140. James Kelly, interview, Washington, May 20, 2006.

141. James Kelly, interview, Washington, May 20, 2006.

142. James Kelly, interview, Beijing, June 26, 2004.

143. Ibid.

144. Philip P. Pan, "N. Korea Says It Can 'Show Flexibility,'" *Washington Post*, June 26, 2004; Soo-Jeong Lee, "Talks on North Korea Nuclear Program End," Associated Press, June 26, 2004.

145. "Chairman's Statement of Third Round of Six-Party Talks," *People's Daily Online*, June 26, 2004 (http://english.peopledaily.com.cn/200406/26/eng20040626_147642.html).

146. "Beicho Joho Shui Atooshi, Tairitsu no Hidane wa Kiezu" ("The Other Parties Urge Both the U.S. and North Korea to Make Concessions. The Roots of Conflict Have Not Disappeared"), *Asahi Shimbun*, June 27, 2004.

147. "DPRK Foreign Ministry Spokesman on Six-Party Talks," Korean Central News Agency, June 28, 2004.

148. Interview with a senior South Korean government official, Seoul, September 4, 2006.

149. Interview with several senior South Korean government officials, Seoul, October 10, 2004; November 29, 2005; and September 4, 2006.

150. Interview with a senior South Korean government official, Seoul, September 4, 2006.

151. Interview with a senior U.S. administration official, Washington, February 24, 2006.

152. Ibid.

153. Phillip P. Pan and Glenn Kessler, "U.S. Revises Proposal at North Korea Nuclear Talks," *Washington Post,* June 24, 2004.

154. Interview with a senior U.S. administration official, Washington, March 1, 2006.

155. E-mail interview with a South Korean government official, January 10, 2007.

156. Interview with a senior U.S. administration official, Washington, March 1, 2006; Nuland was later appointed U.S. permanent representative to the North Atlantic Treaty Organization (NATO).

157. Interview with a senior South Korean government official, Seoul, November 29, 2005.

158. Interview with a senior South Korean government official, Seoul, September 4, 2006; interview with a U.S. administration official, Washington, July 21, 2006.

159. Interview with a Japanese diplomat, Beijing, June 27, 2004.

160. Interview with a U.S. Department of State official, Washington, November 2, 2005.

161. Interview with a senior South Korean government official, Seoul, September 4, 2006.

162. Daily Press Briefing, U.S. Department of State, June 15, 2004 (www.state.gov/r/pa/prs/dpb/2004/33581.htm).

163. "Beicho Joho Shui Atooshi, Tairitsu no Hidane wa Kiezu" ("The Other Parties Urge Both the U.S. and North Korea to Make Concessions. The Roots of Conflict Have Not Disappeared"), *Asahi Shimbun,* June 27, 2004.

164. Interview with a senior South Korean government official, Seoul, September 4, 2006.

165. Interview with a senior U.S. administration official, Washington, June 4, 2004, and September 12, 2006.

166. Interview with a senior U.S. Department of State official, Washington, June 2, 2006; interview with a Japanese diplomat stationed in Beijing, Beijing, June 26, 2004.

167. Track-two diplomacy, or citizen diplomacy, refers to diplomacy conducted through unofficial dialogue, discussions, and even negotiations between private citizens concerning topics that are usually reserved for diplomats—the resolution of an on-going conflict or arms reduction, for instance. It is differentiated from track-one diplomacy, which involves formal discussions between official government representatives.

168. Interview with a senior U.S. administration official, Washington, June 27, 2006.

169. Reconstructed on the basis of a conversation with a Chinese diplomat, February 14, 2006.

170. James Kelly, interview, Washington, May 20, 2006.

171. Interview with a senior U.S. administration official, Washington, August 16, 2006.

172. Interview with a U.S. Department of State official, Washington, August 16, 2006.

173. James Kelly, interview, Seattle, October 18, 2005.

174. Charles L. Pritchard, "North Korea Needs a Personal Touch," *Los Angeles Times,* September 10, 2003.

175. Conversation with a Chinese diplomat, Beijing, April 17, 2006.

176. Interview with a senior South Korean government official, February 8, 2006.

177. Interview with a senior U.S. administration official, Washington, June 27, 2006.

178. Interview with a member of the U.S. delegation, Washington, June 16, 2006.

179. Interview with a U.S. administration official, Washington, August 28, 2006.

180. Interview with a veteran Chinese diplomat, May 15, 2006.

181. Interview with a senior Chinese government official, Tokyo, September 1, 2006; "Liufang Huitan Fangfeiyuan Jishi" ("Six-Party Talks: Fangfeiyuan Document), *Renming Ribao* (*People's Daily*), September 26, 2005.

182. Interview with a U.S. Department of State official, Washington, June 16, 2006.

183. Interview with a Japanese diplomat, Tokyo, February 5, 2004.

184. Interview with a senior U.S. administration official, Washington, August 24, 2004.

185. Ibid.

186. "President Sworn In to Second Term," White House, January 20, 2005 (www.whitehouse.gov/news/releases/2005/01/20050120-1.html).

187. Condoleezza Rice, U.S. Senate Committee on Foreign Relations, *Secretary of State Nomination, Part I: Hearing before the Committee on Foreign Relations,* 109th Cong., 1st sess., January 18, 2005 (http://foreign.senate.gov/testimony/2005/RiceTestimony 050118.pdf).

188. "State of the Union Address," White House, February 2, 2005 (www.whitehouse. gov/news/releases/2005/02/20050202-11.html).

189. Interview with a senior U.S. administration official, Washington, June 27, 2006; interview with a senior South Korean government official, Seoul, July 10, 2006.

190. "DPRK FM on Its Stand to Suspend Its Participation in Six-Party Talks for Indefinite Period," Korean Central News Agency, February 10, 2005.

191. "U.S. Rejects N. Korea's Demand: Washington Refuses to Open One-on-One Talks with Pyongyang," *Los Angeles Times,* February 12, 2005.

192. "North Korea Could Improve Its Security without Nuclear Weapons," remarks by Joseph E. DeTrani, U.S.-China Economic Security Review Commission, March 10, 2005 (http://usinfo.state.gov/xarchives/display.html?p=washfile-english&y=2005&m=March &x=20050311134651ajesrom0.6488153).

193. "Beicho Taiwa de Dakai mo Shusho 'Rokkakoku' Saikai he Yonin" ("Prime Minister [Koizumi] Hopes U.S.-North Korean Dialogue Will Bring About a Breakthrough for Restarting the Six-Party Talks"), *Tokyo Shimbun,* February 15, 2005.

194. Chung Dong-young, interview, Seoul, March 24, 2006.

195. Tadanao Takatsuki, "Misairu Tosai 'Gijutsu wa Nai' Kitachosen Kakude Kankokuga Bunseki" ("North Korea Does Not Have the Capability to Install Nuclear Warheads on Missiles: South Korea's Analysis"), *Asahi Shimbun,* February 16, 2005; "Kitachosen Uran Noshuku Seizo Dekizu Kankoku no Kokka Johoin ga Hokoku" ("North Korea Cannot Produce Enriched Uranium: National Intelligence Agency of South Korea Analysis"), *Yomiuri Shimbun,* February 25, 2005. However, the South Korean National Intelligence Service was reported to acknowledge that North Korea had pursued a uranium enrichment program in its report to the National Assembly in February 2007. "Seoul Believes N. Korea Has Uranium Program," *Chosun Ilbo,* February 21, 2007.

196. Remarks of the deputy secretary general of South Korea's National Security Council on February 29, 2005.

197. Interview with a senior Chinese government official, February 23, 2006.

198. Ibid.

199. Toru Shiraishi, "Rokusha Kyogi Kin Soshoki 'Ridatsu Sezu' Hocho no Chugoku Kokan to Kaidan" ("Kim Jong-il Meets with a High-Ranking Visiting Chinese Official: 'We Will Not Withdraw from the Six-Party Talks"), *Tokyo Shimbun,* February 23, 2005.

200. Pritchard, "The Korean Peninsula and the Role of Multilateral Talks," pp. 25–34.

201. The North Korean Ministry of Foreign Affairs criticized the Bush administration's use of "outpost of tyranny" with the following statement: "On the contrary, they have declared it as their final goal to terminate the tyranny, defined the DPRK, too, as an 'outpost of tyranny' and blustered that they would not rule out the use of force when neces-

sary." "DPRK FM on Its Stand to Suspend Its Participation in Six-Party Talks for Indefinite Period," Korean Central News Agency, February 10, 2005.

202. "Nichibei, Kakusho Naki Keikai Kita-chosen Kaku Jikken" ("The U.S. and Japan Wary of North Korea's Nuclear Test without Solid Evidence"), *Asahi Shimbun,* May 21, 2005.

203. David E. Sanger, "U.S. in Warning to North Korea on Nuclear Test," *New York Times,* May 16, 2005.

204. David E. Sanger," U.S. Warns North Korea against Nuclear Test," *New York Times,* May 6, 2005.

205. "U.S. Stealth Bombers Deployed in South Korea," ABC Online (Australia), July 6, 2005 (www.abc.net.au/news/newsitems/200506/s1386924.htm).

206. "Spokesman for DPRK Foreign Ministry on Bush's Remarks," Korean Central News Agency, June 3, 2005.

207. Interview with a senior U.S. administration official, Washington, August 28, 2006.

208. Interview with a U.S. Department of State official, Washington, August 17, 2006.

209. "Spokesman for DPRK Foreign Ministry on Bush's Remarks," Korean Central News Agency, June 3, 2005.

CHAPTER ELEVEN

1. Christopher R. Hill, "Fourth Round of Six-Party Talks: Hotel Arrival, Beijing," U.S. Department of State, July 24, 2005 (www.state.gov/p/eap/rls/rm/2005/50744.htm).

2. Christopher R. Hill, "Fourth Round of Six-Party Talks: Evening Return to Hotel, Beijing," U.S. Department of State, July 25 and July 26, 2005 (www.state.gov/p/eap/rls/rm/2005/50743.htm).

3. Christopher R. Hill, "Fourth Round of Six-Party Talks: Return to Hotel, Beijing," U.S. Department of State, July 26, 2005. Available at: www.state.gov/p/eap/rls/rm/2005/50614.htm

4. E-mail interview with a member of the U.S. delegation, March 11, 2007.

5. Ibid.

6. Ibid.

7. Jim Yardley, "U.S. Reassures North Korea at Opening of Six-Party Talks," *New York Times,* July 26, 2005.

8. Christopher R. Hill, "U.S. Opening Statement at the Fourth Round of Six-Party Talks, Beijing," U.S. Department of State, July 26, 2005 (www.state.gov/p/eap/rls/rm/2005/50510.htm).

9. Christopher R. Hill, "Fourth Round of Six-Party Talks: Evening Return to Hotel," Beijing, U.S. Department of State, July 29, 2005 (www.state.gov/p/eap/rls/rm/2005/50694.htm).

10. Christopher R. Hill, "Fourth Round of Six-Party Talks: Evening Transit St. Regis Hotel," Beijing, U.S. Department of State, August 1, 2005 (www.state.gov/p/eap/rls/rm/2005/50707.htm).

11. Takao Hishinuma, Beijing, "Rokkakokukyogi, Getsumatsu nimo Saikai Kita 'Heiwariyo' Koshitsu ka" ("The Six-Party Talks May Resume at the End of the Month; North Korea Likely to Stick to 'Peaceful Use' of Its Nuclear Programs"), *Yomiuri Shimbun,* August 9, 2005.

12. Interview with a U.S. Department of State official, Washington, June 14, 2006.

13. Interview with a senior Japanese government official, Tokyo, September 11, 2006; interview with a U.S. Department of State official, Washington, June 14, 2006.

14. Interview with a U.S. Department of State official, Washington, August 17, 2006.

15. Christopher R. Hill, "Fourth Round of Six-Party Talks: Late Evening Transit St. Regis Hotel, Beijing," U.S. Department of State, August 3, 2005 (www.state.gov/p/eap/rls/rm/2005/50798.htm).

16. Interview with a senior Chinese government official, Beijing, September 25, 2006.

17. Interview with a member of the Japanese delegation, Tokyo, September 26, 2006.

18. Christopher R. Hill, "Fourth Round of Six-Party Talks: Evening Transit St. Regis Hotel," U.S. Department of State, August 4, 2005 (www.state.gov/p/eap/rls/rm/2005/50781.htm).

19. Christopher R. Hill, "Fourth Round of Six-Party Talks: Evening Transit St. Regis Hotel, Beijing," U.S. Department of State, August 5, 2005 (www.state.gov/p/eap/rls/rm/2005/50823.htm).

20. Reconstructed on the basis of a conversation with a senior Chinese government official, August 5, 2006.

21. The character for "si" (four) is a homonym for death in Chinese. Christopher R. Hill, "Fourth Round of Six-Party Talks: Early Afternoon Transit St. Regis, Beijing," U.S. Department of State, August 7, 2005 (www.state.gov/p/eap/rls/rm/2005/50869.htm).

22. Ibid.

23. "Goi Yusen, Nokoru Kenen Rokusha Kyogi" ("The Six-Party Talks Highlighted the Consensus but Differences Remain"), *Asahi Shimbun,* September 20, 2005.

24. Barbara Demick, Mark Magnier and Sonni Efron, "N. Korea Sets Condition on Nuclear Pact," *Los Angeles Times,* September 20, 2005.

25. Interview with a White House official, Washington, August 28, 2006.

26. Interview with a senior U.S. administration official, Washington, September 19, 2006.

27. "Goi Yusen, Nokoru Kenen Rokusha Kyogi" ("The Six-Party Talks Highlighted the Consensus, but Differences Remain").

28. Interview with a member of the Japanese delegation, Tokyo, September 26, 2006.

29. Christopher R. Hill, "Resumption of Fourth Round of Six-Party Talks: Evening Transit China World Hotel, September 15, 2005 (www.state.gov/p/eap/rls/rm/2005/53287.htm).

30. Interview with a member of the Japanese delegation, Tokyo, September 26, 2006.

31. E-mail interview with a Chinese diplomat who was involved in the six-party talks, February 9, 2007.

32. Joseph Kahn and David E. Sanger, "U.S. -Korean Deal on Arms Leaves Key Points Open," *New York Times,* September 20, 2005.

33. Interview with a senior South Korean government official, Seoul, October 10, 2005.

34. Interview with a senior Japanese government official, Tokyo, September 11, 2006.

35. Interview with a senior U.S. administration official, Washington, February 24, 2006.

36. Interview with a senior Chinese government official, Beijing, September 25, 2006.

37. Li Po, "Quiet Night Thoughts," in Arthur Cooper, *Li Po and Tu Fu: Poems Selected and Translated with an Introduction and Notes* (Penguin Classics, 1973), as found at www.sacu.org/poetry.html.

38. It is a tradition in China for families to get together and enjoy moon cakes, a baked confection, during the Mid-Autumn Festival; because of that, the moon cake is also called a "family-get-together" cake.

39. "Rokusha Kyogi Uchikiri no Mikata mo" ("The Prospect of Suspension of Six-Party Talks Is Spreading"), *Asahi Shimbun,* September 20, 2005.

40. Interview with a U.S. Department of State official, Washington, June 6, 2006.

41. Interview with a U.S. administration official, Washington, August 17, 2006.

42. Interview with a U.S. Department of State official, Washington, December 19, 2005.

43. Interview with a senior Chinese government official, June 26, 2006.

44. Kahn and Sanger," U.S. -Korean Deal on Arms Leaves Key Points Open."

45. Interview with a senior U.S. administration official, Washington, June 26, 2006.

46. Nobutaka Michimura, interview, Tokyo, September 7, 2006.

47. Ibid.

48. Interview with a U.S. Department of State official, Washington, June 6, 2006; Interview with a senior Japanese government official, Tokyo, September 12, 2006.

49. Interview with a U.S. Department of State official, Washington, November 2, 2005, and August 17, 2006.

50. Ibid.

51. Interview with a senior South Korean government official, Seoul, November 29, 2005.

52. Interview with a U.S. Department of State official, Washington, August 17, 2006.

53. Christopher R. Hill, "Resumption of Fourth Round of Six-Party Talks: Morning Transit, China World Hotel," Beijing, U.S. Department of State, September 19, 2005 (www.state.gov/p/eap/rls/rm/2005/53488.htm).

54. Interview with a senior South Korean government official, Seoul, November 29, 2005.

55. Interview with a U.S. administration official, Washington, August 28, 2006.

56. Interview with a senior Chinese government official, December 13, 2006; interview with a member of the Japanese delegation, Tokyo, September 26, 2006; interview with a member of the U.S. delegation, Washington, August 28, 2006.

57. Interview with a member of the U.S. delegation, Washington, August 28, 2006.

58. "Assistant Secretary of State Christopher R. Hill's Statement at the Closing Plenary of the Fourth Round of the Six-Party Talks," press statement, U.S. Department of State, September 19, 2005 (www.state.gov/r/pa/prs/ps/2005/53499.htm).

59. Interview with a U.S. Department of State official, Washington, March 15, 2006.

60. Interview with a member of the U.S. delegation, Washington, August 28, 2006.

61. Interview with a U.S. Department of State official, Washington, August 17, 2006.

62. "Joint Statement of the Fourth Round of the Six-Party Talks Beijing," U.S. Department of State, September 19, 2005 (www.state.gov/r/pa/prs/ps/2005/53490.htm).

63. Interview with a senior Chinese government official, February 23, 2006.

64. Interview with a senior U.S. administration official, Washington, March 19, 2007; interview with a senior South Korean government official, Washington, March 21, 2007.

65. Interview with a member of the South Korean delegation, February 8, 2006.

66. Interview with a senior U.S. administration official, Washington, March 19, 2007.

67. Interview with a senior U.S. administration official, Washington, August 16, 2006.

68. Interview with a Chinese diplomat, February 23, 2006.

69. "Joint Declaration on the Denuclearization of the Korean Peninsula," U.S. Department of State, January 20, 1992 (www.state.gov/t/ac/rls/or/2004/31011.htm).

70. Interview with a senior Chinese government official, June 26, 2006.

71. Interview with a U.S. Department of State official, Washington, August 17, 2006.

72. Interview with a U.S. Department of State official, Washington, June 14, 2006; interview with a member of the Japanese delegation, Tokyo, September 26, 2006; Glenn Kessler, "What That Accord Really Says," *Washington Post,* September 25, 2005.

73. Interview with a senior U.S. administration official, Washington, June 27 and August 17, 2006.

74. Interview with a senior Chinese government official, June 26, 2006.

75. Interview with a White House official, Washington, June 14, 2006.

76. Interview with a senior Chinese government official, June 26, 2006.

77. Interview with a U.S. Department of State official, Washington, June 14, 2006.

78. Interview with a senior Japanese government official, Tokyo, September 26, 2006; interview with a senior Chinese government official, June 26, 2006.

79. Reconstructed on the basis of a conversation with a Chinese diplomat, August 22, 2005.

80. Christopher R. Hill, "Fourth Round of Six-Party Talks: Evening Return to Hotel," Beijing, U.S. Department of State, July 29, 2005 (www.state.gov/p/eap/rls/rm/2005/50694.htm).

81. Interview with a White House official, Washington, August 28, 2006.

82. "Bush Says U.S. Will Work With Europe to Defuse Iranian Nuclear Issue," Federal Information and News Dispatch, U.S. Department of State, August 9, 2005 (http://usinfo.state.gov/eur/Archive/2005/Aug/09-446966.html).

83. "Rokushakyogi Kita-chosen Daihyo, Bei ni Seisaku Henko wo Yokyu" ("North Korean Negotiator for Six-Party Talks Demanded the U.S. Policy Change"), *Asahi Shimbun,* August 10, 2005.

84. Toshihiko Kasahara, "Rokkakokukyogi: Bei Shuseki Daihyo 'Keisuiro Koshitsu ha Seijiteki'" ("Six-Party Talks: U.S. Chief Negotiator Argued North Korea's Insistence on Light-Water Reactor Is Highly Political"), *Mainichi Shimbun,* September 16, 2005; Ruriko Kubota, "Rokkakokukyogi: Kita, Keisuiro Naze Koshitsu" ("Six-Party Talks: Why North Korea Clings to Light-Water Reactors"), *Sankei Shimbun,* September 16, 2005.

85. Christopher R. Hill, "Resumption of Fourth Round of Six-Party Talks: Evening Transit China World Hotel," Beijing, U.S. Department of State, September 15, 2005 (www.state.gov/p/eap/rls/rm/2005/53287.htm).

86. Interview with a senior U.S. administration official, Washington, August 16, 2006.

87. Interview with a senior Chinese government official, June 26, 2006.

88. Interview with a Chinese diplomat, June 26, 2006; Glenn Kessler, "North Korea Stands Fast on Nuclear Energy Use," *Washington Post,* September 9, 2005.

89. "Spokesman for DPRK Foreign Ministry on Six-Party Talks," Korean Central News Agency, September 20, 2005.

90. Chae-jin Lee, *A Troubled Peace: U.S. Policy and the Two Koreas* (Johns Hopkins University Press, 2006), p. 165.

91. In total, the United States, South Korea, and Japan spent $1.3 billion to finance reactor construction in North Korea. It was estimated that the total project would have cost $4.6 billion had it been completed. Charles L. Pritchard, "North Korea's Nuclear Program: Light-Water Reactor Project," remarks at KEDO Concrete Pouring Ceremony, U.S. Department of State, August 7, 2002; "N. Korean Light-Water Reactor Project Officially Dead," *Chosun Ilbo,* June 1, 2006.

92. Interview with a U.S. Department of State official, Washington, August 17, 2006.

93. Interview with a senior U.S. administration official, Washington, August 16, 2006.

94. Interview with a senior U.S. Department of State official, Washington, August 17, 2006.

95. Interview with a U.S. Department of State official, Washington, August 17, 2006.

96. Interview with a U.S. Department of State official, Washington, June 6, 2006.

97. Ibid.

98. Interview with a senior U.S. Department of Defense official, Washington, December 22, 2005.

99. Ibid.

100. Interview with a member of the U.S. delegation, Washington, May 3, 2006.

101. Interview with a senior Chinese government official, June 26, 2006.

102. Kentaro Kurihara, "Kita-chosen ga Kakuhoki Kakuyaku Rokushakyogi, Hatsu no Kyodoseimei" ("North Korea Promises Nuclear Abandonment; Six-Party Talks Issue First Joint Statement"), *Asahi Shimbun,* September 20, 2005.

103. Interview with a senior Chinese government official, June 26, 2006.

104. Interview with a senior U.S. Department of State official, Washington, August 17, 2006.

105. Interview with a senior Chinese government official, June 26, 2006.

106. Interview with a U.S. Department of State official, Washington, December 27, 2006.

107. Interview with a U.S. Department of Defense official, Washington, December 22, 2006.

108. Interview with a senior Chinese government official, June 26, 2006.

109. Interview with a senior U.S. Department of State official, Washington, November 2, 2006.

110. Interview with a U.S. Department of State official, Washington, November 2, 2006.

111. "Seoul Saved Six-Party Talks: Unification Minister," *Chosun Ilbo,* September 19, 2005.

112. Interview with a veteran Chinese diplomat, June 26, 2006.

113. Interview with a senior Chinese government official, June 26, 2006.

114. Philip Zelikow, interview, Washington, August 16, 2006.

115. Interview with a U.S. Department of State official, Washington, August 17, 2006.

116. "Spokesman for DPRK Foreign Ministry on Six-Party Talks," Korean Central News Agency, September 20, 2005.

117. Steven R. Weisman, "U.S. Says North Korean Demands for Reactor Won't Derail Accord," *New York Times,* September 21, 2005.

118. Interview with a U.S. Department of State official, Washington, August 17, 2006.

119. Interview with a senior U.S. administration official, Washington, August 17, 2006.

120. Interview with a senior South Korean government official, Seoul, September 5, 2006.

121. Interview with a U.S. Department of State official, Washington, August 17, 2006.

122. Interview with a U.S. Department of State official, Washington, June 16, 2006.

123. Interview with a member of the U.S. delegation, Washington, June 14, 2006, and August 17, 2006; interview with a senior U.S. Department of State official, Washington, November 6, 2006.

124. Interview with a U.S. Department of State official, Washington, August 17, 2006.

125. Ibid.

126. Ibid.

127. Interview with a U.S. Department of State official, Washington, June 14, 2006.

128. Interview with a senior U.S. Administration official, Washington, May 30, 2006.

129. Interview with a senior White House official, Washington, May 30, 2006.

130. Interview with a U.S. Department of State official, Washington, June 14, 2006.

131. Conversation with a senior U.S. Department of State official, Washington, June 30, 2006.

132. Interview with a U.S. Department of State official, Washington, June 6, 2006.

133. Interviews with U.S. Department of State officials, Washington, June 14, 2006.

134. Maggie Farley, "N. Korea Revises Nuclear Reactor Demand," *Los Angeles Times,* September 23, 2005.

135. Interview with a U.S. Department of State official, Washington, June 14, 2006.

136. Interview with a senior U.S. administration official, Washington, May 30, 2006.

137. Interviews with senior U.S. administration officials, Washington, November 2, 2006.

138. Interview with a U.S. Department of State official, Washington, August 17, 2006.

139. Interview with a senior U.S. administration official, Washington, May 31, 2006.

140. Ibid.

141. Interview with a U.S. Department of State official, Washington, June 14, 2006.

142. Ibid.

143. Kathleen Hwang, "Smugglers Laundered Cash in Macau, Taiwan," United Press International, August 25, 2005.

144. Glenn R. Simpson, Gordon Fairclough, and Jay Solomon, "U.S. Probes Banks' North Korea Ties," *Wall Street Journal*, September 9, 2005.

145. Anna Fifield and Stephanie Kirchgaessner, "China Freezes N Korean Accounts," *Financial Times*, July 26, 2006.

146. Central Committee Bureau 39 of the Korean Workers' Party runs North Korea's primary foreign exchange–earning businesses, most of them illicit. For more on Bureau 39 see Anthony Spaeth, "Kim's Rackets," *Time*, June 2, 2003 (www.time.com/time/magazine/article/0,9171,455850,00.html).

147. Larry A. Niksch, "Korea: U.S.-Korean Relations: Issues for Congress," *CRS Issue Brief for Congress*, April 14, 2006, p. 13.

148. Interview with a member of the U.S. delegation, Washington, August 17, 2006.

149. Interview with a member of the Japanese delegation, Tokyo, November 25, 2005.

150. Interview with a member of the U.S. delegation, Washington, August 17, 2006.

151. Christopher Hill, keynote speech at the AEI-Maeil Kyungjae seminar, "Sustaining the Alliance: U.S.-Korean Relations in the New Asia," American Enterprise Institute, Washington, February 1, 2006 (www.aei.org/events/eventID.1243/transcript.asp).

152. David Asher, "The North Korean Criminal State, Its Ties to Organized Crime, and the Possibility of WMD Proliferation," *Policy Forum Online* 05-92A, November 15, 2005 (http://nautilus.org/fora/security/0592Asher.html).

153. James Kelly, interview, Washington, May 20, 2006.

154. David Asher, "The Illicit Activities of the Kim Jong-il Regime," Seoul-Washington Forum, Brookings Institution and Sejong Institute, Washington, May 1–2, 2006 (www.brookings.edu/comm/events/20060501_asher.pdf).

155. Marcus Noland, "Economic Integration between North and South Korea," in *Korea's Economy 2000* (Washington: Korean Economic Institute, 2001), p. 69.

156. "President Discusses War on Terror and Upcoming Iraqi Elections," White House, December 12, 2005 (www.whitehouse.gov/news/releases/2005/12/20051212-4.html).

157. Stephen Mihm, "No Ordinary Counterfeit," *New York Times*, July 23, 2006.

158. James Kelly, interview, Washington, September 19, 2006.

159. Interview with a senior U.S. administration official, Washington, August 10, 2006.

160. E-mail interview with a Chinese diplomat, March 5, 2007.

161. James Kelly, interview, Washington, September 19, 2006.

162. Interview with a senior U.S. Treasury official, Washington, August 23, 2006.

163. Conversation with a Chinese diplomat, September 1, 2006; Martin Fackler, "North Korean Counterfeiting Complicates Nuclear Crisis," *New York Times*, January 29, 2006.

164. Reconstructed on the basis of a conversation with a senior member of a Chinese government organization, January 3, 2006; Tadanao Takatsuki and Nobuyoshi Sakajiri, "Kitachosen 'Ittei no Sochi' Dakyoten Saguru Ugoki Nisedorusatsu Mondai" ("North Korea Mentions 'Certain Measures' Regarding the Counterfeit Dollar Issue"), *Asahi Shimbun*, January 18, 2006.

165. Gordon Fairclough, "China Warns of Forgeries," *Wall Street Journal*, March 24, 2006.

166. Interview with a senior U.S. administration official, Washingotn, March 13, 2006.

167. Conversation with a Japanese diplomat, Tokyo, July 3, 2006; interview with a senior U.S. administration official, Washington, August 17, 2006.

168. Intelligence reform following the 9/11 attacks included the Intelligence Reform and Terrorism Prevention Act of 2004, the creation of the Office of the Director of National Intelligence, and, most important, the reorganization of enforcement activities at the Department of the Treasury by combining the Executive Office of Terrorist Financing and Financial Crimes, the Financial Crimes Enforcement Network, and the Office of Foreign Assets Control.

169. Interview with a senior U.S. Treasury Department official, Washington, August 23, 2006.

170. Robert Kimmitt, interview, Washington, September 20, 2006; "Securing Our Future," speech by Gordon Brown, chancellor of the exchequer, at the Royal United Services Institute (RUSI), London, February 13, 2006.

171. Robert Kimmitt, interview, Washington, September 20, 2006.

172. Interview with a senior U.S. administration official, Washington, June 27, 2006; e-mail interview with a Chinese diplomat, March 5, 2007.

173. Interview with a senior U.S. administration official, Washington, June 27, 2006.

174. Interview with a U.S. Department of State official, Washington, December 19, 2005.

175. Interview with a senior U.S. Treasury Department official, Washington, August 23, 2006.

176. E-mail interview with a U.S. administration official, March 11, 2007.

177. Interview with a senior Chinese government official, June 26, 2006.

178. Interview with a senior Chinese government official, Beijing, September 25, 2006.

179. Philip Zelikow, interview, Washington, August 16, 2006.

180. Philip Zelikow, interview, Washington, August 16, 2006.

181. Interview with a senior U.S. administration official, Washington, August 16, 2006.

182. Interview with a senior U.S. Department of State official, Washington, August 17, 2006.

183. Interview with a senior U.S. administration official, Washington, June 2, 2006.

184. "North Korea's Missile Arsenal," *Washington Post*, July 4, 2006.

185. Interview with a U.S. Department of State official, Washington, June 16, 2006.

186. Interview with a White House official, Washington, August 28, 2006.

187. Interview with a U.S. Department of State official, Washington, December 19, 2005.

188. Philip Zelikow, interview, Washington, August 16, 2006.

189. Interview with a senior U.S. administration official, Washington, June 2, 2006.

190. E-mail interview, member of the delegation, March 12, 2007.

191. Elisabeth Bumiller, "White House Letter; Novelist in Chief of Staff's Clothing," *New York Times*, February 18, 2002.

192. Interview with a White House official, Washington, June 26, 2006; interview with a senior administration official, Washington, June 2, 2006.

193. Interview with a senior U.S. administration official, Washington, June 26, 2006.

194. Interview with a senior U.S. administration official, Washington, May 31, 2006.

195. "President Bush Meets with President Hu of the People's Republic of China," White House, April 20, 2006 (www.whitehouse.gov/news/releases/2006/04/20060420-1.html); "President Bush and President Hu of People's Republic of China Participate in

Arrival Ceremony," White House, April 20, 2006 (www.whitehouse.gov/news/releases/2006/04/20060420.html).

196. Interview with a senior U.S. administration official, Washington, May 31, 2006.

197. Interview with a senior Chinese government official, Beijing, September 25, 2006.

198. Interview with a senior U.S. Department of State official, Washington, May 31, 2006.

199. Interview with a U.S. administration official, Washington, June 14, 2006.

200. Philip Zelikow, interview, Washington, August 16, 2006.

201. Interview with a U.S. administration official, Washington, June 6, 2006.

202. Interview with a U.S. Department of State official, Washington, June 6, 2006.

203. Reconstructed on the basis of a conversation with a senior member of a Chinese government organization, Beijing, September 25, 2006.

204. Interview with a senior U.S. administration official, Washington, May 31, 2006.

205. E-mail interview with a Chinese diplomat, March 5, 2007.

206. Conversation with a senior South Korean government official, Tokyo, February 10, 2007.

207. "Joint Declaration on the ROK-U.S. Alliance and Peace on the Korean Peninsula," White House, November 17, 2005 (www.whitehouse.gov/news/releases/2005/11/20051117-6.html).

208. Telephone interview with a senior South Korean government official, October 9, 2006; interview with a senior U.S. administration official, Washington, June 2 and 27, 2006.

209. Lee Jong-soek, interview, Seoul, September 4, 2006.

210. E-mail interview with a senior U.S. Administration official, January 16, 2007.

211. Interview with a U.S. Department of State official, Washington, June 14, 2006.

212. Ibid.

213. Interview with a senior Japanese MOFA official, Tokyo, September 5, 2005.

214. Interview with a Blue House official, Seoul, October 12, 2005.

215. Interview with a White House official, Washington, October 20, 2006.

216. E-mail interview with a member of the U.S. delegation, March 12, 2007.

217. Interview with a senior U.S. administration official, Washington, June 2, 2006.

218. Interview with a U.S. Department of State official, Washington, June 14, 2006.

219. Interview with a senior U.S. administration official, Washington, June 4, 2004.

220. Interview with a member of the U.S. delegation, Washington, May 3, 2006; "S. Korea Pushed U.S. to Give In to N.K.," Korea Times, September 28, 2005.

221. Interview with a senior U.S. administration official, Washington, August 16, 2006.

222. Interview with a senior U.S. administration official, Washington, August 10, 2006.

223. Arata Fujii, interview, Tokyo, October 2, 2003.

224. Interview with a senior U.S. administration official, Washington, June 4, 2004.

225. Interview with a U.S. Department of State official, Washington, June 14, 2006.

226. James Kelly, interview, Seattle, October 18, 2005.

227. Interview with a senior White House official, Washington, October 19, 2005.

228. Interview with a senior South Korean government official, Tokyo, February 12, 2004.

229. Interview with a senior South Korean government official, Seoul, October 10, 2005.

230. Interview with a senior South Korean government official, Tokyo, April 17, 2005.

231. Interview with a South Korean government official, Beijing, June 25, 2004.

232. Interview with a White House official, Washington, August 28, 2006.

233. Reconstructed on the basis of a conversation with a senior South Korean government official, Seoul, October 10, 2005.

234. Interview with a member of the U.S. delegation, Washington, August 28, 2006.

235. Ibid.

236. Interview with a senior South Korean government official, Seoul, September 4, 2006; interview with a senior Chinese government official, Beijing, September 25, 2006.

237. Lee Jong-seok, interview, Seoul, September 4, 2006.

238. Interview with a senior Chinese government official, February 23, 2006.

CHAPTER TWELVE

1. Interview with a senior Chinese government official, Beijing, January 23, 2006; Nobuyoshi Sakajiri, "Kita no 'Shogun Sama' Wagayo no Haru" ("Dear General of the North 'Enjoyed His Stage and His Season'"), *Asahi Shimbun,* January 23, 2006. Kim visited China in May 2000, January 2001, April 2004, and January 2006.

2. Interview with a senior member of a Chinese government organization, Beijing, March 20, 2006.

3. "Kim Jong il May Be Visiting China: Sources," *Yonhap,* January 10, 2006.

4. Philip P. Pan, "North Korean Leader Said On Trip to China, Russia," *Washington Post,* January 11, 2006.

5. "N. Korean leader Arrived in China's Shanghai by Plane: Source," *Yonhap,* January 12, 2006.

6. "N. Korean Leader Tours Tech City of Zhuhai: Hong Kong Media," *Yonhap,* January 15, 2006.

7. Nobuyoshi Sakajiri, "Kita no 'Shogun Sama' wagayo no Haru" ("Dear General of the North 'Enjoyed His Stage and His Season'"), *Asahi Shimbun,* January 23, 2006.

8. Interview with a senior Chinese government official, February 23, 2006.

9. Ibid.

10. Interview with a senior member of a Chinese government organization, Beijing, March 20, 2006.

11. Interview with a senior Chinese government official, Beijing, January 20, 2006.

12. "Kim Jong Il Tours Central and South China," *The People's Korea,* Issue 225, January 28, 2006.

13. Conversation with a Chinese diplomat, September 1, 2006.

14. Interview with a senior Chinese government official, Beijing, March 20, 2006.

15. Conversation with a senior member of a Chinese government organization, Beijing, March 20, 2006.

16. "Premier Wen Jiabao Reaffirms Role of China's Special Economic Zones," Xinhua News Agency, September 14, 2005.

17. "Kim Jong-il Starts Political Leg of Secretive China Trip," *Chosun Ilbo,* January 16, 2006.

18. Interview with a senior Chinese government official, Beijing, January 20, 2006.

19. Kim Jong-il's agenda as well as conduct while he was in China were reconstructed on the basis of conversations with officials of the International Department of the Chinese Communist Party and Foreign Ministry, Beijing, January 20, 2006. The discussion also benefited from independent research conducted by my research assistant, Dr. Li Hu-nan.

20. Reconstructed on the basis of a conversation with a North Korean diplomat, July 14, 2006.

21. Interview with a senior Chinese government official, Beijing, January 20, 2006.

22. Ibid.

23. Ibid.

24. Interview with a senior South Korean government official, Seoul, May 9, 2006.

25. Hwang You-Sung, Beijing, "Kim Jong-il Bangjung Imojomo 'Pyongyang bal Dae-hyung News Naol Got' Beijing Sullung" ("Various Sketches of Kim Jong-il's Visits to China: 'There Must be Big News from Pyongyang'"), *Dong-A Ilbo*, November 3, 2005.

26. Reconstructed on the basis of a conversation with a North Korean diplomat, Beijing, March 18, 2006.

27. "Kim Jong-il Pays Unofficial Visit to China," Korean Central News Agency, January 18, 2006.

28. Interview with a senior Chinese government official, May 15, 2006.

29. Interview with a senior Chinese government official, Beijing, January 20, 2006.

30. Conversation with a member of a Chinese government organization, Beijing, March 20, 2006.

31. "Kim Jong-il Pays Unofficial Visit to China," Korean Central News Agency, January 18, 2006.

32. Reconstructed on the basis of a conversation with a member of a Chinese government organization, Beijing, March 20, 2006.

33. Reconstructed on the basis of a conversation with a senior member of a Chinese government organization, Beijing, March 21, 2006.

34. "'Opening Up' Message Revealed by Kim Jong-il's China Visit," *People's Daily Online*, February 9, 2006.

35. "Kinshonichi Shi Hochu Chugokugawa ga Happyo" ("China Announces Mr. Kim Jong-il's Visit to China"), *Asahi Shimbun*, July 8, 1983.

36. Interview with a Chinese diplomat, June 4, 2004.

37. "North Korea Chief Making 1st Trip to China," *New York Times*, March 3, 1999; Chihiro Kato. "Shanhai heno Tokubetsu Ressha no Tabi: Yowa" ("A Trip to Shanghai on Board a Special Train: Episodes"), *Asahi Shimbun*, February 12, 2001.

38. Chisako Masuo, "To Sho Hei-ki Chugoku no Tai Chosen Hanto Gaiko" ("Chinese Policy toward Korean Peninsula during the Deng Xiaoping Era"), *Ajia Kenkyu (Asia Study)* 48 (2002): 77–101.

39. Reconstructed on the basis of a conversation with a Chinese diplomat, December 9, 2005.

40. Reconstructed on the basis of a conversation with a Chinese diplomat, September 1, 2006.

41. Stephen Haggard and Marcus Noland, *Famine in North Korea: Markets, Aid, and Reform* (Columbia University Press, 2007), p. 1.

42. Ibid., pp. 9 and 59.

43. Jiang Longfan, *Bei Daitoryo Senkyo-go ni okeru Chugoku no Tai-Kita Chosen Seisaku to Chu-Cho Kankei no Tenbo (China's North Korean Policy after the U.S. Presidential Election and the Prospect of China–North Korea Relations)* ERINA Discussion Paper 0502, June 2005 (Niigata, Japan: Economic Research Institute for Northeast Asia, June 2005), pp. 34–35. Stephen Haggard and Marcus Noland, *Famine in North Korea: Markets, Aid, and Reform* (Columbia University Press, 2007), pp. 21–32.

44. Interview with a Chinese government official, Beijing, January 20, 2006.

45. The information was shared by William Perry, who had discussions with Chinese leaders on the Korean situation.

46. Shiro Nakamura and Tadanao Takatsuki, "Hatsu no Gaiko Ganshoku Ryoko Kita-chosen no Kin Soshoki ga Hochu" ("General Secretary Kim Beams in His First 'Diplomatic' Gambit of His Visit to China"), *Asahi Shimbun,* June 2, 2000.

47. Reconstructed on the basis of a conversation with a Chinese expert on the Korean Peninsula, Shanghai, July 30, 2004.

48. Tetsuya Hakoda, "'Shanhai wo Moderu ni Keizai Tokku' Kita Chosen no Kinshonichi Soshoki ga Hochuji Kataru" ("General Secretary Kim Jong-il in His Visit to China Said There Is a Need to Develop an Economic Zone Modeled after Shanghai"), *Asahi Shimbun,* January 27, 2001.

49. "Kim Jong-il Pays Unofficial Visit to China," Korean Central News Agency, April 22, 2004.

50. Kato, "Shanhai eno Tokubetsu Ressha no Tabi: Yowa" ("A Trip to Shanghai on Board a Special Train: Episodes).

51. Interview with a Chinese diplomat, September 1, 2006.

52. Rupert Hoogewerf, "China's Richest," *Forbes,* November 11, 2002.

53. Chihiro Kato, "Oryokuko wo Wataru Tsumetai Kawakaze" ("Cold River Wind Blowing over the Yalu"), *Asahi Shimbun,* December 16, 2002.

54. "Flamboyance, Optimism and Suspicion Swirl around Businessman Tapped for North Korean Venture," Associated Press, October 4, 2002.

55. E-mail interview with a Chinese diplomat, February 5, 2007.

56. Francesco Sisci, "North Korea: Alone Again, Naturally," *Asia Times Online,* December 19, 2002 (www.atimes.com/atimes/China/DL19Ad01.html).

57. Interview with a Chinese diplomat, July 3, 2006.

58. Jiang, *Bei Daitoryo Senkyo-go ni okeru Chugoku no Tai-Kita Chosen Seisaku to Chu-Cho Kankei no Tenbo* (*China's North Korean Policy after the U.S. Presidential Election and the Prospect of China–North Korea Relations*).

59. "Kim Jong-il Pays Unofficial Visit to China," Korean Central News Agency, April 22, 2004.

60. "Kinshonichi Soshoki Rokusha Kyogi Suishin wo Meigen" ("General Secretary Kim Jong-il Stated Clearly the Need to Advance Six-Party Talks"), *Asahi Shimbun,* April 22, 2004.

61. Interview with a senior Chinese government official, Beijing, January 20, 2006.

62. Interview with a senior Chinese government official, February 23, 2006.

63. Reconstructed on the basis of a conversation with a senior member of a Chinese government organization, Beijing, March 20, 2006.

64. Interview with a senior U.S. administration official, Washington, May 31, 2006, and August 16, 2006.

65. Reconstructed on the basis of a conversation with a Chinese expert on the Korean Peninsula, Shenyang, China, July 17, 2006.

66. Philip Zelikow, interview, Washington, August 16, 2006.

67. Conversation with a Shanghai-based Chinese specialist on Korean issues, Shanghai, July 30, 2004.

68. Interview with a senior Chinese government official, Beijing, August 3, 2004.

69. Interview with a Chinese government official, September 15, 2006.

70. Conversation with a North Korean diplomat, Beijing, March 18, 2006.

71. Interview with a senior Chinese government official, February 23, 2006.

72. Interview with two Chinese government officials, Beijing, March 20, 2006, and December 13, 2005.

73. Yoichi Funabashi, "Chugoku wa Kita-Chosen ni Sakana wo Ataeru nodewa Naku Sakana no Tsurikata wo Oshieru Koto ga Dekiruka" ("Can China Teach North Korea How to Catch a Fish instead of Giving It a Fish?"), *Shukan Asahi* (weekly), May 7–14, 2004.

74. Interview with a senior Chinese government official, February 23, 2006.

75. Interview with a senior Chinese government official, Beijing, August 3, 2004.

76. Ibid.

77. Interview with a senior Chinese government official, Beijing, March 20, 2006.

78. Interview with a senior Chinese government official, Boao, China, April 24, 2004.

79. Interview with a senior Chinese government official, May 15, 2006.

80. Interview with a senior Chinese government official, Beijing, August 3, 2004.

81. Madeleine Albright, *Madam Secretary: A Memoir* (New York: Miramax Books, 2003), p. 466.

82. Reconstructed on the basis of a conversation with a North Korean diplomat, March 18, 2006.

83. Robert L. Carlin and Joel S. Wit, "North Korean Reform: Politics, Economics, and Security," Adelphi Paper 382 (Routledge, 2006), p. 45.

84. Takashi Uemura, Seoul, "Kinshonichi Soshoki 'Tepodon Hassha ni Nanokudoru mo" ("General Secretary Kim Admits Spending Several Hundred Million Dollars in Missile Development"), *Asahi Shimbun,* April 25, 1999.

85. Interview with a senior Chinese government official, February 23, 2006.

86. Interview with a senior Chinese government official, Beijing, March 20, 2006.

87. Reconstructed on the basis of a conversation with a North Korean diplomat, March 18, 2006.

88. Charles L. Pritchard, "A Guarantee to Bring Kim into Line," *Financial Times,* October 10, 2003.

89. James Hoare, interview, London, February 6, 2006.

90. Carlin and Wit, "North Korean Reform: Politics, Economics, and Security," p. 31.

91. Ibid., p. 32.

92. Ibid., p. 37.

93. Ibid., p. 38.

94. Ibid., p. 39.

95. Ibid., p. 44.

96. Reconstructed on the basis of a conversation with William Perry, Washington, March 22, 2004. Perry visited Pyongyang in 1999 at the invitation of the president of the standing committee of the Supreme People's Assembly. When Perry met a military officer who had once served as North Korea's minister of defense, the officer referred to Foreign Ministry officials as "those neckties," clearly deprecating them as "weakling diplomats."

97. Interview with a senior South Korean foreign ministry official, Tokyo, April 17, 2005.

98. Lee Jong-seok, "Kita Chosen no Kino, Kyo, Soshite Ashita," ("Yesterday, Today, and Tomorrow of North Korea"), in *Kita Chosen Nenkan—2000-nenban* (*North Korea Annual: 2000*), edited by Yonhap News Agency, quoted in Jiang, *Bei Daitoryo Senkyo-go ni okeru Chugoku no Tai-Kita Chosen Seisaku to Chu-Cho Kankei no Tenbo* (*China's North Korean Policy after the U.S. Presidential Election and the Prospect of China–North Korea Relations*), p. 17.

99. Interview with a Chinese government official, September 29, 2006.

100. Interview with a senior Chinese government official, Beijing, March 20, 2006.

101. Conversation with a Chinese diplomat, February 23, 2006.

102. Weathersby is project leader on research concerning North Korea at the Woodrow Wilson International Center for Scholars in Washington. More information on the Cold War International History Project can be found at www.CWIHP.org.

103. Cold War International History Project, "Conversation between Soviet Ambassador in North Korea Vasily Moskovsky and Soviet specialists in North Korea" (trans. Sergey Radchenko), October 16, 1963 (www.CWIHP.org).

104. Cold War International History Project, "Report, Embassy of Hungary in North Korea to the Hungarian Foreign Ministry" (trans. Balazs Szalontai), March 13, 1967 (www.CWIHP.org).

105. "Pyongyang Long Sought Atomic Bomb," *Wall Street Journal,* May 18, 2005.

106. Interview with a senior Chinese government official, February 23, 2006.

107. Reconstructed on the basis of a conversation with a North Korean diplomat, June 4, 2006.

108. James Kelly, interview, Beijing, June 26, 2004.

109. Nobuyoshi Sakajiri's interview with James Kelly. The author is indebted to Nobuyoshi Sakajiri for permitting his transcription to be quoted in this book.

110. Interview with a senior South Korean government official, Tokyo, July 6, 2006.

111. Interview with a South Korean diplomat, Tokyo, April 17, 2005.

112. Hiroko Imamura. *Kita Chosen: Kyoko no Keizai* (*North Korea: A Fictional Economy*) (Tokyo: Shueisha, 2005), p. 10.

113. Conversations with businessmen in Dandong who do business with North Korea, Dandong, China, July 16, 2006.

114. "Governor Optimistic about Revitalizing Northeast China," *China Daily,* October 1, 2003; "Premier Outlines Plan to Revitalize Rustbelt," *People's Daily,* March 24, 2004.

115. Based on a conversation with Kim Chul, a researcher at the Chinese Academy of Social Sciences, Shenyang, July 17, 2006.

116. Conversations with businessmen in Dandong who do business with North Korea, Dandong, China, July 16, 2006.

117. "New Bridge over Yalu to Link China, DPRK," *People's Daily Online,* March 15, 2002 (http://english.people.com.cn/200203/14/eng20020314_92120.shtml).

118. Reconstructed on the basis of a conversation with a North Korean diplomat, April 16, 2006.

119. Interview with a U.S. Department of Defense official, Washington, April 25, 2006.

120. Ibid.

121. Interview with a senior South Korean government official, Tokyo, July 6, 2006.

122. "KCNA Report on Explosion at Ryongchon Railway Station," Korean Central News Agency, April 24, 2004.

123. The explosion was later determined to have been an accident, but the timing of the accident, the rescheduling of Kim's train, and rumors of a "cellular trigger device" reported by the *Chosun Ilbo* led to the rumors of an assassination attempt. "Rumours Linger over N Korea Blast," *BBC News,* April 24, 2004; Sergey Soukhorukov, "Train Blast Was 'a Plot to Kill North Korea's Leader,'" *Telegraph,* June 13, 2004.

124. Interview with a senior Chinese government official, Boao, China, April 24, 2004.

125. Ibid.

126. "Kim Jong-il Inspects Military Unit: Report," *Yonhap,* January 1, 2005; "North Korea This Week No. 402," *Yonhap,* June 22, 2006.

127. Interview with a senior U.S. administration official, Washington, March 5, 2003; interview with a Japanese government intelligence analyst, Tokyo, February 28, 2007. The Japanese official pointed out that in pictures of Kim Jong-il's inspections, without

exception, military officers accompanying Kim carry no guns. Troops who carry them are instructed to unload. Only Kim Jong-il's security forces are actually armed in Kim's presence.

128. Reconstructed on the basis of a conversation with a Chinese expert on the Korean Peninsula, Tokyo, February 21, 2004.

129. Kim Hee-sang, interview, Seoul, March 22, 2006; Hee Sang Kim, *Korean Security in the 21st Century and Korea-U.S. Relations* (Seoul: Jeonkwang Printing, 2001), p. 289.

130. Interview with a South Korean diplomat, Tokyo, December 14, 2004. In an interview in Tokyo, February 28, 2007, a Japanese government intelligence analyst specializing in North Korea told me that he also heard a similar rumor. He speculated that the story may have flowed from the Zainichi community in Japan (long-time, permanent, typically Korean residents of Japan) to Pyongyang. Lee Ryul, a Korean-Japanese engineer who returned to North Korea in the mid-1960s and eventually defected back to Japan, said that Kim Jong-il was contemplating introducing something like Japan's "symbolic emperor system" into North Korea. Lee Ryul, "Kin Shonichi No Kenryoku Keisho Seshu ha Mohaya Konnan Da" ("Kim Jong-il's Power Succession Is No Longer Possible"), *Ronza*, December 2004, p. 203.

131. Interview with a senior Chinese government official, Beijing, January 20, 2006.

132. Interview with a South Korean government intelligence analyst, Tokyo, July 8, 2006.

133. Interview with a senior Chinese government official, Beijing, January 20, 2006.

134. Ibid.

135. "Kim Dae-jung Urging NK Leader to Visit Seoul," *Korea Times*, February 3, 2006.

136. Kim Dae-jung, interview, Seoul, March 24, 2006.

137. Ibid.

138. Lee Chul, interview; "Rail Head Says Links to North Are Usable," *JoongAng Ilbo*, March 8, 2006.

139. "Kim Dae-jung Won't Ride Reunification Train," *Chosun Ilbo*, May 17, 2006.

140. Conversation with a hotel guest service attendant, Shenzhen, China, July 15, 2006.

141. "Speech of Kim Jong-il at Banquet," Korean Central News Agency, January 18, 2006.

142. Interview with a senior Chinese government official, Beijing, January 20, 2006.

Chapter Thirteen

1. Joseph Bermudez Jr., "North Korea Claims Nuclear Test," *Jane's Defence Weekly*, October 9, 2006.

2. "DPRK Successfully Conducts Underground Nuclear Test," Korean Central News Agency, October 9, 2006.

3. The test took place at 10:36 a.m. local time in North Korea, which was 9:36 p.m. in Washington. David E. Sanger, "North Korea Says It Tested a Nuclear Device Underground," *New York Times*, October 9, 2006.

4. "President Bush's Statement on North Korea Nuclear Test," White House, October 9, 2006 (www.whitehouse.gov/news/releases/2006/10/20061009.html).

5. David Stout and John O'Neil, "North Korea's Claim Is Met with Doubt and Anger," *New York Times*, October 9, 2006.

6. Charter of the United Nations, Chapter VII, June 26, 1945 (www.un.org/aboutun/charter/).

7. "Ambassador John R. Bolton, U.S. Permanent Representative to the United Nations," U.S. Department of State, October 9 2006 (www.state.gov/p/io/rls/rm/73761.htm).

8. "DPRK Foreign Ministry Clarifies Stand on New Measure to Bolster War Deterrent," Korean Central News Agency, October 3, 2006.

9. "N. Korea Nuclear Test Plans a Threat to Peace, Japan Says," Associated Press, October 3, 2006.

10. "U.S. Diplomat Says North Korea Warned Not to Test Nuclear Device," Associated Press, October 3, 2006.

11. "Statement by the President of the Security Council," United Nations Security Council, S/PRST/2006/41, October 6, 2006.

12. "China Resolutely Opposes DPRK's Nuclear Test," *Xinhua Online,* October 9, 2006.

13. Warren Hoge, "China and Russia Stall Sanctions on North Korea," *New York Times,* October 13, 2006.

14. Ibid.

15. Warren Hoge and Sheryl Gay Stolberg, "Bush Rebukes North Korea," *New York Times,* October 10, 2006.

16. UN Security Council Resolution 1718, October 14, 2006.

17. Secretary Rice traveled to Tokyo, Seoul, Beijing, and Moscow.

18. "Kim Jong Il Receives Special Envoy of Chinese President," Korean Central News Agency, October 19, 2006.

19. "Kim Told China: No Plans for Second Nuke Test," *China Daily,* October 24, 2006.

20. "Servicepersons and Pyongyangites Hail Successful Nuclear Test," Korean Central News Agency, October 20, 2006.

21. "'Gyakukokada' Chugoku To Kokumuiin, Seisai ni Hantai" ("State Councilor of China Tang Expresses Opposition to Sanctions, Saying 'They Are Counterproductive'"), *Asahi Shimbun,* July 7, 2006.

22. "DPRK Foreign Ministry Spokesman on Its Missile Launches," Korean Central News Agency, July 6, 2006.

23. Ibid.

24. "China Expresses Serious Concern over DPRK's Missile Test-Firing," Xinhua News Agency, July 5, 2006; "Government Statement on the North Korean Missile Test-Firing," Cheong Wa Dae, July 5, 2006.

25. "Chinese FM Spokeswoman Criticizes Japanese Remarks of 'Preemptive Strike' against DPRK," Xinhua News Agency, July 13, 2006.

26. Interview with a senior U.S. administration official, Washington, August 28, 2006.

27. Norimitsu Onishi, "Missile Tests Divide Seoul from Tokyo," *New York Times,* July 10, 2006; *Kita-Chosen Kuraishisu (North Korean Crisis)* (Tokyo: Nihon Keizai Shimbunsha, 2006), p. 124.

28. "Briefing on Statements by the Key Cabinet Members of the Japanese Government," Cheong Wa Dae, July 11, 2006; "Soaring Feud between Seoul and Tokyo," *Busan Ilbo,* July 12, 2006.

29. Tadanao Takatsuki, "Kankoku, 'Taiwa' Hoshin Kaezu Kita-chosen Misairu Hassha" ("South Korea Maintains Its Stance on Dialogue in Spite of North Korea's Missile Test"), *Asahi Shimbun,* July 9, 2006.

30. Interview with a U.S. administration official, Washington, July 24, 2006.

31. Interview with a senior member of a Chinese government organization, Beijing, July 14, 2006.

32. Interview with a Chinese diplomat, Beijing, September 25, 2006. This diplomat

called attention to the fact that North Korea launched all the missiles over the Sea of Japan/East Sea in the direction of Russia, not Japan. He stressed that North Korea had given careful consideration to its actions, although they may have looked foolhardy.

33. Ibid.

34. Ibid.

35. Interview with a Chinese diplomat, Beijing, September 25, 2006.

36. Interview with a White House official, Washington, August 28, 2006.

37. Richard Lugar, U.S. Senate Committee on Foreign Relations, *North Korea: U.S. Policy Options: Hearing before the Committee on Foreign Relations,* 109th Cong., 2nd sess., July 20, 2006.

38. *Kita-Chosen Kuraishisu (North Korean Crisis)* (Tokyo: Nihon Keizai Shimbun-sha, 2006), p. 124.

39. "Shake Off outdated Concepts of Independence," *Chosun Ilbo,* July 24, 2006.

40. Interview with a senior Japanese government official, Tokyo, July 3, 2006.

41. Junichiro Koizumi, interview, Tokyo, July 5, 2006; "Shusho, Beicho Kyogi Unagasu" ("Prime Minister [Koizumi] Urges [Bush] to Move to U.S.-DPRK Consultations"), *Asahi Shimbun,* July 19, 2006.

42. Interview with a senior Japanese government official, Tokyo, July 3, 2006.

43. Interview with a senior Japanese government official, Tokyo, July 3, 2006.

44. Interview with a Japanese government official, Tokyo, July 3, 2006.

45. Junichiro Koizumi, interview, Tokyo, July 5, 2006.

46. Ibid.

47. Conversation with Junichiro Koizumi, Tokyo, July 5, 2006. Koizumi's term as prime minister and head of the Liberal Democratic Party ended September 26, 2006.

48. The U.S. made a deal with North Korea on the Banco Delta Asia money laundering issue in March 2007. The United States agreed to end its eighteen-month investigation, which determined that North Korea had used the bank for money laundering, by banning U.S. banks from dealing with Banco Delta Asia. Ending the investigation will allow the return, under Macanese law, of the $25 million in North Korean funds held there. It was considered a quid-pro-quo to North Korea's commitment to shut down the Yongbyon nuclear programs and again allow IAEA inspectors on site. However, the deal was criticized because while North Korea has agreed to shut down its reactors, it can turn them back on. Demetri Sevastopulo and Tom Mitchell, "U.S. to Finalise Sanctions on Macao Bank," *Financial Times,* March 13, 2007; Maureen Fan, "Deal on Funds Removes Hurdle to N. Korea Talks," *Washington Post,* March 19, 2007; Helene Cooper and Jim Yardley, "Pact with North Korea Draws Fire From a Wide Range of Critics in U.S.," *New York Times,* February 13, 2007.

49. Colin Powell, interview, Washington, March 31, 2006.

50. North Korea's nuclear test on October 9, 2006, further reinforced the Japanese public's strong antipathy toward North Korea. While Prime Minister Abe enjoyed popularity immediately following North Korea's October 2006 nuclear test, just a couple weeks after his election, the strong position of Abe and his cabinet regarding the abduction issue (discussed in chapter 1) not only has left him isolated vis-à-vis China, South Korea, and Russia but also has complicated Japan's relationship with the United States following the six-party talks in February 2007. Japan has refused to provide direct aid to North Korea until "progress" is made on the abduction issue, which North Korea considers resolved.

51. This has been furthered by Prime Minister Abe's equivocations about Japan's responsibility with respect to the "comfort women" after the U.S. House of Representatives considered a resolution demanding that Japan "formally acknowledge, apologize, and

accept historical responsibility" for its actions during World War II (H. Res. 121, 110th U.S. Congress, 2007–08). Abe later denied that women were coerced into serving as "comfort women" when he said that "testimony to the effect that there had been a hunt for comfort women is a complete fabrication," a refutation that damaged Japan's image abroad. Martin Fackler, "No Apology for Sex Slavery, Japan's Prime Minister Says," *New York Times*, March 6, 2007.

52. China issued a much stronger statement after North Korea conducted a nuclear test in early October 2006. In particular, it included the unusual wording *han ran* (brazenly), which over the past several decades had been used only against Beijing's adversaries—for example, when the United States deployed aircraft carriers to the Taiwan Strait in response to Chinese missile tests there; after the U.S. bombing of China's embassy in Belgrade; and following Koizumi's repeated visits to Yasukuni Shrine. It was the first time that China used such a strong term with a friendly country. One Chinese diplomat noted that when the statement regarding North Korea was issued, it was only the seventh time that the Chinese Foreign Ministry had used the term *han ran* in condemning the actions of another country. E-mail interview with a senior Chinese diplomat, February 5, 2007.

53. Christopher R. Hill, U.S. Senate Committee on Foreign Relations, *North Korea: U.S. Policy Options: Hearing before the Committee on Foreign Relations*, 109th Cong., 2nd sess., July 20, 2006.

54. Interview with a U.S. administration official, Washington, August 28, 2006.

55. James Kelly, interview, Beijing, June 26, 2004.

INTERVIEWEES

Note: Chinese and Korean names have been written with surnames preceding given names, as is customary in East Asia, while Japanese, American, Russian, and other names are written with the surname following the given name.

CHINA

Cui Tiankai
Li Jun
Tang Jiaxuan
Wang Yi
Wu Dawei
Yang Jian
Yang Xiyu
Yang Youming
Zheng Bijian

JAPAN

Shinzo Abe
Ichiro Aizawa
Takeo Akiba
Yukiya Amano
Koreshige Anami
Yutaka Arima
Koro Bessho

Shin Ebihara
Arata Fujii
Yasuo Fukuda
Teijiro Furukawa
Kenji Hiramatsu
Katsuei Hirasawa
Ho Jong Man
Hiroyuki Hosoda
Isao Iijima
Kimihiro Ishikane
Naoki Ito
Takuya Iwamoto
Ryozo Kato
Yoriko Kawaguchi
Chikao Kawai
Yutaka Kawashima
Junichiro Koizumi
Masahiko Komura
Kunihiko Makita
Makoto Matsuda

Daisuke Mibae
Yoshiro Mori
Toshimitsu Motegi
Tomiichi Murayama
Hidenao Nakagawa
Koichiro Nakamura
Kyoko Nakayama
Yoshiji Nogami
Issei Nomura
Hidekazu Okada
Akitaka Saiki
Shinsuke Sugiyama
Kenichiro Sasae
Shigekazu Sato
Seiken Sugiura
Katsuya Suzuki
Kazuhiro Suzuki
Toshiyuki Takano
Yoshinori Takeda
Yukio Takeuchi

Hitoshi Tanaka
Koji Tsuruoka
Mitoji Yabunaka
Shotaro Yachi
Eiji Yamamoto
Tadamichi Yamamoto
Kanji Yamanouchi
Taku Yamazaki

SOUTH KOREA

Ban Ki-moon
Cha Young-koo
Cho Se-hyung
Cho Tae-yong
Choi Sang-yong
Choi Sung-hong
Choi Yong-kil
Choi Young-jin
Chun Yung-woo
Chung Dong-young
Han Sung-joo
Hong Seok-hyun
Jeong Se-hyun
Kim Dae-jung
Kim Hee-sang
Kim Sook
Kim Sung-hwan
Kim Won-jin
Kim Won-soo
Kim Yong-sam
Kwon Chin-ho
Lee Chul
Lee Dong-hwi
Lee Jong-seok
Lee Soo-hyuck
Lee Tae-sik
Lim Dong-won
Moon Chung-in
Park Chan-bong

Park Sun-won
Ra Jong-il
Song Min-soon
Suh Dong-man
Suh Joo-seok
Wi Sung-lac
Yim Sung-joon
Yoo Ihn-tae
Yoon Young-kwan
Yun Byung-se

RUSSIA

Georgy Kunadze
Alexander Losyukov
Alexander Minaev
Igor A. Rogachev
Valery Suhinin
Alexander A. Timonin
Georgy D. Toloraya
Alexander V. Vorontsov
Alexander Zhebin

UNITED KINGDOM

James Hoare

UNITED STATES

Richard L. Armitage
David L. Asher
Samuel R. Berger
John R. Bolton
Robert L. Carlin
Victor D. Cha
Thomas J. Christensen
Richard A. Christenson
Jack D. Crouch
Joseph R. DeTrani
Michael M. Dunn
Evan A. Feigenbaum

Michael J. Finnegan
James J. Foster
Thomas B. Gibbons
Daniel L. Glaser
Michael J. Green
Mark A. Groombridge
Richard N. Haass
Christopher R. Hill
John D. Hill
Thomas C. Hubbard
Charles Jones
Robert G. Joseph
Donald W. Keyser
Charles F. Kartman
James A. Kelly
Tong Kim
Robert M. Kimmitt
Richard P. Lawless
John R. Merrill
James F. Moriarty
Ted Osius
Torkel L. Patterson
Colin L. Powell
Charles L. "Jack"
    Pritchard
Mitchell B. Reiss
Evans J. R. Revere
Anthony J. Ruggiero
David B. Shear
D. Kathleen Stephens
W. David Straub
William H. Tobey
Alexander R. Vershbow
Dennis C. Wilder
Lawrence B. Wilkerson
Stephen J. Yates
Philip D. Zelikow
Robert B. Zoellick

INDEX